For more resources, visit the Web site for

The American Promise

bedfordstmartins.com/roark

FREE Online Study Guide

Get instant feedback on your progress with

- Chapter self-tests
- Key terms review
- Map quizzes
- Timeline activities
- Note-taking outlines

FREE History research and writing help

Refine your research skills and find plenty of good sources with

- Suggested references for each chapter compiled by the textbook authors
- A database of useful images, maps, documents, and more at *Make History*
- A guide to online sources for history
- Help with writing history papers
- A tool for building a bibliography
- Tips on avoiding plagiarism

WASHINGTON
Seattle
Olympia
Mt. Rainier (14,411 ft.; 4,392 m)
Mt. St. Helens (8,366 ft.; 2,550 m)
Portland
Salem
Eugene
OREGON
CASCADE MTS.
COAST RANGES
Columbia River
IDAHO
Boise
Snake River
MONTANA
Helena
Billings
Missouri River
Yellowstone River
NORTH DAKOTA
Bismarck
BADLANDS
SOUTH DAKOTA
Pierre
BLACK HILLS
GREAT PLAINS
WYOMING
ROCKY MOUNTAINS
GREAT DIVIDE BASIN
Cheyenne
NEBRASKA
Platte River
Great Salt Lake
Salt Lake City
UTAH
GREAT BASIN
NEVADA
Carson City
SIERRA NEVADA
Sacramento
Sacramento River
San Francisco
Oakland
San Jose
San Joaquin River
Fresno
Mt. Whitney (14,494 ft.; 4,418 m)
Las Vegas
CALIFORNIA
MOJAVE DESERT
Los Angeles
San Diego
PACIFIC OCEAN
COLORADO
Denver
Mt. Elbert (14,433 ft.; 4,399 m)
Colorado Springs
Pikes Peak (14,110 ft.; 4,301 m)
Colorado River
Arkansas River
KANS
OKLAHO
ARIZONA
Phoenix
Tucson
NEW MEXICO
Santa Fe
Albuquerque
Pecos River
El Paso
Rio Grande
Lubbock
LLANO ESTACADO
TEXAS
EDWARDS PLATEAU
San Antonio
MEXICO
ARCTIC OCEAN
RUSSIA
BROOKS RANGE
ALASKA
Arctic Circle
Yukon River
Mt. McKinley (20,320 ft.; 6,194 m)
ALASKA RANGE
CANADA
Anchorage
Bering Sea
Gulf of Alaska
Juneau
ALEUTIAN ISLANDS
0 250 500 miles
0 250 500 kilometers
HAWAII
Kauai
Niihau
Oahu
Honolulu
Molokai
Lanai
Maui
Kahoolawe
Hawaii
PACIFIC OCEAN
0 50 100 miles
0 50 100 kilometers

CANADA
90°W
80°W
70°W
0
150
300 miles
300 kilometers
N
S
E
W
Lake Superior
Lake Michigan
Lake Huron
Lake Ontario
Lake Erie
St. Lawrence River
Hudson River
MAINE
Augusta
Portland
VERMONT
Burlington
Montpelier
Mt. Washington
(6,288 ft.; 1,917 m)
Concord
Manchester
NEW
HAMPSHIRE
Albany
Boston
MASS.
Hartford
Providence
R.I.
CONNECTICUT
NEW
YORK
Buffalo
New York
Trenton
PENNSYLVANIA
Harrisburg
Philadelphia
NEW JERSEY
Pittsburgh
Dover
Baltimore
DELAWARE
Annapolis
WASHINGTON, D.C.
MARYLAND
Potomac
River
Chesapeake
Bay
Richmond
VIRGINIA
Norfolk
APPALACHIAN MTS.
W.
VA.
Charleston
Wheeling
OHIO
Columbus
Cleveland
Cincinnati
MICHIGAN
Lansing
Detroit
WISCONSIN
Milwaukee
Madison
NNESOTA
St. Paul
nneapolis
IOWA
Des Moines
Chicago
CENTRAL
LOWLAND
INDIANA
Indianapolis
ILLINOIS
Springfield
MISSOURI
Kansas City
St. Louis
Jefferson
City
Ohio River
Louisville
Frankfort
KENTUCKY
Cumberland
River
Knoxville
Mt. Mitchell
(6,684 ft.; 2,037 m)
Nashville
TENNESSEE
Raleigh
NORTH CAROLINA
Charlotte
SOUTH CAROLINA
Columbia
Charleston
TIDEWATER
ATLANTIC
OCEAN
Memphis
ARKANSAS
Little
Rock
Mississippi River
Tennessee River
Atlanta
Birmingham
ALABAMA
GEORGIA
MISSISSIPPI
Jackson
Montgomery
Alabama River
LOUISIANA
Baton Rouge
New Orleans
Jacksonville
Tallahassee
Orlando
FLORIDA
Lake
Okeechobee
Miami
Gulf
of
Mexico
BAHAMAS
CUBA
Tulsa
uston
THE
UNITED STATES
Elevation
Feet
Meters
Over 13,001
Over 3,001
6,561–13,000
2,001–3,000
3,281–6,560
1,001–2,000
1,641–3,280
501–1,000
661–1,640
201–500
0–660
0–200
Below
sea level
Below
sea level
67°W
65°W
ATLANTIC OCEAN
San Juan
PUERTO
RICO
18°N
VIRGIN
ISLANDS
Caribbean Sea
0
50
100 miles
100 kilometers

THE CONTEMPORARY WORLD
80°N
60°N
40°N
20°N
0°
Equator
20°S
40°S
60°S
80°S
160°W
140°W
120°W
100°W
80°W
60°W
40°W
20°W
ALASKA
CANADA
Greenland
(Den.)
ICELAND
UNITED STATES
MEXICO
Hawaii
ATLANTIC
OCEAN
PACIFIC OCEAN
BAHAMAS
DOMINICAN
REPUBLIC
HAITI
CUBA
JAMAICA
BELIZE
Puerto Rico (U.S.)
ST. KITTS AND NEVIS
ANTIGUA AND BARBUDA
Guadeloupe (Fr.)
DOMINICA
Martinique (Fr.)
ST. VINCENT AND THE GRENADINES
ST. LUCIA
BARBADOS
GRENADA
TRINIDAD AND TOBAGO
GUATEMALA
HONDURAS
EL SALVADOR
NICARAGUA
COSTA RICA
PANAMA
VENEZUELA
GUYANA
SURINAME
French Guiana (Fr.)
COLOMBIA
ECUADOR
Galápagos Is.
(Ec.)
PERU
BRAZIL
BOLIVIA
PARAGUAY
CHILE
URUGUAY
ARGENTINA
Falkland Is.
(U.K.)
Easter I.
(Chile)
SAMOA
TONGA
N
E
S
W
0
1,500
3,000 miles
0
1,500
3,000 kilometers
Azores
(Port.)
Canary Is.
(Sp.)
Western Sahara
(Mor.)
CAPE
VERDE
SENEGAL
GAMBIA
GUINEA-BISSAU
GUINEA
SIERRA LEONE
LIBERIA
ATLANTIC
OCEAN

ARCTIC OCEAN
RUSSIAN FEDERATION
SWEDEN
FINLAND
ESTONIA
LATVIA
LITHUANIA
BELARUS
POLAND
CZ.
SLK.
UKRAINE
AUS.
HUNG.
MOLDOVA
SLN.
CR.
ROMANIA
SE.
B.H.
BULGARIA
ITALY
MO.
KO.
MAC.
ALB.
GREECE
GEORGIA
ARMENIA
TURKEY
AZERBAIJAN
MALTA
TUNISIA
CYPRUS
SYRIA
LEBANON
ISRAEL
IRAQ
West Bank
Gaza Strip
JORDAN
IRAN
KUWAIT
BAHRAIN
LIBYA
EGYPT
SAUDI ARABIA
QATAR
UNITED ARAB EMIRATES
OMAN
YEMEN
KAZAKHSTAN
UZBEKISTAN
TURKMENISTAN
KYRGYZSTAN
TAJIKISTAN
AFGHANISTAN
PAKISTAN
MONGOLIA
CHINA
N. KOREA
S. KOREA
JAPAN
NEPAL
BHUTAN
BANGLADESH
INDIA
MYANMAR (BURMA)
LAOS
VIETNAM
THAILAND
CAMBODIA
Taiwan
PHILIPPINES
PACIFIC OCEAN
Mariana Is. (U.S.)
Guam (U.S.)
MARSHALL IS.
CHAD
SUDAN
ERITREA
DJIBOUTI
SOUTH SUDAN
CENTRAL AFRICAN REP.
ETHIOPIA
SOMALIA
CAMEROON
GABON
CONGO
UGANDA
RWANDA
KENYA
DEM. REP. OF THE CONGO
BURUNDI
TANZANIA
COMOROS
SEYCHELLES
ANGOLA
ZAMBIA
MALAWI
ZIMBABWE
MADAGASCAR
NAMIBIA
BOTSWANA
MOZAMBIQUE
SWAZILAND
SOUTH AFRICA
LESOTHO
MAURITIUS
MALDIVES
SRI LANKA
INDIAN OCEAN
BRUNEI
MALAYSIA
SINGAPORE
PALAU
FEDERATED STATES OF MICRONESIA
NAURU
KIRIBATI
INDONESIA
PAPUA NEW GUINEA
TUVALU
SOLOMON IS.
TIMOR LESTE
VANUATU
FIJI
New Caledonia (Fr.)
AUSTRALIA
Tasmania (AUST.)
NEW ZEALAND
ANTARCTICA
20°E
40°E
60°E
80°E
100°E
120°E
140°E
160°E
ABBREVIATIONS
ALB. ALBANIA
AUS. AUSTRIA
BEL. BELGIUM
B.H. BOSNIA AND HERZEGOVINA
CR. CROATIA
CZ. CZECH REPUBLIC
DEN. DENMARK
HUNG. HUNGARY
KO. KOSOVO
LUX. LUXEMBOURG
MAC. MACEDONIA
MO. MONTENEGRO
NETH. NETHERLANDS
SE. SERBIA
SLK. SLOVAKIA
SLN. SLOVENIA
SWITZ. SWITZERLAND

The American Promise

A History of the United States

FIFTH EDITION

The American Promise

A History of the United States

FIFTH EDITION

VOLUME B: 1800–1900

James L. Roark
Emory University

Michael P. Johnson
Johns Hopkins University

Patricia Cline Cohen
University of California, Santa Barbara

Sarah Stage
Arizona State University

Susan M. Hartmann
The Ohio State University

BEDFORD/ST. MARTIN'S
BOSTON ♦ NEW YORK

FOR BEDFORD/ST. MARTIN'S

Publisher for History: Mary Dougherty
Executive Editor for History: William J. Lombardo
Director of Development for History: Jane Knetzger
Developmental Editor: Michelle McSweeney
Senior Production Editor: Bridget Leahy
Assistant Production Manager: Joe Ford
Senior Marketing Manager for U.S. History: Amy Whitaker
Editorial Assistants: Jennifer Jovin and Laura Kintz
Production Assistants: Elise Keller and Victoria Royal
Copy Editor: Linda McLatchie
Indexer: Leoni Z. McVey
Photo Researchers: Pembroke Herbert and Sandi Rygiel, Picture Research Consultants, Inc.
Permissions Manager: Kalina K. Ingham
Senior Art Director: Anna Palchik
Text Designer: Tom Carling, Carling Design, Inc.
Cover Designer: Billy Boardman
Cover Photo: Woman and Men Posing with Giant Log, ca. 1892. A woman and two men pose with a giant log that measured 18 feet in diameter. The log, in Tulare County, California, was measured with a 20-foot saw blade. © CORBIS
Cartography: Mapping Specialists Limited
Composition: Cenveo Publisher Services
Printing and Binding: RR Donnelley and Sons

President: Joan E. Feinberg
Editorial Director: Denise B. Wydra
Director of Marketing: Karen R. Soeltz
Director of Production: Susan W. Brown
Associate Director, Editorial Production: Elise S. Kaiser
Managing Editor: Elizabeth M. Schaaf

Library of Congress Control Number: 2011939422

Manufactured in the United States of America.

7 6 5 4 3 2
f e d c b a

For information, write: Bedford/St. Martin's, 75 Arlington Street, Boston, MA 02116 (617-399-4000)

ISBN: 978–0–312–66312-4 (Combined Edition)
ISBN: 978–0–312–56953-2 (Loose-leaf Edition)
ISBN: 978–0–312–66313-1 (Vol. 1)
ISBN: 978–0–312–56948-8 (Loose-leaf Edition)
ISBN: 978–0–312–66314-8 (Vol. 2)
ISBN: 978–0–312–56946-4 (Loose-leaf Edition)
ISBN: 978–0–312–56954-9 (Vol. A)
ISBN: 978–0–312–56947-1 (Vol. B)
ISBN: 978–0–312–56944-0 (Vol. C)

Acknowledgments: Acknowledgments and copyrights appear at the back of the book on page CR-1, which constitutes an extension of the copyright page. It is a violation of the law to reproduce these selections by any means whatsoever without the written permission of the copyright holder.

Preface

As authors, we continue to be deeply gratified that *The American Promise* is one of the most widely adopted texts for the U.S. history survey, reaching students at all levels and helping instructors in all classroom environments. We know from years of firsthand experience that the survey course is the most difficult to teach and the most difficult to take, and we remain committed to making this book the most teachable and readable introductory American history text available. In creating this fifth edition, we set out to develop a resource that is both recognizable and new.

Our experience as teachers continues to inform every aspect of our text, beginning with its framework. We have found that students need *both* the structure a political narrative provides *and* the insights gained from examining social and cultural experience. To write a comprehensive, balanced account of American history, we focus on the public arena — the place where politics intersects social and cultural developments — to show how Americans confronted the major issues of their day and created far-reaching historical change. To engage students in the American story and to portray fully the diversity of the American experience, we stitch into our narrative the voices of hundreds of contemporaries, provide a vivid and compelling art program, and situate American history in the global world in which students live. To help students read, understand, and remember American history, we provide the best in pedagogical aids. While this edition rests solidly on our original goals and premises, the book has also changed, largely in response to adopters who helped us see new ways that the book could work for their students.

Users of past editions have emphasized the central role that *The American Promise* plays in their introductory courses — both as an in-class tool for them to teach from and as a resource for students to study from independently. Our goal in this fifth edition was to make our text even more successful for all students and instructors, whether they are using it in class or at home, whether in print or online. Within the book's covers, we added more contemporary voices to enliven the narrative, more visuals that promote analytical skills, and more pedagogy to facilitate independent study and class discussion. In an effort to assist instructors to help their students meet specific learning objectives, our new pedagogy highlights historical interrelationships and causality, underscores the importance of global contexts in U.S. history, and models historical thinking.

To extend the text, our array of multimedia and print supplements has never been more abundant or more impressive. A range of options — from video clips to lecture kits on CD-ROM and much more — offers instructors endless combinations to tailor *The American Promise* to fit the needs of their classroom. (See pages xii–xv.) Students of all learning styles have more ways than ever to enhance their traditional textbook experience and make history memorable. The e-book, for example, allows students to zoom in on and more closely examine the text's hundreds of historical photographs and artifacts. The book companion site links to even more primary documents, including images, texts, and audiovisual files, and its Online Study Guide provides Web-based self tests, map exercises, and visual activities. By seamlessly connecting our text to its rich storehouse of digital resources, these supplements help students better understand the people whose ideas and actions shaped their times and whose efforts still affect our lives.

Our title, *The American Promise*, reflects our agreement with playwright Arthur Miller's conviction that the essence of America has been its promise. For millions, the nation has held out the promise of a better life, unfettered worship, equality before the law, representative government, democratic politics, and other freedoms seldom found elsewhere. But none of these promises has come with guarantees. As we see it, much of American history is a continuing struggle over the definition and realization of the nation's promise. Who are we, and what do we want to be? Abraham Lincoln, in the midst of what he termed the "fiery trial" of the Civil

War, pronounced the nation "the last best hope of Earth." Kept alive by countless sacrifices, that hope has been marred by compromises, disappointments, and denials, but it still lives. We believe that our new edition of *The American Promise,* with its increased attention to human agency, will continue to show students that American history is an unfinished story and to make them aware of the legacy of hope bequeathed to them by generations of Americans stretching back more than four centuries, a legacy that is theirs to preserve and build on.

Features

We know that a history survey textbook may be unfamiliar or challenging for many students. The benefit of this full-length format is that we have room to give students *everything* they need to succeed. Our book is designed to pique students' interest and to assist them in every way in their reading, reviewing, and studying for exams. We are pleased to draw your attention to three aspects of our textbook that make *The American Promise* stand out from the crowd — our visual program, pedagogical support, and special features.

Visuals. From the beginning, readers have proclaimed this textbook a visual feast, richly illustrated in ways that extend and reinforce the narrative. The fifth edition offers more than eight hundred contemporaneous **illustrations** — one-third of them new — along with innovative techniques for increasing visual literacy. Twelve new **Visualizing History** features show students how to examine the evidence through a wide spectrum of historic objects, including archaeological artifacts, furniture, paintings, photographs, advertisements, clothing, and political cartoons. In addition, one picture in each chapter includes a special **visual activity caption** that reinforces the skill of image analysis. More than three hundred **artifacts** — from dolls and political buttons to guns and sewing machines — emphasize the importance of material culture in the study of the past and make the historical account tangible.

Our highly regarded and thoroughly redesigned **map program,** with more than 170 maps in all, rests on the old truth that "History is not intelligible without geography." Each chapter offers, on average, four **full-size maps** showing major developments in the narrative and two or three **spot maps** embedded in the narrative that emphasize an area of detail from the discussion. To help students think critically about the role of geography in American history, we include **two critical-thinking map exercises** per chapter. Revised maps in the fifth edition illustrate new scholarship on topics such as the Comanche empire in the American Southwest and highlight recent events in the Middle East. Another unique feature is our brief **Atlas of the Territorial Growth of the United States,** a series of full-color maps at the end of each volume that reveals the changing cartography of the nation.

Throughout the text, a host of tables, figures, and other graphics enhance and reinforce the content. **Thematic chronologies** summarize complex events and highlight key points in the narrative. To support our emphasis on the global context of U.S. history, **Global Comparison figures** showcase data with a focus on transnational connections. In addition, occasional **Promise of Technology** illustrations examine the ramifications — positive and negative — of technological developments in American society and culture.

Pedagogy. As part of our ongoing efforts to make *The American Promise* the most teachable and readable survey text available, we paid renewed attention to imaginative and effective pedagogy. Each chapter begins with a concise but colorful **opening vignette** that invites students into the narrative with lively accounts of individuals or groups who embody the central themes of the chapter. New vignettes in this edition include the Grimké sisters speaking out against slavery, Frederick Jackson Turner proclaiming his frontier hypothesis, migrant mother Frances Owens struggling to survive in the Great Depression, and the experience of Vietnam War veteran Frederick Downs Jr. Each vignette ends with a **narrative overview** of all of the chapter's main topics. Major sections within each chapter have **introductory paragraphs** that preview the subsections that follow and conclude with **review questions** to help students check their comprehension of main ideas. **Running heads** with dates and topical headings remind students of chronology, and **callouts** draw attention to interesting quotations from a wide range of American voices. In addition, **key terms**, set in boldface type and grouped together at the end of the chapter, highlight important people, events, and concepts. All chapters culminate in a **conclusion,** which reexamines central ideas and provides a bridge to the next chapter, and a **Selected Bibliography,** which lists important books to jump-start student research and to show students that our narrative comes from scholarship.

The two-page **Reviewing the Chapter** section at the end of each chapter provides a thorough review guide to ensure student success. A list of **Key Terms**, grouped according to chapter headings, provides a starting point for self study and suggests important relationships among major topics, while an illustrated chapter **Timeline** gives clear chronological overviews of key events. Three sets of questions prompt students to think critically and to make use of the facts they have mastered. **Review Questions,** repeated from within the narrative, focus on a specific topic or event, and **Making Connections** questions prompt students to think about broad developments within the chapter. An **all-new set of Linking to the Past** questions cross-reference developments in earlier chapters, encouraging students to make comparisons, see causality, and understand change over longer periods of time. **Online Study Guide cross-references** at the end of the review section point students to free self-assessment quizzes and other study aids.

Special Features. We have been delighted to learn that students and instructors alike use and enjoy our special features. Many instructors use them for class discussion or homework, and students report that even when the special features are not assigned, they read these features on their own because they find them interesting, informative, and exceptional entry points back into the narrative text itself. Each boxed feature concentrates on a historical thinking skill or a habit of mind. We include features that focus on analyzing written or visual primary source evidence, and other features that pose intriguing questions about the past or America's relation to the world and thereby model historical inquiry, the curiosity at the heart of our discipline. For this edition, we have added a **new Visualizing History** feature to many chapters. Images such as Native American weaponry, Puritan furniture, nineteenth-century paintings, photographs by progressive reformers, early-twentieth-century advertisements, and twenty-first-century political cartoons are all presented as sources for examination. By stressing the importance of historical context and asking critical questions, each of these new features shows students how to mine visual documents for evidence in order to reach conclusions about the past.

Fresh topics and the addition of questions in our four enduring special features further enrich this edition. Each biographical **Seeking the American Promise** essay explores a different promise of America — the promise of home ownership or the promise of higher education, for example — while recognizing that the promises fulfilled for some have meant promises denied to others. New subjects in this edition include indentured servant Anne Orthwood and her struggle in colonial America, progressive reformer Alice Hamilton, World War I servicewoman Nora Saltonstall, Chinese scientist Qian Xuesen and his encounter with anticommunism in America, and Vietnamese immigrant-turned-politician Joseph Cao. In addition to these new topics, all Seeking the American Promise features now conclude with a **new set of Questions for Consideration** that help students explore the subject further and understand its significance within the chapter and the book as a whole.

Each **Documenting the American Promise** feature juxtaposes three or four primary documents to show varying perspectives on a topic or an issue and to provide students with opportunities to build and practice their skills of historical interpretation. Feature introductions and document headnotes contextualize the sources, and **Questions for Analysis and Debate** promote critical thinking about primary sources. New topics in this edition are rich with human drama and include "Hunting Witches in Salem, Massachusetts," "Mill Girls Stand Up to Factory Owners," and "The Press and the Pullman Strike."

Historical Questions essays pose and interpret specific questions of continuing interest in order to demonstrate various methods and perspectives of historical thinking. **New question sets** accompanying each of these features focus on a particular mode of inquiry: **Thinking about Evidence, Thinking about Beliefs and Values,** and **Thinking about Cause and Effect.** New to this edition is the feature "How Did America's First Congress Address the Question of Slavery?"

Beyond America's Borders features consider the reciprocal connections between the United States and the wider world and challenge students to think about the effects of transnational connections over time. With the goal of widening students' perspectives and helping students see that this country did not develop in isolation, these features are enhanced by new end-of-feature questions, **America in a Global Context.** New essays in this edition include "European Nations and the Peace of Paris, 1783" and "Global Prosperity in the 1850s."

Updated Scholarship

We updated the fifth edition in myriad ways to reflect our ongoing effort to offer a comprehensive text that braids all Americans into the national narrative and to frame that national narrative in a more global perspective. To do so, we have paid particular attention to the most recent scholarship and, as always, appreciated and applied many suggestions from our users that keep the book fresh, accurate, and organized in a way that works best for students.

In Volume One, we focused our attention on Native Americans, especially in the West, because of the publication of exciting new scholarship. In Chapter 6, we have incorporated into the narrative more coverage of Indians and their roles in various conflicts between the British and the colonists before the Revolution. Chapter 9 expands the coverage of American conflicts with Indians in the Southwest, adding new material on Creek chief Alexander McGillivray. Chapter 10 greatly increases the coverage of Indians in the West, with a new section devoted to the Osage territory and the impressive Comanche empire known as Comanchería. In addition, several new Visualizing History features — on ancient tools used in Chaco Canyon, on Aztec weaponry and its weaknesses in the face of Spanish steel, on Mohawk clothing and accessories, and on gifts exchanged between Anglos and Indians on the Lewis and Clark trail — highlight the significance of Native American material culture over the centuries.

Volume Two also includes expanded attention to Native Americans — particularly in Chapter 17, where we improved our coverage of Indian schools, assimilation techniques used by whites, and Indian resistance strategies — but our main effort for the fifth edition in the second half of the book has been to do more of what we already do best, and that is to give even more attention to women, African Americans, and the global context of U.S. history. In the narrative, we have added coverage of women as key movers in the rise of the Lost Cause after the Civil War, and we consider the ways in which the GI Bill disproportionately benefited white men after World War II. New features and opening vignettes focus on widely recognized as well as less well-known women who both shaped and were shaped by the American experience: the depression-era struggle of Florence Owens (the face of the famous Dorothea Lange photograph *Migrant Mother*), the workplace reforms set in motion by progressive activist Alice Hamilton, and the World War I service of overseas volunteer Nora Saltonstall. Chapter 16 includes new coverage of the Colfax massacre, arguably the single worst incidence of brutality against African Americans during the Reconstruction era. Chapter 27 provides new coverage of civil rights activism and resistance in northern states, and Chapter 28 increases coverage of black power and urban rebellions across the country. A new Visualizing History feature in Chapter 16 examines the Winslow Homer painting *A Visit from the Old Mistress*.

Because students live in an increasingly global world and need help making connections with the world outside the United States, we have continued our efforts to incorporate the global context of American history throughout the fifth edition. This is particularly evident in Volume Two, where we have expanded coverage of transnational issues in recent decades, such as the 1953 CIA coup in Iran, the U.S. bombing campaign in Vietnam, and U.S. involvement in Afghanistan.

In addition to the many changes noted above, in both volumes we have updated, revised, and improved the fifth edition in response to both new scholarship and requests from instructors. New and expanded coverage areas include, among others, taxation in the pre-Revolutionary period and the early Republic, the Newburgh Conspiracy of the 1780s, the overbuilding of railroads in the West during the Gilded Age, the 1918–1919 global influenza epidemic, finance reform in the 1930s, post–World War II considerations of universal health care, the economic downturn of the late 2000s, the Obama presidency, and the most recent developments in the Middle East.

Acknowledgments

We gratefully acknowledge all of the helpful suggestions from those who have read and taught from previous editions of *The American Promise*, and we hope that our many classroom collaborators will be pleased to see their influence in the fifth edition. In particular, we wish to thank the talented scholars and teachers who gave generously of their time and knowledge to review this book: Patricia Adams, *Chandler-Gilbert Community College*; Susan Agee, *Truckee Meadows Community College*; Jennifer Bertolet, *George Washington University*; Michael Bryan, *Greenville Technical College*; Kim Burdick, *Delaware Technical and Community College*; Monica Butler, *Seminole State College, Sanford*; Andria Crosson, *University of Texas San Antonio*; Lawrence Devaro, *Rowan University and Camden County College*;

Philip DiMare, *California State University, Sacramento*; Dorothy Drinkard-Hawkshawe, *East Tennessee State University*; Edward (Jim) Dudlo, *Brookhaven College*; John Duke, *Alvin Community College*; Aaron Edstrom, *University of Texas El Paso*; Brian Farmer, *Amarillo College*; Rafaele Fierro, *Tunxis Community College*; José Garcia, *University of Central Florida*; Cecilia Gowdy-Wygant, *Front Range Community College Westminster*; William Grose, *Wythevilla Community College*; Stephanie Lee Holyfield, *University of Delaware*; Johanna Hume, *Alvin Community College*; W. Sherman Jackson, *Miami University*; Michael Jacobs, *University of Wisconsin Baraboo/ Sauk County*; Kevin Kern, *University of Akron*; Barbara Martin, *University of Southern Indiana*; Alfonso John Mooney, *University of Oklahoma*; Christopher Paine, *Lake Michigan College*; George Sochan, *Bowie State University*; Joyce Thierer, *Emporia State University*; Kathryn Wells, *Central Piedmont Community College*; Steven White, *Bluegrass Community and Technical College*; and Tom Zeiler, *University of Colorado at Boulder*.

A project as complex as this requires the talents of many individuals. First, we would like to acknowledge our families for their support, forbearance, and toleration of our textbook responsibilities. Pembroke Herbert and Sandi Rygiel of Picture Research Consultants, Inc., contributed their unparalleled knowledge, soaring imagination, and diligent research to make possible the extraordinary illustration program.

We would also like to thank the many people at Bedford/St. Martin's who have been crucial to this project. No one contributed more than freelance developmental editor Michelle McSweeney, who managed the entire revision and oversaw the development of each chapter. The results of her dedication to excellence and commitment to creating the best textbook imaginable are evident on every page. We greatly appreciate the acute intelligence, attention to detail, and limitless tolerance for the authors' eccentricities that Michelle brought to this revision. We thank freelance editors Jan Fitter and Shannon Hunt for their help with the manuscript. Thanks also go to editorial assistant Laura Kintz for her assistance preparing the manuscript and to associate editor Jennifer Jovin, who provided unflagging assistance and who coordinated the supplements. We are also grateful to Jane Knetzger, director of development for history; William J. Lombardo, executive editor for history; and Mary Dougherty, publisher for history, for their support and guidance. For their imaginative and tireless efforts to promote the book, we want to thank Jenna Bookin Barry, Amy Whitaker, John Hunger, Sean Blest, and Stephen Watson. With great skill and professionalism, Bridget Leahy, senior production editor, pulled together the many pieces related to copyediting, design, and composition, with the able assistance of Elise Keller and the guidance of managing editor Elizabeth Schaaf and assistant managing editor John Amburg. Senior production supervisor Joe Ford oversaw the manufacturing of the book. Designer Tom Carling, copyeditor Linda McLatchie, and proofreaders Janet Cocker and Mary Lou Wilshaw-Watts attended to the myriad details that help make the book shine. Leoni McVey provided an outstanding index. The book's gorgeous covers were designed by Billy Boardman. New media editor Marissa Zanetti made sure that *The American Promise* remains at the forefront of technological support for students and instructors. Editorial director Denise Wydra provided helpful advice throughout the course of the project. Finally, Charles H. Christensen, former president, took a personal interest in *The American Promise* from the start, and Joan E. Feinberg, president, guided all editions through every stage of development.

Versions and Supplements

Adopters of *The American Promise* and their students have access to abundant extra resources, including documents, presentation and testing materials, the acclaimed Bedford Series in History and Culture volumes, and much much more. See below for more information, visit the book's catalog site at **bedfordstmartins.com/roark/catalog**, or contact your local Bedford/St. Martin's sales representative.

Get the Right Version for Your Class

To accommodate different course lengths and course budgets, *The American Promise* is available in several different formats, including three-hole punched loose-leaf Budget Books versions and e-books, which are available at a substantial discount.

- **Combined edition** (Chapters 1–31) — available in hardcover, loose-leaf, and e-book formats
- **Volume 1: To 1877** (Chapters 1–16) — available in paperback, loose-leaf, and e-book formats
- **Volume 2: From 1865** (Chapters 16–31) — available in paperback, loose-leaf, and e-book formats
- **Volume A: To 1800** (Chapters 1–10) — available in paperback format
- **Volume B: 1800–1900** (Chapters 10–20) — available in paperback format
- **Volume C: From 1900** (Chapters 21–31) — available in paperback format

The online, interactive **Bedford e-Book** can be examined or purchased at a discount at **bedfordstmartins.com/ebooks**. Your students can also purchase *The American Promise* in other popular e-book formats for computers, tablets, and e-readers.

Online Extras for Students

The book's companion site at **bedfordstmartins.com/roark** gives students a way to read, write, and study, and to find and access quizzes and activities, study aids, and history research and writing help.

FREE **Online Study Guide.** Available at the companion site, this popular resource provides students with quizzes and activities for each chapter, including multiple-choice self-tests that focus on important concepts; flashcards that test students' knowledge of key terms; timeline activities that emphasize causal relationships; and map quizzes intended to strengthen students' geography skills. Instructors can monitor students' progress through an online Quiz Gradebook or receive email updates.

FREE **Research, Writing, and Anti-plagiarism Advice.** Available at the companion site, Bedford's **History Research and Writing Help** includes the textbook authors' **Suggested References** organized by chapter; **History Research and Reference Sources,** with links to history-related databases, indexes, and journals; **More Sources and How to Format a History Paper,** with clear advice on how to integrate primary and secondary sources into research papers and how to cite and format sources correctly; **Build a Bibliography,** a simple Web-based tool known as The Bedford Bibliographer that generates bibliographies in four commonly used documentation styles; and **Tips on Avoiding Plagiarism,** an online tutorial that reviews the consequences of plagiarism and features exercises to help students practice integrating sources and recognize acceptable summaries.

Resources for Instructors

Bedford/St. Martin's has developed a wide range of teaching resources for this book and for this course. They range from lecture and presentation materials and assessment tools to course management options. Most can be downloaded or ordered at **bedfordstmartins.com/roark/catalog.**

HistoryClass for The American Promise. HistoryClass, a Bedford/St. Martin's Online Course

Space, puts the online resources available with this textbook in one convenient and completely customizable course space. There you and your students can access an interactive e-book and primary sources reader; maps, images, documents, and links; chapter review quizzes; interactive multimedia exercises; and research and writing help. In HistoryClass you can get all our premium content and tools and assign, rearrange, and mix them with your own resources. For more information, visit **yourhistoryclass.com**.

Bedford Coursepack for Blackboard, WebCT, Desire2Learn, Angel, Sakai, or Moodle. We have free content to help you integrate our rich content into your course management system. Registered instructors can download coursepacks with no hassle and no strings attached. Content includes our most popular free resources and book-specific content for *The American Promise*. Visit **bedfordstmartins.com/coursepacks** to see a demo, find your version, or download your coursepack.

Instructor's Resource Manual. The instructor's manual offers both experienced and first-time instructors tools for preparing lectures and running discussions. It includes chapter review material, teaching strategies, and a guide to chapter-specific supplements available for the text.

Guide to Changing Editions. Designed to facilitate an instructor's transition from the previous edition of *The American Promise* to the current edition, this guide presents an overview of major changes as well as of changes in each chapter.

Computerized Test Bank. The test bank includes a mix of fresh, carefully crafted multiple-choice, matching, short-answer, and essay questions for each chapter. It also contains the Historical Question, Documenting the American Promise, Seeking the American Promise, and Beyond America's Borders questions from the textbook and model answers for each. The questions appear in Microsoft Word format and in easy-to-use test bank software that allows instructors to easily add, edit, re-sequence, and print questions and answers. Instructors can also export questions into a variety of formats, including WebCT and Blackboard.

***The Bedford Lecture Kit*: Maps, Images, Lecture Outlines, and i>clicker Content.** Look good and save time with *The Bedford Lecture Kit*. These presentation materials are downloadable individually from the Instructor Resources tab at **bedfordstmartins.com/roark/catalog** and are available on *The Bedford Lecture Kit* Instructor's Resource CD-ROM. They provide ready-made and fully customizable PowerPoint multimedia presentations that include lecture outlines with embedded maps, figures, and selected images from the textbook and extra background for instructors. Also available are maps and selected images in JPEG and PowerPoint formats; content for i>clicker, a classroom response system, in Microsoft Word and PowerPoint formats; the *Instructor's Resource Manual* in Microsoft Word format; and outline maps in PDF format for quizzing or handing out. All files are suitable for copying onto transparency acetates.

***Make History* — Free Documents, Maps, Images, and Web Sites.** *Make History* combines the best Web resources with hundreds of maps and images, to make it simple to find the source material you need. Browse the collection of thousands of resources by course or by topic, date, and type. Each item has been carefully chosen and helpfully annotated to make it easy to find exactly what you need. Available at **bedfordstmartins.com/makehistory**.

***Reel Teaching: Film Clips for the U.S. History Survey*.** This DVD provides a large collection of short video clips for classroom presentation. Designed as engaging "lecture launchers" varying in length from 1 to 15 or more minutes, the 59 documentary clips were carefully chosen for use in both semesters of the U.S. survey course. The clips feature compelling images, archival footage, personal narratives, and commentary by noted historians.

***America in Motion: Video Clips for U.S. History*.** Set history in motion with *America in Motion*, an instructor DVD containing dozens of short digital movie files of events in twentieth-century American history. From the wreckage of the battleship *Maine*, to FDR's Fireside Chats, to Oliver North testifying before Congress, *America in Motion* engages students with dynamic scenes from key events and challenges them to think critically. All files are classroom-ready, edited for brevity, and easily integrated with PowerPoint or other presentation software for electronic lectures or assignments. An accompanying guide provides each clip's historical context, ideas for use, and suggested questions.

***The American Promise* via Dallas Tele-Learning Distance Learning Courses.** *The*

American Promise has been selected as the textbook for the award-winning U.S. history video-based courses *Shaping America: U.S. History to 1877* and *Transforming America: U.S. History since 1877* by Dallas TeleLearning at the LeCroy Center for Educational Telecommunications, Dallas County Community College District. Guides for students and instructors fully integrate the narrative of *The American Promise* into each course. For more information on these distance-learning opportunities, visit the Dallas TeleLearning Web site at **http://telelearning.dcccd.edu**, email **learn@dcccd.edu**, or call 972-669-6650.

Videos and Multimedia. A wide assortment of videos and multimedia CD-ROMs on various topics in U.S. History is available to qualified adopters through your Bedford/St. Martin's sales representative.

Package and Save Your Students Money

For information on free packages and discounts up to 50%, visit **bedfordstmartins.com/roark/catalog**, or contact your local Bedford/St. Martin's sales representative.

Bedford e-Book. The e-book for this title, described above, can be packaged with the print text at a discount.

***Reading the American Past,* Fifth Edition.** Edited by Michael P. Johnson, one of the authors of *The American Promise*, and designed to complement the textbook, *Reading the American Past* provides a broad selection of over 150 primary source documents, as well as editorial apparatus to help students understand the sources. Available free when packaged with the print text.

Reading the American Past e-Book. The reader is also available as an e-book. When packaged with the print or electronic version of the textbook, it is available for free.

The Bedford Series in History and Culture. More than one hundred fifty titles in this highly praised series combine first-rate scholarship, historical narrative, and important primary documents for undergraduate courses. Each book is brief, inexpensive, and focused on a specific topic or period. For a complete list of titles, visit **bedfordstmartins.com/history/series**. Package discounts are available.

Rand McNally Atlas of American History. This collection of more than eighty full-color maps illustrates key events and eras from early exploration, settlement, expansion, and immigration to U.S. involvement in wars abroad and on U.S. soil. Introductory pages for each section include a brief overview, timelines, graphs, and photos to quickly establish a historical context. Available for $3.00 when packaged with the print text.

Maps in Context: A Workbook for American History. Written by historical cartography expert Gerald A. Danzer (University of Illinois at Chicago), this skill-building workbook helps students comprehend essential connections between geographic literacy and historical understanding. Organized to correspond to the typical U.S. history survey course, *Maps in Context* presents a wealth of map-centered projects and convenient pop quizzes that give students hands-on experience working with maps. Available free when packaged with the print text.

The Bedford Glossary for U.S. History. This handy supplement for the survey course gives students historically contextualized definitions for hundreds of terms—from *abolitionism* to *zoot suit*—that they will encounter in lectures, reading, and exams. Available free when packaged with the print text.

U.S. History Matters: A Student Guide to World History Online. This resource, written by Alan Gevinson, Kelly Schrum, and the late Roy Rosenzweig (all of George Mason University), provides an illustrated and annotated guide to 250 of the most useful Web sites for student research in U.S. history as well as advice on evaluating and using Internet sources. This essential guide is based on the acclaimed "History Matters" Web site developed by the American Social History Project and the Center for History and New Media. Available free when packaged with the print text.

Trade Books. Titles published by sister companies Hill and Wang; Farrar, Straus and Giroux; Henry Holt and Company; St. Martin's Press; Picador; and Palgrave Macmillan are available at a 50% discount when packaged with Bedford/St. Martin's textbooks. For more information, visit **bedfordstmartins.com/tradeup**.

A Pocket Guide to Writing in History. This portable and affordable reference tool by Mary Lynn Rampolla provides reading, writing, and research advice useful to students in all history courses. Concise yet comprehensive advice on approaching typical history assignments, developing critical reading skills, writing effective history papers, conducting research, using and documenting sources, and avoiding plagiarism—enhanced with practical tips and examples throughout—have made this slim reference a best-seller. Package discounts are available.

A Student's Guide to History. This complete guide to success in any history course provides the practical help students need to be effective. In addition to introducing students to the nature of the discipline, author Jules Benjamin teaches a wide range of skills from preparing for exams to approaching common writing assignments, and explains the research and documentation process with plentiful examples. Package discounts are available.

Going to the Source: The Bedford Reader in American History. Developed by Victoria Bissell Brown and Timothy J. Shannon, this reader's strong pedagogical framework helps students learn how to ask fruitful questions in order to evaluate documents effectively and develop critical reading skills. The reader's wide variety of chapter topics that complement the survey course and its rich diversity of sources—from personal letters to political cartoons—provoke students' interest as it teaches them the skills they need to successfully interrogate historical sources. Package discounts are available.

America Firsthand. With its distinctive focus on ordinary people, this primary documents reader, by Anthony Marcus, John M. Giggie, and David Burner, offers a remarkable range of perspectives on America's history from those who lived it. Popular Points of View sections expose students to different perspectives on a specific event or topic, and Visual Portfolios invite analysis of the visual record. Package discounts are available.

Brief Contents

Contents

CHAPTER 11 The Expanding Republic, 1815–1840 320

CHAPTER 12 The New West and the Free North, 1840–1860 356

CHAPTER 13
The Slave South, 1820–1860 392

CHAPTER 14
The House Divided, 1846–1861 426

CHAPTER 15
The Crucible of War, 1861–1865 460

CHAPTER 16
Reconstruction, 1863–1877 498

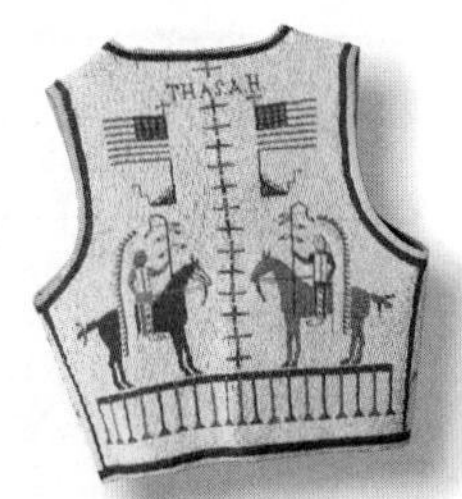

CHAPTER 17
The Contested West, 1865–1900 534

CHAPTER 18
Business and Politics in the Gilded Age, 1865–1900 568

CHAPTER 19
The City and Its Workers, 1870–1900 602

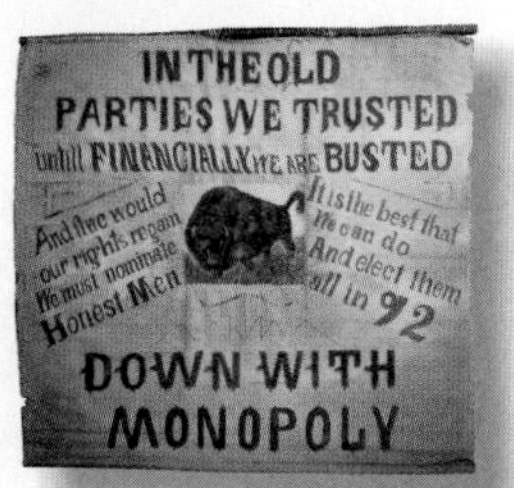

CHAPTER 20
Dissent, Depression, and War, 1890–1900 638

APPENDICES

I. Documents A-1

II. Facts and Figures: Government, Economy, and Demographics A-33

Maps, Figures, and Tables

Maps

Figures and Tables

Special Features

BEYOND AMERICA'S BORDERS

DOCUMENTING THE AMERICAN PROMISE

HISTORICAL QUESTION

THE PROMISE OF TECHNOLOGY

SEEKING THE AMERICAN PROMISE

VISUALIZING HISTORY

The American Promise

A History of the United States

FIFTH EDITION

PATRIOTIC PITCHER, 1800

This earthenware pitcher celebrates American military readiness. A militia officer strikes a springy pose near a cannon that juts out aggressively. Martial words frame the picture and provide a toast: "Success to America Whose Militia Is Better Than Standing Armies." The picture's swagger implies a military preparedness that was in fact woefully off the mark in 1800. Thousands of American-themed pitchers — with eagles and flags, Miss Liberty and George Washington — were marketed by British manufacturers. Pitchers saw daily use wherever people gathered to eat or drink, as in this country tavern scene painted by Philadelphia artist John Lewis Krimmel.

Pitcher: Kahn Fine Antiques/photo courtesy of Antiques and Fine Arts; background: Toledo Museum of Art.

10

Republicans in Power

1800–1824

THE NAME TECUMSEH TRANSLATES AS "SHOOTING STAR," A FITTING name for the Shawnee chief who reached meteoric heights of fame among Indians during Thomas Jefferson's presidency. From Canada to Georgia and west to the Mississippi, Tecumseh was accounted a charismatic leader, for which white Americans praised (and feared) him. Graceful, eloquent, compelling, astute: Tecumseh was all these and more, a gifted natural commander, equal parts politician and warrior.

The Ohio Country, where Tecumseh was born in 1768, was home to some dozen Indian tribes, including the Shawnee, recently displaced from the South. During the Revolutionary War, the region became a battleground with the "Big Knives," as the Shawnee people called the Americans. Tecumseh's childhood was marked by repeated violence and the loss of his father and two brothers in battle. The Revolution's end in 1783 brought no peace to Indian country. American settlers pushed west, and the youthful Tecumseh honed his warrior skills by ambushing pioneers flatboating down the Ohio River. He fought at the battle of Fallen Timbers, a major Indian defeat, but avoided the 1795 negotiations of the Treaty of Greenville, in which half a dozen dispirited tribes ceded much of Ohio to the Big Knives. In frustration, he watched as seven treaties between 1802 and 1805 whittled away more Indian land.

Some Indians, resigned and tired, looked for ways to accommodate, taking up farming, trade, and even intermarriage with the Big Knives. Others spent their treaty payments on alcohol. Tecumseh's younger brother Tenskwatawa led an embittered life of idleness and drink. But Tecumseh rejected accommodation and instead campaigned for a return to ancient ways. Donning traditional animal-skin garb, he traveled around the Great Lakes region after 1805 persuading tribes to join his pan-Indian confederacy. The territorial governor of Indiana, William Henry Harrison, reported, "For four years he has been in constant motion. You see him today on the Wabash, and in a short time hear of him on the shores of Lake Erie or Michigan, or on the banks of the Mississippi, and wherever he goes he makes an impression favorable to his purpose."

Even Tecumseh's dissolute brother was born anew. After a near-death experience in 1805, Tenskwatawa revived and recounted a startling vision of meeting the Master of Life. Renaming himself the Prophet, he urged

Indians everywhere to regard whites as children of the Evil Spirit, destined to be destroyed.

Tecumseh and the Prophet established a new village called Prophetstown, located in present-day Indiana, offering a potent blend of spiritual regeneration and political unity that attracted thousands of followers. Governor Harrison admired and feared Tecumseh, calling him "one of those uncommon geniuses which spring up occasionally to produce revolutions."

President Thomas Jefferson worried about an organized Indian confederacy and its potential for a renewed alliance with the British in Canada. Those worries became a reality during Jefferson's second term in office (1805–1809). Although his first term (1801–1805) brought notable successes, such as the Louisiana Purchase and the Lewis and Clark expedition, his second term was consumed by the threat of war with either Britain or France, in a replay of the late-1790s tensions. When war came in 1812, the enemy was Britain, bolstered by a reenergized Indian-British alliance. Among the causes of the war were insults over international shipping rights and the capture of U.S. vessels. But the war also derived compelling strength from Tecumseh's confederacy. Significant battles pitted U.S. soldiers against Indians in the Great Lakes, Tennessee, and Florida.

Tecumseh
Several portraits of Tecumseh exist, but they all present a different visage, and none of them enjoys verified authenticity. This one perhaps comes closest to how Tecumseh actually looked. It is an 1848 engraving adapted from an earlier drawing that no longer exists, sketched by a French trader in Indiana named Pierre Le Dru in a live sitting with the Indian leader in 1808. The engraver has given Tecumseh a British army officer's uniform, showing that he fought on the British side in the War of 1812. Notice the head covering and the medallion around Tecumseh's neck, marking his Indian identity.
Library of Congress.

In the end, the War of 1812 settled little between the United States and Britain, but it was tragically conclusive for the Indians. Eight hundred warriors led by Tecumseh helped defend Canada against U.S. attacks, but the British did not reciprocate when the Indians were under threat. Tecumseh died on Canadian soil at the battle of the Thames in the fall of 1813. No Indian leader with his star power would emerge again east of the Mississippi.

The briefly unified Indian confederacy under Tecumseh had no counterpart in the young Republic's confederation of states, where widespread unity behind a single leader proved impossible to achieve. Republicans did battle with Federalists during the Jefferson and Madison administrations, but then Federalists doomed their party by opposing the War of 1812. After 1815, they ceased to be a major force in political life. The next two presidents, James Monroe and John Quincy Adams, congratulated themselves on the Federalists' demise and Republican unity, but in fact divisions within their own party were extensive. Wives of politicians increasingly inserted themselves into this dissonant mix, managing their husbands' politicking and enabling them to appear above the fray and maintain the fiction of a nonpartisan state. That it was a fiction became sharply apparent in the most serious political crisis of this period, the Missouri Compromise of 1820.

▸ Jefferson's Presidency

The nerve-wracking election of 1800, decided in the House of Representatives, stoked fears that party divisions would ruin the country. A panicky Federalist newspaper in Connecticut predicted that a victory by **Thomas Jefferson** would produce a bloody civil war and usher in an immoral reign of "murder, robbery, rape, adultery and incest." Similar fears were expressed in the South, where a frightful slave uprising seemed a possible outcome of Jefferson's victory. But nothing nearly so dramatic occurred. Jefferson later called his election the "revolution of 1800," referring to his repudiation of Federalist practices and his cutbacks in military spending and taxes. While he cherished a republican simplicity in governance, he inevitably encountered events that required decisive and sometimes expensive government action. One early example came when pirates repeatedly threatened American ships off the north coast of Africa.

Turbulent Times: Election and Rebellion

The result of the election of 1800 (Map 10.1) remained uncertain from polling times in the late fall to repeated roll call votes in the House of Representatives in February 1801. Federalist John Adams, never secure in his leadership of the Federalist Party, was no longer in the presidential race once it reached the House. Instead, the contest was between Jefferson and his running mate, Senator **Aaron Burr** of New York. Republican voters in the electoral college slipped up, giving Jefferson and Burr an equal number of votes, an outcome possible because of the single balloting to choose both president and vice president. (To fix this problem, the Twelfth Amendment to the Constitution, adopted in 1804, provided for distinct ballots for the two offices.) The vain and ambitious Burr declined to concede, so the sitting Federalist-dominated House of Representatives got to choose the president.

Each state delegation had one vote, and nine were needed to win. Some Federalists preferred Burr, believing that his character flaws made him susceptible to Federalist pressure. But the influential Alexander Hamilton, though no friend of Jefferson, recognized that the high-strung Burr would be more dangerous in the presidency. Jefferson was a "contemptible hypocrite" in Hamilton's opinion, but at least he was not corrupt. Jefferson received the votes of eight states on the first ballot. Thirty-six ballots and six days later, he got the critical ninth vote, as well as a tenth. This election demonstrated a remarkable feature of the new government: No matter how hard fought the campaign, the leadership of the nation could shift from one group to its rivals in a peaceful transfer of power effected by ballots, not bullets.

As the country struggled over its white leadership crisis, a twenty-four-year-old blacksmith named Gabriel, the slave of Thomas Prossor, plotted rebellion in Virginia. Inspired by the Haitian Revolution (see chapter 9), and perhaps directly informed of it by French slaves new to the Richmond area, Gabriel was said to be organizing a thousand slaves to march on the state capital of Richmond and take the governor, James Monroe, hostage. On the appointed day, however, a few nervous slaves went to the authorities with news of **Gabriel's rebellion**, and within days scores of implicated conspirators were jailed and brought to trial.

"I have nothing more to offer than what General Washington would have had to offer, had he been taken by the British and put to trial by them."

— A jailed slave accused of contemplating rebellion

MAP 10.1
The Election of 1800

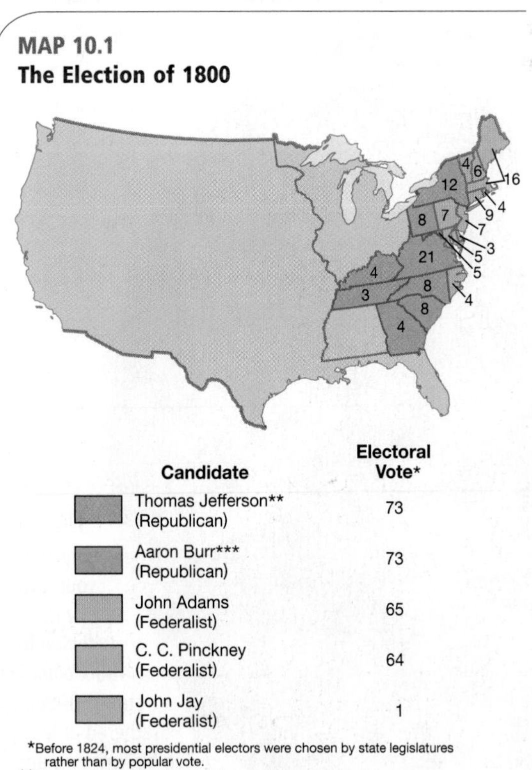

Candidate	Electoral Vote*
Thomas Jefferson** (Republican)	73
Aaron Burr*** (Republican)	73
John Adams (Federalist)	65
C. C. Pinckney (Federalist)	64
John Jay (Federalist)	1

*Before 1824, most presidential electors were chosen by state legislatures rather than by popular vote.
**Chosen president by House of Representatives.
***Chosen vice president by House of Representatives.

Pistols from the Burr-Hamilton Duel
In 1804, Vice President Aaron Burr shot and killed Alexander Hamilton with a .54-caliber pistol. Hamilton had long scorned Burr, and when a newspaper published Hamilton's disdain, Burr felt obliged to avenge his honor. Dueling, fully accepted in the South as an extralegal remedy for insult, had recently been outlawed in northern states. Burr was charged with a misdemeanor in New York, where the challenge was issued, and with homicide in New Jersey, where the duel was fought. After four months as a fugitive in the South, Burr resumed his official duties in Washington. He was never arrested. Courtesy of Chase Manhattan Archives.

One of the jailed rebels compared himself to the most venerated icon of the early Republic: "I have nothing more to offer than what General Washington would have had to offer, had he been taken by the British and put to trial by them." Such talk invoking the specter of a black George Washington worried white Virginians, and in the fall of 1800 twenty-seven black men were hanged for allegedly contemplating rebellion. Finally, Jefferson advised Governor Monroe to halt the hangings. "The world at large will forever condemn us if we indulge a principle of revenge," Jefferson wrote.

The Jeffersonian Vision of Republican Simplicity

Once elected, Thomas Jefferson turned his attention to establishing his administration in clear contrast to the Federalists. For his inauguration, held in the village called Washington City, he dressed in everyday clothing to strike a tone of republican simplicity, and he walked to the Capitol for the modest swearing-in ceremony. As president, he scaled back Federalist building plans for Washington and cut the government budget.

Martha Washington and Abigail Adams had received the wives of government officials at weekly teas, thereby cementing social relations in the governing class. But Jefferson, a longtime widower, disdained female gatherings and avoided the women of Washington City. He abandoned George Washington's practice of holding weekly formal receptions, limiting these drop-in gatherings to just two a year. His preferred social event was the small dinner party with carefully chosen politicos, either all Republicans or all Federalists (and all male). At these intimate dinners, the president exercised influence and strengthened informal relationships that would help him govern.

***Thomas Jefferson,* by John Trumbull**
This miniature portrait of Jefferson was made in the late 1780s, when the young widower lived with his two daughters and their attendant, the slave Sally Hemings. In 1802, a scandal erupted when a journalist charged that Jefferson had fathered several children by Hemings. DNA evidence from 1998, combined with historical evidence about Jefferson's whereabouts at the start of Hemings's six pregnancies, makes a powerful case that Jefferson fathered at least some of her children. Jefferson never commented about Hemings in his writings, and the written record on her side is entirely mute. Two of her four surviving children were allowed to slip away to freedom in the 1820s; the other two were freed in Jefferson's will. Monticello/Thomas Jefferson Memorial Foundation, Inc.

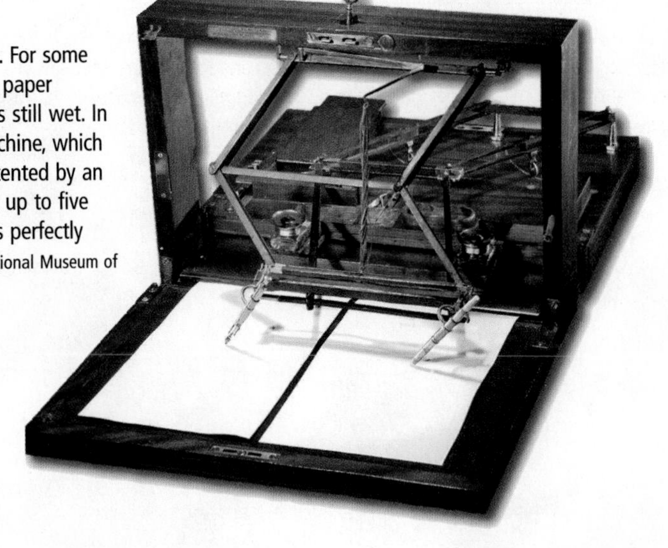

Jefferson's Duplicating Machine
Jefferson wrote tens of thousands of letters during his lifetime. For some years, he made copies of his work by pressing very thin tissue paper against manuscript pages whose patented slow-drying ink was still wet. In 1804, Jefferson acquired his first polygraph, or duplicating machine, which could produce four identical copies of a handwritten page. Patented by an Englishman and a Philadelphian in 1803, the polygraph linked up to five pens. The motion of the first pen, held in Jefferson's hand, was perfectly mimicked by the other pens, poised over tautly held paper. National Museum of American History, Smithsonian Institution, Behring Center.

Jefferson was no Antifederalist. He had supported the Constitution in 1788, despite his concern about the unrestricted reelection allowed to the president. But events of the 1790s had caused him to worry about the stretching of powers in the executive branch. Jefferson had watched with distrust as Hamiltonian policies refinanced the public debt, established a national bank, and secured commercial ties with Britain (see chapter 9). These policies seemed to Jefferson to promote the interests of money-hungry speculators and profiteers at the expense of the rest of the country. Financial schemes that seemed merely to allow rich men to become richer were corrupt and worthless, he believed, and their promotion by the federal government was not authorized by the Constitution. In Jefferson's vision, the source of true liberty in America was the independent farmer, someone who owned and worked his land both for himself and for the market.

Jefferson set out to dismantle Federalist innovations. He reduced the size of the army by a third, preferring "a well-disciplined militia" for defense, and he cut back the navy to just half a dozen ships. With the consent of Congress, he abolished all federal taxes based on population or whiskey. Government revenue would now derive solely from customs duties and the sale of western land. This strategy benefited the South, where three-fifths of the slaves counted for representation but not for taxation now. By the end of his first term, Jefferson had deeply reduced Hamilton's cherished national debt.

A properly limited federal government, according to Jefferson, was responsible merely for running a postal system, maintaining the federal courts, staffing lighthouses, collecting customs duties, and conducting a census once every ten years. The president had one private secretary, a young man named Meriwether Lewis, to help with his correspondence, and Jefferson paid him out of his own pocket. The Department of State employed only 8 people: Secretary James Madison, 6 clerks, and a messenger. The Treasury Department was by far the largest unit, with 73 revenue commissioners, auditors, and clerks, plus 2 watchmen. The entire payroll of the executive branch amounted to a mere 130 people in 1801.

However, one large set of government workers lay beyond Jefferson's command. His predecessor, John Adams, had made 217 last-minute appointments of Federalists to various judicial and military posts. Jefferson refused to honor those "midnight judges" who had not yet been fully processed. One disappointed job seeker, William Marbury, sued the new secretary of state, James Madison, for failure to make good on the appointment. This action gave rise to a landmark Supreme Court case, ***Marbury v. Madison***, decided in 1803. The Court ruled that although Marbury's commission was valid and the new president should have delivered it, the Court could not compel him to do so. What made the case significant was little noted at the time: The Court found that the grounds of Marbury's suit, resting in the Judiciary Act of 1789, were in conflict with the Constitution. For the first time, the Court acted to disallow a law on the grounds that it was unconstitutional.

Dangers Overseas: The Barbary Wars

Jefferson's desire to keep government and the military small met a severe test in the western Mediterranean Sea, where U.S. trading interests ran afoul of local Muslim states, leading to the first formal declaration of war against the United States by a foreign power. For well over a cen-

The Burning of the Frigate *Philadelphia* in Tripoli Harbor, 1804
After losing the warship *Philadelphia* to Tripolitan forces in 1803, American naval leaders decided to destroy it to prevent its use by the so-called pirates of North Africa. Commander Stephen Decatur engineered the daring nighttime raid. With his men concealed below decks of a modest trading vessel, Decatur entered the harbor and had his Arabic-speaking pilot secure permission to tie up next to the *Philadelphia*. The American raiding party quickly boarded, sending the Tripolitan guards into the water to swim to shore. In twenty minutes the warship was ablaze; Decatur departed with only one injured man and no fatalities. The Mariners Museum, Newport News, Virginia.

tury, four Muslim states on the northern coast of Africa — Morocco, Algiers, Tunis, and Tripoli, called the Barbary States by Americans — controlled all Mediterranean shipping traffic by demanding large annual payments (called "tribute") for safe passage. Countries electing not to pay found their ships at risk for seizure, with cargoes plundered and crews captured and sold into slavery. By the mid-1790s, the United States was paying $50,000 a year. About a hundred American merchant ships annually traversed the Mediterranean, trading lumber, tobacco, sugar, and rum for regional delicacies such as raisins, figs, capers, and medicinal opium.

In May 1801, when the pasha (military head) of Tripoli failed to secure a large increase in his tribute, he declared war on the United States. Jefferson had long considered such payments extortion, and he sent four warships to the Mediterranean to protect U.S. shipping. From 1801 to 1803, U.S. frigates engaged in skirmishes with Barbary privateers.

Then, in late 1803, the USS *Philadelphia* ran aground near Tripoli's harbor. Its three-hundred-man crew was captured along with the ship. In retaliation, a U.S. naval ship commanded by Lieutenant Stephen Decatur sailed into the harbor after dark, guided by an Arabic-speaking pilot to fool harbor sentries. Decatur's crew set the *Philadelphia* on fire, rendering the ship useless to its hijackers and making Decatur an instant hero in America. A later foray into the harbor to try to blow up the entire Tripoli fleet with a bomb-laden boat failed when the explosives detonated prematurely, killing eleven Americans.

In 1804, William Eaton, an American officer stationed in Tunis, felt the humiliation of his country's ineffectiveness. He requested a thousand Marines to invade Tripoli, but Secretary of State James Madison rejected the plan and another scheme to ally with the pasha's exiled brother to effect regime change. On his own, Eaton contacted the brother, assembled a force of four hundred men (mostly Greek and Egyptian mercenaries plus his Marines), and marched them over five hundred miles of desert for a surprise attack on Derne, Tripoli's second-largest city. Amazingly, he succeeded. The pasha of Tripoli yielded, released — for a fee — the prisoners taken from the *Philadelphia*, and negotiated a treaty with the United States that terminated tribute. One significant clause of the treaty stipulated that the United States "has in itself no character of enmity against the Laws, Religion or Tranquility of Musselmen [Muslims]" and that "no pretext arising from Religious Opinions, shall ever produce an interruption of the Harmony existing between the two Nations." Peace with the other Barbary States came in a second treaty in 1812.

The **Barbary Wars** of 1801–1805 cost Jefferson's government more money than the tribute demanded. But the honor of the young country was thought to be at stake. At political gatherings, the slogan "Millions for defense, but not a cent for tribute" became a popular toast.

REVIEW How did Jefferson attempt to undo the Federalist innovations of earlier administrations?

▸ Opportunities and Challenges in the West

While Jefferson remained cautious about exercising federal power, he quickly learned that circumstances sometimes required him to enlarge the authority of the presidency. Shifting politics in Europe in 1803 opened an unexpected door to the spectacular purchase from France of the Louisiana Territory. To explore the largely unmarked boundaries of this huge acquisition, Jefferson sent four separate expeditions into the prairie and mountains. The powerful Osage of the Arkansas River valley responded to overtures for an alliance and were soon lavishly welcomed by Jefferson in Washington City, but the even more powerful Comanche of the southern Great Plains stood their ground against all invaders. Meanwhile, the expedition by Lewis and Clark, the longest and northernmost trek of the four launched by Jefferson, mapped U.S. terrain all the way to the Pacific Ocean, giving a boost to expansionist aspirations.

The Louisiana Purchase

When the map of North America was redrawn in 1763, at the end of the Seven Years' War, a large expanse of the territory west of the Mississippi River shifted from France to Spain (see Map 6.2, page 164). Spain never controlled or settled the area centered on the Great Plains, which was already peopled by many Indian tribes, most notably the powerful and expansionist Comanche nation. New Orleans was Spain's principal stronghold in the region, a onetime French city strategically sited on the Mississippi River near its outlet to the Gulf of Mexico. Spain profited modestly from trade taxes it imposed on the small but growing flow of agricultural products shipped down the river from American farms in the western parts of Kentucky and Tennessee (to be sold at New Orleans or Caribbean destinations).

The biggest concern of the Spanish governor of New Orleans was that the sparse population of lower Louisiana was insufficient to ward off an anticipated westward movement of Americans. Spanish officials took steps to encourage European immigration, but only small numbers of Germans and French came. Up the river at St. Louis, the Spanish governor happily welcomed Native American refugees from the Northwest Territory who had been pushed out by what was termed a "plague of locusts" — American settlers — in the 1790s. Hoping that a Spanish-Indian alliance might be able to stop the expected demographic wave, he promised that the Spanish would "receive you in their homes as if you all belonged to our nation." Still, defending many hundreds of miles of the river against Americans on the move was a daunting prospect. "You can't put doors on open country," said an adviser to the Spanish king.

Thus, in 1800 Spain struck a secret deal to return this trans-Mississippi territory to France, in the hopes that a French Louisiana would provide a buffer zone between Spain's more valuable holdings in Mexico and the land-hungry Americans. The French emperor Napoleon accepted the transfer and agreed to Spain's condition that France could not sell Louisiana to anyone without Spain's permission.

From the U.S. perspective, Spain had proved a weak western neighbor, but France was another story. Jefferson was so alarmed by the rumored transfer that he instructed Robert R. Livingston, America's minister in France, to approach the French and offer to buy New Orleans. At first, the French denied they owned the city. But when Livingston hinted that the United States might seize it if buying was not an option, the French negotiator asked him to name his price for the entire Louisiana Territory from the Gulf of Mexico north to Canada. Livingston stalled, and the Frenchman made suggestions: $125 million? $60 million? Livingston shrewdly stalled some more and within days accepted the bargain price of $15 million (Map 10.2).

> **"You can't put doors on open country."**
> — An advisor to the Spanish king

On the verge of war with Britain, France needed both money and friendly neutrality from the United States, and it got both from the quick sale of the Louisiana Territory. In addition, the recent and costly loss of Haiti as a colony made a French presence in New Orleans less feasible as well. But in selling Louisiana to the United States, France had broken its agreement with Spain, which protested that the sale was illegal.

Moreover, there was no consensus on the western border of this land transfer. Spain claimed that the border was about one hundred miles west of the Mississippi River, while in Jefferson's eyes it was some eight hundred miles farther west, defined by the crest of the Rocky Mountains. When Livingston pressured the French negotiator to clarify his country's understanding of the

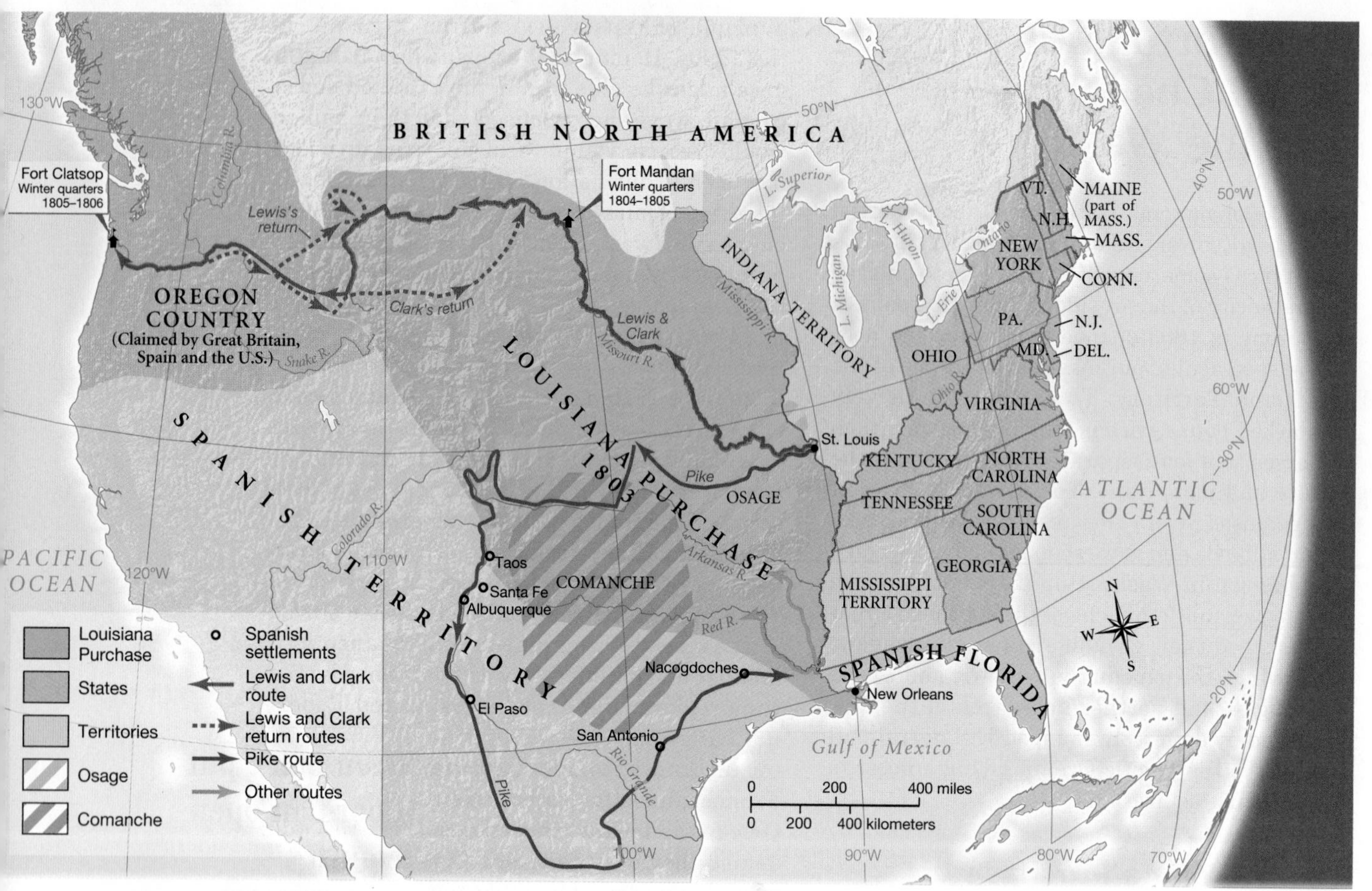

MAP ACTIVITY

Map 10.2 Jefferson's Expeditions in the West, 1804–1806
The Louisiana Purchase of 1803 brought the U.S. a large territory without clear boundaries. Jefferson sent off four scientific expeditions to take stock of the land's possibilities and to assess the degree of potential antagonism from Indian and Spanish inhabitants.

READING THE MAP: How did the size of the newly acquired territory compare to the land area of the existing American states and territories? What natural features of the land might have suggested boundaries for the Louisiana Purchase? Did those natural features coincide with actual patterns of human habitation already in place?
CONNECTIONS: What political events in Europe created the opportunity for the Jefferson administration to purchase Louisiana? How did the acquisition of Louisiana affect Spain's hold on North America?

boundary, the negotiator replied, "I can give you no direction. You have made a noble bargain for yourself, and I suppose you will make the most of it."

Jefferson and most members of Congress were delighted with the **Louisiana Purchase**. In late 1803, the American army took formal control of the Louisiana Territory, and the United States nearly doubled in size — at least on paper. The Spanish inhabitants of New Orleans had relinquished the city to a few French officials just a month before the Americans arrived to claim it, and now many of the Spaniards left for Texas or West Florida (along the Gulf coast), lands still in Spanish hands. One departing Spanish officer expressed his loathing for the "ambitious, restless, lawless, conniving, changeable, and turbulent" Americans, writing, "I am so disgusted with hearing them that I can hardly wait to leave them behind me."

The Lewis and Clark Expedition

Jefferson quickly launched four government-financed expeditions up the river valleys of the new territory to establish relationships with Indian tribes and to determine Spanish influence and presence. The first set out in 1804 to explore the upper reaches of the Missouri River. Jefferson appointed twenty-eight-year-old Meriwether Lewis, his secretary, to head the expedition and instructed him to investigate Indian cultures, to collect plant and animal specimens, and to chart the geography of the West, with particular attention to locating the headwaters of the rivers "running southwardly" to Spain's settlements. (See "Visualizing History," page 298.) The expedition was also charged with scouting locations for military posts, negotiating fur trade agreements, and identifying river routes to the West (see Map 10.2).

For his co-leader, Lewis chose Kentuckian William Clark, a veteran of the 1790s Indian wars. Together, they handpicked a crew of forty-five, including expert rivermen, gunsmiths, hunters, interpreters, a cook, and Clark's slave named York. The explorers left St. Louis in the spring of 1804, working their way northwest up the Missouri River. They camped for the winter at a Mandan village in what is now central North Dakota. The Mandan Indians were familiar with British and French traders from Canada, but the black man York created a sensation. Reportedly, the Indians rubbed moistened fingers over the man's skin to see if the color was painted on.

The following spring, the explorers headed west, accompanied by a sixteen-year-old Shoshoni woman named **Sacajawea**. Kidnapped by Mandans at about age ten, she had been sold to a French trapper as a slave/wife. Hers was not a unique story among Indian women, and such women knew several languages, making them valuable translators and mediators. Further, Sacajawea and her new baby allowed the American expedition to appear peaceful to suspicious tribes. As Lewis wrote in his journal, "No woman ever accompanies a war party of Indians in this quarter."

The **Lewis and Clark expedition** reached the Pacific Ocean at the mouth of the Columbia River in November 1805. When the two leaders returned home the following year, they were greeted as national heroes. They had established favorable relations with dozens of Indian tribes; they had collected invaluable information on the peoples, soils, plants, animals, and geography of the West; and they had inspired a nation of restless explorers and solitary imitators.

Osage and Comanche Indians

The three additional U.S. expeditions set forth between 1804 and 1806 from the Mississippi River to probe the contested southwestern border of the Louisiana Purchase. The first exploring

Comanche Feats of Horsemanship, 1834
Pennsylvania artist George Catlin toured the Great Plains and captured Comanche equestrian warfare in training. "Every young man," Catlin wrote, learned "to drop his body upon the side of his horse at the instant he is passing, effectually screened from his enemies' weapons. . . . [H]e will hang whilst his horse is at fullest speed, carrying with him his bow and his shield, and also his long lance . . . which he will wield upon his enemy as he passes; rising and throwing his arrows over the horse's back, or with equal ease and equal success under the horse's neck."
Smithsonian American Art Museum, Washington, DC/Art Resource, NY.

VISUALIZING HISTORY

Cultural Exchange on the Lewis and Clark Trail

Lewis and Clark carried many gifts for the Indians they anticipated meeting as they traveled up the Missouri River toward the Rocky Mountains. Intended to signal goodwill and respect, some of the gifts held other subtle meanings as well.

Upon encountering new tribes, the explorers presented high-ranking Indian leaders with silver medals bearing the likeness of President Jefferson, in two, three-, or four-inch sizes. Imagine the Indian recipients' reactions. What specific message might the image of the president convey? On what basis do you think the explorers chose to distribute the various sizes?

Thomas Jefferson's Peace Medal, 1801

The explorers traveled with ornamental trinkets ("ear bobs," silk handkerchiefs, ivory combs, ribbons) as well as practical goods (brass buttons, needles and thread, blankets, calico shirts) that demonstrated American manufacturing and handcraft. They carried a few small mirrors and magnifying glasses but on one occasion found that making fire with the latter engendered suspicion, not goodwill. Blue glass beads — portable and inexpensive — were a sought-after gift, leading Clark to observe that beads "may be justly compared to gold and Silver among civilized nations."

Blue Trade Beads

party left from Natchez, Mississippi, and ascended the Red River to the Ouachita River, ending at a hot springs in present-day Arkansas. Two years later, the second group of explorers followed the Red River west into eastern Texas, and the third embarked from St. Louis and traveled west, deep into the Rockies. This third group, led by Zebulon Pike, had gone too far, in the view of the Spaniards: Pike and his men were arrested, taken to northern Mexico, and soon released.

Of the scores of Indian tribes in this lower Great Plains region, two enjoyed reputations for territorial dominance. The **Osage** ruled the land between the Missouri and the lower Arkansas rivers, while the trading and raiding grounds of the **Comanche** stretched from the upper Arkansas River to the Rockies and south into Texas, a vast area called Comanchería. Both were formidable tribes that proved equal to the Spaniards. The Osage accomplished this through careful diplomacy and periodic shows of strength. The Comanche cemented their dominance by expert horsemanship; a brisk trade in guns, captives, and goods; and a constant readiness to employ strong-arm tactics and violence.

Jefferson turned his attention to cultivating the Osage, whose attractive lands (in present-day southern Missouri) beckoned as farmland in America's future. He directed Meriwether Lewis, on his way west, to invite the Osage to Washington City. When the delegation of eleven Osage leaders arrived in 1804, Jefferson greeted them as heads of state, with elaborate ceremonies and generous gifts. He positioned the Osage as equals of the Americans: "The great spirit has given you strength & has given us strength, not that we might hurt one another, but to do each other all the good in our power." Jefferson's goal was to make the Osage a strong trading partner, but he also had firm notions about what items to offer for trade: hoes and ploughs for the men; spinning wheels and looms for the women. These highly gendered tools signified a departure from the native gender system in which women tended crops while men hunted game. As Jefferson saw it, such equipment would bring the Indians the blessings of an agricultural civilization. Diminished reliance on the hunt would reduce the amount of land that tribes needed to sustain their communities. Jefferson expressed his hope that "commerce is the great engine by which we are to coerce them, & not war."

For their part, the Osage wanted Jefferson primarily to provide protection against Indian refugees displaced by American settlers east of the Mississippi. Jefferson's Osage alliance soon

Jefferson pointedly urged Lewis to take small hand-cranked corn mills, to acculturate the native women to American household technology. Indian women, with full charge of corn agriculture and its preparation as food, used mortars and pestles to pulverize dried kernels. Each time Lewis and Clark presented tribal chiefs with a corn mill and demonstrated its use, the recipients professed to be "highly pleased." Yet a year later, a fur trader visiting the Mandan nation wrote, "I saw the remains of an excellent large corn mill, which the foolish fellows had demolished to barb their arrows." Did the explorers perhaps fail in their mission by giving the mill to male leaders instead of to women? Or could this repurposing of the food grinder be read as a rejection by the women themselves of Americans' gendered practices?

Corn Mill Grinder

The explorers received gifts as well. The most impressive was the necklace shown here, made of thirty-five four-inch grizzly bear claws. The explorers encountered a number of Indian men wearing bear claw "collars" (Lewis's term for it). For many tribes, bears were sacred animals, and their claws embodied spiritual power. Grizzlies are large (up to nine hundred pounds) and aggressive, so acquiring so many claws without firearms clearly took extraordinary courage. Can you imagine the impact of wearing such an ornament when meeting visitors from a distant and unknown society? Was it a forceful show of courage and power? Why might Indians bestow this rare necklace on the explorers? Did it honor their manly courage? Or promote a spiritual brotherhood? Or might it have been intended to discourage further shootings of the sacred bears?

Grizzly Bear Claw Necklace

SOURCE: Jefferson's medal: Research Division of the Oklahoma Historical Society; trade beads: Ralph Thompson Collection of the North Dakota Lewis & Clark Bicentennial Foundation, Washburn, ND; corn mill: The Colonial Williamsburg Foundation; bear claw necklace: Peabody Museum, Harvard University, Photo 99-12-10/99700.

proved to be quite expensive, with costs arising from ransoming prisoners, providing defense, brokering treaties, and giving gifts all around. In 1806, a second ceremonial visit to Washington and other eastern cities by a dozen Osage leaders cost the federal government $10,000.

These promising peace initiatives were short-lived. By 1808, intertribal warfare was on the rise, and the governor of the Louisiana Territory declared that the U.S. government no longer had an obligation to protect the Osage. Jefferson's presidency was waning, and soon the practice of whittling away Indian lands through coercive treaties, so familiar to men like Tecumseh, reasserted itself. A treaty in 1808, followed by others in 1818, 1825, and 1839, shrank the Osage lands, and by the 1860s they were forced onto a small region in present-day Oklahoma.

By contrast, the Comanche managed to resist attempts to dominate them. For nearly a century, several branches of the tribe extended control over other tribes and over the Spaniards, holding the latter in check in small settlements clustered around Santa Fe in New Mexico and a few locations in Texas. Maps drawn in Europe marking Spanish ownership of vast North American lands simply did not correspond to the reality on the ground. One sign of Comanche success was their demographic surge during the mid- to late eighteenth century, owing both to their ability to take captives and blend them into their tribe and to their superior command of food resources, especially buffalo.

In 1807, a Comanche delegation arrived at Natchitoches in Louisiana, where a newly appointed U.S. Indian agent entertained them lavishly to demonstrate American power and wealth. In a highly imaginative speech, the agent proclaimed an improbable solidarity with the Comanche: "It is now so long since our Ancestors came from beyond the great Water that we have no remembrance of it. We ourselves are Natives of the Same land that you are, in other words white Indians, we therefore Should feel & live together like brothers & Good Neighbours." The Comanche welcomed the United States as a new trading partner and invited traders to travel into Comanchería to their market fairs. Into the late 1820s, this trade flourished on an extensive scale, with Americans selling weapons, cloth, and household metal goods in exchange for horses, mules, bison, and furs. And despite maps of the United States that showed the Red River just inside the southwestern border of the Louisiana

Purchase, the land from the Red north to the Arkansas River, west of Arkansas, remained under Indian control and thus off-limits to settlement by white Americans until the late nineteenth century (see Map 10.2).

REVIEW Why was Spain concerned that France sold the Louisiana Territory to the United States?

▸ Jefferson, the Madisons, and the War of 1812

Jefferson easily retained the presidency in the election of 1804, with his 162 electoral votes trouncing the 14 won by Federalist Charles Cotesworth Pinckney of South Carolina. Jefferson faced seriously escalating tensions with both France and Britain, leading him to try a novel tactic, an embargo, to stave off war. His Republican secretary of state, James Madison, followed Jefferson as president in 1808, again defeating Pinckney but by a much narrower margin.

Madison continued with a modified embargo, but he broke from Jefferson's all-male style of social networking by involving his gregarious wife, Dolley Madison, in serious politics. Under James Madison's leadership, the country declared war in 1812 on Britain and on Tecumseh's Indian confederacy. The two-year war cost the young nation its White House and its Capitol, but victory was proclaimed at the end nonetheless.

Impressment and Embargo

In 1803, France and Britain went to war, and both repeatedly warned the United States not to ship arms to the other. Britain acted on these threats in 1806, stopping U.S. ships to inspect cargoes for military aid to France and seizing suspected deserters from the British navy, along with many Americans. Ultimately, 2,500 U.S. sailors were "impressed" (taken by force) by the British, who needed them for their war with France. In retaliation against the **impressment** of American sailors, Jefferson convinced Congress to pass a nonimportation law banning a variety of British-made goods, such as leather products, window glass, and beer.

One incident made the usually cautious Jefferson nearly belligerent. In June 1807, the American ship *Chesapeake*, harboring some British deserters, was ordered to stop by the British frigate *Leopard*. The *Chesapeake* refused, and the *Leopard* opened fire, killing three Americans and capturing four alleged deserters— right at the mouth of the Chesapeake Bay, well within U.S. territorial waters. In response, Congress passed the **Embargo Act of 1807**, banning all importation of British goods into the country. Though a drastic measure, the embargo was meant to forestall war and make Britain suffer. All foreign ports were declared off-limits to American merchants to discourage illegal trading through secondary ports. Jefferson was convinced that Britain needed America's agricultural products far more than America needed British goods.

The Embargo Act of 1807 was a disaster. From 1790 to 1807, U.S. exports had increased fivefold, but the embargo brought commerce to a standstill. In New England, the heart of the shipping industry, unemployment rose. Grain plummeted in value, river traffic halted, tobacco rotted in the South, and cotton went unpicked. Protest petitions flooded Washington. The federal government suffered, too, for import duties were a significant source of revenue. Jefferson paid political costs as well and decided not to run for a third term. The Federalist Party, in danger of fading away after its weak showing in the election of 1804, began to revive.

The *Chesapeake* Incident, June 22, 1807

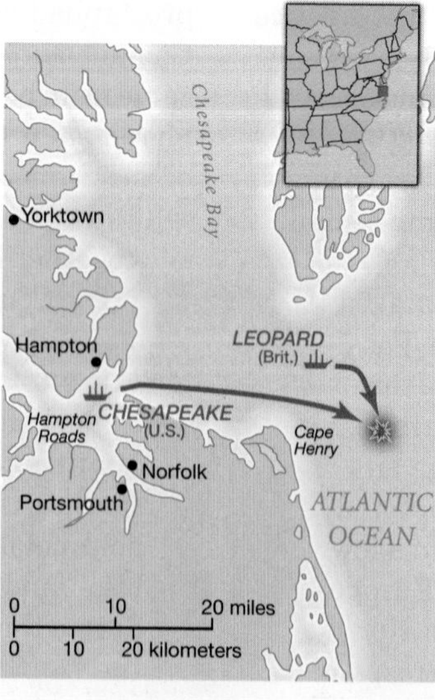

James Madison was chosen to be the Republican candidate by party caucuses — informal political groups that orchestrated the selection of candidates for state and local elections. The Federalist caucuses again chose Pinckney, and in the election he secured 47 electoral votes, compared to 14 in 1804; Madison's total was 122. Support for the Federalists remained centered in New England, whose shipping industry suffered heavy losses in the embargo. The Republicans still held the balance of power nationwide.

***Dolley Madison,* by Gilbert Stuart**
The "presidentress" of the Madison administration sat for this official portrait in 1804. She wears an empire-style dress, at the height of French fashion in 1804 and a style worn by many women at the coronation of the emperor Napoleon in Paris. The hallmarks of such a dress were a light fabric (muslin or chiffon), short sleeves, a high waistline from which the fabric fell straight to the ground, and usually a low, open neckline, as shown here.

Dolley Madison and Social Politics

As wife of the highest-ranking cabinet officer, **Dolley Madison** developed elaborate social networks during her first eight years in Washington. Hers constituted the top level of female politicking in the highly political city, since Jefferson had no First Lady. Although women could not vote and supposedly left politics to men, the female relatives of Washington politicians took on several overtly political functions that greased the wheels of the affairs of state. They networked through dinners, balls, receptions, and the intricate custom of "calling," in which men and women paid brief visits and left calling cards at each other's homes. Webs of friendship and influence in turn facilitated female political lobbying. It was not uncommon for women in this social set to write letters of recommendation for men seeking government work. Hostessing was no trivial or leisured business; it significantly influenced the federal government's patronage system.

When James Madison became president, Dolley Madison, called by some the "presidentress," struck a balance between queenliness and republican openness. She dressed the part in resplendent clothes, choosing a plumed velvet turban for her headdress at her husband's inauguration. She opened three elegant rooms in the executive mansion for a weekly open-house party called "Mrs. Madison's crush" or "squeeze." In contrast to George and Martha Washington's stiff, brief receptions, the Madisons' parties went on for hours, with scores or even hundreds of guests milling about, talking, and eating. Members of Congress, cabinet officers, distinguished guests, envoys from foreign countries, and their womenfolk attended with regularity. The affable and generous Mrs. Madison made her guests comfortable with small talk, but a female partygoer reported that "Mr. Madison had no leisure for the ladies; every moment of his time is engrossed by the crowd of male visitors who court his notice, and after passing the first complimentary salutations, his attention is unavoidably withdrawn to more important objects." His wife's weekly squeeze established informal channels of information and provided crucial political access, a key element of smooth governance.

> **"Mr. Madison had no leisure for the ladies; every moment of his time is engrossed by the crowd of male visitors who court his notice."**
> — A female guest at Mrs. Madison's "squeeze"

In 1810–1811, the Madisons' house acquired its present name, the White House, probably in reference to its white-painted sandstone exterior. The many guests at the weekly parties experienced simultaneously the splendor of the executive mansion and the atmosphere of republicanism that made it accessible to so many. Dolley Madison, ever an enormous political asset to her rather shy husband, understood well the symbolic function of the White House to enhance the power and legitimacy of the presidency.

Tecumseh and Tippecanoe

While the Madisons cemented alliances at home, difficulties with Britain and France overseas and with Indians in the old Northwest continued to increase. The Shawnee chief **Tecumseh** (see pages 289–90) actively solidified his confederacy, while the more northern tribes renewed their ties with supportive British agents and fur traders in Canada, a potential source of food and weapons. If the United States went to war with Britain, there would clearly be serious repercussions on the frontier.

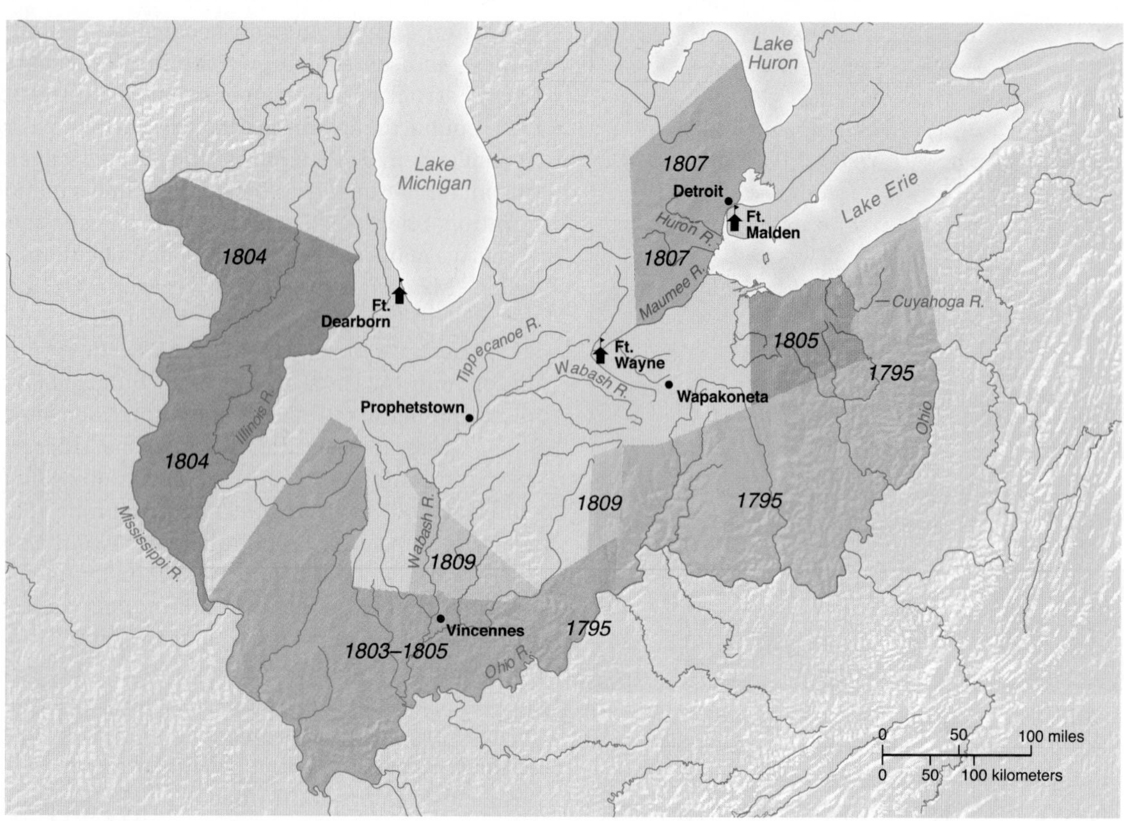

MAP 10.3
Indian Lands Ceded by Treaties in the Northwest Territory, 1795–1809
The Treaty of Greenville (1795) transferred two-thirds of Ohio to the Americans. For more than a decade thereafter, officials such as William Henry Harrison managed to acquire for the United States vast tracts along the Ohio and Mississippi rivers by negotiating with Indians whose authority to speak for their tribes was often unclear or dubious. "Land Cessions in the Old Northwest, 1795–1809." From *Tecumseh: A Life* by John Sugden. Copyright 1997 by John Sugden. Reprinted with the permission of Henry Holt and Company LLC.

Shifting demographics raised the stakes for both sides. The 1810 census counted some 230,000 Americans in Ohio only seven years after it achieved statehood. Another 40,000 Americans inhabited the territories of Indiana, Illinois, and Michigan. The Indian population of the entire region (the old Northwest Territory) was much smaller, probably about 70,000, a number unknown to the Americans but certainly gauged by Tecumseh during his extensive travels.

Up to 1805, Indiana's territorial governor, William Henry Harrison, had negotiated a series of treaties in a divide-and-conquer strategy aimed at extracting Indian lands for paltry payments (Map 10.3). But with the rise to power of Tecumseh and his brother **Tenskwatawa**, the Prophet, Harrison's strategy faltered. A fundamental part of Tecumseh's message was the assertion that all Indian lands were held in common by all the tribes. "No tribe has the right to sell [these lands], even to each other, much less to strangers . . . ," Tecumseh said. "Sell a country! Why not sell the air, the great sea, as well as the earth? Didn't the Great Spirit make them all for the use of his children?" In 1809, while Tecumseh was away on a recruiting trip, Harrison assembled the leaders of the Potawatomi, Miami, and Delaware tribes to negotiate the Treaty of Fort Wayne. After promising (falsely) that this was the last cession of land the United States would seek, Harrison secured three million acres at about two cents per acre.

When he returned, Tecumseh was furious with both Harrison and the tribal leaders. Leaving his brother in charge at Prophetstown on the Tippecanoe River, the Shawnee chief left to seek alliances with tribes in the South. In November 1811, Harrison decided to attack Prophetstown with a thousand men. The two-hour battle resulted in the deaths of sixty-two Americans and forty

Indians before the Prophet's forces fled the town, which Harrison's men set on fire. The **battle of Tippecanoe** was heralded as a glorious victory for the Americans, but Tecumseh was now more ready than ever to make war on the United States.

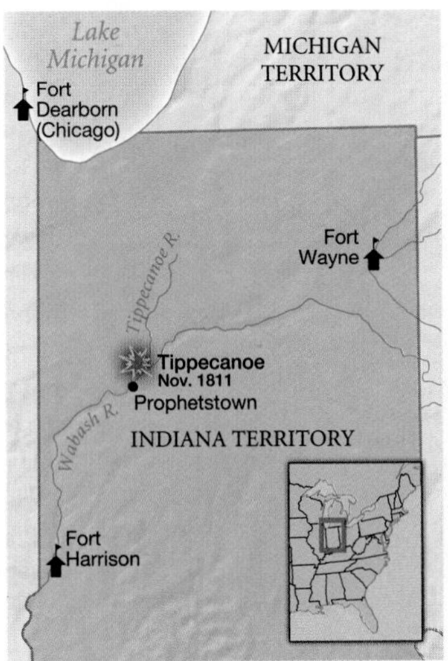

Battle of Tippecanoe, 1811

The War of 1812

The Indian conflicts in the old Northwest soon merged into the wider conflict with Britain, now known as the War of 1812. In 1809, Congress replaced Jefferson's stringent embargo with the Non-Intercourse Act, which prohibited trade only with Britain and France and their colonies, thus restoring trade with other European countries to alleviate somewhat the anguish of shippers, farmers, and planters. By 1811, the country was seriously divided and on the verge of war.

The new Congress seated in March 1811 contained several dozen young Republicans eager to avenge the insults from abroad. Thirty-four-year-old **Henry Clay** from Kentucky and twenty-nine-year-old John C. Calhoun from South Carolina became the center of a group informally known as the **War Hawks**. Mostly lawyers by profession, they came from the West and South and welcomed a war with Britain both to justify attacks on the Indians and to bring an end to impressment. Many were also expansionists, looking to occupy Florida and threaten Canada. Clay was elected Speaker of the House, an extraordinary honor for a newcomer. Calhoun won a seat on the Foreign Relations Committee. The War Hawks approved major defense expenditures, and the army soon quadrupled in size.

In June 1812, Congress declared war on Great Britain in a vote divided along sectional lines: New England and some Middle Atlantic states opposed the war, fearing its effect on commerce, while the South and West were strongly for it. Ironically, Britain had just announced that it would stop the search and seizure of American ships, but the war momentum would not be slowed. The Foreign Relations Committee issued an elaborate justification titled *Report on the Causes and Reasons for War*, written mainly by Calhoun and containing extravagant language about Britain's "lust for power," "unbounded tyranny," and "mad ambition." These were fighting words in a war that was in large measure about insult and honor.

The War Hawks proposed an invasion of Canada, confidently predicting victory in four weeks. Instead, the war lasted two and a half years, and Canada never fell. The northern invasion turned out to be a series of blunders that revealed America's grave unpreparedness for war against the unexpectedly powerful British and Indian forces. Detroit quickly fell, as did Fort Dearborn, site

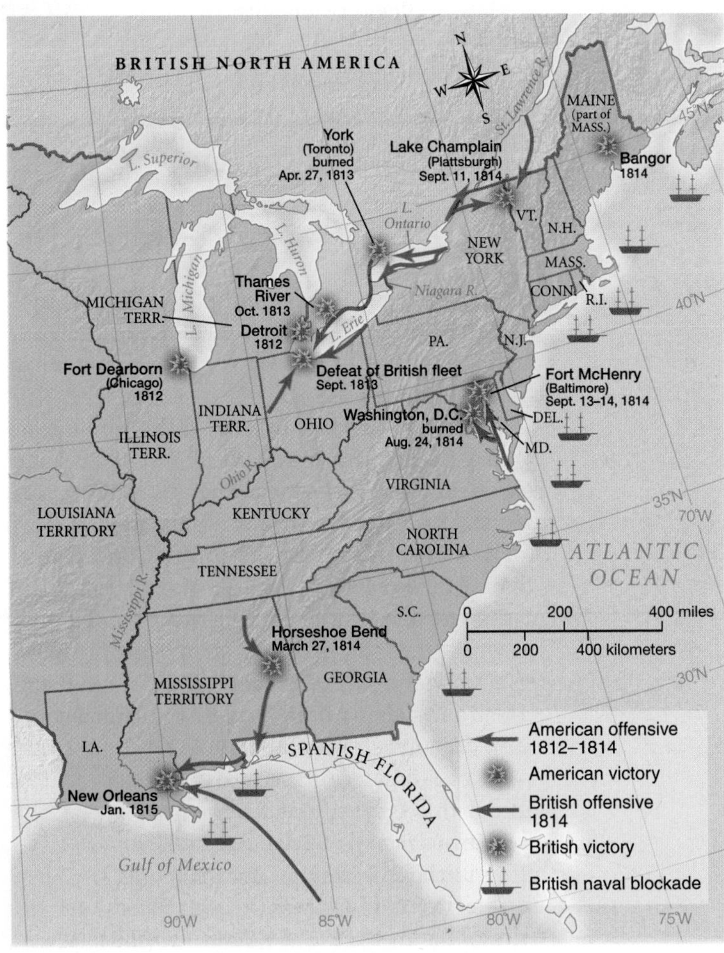

MAP 10.4
The War of 1812
During the War of 1812, battles were fought along the Canadian border and in the Chesapeake region. The most important American victory came in New Orleans two weeks after a peace agreement had been signed in England.

The Burning of Washington City
On August 24, 1814, the British army entered the nation's capital and set government buildings ablaze. This British line engraving celebrates that victory, showing disciplined troops armed with torches. To the left behind the soldiers, the White House burns, as does the round dome of the Capitol in the distance. Some soldiers plundered for trophies of war that night. Shown here is James Madison's personal medicine chest, taken back to England by a British soldier. One of the soldier's descendants returned the souvenir to President Franklin D. Roosevelt in 1939.
Engraving: Anne S. K. Brown Military Collection, Brown University Library; medicine chest: FDR Library.

of the future Chicago (Map 10.4). By the fall of 1812, the outlook was grim.

Worse, the New England states dragged their feet in raising troops, and some New England merchants carried on illegal trade with Britain. While President Madison fumed about Federalist disloyalty, Bostonians drank East India tea in Liverpool cups. The fall presidential election pitted Madison against DeWitt Clinton of New York, nominally a Republican but able to attract the Federalist vote. Clinton picked up all of New England's electoral votes, with the exception of Vermont's, and also took New York, New Jersey, and part of Maryland. Madison won in the electoral college, 128 to 89, but his margin of victory was considerably smaller than in 1808.

In late 1812 and early 1813, the tide began to turn in the Americans' favor. First came some reassuring victories at sea. Then the Americans attacked York (now Toronto) and burned it in April 1813. A few months later, Commodore Oliver Hazard Perry defeated the British fleet at the western end of Lake Erie. Emboldened, General Harrison drove an army into Canada from Detroit and in October 1813 defeated the British and Indians at the battle of the Thames, where Tecumseh was killed.

Creek Indians in the South who had allied with Tecumseh's confederacy were also plunged into all-out war. Some 10,000 living in the Mississippi Territory put up a spirited fight against U.S. forces for ten months in 1813–1814. Even without Tecumseh's recruitment trip of 1811 or the War of 1812, the Creeks had grievances aplenty, sparked by American settlers moving into their territory. Using guns obtained from Spanish Florida, the Creeks mounted a strong defense. But the **Creek War** ended suddenly in March 1814 when a general named Andrew Jackson led 2,500 Tennessee militiamen in a bloody attack called the Battle of Horseshoe Bend. More than 550 Indians were killed, and several hundred more died trying to escape across a river. Later that year, General Jackson extracted from the defeated tribe a treaty relinquishing thousands of square miles of their land to the United States.

Washington City Burns: The British Offensive

In August 1814, British ships sailed into the Chesapeake Bay, landing 5,000 troops and throwing the capital into a panic. Families evacuated, banks hid their money, and government clerks carted away boxes of important papers. Dolley Madison, with dinner for guests cooking over the fire, fled with her husband's papers, leaving several struggling servants to rescue a portrait of George Washington. As the cook related, "When the British did arrive, they ate up the very dinner, and drank the wines, &c.,

that I had prepared for the President's party." Then they torched the White House. They also burned the Capitol, a newspaper office, and a well-stocked arsenal. Instead of trying to hold the city, the British headed north and attacked Baltimore, but a fierce defense by the Maryland militia thwarted that effort.

In another powerful offensive that same month, British troops marched from Canada into New York State, but a series of mistakes cost them a naval skirmish at Plattsburgh on Lake Champlain, and they retreated to Canada. Five months later, another large British army landed in lower Louisiana and, in early January 1815, encountered General Andrew Jackson and his militia just outside New Orleans. Jackson's forces dramatically carried the day. The British suffered between 2,000 and 3,000 casualties, the Americans fewer than 80. Jackson became an instant hero. The **battle of New Orleans** was the most glorious victory the Americans had experienced, allowing some Americans to boast that the United States had won a second war of independence from Britain. No one in the United States knew that negotiators in Europe had signed a peace agreement two weeks earlier.

The Treaty of Ghent, signed in December 1814, settled few of the surface issues that had led to war. Neither country could claim victory, and no land changed hands. Instead, the treaty reflected a mutual agreement to give up certain goals. The Americans dropped their plea for an end to impressments, which in any case subsided as soon as Britain and France ended their war in 1815. They also gave up any claim to Canada. The British agreed to stop all aid to the Indians. Nothing was said about shipping rights. The most concrete result was a plan for a commission to determine the exact boundary between the United States and Canada.

Antiwar Federalists in New England could not gloat over the war's ambiguous conclusion because of an ill-timed and seemingly unpatriotic move on their part. The region's leaders had convened a secret meeting in Hartford, Connecticut, in December 1814 to discuss dramatic measures to curb the South's power. They proposed abolishing the Constitution's three-fifths clause as a basis of representation; requiring a two-thirds vote instead of a simple majority for imposing embargoes, admitting states, or declaring war; limiting the president to one term; and prohibiting the election of successive presidents from the same state. The cumulative aim of these proposals was to reduce the South's political power and break Virginia's lock on the presidency. New England wanted to make sure that no sectional party could again lead the country into war against the clear interests of another. The Federalists at Hartford even discussed secession from the Union but rejected that path. Coming just as peace was achieved, however, the **Hartford Convention** looked very unpatriotic. The Federalist Party never recovered its grip, and within a few years it was reduced to a shadow of its former self, even in New England.

No one really won the War of 1812; however, Americans celebrated as though they had, with parades and fireworks. The war gave rise to a new spirit of nationalism. The paranoia over British tyranny evident in the 1812 declaration of war was laid to rest, replaced by pride in a more equal relationship with the old mother country. Indeed, in 1817 the two countries signed the Rush-Bagot disarmament treaty (named after its two negotiators), which limited each country to a total of four naval vessels, each with just a single cannon, to patrol the vast watery border between them. The Rush-Bagot treaty was perhaps the most successful disarmament treaty for a century to come.

The biggest winners in the War of 1812 were the young men, once called War Hawks, who took up the banner of the Republican Party and carried it in new, expansive directions. These young politicians favored trade, western expansion, internal improvements, and the energetic development of new economic markets. The biggest losers of the war were the Indians. Tecumseh was dead, his brother the Prophet was discredited, the prospects of an Indian confederacy were dashed, the Creeks' large homeland was seized, and the British protectors were gone.

REVIEW Why did Congress declare war on Great Britain in 1812?

▶ Women's Status in the Early Republic

Dolley Madison's pioneering role as "presidentress" showed that at the pinnacles of power, elite women could assume an active presence in civic affairs. But, as with the 1790s cultural compromise that endorsed female education to make women into better wives and mothers (see chapter 9), Mrs. Madison and her female circle practiced politics to further their husbands' careers. There was little talk of the "rights of woman."

From 1800 to 1825, key institutions central to the shaping of women's lives — the legal system, marriage, and religion — proved fairly resistant to change. State legislatures and the courts maintained the legal dependency of married white women in a country whose defining characteristic for men was independence. Marriage laws for whites continued to support unequal power between men and women, while religious organizations reconsidered the role of women in church governance in the face of rising church membership rates for women. The most dramatic opportunity for women came with the flowering of female academies whose rigorous curricula fostered high-level literacy and rational thought. Even when advertised as institutions to prepare girls to be intelligent mothers, many academies built up their students' self-confidence and implanted expectations that their mental training would find a use beyond the kitchen and nursery.

Women and the Law

The Anglo-American view of women, embedded in English common law, was that wives had no independent legal or political personhood. The legal doctrine of ***feme covert*** (covered woman) held that a wife's civic life was completely subsumed by her husband's. A wife was obligated to obey her husband; her property was his, her domestic and sexual services were his, and even their children were legally his. Women had no right to keep their wages, to make contracts, or to sue or be sued.

State legislatures generally passed up the opportunity to rewrite the laws of domestic relations even though they redrafted other British laws in light of republican principles. Lawyers never paused to defend, much less to challenge, the assumption that unequal power relations lay at the heart of marriage.

The one aspect of family law that changed in the early Republic was divorce. Before the Revolution, only New England jurisdictions recognized a limited right to divorce; by 1820, every state except South Carolina did so. However, divorce was uncommon and in many states could be obtained only by petition to the state's legislature, a daunting obstacle for many ordinary people. A mutual wish to terminate a marriage was never sufficient grounds for a legal divorce. A New York judge affirmed that "it would be aiming a deadly blow at public morals to decree a dissolution of the marriage contract merely because the parties requested it. Divorces should never be allowed, except for the protection of the innocent party, and for the punishment of the guilty." States upheld the institution of marriage both to protect persons they thought of as naturally dependent (women and children) and to regulate the use and inheritance of property. (Unofficial self-divorce, desertion, and bigamy were remedies that ordinary people sometimes chose to get around the law, but all were socially unacceptable.) Legal enforcement of marriage as an unequal relationship played a major role in maintaining gender inequality in the nineteenth century.

Single adult women could own and convey property, make contracts, initiate lawsuits, and pay taxes. They could not vote (except in New Jersey before 1807), serve on juries, or practice law, so their civil status was limited. Single women's economic status was often limited as well, by custom as much as by law. Job prospects were few and low-paying. Unless they had inherited adequate property or could live with married siblings, single adult women in the early Republic very often were poor.

None of the legal institutions that structured white gender relations applied to black slaves. As property themselves, under the jurisdiction of slave owners, they could not freely consent to any contractual obligations, including marriage. The protective features of state-sponsored unions were thus denied to black men and women in slavery. But this also meant that slave unions did not establish unequal power relations between partners backed by the force of law, as did marriages among the free.

Women and Church Governance

In most Protestant denominations around 1800, white women made up the majority of congregants. Yet church leadership of most denominations rested in men's hands. There were some exceptions, however. In Baptist congregations in New England, women served along with men on church governance committees, deciding on the admission of new members, voting on hiring ministers, and even debating doctrinal points. Quakers, too, had a history of recognizing women's spiritual talents. Some were accorded the status of minister, capable of leading and speaking in Quaker meetings.

Between 1790 and 1820, a small and highly unusual set of women actively engaged in open preaching. Most were from Freewill Baptist

Women and the Church: Jemima Wilkinson
In this early woodcut, Jemima Wilkinson, "the Publick Universal Friend," wears a clerical collar and body-obscuring robe, in keeping with the claim that the former Jemima was now a person without gender. With hair pulled back tight on the head and curled at the neck in a masculine style of the 1790s, was Wilkinson masculinized, or did the "Universal Friend" truly transcend gender? Rhode Island Historical Society.

groups centered in New England and upstate New York. Others came from small Methodist sects, and yet others rejected any formal religious affiliation. Probably fewer than a hundred such women existed, but several dozen traveled beyond their local communities, creating converts and controversy. They spoke from the heart, without prepared speeches, often exhibiting trances and claiming to exhort (counsel or warn) rather than to preach.

The best-known exhorting woman was **Jemima Wilkinson**, who called herself "the Publick Universal Friend." After a near-death experience from a high fever, Wilkinson proclaimed her body no longer female or male but the incarnation of the "Spirit of Light." She dressed in men's clothes, wore her hair in a masculine style, shunned gender-specific pronouns, and preached openly in Rhode Island and Philadelphia. In the early nineteenth century, Wilkinson established a town called New Jerusalem in western New York with some 250 followers. Her fame was sustained by periodic newspaper articles that fed public curiosity about her lifelong transvestism and her unfeminine forcefulness.

The decades from 1790 to the 1820s marked a period of unusual confusion, ferment, and creativity in American religion. New denominations blossomed, new styles of religiosity gripped adherents, and an extensive periodical press devoted to religion popularized all manner of theological and institutional innovations. In such a climate, the age-old tradition of gender subordination came into question here and there among the most radically democratic of the churches. But the presumption of male authority over women was deeply entrenched in American culture. Even denominations that had allowed women to participate in church governance began to pull back, and most churches reinstated patterns of hierarchy along gender lines.

Female Education

First in the North and then in the South, states and localities began investing in public schools to foster an educated citizenry deemed essential to the healthy functioning of a republic. Young girls attended district schools, sometimes along with boys or, in rural areas, more often in separate summer sessions. Basic literacy and numeracy formed the curriculum taught to white children aged roughly six to eleven. By 1830, girls had made rapid gains, in many places approaching male literacy rates. (Far fewer schools addressed the needs of free black children, whether male or female.)

More advanced female education came from a growing number of private academies. Judith Sargent Murray, the Massachusetts author who had called for equality of the sexes around 1790 (see chapter 9), predicted in 1800 that "a new era in female history" would emerge because "**female academies** are everywhere establishing." Some dozen female academies were established in the 1790s, and by 1830 that number had grown to nearly two hundred. Candidates for admission were primarily daughters of elite families as well as those of middling families with elite or intellectual aspirations, such as ministers' daughters.

SEEKING THE AMERICAN PROMISE

One Woman's Quest to Provide Higher Education for Women

Talented young men seeking the mental enrichment and career boost of higher education saw their opportunities expand rapidly in the early Republic. By 1830, six dozen private and state-chartered institutions offered them training in science, history, religion, literature, and philosophy. Yet not a single one admitted females.

With the spread of district schools and female academies, however, the number of girls trained for advanced study was on the rise. The winning rationale for female education — that mothers molded the character of rising generations — worked well to justify basic schooling. But a highly intellectual woman, negatively termed a "bluestocking," was thought to put her very femininity at risk. Some critics sounded a more practical note: "When girls become scholars, who is to make the puddings and pies?"

The academic aspirations of Emma Hart — born in Connecticut in 1787 as the sixteenth in a farm family of seventeen children — were encouraged by her father, who read Shakespeare at night to his large brood. After graduating from the local district school and then an academy for girls, Emma taught for a term at the district school before moving to Vermont to head the Middlebury Female Academy, founded in 1800. There, she taught sixty adolescents in an underheated building.

Emma ran the academy for two years until her marriage in 1809 to an established Middlebury physician and banker named John Willard. Marriage for white women usually brought an end to employment outside the home. Yet despite caring for a baby and attending to her domestic duties, Emma found time to read books from her husband's well-stocked library. She read widely, from political philosophy to medical treatises, physiology texts, and even Euclid's geometry.

Four years into their marriage, John Willard suffered severe financial losses. This turn of events led Emma Willard to open an advanced girls' school in her home. She patterned her courses on those at nearby Middlebury College for men, and her rigorous curriculum soon drew students from all over the Northeast. One satisfied father with political connections persuaded the Willards to relocate to his home state of New York with the promise to help them secure state funding for a school.

Emma drew up a formal proposal in 1819, arguing that advanced female education would both enhance motherhood and supply excellent teachers needed for a projected state-supported school system. Though her proposal was endorsed by Governor DeWitt Clinton, John Adams, and Thomas Jefferson, the New York assembly failed to fund Willard's school. Local citizens in Troy supplied Willard with a building, however, and in 1821 the Troy Female Seminary opened with students coming from many states. Willard deliberately chose the modest term "seminary" instead of "college," which was "the province of the men." Yet her rigorous curriculum did include "masculine" subjects such as Latin, Greek, mathematics, and science in addition to modern languages and

The three-year curriculum included both ornamental arts and solid academics. The former strengthened female gentility: drawing, needlework, music, and French conversation. The academic subjects included English grammar, literature, history, the natural sciences, geography, and elocution (the art of effective public speaking). Academy catalogs show that, by the 1820s, the courses and reading lists at the top female academies equaled those at male colleges such as Harvard, Yale, Dartmouth, and Princeton. The girls at these academies studied Latin, rhetoric, logic, theology, moral philosophy, algebra, geometry, and even chemistry and physics.

Two of the best-known female academies were the Troy Female Seminary in New York, founded by Emma Willard in 1821, and the Hartford Seminary in Connecticut, founded by Catharine Beecher in 1822. (See "Seeking the American Promise," page 308.) Unlike theological seminaries that trained men for the clergy, Troy and Hartford prepared their female students to teach, on the grounds that women made better teachers than did men. Author Harriet Beecher Stowe, educated at her sister's school and then a teacher there, agreed: "If men have more knowledge they have less talent at communicating it. Nor have they the patience, the long-suffering, and gentleness necessary to superintend the formation of character."

literature. Willard taught geometry and trigonometry herself and hired other teachers for classes in astronomy, botany, geology, chemistry, and zoology. She soon forged a cooperative alliance with the neighboring Rensselaer Polytechnic Institute. In direct emulation of Harvard and Princeton, her seminary also offered a required course in moral philosophy, which Willard herself taught to all senior students using the same texts employed at the male colleges.

Willard invited the public to weeklong examinations, where students solved algebra problems and geometry proofs on chalkboards and gave twenty-minute discourses on history and philosophy. Educated men were particularly encouraged to question the students, to put to rest any "lurking suspicion, that the learning which a female possesses must be superficial." One minister was astonished, and pleased, to see "Euclid discussed by female lips." By emphasizing geometry, Willard vindicated her claim that women could equal men in logic. But she took pains to make sure her students preserved "feminine delicacy" and avoided "the least indelicacy of language or behavior, such as too much exposure of the person."

More than the rigorous curriculum inspired these young women. Willard was an exemplary role model, beloved by many of her students for her dedication and confidence. A student named Elizabeth Cady, who attended the seminary in the 1830s and later became an important figure in the woman's rights movement, recalled that Willard had a "profound self respect (a rare quality in a woman) which gave her a dignity truly regal." Willard graciously gave much of the credit to her unusually supportive husband: "He entered into the full spirit of my views, with a disinterested zeal for the sex whom, as he had come to believe, his own had unjustly neglected."

The Troy Female Seminary flourished; it still exists today as the Emma Willard School. From 1821 to 1871, more than 12,000 girls attended; it was larger than most men's colleges. Ministers' daughters received a discount on tuition, and many girls were allowed to defer payment until they were wage-earning teachers. Nearly 5,000 graduates in the first fifty years became teachers, and some 150 directed their own schools scattered across the nation. When the marquis de Lafayette, aging hero of the American Revolution, visited Willard's school in 1824, he pronounced it a "Female University." Surely, Willard took pleasure in his recognition of her success.

Portrait of Emma Willard
Emma Hart Willard's calm composure shines through in this portrait. Emma Willard School.

Questions for Consideration

1. How did Emma Willard's own life demonstrate the importance of female education for a family's financial security?
2. Compare the occupation of Emma Willard with that of Dolley Madison. In what ways were these women similar? How did they differ?

The most immediate value of advanced female education lay in the self-cultivation and confidence it provided. Following the model of male colleges, female graduation exercises showcased speeches and recitations performed in front of a mixed-sex audience of family, friends, and local notables. Here, the young women's elocution studies paid off; they had learned the art of persuasion along with correct pronunciation and the skill of fluent speaking. Academies also took care to promote a pleasing female modesty. Female pedantry or intellectual immodesty triggered the stereotype of the "bluestocking," a British term of hostility for a too-learned woman doomed to fail in the marriage market.

By the mid-1820s, the total annual enrollment at the female academies and seminaries equaled enrollment at the near six dozen male colleges in the United States. Both groups accounted for only about 1 percent of their age cohorts in the country at large, indicating that advanced education was clearly limited to a privileged few. Among the men, this group disproportionately filled the future rosters of ministers, lawyers, judges, and political leaders. Most female graduates in time married and raised families, but first many of them became teachers at academies and district schools. A large number also became authors, contributing essays and poetry to newspapers,

An Academy Student's Embroidery
Girls in the burgeoning female academies studied grammar, history, geography, arithmetic, French, and sometimes Greek, Latin, and geometry, although study of ancient languages and abstruse math was sometimes criticized as an intrusion into male domains. Female students also learned ornamental sewing. This work of silk embroidery comes from South Carolina and probably dates from around 1800–1810, judging from the high-waisted dress style. It shows an accomplished student, with map and globe on the table. What do you think would be more challenging for a 14-year-old girl: to learn basic arithmetic or to embroider so expertly? Rivers Collection, Charleston.

editing periodicals, and publishing novels. The new attention to the training of female minds laid the foundation for major changes in the gender system as girl students of the 1810s matured into adult women of the 1830s.

REVIEW How did the civil status of American women and men differ in the early Republic?

▶ Monroe and Adams

With the elections of 1816 and 1820, Virginians continued their hold on the presidency. In 1816, **James Monroe** beat Federalist Rufus King of New York, garnering 183 electoral votes to King's 34. In 1820, the Republican Monroe was reelected with all but one electoral vote. The collapse of the Federalist Party ushered in an apparent period of one-party rule, but politics remained highly contentious. At the state level, increasing voter engagement sparked a drive for universal white male suffrage.

Many factors promoted increased partisanship. Monroe and his aloof wife, Elizabeth, sharply curtailed social gatherings at the White House, driving the hard work of social networking into competing channels. Ill feelings were stirred by a sectional crisis over the admission of Missouri to the Union, and foreign policy questions involving European claims to Latin America animated sharp disagreements as well. The election of 1824 brought forth an abundance of candidates, all claiming to be Republicans. The winner was John Quincy Adams in an election decided by the House of Representatives and, many believed, a backroom bargain. Put to the test of practical circumstances, the one-party political system failed and then fractured.

From Property to Democracy

Up to 1820, presidential elections occurred in the electoral college, at a remove from ordinary voters. The excitement generated by state elections, however, created an insistent pressure for greater democratization of presidential elections.

In the 1780s, twelve of the original thirteen states enacted property qualifications based on the time-honored theory that only male freeholders — landowners, as distinct from tenants or servants — had sufficient independence of mind to be entrusted with the vote. Of course, not everyone accepted that restricted idea of the people's role in government (see chapter 8). In the 1790s, Vermont became the first state to enfranchise all adult males, and four other states soon broadened suffrage considerably by allowing all male taxpayers to vote, a status that could be triggered simply by owning a cow, since local property taxes were an ever-present and generally nonburdensome reality. Between 1800 and 1830, greater democratization became a lively issue both in established states and in new states emerging in the West.

In the established states, lively newspaper exchanges and petition campaigns pushed state after state to hold constitutional conventions, where questions of suffrage, balloting procedures, apportionment, and representation were hotly debated. Both political philosophy and practical politics were entwined in these debates: Who are "the people" in a government founded on popular sovereignty, and whose party or interest group gains the most from expanded suffrage?

In new states, small populations together with yet smaller numbers of large property owners meant that few men could vote under typical restrictive property qualifications. Congress initially set a fifty-acre freehold as the threshold

VISUAL ACTIVITY

"We Owe Allegiance to No Crown"

John A. Woodside, a Philadelphia sign painter, made his living creating advertisements and ornamental pictures for hotels, taverns, and city fire engines. He specialized in promotional paintings conveying a booster spirit, especially heroic scenes on banners to be carried in parades. At some point in his decades-long career, which ran from about 1815 to 1850, he created this scene of a youthful sailor being crowned with a laurel wreath, the ancient Greek symbol of victory, by a breezy Miss Liberty (identified by the liberty cap she carries on a stick).

READING THE IMAGE: : What might the chain at the sailor's feet indicate? What do you think the slogan on the banner means? What do you see in the picture that would help date it? (Hint: examine the flag. And for the truly curious, consider the history of men's facial hair styles.)

CONNECTIONS: How and why does the painting reference the War of 1812? Regardless of the painting's date, what message do you think Woodside is trying to convey here?

Picture Research Consultants & Archives.

for voting, but in Illinois fewer than three hundred men met that test at the time of statehood. When Indiana, Illinois, and Mississippi became states, their constitutions granted suffrage to all taxpayers. Five additional new western states abandoned property and taxpayer qualifications altogether.

The most heated battles over suffrage occurred in eastern states, where expanding numbers of commercial men, renters, and mortgage holders of all classes contended with entrenched landed elites who, not surprisingly, favored the status quo. Still, by 1820, half a dozen states passed suffrage reform. Some stopped short of complete male suffrage, instead tying the vote to tax status or militia service. In the remainder of the states, the defenders of landed property qualifications managed to delay expanded suffrage for two more decades. But it was increasingly hard to persuade the disfranchised that landowners alone had a stake in government. Proponents of the status quo began to argue instead that the "industry and good habits" necessary to achieve a propertied status in life were what gave landowners the right character to vote. Opponents fired back blistering attacks. One delegate to New York's constitutional convention said, "More integrity and more patriotism are generally found in the labouring class of the community than in the higher orders." Owning land was no more predictive of wisdom and good character than it was of a person's height or strength, said another observer.

Both sides of the debate generally agreed that character mattered, and many ideas for ensuring an electorate of proper wisdom came up for discussion. The exclusion of paupers and felons convicted of "infamous crimes" found favor in legislation in many states. Literacy tests and raising the voting age to a figure in the thirties were debated but ultimately discarded. The exclusion of women required no discussion in the constitutional conventions, so firm was the legal power of *feme covert*. But in one exceptional moment, at the Virginia convention in 1829, a delegate wondered aloud why unmarried women over the age of twenty-one could not vote; he was quickly silenced with the argument that all women lacked the "free agency and intelligence" necessary for wise voting.

Free black men's enfranchisement was another story, generating much discussion at all the conventions. Under existing freehold qualifications, a small number of propertied black men could vote; universal or taxpayer suffrage would inevitably enfranchise many more. Many delegates at the various state conventions spoke against that extension, claiming that blacks as a race lacked prudence, independence, and knowledge. With the exception of New York, which

***The House of Representatives*, by Samuel F. B. Morse, 1822**
In this large chamber, arising in 1815–1819 from the ashes of the old Capitol, Congress debated the various Missouri statehood bills. Built in a grand classical style, the room had towering marble columns and a cast-steel dome. A window in the dome provided natural light; the oil chandelier, lowered and lighted by hand, permitted evening sessions. Unfortunately, echoes bouncing off the smooth dome ruined the room's acoustics. Various fixes were tried — hanging draperies, rearranging the desks. In 1850 Congress finally authorized a bigger chamber. The room shown here is now called Statuary Hall, where Capitol visitors can experience for themselves the poor acoustics. Samuel F. B. Morse, *The House of Representatives*, completed 1822; probably reworked 1823; oil on canvas, 86-7/8 x 130-5/8 inches. The Corcoran Gallery of Art, Washington, D.C., Museum Purchase, Gallery Fund 11.14.

retained the existing property qualification for black voters as it removed it for whites, the general pattern was one of expanded suffrage for whites and a total eclipse of suffrage for blacks.

The Missouri Compromise

The politics of race produced the most divisive issue during Monroe's term. In February 1819, Missouri—so recently the territory of the powerful Osage Indians—applied for statehood. Since 1815, four other states had joined the Union (Indiana, Mississippi, Illinois, and Alabama) following the blueprint laid out by the Northwest Ordinance of 1787. But Missouri posed a problem. Although much of its area was on the same latitude as the free state of Illinois, its territorial population included ten thousand slaves brought there by southern planters.

Missouri's unusual combination of geography and demography led a New York congressman, James Tallmadge Jr., to propose two amendments to the statehood bill. The first stipulated that slaves born in Missouri after statehood would be free at age twenty-five, and the second declared that no new slaves could be imported into the state. Tallmadge's model was New York's gradual emancipation law of 1799 (see chapter 8). It did not strip slave owners of their current property, and it allowed them full use of the labor of newborn slaves well into their prime productive years. Still, southern congressmen objected because in the long run the amendments would make Missouri a free state, presumably no longer allied with southern economic and political interests. Just as southern economic power rested on slave labor, southern political power drew extra strength from the slave population because of the three-fifths rule. In 1820, the South owed seventeen of its seats in the House of Representatives to its slave population.

Tallmadge's amendments passed in the House by a close and sharply sectional vote of North against South. The ferocious debate led a Georgia representative to observe that the question had started "a fire which all the waters of the ocean could not extinguish. It can be extinguished only in blood." The Senate, with an even number of slave and free states, voted down the amendments, and Missouri statehood was postponed until the next congressional term.

In 1820, a compromise emerged. Maine, once part of Massachusetts, applied for statehood as a free state, balancing against Missouri as a slave state. The Senate further agreed that the southern boundary of Missouri — latitude 36°30' — extended west, would become the permanent line dividing slave from free states, guaranteeing the North a large area where slavery was banned (Map 10.5). The House also approved the **Missouri Compromise**, thanks to expert deal brokering by Kentucky's Henry Clay, who earned the nickname "the Great Pacificator" for his superb negotiating skills. The whole package passed because seventeen northern congressmen decided that minimizing sectional conflict was the best course and voted with the South.

President Monroe and former president Jefferson at first worried that the Missouri crisis would reinvigorate the Federalist Party as the party of the North. But even ex-Federalists agreed that the split between free and slave states was too dangerous a fault line to be permitted to become a shaper of national politics. When new parties did develop in the 1830s, they

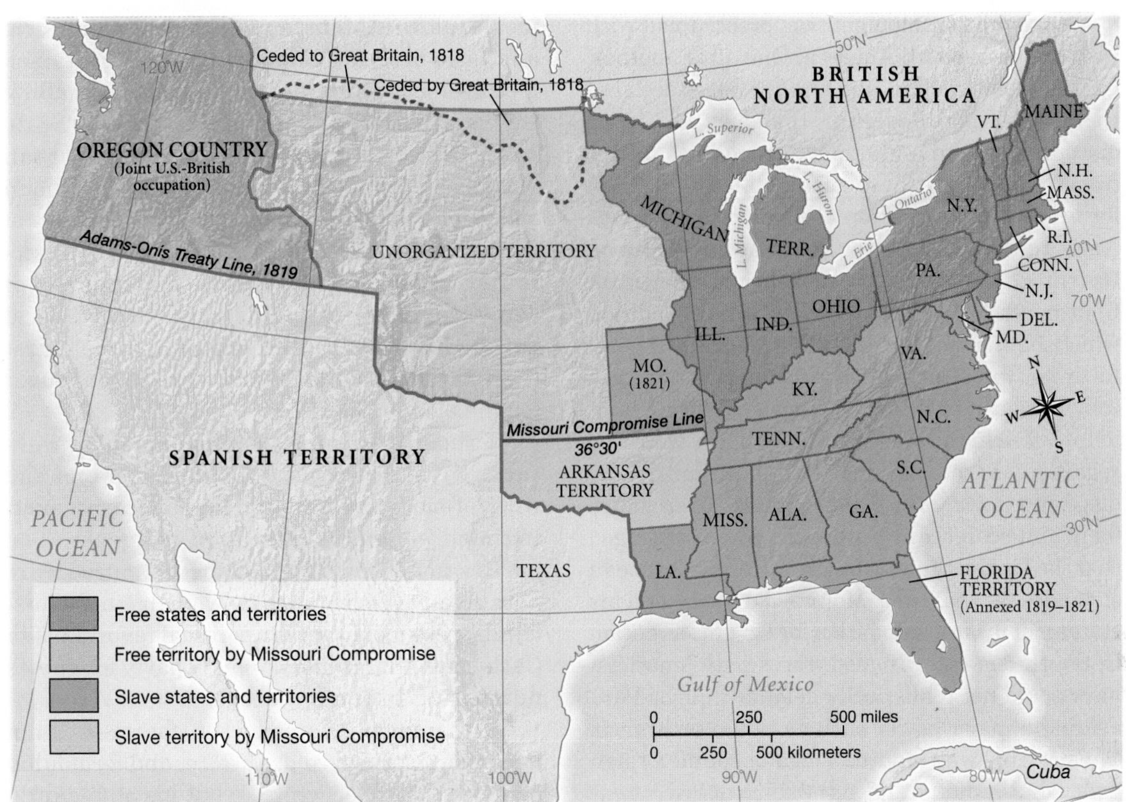

MAP ACTIVITY

Map 10.5 The Missouri Compromise, 1820

After a difficult battle in Congress, Missouri entered the Union in 1821 as part of a package of compromises. Maine was admitted as a free state to balance slavery in Missouri, and a line drawn at latitude 36°30' put most of the rest of the Louisiana Territory off-limits to slavery in the future.

READING THE MAP: How many free and how many slave states were there prior to the Missouri Compromise? What did the admission of Missouri as a slave state threaten to do?

CONNECTIONS: Who precipitated the crisis over Missouri, what did he propose, and where did the idea come from? Who proposed the Missouri Compromise, and who benefited from it?

took pains to bridge geography, each party developing a presence in both North and South. Monroe and Jefferson also worried about the future of slavery. Both understood slavery to be deeply problematic, but, as Jefferson said, "we have the wolf by the ears, and we can neither hold him, nor safely let him go. Justice is in one scale, and self-preservation in the other."

The Monroe Doctrine

As Congress struggled with the slavery issue, new foreign policy challenges also arose. In 1816, U.S. troops led by General Andrew Jackson invaded Spanish Florida in search of Seminole Indians harboring escaped slaves. Once there, Jackson declared himself the commander of northern Florida, demonstrating his power in 1818 by executing two British men who he claimed were dangerous enemies. In asserting rule over the territory, and surely in executing the two British subjects on Spanish land, Jackson had gone too far. Privately, President Monroe was distressed and pondered court-martialing Jackson, prevented only by Jackson's immense popularity as the hero of the battle of New Orleans. Instead, John Quincy Adams, the secretary of state, negotiated with Spain the Adams-Onís Treaty, which delivered all of Florida to the United States in 1819 and finally settled the disputed borders of the Louisiana Purchase. In exchange, the Americans agreed to abandon any claim to Texas or Cuba. Southerners viewed this as a large concession, having eyed both places as potential acquisitions for future slave states.

Spain at that moment was preoccupied with its colonies in South America. One after another, Chile, Colombia, Peru, and finally Mexico declared themselves independent in the early 1820s. To discourage Spain and other European countries from reconquering these colonies, Monroe in 1823 formulated a declaration of principles on South America, known in later years as the **Monroe Doctrine**. The president warned that "the American Continents, by the free and independent condition which they have assumed and maintain, are henceforth not to be considered as subjects for future colonization by any European power." Any attempt to interfere in the Western Hemisphere would be regarded as "the manifestation of an unfriendly disposition towards the United States." In exchange for noninterference by Europeans, Monroe pledged that the United States would stay out of European struggles. At that time, Monroe did not intend his statement to lay a foundation for U.S. intervention in South America. Indeed, the small American navy could not realistically defend Chile or Peru against a major power such as Spain or France. The doctrine was Monroe's idea of sound foreign policy, but it did not have the force of law.

The Election of 1824

Monroe's nonpartisan administration was the last of its kind, a throwback to eighteenth-century ideals, as was Monroe, with his powdered wig and knee breeches. Monroe's cabinet contained men of sharply different philosophies, all calling themselves Republicans. Secretary of State **John Quincy Adams** represented the urban Northeast; South Carolinian John C. Calhoun spoke for the planter aristocracy as secretary of war; and William H. Crawford of Georgia, secretary of the treasury, was a proponent of Jeffersonian states' rights and limited federal power. Even before the end of Monroe's first term, these men and others began to maneuver for the election of 1824.

Crucially helping them to maneuver were their wives, who accomplished some of the work of modern campaign managers by courting men — and women — of influence. The parties not thrown by Elizabeth Monroe were now given all over town by women whose husbands were jockeying for political favor. Louisa Catherine Adams had a weekly party for guests numbering in the hundreds.

The somber Adams lacked charm — "I am a man of reserved, cold, austere, and forbidding manners," he once wrote — but his abundantly charming (and hardworking) wife made up for that. She attended to the etiquette of social calls, sometimes making two dozen in a morning, and counted sixty-eight members of Congress as her regular guests. This was smart politics, in case

Election Sewing or Trinket Boxes from 1824

Women could express their support for a presidential candidate by purchasing a sewing box emblazoned with his face. On the left is a box with John Quincy Adams's picture inside the cover; the top of the box (not visible here) has a velvet pincushion printed with the slogan "Be Firm for Adams." The competing box on the right features Andrew Jackson's likeness under glass on top of the cover. The lithographic portrait was hand-colored with watercolors. Notice that Jackson is shown in his military uniform, with the title of general and a rather younger-looking face than he actually had in 1824. Collection of Janice L. and David J. Frent.

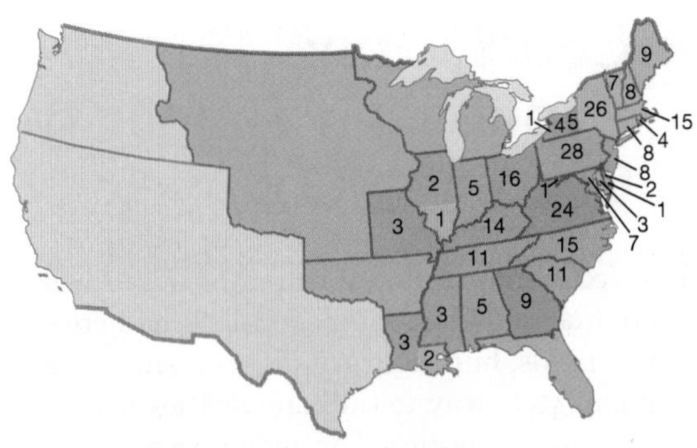

	Candidate*	Electoral Vote	Popular Vote	Percent of Popular Vote
	John Q. Adams	84	108,740	30.5
	Andrew Jackson	99	153,544	43.1
	Henry Clay	37	47,136	13.2
	W. H. Crawford	41	46,618	13.1

*No distinct political parties

Note: Because no candidate garnered a majority in the electoral college, the election was decided in the House of Representatives. Although Clay was eliminated from the running, as Speaker of the House he influenced the final decision in favor of Adams.

MAP 10.6
The Election of 1824

the House of Representatives wound up deciding the 1824 election — which it did.

John Quincy Adams (as well as Louisa Catherine) was ambitious for the presidency, but so were others. Candidate Henry Clay, Speaker of the House and negotiator of the Treaty of Ghent with Britain in 1814, promoted a new "American System," a package of protective tariffs to encourage manufacturing and federal expenditures for internal improvements such as roads and canals. Treasurer William Crawford was a favorite of Republicans from Virginia and New York, even after he suffered an incapacitating stroke in mid-1824. Calhoun was another serious contender, having served in Congress and in several cabinets. A southern planter, he attracted northern support for his backing of internal improvements and protective tariffs.

The final candidate was an outsider and a latecomer: General **Andrew Jackson** of Tennessee. Jackson had far less national political experience than the others, but he enjoyed great celebrity from his military career. In 1824, on the anniversary of the battle of New Orleans, the Adamses threw a spectacular ball in his honor, hoping that some of Jackson's charisma would rub off on Adams, who was not yet thinking of Jackson as a rival for office. Not long after, Jackson's supporters put his name forward for the presidency, and voters in the West and South reacted with enthusiasm. Adams was dismayed, while Calhoun dropped out of the race and shifted his attention to winning the vice presidency.

Along with democratizing the vote, eighteen states (out of the full twenty-four) had put the power to choose members of the electoral college directly in the hands of voters, making the 1824 election the first one to have a popular vote tally for the presidency. Jackson proved by far to be the most popular candidate, winning 153,544 votes. Adams was second with 108,740, Clay won 47,136 votes, and the debilitated Crawford garnered 46,618. This was not a large turnout, probably amounting to just over a quarter of adult white males. Nevertheless, the election of 1824 marked a new departure in choosing presidents. Partisanship energized the electorate; apathy and a low voter turnout would not recur until the twentieth century.

In the electoral college, Jackson received 99 votes, Adams 84, Crawford 41, and Clay 37 (Map 10.6). Jackson lacked a majority, so the House of Representatives stepped in for the second time in U.S. history. Each congressional delegation had one vote; according to the Constitution's Twelfth Amendment, passed in 1804, only the top three candidates joined the runoff. Thus Henry Clay was out of the race and in a position to bestow his support on another candidate.

Jackson's supporters later characterized the election of 1824 as the "corrupt bargain." Clay backed Adams, and Adams won by one vote in the House in February 1825. Clay's support made sense on several levels. Despite strong mutual dislike, he and Adams agreed on issues such as federal support to build roads and canals. Moreover, Clay was uneasy with Jackson's volatile temperament and unstated political views and with Crawford's diminished capacity. What made Clay's decision look "corrupt" was that immediately after the election, Adams offered to appoint Clay secretary of state — and Clay accepted.

In fact, there probably was no concrete bargain; Adams's subsequent cabinet appointments demonstrated his lack of political astuteness. But Andrew Jackson felt that the election had been stolen from him, and he wrote bitterly that "the Judas of the West [Clay] has closed the contract and will receive the thirty pieces of silver."

The Adams Administration

John Quincy Adams, like his father, was a one-term president. His career had been built on diplomacy, not electoral politics, and despite his wife's deftness in the art of political influence, his own political horse sense was not well developed. With his cabinet choices, he welcomed his opposition into his inner circle. He asked Crawford to stay on in the Treasury. He retained an openly pro-Jackson postmaster general even though that position controlled thousands of nationwide patronage appointments. He even asked Jackson to become secretary of war. With Calhoun as vice president (elected without opposition by the electoral college) and Clay at the State Department, the whole argumentative crew would have been thrust into the executive branch. Crawford and Jackson had the good sense to decline the appointments.

Adams had lofty ideas for federal action during his presidency, and the plan he put before Congress was so sweeping that it took Henry Clay aback. Adams called for federally built roads, canals, and harbors. He proposed a national university in Washington as well as government-sponsored scientific research. He wanted to build observatories to advance astronomical knowledge and to promote precision in timekeeping, and he backed a decimal-based system of weights and measures. In all these endeavors, Adams believed he was continuing the legacy of Jefferson and Madison, using the powers of government to advance knowledge. But his opponents feared he was too Hamiltonian, using federal power inappropriately to advance commercial interests.

Whether he was more truly Federalist or Republican was a moot point. Lacking the give-and-take political skills required to gain congressional support, Adams was unable to implement much of his program. He scorned the idea of courting voters to gain support and using the patronage system to enhance his power. He often made appointments (to posts such as customs collectors) to placate enemies rather than to reward friends. A story of a toast offered to the president may well have been mythical, but as humorous folklore it made the rounds during his term and came to summarize Adams's precarious hold on leadership. A dignitary raised a glass and said, "May he strike confusion to his foes," to which another voice scornfully chimed in, "as he has already done to his friends."

REVIEW How did the collapse of the Federalist Party influence the administrations of James Monroe and John Quincy Adams?

▸ Conclusion: Republican Simplicity Becomes Complex

The Jeffersonian Republicans at first tried to undo much of what the Federalists had created in the 1790s, but their promise of a simpler government gave way to the complexities of domestic and foreign issues. The sudden acquisition of the Louisiana Purchase promised land and opportunity to settlers but first required intricate federal-level dealings with powerful western Indians. British impressments of American sailors challenged Jefferson and Madison to stand up to the onetime mother country, culminating in the War of 1812. Fighting both the British and their Indian allies, the Americans engaged in two years of inconclusive battles, mostly on American soil. Their eventual triumph at the battle of New Orleans allowed them the illusion that they had fought a second war of independence.

The War of 1812 was the Indians' second lost war for independence. Tecumseh's vision of an unprecedentedly large confederacy of Indian tribes that would halt westward expansion by white Americans was cut short by the war and by his death. When Canada was under attack, the British valued its defense more than they valued their promises to help the Indians.

The war elevated to national prominence General Andrew Jackson, whose popularity with voters in the 1824 election surprised traditional politicians (and their politically astute wives) and threw the one-party rule of Republicans into a tailspin. New western states with more lenient voter qualifications and eastern states with reformed suffrage laws further eroded the old political elite. Appeals to the mass of white male voters would be the hallmark of all nineteenth-century elections after 1824. In such a system, John Quincy Adams and men like him were at a great disadvantage.

Ordinary American women, whether white or free black, had no place in government. Male legislatures maintained women's *feme covert* status, keeping wives dependent on husbands. A few women claimed greater personal autonomy through religion, while many others benefited from expanded female schooling in schools and academies. These increasingly substantial gains in education would blossom into a major transformation of gender starting in the 1830s and 1840s.

Amid the turmoil of the early Republic, two events in particular sparked developments that would prove momentous in later decades. The bitter debate over slavery that surrounded the Missouri Compromise accentuated the serious divisions between northern and southern states — divisions that would only widen in the decades to come. And Jefferson's long embargo and Madison's wartime trade stoppage gave a big boost to American manufacturing by removing competition with British factories. When peace returned in 1815, the years of independent development burst forth into a period of sustained economic growth that continued nearly unabated into the mid-nineteenth century.

▶ Selected Bibliography

Politics

Andrew Burstein and Nancy Isenberg, *Madison and Jefferson* (2010).
Saul Cornell, *The Other Founders: Anti-Federalism and the Dissenting Tradition in America, 1788–1828* (1999).
Joseph J. Ellis, *American Sphinx: The Character of Thomas Jefferson* (1997).
Joanne B. Freeman, *Affairs of Honor: National Politics in the New Republic* (2001).
Nancy Isenberg, *Fallen Founder: The Life of Aaron Burr* (2008).
Alexander Keyssar, *The Right to Vote: The Contested History of Democracy in the United States* (2000).
Jon Kukla, *A Wilderness So Immense: The Louisiana Purchase and the Destiny of America* (2003).
Jeffrey L. Pasley, Andrew W. Robertson, and David Waldstreicher, *Beyond the Founders: New Approaches to the Political History of the Early American Republic* (2003).
Stephen Watts, *The Republic Reborn: War and the Making of Liberal America, 1790–1820* (1987).
Sean Wilentz, *The Rise of American Democracy: Jefferson to Lincoln* (2005).
Richard Zacks, *The Pirate Coast: Thomas Jefferson, the First Marines, and the Secret Mission of 1805* (2006).

Indians, the War of 1812, and the West

Stephen E. Ambrose, *Undaunted Courage: Meriwether Lewis, Thomas Jefferson, and the Opening of the American West* (1996).
Carl Benn, *The Iroquois in the War of 1812* (1998).
James F. Brooks, *Captives and Cousins: Slavery, Kinship, and Community in the Southwest Borderlands* (2002).
Kathleen DuVal, *The Native Ground: Indians and Colonists in the Heart of the Continent* (2007).
R. David Edmunds, *Tecumseh and the Quest for Indian Leadership* (1984).
Albert Furtwangler, *Acts of Discovery: Visions of America in the Lewis and Clark Journals* (1993).
Pekka Hämäläinen, *The Comanche Empire* (2009).
John Sugden, *Tecumseh: A Life* (1997).
Alan Taylor, *The Civil War of 1812: American Citizens, British Subjects, Irish Rebels, and Indian Allies* (2010).
Richard White, *The Middle Ground: Indians, Empires, and Republics in the Great Lakes Region, 1650–1815* (1991).

Slavery

Douglas Egerton, *Gabriel's Rebellion* (1993).
Annette Gordon-Reed, *The Hemingses of Monticello: An American Family* (2009).
James Oliver Horton and Lois E. Horton, *In Hope of Liberty: Culture, Community, and Protest among Northern Free Blacks, 1700–1860* (1997).
Gary B. Nash, *Forging Freedom: The Formation of Philadelphia's Black Community, 1720–1840* (1988).
Shane White, *Somewhat More Independent: The End of Slavery in New York City, 1710–1810* (1991).

Women, Marriage, and Religion

Catherine Allgor, *Parlor Politics: In Which the Ladies of Washington Help Build a City and a Government* (2000).
Norma Basch, *Framing American Divorce: From the Revolutionary Generation to the Victorians* (1999).
Norma Basch, *In the Eyes of the Law: Women, Marriage, and Property in Nineteenth-Century New York* (1982).
Catherine A. Brekus, *Strangers and Pilgrims: Female Preaching in America, 1740–1845* (1998).
Nancy Cott, *Public Vows: A History of Marriage and the Nation* (2001).
Susan Juster, *Disorderly Women: Sexual Politics and Evangelicalism in Revolutionary New England* (1994).
Mary Kelley, *Learning to Stand and Speak: Women, Education, and Public Life in America's Republic* (2006).
Susan E. Klepp, *Revolutionary Conceptions: Women, Fertility, and Family Limitation in America, 1760–1820* (2009).
Mary Beth Sievens, *Stray Wives: Marital Conflict in Early National New England* (2005).

▶ **For more books about topics in this chapter,** see the Online Bibliography at **bedfordstmartins.com/roark.**

▶ **For additional primary sources from this period,** see Michael Johnson, ed., *Reading the American Past*, Fifth Edition.

▶ **For Web sites, images, and documents related to topics and places in this chapter,** visit Make History at **bedfordstmartins.com/roark.**

Reviewing Chapter 10

KEY TERMS

Explain each term's significance.

Jefferson's Presidency

- Thomas Jefferson (p. 291)
- Aaron Burr (p. 291)
- Gabriel's rebellion (p. 291)
- *Marbury v. Madison* (p. 293)
- Barbary Wars (p. 294)

Opportunities and Challenges in the West

- Louisiana Purchase (p. 296)
- Sacajawea (p. 297)
- Lewis and Clark expedition (p. 297)
- Osage (p. 298)
- Comanche (p. 298)

Jefferson, the Madisons, and the War of 1812

- Impressment (p. 300)
- Embargo Act of 1807 (p. 300)
- Dolley Madison (p. 301)
- Tecumseh (p. 301)
- Tenskwatawa (p. 302)
- battle of Tippecanoe (p. 303)
- Henry Clay (p. 303)
- War Hawks (p. 303)
- Creek War (p. 304)
- battle of New Orleans (p. 305)
- Hartford Convention (p. 305)

Women's Status in the Early Republic

- *feme covert* (p. 306)
- Jemima Wilkinson (p. 307)
- female academies (p. 307)

Monroe and Adams

- James Monroe (p. 310)
- Missouri Compromise (p. 312)
- Monroe Doctrine (p. 314)
- John Quincy Adams (p. 314)
- Andrew Jackson (p. 315)

REVIEW QUESTIONS

Use key terms and dates to support your answer.

1. How did Jefferson attempt to undo the Federalist innovations of earlier administrations? (pp. 291–294)
2. Why was Spain concerned that France sold the Louisiana Territory to the United States? (pp. 295–300)
3. Why did Congress declare war on Great Britain in 1812? (pp. 300–305)
4. How did the civil status of American women and men differ in the early Republic? (pp. 305–310)
5. How did the collapse of the Federalist Party influence the administrations of James Monroe and John Quincy Adams? (pp. 310–316)

MAKING CONNECTIONS

Draw on key terms, the timeline, and review questions.

1. When Jefferson assumed the presidency following the election of 1800, he expected to transform the national government. Describe his republican vision and his successes and failures in implementing it. Did subsequent Republican presidents advance the same objectives?
2. How did the United States expand and strengthen its control of territory in North America in the early nineteenth century? In your answer, discuss the roles of diplomacy, military action, and political leadership in contributing to this development.
3. Regional tensions emerged as a serious danger to the American political system in the early nineteenth century. Discuss specific conflicts that had regional dimensions. How did Americans resolve, or fail to resolve, these tensions?
4. Although the United States denied its female citizens equality in public life, some women were able to exert considerable influence. How did they do so? In your answer, discuss the legal, political, and educational status of women in the early Republic.

LINKING TO THE PAST

Link events in this chapter to earlier events.

1. Compare the British-Indian alliance in the Revolutionary War with the British-Indian alliance in the War of 1812. Were there any reasons for men like Tecumseh to think that the alliance might work out better the second time? (See chapter 7.)
2. How do you think the Federalist supporters of the Constitution in 1787–1788 felt about the steady decline in states' property qualifications for male voters that occurred between 1800 and 1824? Did the democratization of voting necessarily undermine the Constitution's restrictions on direct democracy in the federal government? (See chapter 8.)

▶ For practice quizzes and other study tools, visit the Online Study Guide at bedfordstmartins.com/roark.

TIMELINE 1800–1825

1800	• Republicans Thomas Jefferson and Aaron Burr tie in electoral college. • Fears of slave rebellion led by Gabriel in Virginia result in twenty-seven executions.
1801	• House of Representatives elects Thomas Jefferson president after thirty-six ballots. • Pasha of Tripoli declares war on United States.
1803	• *Marbury v. Madison.* • Britain and France each warn United States not to ship war-related goods to the other. • United States purchases Louisiana Territory.
1804	• U.S. Marines and foreign mercenaries under William Eaton take Derne, Tripoli. • President Jefferson meets with Osage leaders in Washington City.
1804–1806	• Lewis and Clark expedition travels from St. Louis to Pacific Ocean.
1807	• British attack and search *Chesapeake.* • Embargo Act. • United States establishes trade with Comanche Indians.
1808	• Republican James Madison elected president; Dolley Madison soon dubbed "presidentress."
1809	• Treaty of Fort Wayne. • Non-Intercourse Act.
1811	• Battle of Tippecanoe.
1812	• United States declares war on Great Britain.
1813	• Tecumseh dies at battle of the Thames.
1814	• British attack Washington City. • Treaty of Ghent. • New England Federalists meet at Hartford Convention.
1815	• Battle of New Orleans.
1816	• Republican James Monroe elected president.
1819	• Adams-Onís Treaty.
1820	• Missouri Compromise.
1823	• Monroe Doctrine asserted.
1825	• John Quincy Adams elected president by House of Representatives.

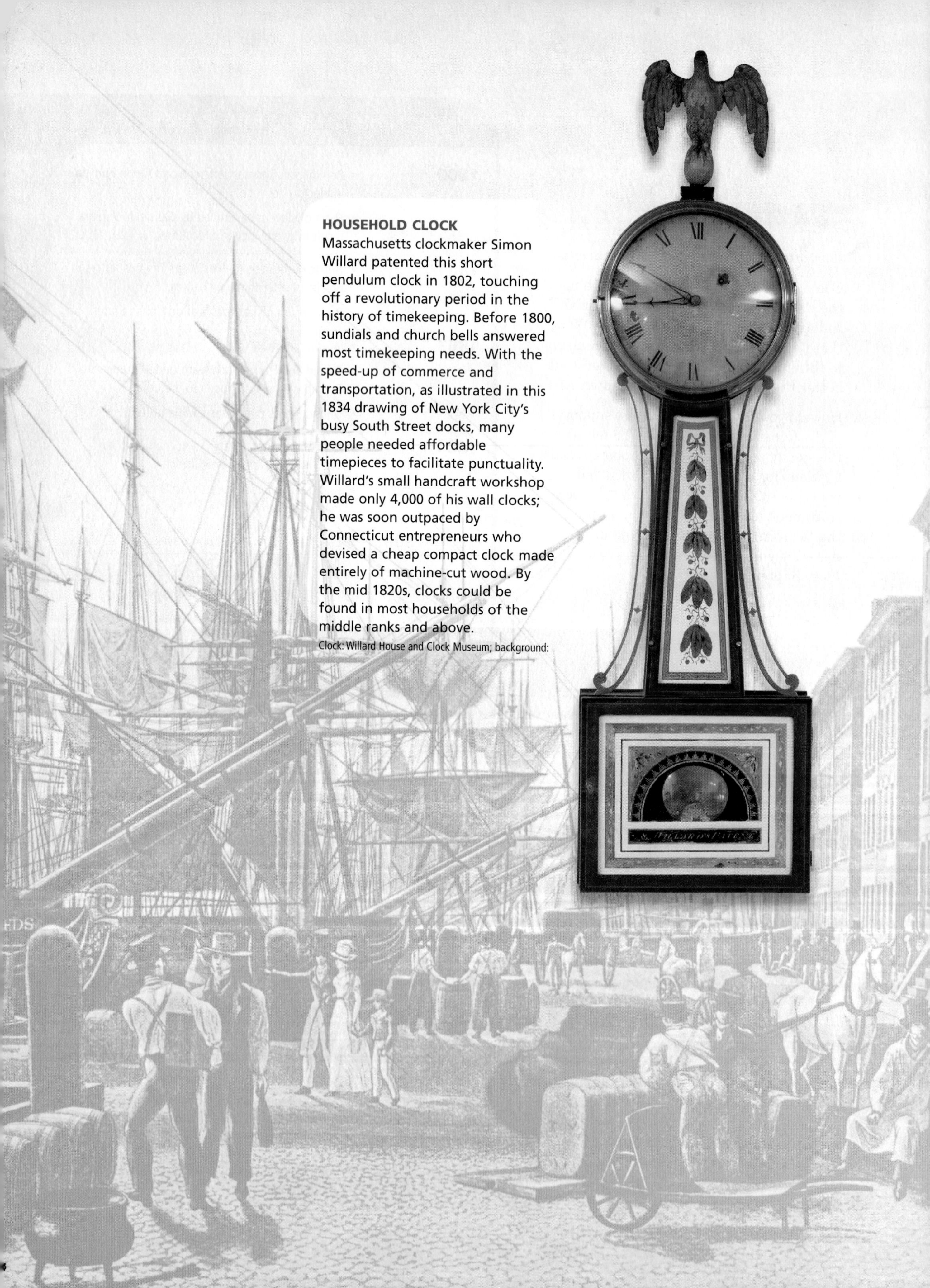

HOUSEHOLD CLOCK

Massachusetts clockmaker Simon Willard patented this short pendulum clock in 1802, touching off a revolutionary period in the history of timekeeping. Before 1800, sundials and church bells answered most timekeeping needs. With the speed-up of commerce and transportation, as illustrated in this 1834 drawing of New York City's busy South Street docks, many people needed affordable timepieces to facilitate punctuality. Willard's small handcraft workshop made only 4,000 of his wall clocks; he was soon outpaced by Connecticut entrepreneurs who devised a cheap compact clock made entirely of machine-cut wood. By the mid 1820s, clocks could be found in most households of the middle ranks and above.

Clock: Willard House and Clock Museum; background:

11

The Expanding Republic

1815–1840

IN 1837, LARGE AUDIENCES THROUGHOUT MASSACHUSETTS WITNESSED the astonishing spectacle of two sisters from a wealthy southern family delivering long, impassioned speeches about the evils of slavery. Sarah and Angelina Grimké showed no fear or hesitation. They were women on a mission, channeling a higher power to authorize their outspokenness. As Angelina, thirty-two, wrote to a friend after one event: "Whilst in the act of speaking I am favored to forget little 'I' entirely & to feel altogether hid behind the great cause I am pleading. Were it not for this feeling, I know not how I could face such audiences without embarrassment." In their seventy-nine speaking engagements, some forty thousand women — and men — came to hear them.

Not much in their family background predicted the sisters' radical break with tradition. And radical it was: The abolitionist movement was in its infancy in the 1830s, centered around Boston editor William Lloyd Garrison, who demanded an immediate end to slavery. Nearly as radical as Garrison, the Grimké sisters had crossed a gender line by speaking their own unscripted words of moral politics in front of mixed-sex audiences.

The Grimké sisters grew up in Charleston, South Carolina, in a prominent family whose wealth derived from slavery. With a dozen siblings, an invalid mother, and a busy father — he was chief justice of the State Supreme Court — the two sisters evaded familial surveillance enough to develop independent minds and explore alternative churches that opposed slavery. By the late 1820s, both sisters had moved to Philadelphia and joined the Quakers' Society of Friends.

Until 1835, they refrained from activism and remained aloof from Philadelphia's growing antislavery community. That year, the British abolitionist George Thompson lectured in town, inspiring Angelina to write to Garrison, describing herself as a white southern exile from slavery. When Garrison published her letter in his weekly paper, the *Liberator*, her rare voice of personal testimony caused a great stir. Angelina next wrote *An Appeal to the Christian Women of the South*, urging southern women to take political action against slavery; Charleston postmasters burned copies sent by mail. A year later, she issued *An Appeal to the Women of the Nominally Free States*, setting forth the ideas that would be articulated on her Massachusetts lecture tour.

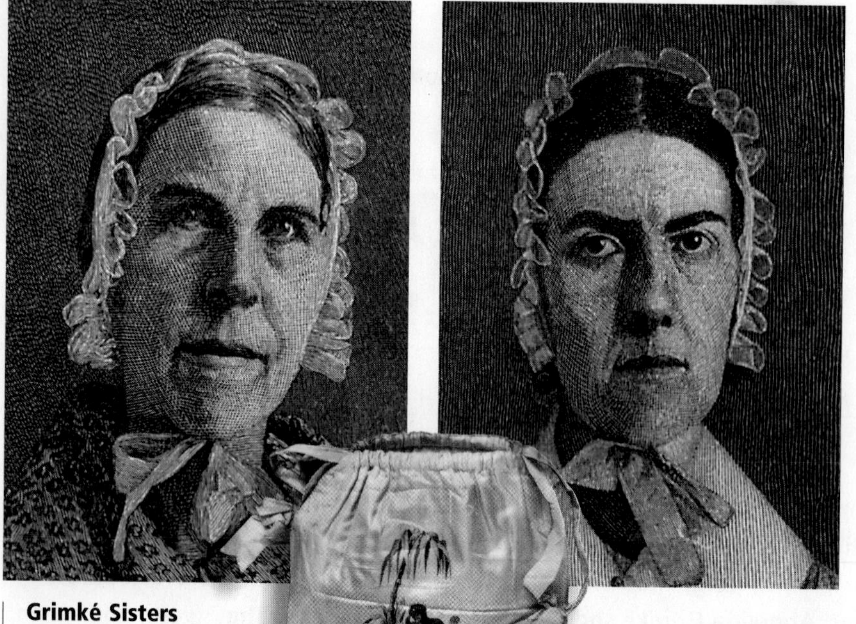

Grimké Sisters
Sarah M. and Angelina E. Grimké sat for these portraits probably sometime around 1840, when Sarah was 48 and Angelina was 35. Quaker women typically wore plain headdresses, but these day caps—sheer fabric with ruffles—are not very austere. Such caps were common indoor wear, to keep hair in place and protected, while outdoors, a large-brimmed sun-screening bonnet would go over the cap. The thousands of abolitionist women who did not take to lecture platforms instead contributed major financial support to the movement by making handcraft items, such as this silk drawstring purse, and selling them at giant fairs. Portraits: Library of Congress; purse: The Daughters of the American Revolution Museum, Washington, D.C., Gift of Mrs. Erwin L. Broecker.

The extended tour of Massachusetts caused a sensation and led to a doubling of membership in northern antislavery societies. Newspapers and state church leaders fiercely debated the Grimkés' position. And the issue of women's right to speak in public was open for full examination. The Grimké sisters defended their stand: "Whatever is morally right for a man to do is morally right for a woman to do," Angelina wrote. "I recognize no rights but human rights." Sarah produced a set of essays titled *Letters on the Equality of the Sexes* (1838), the first American treatise asserting women's equality with men.

The Grimké sisters' innovative radicalism was part of a vibrant, contested public life that came alive in the United States of the 1830s. This decade — often summed up as the Age of Jackson, in honor of the two-term president who left his distinctive mark on the period — was a time of rapid economic, political, and social change. Andrew Jackson's bold self-confidence mirrored the new confidence of American society in the years after 1815. An entrepreneurial spirit gripped the country, producing a market revolution of unprecedented scale. Old social hierarchies eroded; ordinary men dreamed of moving high up the ladder of success. Stunning advances in transportation and economic productivity fueled such dreams and propelled thousands to travel west or to cities. Urban growth and technological change fostered the diffusion of a distinctive and lively public culture, spread mainly through the increased circulation of newspapers and also by thousands of public lecturers, like the Grimké sisters, allowing popular opinions to coalesce and intensify.

Expanded communication transformed politics dramatically. Sharp disagreements over the best way to promote individual liberty, economic opportunity, and national prosperity in the new market economy defined key differences between presidential candidates in the election of 1828. By the early 1830s, these political differences were embedded in new political parties, which attracted increasing numbers of white male voters into their ranks. Religion became democratized as well. A nationwide evangelical revival brought its adherents the certainty that salvation was now available to all and that the moral perfection of society was within reach.

But perfection proved elusive. Steamboats blew up, banks and businesses periodically collapsed, alcoholism rates soared, Indians were killed or relocated farther west, and slavery continued to expand. The brash confidence that turned some people into rugged, self-promoting individuals inspired others to think about the human costs of rapid economic expansion and thus about reforming society in dramatic ways. The common denominator was a faith that people and societies could shape their own destinies.

▸ The Market Revolution

The return of peace in 1815 unleashed powerful forces that revolutionized the organization of the economy. Spectacular changes in transportation facilitated the movement of commodities, information, and people, while textile mills and other factories created many new jobs, especially for young unmarried women. Innovations in banking, legal practices, and tariff policies promoted swift economic growth.

This was not yet an industrial revolution, as was beginning in Britain, but rather a market revolution fueled by traditional sources — water, wood, beasts of burden, and human muscle. What was new was the accelerated pace of economic activity and the scale of the distribution of goods. Men and women were drawn out of old patterns of rural self-sufficiency into the wider realm of national market relations. At the same time, the nation's money supply enlarged considerably, leading to speculative investments in commerce, manufacturing, transportation, and land. The new nature and scale of production and consumption changed Americans' economic behavior, attitudes, and expectations. But in 1819 and again in 1837 and 1839, serious crashes of the economy punctured their optimistic expectations.

Improvements in Transportation

Before 1815, transportation in the United States was slow and expensive; it cost as much to ship a crate over thirty miles of domestic roads as it did to send it across the Atlantic Ocean. A stagecoach trip from Boston to New York took four days. But between 1815 and 1840, networks of roads, canals, steamboats, and finally railroads dramatically raised the speed and lowered the cost of travel (Map 11.1).

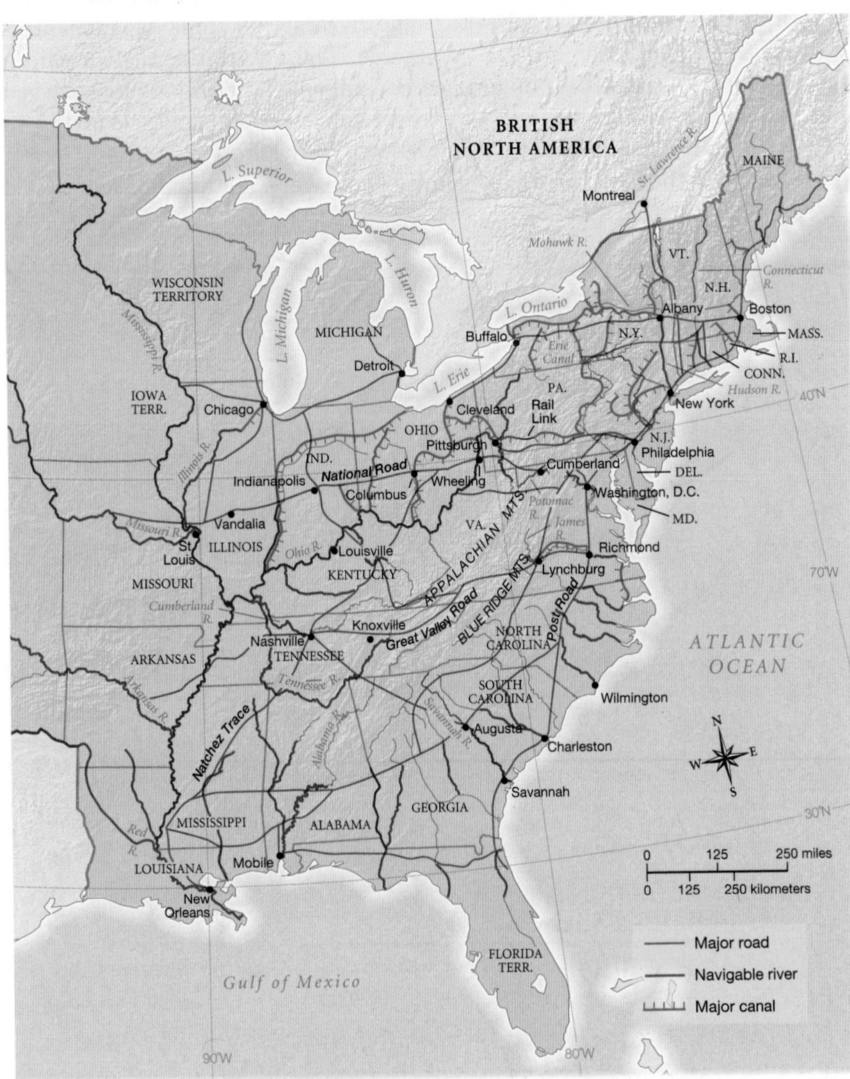

MAP ACTIVITY

Map 11.1 Routes of Transportation in 1840

By the 1830s, transportation advances had cut travel times significantly. By way of the Erie Canal, goods and people could move from New York City to Buffalo in four days, a trip that had taken two weeks by road in 1800. Similarly, the trip from New York to New Orleans, which had taken four weeks in 1800, could now be accomplished in less than half that time on steamboats plying the western rivers.

READING THE MAP: In what parts of the country were canals built most extensively? Were most of them within a single state's borders, or did they encourage interstate travel and shipping?

CONNECTIONS: What impact did the Erie Canal have on the development of New York City? How did improvements in transportation affect urbanization in other parts of the country?

Improved transportation moved goods into wider markets. It moved passengers, too, broadening their horizons and allowing young people as well as adults to take up new employment in cities or factory towns. Transportation also facilitated the flow of political information via the U.S. mail with its bargain postal rates for newspapers, periodicals, and books. Enhanced public transport was expensive and produced uneven economic benefits, so presidents from Jefferson to Monroe were reluctant to fund it with federal dollars. Only the National Road, begun in 1806, was government sponsored. By 1818, it linked Baltimore with Wheeling, in western Virginia. In all other cases, private investors pooled resources and chartered transport companies, receiving significant subsidies and monopoly rights from state governments. Turnpike and roadway mileage increased dramatically after 1815, reducing shipping costs. Stagecoach companies proliferated, and travel time on main routes was cut in half.

Water travel was similarly transformed. In 1807, Robert Fulton's steam-propelled boat, the *Clermont*, churned up the Hudson River from New York City to Albany, touching off a steamboat craze. By 1820, a dozen boats left New York City daily, and scores more operated on midwestern rivers and the Great Lakes. By the early 1830s, more than seven hundred steamboats were in operation on the Ohio and Mississippi rivers. A voyager on one of the first steamboats to go down the Mississippi reported that the Chickasaw Indians called the vessel a "fire canoe" and considered it "an omen of evil."

Indeed, steamboats were not benign advances. The urgency to cut travel time for competitive gain over rival steamboat companies — or to win impromptu races — led to overstoked furnaces, sudden boiler explosions, and terrible mass fatalities. An investigation of an accident near Cincinnati in 1838, in which 150 passengers were killed, charged: "Such disasters have their foundation in the present mammoth evil of our country, an inordinate love of gain. We are not satisfied with getting rich, but we must get rich in a day. We are not satisfied with traveling at a speed of ten miles an hour, but we must fly." By that year, nearly three thousand Americans had been killed in steamboat accidents, leading to initial federal attempts — at first unsuccessful — to regulate safety on ships used for interstate commerce. The environment also paid a huge price: Steamboats had to load fuel — "wood up" — every twenty miles or so, resulting in mass deforestation. By the 1830s, the banks of many main rivers were denuded of trees, and

THE PROMISE OF TECHNOLOGY

Early Steamboats

The American traveling public fell in love with steamboats for their speed and power. People and products could now go upriver, against the current, under the enthralling and modern power of steam. On every boat, a furnace heated water under pressure in a boiler to produce that steam, powering an engine that drove large paddlewheels. However, with innovation came risk. Between 1811 and 1851, accidents destroyed nearly a thousand boats, a third of all steam vessels built in that period, and killed a total of several thousand travelers. Fires and boiler explosions made for horrifying spectacles, as this lithograph by the famed printmakers Currier and Ives attests. In 1840, the *Lexington* caught fire in Long Island Sound. Despite having the latest safety features, only 4 people survived; many of the 139 victims froze to death in the icy winter waters. How did Americans' fondness for steamboats reflect the attitudes of this era? The Mariners Museum, Newport News, VA.

The Erie Canal at Lockport The Erie Canal, completed in 1825, struck many as the eighth wonder of the world, both for its length of 350 miles and for its impressive elevation, requiring the construction of eighty-three locks. The biggest engineering challenge came at Lockport, twenty miles from Buffalo, where the canal had to traverse a steep slate escarpment. Work crews — mostly immigrant Irishmen — used gunpowder and grueling physical labor to blast the deep artificial gorge shown here. Next, a series of double locks was constructed to move boats in stages up and down the 60-foot elevation. Department of Rare Books and Special Collections, Rush Rhees Library, University of Rochester.

forests miles back from the rivers fell to the ax. Wood combustion transferred the carbon stored in trees into the atmosphere, creating America's first significant air pollution.

Canals were another major innovation of the transportation revolution. These shallow highways of water allowed passage for boats pulled by mules. Travel was slow — less than five miles per hour — but the low-friction water enabled one mule to pull a fifty-ton barge. Pennsylvania in 1815 and New York in 1817 commenced major state-sponsored canal enterprises. Pennsylvania's Schuylkill Canal stretched 108 miles west from Philadelphia when it was completed in 1826. Much more impressive was the **Erie Canal**, finished in 1825, covering 350 miles between Albany and Buffalo and linking the port of New York City with the entire Great Lakes region. Wheat and flour moved east, household goods and tools moved west, and passengers went in both directions. By the 1830s, the cost of shipping by canal fell to less than one-tenth of the cost of overland transport, and New York City quickly blossomed into the premier commercial city in the United States.

In the 1830s, private railroad companies began to give canals competition. The nation's first railroad, the Baltimore and Ohio, laid thirteen miles of track in 1829. During the 1830s, three thousand more miles of track materialized nationwide, the result of a speculative fever in railroad construction masterminded by bankers, locomotive manufacturers, and state legislators who provided subsidies, charters, and land rights-of-way. Rail lines in the 1830s were generally short, on the order of twenty to one hundred miles. They did not yet provide an efficient distribution system for goods, but passengers flocked to experience the marvelous speeds of fifteen to twenty miles per hour. Railroads and other advances in transportation made possible enormous change by unifying the country culturally and economically.

Factories, Workingwomen, and Wage Labor

Transportation advances promoted the expansion of manufacturing after 1815, creating an ever-expanding market for goods. The two leading industries, textiles and shoes, altered methods of production and labor relations. Textile production was greatly spurred by the development of water-driven machinery built near fast-coursing rivers. Shoe manufacturing, still using the power and skill of human hands, involved only a reorganization of production. Both industries pulled young women into wage-earning labor for the first time.

The earliest factory was built by English immigrant Samuel Slater in Pawtucket, Rhode Island, in the 1790s. It featured a mechanical spinning machine that produced thread and yarn. By 1815, nearly 170 spinning mills had been built along New England rivers. In British manufacturing cities, entire families worked in low-wage, health-threatening factories. By contrast, American factories targeted young women as employees; they were cheap to hire because of their limited employment options. Mill girls would "retire" to marriage, replaced by fresh recruits earning beginners' wages.

In 1821, a group of Boston entrepreneurs founded the town of Lowell on the Merrimack River, centralizing all aspects of cloth production: combing, shrinking, spinning, weaving, and dyeing. By 1836, the eight mills in Lowell employed more than five thousand young women, who lived in carefully managed company-owned boardinghouses. Corporation rules at the **Lowell mills** required church attendance and prohibited drinking and unsupervised courtship; dorms were locked at 10 P.M. A typical mill worker earned $2 to $3 for a seventy-hour week, more than a seamstress or domestic servant could earn but less than a young man's wages. The job consisted of tending noisy power looms in rooms kept hot and humid, ideal for thread but not for people.

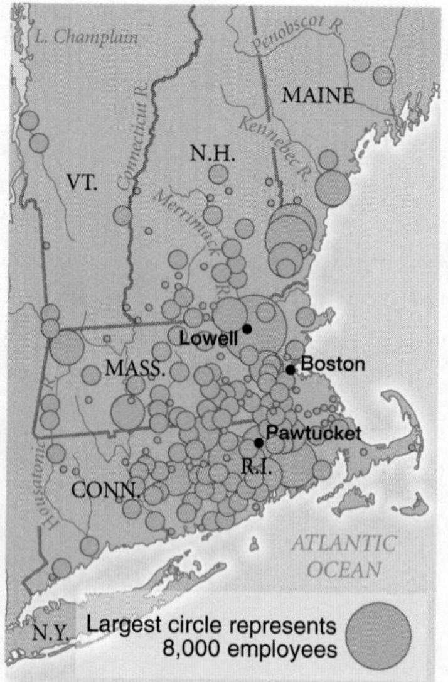

Cotton Textile Industry, ca. 1840

Despite the discomforts, young women embraced factory work as a means to earn spending money and build savings before marriage; several banks in town held the nest eggs of thousands of workers. Also welcome was the unprecedented, though still limited, personal freedom of living in an all-female social space, away from parents and domestic tasks. In the evening, the women could engage in self-improvement activities, such as writing for the company's periodical, the *Lowell Offering*, or attending lectures on literary, scientific, or even political topics. In 1837, 1,500 mill girls squeezed into Lowell's city hall to hear the Grimké sisters speak about the evils of slavery.

In the mid-1830s, worldwide growth and competition in the cotton market impelled mill owners to speed up work and decrease wages. The workers protested, emboldened by their communal living arrangement and by their relative independence as temporary employees. In 1834 and again in 1836, hundreds of women at Lowell went out on strike (see "Documenting the American Promise," page 328). All over New England, female mill workers led strikes and formed unions. In 1834, mill workers in Dover, New Hampshire, denounced their

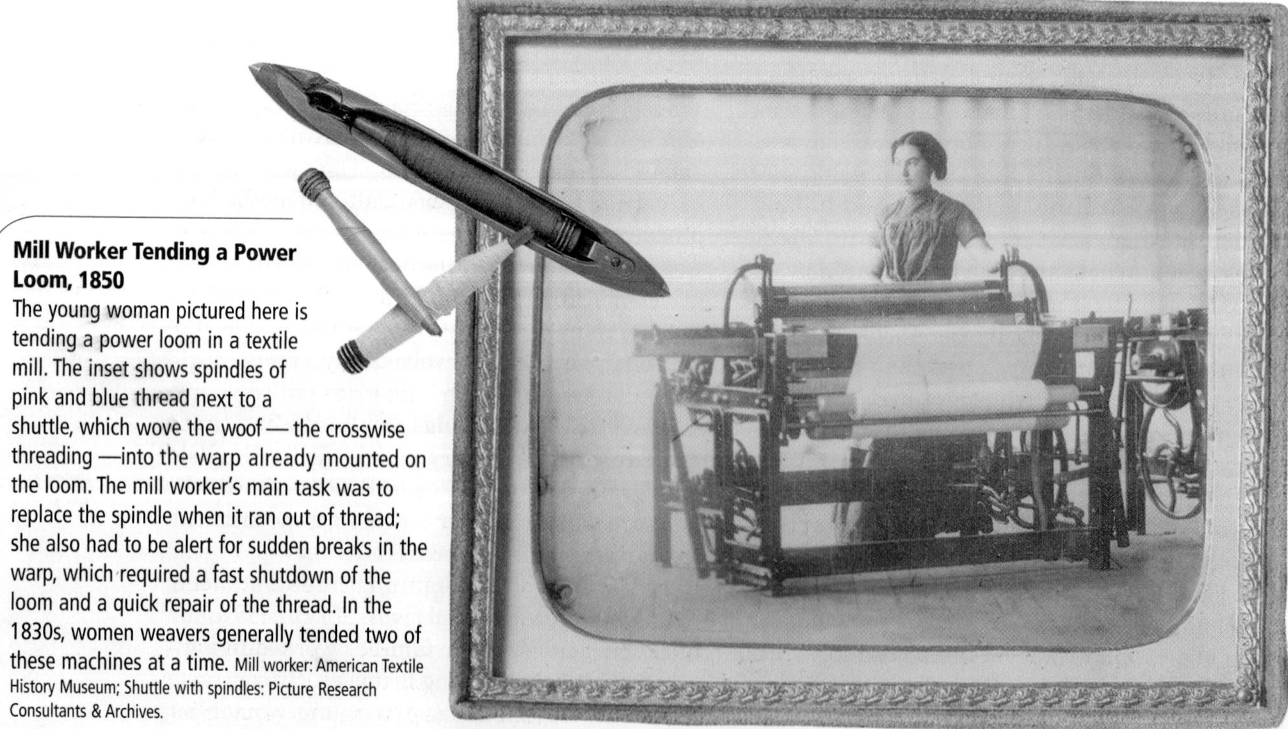

Mill Worker Tending a Power Loom, 1850

The young woman pictured here is tending a power loom in a textile mill. The inset shows spindles of pink and blue thread next to a shuttle, which wove the woof — the crosswise threading —into the warp already mounted on the loom. The mill worker's main task was to replace the spindle when it ran out of thread; she also had to be alert for sudden breaks in the warp, which required a fast shutdown of the loom and a quick repair of the thread. In the 1830s, women weavers generally tended two of these machines at a time. Mill worker: American Textile History Museum; Shuttle with spindles: Picture Research Consultants & Archives.

owners for trying to turn them into "slaves": "However freely the epithet of 'factory slaves' may be bestowed upon us, we will never deserve it by a base and cringing submission to proud wealth or haughty insolence." Their assertiveness surprised many, but ultimately the ease of replacing them undermined their bargaining power, and owners in the 1840s began to shift to immigrant families as their primary labor source.

The shoe manufacturing industry centered in eastern New England reorganized production and hired women, including wives, as shoebinders. Male shoemakers still cut the leather and made the soles in shops, but female shoebinders working from home now stitched the upper parts of the shoes. Working from home meant that wives could contribute to family income — unusual for most wives in that period — and still perform their domestic chores.

In the economically turbulent 1830s, shoebinder wages fell. Unlike mill workers, female shoebinders worked in isolation, a serious hindrance to organized protest. In Lynn, Massachusetts, a major shoemaking center, women used female church networks to organize resistance, communicating via religious newspapers. The Lynn shoebinders who demanded higher wages in 1834 built on a collective sense of themselves as women, even though they did not work together daily. "Equal rights should be extended to all — to the weaker sex as well as the stronger," they wrote in a document establishing the Female Society of Lynn.

In the end, the Lynn shoebinders' protests failed to achieve wage increases. At-home workers all over New England continued to accept low wages, and even in Lynn many women shied away from organized protest, preferring to situate their work in the context of family duty (helping their husbands to finish the shoes) instead of market relations.

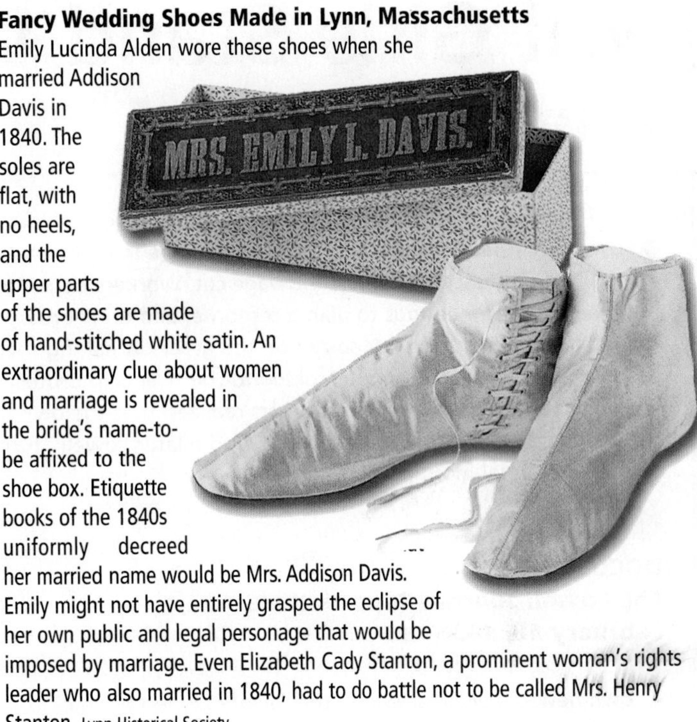

Fancy Wedding Shoes Made in Lynn, Massachusetts
Emily Lucinda Alden wore these shoes when she married Addison Davis in 1840. The soles are flat, with no heels, and the upper parts of the shoes are made of hand-stitched white satin. An extraordinary clue about women and marriage is revealed in the bride's name-to-be affixed to the shoe box. Etiquette books of the 1840s uniformly decreed her married name would be Mrs. Addison Davis. Emily might not have entirely grasped the eclipse of her own public and legal personage that would be imposed by marriage. Even Elizabeth Cady Stanton, a prominent woman's rights leader who also married in 1840, had to do battle not to be called Mrs. Henry Stanton. Lynn Historical Society.

Bankers and Lawyers

Entrepreneurs like the Lowell factory owners relied on innovations in the banking system to finance their ventures. Between 1814 and 1816, the number of state-chartered banks in the United States more than doubled from fewer than 90 to 208. By 1830, there were 330, and by 1840 hundreds more. Banks stimulated the economy by making loans to merchants and manufacturers and by enlarging the money supply. Borrowers were issued loans in the form of banknotes — certificates unique to each bank — that were used as money for all transactions. Neither federal nor state governments issued paper money, so banknotes became the country's currency.

In theory, a note could always be traded in at a bank for its hard-money equivalent in gold or silver, a transaction known as a "**specie payment**." A note from a solid local bank might be worth exactly what it was written for, but the face value of a note from a distant or questionable bank would be discounted. Buying and selling banknotes in this era required knowledge and caution. Not surprisingly, counterfeiting flourished.

Bankers exercised great power over the economy, deciding who would get loans and what the discount rates would be. The most powerful bankers sat on the board of directors for the **second Bank of the United States**, headquartered in Philadelphia and featuring eighteen branches throughout the country. The twenty-year charter of the first Bank of the United States had expired in 1811, and the second Bank of the United States opened for business in 1816 under another twenty-year charter. The rechartering of this bank would become a major issue in the 1832 presidential campaign.

Accompanying the market revolution was a revolution in commercial law, fashioned by politicians to enhance the prospects of private investment. In 1811, states started to rewrite their laws of incorporation (allowing the chartering

Mill Girls Stand Up to Factory Owners, 1834

Lowell's first large "turn out" by mill girls came in February 1834, after the factory owners announced a 15 percent wage cut. Workers began to circulate petitions and hold female-only meetings to plan a response, and on February 14 hundreds walked off the job. Newspaper accounts seized on the groundbreaking spectacle of young women, thought to be docile and polite, taking to the streets in protest. Four days later, the strike fizzled when the inexperienced workers realized that the owners could ignore and easily replace them. But lessons were learned, and a later Lowell "turn out," in 1836, was sustained for several months.

DOCUMENT 1
The Lowell Journal Reports the Strike, February 18, 1834

A town newspaper favorable to the factory owners characterized the work stoppage as a delusional farce led by a small number of "wicked girls."

THE FACTORY GIRLS.—It has become known, from rumor, that a considerable number of the girls employed in the mills of this town turned out on Friday last, to prevent a reduction in wages. . . . It was proposed, some time since, to make a very small reduction in the wages of all of the hands on the first of March, and notices to that effect were posted in the mills. . . .

Upon this, several wicked and malicious girls . . . undertook to get up a *turn out*, with a view to threaten the agents with an entire stoppage of the works, in order to exact the higher rates of wages. . . . On Friday and Saturday from 800 to 1000 girls revolted under the most laughable delusions, that mischief could invent. The first day, processions were formed of about 700 girls, who listened to sundry stimulative exhortations, . . . and marched through the streets, ankle-deep in mud, with waving handkerchiefs and scarfs, and signals of beckonings to all who kept the peace, and conducted wisely. Saturday became a day of repentance to many; and they would gladly have returned to their business, but for a pledge, cunningly devised, that each who did so, should forfeit five dollars to the rebels. The Sabbath afforded opportunity for a little more cool reflection, and on Monday morning, a large concourse attended by a parcel of idle men and boys, heard another speech, . . . which was followed by a well-timed prayer and a judicious exhortation from a clergyman of the Methodist persuasion. The result of the whole matter is, that a few of the ring-leaders are refused entrance into the mills, and most of the disaffected, having learned the truth, and becoming sensible of the wicked misrepresentations of which they had nearly been the victims, are returning to their work, ready to take a diminished price, and continue to labor at wages which will give them from one and a half, to two and a half dollars per week, more than their board. — This, to be sure, is not so much as they have had in past times, nor so much as we hope they will soon have again, but it is more than they can get in any other occupation in New England.

The most amusing part of the farce, for it deserves no other name, was the eagerness with which an attempt was made to break the banks. A large sum, in the total, was withdrawn from the Savings' Bank, which, in addition to wages due, was presented at the Lowell and Rail Road Banks for specie — a flock of girls about as numerous and dense as the wild pigeons of the West, thronged the counters and pocketed the hard cash. The Banks, notwithstanding the severe pressure outside their counters have felt none within, and the public generally, and the factory girls in particular, are still invited to call.

SOURCE: *The Lowell Journal*, February 18, 1834, as reprinted in the *New-York Spectator*, March 6, 1834. Gale Database, "Nineteenth-century U.S. Newspapers."

DOCUMENT 2
Anonymous Mill Girls, "Union Is Power"

A position paper, quickly drafted, framed the strikers' goals in terms of "rights" and appealed to the patriotic spirit of the American Revolution and their heritage as "daughters of freemen" to justify their actions.

Our present object is to have union and exertion, and we remain in possession of our own unquestionable rights. We circulate this paper, wishing to obtain the names of all who imbibe the spirit of our patriotic ancestors, who preferred privation to bondage, and parted with all that renders life desirable — and even life itself — to procure independence for their children. The oppressing hand of avarice would enslave us; and to gain their object, they very gravely tell us of the pressure of the times; this we are already sensible of, and deplore it. If any are in want of assistance, the Ladies will be compassionate, and assist them; but we prefer to have the disposing of our charities in our own hands; and as we are free, we would remain in possession of what kind Providence has bestowed upon us, and remain daughters of freemen still.

All who patronize this effort, we wish to have discontinue their labors until terms of reconciliation are made.

Resolved, That we will not go back into the mills to work unless our wages are continued to us as they have been.

Resolved, That none of us will go back unless they receive us all as one.

Resolved, That if any have not money enough to carry them home, that they shall be supplied.

SOURCE: Printed in *The Man*, February 22, 1834. Published in New York City by G. H. Evans. American Periodicals Series Online.

DOCUMENT 3
Support from Workingmen, March, 1834

Periodicals aimed at working-class men championed the striking women of Lowell.

Some of the Eastern papers severely censure the Lowell girls for their recent "Turn out," and for not submitting to the reduction announced by their employers. Those females had as good a right to fix a price on their labor, and to refuse to reduce it, as their employers have to fix a price on their manufactures, and if they were to resign that right, they would be altogether at the mercy of their employers. . . .

The price of female labor is already too low, and the amount of labor that females have to perform too great. Many of those young women . . . must, out of their small earning, which rarely exceeds two dollars and fifty cents a week, provide board and clothing, and lay by something to support themselves when they are sick or unemployed.

SOURCE: *The National Trades' Union* (published weekly by the General Trades' Union of the City of New York), as reprinted in the *Workingman's Advocate* (New York), March 8, 1834. American Periodical Series Online.

DOCUMENT 4
A Strike Leader Speaks Out, mid-March, 1834

A month later, one of the leaders explained that the strike was caused not only by reduced wages but also by anger at the insolence and tyranny of wealthy factory owners. Her remarks were published in a New York daily, The Man, *a paper established in 1834 to advocate for workingmen's issues.*

The Lowell Girls have been censured in no measured terms by the Federal press of the east, for the "turn out.". . . One of the girls has turned round on her accusers, and while she does not outstep the modesty of her sex, her spirit would do credit to any parentage in these or other days. Hear the yankee girl:

"We do not estimate our *Liberty* by dollars and cents; consequently it was not the reduction of *wages* alone which caused the excitement, but that *haughty, overbearing disposition* — that *purse proud insolence*, which was becoming more and more apparent — that spirit of tyranny so manifest at present among the *avaricious* and wealthy manufacturers of this and the old country.

"I have only to add, that if the proprietors and agents are not satisfied with alluring us from our homes — from the peaceful abodes of our childhood, under the false promises of a great reward, and then casting us upon the world, . . . merely because we would not be slaves — . . . let them bring down upon us the whole influence of the *rich* and *noble*, the *proud* and the *mighty*, all piled upon the *United States Bank* — steep us in poverty to the very dregs, but we beseech them not to asperse our characters, or *stigmatize* us as *disorderly* persons. Grant us this favor, and give us the privilege of breathing the air of freedom in its *purity*, and we will be content."

SOURCE: *The Man*, March 20, 1834. Published in New York City by G. H. Evans. American Periodicals Series Online.

Questions for Analysis and Debate

1. Does the *Lowell Journal* adequately explain how a few "ringleaders" could motivate over eight hundred female workers to engage in street protests and a run on the local banks?

2. In the strikers' statement of purpose, what is the significance of the references to Revolutionary-era ideals of independence and liberty and the phrase "daughters of freemen"? What did their final resolution promise? Do these young women feel subordinate and deferential to the factory owners? Were they in fact subordinates?

3. What do the several references to banks and money tell us about the class dimensions of this situation? How did the *Lowell Journal* excuse the wage reduction? What did the strike leader mean by "purse proud insolence"?

of businesses by states), and the number of corporations expanded rapidly, from about twenty in 1800 to eighteen hundred by 1817. Incorporation protected individual investors from being held liable for corporate debts. State lawmakers also wrote laws of eminent domain, empowering states to buy land for roads and canals even from unwilling sellers. In such ways, entrepreneurial lawyers of the 1820s and 1830s created the legal foundation for an economy that favored ambitious individuals interested in maximizing their own wealth.

Not everyone applauded these developments. The skillful lawyer-turned-politician **Andrew Jackson** spoke for a large and mistrustful segment of the population when he warned about the potential abuses of power "which the moneyed interest derives from a paper currency which they are able to control, from the multitude of corporations with exclusive privileges which they have succeeded in obtaining in the different states, and which are employed altogether for their benefit." Jacksonians believed that ending government-granted privileges was the way to maximize individual liberty and economic opportunity.

Booms and Busts

One aspect of the economy that the lawyer-politicians could not control was the threat of financial collapse. The boom years from 1815 to 1818 exhibited a volatility that resulted in the first sharp, large-scale economic downturn in U.S. history. Americans called this downturn a "panic," and the pattern was repeated in the 1830s. Rapidly rising consumer demand stimulated price increases, and speculative investment opportunities offering the possibility of high payoffs abounded — in bank stocks, western land sales, urban real estate, and commodities markets. High inflation made some people wealthy but created hardships for workers on fixed incomes.

> "[Credit is like] a man pissing in his breeches on a cold day to keep his arse warm — very comfortable at first but I dare say . . . you know how it feels afterwards."
> — A farmer in debt in 1819

When the bubble burst in 1819, the overnight rich suddenly became the overnight poor. Some blamed the **panic of 1819** on the second Bank of the United States for failing to control state banks that had suspended specie payments in their eagerness to expand the economic bubble. By mid-1818, when the Bank of the United States called in its loans and insisted that the state banks do likewise, the contracting of the money supply sent tremors throughout the economy. The crunch was made worse by a financial crisis in Europe in the spring of 1819. Overseas, prices for American cotton, tobacco, and wheat plummeted by more than 50 percent. Thus, when the banks began to call in their outstanding loans, American debtors involved in the commodities trade could not come up with the money. Business and personal bankruptcies skyrocketed. The intricate web of credit and debt relationships meant that almost everyone with even a toehold in the new commercial economy was affected by the panic. Thousands of Americans lost their savings and property, and unemployment estimates suggest that half a million people lost their jobs.

Recovery took several years. Unemployment declined, but bitterness lingered, ready to be stirred up by politicians in the decades to come. The dangers of a system dependent on extensive credit were now clear. In one folksy formulation that circulated around 1820, a farmer compared credit to "a man pissing in his breeches on a cold day to keep his arse warm — very comfortable at first but I dare say . . . you know how it feels afterwards."

By the mid-1820s, the economy was back on track, driven by increases in productivity, consumer demand for goods, and international trade, as well as a restless and calculating people moving goods, human labor, and investment capital in expanding circles of commerce. Despite the panic of 1819, credit financing continued to fuel the system. With the growth of manufacturing and transportation networks, buyers and sellers operated in a much larger arena, using credit transactions on paper instead of moving actual (and scarce) hard money around. A merchant in Ohio who bought goods in New York City on credit hoped to repay the loan with interest when he sold the merchandise — often on credit — for a profit. Slave owners might obtain loans to purchase additional land or slaves, using currently owned slaves as collateral. A network of credit and debt relations grew dense by the 1830s in a system that encouraged speculation and risk taking. A pervasive optimism about continued growth supported the elaborate system, but a single business failure could produce many innocent victims. Well after the panic of 1819, an undercurrent of anxiety about rapid economic change continued to shape the political views of many Americans.

REVIEW Why did the United States experience a market revolution after 1815?

▶ The Spread of Democracy

Just as the market revolution held out the promise, if not the reality, of economic opportunity for all who worked, the political transformation of the 1830s held out the promise of political opportunity for hundreds of thousands of new voters. During Andrew Jackson's presidency (1829–1837), the second American party system took shape. Not until 1836, however, would the parties have distinct names and consistent programs transcending the particular personalities running for office. Over those years, more men could and did vote, responding to new methods of arousing voter interest. In 1828, Jackson's charismatic personality defined his party, and his victory over incumbent president John Quincy Adams turned on questions of character. Once in office, Jackson championed ordinary citizens against the power elite — democracy versus aristocracy, in Jackson's terminology. A lasting contribution of the Jackson years was the notion that politicians needed to have the common touch in their dealings with voters.

Popular Politics and Partisan Identity

The election of 1828 was the first presidential contest in which the popular vote determined the outcome. In twenty-two out of twenty-four states, voters — not state legislatures — designated the number of electors committed to a particular candidate. More than a million voters participated, three times the number in 1824 and nearly half the free male population, reflecting the high stakes that voters perceived in the Adams-Jackson rematch. Throughout the 1830s, voter turnout continued to rise and reached 70 percent in some localities, partly because of the disappearance of property qualifications in all but three states and partly because of heightened political interest.

The 1828 election inaugurated new campaign styles. State-level candidates routinely gave speeches at rallies, picnics, and banquets. Adams and Jackson still declined such appearances as undignified, but **Henry Clay** of Kentucky, campaigning for Adams, earned the nickname "the Barbecue Orator." Campaign rhetoric became more informal and even blunt. The Jackson camp established many Hickory Clubs, trading on Jackson's popular nickname, "Old Hickory," from a common Tennessee tree suggesting resilience and toughness. (Jackson was the first presidential candidate to have an affectionate and widely used nickname.)

TABLE 11.1 THE GROWTH OF NEWSPAPERS, 1820–1840

	1820	1830	1835	1840
U.S. population (in millions)	9.6	12.8	15.0	17.1
Number of newspapers published	500	800	1,200	1,400
Daily newspapers	42	65	—	138

Partisan newspapers in ever-larger numbers defined issues and publicized political personalities as never before. Improved printing technology and rising literacy rates fueled a great expansion of newspapers of all kinds (Table 11.1). Party leaders dispensed subsidies and other favors to secure the support of papers, even in remote towns and villages. In New York State, where party development was most advanced, a pro-Jackson group called the Bucktails controlled fifty weekly publications. Stories from the leading Jacksonian paper in Washington, D.C., were reprinted two days later in a Boston or Cincinnati paper, for example, as fast as the mail stage could carry them. Presidential campaigns were now coordinated in a national arena.

Politicians at first identified themselves as Jackson or Adams men, honoring the fiction of Republican Party unity. By 1832, however, the terminology had evolved to National Republicans, who favored federal action to promote commercial development, and Democratic Republicans, who promised to be responsive to the will of the majority. Between 1834 and 1836, National Republicans came to be called **Whigs**, while Jackson's party became simply the **Democrats**.

The Election of 1828 and the Character Issue

The campaign of 1828 was the first national election in which scandal and character questions reigned supreme. They became central issues because voters used them to comprehend the kind of public official each man would make. Character issues conveyed in shorthand larger questions about morality, honor, and discipline. Jackson and Adams presented two radically different styles of manhood.

John Quincy Adams was vilified by his opponents as an elitist, a bookish academic, and even a monarchist. Critics pointed to his White House billiard table and ivory chess set as symbols of his aristocratic degeneracy. They also attacked

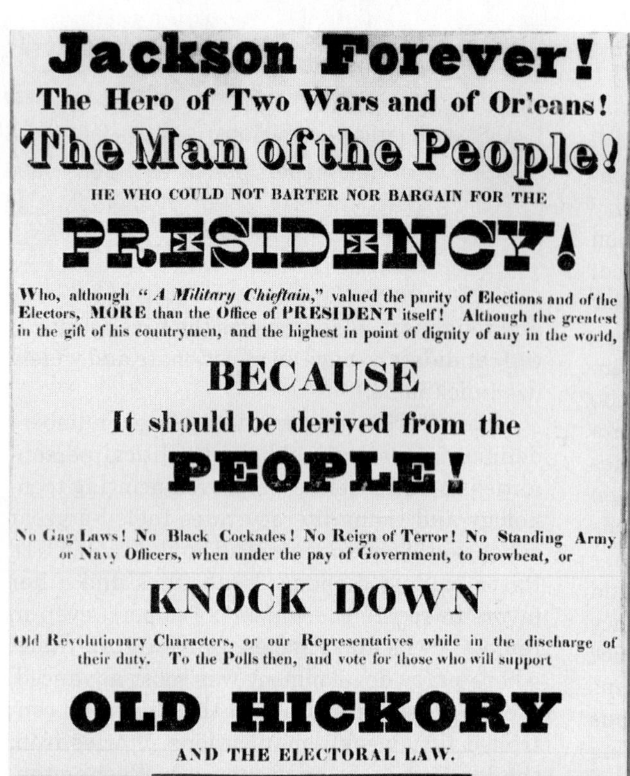

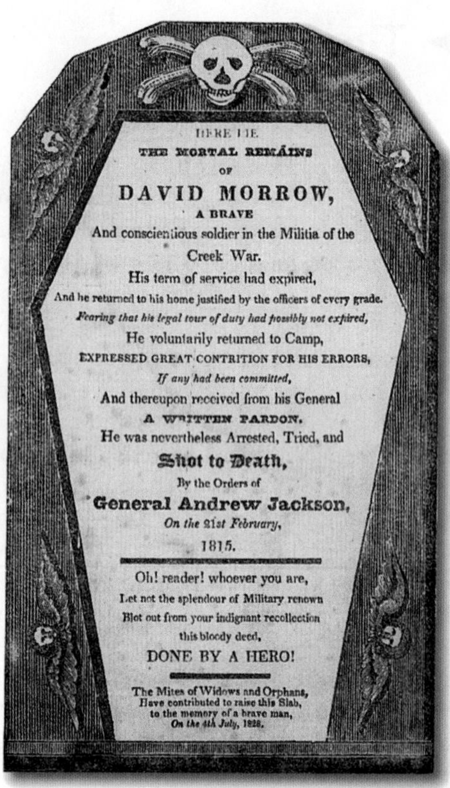

Campaign Posters from 1828
The poster on the left praises Andrew Jackson as a war hero and "man of the people" and reminds readers that Jackson, who won the popular vote in 1824, did not stoop to "bargain for the presidency," as John Quincy Adams presumably had in his dealings with Henry Clay (see chapter 10). The poster with the ominous tombstone and coffin graphics accuses Jackson of an unjustified killing of a Kentucky militiaman (one of six executed) during the Creek War in 1815. The text implores readers to think of the "hero" as a man capable of "this bloody deed."
Pro-Jackson broadside: © Collection of the New-York Historical Society; anti-Jackson broadside: Smithsonian Institution, Washington, D.C.

his "corrupt bargain" of 1824 — the alleged election deal between Adams and Henry Clay (see chapter 10). Adams's supporters returned fire with fire. They played on Jackson's fatherless childhood to portray him as the bastard son of a prostitute. Worse, the cloudy circumstances around his marriage to Rachel Donelson Robards in 1791 gave rise to the story that Jackson was a seducer and an adulterer, having married a woman whose divorce from her first husband was not entirely legal. Pro-Adams newspapers howled that Jackson was sinful and impulsive, while portraying Adams as pious, learned, and virtuous.

Editors in favor of Adams played up Jackson's violent temper, as evidenced by his participation in many duels, brawls, and canings. Jackson's supporters used the same stories to project Old Hickory as a tough frontier hero who knew how to command obedience. As for learning, Jackson's rough frontier education gave him a "natural sense," wrote a Boston editor, that "can never be acquired by reading books — it can only be acquired, in perfection, by reading men." Jackson won a sweeping victory, with 56 percent of the popular vote and 178 electoral votes to Adams's 83 (Map 11.2). Old Hickory took most of the South and West and carried Pennsylvania and New York as well; Adams carried the remainder of the East. Jackson's vice president was **John C. Calhoun**, who had just served as vice president under Adams but had broken with Adams's policies.

After 1828, national politicians no longer deplored the existence of political parties. They were coming to see that parties mobilized and delivered voters, sharpened candidates' differences, and created party loyalty that surpassed loyalty to individual candidates and elections. Adams and Jackson clearly symbolized the competing ideas of the emerging parties: a moralistic, top-down party (the Whigs) ready to make major decisions to promote economic growth competing against a contentious, energetic party (the Democrats) ready to embrace liberty-loving individualism.

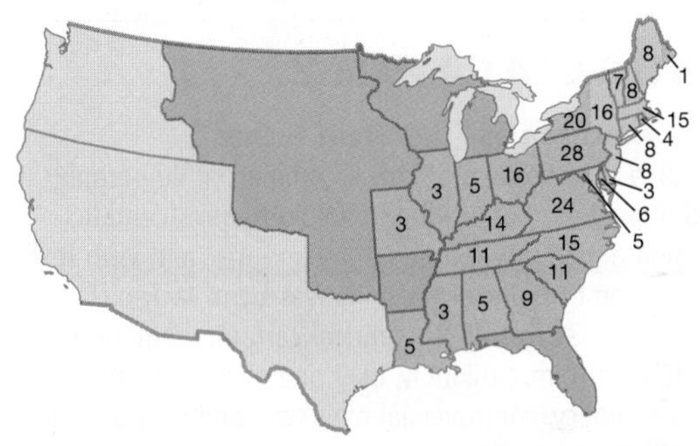

Candidate	Electoral Vote	Popular Vote	Percent of Popular Vote
Andrew Jackson (Democratic Republican)	178	647,286	56
John Q. Adams (National Republican)	83	508,064	44

MAP 11.2
The Election of 1828

Jackson's Democratic Agenda

Before the inauguration in March 1829, Rachel Jackson died. Certain that the ugly campaign had hastened his wife's death, the president went into deep mourning, his depression worsened by constant pain from a bullet still lodged in his chest from an 1806 duel and by mercury poisoning from the medicines he took. Aged sixty-two, Jackson carried only 140 pounds on his six-foot-one frame. His adversaries doubted that he would make it to a second term. His supporters, however, went wild at the inauguration. Thousands cheered his ten-minute inaugural address, the shortest in history. An open reception at the White House turned into a near riot as well-wishers jammed the premises, used windows as doors, stood on furniture for a better view of the great man, and broke thousands of dollars' worth of china and glasses.

During his presidency, Jackson continued to offer unprecedented hospitality to the public. Twenty spittoons newly installed in the East Room of the White House accommodated the tobacco chewers among the throngs that arrived daily to see the president. The courteous Jackson, committed to his image as president of the "common man," held audiences with unannounced visitors throughout his two terms.

Past presidents had tried to lessen party conflict by including men of different factions in their cabinets, but Jackson would have only loyalists, a political tactic followed by most later presidents. For secretary of state, the key job, he tapped New Yorker Martin Van Buren, one of the shrewdest politicians of the day. Throughout the federal government, from postal clerks to ambassadors, Jackson replaced competent civil servants with party loyalists. "To the victor belong the spoils," said a Democratic senator from New York, expressing approval of patronage-driven appointments. Jackson's appointment practices became known as the **spoils system**; it was a concept the president strenuously defended.

Jackson's agenda quickly emerged. Fearing that intervention in the economy inevitably favored some groups at the expense of others, Jackson favored a Jeffersonian limited federal government. He therefore opposed federal support of transportation and grants of monopolies and charters that benefited wealthy investors. Like Jefferson, he anticipated the rapid settlement of the country's interior, where land sales would spread economic democracy to settlers. Thus, establishing a federal policy to remove the Indians from this area had high priority. Unlike Jefferson, Jackson exercised his presidential veto power over Congress. In 1830, he vetoed a highway project in Maysville, Kentucky — Henry Clay's home state — that Congress had backed. The Maysville Road veto articulated Jackson's principled stand that citizens' tax dollars could be spent only on projects of a "general, not local" character. In all, Jackson used the veto twelve times; all previous presidents combined had exercised that right a total of nine times.

"To the victor belong the spoils."
— A Democratic senator from New York, praising patronage appointments

REVIEW Why did Andrew Jackson defeat John Quincy Adams so dramatically in the 1828 election?

▸ Jackson Defines the Democratic Party

In his two terms as president, Andrew Jackson worked to implement his vision of a politics of opportunity for all white men. To open land for white settlement, he favored the relocation of all eastern Indian tribes. He dramatically confronted John C. Calhoun and South Carolina when that state tried to nullify the tariff of 1828. Disapproving of all government-granted privilege, Jackson challenged what he called the "monster" Bank of the United States and took it down to defeat. In all this, he greatly enhanced the power of the presidency.

VISUAL ACTIVITY

Andrew Jackson as "the Great Father"

In 1828, a new process of cheap commercial lithography found immediate application in a colorful presidential campaign aimed at capturing popular votes, and with it, a rich tradition of political cartoons was born. Jackson inspired at least five dozen satirical cartoons centering on caricatures of him. Strikingly, only one of them featured his Indian policy, controversial as it was, and only a single copy still exists. At some point, this cartoon was cropped at the bottom and top, and thus we do not have the cartoonist's caption or signature, both important for more fully understanding the artist's intent. Still, the sarcastic visual humor of Jackson cradling Indians packs an immediate punch. William L. Clements Library.

READING THE IMAGE: Examine the body language conveyed in the various characters' poses. Are the Indians depicted as children or as powerless, miniature adults? What is going on in the picture on the wall?

CONNECTIONS: Does the cartoon suggest that Jackson offers protection to Indians? What does the picture on the wall contribute to our understanding of the artist's opinion of Jackson's Indian removal policy?

Indian Policy and the Trail of Tears

Probably nothing defined Jackson's presidency more than his efforts to solve what he saw as the Indian problem. Thousands of Indians lived in the South and the old Northwest, and many remained in New England and New York. In his first message to Congress in 1829, Jackson, who rose to fame fighting the Creek and Seminole tribes in the 1810s, declared that removing the Indians to territory west of the Mississippi was the only way to save them. White civilization destroyed Indian resources and thus doomed the Indians, he claimed: "That this fate surely awaits them if they remain within the limits of the states does not admit of a doubt. Humanity and national honor demand that every effort should be made to avert so great a calamity." Jackson never publicly wavered from this seemingly noble theme, returning to it in his next seven annual messages.

Prior administrations had experimented with different Indian policies. Starting in 1819, Congress funded missionary associations eager to "civilize" native peoples by converting them to Christianity and encouraging English literacy and agricultural practices. Missionaries also promoted white gender customs, but Indian women were reluctant to embrace practices that accorded them less power than their tribal systems did. The federal government had also pursued aggressive treaty making with many tribes, dealing with the Indians as foreign nations (see chapters 9 and 10).

Privately, Jackson thought it was "absurd" to treat the Indians as foreigners; he saw them as subjects of the United States. Jackson also did not approve of assimilation; that way lay extinction, he said. Removal was the answer. Congress backed Jackson's goal and passed the **Indian Removal Act of 1830**, appropriating $500,000 to relocate eastern tribes west of the Mississippi. About 100 million acres of eastern land would be vacated for eventual white settlement under this act authorizing ethnic expulsion (Map 11.3).

Jackson's frequent claim that removal would save the Indians from extinction was in part formulated in response to the widespread controversy generated by the Indian Removal Act. Newspapers, public lecturers, and local clubs debated the expulsion law, and public opinion, especially in the North, was heated. "One would think that the guilt of African slavery was enough for the nation to bear, without the additional

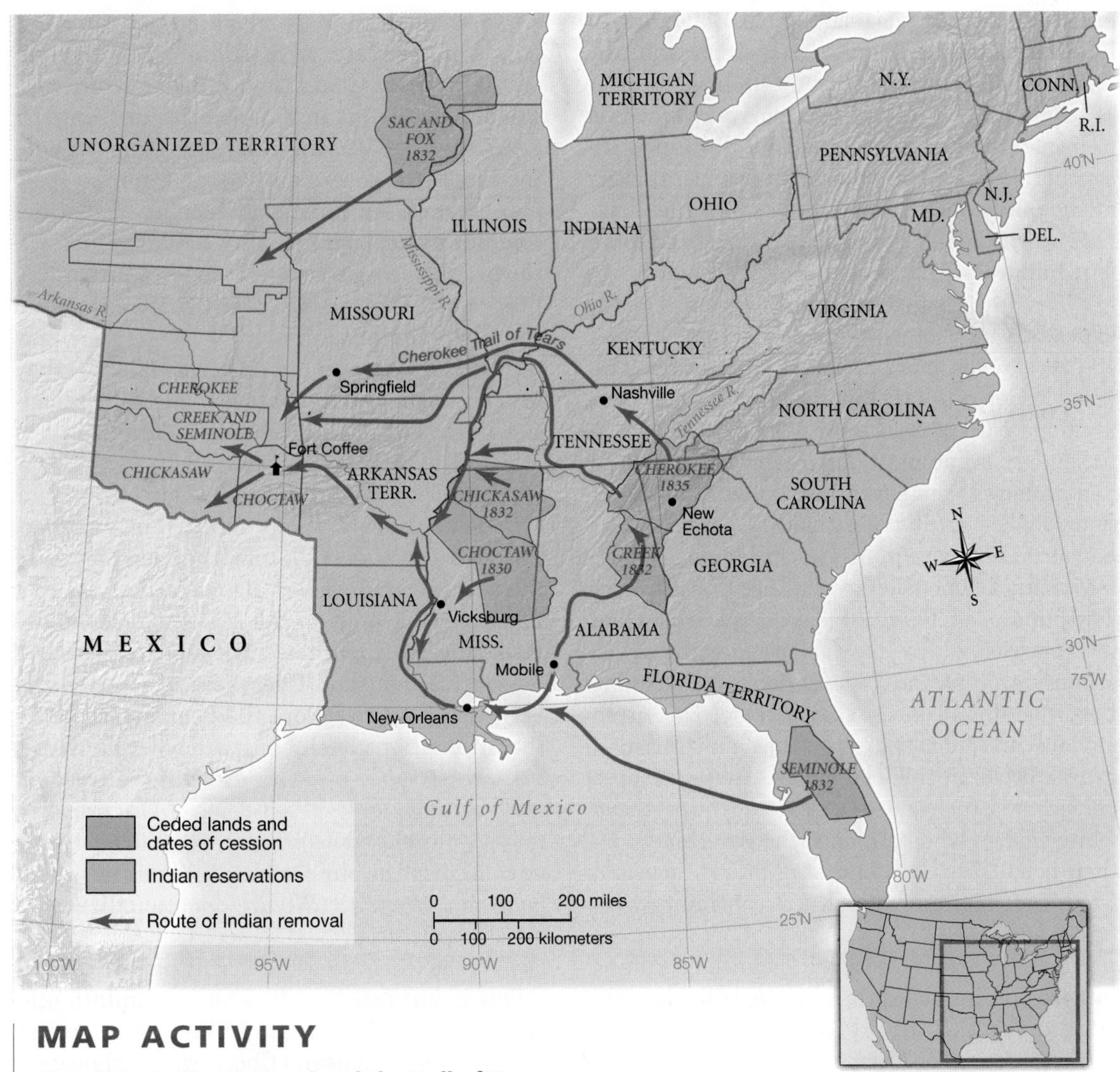

MAP ACTIVITY

Map 11.3 Indian Removal and the Trail of Tears

The federal government under President Andrew Jackson pursued a vigorous policy of Indian removal in the 1830s. Tribes were forcibly moved west to land known as Indian Territory (present-day Oklahoma). In 1838, as many as a quarter of the Cherokee Indians died on the route known as the Trail of Tears.

READING THE MAP: From which states were most of the Native Americans removed? Through which states did the Trail of Tears go?

CONNECTIONS: Before Jackson's presidency, how did the federal government view Native Americans, and what policy initiatives were undertaken by the government and private groups? How did Jackson change the government's policy toward Native Americans?

crime of injustice to the aborigines," one writer declared in 1829. In an unprecedented move, thousands of northern white women signed petitions opposing the removal policy. The right to petition for redress of grievances, part of the Constitution's First Amendment, had long been used by individual women acting on a personal cause — say, a military widow requesting her husband's pension. But mass petitioning by women was something new; it directly challenged the prevailing assumption that women could not be political actors. Between 1830 and 1832, women's petitions rolled into Washington, arguing specifically that the Cherokee Indians of Georgia were a sovereign people on the road to Christianity and entitled to stay on their land. Jackson ignored the petitions.

For the northern tribes, their numbers diminished by years of war, gradual removal was already well under way. But not all the Indians went quietly. In 1832 in western Illinois, Black Hawk, a leader of the Sauk and Fox Indians who had fought in alliance with Tecumseh in the War of 1812 (see chapter 10), resisted removal. Volunteer militias attacked and chased the Indians into southern Wisconsin, where, after several skirmishes and a deadly battle (later called the Black Hawk War), Black Hawk was captured and some four hundred of his people were massacred.

The large southern tribes — the Creek, Chickasaw, Choctaw, Seminole, and Cherokee — proved even more resistant to removal. The tribal leadership of the Cherokee in Georgia chose a unique path of resistance by taking their case to the U.S. Supreme Court. Georgia Cherokees had already taken several assimilationist steps. Spurred by dedicated missionaries, these leaders had incorporated written laws, including, in 1827, a constitution modeled on the U.S. Constitution. Two hundred of the wealthiest Cherokee men had intermarried with whites, adopting white styles of housing, dress, and cotton agriculture, including the ownership of slaves. They developed a written alphabet and published a newspaper and Christian prayer books in their language. These features helped make their cause attractive to the northern white women who petitioned the government on their behalf. Yet most of the seventeen thousand Cherokees maintained cultural continuity with past traditions.

In 1831, when Georgia announced its plans to seize all Cherokee property, the tribal leaders asked the U.S. Supreme Court to restrain Georgia. The Court held that the Cherokee people lacked standing to sue, not being citizens of either the United States or any foreign state. In the Court's view, tribes residing within U.S. boundaries were "domestic dependent nations," in effect wards of the state. A year later, they brought suit again, this time using an ally, a white missionary, as their stand-in plaintiff. In *Worcester v. Georgia* (1832), the Supreme Court upheld the territorial sovereignty of the Cherokee people, recognizing their existence as "a distinct community, occupying its own territory, in which the laws of Georgia can have no force." An angry President Jackson ignored the Court and pressed the Cherokee tribe to move west: "If they now refuse to accept the liberal terms offered, they can only be liable for whatever evils and difficulties may arise. I feel conscious of having done my duty to my red children."

The Cherokee tribe remained in Georgia for two more years without significant violence. Then, in 1835, a small, unauthorized faction of the acculturated leaders signed a treaty selling all the tribal lands to the state, which rapidly resold the land to whites. Chief John Ross, backed by several thousand Cherokees, petitioned the U.S. Congress to ignore the bogus treaty. "By the stipulations of this instrument," he wrote, "we are stripped of every attribute of freedom and eligibility for legal self-defense. Our property may be plundered before our eyes; violence may be committed on our persons; even our lives may be taken away. . . . We are denationalized; we are disfranchised."

As the Cherokees stubbornly held out, other tribes capitulated to Jackson's mandate and endured forcible relocation. Fifteen thousand Creek, twelve thousand Choctaw, five thousand Chickasaw, and several thousand Seminole Indians moved to Indian Territory (which became the state of Oklahoma in 1907). In his farewell address to the nation in 1837, Jackson assured white listeners of his faith in the humanitarian benefits of Indian removal: "This unhappy race . . . are now placed in a situation where we may well hope that they will share in the blessings of civilization and be saved from the degradation and destruction to which they were rapidly hastening while they remained in the states."

When the Cherokees refused to move by the voluntary evacuation deadline of May 1838, Jackson's successor, Martin Van Buren, sent federal troops to remove them. Under armed guard, the Cherokees embarked on a 1,200-mile journey west that came to be called the **Trail of Tears**. A newspaperman in Kentucky described the forced march: "Even aged females, apparently, nearly ready to drop into the grave, were traveling with heavy burdens attached to the back. . . . They buried fourteen to fifteen at every

Cherokee Deer Hide Coat
Durable, supple, and nearly airtight, tanned deer hides made excellent clothing material. This knee-length coat, decorated with red paint, red buttons, and fringe, has extra layers of hide on the shoulders for additional protection against rain and snow. It dates from the first quarter of the nineteenth century and was still in the possession of Cherokees in Oklahoma in the 1930s. It seems entirely plausible to surmise that it traveled to Oklahoma with its owner on the Trail of Tears in 1838. Courtesy, Museum of the American Indian, Smithsonian Institution, Washington, D.C.

stopping place." Nearly a quarter of the Cherokees died en route from the hardship. Perhaps Jackson had genuinely believed that exile to the West was necessary to save Indian cultures from destruction. But for the forcibly removed tribes, the costs of relocation were high.

The Tariff of Abominations and Nullification

Jackson's Indian policy happened to harmonize with the principle of states' rights; the president supported Georgia's right to ignore the Supreme Court's decision in *Worcester v. Georgia*. But in another pressing question of states' rights, Jackson contested South Carolina's attempt to ignore federal tariff policy.

Federal tariffs as high as 33 percent on imports such as textiles and iron goods had been passed in 1816 and again in 1824 in an effort to shelter new American manufacturers from foreign competition. Some southern congressmen opposed the steep tariffs, fearing they would reduce overseas shipping and thereby hurt cotton exports. In 1828, Congress passed a revised tariff that came to be known as the **Tariff of Abominations**. A bundle of conflicting duties, some as high as 50 percent, the legislation contained provisions that pleased and angered every economic and sectional interest.

South Carolina in particular suffered from the Tariff of Abominations. Worldwide prices for cotton had declined in the late 1820s, and the falloff in shipping caused by the high tariffs further hurt the South. In 1828, a group of South Carolina politicians headed by John C. Calhoun advanced a doctrine called **nullification**. The Union, they argued, was a confederation of states that had yielded some but not all power to the federal government. When Congress overstepped its powers, states had the right to nullify Congress's acts. As precedents, they pointed to the Virginia and Kentucky Resolutions of 1798, intended to invalidate the Alien and Sedition Acts (see chapter 9). Congress had erred in using tariff policy to benefit specific industries, they claimed; tariffs should be used only to raise revenue.

On assuming the presidency in 1829, Jackson ignored the South Carolina statement of nullification and shut out Calhoun, his new vice president, from influence or power. Tariff revisions in early 1832 brought little relief to the South. Sensing futility, Calhoun resigned the vice presidency and became a senator to better serve his state. Finally, strained to their limit, South Carolina leaders took the radical step of declaring federal tariffs null and void in their state as of February 1, 1833. The constitutional crisis was out in the open.

Opting for a dramatic confrontation, Jackson sent armed ships to Charleston harbor and threatened to invade the state. He pushed through Congress the Force Bill, defining South Carolina's stance as treason and authorizing military action to collect federal tariffs. At the same time, Congress moved quickly to pass a revised tariff that was more acceptable to the South. The conciliating Senator Henry Clay rallied support for a moderate bill that gradually reduced tariffs down to the 1816 level. On March 1, 1833, Congress passed both the new tariff and the Force Bill. In response, South Carolina withdrew its nullification of the old tariff — and then nullified the Force Bill. It was a symbolic gesture, since Jackson's show of muscle was no longer necessary. Both sides were satisfied: Federal power had prevailed over an assertion of states' rights, and South Carolina got the lower tariff it wanted.

Yet the question of federal power versus states' rights was far from settled. The implied threat behind nullification was secession, a position articulated in 1832 by some South Carolinians whose concerns went beyond tariff policy. In the 1830s, the political moratorium on discussions of slavery agreed on at the time of the Missouri Compromise (see chapter 10) was coming unglued, and new northern voices opposed to slavery gained increasing attention. If and when a northern-dominated federal government decided to end slavery, the South Carolinians thought, the South should nullify such laws or else remove itself from the Union.

The Bank War and Economic Boom

Along with the tariff and nullification, President Jackson fought another political battle, over the Bank of the United States. After riding out the panic of 1819, the bank finally prospered. With twenty-nine branches, it handled the federal government's deposits, extended credit and loans, and issued banknotes — by 1830, the most stable currency in the country. Jackson, however, did not find the bank's functions sufficiently valuable to offset his criticism of the concept of a national bank: that it concentrated undue economic power in the hands of a few.

National Republican (Whig) senators Daniel Webster and Henry Clay decided to force the issue.

They convinced the bank to apply for charter renewal in 1832, well before the fall election, even though the existing charter ran until 1836. They fully expected that Congress's renewal would force Jackson to follow through on his rhetoric with a veto, that the unpopular veto would cause Jackson to lose the election, and that the bank would survive on an override vote by a new Congress swept into power on the anti-Jackson tide.

At first, the plan seemed to work. The bank applied for rechartering, Congress voted to renew, and Jackson, angry over being manipulated, issued his veto. But it was a brilliantly written veto, full of fierce language about the privileges of the moneyed elite who oppressed the democratic masses in order to enrich themselves. "Many of our rich men have not been content with equal protection and equal benefits, but have besought us to make them richer by act of Congress," Jackson wrote.

Clay and his supporters found Jackson's economic ideas and his language of class antagonism so absurd that they distributed thousands of copies of the bank veto as campaign material for their own party. A confident Henry Clay headed his party's ticket for the presidency. But the plan backfired. Jackson's translation of the bank controversy into a language of class antagonism and egalitarian ideals resonated with many Americans. Old Hickory won the election easily, gaining 55 percent of the popular vote and 219 electoral votes to Clay's 49. Jackson's party still controlled Congress, so no override was possible. The second Bank of the United States would cease to exist after 1836. Distraught over the election, Clay condemned the "reign of Jackson," which he termed a "reign of corruption." "The dark cloud," he wrote, "has become more dense, more menacing, more alarming."

Confirming Clay's fears, Jackson took steps to destroy the bank sooner than 1836. Calling it a "monster," he ordered the sizable federal deposits to be removed from its vaults and redeposited into Democratic-inclined state banks. In retaliation, the Bank of the United States raised interest rates and called in loans. This action caused a brief decline in the economy in 1833 and actually enhanced Jackson's claim that the bank was too powerful for the good of the country.

Unleashed and unregulated, the economy went into high gear in 1834. Just at this moment, an excess of silver from Mexican mines made its way into American banks, giving bankers license to print ever more banknotes. From 1834 to 1837, inflation soared; prices of basic goods rose more than 50 percent. States quickly chartered hundreds of new private banks, each issuing its own banknotes. Entrepreneurs borrowed and invested money, and the webs of credit and debt relationships that were the hallmark of the American economy grew denser yet.

The market in western land sales also heated up. In 1834, about 4.5 million acres of the public domain had been sold, the highest annual volume since 1818. By 1836, the total reached an astonishing 20 million acres (Figure 11.1). Some of this was southern land in Mississippi and Louisiana, which slave owners rushed to bring under cultivation, but much more was in the North, where land offices were deluged with buyers. The Jackson administration worried that the purchasers were overwhelmingly eastern capitalist land speculators instead of independent farmers intending to settle on the land.

In one respect, the economy attained an admirable goal: The national debt disappeared, and from 1835 to 1837, for the only time in American history, the government had a monetary surplus. But much of that surplus consisted of questionable bank currencies — "bloated, diseased" currencies, in Jackson's vivid terminology. While the boom was on, however, few stopped to worry about the consequences if and when the bubble burst.

REVIEW Why did Jackson promote Indian removal?

FIGURE 11.1 Western Land Sales, 1810–1860
Land sales peaked in the 1810s, 1830s, and 1850s as Americans rushed to speculate in western land sold by the federal government. The surges in 1818 and 1836 demonstrate the volatile, speculative economy that suddenly collapsed in the panics of 1819 and 1837.

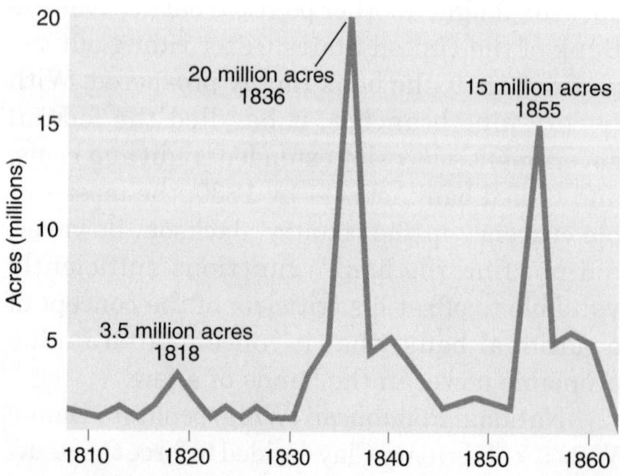

▶ Cultural Shifts, Religion, and Reform

The growing economy, booming by the mid-1830s, transformed social and cultural life. For many families, especially in the commercialized Northeast, standards of living rose, consumption patterns changed, and the nature and location of work were altered. All this had a direct impact on the duties of men and women and on the training of youths for the economy of the future.

Along with economic change came an unprecedented revival of evangelical religion known as the Second Great Awakening. Just as universal male suffrage allowed all white men to vote, democratized religion offered salvation to all who embraced it. Among the most serious adherents of evangelical Protestantism were men and women of the new merchant classes, whose self-discipline in pursuing market ambitions meshed well with the message of self-discipline in pursuit of spiritual perfection. Not content with individual perfection, many of these people sought to perfect society as well, by defining excessive alcohol consumption, nonmarital sex, and slavery as three major evils of modern life in need of correction.

The Family and Separate Spheres

The centerpiece of new ideas about gender relations was the notion that husbands found their status and authority in the new world of work, leaving wives to tend the hearth and home. Sermons, advice books, periodicals, and novels reinforced the idea that men and women inhabited **separate spheres** and had separate duties. "To woman it belongs . . . to elevate the intellectual character of her household [and] to kindle the fires of mental activity in childhood," wrote Mrs. A. J. Graves in a popular book titled *Advice to American Women*. For men, by contrast, "the absorbing passion for gain, and the pressing demands of business, engross their whole attention." In particular, the home, now said to be the exclusive domain of women, was sentimentalized as the source of intimacy, love, and safety, a refuge from the cruel and competitive world of market relations.

Images of the Family at Home
Hundreds of itinerant amateur artists journeyed the back roads and small villages of antebellum America, earning a modest living painting individuals and families. This picture from the 1830s exhibits a common convention—the arrangement of family members by age and by sex, as if to emphasize the ideal of separate spheres. In contrast, the handpainted snuff box depicts a cozy and more realistic scene where a husband rocks the cradle while his wife lies in bed, perhaps recuperating from childbirth. Note the scampering pets, the kettle on the stove, and the chamber pot under the bed, all emblems of unvarnished everyday life. Portrait: Museum of Fine Arts, Boston, Gift of Maxim Karolik for the M. and M. Karolik Collection of American Watercolors and Drawings, 1800–1875; snuff box: Historic Deerfield, photo by Penny Leveritt.

	Nineteenth Century		Twentieth Century		
	1800	*1850*	*1900*	*1960*	*2000*
United States	21	23	23	20	25
England	20	24	24	22	28
Netherlands	—	28	26	25	28
Russia	—	19	—	25	22

Note: Dates are approximate. Dashes indicate a lack of reliable information.

FIGURE 11.2 GLOBAL COMPARISON: Changing Trends in Age at First Marriage for Women
Average age at first marriage is a remarkably complex indicator of social, economic, and cultural factors. In general, women marry younger if existing conditions provide young couples with early financial support: abundant affordable farmland, coresidence with parents, or steady employment for men. Factors that postpone marriage include a lack of farmland, deterioration in male employment prospects, a changed economy requiring more years of pre-job education and training, or enhanced employment for women that makes the job market more attractive than the marriage market. In Europe and the United States, women's age at marriage rose steeply in the nineteenth century. The northeastern United States led the way in the 1820s and 1830s. Can you suggest reasons why? Population experts note that rising age at first marriage is often accompanied by rising rates of nonmarriage, sometimes as high as 20 percent. How might these two trends be connected?

Some new aspects of society gave substance to this formulation of separate spheres. Men's work was undergoing profound change after 1815 and increasingly brought cash to the household, especially in the manufacturing and urban Northeast. Farmers and tradesmen sold products in a market, and bankers, bookkeepers, shoemakers, and canal diggers earned regular salaries or wages. Furthermore, many men now worked away from the home, at an office or a store.

A woman's domestic role was more complicated than the cultural prescriptions indicated (Figure 11.2). Although the vast majority of married white women did not hold paying jobs, their homes required time-consuming labor. But the advice books treated housework as a loving familial duty, thus rendering it invisible in an economy that evaluated work by how much cash it generated. In reality, wives contributed directly to family income in many ways. Some took in boarders; others earned pay for shoebinding or needlework done at home. Wives in the poorest classes, including most free black wives, did not have the luxury of husbands earning adequate wages; for them, wage-paying work as servants or laundresses helped augment family income.

"Females can be educated cheaper, quicker, and better, and will teach cheaper after they are qualified."
— A Massachusetts report on education

Idealized notions about the feminine home and the masculine workplace gained acceptance in the 1830s (and well beyond) because of the cultural ascendancy of the commercialized Northeast, with its domination of book and periodical publication. Men seeking manhood through work and pay could embrace competition and acquisitiveness, while women established femininity through dutiful service to home and family. This particular formulation of gender difference helped smooth the path for the first generation of Americans experiencing the market revolution, and both men and women of the middle classes benefited. Men were set free to pursue wealth, and women gained moral authority within the home. Beyond white families of the middle and upper classes, however, these new gender ideals had limited applicability. And new voices like those of the Grimké sisters challenged whether "virtue" and "duty" had separate masculine and feminine manifestations. Despite their apparent authority in printed material of the period, these gender ideals were never all-pervasive.

The Education and Training of Youths

The market economy required expanded opportunities for training youths of both sexes. By the 1830s, in both the North and the South,

Women Graduates of Oberlin College, Class of 1855
Oberlin College, founded in Ohio by evangelical and abolitionist activists in the 1830s, admitted men and women, both white and black. In the early years, the black students were all male, and the women students, who attended classes in the separate Ladies' Department, were all white. By 1855, as this daguerreotype shows, black women had integrated the Ladies' Department. Each student is dressed in the latest fashion: a dark taffeta dress with a detachable white lace collar. Hairstyles were similarly uniform in the 1850s: hair parted down the middle, dressed with oil, and lustrously coiled over the ears. Oberlin College Archives, Oberlin, OH.

state-supported public school systems were the norm, designed to produce pupils of both sexes able, by age twelve to fourteen, to read, write, and participate in marketplace calculations. Literacy rates for white females climbed dramatically, rivaling the rates for white males for the first time. The fact that taxpayers paid for children's education created an incentive to seek an inexpensive teaching force. By the 1830s, school districts replaced male teachers with young females, for, as a Massachusetts report on education put it, "females can be educated cheaper, quicker, and better, and will teach cheaper after they are qualified." Many were trained in private female academies, now numbering in the hundreds (see chapter 10).

Advanced education continued to expand in the 1830s, with an additional two dozen colleges for men and several more female seminaries offering education on a par with the male colleges. Mount Holyoke Seminary in western Massachusetts, founded by educator Mary Lyon in 1837, developed a rigorous scientific curriculum, and Oberlin College in Ohio, founded by Presbyterians in 1835, became the first coeducational college when it opened its doors to women in 1837. Oberlin's goal was to train young men for the ministry and to prepare young women to be ministers' wives.

Still, only a very small percentage of young people attended institutions of higher learning. The vast majority of male youths left public school at age fourteen to apprentice in specific trades or to embark on business careers by seeking entry-level clerkships, abundant in the growing urban centers. Young women headed for mill towns or cities in unprecedented numbers, seeking work in the expanding service sector as seamstresses and domestic servants. Changes in patterns of youth employment meant that large numbers of youngsters escaped the watchful eyes of their parents. Moralists fretted about the dangers of unsupervised youths, and following the lead of the Lowell mill owners, some established apprentices' libraries and uplifting lecture series to keep young people honorably occupied. Advice books published by the hundreds instructed youths in the virtues of hard work and delayed gratification.

The Second Great Awakening

A newly invigorated version of Protestantism gained momentum in the 1820s and 1830s as the economy reshaped gender and age relations. The earliest manifestations of this fervent piety, which historians call the **Second Great Awakening**, appeared in 1801 in Kentucky, when a crowd of ten thousand people camped out on a hillside at Cane Ridge for a revival meeting that lasted several weeks. By the 1810s and 1820s, "camp meetings" had spread to the Atlantic seaboard states. The outdoor settings permitted huge attendance, intensifying the emotional impact of the revival.

The gatherings attracted women and men hungry for a more immediate access to spiritual peace, one not requiring years of soul-searching. One eyewitness reported that "some of the people were singing, others praying, some crying for mercy. . . . At one time I saw at least five hundred swept down in a moment as if a battery of a thousand guns had been opened upon them, and then immediately followed shrieks and shouts that rent the very heavens."

From 1800 to 1820, church membership doubled in the United States, much of it among the evangelical groups. Methodists, Baptists, and Presbyterians formed the core of the new movement; Episcopalians, Congregationalists, Unitarians, Dutch Reformed, Lutherans, and Catholics maintained strong skepticism about the emotional enthusiasm. Women more than men were attracted to the evangelical movement, and wives and mothers typically recruited husbands and sons to join them.

The leading exemplar of the Second Great Awakening was a lawyer turned minister named **Charles Grandison Finney**. Finney lived in western New York, where the completion of the Erie Canal in 1825 fundamentally altered the social and economic landscape overnight. Towns swelled with new inhabitants who brought remarkable prosperity along with other, less admirable side effects, such as prostitution, drinking, and gaming. Finney saw New York canal towns as especially ripe for evangelical awakening. In Rochester, he sustained a six-month revival through the winter of 1830–31, generating thousands of converts.

Finney's message was directed primarily at the business classes. He argued that a reign of Christian perfection loomed, one that required public-spirited outreach to the less-than-perfect to foster their salvation. Evangelicals promoted Sunday schools to bring piety to children; they battled to honor the Sabbath by ending mail delivery, stopping public transport, and closing shops on Sundays. Many women formed missionary societies that distributed millions of Bibles and religious tracts. Through such avenues, evangelical religion offered women expanded spheres of influence. Finney adopted the tactics of Jacksonian-era politicians — publicity, argumentation, rallies, and speeches — to sell his cause. His object, he said, was to get Americans to "vote in the Lord Jesus Christ as the governor of the Universe."

Sunday School

In the 1820s, American Protestantism embraced the idea of Sunday Schools for indigent children, and by 1832, the American Sunday School Union formed to generate curriculum materials for what had quickly become a popular nationwide movement. Leadership came from coalitions of lay people mainly from the newly awakened variety of Protestant churches, while teachers both male and female usually volunteered their labor. The target student population consisted of poor children both white and free black, many of whom worked six days a week and had only the Sabbath free for schooling. The schools imparted basic literacy along with an education in Christianity. The Granger Collection, NYC.

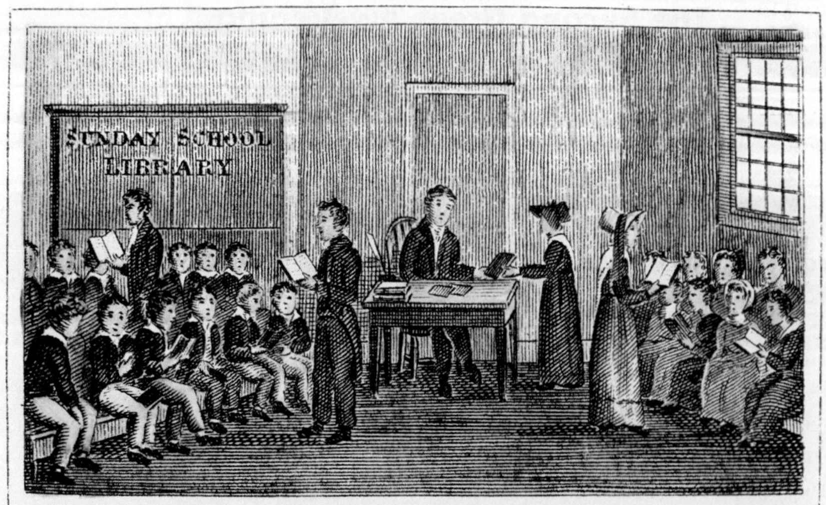

The Temperance Movement and the Campaign for Moral Reform

The evangelical disposition — a combination of faith, energy, self-discipline, and righteousness — animated vigorous campaigns to eliminate alcohol abuse and eradicate sexual sin. Millions of Americans took the temperance pledge to abstain from strong drink, and thousands became involved in efforts to end prostitution.

Alcohol consumption had risen steadily in the decades up to 1830, when the average person over age thirteen annually consumed an astonishing nine gallons of hard liquor plus thirty gallons of hard cider, beer, and wine. All classes imbibed. A lively saloon culture fostered masculine camaraderie along with extensive alcohol consumption among laborers, while in elite homes the after-dinner whiskey or sherry was commonplace. Colleges before 1820 routinely served students a pint of ale with meals, and the military included rum in the daily ration.

Organized opposition to drinking first surfaced in the 1810s among health and religious reformers. In 1826, Lyman Beecher, a Connecticut minister of an "awakened" church, founded the **American Temperance Society**, which warned that drinking led to poverty, idleness, crime, and family violence. Adopting the methods of evangelical ministers, temperance lecturers traveled the country expounding the damage of drink. By 1833, some six thousand local affiliates of the American Temperance Society boasted more than a million members. Middle-class drinking began a steep decline. One powerful tool of persuasion was the temperance pledge, which many business owners began to require of employees.

"Signing the Pledge"
This lithograph from the 1840s captures and celebrates a hard-won moment in the life of a hard-luck (but fictive) family. A temperance worker convinces the man of the household to give his solemn word to abstain from all alcohol, while his wife exhibits prayerful gratitude. What message does this picture send about the consequences of alcohol abuse? And about the possibilities of redemption? The temperance pledge was a major tool used by anti-alcohol advocates to curb drinking: Could it have really worked? Consider the power of religious oaths in a society infused with religious belief. The Granger Collection, NYC.

In 1836, leaders of the temperance movement regrouped into a new society, the American Temperance Union, which demanded total abstinence from its adherents. The intensified war against alcohol moved beyond individual moral suasion into the realm of politics as reformers sought to deny taverns liquor licenses. By 1845, temperance advocates had put an impressive dent in alcohol consumption, which diminished to one-quarter of the per capita consumption of 1830. In 1851, Maine became the first state to ban entirely the manufacture and sale of all alcoholic beverages.

More controversial than temperance was a social movement called "moral reform," which first aimed at public morals in general but quickly narrowed to a campaign to eradicate sexual sin. In 1833, a group of Finneyite women started the New York Female Moral Reform Society. Its members insisted that uncontrolled male sexual expression posed a serious threat to society in general and to women in particular. The society's nationally distributed newspaper, the *Advocate of Moral Reform*, was the first major paper in the country that was written, edited, and typeset by women. In it, they condemned men who visited brothels or seduced innocent women. Within five years, more than four thousand auxiliary groups of women had sprung up, mostly in New England, New York, Pennsylvania, and Ohio.

In its analysis of the causes of licentiousness and its conviction that women had a duty to speak out about unspeakable things, the Moral Reform Society pushed the limits of what even the men in the evangelical movement could tolerate. Yet these women did not regard themselves as radicals. They were simply pursuing the logic of a gender system that defined home protection and morality as women's special sphere and a religious conviction that called for the eradication of sin.

Organizing against Slavery

More radical still was the movement in the 1830s to abolish the sin of slavery. The abolitionist movement had its roots in Great Britain in the late 1700s. (See "Beyond America's Borders," page 344.) Previously, the American Colonization Society, founded in 1817 by Maryland and Virginia planters, aimed to promote gradual individual emancipation of slaves followed by colonization in Africa. By the early 1820s, several thousand ex-slaves had been transported to Liberia on the West African coast. But not surprisingly, newly freed men and women often were not eager to emigrate; their African roots were three or more generations in the past. Colonization was too gradual (and expensive) to have much impact on American slavery.

BEYOND AMERICA'S BORDERS

Transatlantic Abolition

Abolitionism blossomed in the United States in the 1830s, but its roots stretched back to the 1780s in Britain and America. Developments in both countries led to a transatlantic antislavery movement with shared ideas, strategies, activists, songs, and, eventually, victories.

An important source of antislavery sentiment derived from the Quaker religion, with its deep convictions regarding human equality. But moral sentiment alone does not make a political movement. English Quakers, customarily an apolitical group, awoke to sudden antislavery zeal in 1783, triggered in part by the loss of the imperial war for America and the debate it spurred about citizenship and slavery. The end of the war also brought a delegation of Philadelphia Quakers to meet with the London group, and an immediate result was the first petition requesting that Parliament abolish the slave trade.

The English Quakers, now joined by a scattering of evangelical Anglicans and Methodists, formed the Society for Effecting the Abolition of the Slave Trade in 1787 and in just five years became a force to be reckoned with. They amassed thousands of signatures on petitions to Parliament. They organized a boycott of slave-produced sugar from the British West Indies that involved 300,000 Britons. (Women, the traditional cooks of English families, were essential to the effort.) In 1789, the society scored a publicity coup by publishing two chilling illustrations of slave ships stacked with human cargo. These images, reprinted by the thousands, created a sensation. The society mobilized the resulting groundswell of antislavery sentiment to pressure Parliament once again. A sympathetic member of that body, the Methodist William Wilberforce, brought the anti–slave trade issue to a debate and vote in 1791; it lost.

Meanwhile, Pennsylvania Quakers in 1784 launched their own Society for Promoting the Abolition of Slavery, which worked to end slavery in that state and petitioned the confederation congress — unsuccessfully — to end American participation in the international slave trade. When the First Congress met in 1790, this antislavery society delivered two petitions in quick succession, one to ban the slave trade and a second to ban slavery itself (see chapter 9, "Historical Question," page 262). In rejecting both petitions, Congress pointed to the U.S. Constitution's clause that prohibited federal regulation of the trade before 1808.

The antislavery movement also took root in France, with the founding of the Société des Amis des Noirs (Society of the Friends of Blacks) in 1788. Inspired by Quaker groups in London and Philadelphia, the Société sent petitions to the French National Assembly. All three antislavery groups, in close communication, agreed that ending the slave trade was the critical first step in abolishing slavery. That goal was achieved once the revolution of *liberté and égalité* came to France; a 1794 decree of the National Assembly freed all French colonial slaves and termed them citizens.

Success came more slowly in Britain and America. In 1807, Parliament finally made it illegal for British ships to transport Africans into slavery. A year later, the United States also banned the international slave trade. The rapid natural increase of the African American population made passage of this law relatively easy. Older slave states along the coast supported the ban because it actually increased the value of their native-born slaves who were sold and transported west in the domestic slave trade.

Around 1830, northern challenges to slavery surfaced with increasing frequency and resolve, beginning in free black communities. In 1829, a Boston printer named David Walker published *An Appeal . . . to the Coloured Citizens of the World*, which condemned racism, invoked the egalitarian language of the Declaration of Independence, and hinted at racial violence if whites did not change their prejudiced ways. In 1830, at the inaugural National Negro Convention meeting in Philadelphia, forty blacks from nine states discussed the racism of American society and proposed emigration to Canada. In 1832 and 1833, a twenty-eight-year-old black woman named **Maria Stewart** delivered public lectures on slavery and racial prejudice to black audiences in Boston.

Although Stewart's arguments against slavery were welcomed, her voice — that of a woman — created problems even among her sympathetic audiences. Few American-born women had yet engaged in public speaking beyond theatrical performances or religious prophesying. Stewart was breaking a social taboo, an offense made more challenging by her statements suggesting that black women should rise above housework:

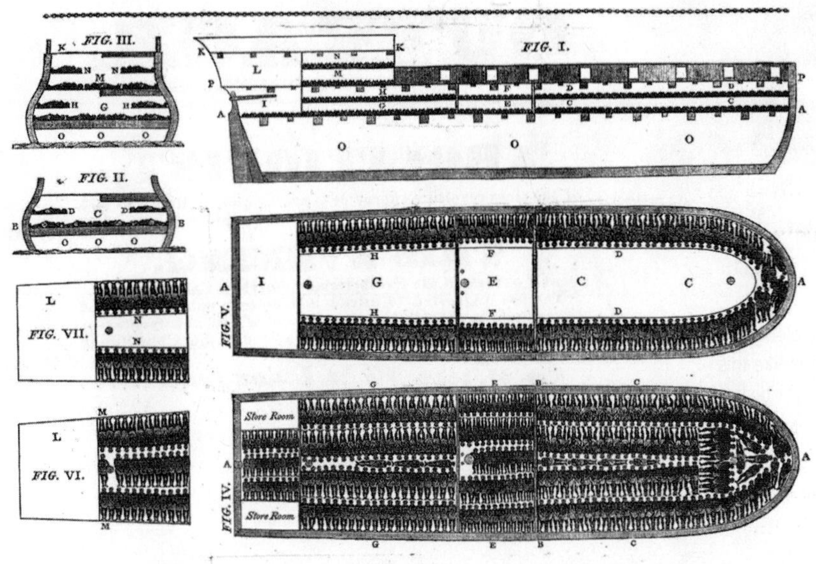

Description of a Slave Ship
This powerful and often-reprinted image combines a precise technical rendering of a British ship (normally evoking pride in Britons) with the horrors of a crowded mass of dark human flesh. Peabody Essex Museum, Salem, MA.

British antislavery forces took a new tack in the 1820s, when women became active and pushed beyond the ban on trade. Quaker widow Elizabeth Heyrick authored *Immediate Not Gradual Abolition* in 1824, prompting the formation of scores of all-women societies. American women abolitionists soon followed suit. Abolitionists again bombarded Parliament with a massive petition campaign, and 30 percent of the 1.3 million signatures submitted in 1833 were women's. That year, Parliament finally passed the Abolition of Slavery Act, which freed all slave children under age six and gradually phased out slavery for everyone older during a four-year apprenticeship. The act also provided financial compensation for owners (£20 million), a key proviso made possible by the relatively small number of slave owners in the British slaveholding colonies.

The success of the British movement generated even greater transatlantic communication. In 1840, British and American abolitionists came together in full force at the World Anti-Slavery Convention in London. Most of the 409 delegates were from Britain and the West Indies, although 53 Americans and half a dozen French delegates also attended. Ten days of meetings produced speeches and reports on the worldwide practice of slavery, along with debates over various economic and religious strategies to end it. A key plan was to publicize throughout America the British movement's success in achieving emancipation. The delegates closed their meeting fully energized by their international congress, called to propose international solutions to an international problem.

America in a Global Context

1. What were some of the tactics that British abolitionists used to advance their cause?
2. What factors help explain why the emancipation of slaves came earliest in France, and then four decades later in Britain and seven decades later in the United States?

"How long shall the fair daughters of Africa be compelled to bury their minds and talents beneath a load of iron pots and kettles?" She retired from the platform in 1833 but took up writing and published her lectures in a national publication called the *Liberator*, giving them much wider circulation.

The *Liberator*, founded in 1831 in Boston, took antislavery agitation to new heights. Its founder and editor, an uncompromising twenty-six-year-old white printer named **William Lloyd Garrison**, advocated immediate abolition: "On this subject, I do not wish to think, or speak, or write, with moderation. No! No! Tell a man whose house is on fire to give a moderate alarm; tell him to moderately rescue his wife from the hands of the ravisher; tell the mother to gradually extricate her babe from the fire into which it has fallen; — but urge me not to use moderation in a cause like the present." In 1832, Garrison's supporters started the New England Anti-Slavery Society.

Similar groups were organized in Philadelphia and New York in 1833. Soon a dozen antislavery newspapers and scores of antislavery lecturers were spreading the word and inspiring

OUTRAGE.

Fellow Citizens,

AN

ABOLITIONIST,

of the most revolting character is among you, exciting the feelings of the North against the South. A seditious Lecture is to be delivered

THIS EVENING,

at 7 o'clock, at the Presbyterian Church in Cannon-street.

You are requested to attend and unite in putting down and silencing by peaceable means this *tool of evil and fanaticism.*

Let the rights of the States guaranteed by the Constitution *be protected.*

Feb. 27, 1837. *The Union forever!*

Controversy over Abolitionism Mob violence erupted in northern cities with regularity when abolitionist speakers came to town. This 1837 poster from Poughkeepsie, New York, exemplifies the inflammatory language that kindled riots. The abolitionist speaker is framed as seditious, evil, and fanatical, while the citizens are called to the noble task of defending the Constitution and the Union. Antislavery societies raised money to support these lecture tours, one way being the weekly pledge. Families committed to the cause kept a contribution box like this one, inscribed with biblical passages and the symbolic yet disturbing image of the slave in chains. Poster: Library of Congress; box: Boston Public Library/Rare Books Department—Courtesy of the Trustees.

the formation of new local societies, which numbered thirteen hundred by 1837. Confined entirely to the North, their membership totaled a quarter of a million men and women.

Many white northerners, even those who opposed slavery as a blot on the country's ideals, were not prepared to embrace the abolitionist call for emancipation. From 1834 to 1838, there were more than a hundred eruptions of serious mob violence against abolitionists and free blacks. On one occasion, antislavery headquarters in Philadelphia and a black church and orphanage were burned to the ground. In another incident, Illinois abolitionist editor Elijah Lovejoy was killed by a rioting crowd attempting to destroy his printing press.

Women played a prominent role in abolition, just as they did in moral reform and evangelical religion. They formed women's auxiliaries and held fairs to sell handmade crafts to support male lecturers in the field. They circulated antislavery petitions, presented to the U.S. Congress with tens of thousands of their signatures. Up to 1835, women's petitions were framed as respectful memorials to Congress about the evils of slavery, but by mid-decade these petitions used urgent language to call for political action, instructing Congress to outlaw slavery in the District of Columbia (the only area under Congress's sole power). By such fervent tactics, antislavery women asserted their claim to be heard on political issues independently of their husbands and fathers.

Garrison particularly welcomed women's activity, despite the potential for danger. The 1837 Massachusetts speaking tour of the **Grimké sisters** (see pages 321–322) brought out respectful audiences of thousands but also drew intimidation from some quarters. The state leaders of the Congregational Church banned the sisters from speaking in their churches. They claimed that while a modest woman deserved deference and protection, an immodest woman presumptuously instructing men in public forfeited her privileges and invited male attack. "When she assumes the place and tone of man as a public reformer, our care and protection of her seem unnecessary; we put ourselves in self-defence against her . . . her character becomes unnatural." Serious violence occurred in 1838, when a mob attacked a female antislavery convention in Philadelphia. Rocks shattered windows as Angelina Grimké gave her speech, and after the women vacated the building, it was burned to the ground.

In the late 1830s, the cause of abolition divided the nation as no other issue did. Even among abolitionists, significant divisions emerged. The Grimké sisters, radicalized by the public reaction to their speaking tour, began to write and speak about woman's rights. Angelina Grimké compared the silencing of women to the silencing of slaves: "The denial of our duty to act, is a bold denial of our right to act; and if *we* have no right to act, then may we well be termed 'the white slaves of the North' — for, like our brethren in bonds, we must seal our lips in silence and despair." The Grimkés were opposed by moderate abolitionists who were unwilling to mix the new and controversial issue of woman's rights with their first cause, the rights of blacks. A few radical men, such as Garrison, embraced woman's rights fully, working to get women some leadership positions in the national antislavery group.

The many men and women active in reform movements in the 1830s found their initial inspiration in evangelical Protestantism's dual message: Salvation was open to all, and society needed to be perfected. Their activist mentality squared well with the interventionist tendencies of the party forming in opposition to Andrew Jackson's Democrats. Generally, reformers gravitated toward the Whig Party, the males as voters and the females as rallying supporters in the 1830s campaigns.

REVIEW How did evangelical Protestantism contribute to the social reform movements of the 1830s?

▸ Van Buren's One-Term Presidency

By the mid-1830s, a vibrant and tumultuous political culture occupied center stage in American life. A colorful military hero had left his stamp on the nation, but Andrew Jackson was too ill to stand for a third term. His vice president and handpicked successor, the northerner Martin Van Buren, inherited a strong Democratic organization, but he faced doubts from slave-owning Jacksonians and outright opposition from increasingly combative Whigs. Abolitionist tactics had pushed slavery into the political debate, but Van Buren managed to defuse that conflict somewhat and even use it to his advantage. What could not be forestalled, however, was the collapse of the economic boom so celebrated by both Democrats and Whigs. The shattering panic of 1837, followed by another panic in 1839, brought the country its worst economic depression yet.

The Politics of Slavery

Sophisticated party organization was the specialty of **Martin Van Buren**. Nicknamed "the Little Magician" for his consummate political skills, the New Yorker had built his career by pioneering many of the loyalty-enhancing techniques the Democrats used in the 1830s. First a senator and then governor, Van Buren became Jackson's secretary of state and then his running mate in 1832, replacing John C. Calhoun. His eight years in the volatile Jackson administration required the full measure of his political deftness as he sought repeatedly to save Jackson from both his enemies and his own obstinacy.

Jackson clearly favored Van Buren for the nomination in 1836, but starting in 1832, the major political parties had developed nominating conventions to choose their candidates. In 1835, Van Buren got the convention nod unanimously, to the dismay of his archrival, Calhoun, who then worked to discredit Van Buren among southern proslavery Democrats. Van Buren spent months assuring them that he was a "northern man with southern principles." This was not hard, since his Dutch family hailed from the Hudson River counties where New York slavery had once flourished, and his own family had owned at least one slave as late as the 1810s, although he chose not to broadcast that fact. (Slavery was only gradually phased out in New York starting in 1799.) Calhoun's partisans whipped up controversy over Van Buren's support of suffrage for New York's propertied free blacks at the 1821 state convention on suffrage. Van Buren's partisans countered by emphasizing that the Little Magician had argued that the mass of "poor, degraded blacks" were incapable of voting; he had merely favored retaining the existing stiff property qualifications for the handful of elite blacks who had always voted in New York, while simultaneously removing all such qualifications for white men.

Calhoun was able to stir up trouble for Van Buren because southerners were becoming increasingly alarmed by the rise of northern antislavery sentiment. When, in late 1835, abolitionists prepared to circulate in the South a million pamphlets condemning slavery, a mailbag of their literature was hijacked at the post office in Charleston, South Carolina, and ceremoniously burned along with effigies of leading abolitionists. President Jackson condemned the theft but issued approval for individual postmasters to exercise their own judgment about whether to allow incendiary materials to reach their destination. Abolitionists saw this as censorship of the mail.

> **"The South already turns pale at the number [of antislavery petitions] sent."**
> — ANGELINA GRIMKÉ

The petitioning tactics of abolitionists escalated sectional tensions. As petitions demanding that Congress "purify" the District of Columbia by outlawing slavery grew into the hundreds, proslavery congressmen sought to short-circuit the appeals by passing a "gag rule" in 1836. The gag rule prohibited entering the documents into the public record on the

SEEKING THE AMERICAN PROMISE

Going Ahead or Gone to Smash: An Entrepreneur Struggles in the 1830s

The spectacular economic boom of the 1830s gave life to the dream of get-rich-quick entrepreneurship. America's newfound abundance and progress promised a level of comfort and even opulence previously unimagined. A new slang term, *go-aheadism*, captured the enthusiasm of the day. But this cocky confidence also had a downside, identified by a New York diarist who lamented that *go-aheadism* had made Americans "the most careless, reckless, headlong people on the face of the earth." Soon enough, a rich vocabulary also defined business failure: *gone to smash, fizzled, wiped out, busted, up a tree,* and *GTT* — for "gone to Texas," a location outside the United States (until 1845) and therefore out of reach of U.S. law.

Benjamin Rathbun epitomized both *go-aheadism* and *gone to smash* failure in the turbulent 1830s. A shy man who was never seen to smile, he shrewdly identified Buffalo, New York, as the perfect location for his new business venture, an opulent hotel. Buffalo, a boomtown, linked the Erie Canal with the Great Lakes, where scores of steamboats departed daily for the interior of the country. The town's population nearly doubled from 1830 to 1835, and then doubled again, to eighteen thousand inhabitants, by 1840. Fueling this boom were brokerage houses that lined Buffalo's streets, lending money at high interest rates to borrowers speculating in real estate and business.

The success of the Eagle Hotel enabled Rathbun to become Buffalo's biggest self-made man. In eight years, he built a vast empire of real estate, building construction, banks, stores, and transportation. More than two thousand employees — more than a third of all adult males in Buffalo — were on his payroll. This empire required business acumen, astute management, and a steady influx of borrowed banknotes issued by New York City creditors. Rathbun's trusted younger brother, Lyman, headed financial operations, while Rathbun kept his eye on the big picture: designing the grand architecture of Buffalo (ninety-nine buildings) and buying up all the land on the American side of Niagara Falls for profitable resale. Some people even said that Rathbun owned the falls themselves.

Collapse came suddenly in 1836. Rathbun learned that his creditors in New York City had lost faith in him and were selling his IOUs to brokers at a steep discount, a process known as "note shaving." To cover the much higher interest rates charged by the new note holders, the Rathbuns negotiated more loans, supposedly backed by a dozen cosigners from the Buffalo business community guaranteeing payment if the brothers failed. When Rathbun applied for a $500,000 loan in an attempt to consolidate his debt, the dozen endorsements were revealed to be forgeries. Benjamin Rathbun was convicted of fraud and sentenced to five years' hard labor in state prison; brother Lyman disappeared with trunks full of money — "GTT," many people said.

Rathbun's spectacular failure plunged Buffalo into a severe depression eight months in advance of the panic of 1837. Although deliberate fraud brought him down, his *wipe-out* highlighted the inherent difficulties in an economy of note shaving and discounting, where loans of millions of dollars were granted on the basis of a few signatures. Historians calculate that something like one-fifth of all businessmen in the 1830s *fizzled* or went *up a tree*.

Massive failures in the five years after 1837 led to two striking innovations in business law and loan practices. First, the federal government passed the U.S. Bankruptcy Act of 1841, a controversial and short-term law that enabled failed debtors to wipe debts away legally, paying creditors a fraction of what was owed. Debtors gained release from crushing

grounds that what the abolitionists prayed for was unconstitutional and, further, an assault on the rights of white southerners, as one South Carolina representative put it. Abolitionists like the Grimké sisters considered the gag rule to be an abridgment of free speech. They also argued that, tabled or not, the petitions were effective. "The South already turns pale at the number sent," Angelina Grimké said in a speech exhorting more petitions to be circulated.

Van Buren shrewdly seized on both mail censorship and the gag rule to express his prosouthern sympathies. Abolitionists were "fanatics," he repeatedly claimed, possibly under the influence of "foreign agents" (British abolitionists). He dismissed the issue of abolition in the District of

The Eagle Hotel, Buffalo, 1825
Benjamin Rathbun (shown here scowling) bought this three-story building in 1825, doubled it in size with a building behind it, and turned it into the finest hotel west of New York City. Located on Main Street in Buffalo, the Eagle became the meeting place for all civic and professional groups in early Buffalo. The marquis de Lafayette, French hero of the American Revolution, stayed at the Eagle in 1825 on his U.S. tour. *The Picture Book of Earlier Buffalo,* Frank H. Severance, vol. 16, 1912, page 161.

debt but had to endure the humiliation of having notices of their bankruptcies printed in the newspapers.

Second, the credit rating industry was born in 1841 when a failed businessman opened the Mercantile Agency in New York City. For a $50 subscription fee, lenders could tap into large books containing confidential information gathered by hundreds of agents around the country who assessed the creditworthiness of local businessmen. Church (and saloon) attendance, family stability, and punctuality were often factors in grading businessmen's reputations for prudence and reliability.

Had it been in existence in 1836, the Mercantile Agency might have unmasked Rathbun's fraud through semiannual checks on his reputation. The Bankruptcy Act no doubt helped the many debt-saddled Buffalo men who had been caught out by Rathbun's failure. His liquidated estate paid out first to the thousands of workers on his payroll, second to the lawyers, and third to preferred creditors, leaving hundreds of thousands of dollars of debt unpaid.

When Rathbun left prison in 1843, he rejoined his wife, now running a boardinghouse in Buffalo to make ends meet. Soon the Rathbuns moved to New York City, where the onetime proprietor of Buffalo's Eagle Hotel returned to his first occupation. With financial help from cousins, he leased a building for the first in a series of increasingly seedy hotels that he ran until his death.

Questions for Consideration

1. What factors led to the Rathbuns' downfall?
2. How did the new credit rating agency, established in reaction to the panic of 1837, intend to prevent economic crises?

Columbia as "inexpedient" and promised that if he was elected president, he would not allow any interference in southern "domestic institutions."

Elections and Panics

Although the elections of 1824, 1828, and 1832 clearly bore the stamp of Jackson's personality, by 1836 the party apparatus was sufficiently developed to give Van Buren, a backroom politician, a shot at the presidency. Local and state committees existed throughout the country. Democratic candidates ran in every state election, succeeding even in the old Federalist stronghold of New England. More than four hundred newspapers self-identified as Democratic partisans.

The Whigs had also built state-level organizations and newspaper loyalty. They had no top contender with nationwide support, so three regional candidates opposed Van Buren. Senator Daniel Webster of Massachusetts could deliver New England, home to reformers, merchants, and manufacturers; Senator Hugh Lawson White of Tennessee attracted proslavery voters still suspicious of the northern Magician; and the aging General William Henry Harrison, now residing in Ohio and remembered for his Indian war heroics in 1811, pulled in the western anti-Indian vote. Not one of the three candidates had the ability to win the presidency, but together they came close to denying Van Buren a majority vote. Van Burenites called the three-Whig strategy a deliberate plot to derail the election and move it to the House of Representatives.

In the end, Van Buren won with 170 electoral votes, while the other three received a total of 113. The popular vote told a somewhat different story. Van Buren's narrow majorities, where he won, were far below those Jackson had commanded. Although Van Buren had pulled together a national Democratic Party with wins in both the North and the South, he had done it at the cost of committing northern Democrats to the proslavery agenda. And running three candidates had maximized the Whigs' success by drawing Whigs into office at the state level.

When Van Buren took office in March 1837, the financial markets were already quaking; by April, the country was plunged into crisis. The causes of the **panic of 1837** were multiple and far-ranging. Bad harvests in Europe and a large trade imbalance between Britain and the United States caused the Bank of England to start calling in loans to American merchants. Failures in various crop markets and a 30 percent downturn in international cotton prices fed the growing

The Panic of 1837
A sad family with an unemployed father faces sudden privation in this cartoon showing the consequences of the panic of 1837. The wife and children complain of hunger, the house is stripped nearly bare, and rent collectors loom in the doorway. Faint pictures on the wall show Andrew Jackson and Martin Van Buren presiding over the economic devastation of the family. The only support system for the unemployed in 1837 was the local almshouse, where families were split up and living conditions were harsh. Library of Congress.

disaster. Cotton merchants in the South could no longer meet their obligations to New York creditors, whose firms began to fail — ninety-eight of them in March and April 1837 alone. Frightened citizens thronged the banks to try to get their money out, and businesses rushed to liquefy their remaining assets to pay off debts. Prices of stocks, bonds, and real estate fell 30 to 40 percent. The familiar events of the panic of 1819 unfolded again, with terrifying rapidity, and the credit market tumbled like a house of cards. Newspapers describing the economic free fall generally used the language of emotional states — excitement, anxiety, terror, panic. Such words focused on human reactions to the crisis rather than on the structural features of the economy that had interacted to amplify the downturn. The vocabulary for understanding the wider economy was still quite limited, making it hard to track the bigger picture of the workings of capitalism. (See "Seeking the American Promise," page 348.)

Instead, many observers looked to politics, religion, and character flaws to explain the crisis. Some Whig leaders were certain that Jackson's antibank and hard-money policies were responsible for the ruin. New Yorker Philip Hone, a wealthy Whig, called the Jackson administration "the most disastrous in the annals of the country" for its "wicked interference" in banking and monetary matters. Others framed the devastation as retribution for an immoral frenzy of speculation that had gripped the nation. A religious periodical in Boston hoped that Americans would now moderate their greed: "We were getting to think that there was no end to the wealth, and could be no check to the progress of our country; that economy was not needed, that prudence was weakness." In this view, the panic was a wakeup call, a blessing in disguise. Others identified the competitive, profit-maximizing capitalist system as the cause and looked to Britain and France for new socialist ideas calling for the common ownership of the means of production. American socialists, though few in number, were vocal and imaginative, and in the early 1840s several thousand developed utopian alternative communities (as discussed in chapter 12).

The panic of 1837 subsided by 1838, but in 1839 another run on the banks and ripples of business failures deflated the economy, creating a second panic. President Van Buren called a special session of Congress to consider creating an independent treasury system to perform some of the functions of the defunct Bank of the United States. Such a system, funded by government deposits, would deal only in hard money and would exert a powerful moderating influence on inflation and the credit market. But Van Buren encountered strong resistance in Congress, even among Democrats. The treasury system finally won approval in 1840, but by then Van Buren's chances of winning a second term in office were virtually nil.

In 1840, the Whigs settled on **William Henry Harrison** to oppose Van Buren. The campaign drew on voter involvement as no other presidential campaign ever had. The Whigs borrowed tricks from the Democrats: Harrison was touted as a common man born in a log cabin (in reality, he was born on a Virginia plantation), and raucous campaign parades featured toy log cabins held aloft. His Indian-fighting days, now thirty years behind him, were played up to give him a Jacksonian aura. Whigs staged festive rallies around the country, drumming up mass appeal with candlelight parades and song shows, and women participated in rallies as never before. Some 78 percent of eligible voters cast ballots — the highest percentage ever in American history.

Harrison took 53 percent of the popular vote and won a resounding 234 electoral college votes to Van Buren's 60. A Democratic editor lamented, "We have taught them how to conquer us!"

REVIEW How did slavery figure as a campaign issue in the election of 1836?

Conclusion: The Age of Jackson or the Era of Reform?

Harrison's election closed a decade that had brought the common man and democracy to the forefront of American politics. Economic transformations loom large in explaining the fast-paced changes of the 1830s. Transportation advances put goods and people in circulation, augmenting urban growth and helping to create a national culture, and water-powered manufacturing began to change the face of wage labor. Trade and banking mushroomed, and western land once occupied by Indians was auctioned off in a landslide of sales. Two periods of economic downturn — including the panic of 1819 and the panics of 1837 and

1839—offered sobering lessons about speculative fever.

For many people, Andrew Jackson symbolized this age of opportunity. His fame as an aggressive general, Indian fighter, champion of the common man, and defender of slavery attracted growing numbers of voters to the emergent Democratic Party, which championed personal liberty, free competition, and egalitarian opportunity for all white men.

Jackson's constituency was challenged by a small but vocal segment of the population troubled by serious moral problems that Jacksonians preferred to ignore. Reformers drew sustenance from the message of the Second Great Awakening: that all men and women were free to choose salvation and that personal and societal sins could be overcome. Reformers targeted personal vices (illicit sex and intemperance) and social problems (prostitution, poverty, and slavery) and joined forces with evangelicals and wealthy lawyers and merchants (North and South) who appreciated a national bank and protective tariffs. The Whig Party was the party of activist moralism and state-sponsored entrepreneurship. Whig voters were, of course, male, but thousands of reform-minded women broke new ground by signing political petitions on the issues of Indian removal and slavery. A few exceptional women, like Sarah and Angelina Grimké, captured the national limelight by offering powerful testimony against slavery and in the process pioneering new pathways for women to contribute a moral voice to politics.

National politics in the 1830s were more divisive than at any time since the 1790s. The new party system of Democrats and Whigs reached far deeper into the electorate than had the Federalists and Republicans. Stagecoaches and steamboats carried newspapers from the cities to the backwoods, politicizing voters and creating party loyalty. Politics acquired immediacy and excitement, causing nearly four out of five white men to cast ballots in 1840.

High rates of voter participation would continue into the 1840s and 1850s. Unprecedented urban growth, westward expansion, and early industrialism marked those decades, sustaining the Democrat-Whig split in the electorate. But critiques of slavery, concerns for free labor, and an emerging protest against women's second-class citizenship complicated the political scene of the 1840s, leading to third-party political movements. One of these third parties, called the Republican Party, would achieve dominance in 1860 with the election of an Illinois lawyer, Abraham Lincoln, to the presidency.

▸ Selected Bibliography

The Market Revolution

Edward J. Balleisen, *Navigating Failure: Bankruptcy and Commercial Society in Antebellum America* (2001).

Mary H. Blewett, *Men, Women, and Work: Class, Gender, and Protest in the New England Shoe Industry, 1780–1910* (1988).

Jeanne Boydston, *Home and Work: Housework, Wages, and the Ideology of Labor in the Early Republic* (1990).

Thomas Dublin, *Transforming Women's Work: New England Lives in the Industrial Revolution* (1994).

John Lauritz Larson, *The Market Revolution in America: Liberty, Ambition, and the Eclipse of the Common Good* (2009).

Stephen Mihm, *A Nation of Counterfeiters: Capitalists, Con Men, and the Making of the United States* (2009).

Seth Rockman, *Scraping By: Wage Labor, Slavery, and Survival in Early Baltimore* (2008).

Charles G. Sellers, *The Market Revolution: Jacksonian America, 1815–1846* (1991).

Carol Sheriff, *The Artificial River: The Erie Canal and the Paradox of Progress, 1817–1862* (1996).

Politics

Andrew Burstein, *The Passions of Andrew Jackson* (2003).

John Ehle, *Trail of Tears: The Rise and Fall of the Cherokee Nation* (1997).

Daniel Walker Howe, *What Hath God Wrought: The Transformation of America, 1815–1845* (2009).

Jon Meacham, *American Lion: Andrew Jackson in the White House* (2009).

Sean Michael O'Brien, *In Bitterness and in Tears: Andrew Jackson's Destruction of the Creeks and Seminoles* (2003).

Theda Perdue, *Cherokee Women: Gender and Culture Change, 1700–1835* (1998).

Merrill D. Peterson, *The Great Triumvirate: Webster, Clay, and Calhoun* (1987).

Sean Wilentz, *The Rise of American Democracy, Jefferson to Lincoln* (2005).

Culture, Religion, and Reform

Bruce Dorsey, *Reforming Men and Women: Gender in the Antebellum City* (2002).

Lori D. Ginzberg, *Women and the Work of Benevolence: Morality, Politics, and Class in the Nineteenth-Century United States* (1990).
Nathan O. Hatch, *The Democratization of American Christianity* (1991).
Julie Roy Jeffrey, *The Great Silent Army of Abolitionism: Ordinary Women in the Antislavery Movement* (1998).
Richard R. John, *Spreading the News: The American Postal System from Franklin to Morse* (1995).
Catherine E. Kelly, *In the New England Fashion: Reshaping Women's Lives in the Nineteenth Century* (1999).
Bruce Laurie, *Beyond Garrison: Antislavery and Social Reform* (2005).
Gerda Lerner, *The Grimké Sisters from South Carolina: Pioneers for Women's Rights and Abolition* (2009).
Richard S. Newman, *The Transformation of American Abolitionism: Fighting Slavery in the Early Republic* (2002).
Mark Perry, *Lift Up Thy Voice: The Grimké Family's Journey from Slaveholders to Civil Rights Leaders* (2002).
Alisse Portnoy, *Their Right to Speak: Women's Activism in the Indian and Slave Debates* (2005).
Patrick Rael, *Black Identity and Black Protest in the Antebellum North* (2002).
Stacey M. Robertson, *Hearts Beating for Liberty: Women Abolitionists in the Old Northwest* (2010).
Scott A. Sandage, *Born Losers: A History of Failure in America* (2005).
Kathryn Kish Sklar and James Brewer Stewart, *Women's Rights and Transatlantic Slavery in the Era of Emancipation* (2007).
Richard B. Stott, *Jolly Fellows: Male Milieus in Mid-Nineteenth Century America* (2009).
Daniel S. Wright, *"The First of Causes to Our Sex": The Female Moral Reform Movement in the Antebellum Northeast, 1834–1848* (2006).
Ronald J. Zboray, *Literary Dollars and Social Sense: A People's History of the Mass Market Book* (2005).

▶ **FOR MORE BOOKS ABOUT TOPICS IN THIS CHAPTER,** see the Online Bibliography at **bedfordstmartins.com/roark.**

▶ **FOR ADDITIONAL PRIMARY SOURCES FROM THIS PERIOD,** see Michael Johnson, ed., *Reading the American Past*, Fifth Edition.

▶ **FOR WEB SITES, IMAGES, AND DOCUMENTS RELATED TO TOPICS AND PLACES IN THIS CHAPTER,** visit Make History at **bedfordstmartins.com/roark.**

Reviewing Chapter 11

KEY TERMS

Explain each term's significance.

The Market Revolution

- Erie Canal (p. 325)
- Lowell mills (p. 326)
- specie payment (p. 327)
- second Bank of the United States (p. 327)
- Andrew Jackson (p. 330)
- panic of 1819 (p. 330)

The Spread of Democracy

- Henry Clay (p. 331)
- Whigs (p. 331)
- Democrats (p. 331)
- John C. Calhoun (p. 332)
- spoils system (p. 333)

Jackson Defines the Democratic Party

- Indian Removal Act of 1830 (p. 334)
- Trail of Tears (p. 336)
- Tariff of Abominations (p. 337)
- nullification (p. 337)

Cultural Shifts, Religion, and Reform

- separate spheres (p. 339)
- Second Great Awakening (p. 341)
- Charles Grandison Finney (p. 342)
- American Temperance Society (p. 343)
- Maria Stewart (p. 344)
- William Lloyd Garrison (p. 345)
- Grimké sisters (p. 346)

Van Buren's One-Term Presidency

- Martin Van Buren (p. 347)
- panic of 1837 (p. 350)
- William Henry Harrison (p. 351)

REVIEW QUESTIONS

Use key terms and dates to support your answer.

1. Why did the United States experience a market revolution after 1815? (pp. 323–330)
2. Why did Andrew Jackson defeat John Quincy Adams so dramatically in the 1828 election? (pp. 331–333)
3. Why did Jackson promote Indian removal? (pp. 333–339)
4. How did evangelical Protestantism contribute to the social reform movements of the 1830s? (pp. 339–347)
5. How did slavery figure as a campaign issue in the election of 1836? (pp. 347–351)

MAKING CONNECTIONS

Draw on key terms, the timeline, and review questions.

1. Describe the market revolution that began in the 1810s. How did it affect Americans' work and domestic lives? In your answer, be sure to consider how gender contributed to these developments.
2. Andrew Jackson's presidency coincided with important changes in American politics. Discuss how Jackson benefited from, and contributed to, the vibrant political culture of the 1830s. Cite specific national developments in your answer.
3. Describe Andrew Jackson's response to the "Indian problem" during his presidency. How did his policies revise or continue earlier federal policies toward Native Americans? How did Native Americans respond to Jackson's actions?
4. While a volatile economy buffeted the United States in the 1830s, some Americans looked to reform the nation. Discuss the objectives and strategies of two reform movements. What was the relationship of these reform movements to larger political and economic trends of the 1830s?

LINKING TO THE PAST

Link events in this chapter to earlier events.

1. How were the economic circumstances and social anxieties that gave rise to the Second Great Awakening similar to, and different from, those that encouraged the First Great Awakening? (See chapter 5.)
2. Compare the development of political parties in the 1790s (Federalists and Republicans) with the second development of parties in the 1830s (Whigs and Democrats). Were the parties of the 1830s in any way the descendants of the two of the 1790s? Or were they completely different? (See chapter 9.)

▶ FOR PRACTICE QUIZZES AND OTHER STUDY TOOLS, see the Online Study Guide at **bedfordstmartins.com/roark.**

TIMELINE 1807–1840

1807	• Robert Fulton's *Clermont* sets off steamboat craze.
1816	• Second Bank of the United States chartered.
1817	• American Colonization Society founded.
1818	• National Road links Baltimore to western Virginia.
1819	• Economic panic.
1821	• Mill town of Lowell, Massachusetts, founded.
1825	• Erie Canal completed in New York.
1826	• American Temperance Society founded. • Schuylkill Canal completed in Pennsylvania.
1828	• Congress passes Tariff of Abominations. • Democrat Andrew Jackson elected president.
1829	• David Walker's *Appeal . . . to the Coloured Citizens of the World* published. • Baltimore and Ohio Railroad begun.
1830	• Indian Removal Act. • Women's petitions for Indian rights begin.
1830–1831	• Charles Grandison Finney preaches in Rochester, New York.
1831	• William Lloyd Garrison starts *Liberator*.
1832	• Massacre of Sauk and Fox Indians led by Chief Black Hawk. • *Worcester v. Georgia*. • Jackson vetoes charter renewal of Bank of the United States. • New England Anti-Slavery Society founded.
1833	• Nullification of federal tariffs declared in South Carolina. • New York and Philadelphia antislavery societies founded. • New York Female Moral Reform Society founded.
1834	• Female mill workers strike in Lowell, Massachusetts, and again in 1836.
1836	• Democrat Martin Van Buren elected president. • American Temperance Union founded.
1837	• Economic panic.
1838	• Trail of Tears: Cherokees forced to relocate west.
1839	• Economic panic.
1840	• Whig William Henry Harrison elected president.

GOLD NUGGET

Gold! Nuggets like this one scooped from a California river drove easterners crazy with excitement. The quarter of a million men who joined the gold rush in the five years after gold's discovery in 1848 sought to escape routine jobs and mundane lives by "making their pile" in California. The great rush for western riches fulfilled the hopes of only a few, but the rest participated in one of the great adventures of the nineteenth century and rarely regretted their experiences. The background image reminds us that gold mining meant hard work.

Nugget: Collection of the Oakland Museum of California; background: Library of Congress.

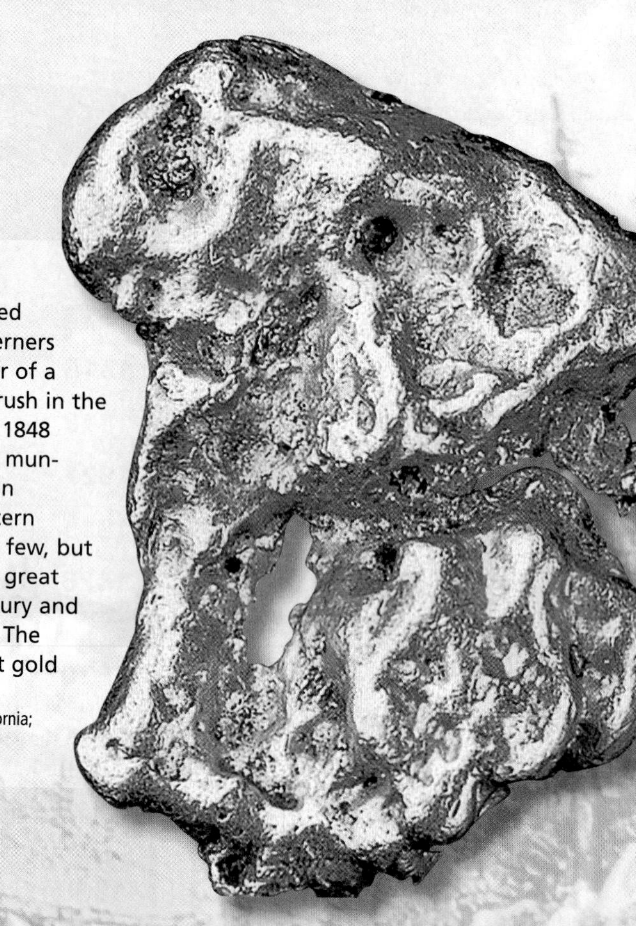

12

The New West and the Free North

1840–1860

EARLY IN NOVEMBER 1842, ABRAHAM LINCOLN AND HIS NEW WIFE, Mary, moved into their first home in Springfield, Illinois, a rented room measuring eight by fourteen feet on the second floor of the Globe Tavern. The small, noisy room above the tavern and next door to a blacksmith shop was the nicest place that Abraham Lincoln had ever lived. It was the worst place that Mary Todd Lincoln had ever inhabited. She grew up in Lexington, Kentucky, attended by slaves in the elegant home of her father, a prosperous merchant, banker, and politician. In March 1861, nineteen years after their marriage, the Lincolns moved into what would prove to be their last home, the presidential mansion in Washington, D.C.

Abraham Lincoln climbed from the Globe Tavern to the White House by relentless work, unslaked ambition, and immense talent — traits he had honed since boyhood. Lincoln and many others celebrated his rise from humble origins as an example of the opportunities that beckoned in the free-labor economy of the North and West. They attributed his spectacular ascent to his individual qualities and tended to ignore the help he received from Mary and many others.

Born in a Kentucky log cabin in 1809, Lincoln grew up on small, struggling farms as his family migrated west. His father, Thomas Lincoln, who had been born in Virginia, never learned to read and, as his son recalled, "never did more in the way of writing than to bunglingly sign his own name." Lincoln's mother, Nancy, could neither read nor write. In December 1816, Thomas Lincoln moved his young family from Kentucky to the Indiana wilderness. On the Indiana farmstead, Abraham learned the arts of agriculture practiced by families throughout the nation. Although only eight years old, he "had an axe put into his hands at once" and used it "almost constantly" for the next fifteen years, as he recalled later. When he could be spared from work, the boy attended school, less than a year in all. "There was absolutely nothing to excite ambition for education," Lincoln recollected. In contrast, Mary Todd received ten years of schooling in Lexington's best private academies for young women.

In 1830, Thomas Lincoln decided to move farther west. The Lincolns hitched up the family oxen and headed to central Illinois. The next spring, Thomas moved yet again, but this time Abraham stayed behind and set out on his own, a "friendless, uneducated, penniless boy," as he described himself.

By dogged striving, Abraham Lincoln gained an education and the respect of his Illinois neighbors, although a steady income eluded him for years. Mary Todd had many suitors, including Stephen A. Douglas, Lincoln's eventual political rival. After she married Lincoln, she said, "Intellectually my husband towers above Douglas . . . [and he] has no equal in the United States." The newlyweds received help from Mary's father, including eighty acres of land and a yearly allowance of about $1,100 for six years that helped them move out of their room above the Globe Tavern and into their own home. Abraham eventually built a thriving law practice in Springfield, Illinois, and served in the state legislature and then in Congress. Mary helped him in many ways, rearing their sons, tending their household, and integrating him into her wealthy and influential extended family in Illinois and Kentucky. Mary also shared Abraham's keen interest in politics and ambition for power. With Mary's support, Abraham's striving ultimately propelled them into the White House, where he became the first president born west of the Appalachian Mountains.

Like Lincoln, millions of Americans believed they could make something of themselves, whatever their origins, so long as they were willing to work. Individuals who refused to work — who were lazy, undisciplined, or foolish — had only themselves to blame if they failed. Work was a prerequisite for success, not a guarantee. This emphasis on work highlighted the individual efforts of men and tended to slight the many crucial contributions of women, family members, neighbors, and friends to the successes of men like Lincoln. In addition, the rewards of work were skewed toward white men and away from women and free African Americans. Nonetheless, the promise of such rewards spurred efforts that shaped the contours of America, pushing the boundaries of the nation ever westward to the Pacific Ocean. The nation's economic, political, and geographic expansion raised anew the question of whether slavery should also move west, the question that Lincoln and other Americans confronted again and again following the Mexican-American War, yet another outgrowth of the nation's ceaseless westward movement.

Lincoln's Log Cabin and Springfield Home
Abraham Lincoln grew up in Indiana between 1816, when he was eight years old, and 1830, when he became twenty-one. In Indiana, Lincoln, his father, his stepmother, and assorted kinfolk lived in the log cabin shown here. After moving to Illinois and becoming a successful lawyer and politician in Springfield, Lincoln and his wife Mary moved in 1844 to the home shown here. The contrast between the rustic log cabin and the spacious home highlights the opportunities the free labor system offered to all Americans, according to Lincoln. Log cabin: Meserve-Kunhandt collection; Springfield home: © Bettmann/Corbis.

▶ Economic and Industrial Evolution

During the 1840s and 1850s, Americans experienced a profound economic transformation whose roots reached back to the beginning of the nineteenth century. Since 1800, the total output of the U.S. economy had multiplied twelvefold. Four fundamental changes in American society fueled this remarkable economic growth. First, millions of Americans moved from farms to towns and cities, Abraham Lincoln among them. Second, factory workers (primarily in towns and cities) increased to about 20 percent of the labor force by 1860. Third, a shift from water power to steam as a source of energy raised productivity, especially in factories and transportation. Railroads in particular harnessed steam power, speeding transport and cutting costs. Fourth, agricultural productivity nearly doubled during Lincoln's lifetime, spurring the nation's economic growth more than any other factor.

Historians often refer to this cascade of changes as an industrial revolution. However, these changes did not cause an abrupt discontinuity in America's economy or society, which remained overwhelmingly agricultural. Old methods of production continued alongside the new. The changes in the American economy during the 1840s and 1850s might better be termed "industrial evolution."

Agriculture and Land Policy

While cities, factories, and steam engines multiplied throughout the North and West, the foundation of the United States' economic growth lay in agriculture. A French traveler in the United States noted that Americans had "a general feeling of hatred against trees." Although the traveler exaggerated, his observation contained an important truth. Trees limited agricultural productivity because farmers had to spend a great deal of time and energy clearing land for planting. As farmers pushed westward in a quest for cheap land, they encountered the Midwest's comparatively treeless prairie, where they could spend less time with an ax and more time with a plow and hoe. Rich prairie soils yielded bumper crops, enticing farmers such as the Lincolns to migrate to the Midwest by the tens of thousands between 1830 and 1860. The populations of Indiana, Illinois, Michigan, Wisconsin, and Iowa exploded tenfold between 1830 and 1860, four times faster than the growth of the nation as a whole. Lincoln's home state of Illinois added more people during the 1850s than any other state in the Union.

Labor-saving improvements in farm implements also boosted agricultural productivity. Inventors tinkered to craft stronger, more efficient plows to furrow the earth with as little effort as possible. In 1837, **John Deere** made a strong, smooth steel plow that sliced through prairie soil so cleanly that farmers called it the "singing plow." Deere's company became the leading plow manufacturer in the Midwest, turning out more than ten thousand plows a year by the late 1850s. Humans and animals (rather than steam) provided the energy for plowing, but better plows permitted farmers to break more ground and plant more crops.

Improvements in wheat harvesting also increased farmers' productivity. In 1850, most farmers harvested wheat by hand, cutting two or three acres a day with backbreaking labor. In the 1840s, Cyrus McCormick and others experimented with designs for **mechanical reapers**, and by the 1850s a McCormick reaper that cost between $100 and $150 allowed a farmer to harvest twelve acres a day. Farmers had purchased about eighty thousand reapers by 1860, but most continued to cut their grain by hand. Still, improved reapers and plows, usually powered by horses or oxen, allowed farmers to cultivate more land, doubling the corn and wheat harvests between 1840 and 1860.

> **"There is . . . in America a general feeling of hatred against trees."**
>
> — A French visitor to the United States

Federal land policy made possible the agricultural productivity that fueled the nation's economy. Up to 1860, the United States continued to be land-rich and labor-poor. Territorial acquisitions made the nation a great deal richer in land, adding more than a billion acres with the Louisiana Purchase (see chapter 10) and the annexation of Florida, Oregon, and vast territories following the Mexican-American War. The federal government made most of this land available for purchase to attract settlers and to generate revenue. Wily speculators found ways to claim large tracts of the most desirable plots and sell them to settlers at a generous markup. But millions of ordinary farmers bought federal land for just $1.25 an acre, or $50 for a forty-acre farm that could support a family. Millions of other farmers squatted on unclaimed federal land, carved

Harvesting Grain with Cradles
This late-nineteenth-century painting shows a grain harvest during the mid-nineteenth century at Bishop Hill, Illinois, a Swedish community where the artist, Olof Krans, and his parents settled in 1850. The men swing cradles, slowly cutting a swath through the grain; the women gather the cut grain into sheaves to be hauled away later for threshing. Although most Bishop Hill farmers had only a few family members and a hired hand or two, they could call upon the labor of the many men and women from the community at harvest time. Notice that all the work is done by hand; there is no machine in sight. Bishop Hill State Historic Site, Illinois Historic Preservation Agency.

out farms, and, if they still lacked funds to buy the land after a few years, usually moved farther west to squat on federal land elsewhere. By making land available to millions of Americans on relatively easy terms, the federal government achieved the goal of attracting settlers to the new territories in the West, which in due course joined the Union as new states. Above all, federal land policy facilitated the increase in agricultural productivity that underlay the nation's impressive economic growth.

Manufacturing and Mechanization

Changes in manufacturing arose from the nation's land-rich, labor-poor economy. European countries had land-poor, labor-rich economies; there, meager opportunities in agriculture kept factory laborers plentiful and wages low. In the United States, western expansion and government land policies buoyed agriculture, keeping millions of people on the farm — 80 percent of the nation's 31 million people lived in rural areas in 1860 — and thereby limiting the supply of workers for manufacturing and elevating wages. Because of this relative shortage of workers, American manufacturers searched constantly for ways to save labor.

Mechanization allowed manufacturers to produce more with less labor. In general, factory workers produced twice as much (per unit of labor) as agricultural workers. The practice of manufacturing and then assembling interchangeable parts spread from gun making to other industries and became known as the **American system**. Standardized parts produced by machine allowed manufacturers to employ unskilled workers, who were much cheaper and more readily available than highly trained craftsmen. A visitor to a Springfield, Massachusetts, gun factory in 1842 noted, for example, that standardized parts made the trained gunsmith's "skill of the eye and the hand, [previously] acquired by practice alone . . . no longer indispensable." Even in heavily mechanized industries, few factories had more than twenty or thirty employees.

Manufacturing and agriculture meshed into a dynamic national economy. New England led the nation in manufacturing, shipping goods such as guns, clocks, plows, and axes west and south, while southern and western states sent commodities such as wheat, pork, whiskey, tobacco, and cotton north and east. In the 1840s, mines in Pennsylvania, Ohio, and elsewhere began to produce millions of tons of coal for industrial fuel, accelerating the shift to steam power. Between 1840 and 1860, coal production multiplied eightfold, cutting prices in half and permitting coal-fired steam engines to power ever more factories, railroads, and ships. Even so, by 1860 coal accounted for less than a fifth of the nation's energy consumption while, in manufacturing, people and work animals provided thirty times more energy than steam did.

American manufacturers specialized in producing for the gigantic domestic market rather than for export. British goods dominated the international market and, on the whole, were cheaper and better than American-made products. U.S. manufacturers supported tariffs to minimize British competition, but their best protection from British competitors was to strive harder to please their American customers, most of them farmers. The burgeoning national economy was further fueled by the growth of the railroads, which served to link farmers and factories in new ways.

Railroads: Breaking the Bonds of Nature

A Swedish visitor in 1849 noticed that American schoolboys drew sketches of locomotives, always in motion, belching smoke. Railroads captured Americans' imagination because they seemed to break the bonds of nature. (See "Visualizing History," page 364.) When canals and rivers froze in winter or became impassable during summer droughts, trains steamed ahead. When becalmed sailing ships went nowhere, locomotives kept on chugging, averaging more than twenty miles an hour during the 1850s. Above all, railroads gave cities not blessed with canals or navigable rivers a way to compete for rural trade.

In 1850, trains steamed along 9,000 miles of track, almost two-thirds of it in New England and the Middle Atlantic states. By 1860, several railroads spanned the Mississippi River, connecting frontier farmers to the nation's 30,000 miles of track, approximately as much as in all of the rest of the world combined (Map 12.1). In 1857, for example, France had 3,700 miles of track; England and Wales had 6,400 miles. The massive expansion of American railroads helped catapult

THE PROMISE OF TECHNOLOGY

The Telegraph

Samuel F. B. Morse is credited with inventing the telegraph because of his patent in June 1840, but, as one contemporary observed, Morse's talent consisted of "combining and applying the discoveries of others in the invention of a particular instrument and process for telegraphic purposes." Morse sent the first message in 1844 on this telegraph using a code he devised that represented each letter and number with dots and dashes. With a series of taps on a telegraph key, operators sent short and long pulses of electricity. By 1846, most eastern cities were connected by telegraph. By 1850, of the states east of the Mississippi River, only Florida remained without it. More than fifty thousand miles of wires webbed the nation by 1861, when the telegraph reached California. The telegraph obliterated distance, and cheap, efficient, and fast communication changed American businesses, newspapers, government, and everyday life. The telegraph made it possible to synchronize clocks, which in turn allowed railroads to run safely according to precise schedules. Newspapers could gather information from around the country and have it in the headlines within hours. On a personal level, families across the continent could communicate more quickly than letter writing allowed. The telegraph met the needs of the vigorous, sprawling nation. Division of Political History, Smithsonian Institution, Washington, D.C.

MAP ACTIVITY

Map 12.1 Railroads in 1860

Railroads were a crucial component of the revolutions in transportation and communications that transformed nineteenth-century America. The railroad system reflected the differences in the economies of the North and South.

READING THE MAP: In which sections of the country was most of the railroad track laid by the middle of the nineteenth century? What cities served as the busiest railroad hubs?

CONNECTIONS: How did the expansion of railroad networks affect the American economy? Why was the U.S. government willing to grant more than twenty million acres of public land to the private corporations that ran the railroads?

the nation into position as the world's second-greatest industrial power, after Great Britain.

In addition to speeding transportation, railroads propelled the growth of other industries, such as iron and communications. Iron production grew five times faster than the population during the decades up to 1860, in part to meet railroads' demand. Railroads also stimulated the fledgling telegraph industry. In 1844, **Samuel F. B. Morse** persuasively demonstrated the potential of his telegraph by transmitting a series of dots and dashes that instantly conveyed an electronic message along forty miles of wire strung between Washington, D.C., and Baltimore. By

1861, more than fifty thousand miles of wire stretched across the continent to the Pacific Ocean, often alongside railroad tracks, making trains safer and more efficient and accelerating communications of all sorts.

In contrast to the government ownership of railroads common in other industrial nations, private corporations built and owned almost all American railroads. But the railroads received massive government aid, especially federal land grants. Up to 1850, the federal government had granted a total of seven million acres of federal land to various turnpike, highway, and canal projects. In 1850, Congress approved a precedent-setting grant to railroads of six square miles of federal land for each mile of track laid. By 1860, Congress had granted railroads more than twenty million acres of federal land, thereby underwriting construction costs and promoting the expansion of the rail network, the settlement of federal land, and the integration of the domestic market.

The railroad boom of the 1850s signaled the growing industrial might of the American economy. An Illinois farmer praised railroads' "cheap and easy conveyance of commodities to foreign markets." Like other industries, railroads succeeded because they served both farms and cities. But transportation was not revolutionized overnight. Most Americans in 1860 were still far more familiar with horses than with locomotives. And even by 1875, trains carried only about one-third of the mail; most of the rest still went by stagecoach or horseback.

The economy of the 1840s and 1850s linked an expanding, westward-moving population in farms and cities with muscles, animals, machines, steam, and railroads. Abraham Lincoln cut trees, planted corn, and split rails as a young man before he moved to Springfield, Illinois, and became a successful attorney who defended, among others, railroad corporations. His mobility — westward, from farm to city, from manual to mental labor, and upward — illustrated the direction of economic change and the opportunities that beckoned enterprising individuals.

REVIEW Why did the United States become a leading industrial power in the nineteenth century?

▸ Free Labor: Promise and Reality

The nation's impressive economic performance did not reward all Americans equally. Native-born white men tended to do better than immigrants. With few exceptions, women were excluded from opportunities open to men. Tens of thousands of women worked as seamstresses, laundresses,

Hiring a Domestic Servant
This 1849 painting portrays a middle-class woman (seated) at an employment office looking over women to hire as domestic servants. The employment agent (center) advertised his services in the newspaper (crumpled on the floor) and attracted a supply of poor women seeking jobs. The agent appears to be explaining the qualifications of the two standing women. The middle-class woman would want a servant who knew how to do domestic chores and was obedient, honest, and virtuous. While the agent talks, the two women for hire appear uncomfortable and look away from their potential boss.

VISUALIZING HISTORY

The Path of Progress

Westward the Star of Empire Takes Its Way — near Council Bluffs, Iowa

domestic servants, factory hands, and teachers but had little opportunity to aspire to higher-paying jobs. In the North and West, slavery was slowly eliminated in the half century after the American Revolution, but most free African Americans were relegated to dead-end jobs as laborers and servants. Discrimination against immigrants, women, and free blacks did not trouble most white men. With certain notable exceptions, they considered it proper and just.

The Free-Labor Ideal

During the 1840s and 1850s, leaders throughout the North and West emphasized a set of ideas that seemed to explain why the changes under way in their society benefited some people more than others. They referred again and again to the advantages of what they termed *free labor*. (The word *free* referred to laborers who were not slaves. It did not mean laborers who worked for nothing.) By the 1850s, free-labor ideas described a social and economic ideal that accounted for both the successes and the shortcomings of the economy and society taking shape in the North and West.

Spokesmen for the **free-labor ideal** celebrated hard work, self-reliance, and independence. They proclaimed that the door to success was open not just to those who inherited wealth or status but also to self-made men such as Abraham Lincoln. Free labor, Lincoln argued, was "the just and generous, and prosperous system, which opens the way for all — gives hope to all, and energy, and progress, and improvement of condition to all." Free labor permitted farmers and artisans to enjoy the products of their own labor, and it also benefited wageworkers. "The prudent, penniless beginner in the world," Lincoln asserted, "labors for wages awhile, saves a surplus with which to buy tools or land, for himself; then labors on his own account another while, and at

This painting depicts a mid-nineteenth-century landscape of agricultural and industrial progress. Created by Andrew Melrose to celebrate the recently built railroad connecting Chicago and Council Bluffs, Iowa, almost four hundred miles to the west, the painting contrasts the irregularity of nature with the new principles of order imposed on the natural landscape by human beings.

Detail of Farmhouse

What principles of order are suggested by the locomotive and the railroad tracks? How do they contrast with the natural order represented by the forest on the right side of the painting, by the rock-studded vegetation on either side of the rail bed, and by the deer scampering across the tracks?

The locomotive barreling down the tracks is barely visible behind its blazing headlight, which illuminates the way forward and startles the deer accustomed to shadowed hiding places in the forest. What does the contrast between the immense power of the locomotive and the skittish, vulnerable deer suggest about industrial progress? Likewise, how do the speed, direction, and glaring headlight of the locomotive contrast with the obstacles to progress in the painting? Are the deer headed toward progress? Why or why not?

The left side of the painting shows a frontier farm cultivated by a family standing in the shadow of the log cabin. How do the principles of agricultural order represented by the farm compare with those of the industrial order represented by the railroad and the natural order represented by the forest? What attributes of familial order are visible in the depiction of the farm? Do these attributes differ from the attributes of order among the deer?

To what extent does the farm suggest agricultural progress? Why have so many trees been chopped down? Why are the stumps littering the fields? What do these farming practices suggest about the farm family's attitudes toward nature?

Notice that the family is not watching the natural beauty of the setting sun bathing the landscape in a golden twilight but instead is looking toward the artificial light of the locomotive. Why might they have gathered outside their cabin to watch the train? What does their interest in the locomotive suggest about their attitudes toward the railroad?

The smoke rises vertically from the chimney of the log cabin, yet it trails backward from the smokestack of the locomotive. What does this contrast suggest about the differences between agricultural and industrial progress?

Detail of Deer Crossing Tracks

Overall, what does this painting suggest about the benefits and costs of progress for the farm family, the forest, the deer, the railroad, and American society in general?

SOURCE: Museum of the American West, Autry National Center.

length hires another new beginner to help him." Wage labor, he claimed, was the first rung on the ladder toward self-employment and eventually hiring others.

The free-labor ideal affirmed an egalitarian vision of human potential. Lincoln and other spokesmen stressed the importance of **universal education** to permit "heads and hands [to] cooperate as friends" (Figure 12.1). Throughout the North and West, communities supported public schools to make the rudiments of learning available to young children. By 1860, many cities and towns had public schools that boasted that up to 80 percent of children ages seven to thirteen attended school at least for a few weeks each year. In rural areas, where the labor of children was more difficult to spare, schools typically enrolled no more than half the school-age children. Lessons included more than arithmetic, penmanship, and a smattering of other subjects. Textbooks and teachers — most of whom were young women — drummed into students the lessons of the free-labor system: self-reliance, discipline, and, above all else, hard work. "Remember that all the ignorance, degradation, and misery in the world is the result of indolence and vice," one textbook intoned. Both in and outside school, free-labor ideology emphasized labor as much as freedom.

Economic Inequality

The free-labor ideal made sense to many Americans, especially in the North and West, because it seemed to describe their own experiences. Lincoln frequently referred to his humble beginnings as a hired laborer and implicitly invited his listeners to consider how far he had come. In 1860, his assets of $17,000 easily placed him in the wealthiest 5 percent of the population. The opportunities presented by the expanding economy made a few men much, much richer. In 1860, the nation

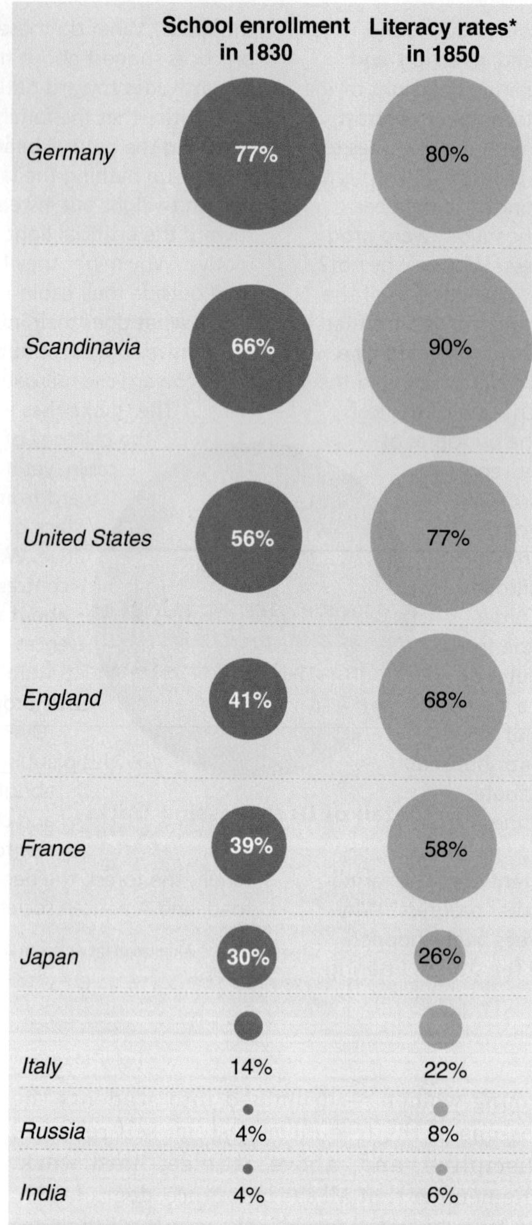

FIGURE 12.1 GLOBAL COMPARISON: Nineteenth-Century School Enrollment and Literacy Rates
In the first half of the nineteenth century, school enrollment and literacy rates in northern and western Europe and the United States were high compared to those in the rest of the world. U.S. figures would be even higher but for the South, where less than 10 percent of black slaves were literate and whites were less likely to attend school than in the North. The ability to read and write facilitates communication, business transactions, acquisition of skills, and perhaps even greater openness to change, all building blocks of rapid economic growth. But mass literacy has not always been a prerequisite for economic development. When England underwent industrialization between 1780 and 1830, less than half of the nation's children attended school. By 1850, England was the world's greatest industrial power, but where did it rank in literacy?

had about forty millionaires. Most Americans, however, measured success in more modest terms. The average wealth of adult white men in the North in 1860 barely topped $2,000. Nearly half of American men had no wealth at all; about 60 percent owned no land. Because property possessed by married women was normally considered to belong to their husbands, women typically had less wealth than men. Free African Americans had still less; 90 percent of them were propertyless. (See "Beyond America's Borders," page 368.)

Free-labor spokesmen considered these economic inequalities a natural outgrowth of freedom — the inevitable result of some individuals being both luckier and more able and willing to work. These inequalities also demonstrate the gap between the promise and the performance of the free-labor ideal. Economic growth permitted many men to move from being landless squatters to landowning farmers and from being hired laborers to independent, self-employed producers. But many more Americans remained behind, landless and working for wages. Even those who realized their aspirations often had a precarious hold on their independence. Bad debts, market volatility, crop failure, sickness, or death could quickly eliminate a family's gains.

Seeking out new opportunities in pursuit of free-labor ideals created restless social and geographic mobility. While fortunate people such as Abraham Lincoln rose far beyond their social origins, others shared the misfortune of a merchant who, an observer noted, "has been on the sinking list all his life." In search of better prospects, roughly two-thirds of the rural population moved every decade, and population turnover in cities was even greater. This constant coming and going weakened community ties to neighbors and friends and threw individuals even more on their own resources in times of trouble.

Immigrants and the Free-Labor Ladder

The risks and uncertainties of free labor did not deter millions of immigrants from entering the United States during the 1840s and 1850s. Almost 4.5 million immigrants arrived between 1840 and 1860, six times more than had come during the previous two decades (Figure 12.2). By 1860, foreign-born residents made up about one-eighth of the U.S. population, a fraction that held steady well into the twentieth century.

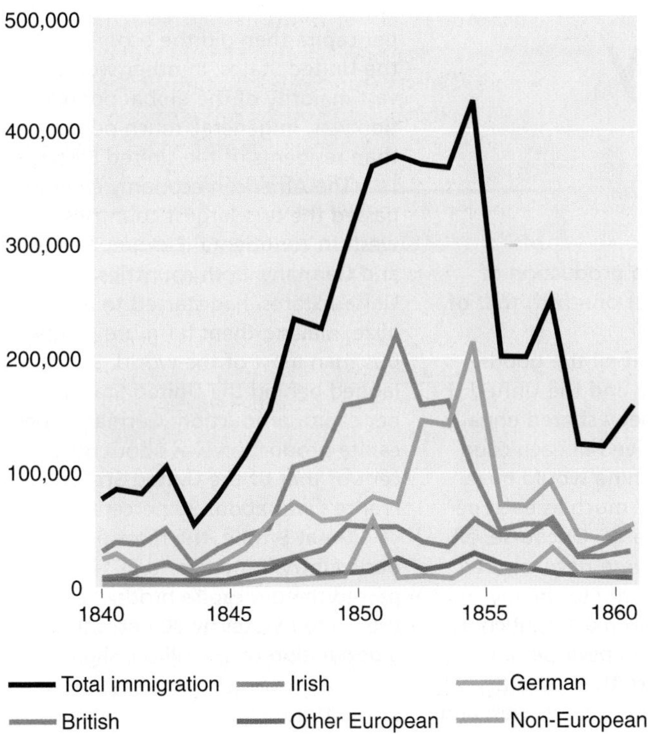

FIGURE 12.2 Antebellum Immigration, 1840–1860
After increasing gradually for several decades, immigration shot up in the mid-1840s. Between 1848 and 1860, nearly 3.5 million immigrants entered the United States.

Nearly three-fourths of the immigrants who arrived in the United States between 1840 and 1860 came from either Germany or Ireland. The majority of the 1.4 million Germans who entered during these years were skilled tradesmen and their families. Roughly a quarter were farmers, some of whom settled in Texas. German butchers, bakers, beer makers, carpenters, shopkeepers, and machinists settled mostly in the Midwest, often congregating in cities. On the whole, German Americans were often Protestants and occupied the middle stratum of independent producers celebrated by free-labor spokesmen; relatively few worked as wage laborers or domestic servants.

Irish immigrants, in contrast, entered at the bottom of the free-labor ladder and struggled to climb up. Nearly 1.7 million Irish immigrants arrived between 1840 and 1860, nearly all of them desperately poor and often weakened by hunger and disease. Potato blight struck Ireland in 1845 and returned repeatedly in subsequent years, spreading a catastrophic famine throughout the island. Many of the lucky ones crowded into the holds of ships and set out for America, where

A German Immigrant in New York
This 1855 painting depicts a German immigrant in New York City asking directions from an African American man who is cutting firewood. Like many other German immigrants, the man shown here appears relatively well off. Compare his clothing with that of the sawyer and the white laborer on the right. Unlike most Irish immigrants, who arrived without family members, the German immigrant is accompanied by his daughter and son. The German appears to be speaking respectfully to the black sawyer, suggesting that he did not fully share assumptions of white supremacy common among native-born white working men. North Carolina Museum of Art, Raleigh, purchased with funds from the State of North Carolina (52.9.2).

BEYOND AMERICA'S BORDERS

Global Prosperity in the 1850s

By the 1850s, the U.S. economy had achieved a remarkable economic transformation. In 1801, when president-elect Thomas Jefferson rode horseback the 180 miles from his home in Monticello, Virginia, to Washington, D.C., he and his horse had to swim across several rivers that lacked bridges or ferries. In 1861, when president-elect Abraham Lincoln traveled more than 1,000 miles to Washington from his home in Springfield, Illinois, he did not need to get wet swimming across rivers. He rode the entire way on railroads. The changes that made Lincoln's journey possible created an American economy that produced more goods and services per capita than that of any other country in the world, except one — Great Britain.

In the 1850s, some countries in the world produced more total goods and services than the United States. But since they had much larger populations than the United States, they produced much less per capita. For example, China produced huge quantities of goods and services, roughly four times more than the United States did. But since the Chinese population was about twenty times greater than that of the United States, the per capita production of China was only about one-fifth that of the United States.

In other words, if all the goods and services in China and the United States in 1850 had been shared equally by the people who lived in each country, each person in China would have had only one-fifth as much as each person in the United States. Of course, all goods and services were never shared equally in either country (or in any other country for that matter). Rich people had more than poor people; landowners had more than laborers; slave owners had more than slaves; and so on. Still, per capita production can serve as an imperfect but revealing indicator of the general prosperity of a country's economy.

Like China, African countries were about one-fifth as prosperous as the United States. India, Japan, Mexico, and Brazil had somewhat more prosperous economies, with per capita production about one-third that of the United States. European countries such as Russia, Spain, and Italy were about half as prosperous as the United States. Overall, more than 90 percent of the people in the world in 1850 lived in countries whose economies produced half or less (much less, for most people) per capita than did the economy of the United States. In other words, the vast majority of the global population was, in general, much poorer than residents of the United States.

The American economy even surpassed the two largest countries of western continental Europe, France and Germany. Both countries, like the United States, had started to industrialize, making them far more prosperous than most of the world. But they lagged behind the United States in per capita production. Germany's per capita production was about 80 percent of that of the United States; France's was about 90 percent.

Great Britain, the most prosperous country in the world in 1850, surpassed the per capita production of the United States by 30 percent. With a population of 21 million, slightly fewer than the 23 million residents of the United States, Britain produced a whopping 45 percent of the world's manufactured goods.

Many factors contributed to Britain's economic leadership, but three were especially important. First, most people in Britain had moved to towns and cities by 1850. Rural folks made up only 22 percent of Britain's population, compared to 85 percent of the U.S. population. Many urban dwellers worked in industries that, in general, were more productive than agriculture, boosting British output. Second, wages were relatively high in Britain, giving manufacturers a big incentive to replace costly labor with machinery. Although machinery

they congregated in northeastern cities. As one immigrant group declared, "All we want is to get out of Ireland; we must be better anywhere than here." Death trailed after them. So many died crossing the Atlantic that ships from Ireland were often termed "coffin ships."

Roughly three out of four Irish immigrants worked as laborers or domestic servants. Irish men dug canals, loaded ships, laid railroad track, and did odd jobs while Irish women worked in the homes of others — cooking, washing and ironing, minding children, and cleaning house. Almost all Irish immigrants were Catholic, a fact that set them apart from the overwhelmingly Protestant native-born residents. Many natives regarded the Irish as hard-drinking, unruly, half-civilized folk. Such views lay behind the discrimination reflected in job announcements that commonly stated, "No Irish need apply." Despite such prejudices, native residents hired Irish immigrants because they accepted low pay and worked hard.

Poverty and Prosperity
This poverty-stricken family living in a barren attic has somehow been noticed by the prosperous couple entering the door bearing blankets and parcels probably containing food. With three young children and an infant at his wife's breast, the poor man looks dejected and ashamed, probably because he could not work with an injured arm. The charity provided by the benevolent couple offered a small measure of temporary relief, but it did not promise a long-term solution to the poor family's plight. The clothing and bodily postures in the painting highlight the contrast between poverty and prosperity in the mid-nineteenth century.
The Granger Collection, NYC.

required capital outlays to set up and maintain, it was far more efficient and tireless than wageworkers.

Manufacturers in both Britain and the United States had similar incentives to industrialize, but British producers did so first and with far greater effectiveness than did those in the United States, in large measure because Britain had a cheap and nearly inexhaustible source of energy — coal, the third crucial factor in Britain's economic leadership. Britain had a unique endowment of coal resources that could be mined relatively inexpensively, making coal prices much lower than in the rest of the world. Low coal prices gave manufacturers a cheap energy source, making it less costly for them to adopt innovative industrial techniques that boosted production — such as steam power. In 1850, coal consumption in Britain was ten times greater than in France and seven times greater than in Germany and the United States. Britain's unique combination of cheap energy, high wages, and a large urban population helped make it the most productive and prosperous country in the world in 1850.

America in a Global Context

1. In 1850, how did U.S. prosperity compare to that in the rest of the world?
2. Why did Britain have the world's leading economy in 1850?
3. To what extent is per capita production a misleading measure of prosperity? Can you think of better measures?
4. What questions does the pattern of global prosperity and poverty in 1850 raise about immigration to the United States?

In America's labor-poor economy, Irish laborers could earn more in one day than in several weeks in Ireland, where opportunities were often scarce. In America, one immigrant explained in 1853, there was "plenty of work and plenty of wages plenty to eat and no land lords thats enough what more does a man want." But some immigrants wanted more, especially respect and decent working conditions. One immigrant complained that he was "a slave for the Americans as the generality of the Irish . . . are."

Such testimony illustrates that the free-labor system, whether for immigrants or native-born laborers, often did not live up to the optimistic vision outlined by Abraham Lincoln and others. Many wage laborers could not realistically aspire to become independent, self-sufficient property holders, despite the claims of free-labor proponents.

REVIEW How did the free-labor ideal account for economic inequality?

▶ The Westward Movement

The nation's swelling population, booming economy, and boundless confidence propelled a new era of rapid westward migration beginning in the 1840s. Until then, the overwhelming majority of Americans lived east of the Mississippi River. Native Americans inhabited the plains, deserts, and rugged coasts to the west. The British claimed the Oregon Country, and the Mexican flag flew over the vast expanse of the Southwest. But by 1850, the nation's limits pushed far beyond the boundaries of the 1803 Louisiana Purchase. The United States stretched to the Pacific and had more than doubled in size. By 1860, the great migration had carried four million Americans west of the Mississippi River.

Frontier settlers took the land and then, with the exception of the Mormons, lobbied their government to acquire the territory they had settled. The human cost of aggressive expansionism was high. The young Mexican nation lost a war and half of its territory. Two centuries of Indian wars east of the Mississippi ended during the 1830s, but the fierce struggle between native inhabitants and invaders continued for another half century in the West. Americans believed it was their destiny to conquer the continent.

Manifest Destiny

Most Americans believed that the superiority of their institutions and white culture bestowed on them a God-given right to spread their civilization across the continent. They imagined the West as a howling wilderness, empty and undeveloped. If they recognized Indians and Mexicans at all, they dismissed them as primitive drags on progress who would have to be redeemed, shoved aside, or exterminated. The West provided young men especially an arena in which to "show their manhood." The sense of uniqueness and mission was as old as the Puritans, but by the 1840s the conviction of superiority had been bolstered by the United States' amazing success. Most Americans believed that the West needed the civilizing power of the hammer and the plow, the ballot box and the pulpit, which had transformed the East.

In 1845, a New York political journal edited by John L. O'Sullivan coined the term ***manifest destiny*** as the latest justification for white settlers to take the land they coveted. O'Sullivan called on Americans to resist any foreign power — British, French, or Mexican — that attempted to thwart "the fulfillment of our manifest destiny to overspread the continent allotted by Providence for the free development of our yearly multiplying millions . . . [and] for the development of the great experiment of liberty and federative self-government entrusted to us." Almost overnight, the magic phrase *manifest destiny* swept the nation and provided an ideological shield for conquering the West.

As important as national pride and racial arrogance were to manifest destiny, economic gain made up its core. Land hunger drew hundreds of thousands of average Americans westward. Some politicians, moreover, had become convinced that national prosperity depended on capturing the rich trade of the Far East. To trade with Asia, the United States needed the Pacific coast ports that stretched from San Diego to Puget Sound. "The sun of civilization must shine across the sea: socially and commercially," Missouri senator Thomas Hart Benton declared. The United States and Asia must "talk together, and trade together. Commerce is a great civilizer." In the 1840s, American economic expansion came wrapped in the rhetoric of uplift and civilization.

Oregon and the Overland Trail

The Oregon Country — a vast region bounded on the west by the Pacific Ocean, on the east by the Rocky Mountains, on the south by the forty-second parallel, and on the north by Russian Alaska — caused the pulse of American expansionists to race. But the British also coveted the area. They argued that their claim lay with Sir Francis Drake's discovery of the Oregon coast in 1579. Americans countered with historic claims of their own. Unable to agree, the United States and Great Britain decided in 1818 on "joint occupation" that would leave Oregon "free and open" to settlement by both countries. A handful of American fur traders and "mountain men" roamed the region in the 1820s.

By the late 1830s, settlers began to trickle along the **Oregon Trail**, following a trail blazed by the mountain men (Map 12.2). The first wagon trains headed west in 1841, and by 1843 about 1,000 emigrants a year set out from Independence, Missouri. By 1869, when the first transcontinental railroad was completed, approximately 350,000 migrants had traveled west to the Pacific in wagon trains.

Emigrants encountered the Plains Indians, a quarter of a million Native Americans scattered over the area between the Mississippi River and

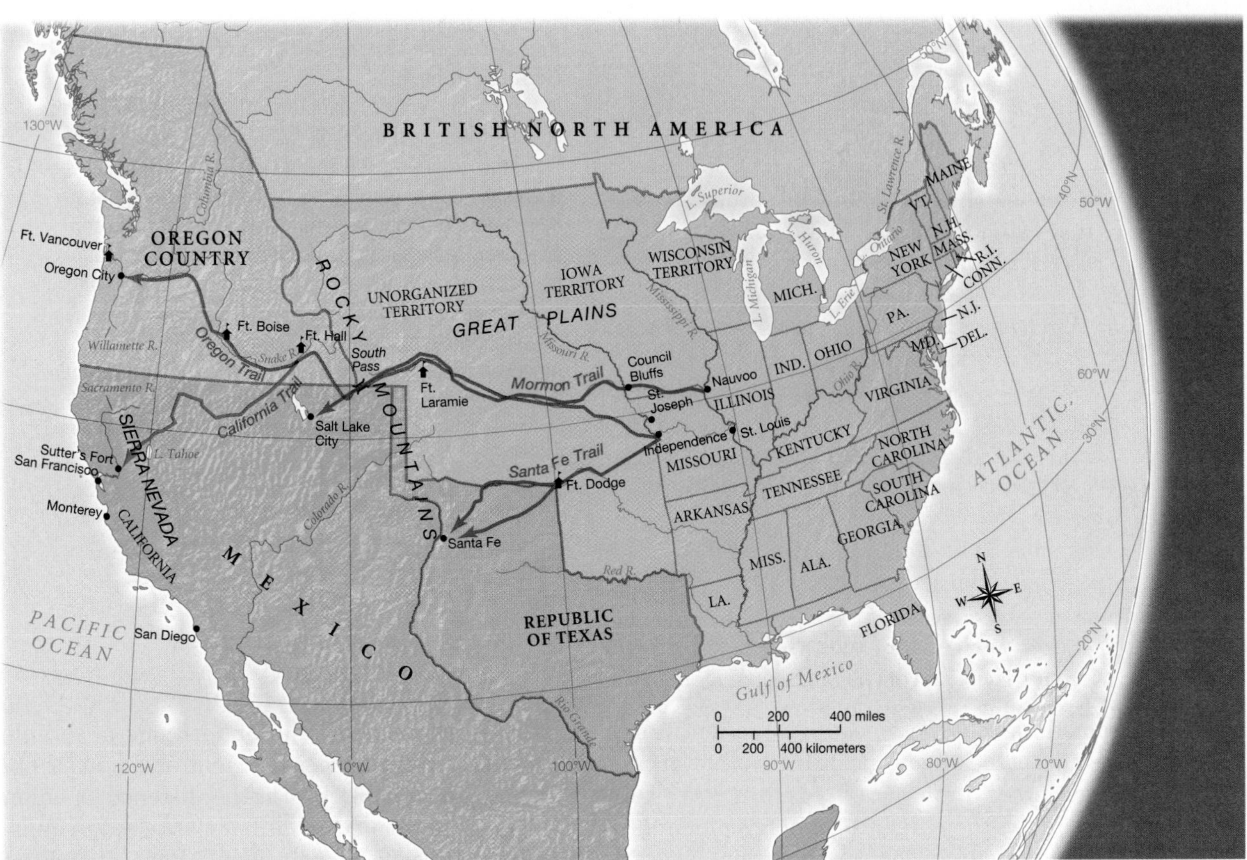

MAP 12.2
Major Trails West
In the 1830s, wagon trains began snaking their way to the Southwest and the Pacific coast. Deep ruts, some of which can still be seen today, soon marked the most popular routes.

the Rocky Mountains. Some were farmers who lived peaceful, sedentary lives, but a majority — the Sioux, Cheyenne, Shoshoni, and Arapaho of the central plains and the Kiowa, Wichita, and Comanche of the southern plains — were horse-mounted, nomadic, nonagricultural peoples whose warriors symbolized the "savage Indian" in the minds of whites.

Horses, which had been brought to North America by Spaniards in the sixteenth century, permitted the Plains tribes to become highly mobile hunters of buffalo. They came to depend on buffalo for nearly everything — food, clothing, shelter, and fuel. Competition for buffalo led to war between the tribes. Young men were introduced to warfare early, learning to ride ponies at breakneck speed while firing off arrows and, later, rifles with astounding accuracy. "A Comanche on his feet is out of his element," observed western artist George Catlin, "but the moment he lays his hands upon his horse, his *face* even becomes handsome, and he gracefully flies away like a different being."

The Plains Indians struck fear in the hearts of whites on the wagon trains. But Native Americans had far more to fear from whites. Indians killed fewer than four hundred emigrants on the trail between 1840 and 1860, while whites brought alcohol and deadly epidemics of smallpox, measles, cholera, and scarlet fever. Moreover, white hunters slaughtered buffalo for the international hide market and sometimes just for sport. The buffalo still numbered some twelve million in 1860, but the herds were shrinking rapidly, intensifying conflict among the Plains tribes.

"A woman that can not endure almost as much as a horse has no business here."
— An Oregon settler

Emigrants insisted that the federal government provide them with more protection. The government constructed a chain of forts along the Oregon Trail (see Map 12.2). More important, it adopted a new Indian policy: "concentration." In 1851, the government called the Plains tribes to a conference at Fort Laramie, Wyoming. Some ten thousand Indians showed up, hopeful that

***Kee-O-Kuk, the Watchful Fox, Chief of the Tribe*, by George Catlin, 1835**
In the 1830s, Pennsylvania-born artist George Catlin traveled the West painting Native Americans. Catlin was the first artist to portray Indians in their own environments and one of the few to present them as human beings, not savages. Convinced that western Indian cultures would soon disappear, Catlin sought to document Indian life through hundreds of paintings and prints. Keokuk, chief of the Sauk and Fox, struggled with the warrior Black Hawk (see chapter 11) about how to deal with whites. Black Hawk fought American expansion; Keokuk believed that war was fruitless and signed over land in Illinois, Missouri, and Wisconsin.
Smithsonian American Art Institution, Washington, D.C. Gift of Mrs. Joseph Harrison Jr.

something could be done to protect them from the ravages of the wagon trains. Instead, government negotiators at the **Fort Laramie conference** persuaded the chiefs to sign agreements that cleared a wide corridor for wagon trains by restricting Native Americans to specific areas that whites promised they would never violate. This policy of concentration became the seedbed for the subsequent policy of reservations. But whites would not keep out of Indian territory, and Indians would not easily give up their traditional ways of life. Struggle for control of the West meant warfare for decades to come.

Still, Indians threatened emigrants less than life on the trail did. The men, women, and children who headed west each spring could count on at least six months of grueling travel. With nearly two thousand miles to go and traveling no more than fifteen miles a day, the pioneers endured parching heat, drought, treacherous rivers, disease, physical and emotional exhaustion, and, if the snows closed the mountain passes before they got through, freezing and starvation. Women sometimes faced the dangers of trailside childbirth. It was said that a person could walk from Missouri to the Pacific stepping only on the graves of those who had died heading west. Such tribulations led one miserable woman, trying to keep her children dry in a rainstorm and to calm them as they listened to Indian shouts, to wonder "what had possessed my husband, anyway, that he should have thought of bringing us away out through this God forsaken country."

Men usually found Oregon "one of the greatest countries in the world." From "the Cascade mountains to the Pacific, the whole country can be cultivated," exclaimed one eager settler. When women reached Oregon, they found that neighbors were scarce and things were in a "primitive state." One young wife arrived with only her husband, one stew kettle, and three knives. Necessity blurred the traditional division between men's and women's work. "I am maid of all traids," one busy woman remarked in 1853. Work seemed unending. "I am a very old woman," declared twenty-nine-year-old Sarah Everett. "My face is thin sunken and wrinkled, my hands bony withered and hard." Another settler observed, "A woman that can not endure almost as much as a horse has no business here." Yet despite the ordeal of the trail and the difficulties of starting from scratch, emigrants kept coming.

Plains Indians and Trails West in the 1840s and 1850s

VISUAL ACTIVITY

Pioneer Family on the Trail West

In 1860, W. G. Chamberlain photographed these unidentified travelers momentarily at rest by the upper Arkansas River in Colorado. We do not know their fates, but we can only hope that they fared better than the Sager family. Henry and Naomi Sager and their six children set out from St. Joseph, Missouri, in 1844. "Father," one of Henry and Naomi's daughters remembered, "was one of those restless men who are not content to remain in one place long at a time. [He] had been talking of going to Texas. But mother, hearing much said about the healthfulness of Oregon, preferred to go there." Still far from Oregon, Henry Sager died of fever. Twenty-six days later, Naomi died, leaving seven children, the last delivered on the trail. The Sager children, under the care of other families in the wagon train, pressed on. After traveling two thousand miles in seven months, the migrants arrived in Oregon, where Marcus and Narcissa Whitman, whose own daughter had drowned, adopted all seven of the Sager children. Denver Public Library, Western History Division # F3226.

READING THE IMAGE: Based on this photograph, what were some of the difficulties faced by pioneers traveling west?

CONNECTIONS: How did wagon trains change the western United States?

The Mormon Exodus

Not every wagon train heading west was bound for the Pacific Slope. One remarkable group of religious emigrants halted near the Great Salt Lake in what was then Mexican territory. The **Mormons** deliberately chose the remote site as a refuge. After years of persecution in the East, they fled west to find religious freedom and communal security.

In 1820, an upstate New York farm boy named **Joseph Smith Jr.** had begun to experience revelations that were followed, he said, by a visit from an angel who led him to golden tablets buried near his home. With the aid of magic stones, he translated the mysterious language on the tablets to produce *The Book of Mormon*, which he published in 1830. It told the story of an ancient Hebrew civilization in the New World and predicted the appearance of an American prophet who would reestablish Jesus Christ's undefiled kingdom in America. Converts, attracted to the promise of a pure faith in the midst of antebellum America's social turmoil and rampant materialism, flocked to the new Church of Jesus Christ of Latter-Day Saints (the Mormons).

Neighbors branded Mormons heretics and drove Smith and his followers from New York to Ohio, then to Missouri, and finally in 1839 to Nauvoo, Illinois, where they built a prosperous community. But a rift in the church developed after Smith sanctioned "plural marriage" (polygamy). Non-Mormons caught wind of the controversy and eventually arrested Smith and his brother. On June 27, 1844, a mob stormed the jail and shot both men dead.

The embattled church turned to an extraordinary new leader, **Brigham Young**, who oversaw a great exodus. In 1846, traveling in 3,700 wagons, 12,000 Mormons made their way to eastern Iowa, then the following year to their new home beside the Great Salt Lake. Young described the region as a barren waste, "the paradise of the lizard, the cricket and the rattlesnake." Within ten years, however, the Mormons developed an irrigation system that made the desert bloom. Under Young's stern leadership, the Mormons built a thriving community using cooperative labor, not the individualistic and competitive enterprise common among most emigrants.

In 1850, the Mormon kingdom was annexed to the United States as Utah Territory. The nation's attention focused on Utah in 1852 when Brigham Young announced that many Mormons practiced polygamy. Although only one Mormon man in five had more than one wife (Young had twenty-three), Young's statement caused a popular outcry that forced the U.S. government to establish its authority in Utah. In 1857, 2,500 U.S. troops invaded Salt Lake City in what was known as the Mormon War. The bloodless occupation illustrated that most Americans viewed the Mormons as a threat to American morality, law, and institutions. The invasion did not dislodge the Mormon Church from its central place in Utah, however, and for years to come, most Americans perceived the Mormon settlement as strange and suitably isolated.

The Mexican Borderlands

In the Mexican Southwest, westward-moving Anglo-American pioneers confronted northern-moving Spanish-speaking frontiersmen. On this frontier as elsewhere, national cultures, interests, and aspirations collided. Since 1821, when Mexico won its independence from Spain, the Mexican flag had flown over the vast expanse that stretched from the Gulf of Mexico to the Pacific and from the Oregon Country to Guatemala (Map 12.3). But Mexico's northern provinces were sparsely populated, and the young nation was plagued by civil wars, economic crises, quarrels with the Roman Catholic Church, and devastating raids by the Comanche, Apache, and Kiowa. Mexico found it increasingly difficult to defend its borderlands, especially when faced with a northern neighbor convinced of its superiority and bent on territorial acquisition.

The American assault began quietly. In the 1820s, Anglo-American trappers, traders, and settlers drifted into Mexico's far northern provinces. Santa Fe, a remote outpost in the province of New Mexico, became a magnet for American

Mormon Family
The rest of America found the Mormon practice of polygamy deeply offensive. Five years after American troops occupied Utah in 1857, President Abraham Lincoln signed anti-polygamy legislation, and in 1890 the Mormons officially abandoned plural marriages. But in this photograph from Salt Lake City in the 1850s, a husband, his three wives, and their five children sit proudly for a family portrait. No matter national opinion, they clearly are at ease with their unusual family constellation. ©The Church of Jesus Christ of Latter Day Saints, Intellectual Property Division.

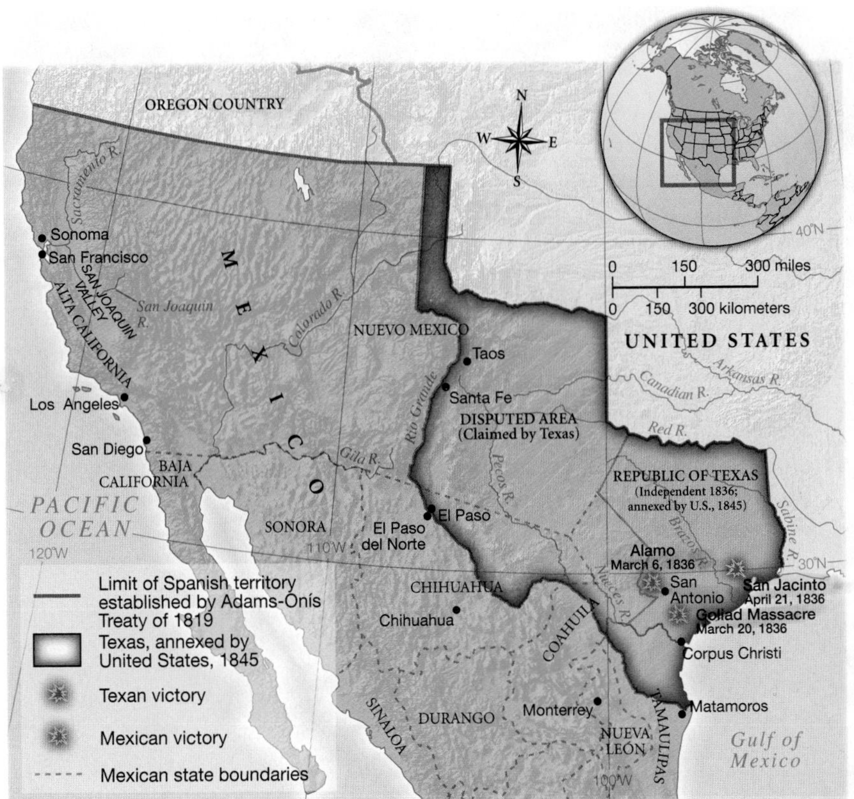

MAP 12.3
Texas and Mexico in the 1830s
As Americans spilled into lightly populated and loosely governed northern Mexico, Texas and then other Mexican provinces became contested territory.

enterprise. Each spring, American traders gathered at Independence, Missouri, for the long trek southwest along the Santa Fe Trail (see Map 12.2). They crammed their wagons with inexpensive American manufactured goods and returned home with Mexican silver, furs, and mules.

The Mexican province of Texas attracted a flood of Americans who had settlement, not long-distance trade, on their minds (see Map 12.3). Wanting to populate and develop its northern territory, the Mexican government granted the American **Stephen F. Austin** a huge tract of land along the Brazos River. In the 1820s, Austin became the first Anglo-American *empresario* (colonization agent) in Texas, offering land at only ten cents an acre. Thousands of Americans poured across the border. Most were Southerners who brought cotton and slaves with them.

By the 1830s, the settlers had established a thriving plantation economy in Texas. Americans numbered 35,000, while the *Tejano* (Spanish-speaking) population was less than 8,000. Few Anglo-American settlers were Roman Catholic, spoke Spanish, or cared about assimilating into Mexican culture. Afraid of losing Texas to the new arrivals, the Mexican government in 1830 banned further immigration to Texas from the United States and outlawed the introduction of additional slaves. The Anglo-Americans made it clear that they wanted to be rid of the "despotism of the sword and the priesthood" and to govern themselves. In Mexico City, however, General **Antonio López de Santa Anna** seized political power and set about restoring order to the northern frontier.

When the Texan settlers rebelled, Santa Anna ordered the Mexican army northward. In February 1836, the army arrived at the outskirts of San Antonio. Commanded by Colonel William B. Travis from Alabama, the rebels included the Tennessee frontiersman Davy Crockett and the Louisiana adventurer James Bowie, as well as a handful of Tejanos. They took refuge in a former Franciscan mission known as the Alamo. Santa Anna sent wave after wave of his 2,000-man army crashing against the walls until the attackers finally broke through and killed all 187 rebels. A few weeks later, outside the small town of Goliad, Mexican forces captured a

Texas War for Independence, 1836

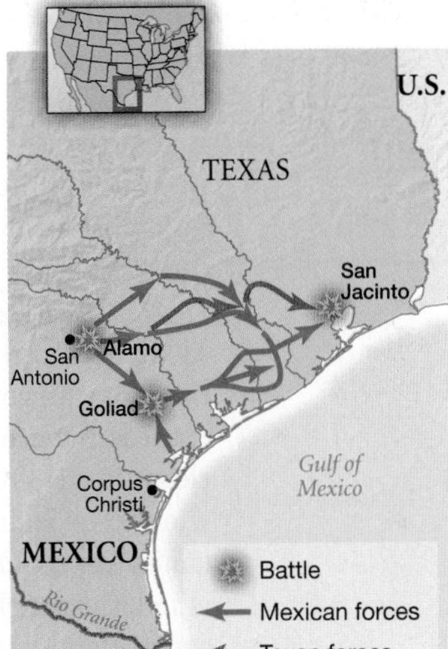

***Fandango*, by Theodore Gentilz, 1844**
Although Spanish and Mexican authorities failed to entice many Hispanic settlers to distant provinces such as Texas, a small and resourceful Tejano community managed to develop a ranching economy in the harsh frontier conditions. The largest Hispanic population was concentrated in the vicinity of San Antonio, where settlers reproduced as best they could the cultural traditions they carried with them. Here, a group of animated, well-dressed men and women perform a Spanish dance called the fandango while musicians play in triple time. Daughters of the Republic of Texas Library, Alamo Collection.

garrison of Texans. Mexican firing squads executed almost 400 of the men as "pirates and outlaws." In April 1836, at San Jacinto, General Sam Houston's army adopted the massacre of Goliad as a battle cry and crushed Santa Anna's troops in a surprise attack. The Texans had succeeded in establishing the **Lone Star Republic**, and the following year the United States recognized the independence of Texas from Mexico.

Earlier, in 1824, in an effort to increase Mexican migration to the province of California, the Mexican government granted *ranchos* — huge estates devoted to cattle raising — to new settlers. *Rancheros* ruled over near-feudal empires worked by Indians whose condition sometimes approached that of slaves. Not satisfied, the rancheros coveted the vast lands controlled by the Franciscan missions. In 1834, they persuaded the Mexican government to confiscate the missions and make their lands available to new settlement, a development that accelerated the decline of the California Indians. Devastated by disease, the Indians, who had numbered approximately 300,000 when the Spanish arrived in 1769, had declined to half that number by 1846.

Despite the efforts of the Mexican government, California in 1840 had a population of only 7,000 Mexican settlers. Non-Mexican settlers numbered only 380, but among them were Americans who championed manifest destiny. They sought to woo American emigrants to California. In the 1840s, wagon after wagon left the Oregon Trail to head southwest on the California Trail (see Map 12.2). As the trickle of Americans became a river, Mexican officials grew alarmed. As a New York newspaper put it in 1845, "Let the tide of emigration flow toward California and the American population will soon be sufficiently numerous to play the Texas game." Only a few Americans in California wanted a war for independence, but many dreamed of living again under the U.S. flag.

The U.S. government made no secret of its desire to acquire California. In 1835, President Andrew Jackson tried unsuccessfully to purchase it. In 1846, American settlers in the Sacramento Valley took matters into their own hands. Prodded by John C. Frémont, a former army captain and explorer who had arrived with a party of sixty buckskin-clad frontiersmen spoiling for a fight, the Californians raised an independence movement known as the Bear Flag Revolt. By then, James K. Polk, a champion of aggressive expansion, sat in the White House.

REVIEW Why did westward migration expand dramatically in the mid-nineteenth century?

▶ Expansion and the Mexican-American War

Although emigrants acted as the advance guard of American empire, there was nothing automatic about the U.S. annexation of territory in the West. Acquiring territory required political action. In the 1840s, the politics of expansion became entangled with sectionalism and the slavery question. Texas, Oregon, and the Mexican borderlands also thrust the United States into dangerous diplomatic crises with Great Britain and Mexico.

Aggravation between Mexico and the United States escalated to open antagonism in 1845 when the United States annexed Texas. Absorbing territory still claimed by Mexico ruptured diplomatic relations between the two countries and set the stage for war. But it was President James K. Polk's insistence on having Mexico's other northern provinces that made war certain. The war was not as easy as Polk anticipated, but it ended in American victory and the acquisition of a new American West. One of the nation's new territories, California, proved immediately profitable; the discovery of gold prompted a massive wave of emigration to the western coast, a rush that nearly destroyed Native American and Californio society.

The Politics of Expansion

Texans had sought admission to the Union almost since winning their independence from Mexico in 1836. Almost constant border warfare between Mexico and the Republic of Texas in the decade following the revolution underscored the precarious nature of independence. It also made clear that annexing Texas to the United States risked precipitating war, for Mexico had never relinquished its claim to its lost province. But any suggestion of adding another slave state to the Union outraged most Northerners, who applauded westward expansion but imagined the expansion of liberty, not slavery.

President **John Tyler**, who became president in April 1841 when William Henry Harrison died one month after taking office, understood that Texas was a dangerous issue. Adding to the danger, Great Britain began sniffing around Texas, apparently contemplating adding the young republic to its growing empire. Tyler, an ardent expansionist, decided to risk annexing the Lone Star Republic. However, when he laid an annexation treaty before the Senate in 1844, howls of protest erupted across the North. Future Massachusetts senator Charles Sumner deplored the "insidious" plan to annex Texas and carve from it "great slaveholding states." The Senate soundly rejected the treaty, and it appeared that Tyler had succeeded only in inflaming sectional conflict.

Polk and Dallas Banner, 1844

In 1844, Democratic presidential nominee James K. Polk and vice presidential nominee George M. Dallas campaigned under this cotton banner. The extra star spilling over into the red and white stripes symbolizes Polk's vigorous support for annexing the huge slave republic of Texas, which had declared its independence from Mexico eight years earlier. Henry Clay, Polk's Whig opponent, ran under a banner that was similar but conspicuously lacked the additional star. Collection of Janice L. and David J. Frent.

The issue of Texas had not died down by the 1844 election. In an effort to appeal to northern voters, the Whig nominee for president, **Henry Clay**, came out against annexation of Texas. "Annexation and war with Mexico are identical," he declared. The Democrats chose Tennessean **James K. Polk**, a passionate expansionist who vigorously backed annexation. To make annexation palatable to Northerners, the Democrats shrewdly yoked Texas to Oregon, thus tapping the desire for expansion in the free states of the North as well as in the slave states of the South. The Democratic platform called for the "reannexation of Texas" and the "reoccupation of Oregon." The suggestion that the United States was merely reasserting existing rights was poor history but good politics.

When Clay finally recognized the popularity of expansion, he waffled, hinting that he might accept the annexation of Texas after all. His retreat succeeded only in alienating antislavery opinion in the North. James G. Birney, the candidate of the fledgling Liberty Party, picked up the votes of thousands of disillusioned Clay supporters. In the November election, Polk received 170 electoral votes and Clay 105. New York's 35 electoral votes proved critical to Clay's defeat. A shift of just one-third of Birney's 15,000 votes to Clay would have given Clay the state and the presidency.

In his inaugural address on March 4, 1845, Polk underscored his faith in America's manifest destiny. "This heaven-favored land," he proclaimed, enjoyed the "most admirable and wisest system of well-regulated self-government . . . ever devised by human minds." He asked, "Who shall assign limits to the achievements of free minds and free hands under the protection of this glorious Union?"

The nation did not have to wait for Polk's inauguration to see results from his victory. One month after the election, President Tyler announced that the triumph of the Democratic Party provided a mandate for the annexation of Texas "promptly and immediately." In February 1845, after a fierce debate between antislavery and proslavery forces, Congress approved a joint resolution offering the Republic of Texas admission to the United States. Texas entered as the fifteenth slave state.

Tyler delivered Texas, but Polk had promised Oregon, too. Westerners particularly demanded that the new president make good on the Democrats' pledge "Fifty-four Forty or Fight" —that is, all of Oregon, right up to Alaska (54°40′ was the southern latitude of Russian Alaska). But Polk was close to war with Mexico and could not afford a war with Britain over U.S. claims in Canada. He renewed an old offer to divide Oregon along the forty-ninth parallel. When Britain accepted the compromise, some Americans cried betrayal, but most celebrated the agreement that gave the nation an enormous territory peacefully. When the Senate finally approved the treaty in June 1846, the United States and Mexico were already at war.

The Mexican-American War, 1846–1848

From the day he entered the White House, Polk craved Mexico's remaining northern provinces: California and New Mexico, land that today makes up California, Nevada, Utah, most of New Mexico and Arizona, and parts of Wyoming and Colorado. Since the 1830s, Comanches, Kiowas, Apaches, and others had attacked Mexican ranches and towns, killing thousands, and the Polk administration invoked Mexico's inability to control its northern provinces to denigrate its claims to them. Polk hoped to buy the territory, but when the Mexicans refused to sell, he concluded that military force would be needed to realize the United States' manifest destiny.

Polk had already ordered General **Zachary Taylor** to march his 4,000-man army 150 miles south from its position on the Nueces River, the southern boundary of Texas according to the Mexicans, to the banks of the Rio Grande, the boundary claimed by Texans (Map 12.4). Viewing the American advance as aggression, the Mexican general in Matamoros ordered Taylor back to the Nueces. Taylor refused, and on April 25, 1846, Mexican cavalry attacked a party of American soldiers, killing or wounding sixteen and capturing the rest. Even before news of the battle arrived in Washington, Polk had obtained his cabinet's approval of a war message.

On May 11, the president told Congress, "Mexico has passed the boundary of the United States, has invaded our territory, and shed American blood upon American soil." Thus "war exists, and, notwithstanding all our efforts to avoid it, exists by the act of Mexico herself." Congress passed a declaration of war and began raising an army. Despite years of saber rattling toward Mexico and Britain, the U.S. Army was pitifully small, only 8,600 soldiers. Faced with the nation's first foreign war, against a Mexican army that numbered more than 30,000, Polk called for volunteers. Eventually, more than 112,000 white Americans (40 percent of whom

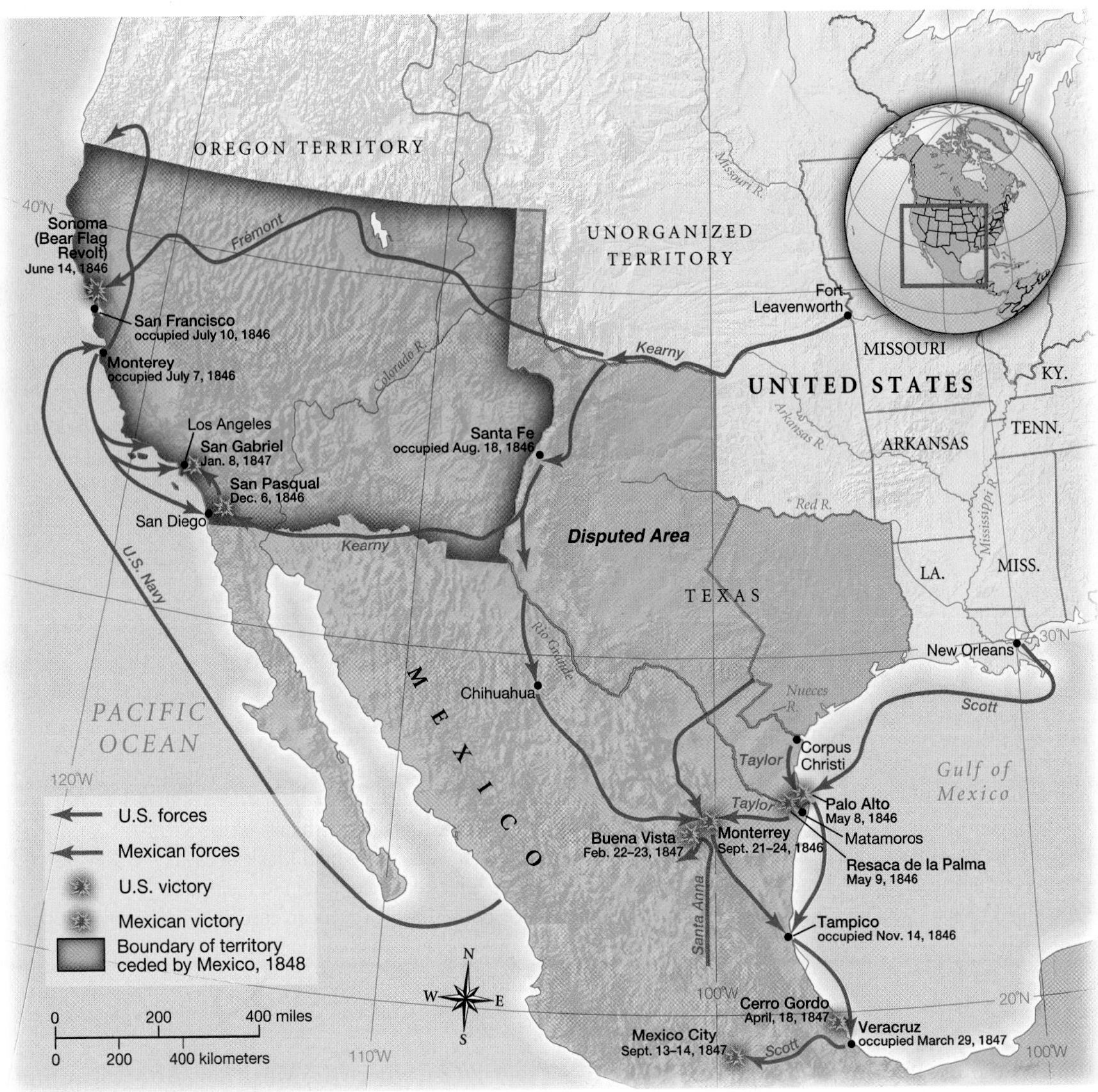

MAP 12.4
The Mexican-American War, 1846–1848
American and Mexican soldiers skirmished across much of northern Mexico, but the major battles took place between the Rio Grande and Mexico City.

were immigrants; blacks were banned) joined the army to fight in Mexico.

Despite the flood of volunteers, the war divided the nation. Northern Whigs in particular condemned the war. The Massachusetts legislature claimed that the war was being fought for the "triple object of extending slavery, of strengthening the slave power, and of obtaining control of the free states." On January 12, 1848, a gangly freshman Whig representative from Illinois rose in the House of Representatives to deliver his first important speech in Congress. Before Abraham Lincoln sat down, he had questioned Polk's intelligence, honesty, and sanity. The president ignored the upstart representative, but antislavery, antiwar Whigs kept up the attack throughout the conflict. In their effort to undercut national support, they labeled it "Mr. Polk's War."

Since most Americans backed the war, it was not really Polk's war, but the president acted as if it were and directed the war personally. He planned a short war in which U.S. armies would occupy Mexico's northern provinces and defeat the Mexican army in a decisive battle or two, after which Mexico would sue for peace and the United States would keep the territory its armies occupied.

At first, Polk's strategy seemed to work. In May 1846, Zachary Taylor's troops drove south from the Rio Grande and routed the Mexican army, first at Palo Alto, then at Resaca de la

***Batalla del Sacramento*, by Julio Michaud y Thomas**
Most images of the Mexican-American War were created by artists from the United States, but Mexicans also recorded the war. In this hand-colored lithograph, Mexican artist Julio Michaud y Thomas depicts the February 1847 battle in which 1,100 American troops engaged 3,000 Mexicans on the banks of the Sacramento River near Chihuahua. Michaud accurately portrays the first moments of the bold Mexican cavalry charge, but American artillery forced the Mexican lancers to retreat, with "great confusion in their ranks." When the fighting ended, the Mexicans had suffered some 700 casualties, while American casualties amounted to about a half dozen. Yale Collection of Western Americana, Beinecke Rare Book and Manuscript Library.

Palma (see Map 12.4). "Old Rough and Ready," as Taylor was affectionately known among his adoring troops, became an instant war hero. Polk rewarded Taylor for his victories by making him commander of the Mexican campaign.

> **"I can assure you that fighting is the least dangerous & arduous part of a soldier's life."**
> — An American soldier in the Mexican-American War

A second prong of the campaign centered on Colonel Stephen Watts Kearny, who led a 1,700-man army from Missouri into New Mexico. Without firing a shot, U.S. forces took Santa Fe in August 1846. Kearny then marched into San Diego three months later, encountering a major Mexican rebellion against American rule. In January 1847, after several clashes and severe losses, the U.S. forces occupied Los Angeles. California and New Mexico were in American hands.

By then, Taylor had driven deep into the interior of Mexico. In September 1846, after house-to-house fighting, he took the city of Monterrey. Taylor then pushed his 5,000 troops southwest, where the Mexican hero of the Alamo, General Antonio López de Santa Anna, was concentrating an army of 21,000. On February 23, 1847, Santa Anna's troops attacked Taylor at Buena Vista. Superior American artillery and accurate musket fire won the day, but the Americans suffered heavy casualties, including Henry Clay Jr., the son of the man who had opposed Texas annexation for fear it would precipitate war. The Mexicans suffered even greater losses (some 3,400 dead, wounded, and missing, compared with 650 Americans). During the night, Santa Anna withdrew his battered army, much to the "profound disgust of the troops," one Mexican officer remembered. "They are filled with grief that they were going to lose the benefit of all the sacrifices that they had made; that the conquered field would be abandoned, and that the victory would be given to the enemy."

The series of uninterrupted victories in northern Mexico fed the American troops' sense of invincibility. "No American force has ever thought of being defeated by any amount of Mexican troops," one soldier declared. The Americans worried about other hazards, however. "I can assure you that fighting is the least dangerous & arduous part of a soldier's life," one young man declared. Letters home told of torturous marches across arid wastes alive with tarantulas, scorpions, and rattlesnakes. Others recounted dysentery, malaria, smallpox, cholera, and yellow fever. Of the 13,000 American soldiers who died (some 50,000 Mexicans perished), fewer than 2,000 fell to Mexican bullets and shells. Disease killed most of the others. Medicine was so primitive that, as one Tennessee man observed, "nearly all who take sick die."

Mexican Family
This family had its portrait taken in 1847, in the middle of the war. Where were the adult males? Mexican civilians were vulnerable to atrocities committed by the invading army, a large part of which were volunteers who received little training and resisted discipline. The "lawless Volunteers stop at no outrage," Brigadier General William Worth declared. "Innocent blood has been basely, cowardly, and barbarously shed in cold blood." Generals Zachary Taylor and Winfield Scott gradually tamed the volunteers with stern military justice.
Unknown photographer. Daguerrotype, ca. 1947, 2-7/8 x 3/16 inches, Amon Carter Museum, Fort Worth, Texas, P1981.65.18.

Victory in Mexico

Although the Americans won battle after battle, President Polk's strategy misfired. Despite heavy losses on the battlefield, Mexico refused to trade land for peace. One American soldier captured the Mexican mood: "They cannot submit to be deprived of California after the loss of Texas, and nothing but the conquest of their Capital will force them to such a humiliation." Polk had arrived at the same conclusion. While Taylor occupied the north, General **Winfield Scott** would land an army on the Gulf coast of Mexico and march 250 miles inland to Mexico City. Polk's plan entailed enormous risk because Scott would have to cut himself off from supplies and lead his men deep into enemy country against a much larger army.

An amphibious landing on March 9, 1847, near Veracruz put some 10,000 American troops ashore. After a siege of two weeks and furious shelling, Veracruz surrendered. In April 1847, Scott's forces moved westward, following the path blazed more than three centuries earlier by Hernán Cortés to "the halls of Montezuma" (see chapter 2).

After the defeat at Buena Vista, Santa Anna had returned to Mexico City, where he rallied his ragged troops and marched them east to set a trap for Scott in the mountain pass at Cerro Gordo. Knifing through Mexican lines, the Americans almost captured Santa Anna, who fled the field on foot. So complete was the victory that Scott gloated to Taylor, "Mexico no longer has an army." But Santa Anna, ever resilient, again rallied the Mexican army. Some 30,000 troops took up defensive positions on the outskirts of Mexico City and began melting down church bells to cast new cannons.

In August 1847, Scott began his assault on the Mexican capital. The fighting proved the most brutal of the war. Santa Anna backed his army into the city, fighting each step of the way. At the battle of Churubusco, the Mexicans took 4,000 casualties in a single day and the Americans more than 1,000. At the castle of Chapultepec, American troops scaled the walls and fought the Mexican defenders hand to hand. After Chapultepec, Mexico City officials persuaded Santa Anna to evacuate the city to save it from destruction, and on September 14, 1847, Scott rode in triumphantly.

On February 2, 1848, American and Mexican officials signed the **Treaty of Guadalupe Hidalgo** in Mexico City. Mexico agreed to give up all claims to Texas north of the Rio Grande and to cede the provinces of New Mexico and California — more than 500,000 square miles — to the United States (see Map 12.4). The United States agreed to pay Mexico $15 million and to assume $3.25 million in claims that American citizens had against Mexico. In March 1848, the Senate ratified the treaty. Polk had his Rio Grande border, his Pacific ports, and all the land that lay between.

MAP ACTIVITY

MAP 12.5 Territorial Expansion by 1860
Less than a century after its founding, the United States spread from the Atlantic seaboard to the Pacific coast. War, purchase, and diplomacy had gained a continent.

READING THE MAP: List the countries from which the United States acquired land. Which nation lost the most land because of U.S. expansion?

CONNECTIONS: Who coined the phrase *manifest destiny*? When? What does it mean? What areas targeted for expansion were the subjects of debate during the presidential campaign of 1844?

The American triumph had enormous consequences. Less than three-quarters of a century after its founding, the United States had achieved its self-proclaimed manifest destiny to stretch from the Atlantic to the Pacific (Map 12.5). It would enter the industrial age with vast new natural resources and a two-ocean economy, while Mexico faced a sharply diminished economic future.

Golden California

Another consequence of the Mexican defeat was that California gold poured into American, not Mexican, pockets. In January 1848, just weeks before the formal transfer of territory, James Marshall discovered gold in the American River in the foothills of the Sierra Nevada. Marshall's discovery set off the **California gold rush**, one of the wildest mining stampedes in the world's history. Between 1849 and 1852, more than 250,000 "forty-niners," as the would-be miners were known, descended on the Golden State. In less than two years, Marshall's discovery transformed California from foreign territory to statehood.

Gold fever quickly spread around the world. A stream of men of various races and nationalities, all bent on getting rich, remade the quiet California world of Mexican ranches into a raucous, roaring mining and town economy. Only a few struck it rich, and life in the goldfields was nasty, brutish, and often short. Men faced miserable living conditions, sometimes sheltering in holes and brush lean-tos. They also faced cholera and scurvy, exorbitant prices for food (eggs cost a dollar apiece), deadly encounters with claim jumpers, and endless backbreaking labor. An individual with gold in his pocket could find only temporary relief in the saloons, card games, dogfights, gambling dens, and brothels that flourished in the mining camps.

By 1853, San Francisco had grown into a raw, booming city of 50,000 that depended as much on gold as did the mining camps inland. Like the towns that dotted the San Joaquin and Sacramento valleys, it suffered from overcrowding, fire, crime, and violence. But enterprising individuals had learned that there was money to be made tending to the needs of the miners. Hotels, saloons, restaurants, laundries, and stores of all kinds exchanged services and goods for miners' gold.

In 1851, the Committee of Vigilance determined to bring order to the city. Members pledged that "no thief, burglar, incendiary or assassin shall escape punishment, either by the quibbles of the law, the insecurity of prisons, the carelessness or corruption of the police, or a laxity of those who pretended to administer justice." Lynchings proved that the committee meant business. In time, merchants, tradesmen, and professionals made the city their home and brought their families from back east. Gunfights declined, but many years would pass before anyone pacified San Francisco.

Miner with Pick, Pan, and Shovel
This young man exhibits the spirit of individual effort that was the foundation of free-labor ideals. Posing with a pick and shovel to loosen gold-bearing deposits and a pan to wash away debris, the man appears determined to succeed as a miner by his own muscles and sweat. Hard work with these tools, the picture suggests, promised rewards and maybe riches. Collection of Matthew Isenburg.

Establishing civic order was made more difficult by California's diversity and Anglo bigotry. The Chinese attracted special scrutiny. By 1851, 25,000 Chinese lived in California, and their religion, language, dress, queues (long pigtails), eating habits, and recreational use of opium convinced many Anglos that they were not fit citizens of the Golden State. In 1850, the California legislature passed the Foreign Miners' Tax Law, which levied high taxes on non-Americans to drive them from the goldfields, except as hired laborers working on claims owned by Americans. The Chinese were segregated residentially and occupationally and made ineligible for citizenship. Along with blacks and Indians, Chinese were denied public education and the right to testify in court.

As early as 1852, opponents demanded a halt to Chinese immigration. Chinese leaders in San Francisco fought back. Admitting deep cultural differences, they insisted that "in the important matters we are good men. We honor our parents; we take care of our children; we are industrious and peaceable; we trade much; we are trusted for small and large sums; we pay our debts; and are honest, and of course must tell the truth." Their protestations offered little protection, however, and racial violence grew.

Anglo-American prospectors asserted their dominance over other groups, especially Native Americans and the Californios, Spanish and Mexican settlers who had lived in California for decades. Despite the U.S. government's pledge to protect Mexican and Spanish land titles after the cession of 1848, Americans took the land of the rancheros and through discriminatory legislation pushed Hispanic professionals, merchants, and artisans into the ranks of unskilled labor. Mariano Vallejo, a leading Californio, said of the forty-niners, "The good ones were few and the wicked many."

For Indians, the gold rush was catastrophic. Numbering about 150,000 in 1848, the Indian population of California fell to 25,000 by 1854. Starvation, disease, and a declining birthrate took a heavy toll. Indians also fell victim to wholesale murder. The nineteenth-century historian Hubert Howe Bancroft described

Chinese Man
This daguerreotype of an unidentified Chinese man was made by Isaac Wallace Baker, a photographer who traveled through California's mining camps in his wagon studio. One of the earliest known portraits of an Asian in California, the portrait shows a proud man boldly displaying his queue (long braid). This was almost certainly an act of defiance, for Anglos ridiculed Chinese cultural traditions, and vigilantes chased down men who wore queues. Collection of the Oakland Museum of California, Gift of Anonymous Donor.

white behavior toward Indians during the gold rush as "one of the last human hunts of civilization, and the basest and most brutal of them all." To survive, Indians moved to the most remote areas of the state and tried to stay out of the way.

The forty-niners created dazzling wealth: In 1852, 81 million ounces of gold, nearly half of the world's production, came from California. However, most forty-niners eventually took up farming, opened small businesses, or worked for wages for the corporations that took over the mining industry. Others looked beyond the land, for California's ports were connected to a vast trade network throughout the Pacific. Americans traded furs, hides, and lumber and engaged in whaling and the China trade in tea, silk, and porcelain. Still, as California's first congressional representative observed, the state was separated "by thousands of miles of plains, deserts, and almost impossible mountains" from the rest of the Union. Some dreamers imagined a railroad that would someday connect the Golden State with the thriving agriculture and industry of the East. Others imagined a country transformed not by transportation but by progressive individual and institutional reform.

REVIEW Why was the annexation of Texas such a controversial policy?

▸ Reforming Self and Society

While manifest destiny, the Mexican-American War, and the California gold rush transformed the nation's boundaries, many Americans sought personal and social reform. The emphasis on self-discipline and individual effort at the core of the free-labor ideal led Americans to believe that insufficient self-control caused the major social problems of the era. Evangelical Protestants struggled to control individuals' propensity to sin. Temperance advocates exhorted drinkers to control their urge for alcohol. In the midst of the worldly disruptions of geographic expansion and economic change, about one-third of Americans belonged to a church in 1850. Although many — like Abraham Lincoln — remained outside churches, the influence of evangelical religion reached far beyond church members.

The evangelical temperament — a conviction of righteousness coupled with energy, self-discipline, and faith that the world could be improved — animated most reformers. However, a few activists pointed out that certain fundamental injustices lay beyond the reach of individual self-control. Transcendentalists and utopians believed that perfection could be attained only by rejecting the competitive, individualistic values of mainstream society. Woman's rights activists and abolitionists sought to reverse the subordination of women and to eliminate the enslavement of blacks by changing laws and social institutions as well as attitudes and customs. They confronted the daunting challenge of repudiating widespread assumptions about male supremacy and white supremacy and somehow challenging the entrenched institutions that reinforced those assumptions: the family and slavery.

The Mansion of Happiness
Unlike the modern day board game Monopoly, which encourages players to greedily amass real estate and wealth, The Mansion of Happiness, designed by a minister in 1843, rewarded players for traits of pious, middle-class respectability. Players spun a small top to determine how many spaces to advance. Players who landed on spaces labeled Piety, Chastity, or Temperance, got to advance six more spaces. Landing on Idleness sent a player back to Industry. A player who settled on Passion had to return to the water to cool off. The winner made it to the central Mansion of Happiness: Heaven. Rare Book & Special Collections Division, Library of Congress.

The Pursuit of Perfection: Transcendentalists and Utopians

A group of New England writers who came to be known as transcendentalists believed that individuals should conform neither to the dictates of the materialistic world nor to the dogma of formal religion. Instead, people should look within themselves for truth and guidance. The leading transcendentalist, Ralph Waldo Emerson — an essayist, poet, and lecturer — proclaimed that the power of the solitary individual was nearly limitless. Henry David Thoreau, Margaret Fuller, and other transcendentalists agreed with Emerson that "if the single man plant himself indomitably on his instincts, and there abide, the huge world will come round to him." In many ways, the inward gaze and confident egoism of **transcendentalism** represented less an alternative to mainstream values than an exaggerated form of the rampant individualism of the age.

Unlike transcendentalists who sought to turn inward, a few reformers tried to change the world by organizing utopian communities as alternatives to prevailing social arrangements. Although these communities never attracted more than a few thousand people, the activities of their members demonstrated both dissatisfaction with the larger society and their efforts to realize their visions of perfection.

Some communities set out to become models of perfection whose success would point the way toward a better life for everyone. During the 1840s, more than two dozen communities organized themselves around the ideas of Charles

Fourier, a French critic of contemporary society. Members of **Fourierist phalanxes**, as these communities were called, believed that individualism and competition were evils that denied the basic truth that "men . . . are brothers and not competitors." Phalanxes aspired to replace competition with harmonious cooperation based on communal ownership of property. But Fourierist communities failed to realize their lofty goals, and few survived more than two or three years.

The **Oneida community** went beyond the Fourierist notion of communalism. John Humphrey Noyes, the charismatic leader of Oneida, believed that American society's commitment to private property made people greedy and selfish. Noyes claimed that the root of private property lay in marriage, in men's conviction that their wives were their exclusive property. Drawing from a substantial inheritance, Noyes organized the Oneida community in New York in 1848 to abolish marital property rights through the practice of what he called "complex marriage." Sexual intercourse was not restricted to married couples but was permitted between any consenting man and woman in the community. Noyes also required all members to relinquish their economic property to the community, which developed a lucrative business manufacturing animal traps. Oneida's sexual and economic communalism attracted several hundred members, but most of their neighbors considered Oneidans adulterers, blasphemers, and worse. Yet the practices that set Oneida apart from its mainstream neighbors strengthened the community, and it survived long after the Civil War.

Bloomers and Woman's Emancipation

This 1851 British cartoon lampoons bloomers, the trouserlike garment worn beneath shortened skirts by two cigar-smoking American women. Bloomers were invented in the United States as an alternative to the uncomfortable, confining, and awkward dresses worn by fashionable women, suggested here by the clothing of the "respectable" women on the right. In the 1850s, Elizabeth Cady Stanton and other woman's rights activists wore bloomers and urged all American women to do likewise. Ridiculed as unfeminine by critics, American reformers eventually abandoned bloomers and focused on more important woman's rights issues. The "bloomerism" controversy illustrates the immense power of conventional notions of femininity confronted by woman's rights advocates. Miriam and Ira D. Wallach Division of Art, Prints, and Photographs, The New York Public Library. Astor, Lenox, and Tilden Foundations.

Woman's Rights Activists

Women participated in the many reform activities that grew out of evangelical churches. Women church members outnumbered men two to one and worked to put their religious ideas into practice by joining peace, temperance, antislavery, and other societies. Involvement in reform organizations gave a few women activists practical experience in such political arts as speaking in public, running a meeting, drafting resolutions, and circulating petitions. Along with such experience came confidence. The abolitionist Lydia Maria Child pointed out in 1841 that "those who urged women to become missionaries and form tract societies . . . have changed the household utensil to a living energetic being and they have no spell to turn it into a broom again."

In 1848, about three hundred reformers led by **Elizabeth Cady Stanton** and Lucretia Mott gathered at Seneca Falls, New York, for the first national woman's rights convention in the United States. As Stanton recalled, "The general discontent I felt with women's portion as wife, mother, housekeeper, physician, and spiritual guide, [and] the wearied anxious look of the majority of women impressed me with a strong feeling that some active measure should be taken to right the wrongs of society in general, and of women in particular." The **Seneca Falls Declaration of Sentiments** set an ambitious agenda to demand civil liberties for women and to right the wrongs of society. The declaration proclaimed that "the history of mankind is a history of repeated injuries and usurpations on the part of man toward woman, having in direct object the establishment of an absolute tyranny over her." In the style of the Declaration of Independence (see appendix I, page A-1), the Seneca Falls declaration demanded that women "have immediate admission to all the rights and privileges which belong to them as citizens of the United States," particularly the "inalienable right to the elective franchise."

Nearly two dozen other woman's rights conventions assembled before 1860, repeatedly calling for suffrage and an end to discrimination against women. But women had difficulty receiving a respectful hearing, much less achieving legislative action. Even so, the Seneca Falls declaration served as a pathbreaking manifesto of dissent against male supremacy and of support for woman suffrage, and it inspired many women to challenge the barriers that limited their opportunities.

Stanton and other activists sought fair pay and expanded employment opportunities for women by appealing to free-labor ideology. Woman's rights advocate Paula Wright Davis urged Americans to stop discriminating against able and enterprising women: "Let [women] . . . open a Store, . . . plant and tend an Orchard, . . . learn any of the lighter mechanical Trades, . . . study for a Profession, . . . be called to the lecture-room, [and] . . . the Temperance rostrum . . . [and] let her be appointed [to serve in the Post Office]." Some women pioneered in these and many other occupations during the 1840s and 1850s. Woman's rights activists also succeeded in protecting married women's rights to their own wages and property in New York in 1860. But discrimination against women persisted, as most men believed that free-labor ideology required no compromise of male supremacy.

Abolitionists and the American Ideal

During the 1840s and 1850s, abolitionists continued to struggle to draw the nation's attention to the plight of slaves and the need for emancipation. Former slaves **Frederick Douglass**, Henry Bibb, and Sojourner Truth lectured to reform audiences throughout the North about the cruelties of slavery. Abolitionists published newspapers, held conventions, and petitioned Congress, but they never attracted a mass following among white Americans. Many white Northerners became convinced that slavery was wrong, but they still believed that blacks were inferior. Many other white Northerners shared the common view of white Southerners that slavery was necessary and even desirable. The westward extension of the nation during the 1840s offered abolitionists an opportunity to link their unpopular ideal to a goal that many white Northerners found much more attractive — limiting the geographic expansion of slavery, an issue that moved to the center of national politics during the 1850s (as discussed in chapter 14).

Black leaders rose to prominence in the abolitionist movement during the 1840s and 1850s. African Americans had actively opposed slavery for decades, but a new generation of leaders came to the forefront in these years. Frederick Douglass, Henry Highland Garnet, William Wells Brown, Martin R. Delany, and others became impatient with white abolitionists' appeals to the conscience of the white majority. In 1843, Garnet urged slaves to choose "Liberty or Death"

Abolitionist Meeting
This rare daguerreotype was made by Ezra Greenleaf Weld in August 1850 at an abolitionist meeting in Cazenovia, New York. Frederick Douglass, who had escaped from slavery in Maryland twelve years earlier, is seated on the platform next to the woman at the table. One of the nation's most brilliant and eloquent abolitionists, Douglass also supported equal rights for women. The man behind Douglass is Gerrit Smith, a wealthy and militant abolitionist whose funds supported many reform activities. Notice the two black women on either side of Smith and the white woman next to Douglass. Most white Americans considered such voluntary racial proximity scandalous and promiscuous. Collection of the J. Paul Getty Museum, Malibu, CA.

and rise in insurrection against their masters, an idea that alienated almost all white people and carried little influence among slaves. To express their own uncompromising ideas, black abolitionists founded their own newspapers and held their own antislavery conventions, although they still cooperated with sympathetic whites.

The commitment of black abolitionists to battling slavery grew out of their own experiences with white supremacy. The 250,000 free African Americans in the North and West constituted less than 2 percent of the total population in 1860. They confronted the humiliations of racial discrimination in nearly every arena of daily life. Only Maine, Massachusetts, New Hampshire, and Vermont permitted black men to vote; New York imposed a special property-holding requirement on black—but not white—voters, effectively excluding most black men from the franchise. The pervasive racial discrimination both handicapped and energized black abolitionists. Some cooperated with the efforts of the **American Colonization Society** to send freed slaves and other black Americans to Liberia in West Africa. Others sought to move to Canada, Haiti, or elsewhere. They were convinced that, as an African American from Michigan wrote, "it is impracticable, not to say impossible, for the whites and blacks to live together, and upon terms of social and civil equality, under the same government." Most black American leaders refused to embrace emigration and worked against racial prejudice in their own communities, organizing campaigns against segregation, particularly in transportation and education. Their most notable success came in 1855 when Massachusetts integrated its public schools. Elsewhere, white supremacy continued unabated.

Outside the public spotlight, free African Americans in the North and West contributed to the antislavery cause by quietly aiding fugitive slaves. **Harriet Tubman** escaped from slavery in Maryland in 1849 and repeatedly risked her freedom and her life to return to the South to escort slaves to freedom. When the opportunity arose, free blacks in the North provided fugitive slaves with food, a safe place to rest, and a helping hand. An outgrowth of the antislavery sentiment and opposition to white supremacy that unified nearly all African Americans in the North, this "**underground railroad**" ran mainly through black neighborhoods, black churches, and black homes.

REVIEW Why were women especially prominent in many nineteenth-century reform efforts?

▸ Conclusion: Free Labor, Free Men

During the 1840s and 1850s, a cluster of interrelated developments—population growth, steam power, railroads, and the growing mechanization of agriculture and manufacturing—meant greater economic productivity, a burst of output from farms and factories, and prosperity for many. Diplomacy with Great Britain and war with Mexico handed the United States 1.2 million square miles and more than 1,000 miles of Pacific coastline. One prize of manifest destiny, California, almost immediately rewarded its new owners with tons of gold. To most Americans, new territory and vast riches were appropriate accompaniments to the nation's stunning economic progress and superior institutions.

To Northerners, industrial evolution confirmed the choice they had made to eliminate slavery and promote free labor as the key to independence, equality, and prosperity. Like Abraham Lincoln, millions of Americans could point to their personal experiences as evidence of the practical truth of the free-labor ideal. But millions of others had different stories to tell. They knew that in the free-labor system, poverty and wealth continued to rub shoulders. By 1860, more than half of the nation's free-labor workforce toiled for someone else. Free-labor enthusiasts denied that the problems were inherent in the country's social and economic systems. Instead, they argued, most social ills—including poverty and dependency—sprang from individual deficiencies. Consequently, many reformers focused on personal self-control and discipline, on avoiding sin and alcohol. Other reformers focused on woman's rights and the abolition of slavery. They challenged widespread conceptions of male supremacy and black inferiority, but neither group managed to overcome the prevailing free-labor ideology based on individualism, racial prejudice, and notions of male superiority.

By midcentury, half of the nation had prohibited slavery, and half permitted it. The North and the South were animated by different economic interests, cultural values, and political aims. Each celebrated its regional identity and increasingly disparaged that of the other. Not even the victory over Mexico could bridge the deepening divide between North and South.

▸ Selected Bibliography

The Economy and Free Labor

Jeanne Boydston, *Home and Work: Housework, Wages, and the Ideology of Labor in the Early Republic* (1990).

J. Matthew Gallman, *Receiving Erin's Children: Philadelphia, Liverpool, and the Irish Famine Migration, 1854–1855* (2000).

Jonathan A. Glickstein, *Concepts of Free Labor in the Antebellum United States* (1991).

Donald R. Hoke, *Ingenious Yankees: The Rise of the American System of Manufactures in the Private Sector* (1990).

Jonathan Hughes and Louis P. Cain, *American Economic History* (2011).

Robert A. Margo, *Wages and Labor Markets in the United States, 1820–1860* (2000).

David R. Meyer, *The Roots of American Industrialization* (2003).

Scott A. Sandage, *Born Losers: A History of Failure in America* (2005).

Kenneth J. Winkle, *The Young Eagle: The Rise of Abraham Lincoln* (2001).

Westward Expansion and the Mexican-American War

H. W. Brand, *Lone Star Nation* (2004).

Christopher Corbett, *The Poker Bride: The First Chinese in the Wild West* (2009).

David Dary, *The Oregon Trail: An American Saga* (2004).

Brian DeLay, *War of a Thousand Deserts: Indian Raids and the U.S.-Mexican War* (2008).

Jared Farmer, *On Zion's Mount: Mormons, Indians, and the American Landscape* (2008).

Paul W. Foos, *A Short, Offhand, Killing Affair: Soldiers and Social Conflict during the Mexican-American War* (2002).

Amy S. Greenberg, *Manifest Manhood and the Antebellum American Empire* (2005).

Timothy J. Henderson, *A Glorious Defeat: Mexico and Its War with the United States* (2007).

Benjamin Heber Johnson, *Revolution in Texas: How a Forgotten Rebellion and Its Bloody Suppression Turned Mexicans into Americans* (2003).

Susan Lee Johnson, *Roaring Camp: The Social World of the California Gold Rush* (2000).

Robert W. Merry, *A Country of Vast Designs: James K. Polk, the Mexican War, and the Conquest of the American Continent* (2009).

Gregory H. Nobles, *American Frontiers: Cultural Encounters and Continental Conquest* (1997).

Malcolm Rohrbough, *Days of Gold: The California Gold Rush and the American Nation* (1997).

James A. Sandos, *Converting California: Indians and Franciscans in the Missions* (2004).

Joel H. Sibley, *Storm over Texas: The Annexation Controversy and the Road to Civil War* (2005).

Richard White, *"It's Your Misfortune and None of My Own": A New History of the American West* (1993).

Richard Bruce Winders, *Mr. Polk's Army: The American Military Experience in the Mexican War* (1997).

Antebellum Culture and Reform

Bruce Dorsey, *Reforming Men and Women: Gender in the Antebellum City* (2002).

Lori D. Ginzberg, *Elizabeth Cady Stanton: An American Life* (2009).

Bruce Laurie, *Beyond Garrison: Antislavery and Social Reform* (2005).

Sally McMillen, *Seneca Falls and the Origins of the Women's Rights Movement* (2008).

Patrick Rael, *Black Identity and Black Protest in the Antebellum North* (2002).

Susan M. Ryan, *The Grammar of Good Intentions: Race and the Antebellum Culture of Benevolence* (2003).

Beth A. Salerno, *Sister Societies: Women's Antislavery Organizations in Antebellum America* (2005).

Susan Zaeske, *Signatures of Citizenship: Petitioning, Antislavery, and Women's Political Identity* (2003).

▸ **For more books about topics in this chapter,** see the Online Bibliography at **bedfordstmartins.com/roark.**

▸ **For additional primary sources from this period,** see Michael Johnson, ed., *Reading the American Past*, Fifth Edition.

▸ **For Web sites, images, and documents related to topics and places in this chapter,** visit Make History at **bedfordstmartins.com/roark.**

Reviewing Chapter 12

KEY TERMS

Explain each term's significance.

Economic and Industrial Evolution

- John Deere (p. 359)
- mechanical reapers (p. 359)
- American system (p. 360)
- Samuel F. B. Morse (p. 362)

Free Labor: Promise and Reality

- free-labor ideal (p. 364)
- universal education (p. 365)

The Westward Movement

- manifest destiny (p. 370)
- Oregon Trail (p. 370)
- Fort Laramie conference (p. 372)
- Mormons (p. 373)
- Joseph Smith Jr. (p. 373)
- Brigham Young (p. 374)
- Stephen F. Austin (p. 375)
- Antonio López de Santa Anna (p. 375)
- Lone Star Republic (p. 376)

Expansion and the Mexican-American War

- John Tyler (p. 377)
- Henry Clay (p. 378)
- James K. Polk (p. 378)
- Zachary Taylor (p. 378)
- Winfield Scott (p. 381)
- Treaty of Guadalupe Hidalgo (p. 381)
- California gold rush (p. 382)

Reforming Self and Society

- transcendentalism (p. 385)
- Fourierist phalanxes (p. 386)
- Oneida community (p. 386)
- Elizabeth Cady Stanton (p. 386)
- Seneca Falls Declaration of Sentiments (p. 386)
- Frederick Douglass (p. 387)
- American Colonization Society (p. 388)
- Harriet Tubman (p. 388)
- underground railroad (p. 388)

REVIEW QUESTIONS

Use key terms and dates to support your answer.

1. Why did the United States become a leading industrial power in the nineteenth century? (pp. 359–363)
2. How did the free-labor ideal account for economic inequality? (pp. 363–369)
3. Why did westward migration expand dramatically in the mid-nineteenth century? (pp. 370–377)
4. Why was the annexation of Texas such a controversial policy? (pp. 377–384)
5. Why were women especially prominent in many nineteenth-century reform efforts? (pp. 384–388)

MAKING CONNECTIONS

Draw on key terms, the timeline, and review questions.

1. Varied political, economic, and technological factors promoted westward migration in the mid-nineteenth century. Considering these factors, discuss migration to two different regions (for instance, Texas, Oregon, Utah, or California). What drew migrants to the regions? How did the U.S. government contribute to their efforts?
2. How did the ideology of manifest destiny contribute to the mid-nineteenth-century drive for expansion? Discuss its implications for individual migrants and the nation. In your answer, consider how manifest destiny built on, or revised, earlier understandings of the nation's history and racial politics.
3. The Mexican-American War reshaped U.S. borders and more. Discuss the consequences of the war for national political and economic developments in subsequent decades. What resources did the new territory give the United States? How did debate over annexation revive older political disputes?
4. Some nineteenth-century reform movements drew on the free-labor ideal, while others challenged it. Discuss the free-labor ideal in relation to two reform movements (such as abolitionism and utopian communalism). How did the reform movements draw on the ideal to pursue specific reforms? How did these minority movements try to influence national developments?

LINKING TO THE PAST

Link events in this chapter to earlier events.

1. In what ways were the North's economy, society, and political structure during the 1840s and 1850s shaped by the American Revolution and the Constitution? (See chapters 7 and 8.)
2. The nation's mighty push westward in the 1840s and 1850s extended a history of expansion that was as old as the nation itself. How was expansion to the West between 1840 and 1860 similar to and different from expansion between 1800 and 1820? (See chapter 10.)

▶ **For practice quizzes and other study tools**, visit the Online Study Guide at **bedfordstmartins.com/roark.**

TIMELINE 1830–1861

1830	• Joseph Smith Jr. publishes *The Book of Mormon.*
1836	• Battle of the Alamo. • Texas declares independence from Mexico.
1837	• John Deere patents steel plow.
1840s	• Practical mechanical reapers created. • Fourierist phalanxes founded.
1841	• First wagon trains head west on Oregon Trail. • Vice President John Tyler becomes president when William Henry Harrison dies.
1844	• Democrat James K. Polk elected president. • Samuel F. B. Morse demonstrates telegraph.
1845	• Term *manifest destiny* coined. • United States annexes Texas, which enters Union as slave state. • Potato blight in Ireland spurs immigration to United States.
1846	• Bear Flag Revolt in California. • Congress declares war on Mexico. • United States and Great Britain agree to divide Oregon Country.
1847	• Mormons settle in Utah.
1848	• Treaty of Guadalupe Hidalgo. • Oneida community organized in New York. • First U.S. woman's rights convention takes place at Seneca Falls, New York.
1849	• California gold rush begins.
1850	• Mormon community annexed to United States as Utah Territory. • Congress grants railroads six square miles of land for every mile of track laid.
1851	• Conference at Fort Laramie, Wyoming, marks the beginning of government policy of Indian concentration.
1855	• Massachusetts integrates public schools.
1857	• U.S. troops invade Salt Lake City in Mormon War.
1861	• California connected to rest of nation by telegraph.

CLAY JUG

Enslaved African American potters created tens of thousands of ceramic pots to hold water and store food. Renowned South Carolina slave potter, Dave, created this three-foot-tall pot in 1857. Although teaching slaves to read and write was illegal, Dave usually signed his work; he also inscribed some of his pots with verse. “I wonder where is all my relations / Friendship to all and every nation” probably refers to the slave sales that sent some of his family to Louisiana. While Dave worked in his potter’s shed, most slaves toiled in cotton fields.

Jug: Collection of McKissick Museum, University of South Carolina; background image: Schomburg Center for Research in Black Culture / General Research and Reference Division / The New York Public Library.

13 The Slave South 1820–1860

NAT TURNER WAS BORN A SLAVE IN SOUTHAMPTON COUNTY, VIRGINIA, in October 1800. People in his neighborhood claimed that he had always been different. His parents noticed special marks on his body, which they said were signs that he was "intended for some great purpose." His master said that he learned to read without being taught. As an adolescent, he adopted an austere lifestyle of Christian devotion and fasting. In his twenties, he received visits from the "Spirit," the same spirit, he believed, that had spoken to the ancient prophets. In time, Nat Turner began to interpret these things to mean that God had appointed him an instrument of divine vengeance for the sin of slaveholding.

In the early morning of August 22, 1831, he set out with six trusted friends — Hark, Henry, Sam, Nelson, Will, and Jack — to punish slave owners. Turner struck the first blow, an ax to the head of his master, Joseph Travis. The rebels killed all of the white men, women, and children they encountered. By noon, they had visited eleven farms and slaughtered fifty-seven whites. Along the way, they had added fifty or sixty men to their army. Word spread quickly, and soon the militia and hundreds of local whites gathered. By the next day, whites had captured or killed all of the rebels except Turner, who hid out for about ten weeks before being captured in nearby woods. Within a week, he was tried, convicted, and executed. By then, forty-five slaves had stood trial, twenty had been convicted and hanged, and another ten had been banished from Virginia. Frenzied whites had killed another hundred or more blacks — insurgents and innocent bystanders — in their counterattack against the rebellion.

Virginia's bewildered governor, John Floyd, struggled to understand why Turner's band of "assassins and murderers" assaulted the "unsuspecting and defenseless" citizens of "one of the fairest counties" of the state. White Virginians prided themselves on having the "mildest" slavery in the South, but sixty black rebels on a rampage challenged the comforting theory of the contented slave. Nonetheless, whites found explanations that allowed them to feel safer. They placed the blame on outside agitators. In 1829, David Walker, a freeborn black man living in Boston, had published his *Appeal . . . to the Coloured Citizens of the World*, an invitation to slaves to rise up in bloody rebellion, and copies had fallen into the hands of Virginia slaves. Moreover, on January 1, 1831, in Boston, the Massachusetts

Horrid Massacre in Virginia
No contemporary images of Nat Turner are known to exist. This woodcut simply imagines the rebellion as a nightmare in which black brutes took the lives of innocent whites. Although there was never another rebellion as large as Turner's, images of black violence continued to haunt white imaginations.
Library of Congress.

abolitionist William Lloyd Garrison had published the first issue of the *Liberator*, his fiery newspaper (see chapter 11). White Virginians also dismissed the rebellion's leader, Nat Turner, as insane. "He is a complete fanatic, or plays his part admirably," wrote Thomas R. Gray, the lawyer who was assigned to defend Turner.

In the months following the insurrection, the Virginia legislature reaffirmed the state's determination to preserve black bondage by passing laws that strengthened the institution of slavery and further restricted free blacks. A professor at the College of William and Mary, Thomas R. Dew, published a vigorous defense of slavery that became the bible of Southerners' proslavery arguments. More than ever, the nation was divided along the Mason-Dixon line, the surveyors' mark that in colonial times had established the boundary between Maryland and Pennsylvania but half a century later divided the free North and the slave South.

Black slavery increasingly molded the South into a distinctive region. In the decades after 1820, Southerners, like Northerners, raced westward, but unlike Northerners who spread small farms, manufacturing, and free labor, Southerners spread slavery, cotton, and plantations. Geographic expansion meant that slavery became more vigorous and more profitable than ever, embraced more people, and increased the South's political power. Antebellum Southerners included diverse people who at times found themselves at odds with one another — not only slaves and free people but also women and men; Indians, Africans, and Europeans; and aristocrats and common folk. Nevertheless, beneath this diversity, a distinctively southern society and culture were forming. The South became a slave society, and most white Southerners were proud of it.

▶ The Growing Distinctiveness of the South

From the earliest settlements, inhabitants of the southern colonies had shared a great deal with northern colonists. Most whites in both sections were British and Protestant, spoke a common language, and shared an exuberant pride in their victorious revolution against British rule. The creation of the new nation under the Constitution in 1789 forged political ties that bound all Americans. The beginnings of a national economy fostered economic interdependence and communication across regional boundaries. White Americans everywhere celebrated the achievements of the prosperous young nation, and they looked forward to its seemingly boundless future.

Despite these national similarities, Southerners and Northerners grew increasingly different. The French political observer Alexis de Tocqueville believed he knew why. "I could easily prove," he asserted in 1831, "that almost all the differences which may be noticed between the character of the Americans in the Southern and Northern states have originated in slavery." Slavery made the South different, and it was the differences between the North and South, not the similarities, that increasingly shaped antebellum American history.

Cotton Kingdom, Slave Empire

In the first half of the nineteenth century, millions of Americans migrated west. In the South, the stampede began after the Creek War of 1813–1814, which divested the Creek Indians of 24 million acres and initiated the government campaign to remove Indian people living east of the Mississippi River to the West (see chapters 10 and 11). Hard-driving slaveholders seeking virgin acreage for new plantations, striving farmers looking for patches of cheap land for small farms, herders and drovers pushing their hogs and cattle toward fresh pastures — anyone who was restless and ambitious felt the pull of Indian land.

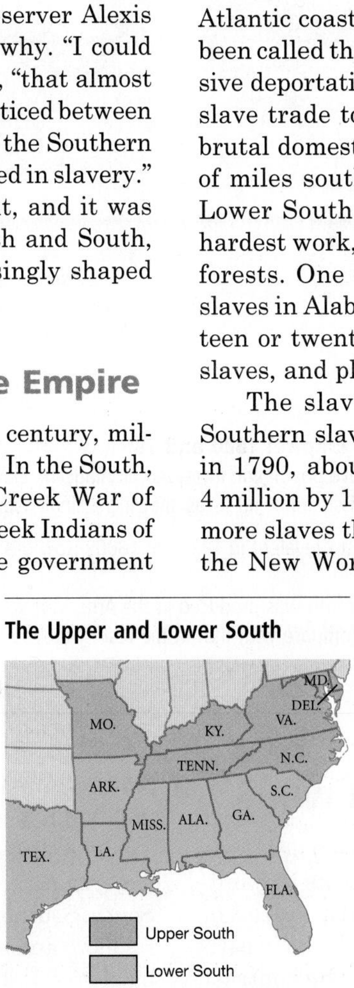

But more than anything it was cotton that propelled Southerners westward. South of the **Mason-Dixon line**, climate and geography were ideally suited for the cultivation of cotton. Cotton's requirements are minimal: two hundred frost-free days from planting to picking, and plentiful rain, conditions found in much of the South. By the 1830s, cotton fields stretched from the Atlantic seaboard to central Texas. Heavy migration led to statehood for Arkansas in 1836 and for Texas and Florida in 1845. Production soared from 300,000 bales in 1830 to nearly 5 million in 1860, when the South produced three-fourths of the world's supply. The South — especially that tier of states from South Carolina west to Texas called the Lower South — had become the **cotton kingdom** (Map 13.1).

The cotton kingdom was also a slave empire. The South's cotton boom rested on the backs of slaves, most of whom toiled in gangs under the direct supervision of whites. As cotton agriculture expanded westward, whites shipped more than a million enslaved men and women from the Atlantic coast across the continent in what has been called the "Second Middle Passage," a massive deportation that dwarfed the transatlantic slave trade to North America. Victims of this brutal domestic slave trade marched hundreds of miles southwest to new plantations in the Lower South. The earliest arrivals faced the hardest work, literally cutting plantations from forests. One observer noted that young male slaves in Alabama who were no more than nineteen or twenty looked twice their age. Cotton, slaves, and plantations moved west together.

The slave population grew enormously. Southern slaves numbered fewer than 700,000 in 1790, about 2 million in 1830, and almost 4 million by 1860. By 1860, the South contained more slaves than all the other slave societies in the New World combined. The extraordinary growth was not the result of the importation of slaves, which the federal government outlawed in 1808. Instead, the slave population grew through natural reproduction; by midcentury, most U.S. slaves were native-born Southerners. In comparison, Cuba and Brazil, slave societies that kept their slave trades open until the mid-nineteenth century, had more African-born slaves and thus stronger ties to Africa.

The Upper and Lower South

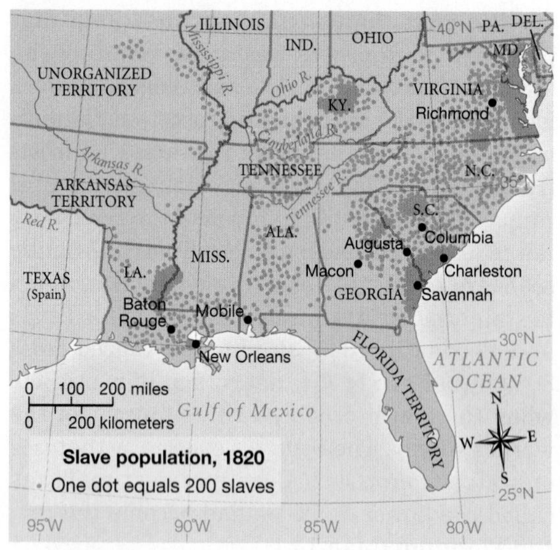

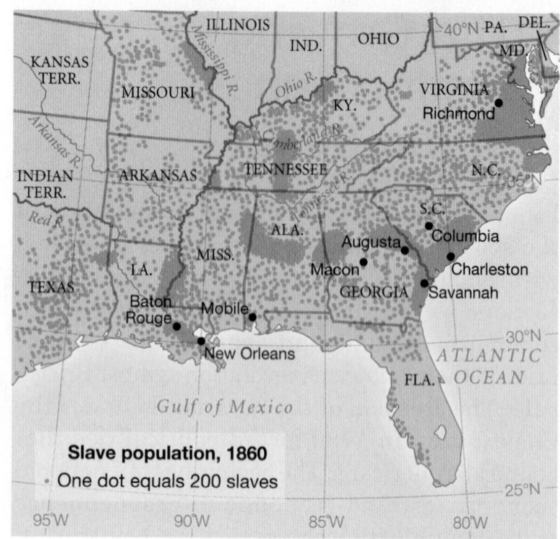

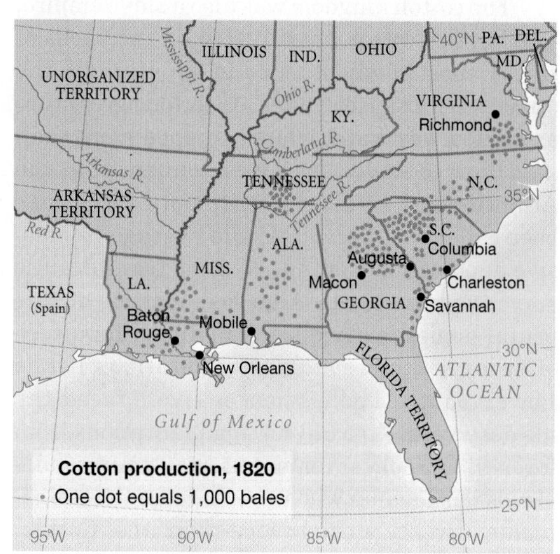

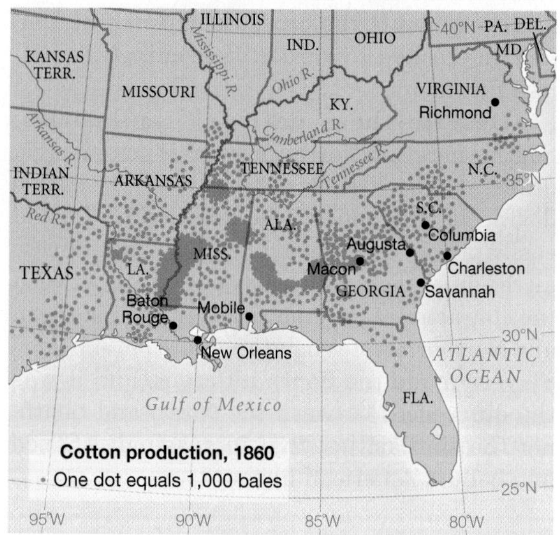

MAP ACTIVITY

Map 13.1 Cotton Kingdom, Slave Empire: 1820 and 1860

As the production of cotton soared, the slave population increased dramatically. Slaves continued to toil in tobacco and rice fields, but in Alabama, Mississippi, and Texas, they increasingly worked on cotton plantations.

READING THE MAP: Where was slavery most prevalent in 1820? In 1860? How did the spread of slavery compare with the spread of cotton?

CONNECTIONS: How much of the world's cotton was produced in the American South in 1860? How did the number of slaves in the American South compare with that in the rest of the world? What does this suggest about the South's cotton kingdom?

The South in Black and White

By 1860, one in every three Southerners was black (approximately 4 million blacks to 8 million whites). In the Lower South states of Mississippi and South Carolina, blacks constituted the majority (Figure 13.1). The contrast with the North was striking: In 1860, only one Northerner in seventy-six was black (about 250,000 blacks to 19 million whites).

The presence of large numbers of African Americans had profound consequences for the South. Southern culture — language, food, music, religion, and even accents — was in part shaped by blacks. But the most direct consequence of the South's biracialism was southern whites' commit-

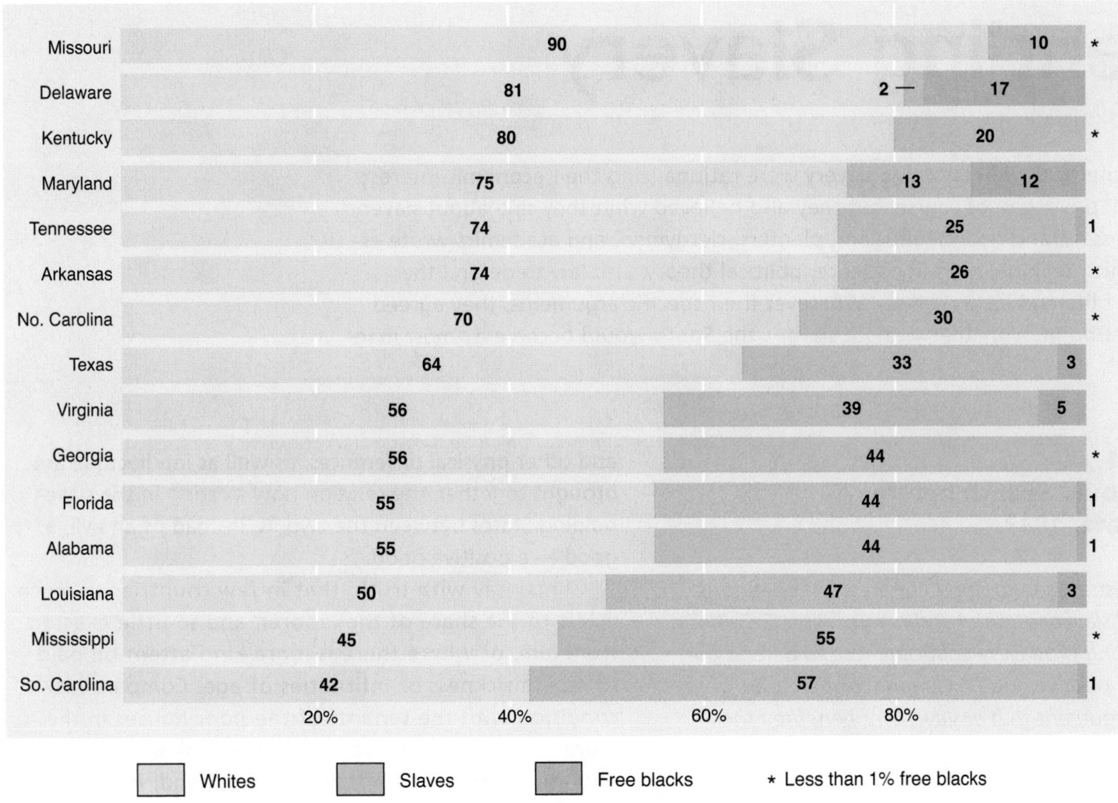

FIGURE 13.1 Black and White Populations in the South, 1860
Blacks represented a much larger fraction of the population in the South than in the North, but considerable variation existed from state to state. Only one Missourian in ten, for example, was black, while Mississippi and South Carolina had black majorities. States in the Upper South were "whiter" than states in the Lower South, despite the Upper South's greater number of free blacks.

ment to white supremacy. Northern whites believed in racial superiority, too, but their dedication to white supremacy lacked the intensity and urgency increasingly felt by white Southerners who lived among millions of blacks who had every reason to hate them and to strike back, as Nat Turner had.

After 1820, attacks on slavery — from blacks and a handful of white Southerners opposed to slavery and from Northern abolitionists — jolted southern slaveholders into a distressing awareness that they lived in a dangerous world. As the only slave society embedded in an egalitarian, democratic republic, the South made extraordinary efforts to strengthen slavery. In the 1820s and 1830s, state legislatures constructed **slave codes** (laws) that required the total submission of slaves. As the Louisiana code stated, a slave "owes his master . . . a respect without bounds, and an absolute obedience." The laws also underlined the authority of all whites, not just masters. Any white could "correct" slaves who did not stay "in their place."

Intellectuals joined legislators in the campaign to strengthen slavery. The South's academics, writers, and clergy employed every imaginable defense. They argued that in the South slaves were legal property, and wasn't the protection of property the bedrock of American liberty? History also endorsed slavery, they claimed. Weren't the great civilizations — such as those of the Hebrews, Greeks, and Romans — slave societies? They claimed that the Bible, properly interpreted, also sanctioned slavery. Old Testament patriarchs owned slaves, they observed, and in the New Testament, Paul returned the runaway slave Onesimus to his master. Proslavery spokesmen played on the fears of Northerners and Southerners alike by charging that giving blacks equal rights would lead to the sexual mixing of the races, or **miscegenation**.

Another of slavery's champions, George Fitzhugh of Virginia, attacked the North's free-labor economy and society. He claimed that behind the North's grand slogans lay a heartless

DOCUMENTING THE AMERICAN PROMISE

Defending Slavery

White Southerners who defended slavery were rationalizing their economic interests and racial privileges, of course, but they also believed what they said about slavery being just, necessary, and godly. Politicians, planters, clergymen, and academics wrote essays on economics, religion, morality, science, political theory, and law to defend the southern way of life and justify slavery. Whatever their specific arguments, they agreed with the *Charleston Mercury* that without slavery, the South would become a "most magnificent jungle."

DOCUMENT 1
John C. Calhoun, Speech before the U.S. Senate, 1837

When abolitionists began to flood Congress with petitions that denounced slavery as sinful and odious, John C. Calhoun, the South's leading proslavery politician, rose to defend the institution as "a positive good." Calhoun devoted part of his speech to the argument that enslavement benefited the slaves themselves.

Be it good or bad, it [slavery] has grown up with our society and institutions, and is so interwoven with them, that to destroy it would be to destroy us as a people. But let me not be understood as admitting, even by implication, that the existing relations between the two races in the slaveholding States is an evil: far otherwise; I hold it to be a good, as it has thus far proved to be to both, and will continue to prove so if not disturbed by the fell spirit of abolition. I appeal to facts. Never before has the black race of Central Africa, from the dawn of history to the present day, attained a condition so civilized and so improved, not only physically, but morally and intellectually. It came to us in a low, degraded, and savage condition, and in the course of a few generations, it has grown up under the fostering care of our institutions, reviled they have been, to its present comparatively civilized condition. This, with the rapid increase of numbers, is conclusive proof of the general happiness of the race, in spite of all the exaggerated tales to the contrary. . . .

I hold that in the present state of civilization, where two races of different origin, and distinguished by color, and other physical differences, as well as intellectual, are brought together, the relation now existing in the slaveholding States between the two, is, instead of an evil, a good — a positive good. . . .

I may say with truth, that in few countries so much is left to the share of the laborer, and so little exacted from him, or where there is more kind attention paid to him in sickness or infirmities of age. Compare his condition with the tenants of the poor houses in the more civilized portions of Europe — look at the sick, and the old and infirm slave, on one hand, in the midst of his family and friends, under the kind superintending care of his master and mistress, and compare it with the forlorn and wretched condition of the pauper in the poor house.

SOURCE: John C. Calhoun, "Speech on the Reception of Abolition Petitions, Delivered in the Senate, February 6th, 1837," in *Speeches of John C. Calhoun, Delivered in the House of Representatives and in the Senate of the United States*. Edited by Richard K. Cralle (Appleton, 1853), 625–33.

DOCUMENT 2
William Harper, *Memoir on Slavery*, 1837

Unlike Calhoun, who defended slavery by pointing to what he considered slavery's concrete benefits for blacks, William Harper — judge, politician, and academic — defended slavery by denouncing abolitionists, particularly the "atrocious philosophy" of "natural equality and inalienable rights" that they used to support their attacks on slavery.

philosophy: "Every man for himself, and the devil take the hindmost." Gouging capitalists exploited wageworkers unmercifully, Fitzhugh declared, and he contrasted the North's vicious free-labor system with the humane relations that he said prevailed between masters and slaves because slaves were valuable capital that masters sought to protect.

But at the heart of the defense of slavery lay the claim of black inferiority. Black enslavement was both necessary and proper, slavery's defenders argued, because Africans were lesser

All men are born free and equal. Is it not palpably nearer the truth to say that no man was ever born free, and that no two men were ever born equal? . . . Wealth and poverty, fame or obscurity, strength or weakness, knowledge or ignorance, ease or labor, power or subjection, mark the endless diversity in the condition of men. . . .

It is the order of nature and of God, that the being of superior faculties and knowledge, and therefore of superior power, should control and dispose of those who are inferior. It is as much in the order of nature, that men should enslave each other, as that other animals should prey upon each other. I admit that he does this under the highest moral responsibility, and is most guilty if he wantonly inflicts misery or privation on beings more capable of enjoyment or suffering than brutes, without necessity or any view to the great good which is to result. . . .

Moralists have denounced the injustice and cruelty which have been practiced towards our aboriginal Indians, by which they have been driven from their native seats and exterminated.

. . . No doubt, much fraud and injustice has been practiced in the circumstances and manner of their removal. Yet who has contended that civilized man had no moral right to possess himself of the country? That he was bound to leave this wide and fertile continent, which is capable of sustaining uncounted myriads of a civilized race, to a few roving and ignorant barbarians? Yet if any thing is certain, it is certain that there were no means by which he could possess the country, without exterminating or enslaving them. Slave and civilized man cannot live together, and the savage can only be tamed by being enslaved or by having slaves.

SOURCE: William Harper, *Memoir of Slavery* (J. S. Burges, 1838).

DOCUMENT 3
Thornton Stringfellow, "The Bible Argument: or, Slavery in the Light of Divine Revelation," 1856

Reverend Thornton Stringfellow, a Baptist minister from Virginia, offered a defense of human bondage based on his reading of the Bible. In these passages, he makes a case that Jesus himself approved of the relationship between master and slave.

Jesus Christ recognized this institution [slavery] as one that was lawful among men, and regulated its relative duties. . . . I affirm then, first, (and no man denies,) that Jesus Christ has not abolished slavery by a prohibitory command: and second, I affirm, he has introduced no new moral principle which can work its destruction, under the gospel dispensation; and that the principle relied on for this purpose, is a fundamental principle of the Mosaic law, under which slavery was instituted by Jehovah himself. . . .

To the church at Colosse, a city of Phrygia, in the lesser Asia, Paul in his letter to them, recognizes the three relations of wives and husbands, parents and children, servants and masters, as relations existing among the members . . . and to the servants and masters he thus writes: "Servants obey in all things your masters, according to the flesh: not with eye service, as men pleasers, but in singleness of heart, fearing God: and whatsoever you do, do it heartily, as to the Lord and not unto men; knowing that of the Lord ye shall receive the reward of the inheritance, for ye serve the Lord Christ. . . . Masters give unto your servants that which is just and equal, knowing that you also have a master in heaven."

SOURCE: *Slavery Defended: The Views of the Old South* by Eric L. McKitrick, editor. Published by Prentice-Hall, 1963. Reprinted with permission. *Cotton Is King and Pro-Slavery Arguments* by Thornton Stringfellow (Pritchard, Abbott & Loomis, 1860), 459–546.

Questions for Analysis and Debate

1. According to John C. Calhoun, what were slavery's chief benefits for blacks? How did his proslavery convictions shape his argument?
2. Why do you suppose William Harper interjected Americans' treatment of Indians into his defense of slavery?
3. According to Thornton Stringfellow, the Bible instructs both masters and slaves about their duties. What are their respective obligations?

beings. Rather than exploitative, slavery was a mass civilizing effort that lifted lowly blacks from barbarism and savagery, taught them disciplined work, and converted them to soul-saving Christianity. According to Virginian **Thomas R. Dew**, most slaves were grateful. He declared that "the slaves of a good master are his warmest, most constant, and most devoted friends."

Whites gradually moved away from defending slavery as a "necessary evil"— the halfhearted argument popular at the time of the American Revolution — and toward an aggressive defense

The Fruits of Amalgamation
In this lithograph from 1839, Edward W. Clay of Philadelphia attacked abolitionists by imagining the miscegenation (also known as "amalgamation") that would come from their misguided campaign. He drew a beautiful white woman, her two black children, and her dark-skinned, ridiculously overdressed husband, resting his feet in his wife's lap. The couple is attended by a white servant. Another interracial couple has come calling. Abolitionists denied the charge of amalgamation and pointed to the lasciviousness of southern slaveholders as the true source of racial mixing in antebellum America. Courtesy, American Antiquarian Society.

of slavery as a "positive good." **John C. Calhoun**, an influential southern politician, declared that in the states where slavery had been abolished, "the condition of the African, instead of being improved, has become worse," while in the slave states, the Africans "have improved greatly in every respect." (See "Documenting the American Promise," page 398.)

Black slavery encouraged southern whites to unify around race rather than to divide by class. The grubbiest, most tobacco-stained white man could proudly proclaim his superiority to all blacks and his equality with the most refined southern patrician. Because of racial slavery, Georgia attorney Thomas R. R. Cobb observed, every white Southerner "feels that he belongs to an elevated class. It matters not that he is no slaveholder; he is not of the inferior race; he is a freeborn citizen." Consequently, the "poorest meets the richest as an equal; sits at his table with him; salutes him as a neighbor; meets him in every public assembly, and stands on the same social platform." In the South, Cobb boasted, "there is no war of classes."

In reality, slavery did not create perfect harmony among whites or ease every strain along class lines. But by providing every white Southerner membership in the ruling race, slavery helped whites bridge differences in wealth, education, and culture.

The Plantation Economy

As important as slavery was in unifying white Southerners, only about a quarter of the white population lived in slaveholding families. Most slaveholders owned fewer than five slaves. Only about 12 percent of slave owners owned twenty or more, the number of slaves that historians consider necessary to distinguish a **planter** from a farmer. Despite their small numbers, planters dominated the southern economy. In 1860, 52 percent of the South's slaves lived and worked on **plantations**. Plantation slaves produced more than 75 percent of the South's export crops, the backbone of the region's economy. Slavery was dying elsewhere in the New World (only Brazil and Cuba still defended slavery at midcentury), but slave plantations increasingly dominated southern agriculture.

The South's major cash crops — tobacco, sugar, rice, and cotton — grew on plantations (Map 13.2). Tobacco, the original plantation crop in North America, had shifted westward in the nineteenth century from the Chesapeake to Tennessee and Kentucky. Large-scale sugar production began in 1795, when Étienne de Boré built a modern sugar mill in what is today New Orleans, and sugar plantations were confined almost entirely to Louisiana. Commercial rice production began in the seventeenth century, and like sugar, rice was confined to a small geographic area, a narrow strip of coast stretching from the Carolinas into Georgia.

Tobacco, sugar, and rice were labor-intensive crops that relied on large numbers of slaves to do the backbreaking work. Most phases of tobacco cultivation — planting, transporting, thinning, picking off caterpillars, cutting, drying, packing — required laborers to stoop or bend down. Work on sugarcane plantations was particularly physically demanding. During the harvest, slaves worked eighteen hours a day, and so hard was the slaves' task that one visitor concluded that "nothing but 'involuntary servitude' could go through the toil and suffering required to produce sugar." Working in water and mud in the heat of a Carolina summer regularly threatened slaves engaged in rice production with malaria, yellow fever, and other diseases.

But by the nineteenth century, cotton was king of the South's plantation crops. Cotton became commercially significant in the 1790s after the invention of a new cotton gin by Eli Whitney dramatically increased the production of raw cotton (see chapter 9). Cotton was relatively easy to grow and took little capital to get started — just enough to purchase land, seed, and simple tools. Thus, small farmers as well as planters grew cotton. But planters, whose fields were worked by gangs of slaves, produced three-quarters of the South's cotton, and cotton made planters rich.

Plantation slavery also enriched the nation. By 1840, cotton accounted for more than 60 percent of American exports. Most of the cotton was shipped to Great Britain, the world's largest manufacturer of cotton textiles. Much of the profit from the sale of cotton overseas returned to planters, but some went to northern middlemen who bought, sold, insured, warehoused, and shipped cotton to the mills in Great Britain and

"Nothing but 'involuntary servitude' could go through the toil and suffering required to produce sugar."
— A visitor to a sugarcane plantation

MAP ACTIVITY

Map 13.2 The Agricultural Economy of the South, 1860
Cotton dominated the South's agricultural economy, but the region grew a variety of crops and was largely self-sufficient in foodstuffs.

READING THE MAP: In what type of geographic areas were rice and sugar grown? After cotton, what crop commanded the greatest agricultural area in the South? In which region of the South was this crop predominantly found?
CONNECTIONS: What role did the South play in the U.S. economy in 1860? How did the economy of the South differ from that of the North?

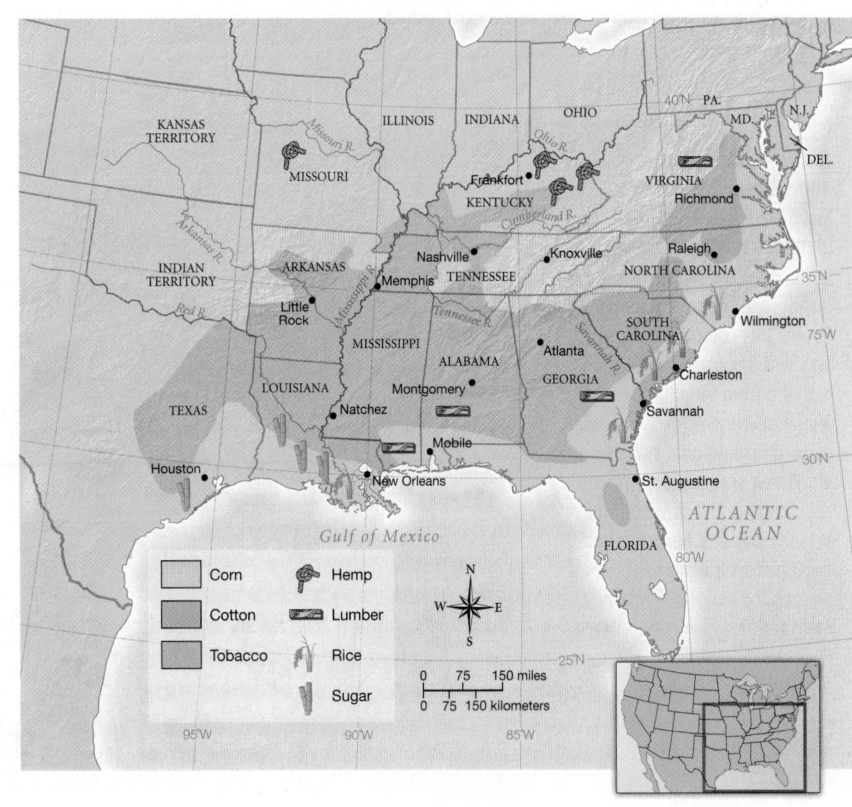

THE PROMISE OF TECHNOLOGY

The Cotton Gin

Machines for separating cotton fibers from seeds that clung to the fiber — cotton gins (the word *gin* is short for *engine*) — had been around for centuries, but none cleaned cotton quickly and efficiently. In 1793, Eli Whitney, a young New Englander living on a Georgia plantation, built a simple little device that was crude but effective. It was not much more than wire teeth set in a wooden cylinder that, when rotated, reached through narrow slats to pull cotton fibers away from the sticky seeds while a brush swept the fibers from the revolving teeth. News of the invention spread like wildfire. The cotton gin enabled southern farmers to supply huge quantities of clean cotton for the world market. Planters in particular profited hugely as cotton pushed out indigo, then tobacco, as the South's major cash crop. The commercial production of cotton eventually bound millions of African Americans to slavery. Why did the cotton gin have such different consequences for planters and for slaves? Smithsonian Institution, National Museum of American History, Behring Center.

elsewhere. As one New York merchant observed, "Cotton has enriched all through whose hands it has passed." As middlemen invested their profits in the booming northern economy, industrial development received a burst of much-needed capital. Furthermore, southern plantations benefited northern industry by providing an important market for textiles, agricultural tools, and other manufactured goods.

The economies of the North and South steadily diverged. While the North developed a mixed economy — agriculture, commerce, and manufacturing — the South remained overwhelmingly agricultural. Year after year, planters funneled the profits they earned from land and slaves back into more land and more slaves. With its capital flowing into agriculture, the South did not develop many factories. By 1860, only 10

Slave Traders: Sold to Tennessee
Slave trading — or "Negro speculation," as it was called by contemporaries — was a booming business in the antebellum South. This color drawing by Lewis Miller portrays slaves walking from Virginia to Tennessee under the watchful eyes of professional slave traders. A few children accompany the adults, some of whom may be their parents. Forced migrations almost always resulted in the separation of black family members. Abby Aldrich Rockefeller Folk Art Center, Williamsburg, VA.

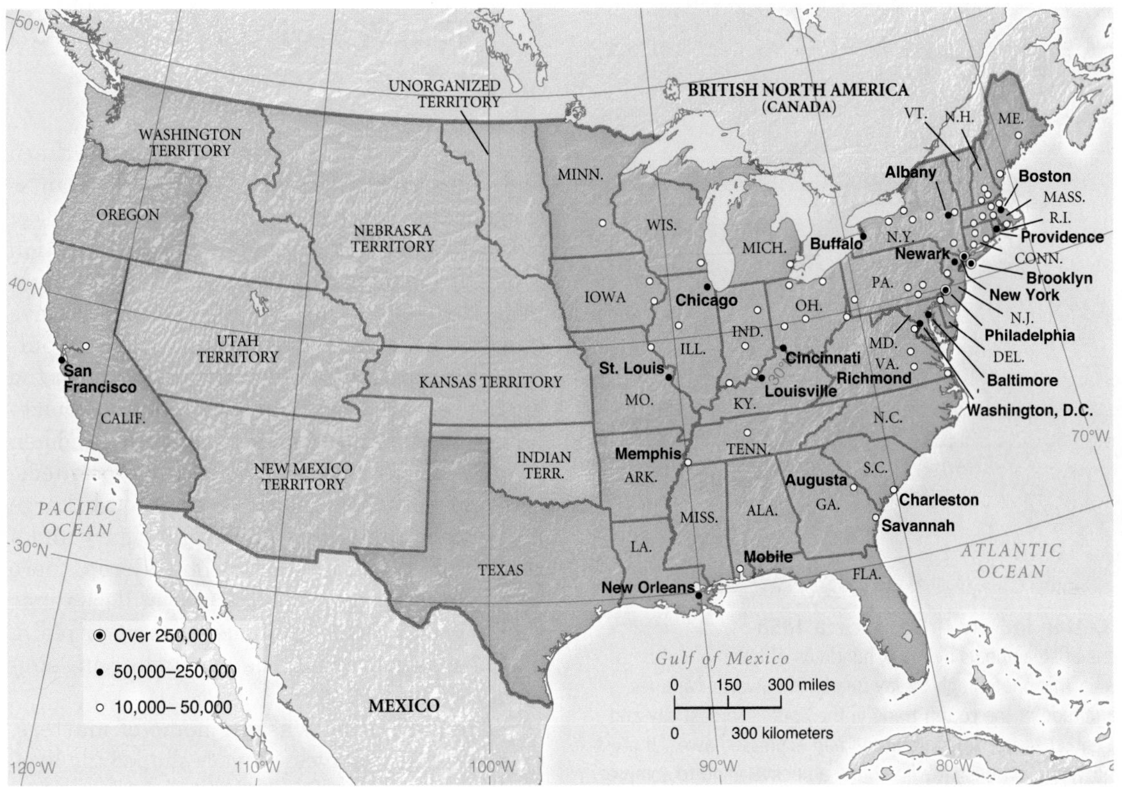

MAP 13.3
Major Cities in 1860
By 1860, northern cities were more numerous and larger than southern cities. In the slave states, cities were usually seaports or river ports that served the needs of agriculture, especially cotton.

percent of the nation's industrial workers lived in the South. Some cotton mills sprang up, but the region that produced 100 percent of the nation's cotton manufactured less than 7 percent of its cotton textiles.

Without significant economic diversification, the South developed fewer cities than the North and West (Map 13.3). In 1860, it was the least urban region in the country. Whereas nearly 37 percent of New England's population lived in cities, less than 12 percent of Southerners were urban dwellers. Southern cities were mostly port cities and were busy principally with exporting the agricultural products of plantations in the interior. Urban merchants provided agriculture with indispensable services, such as hauling, insuring, and selling cotton, rice, and sugar, but they were the tail on the plantation dog.

Immigrants as a Percentage of State Populations, 1860

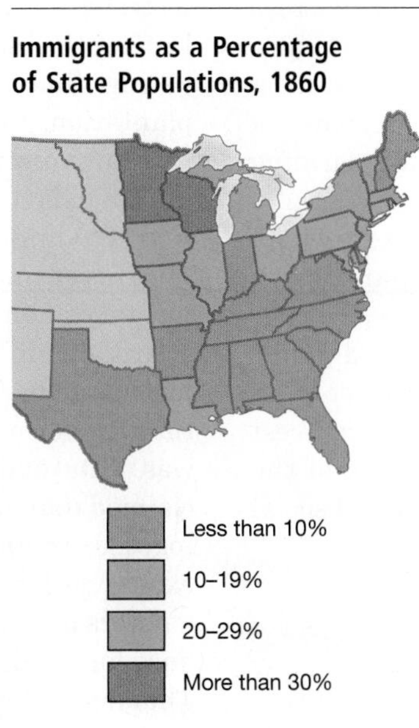

Because the South had so few cities and industrial jobs, it attracted small numbers of European immigrants. Seeking economic opportunity, not competition with slaves (whose labor would keep wages low), immigrants steered northward. In 1860, 13 percent of all Americans were born abroad. But in nine of the fifteen slave states, only 2 percent or less of the population was foreign-born.

Not every Southerner celebrated the region's commitment to cotton and slaves. Critics bemoaned what one called the "deplorable scarcity" of factories. Diversification, reformers promised, would make the South economically independent and more prosperous. State governments encouraged economic development by helping to create banking systems that supplied credit for a wide range of projects and by constructing railroads, but they

Steamboats and Cotton in New Orleans, circa 1858
Smokestacks of dozens of steamboats overlook hundreds of bales of cotton at the foot of Canal Street. This photograph by Jay Dearborn Edwards captures something of the magnitude of the cotton trade in the South's largest city and major port. A decade earlier, visitor Solon Robinson had expressed awe: "It must be seen to be believed; and even then, it will require an active mind to comprehend acres of cotton bales standing upon the levee. . . ." Amid the sea of cotton, few Southerners doubted that cotton was king. Historic New Orleans Collection.

failed to create some of the essential services modern economies required. By the mid-nineteenth century, for example, no southern legislature had created a statewide public school system. Planters failed to see any benefit in educating the children of small farmers, especially with their tax money. Despite the flurry of railroad building, the South's mileage in 1860 was less than half that of the North. Moreover, whereas railroads crisscrossed the North carrying manufactured goods and agricultural products, most railroads in the South were short stretches of track that ran from port cities back into farming areas in order to transport cotton.

Northerners claimed that slavery was a backward labor system, and compared with Northerners, Southerners invested less of their capital in industry, transportation, and public education. But planters' pockets were never fuller than in the 1850s. Planters' decisions to reinvest in agriculture ensured the momentum of the plantation economy and the political and social relationships rooted in it.

REVIEW Why did the nineteenth-century southern economy remain primarily agricultural?

▸ Masters and Mistresses in the Big House

Nowhere was the contrast between northern and southern life more vivid than on the plantations of the South. Located on a patchwork of cleared fields and dense forests, a plantation typically included a "big house," where the plantation owner and his family lived, and a slave quarter. Scattered about were numerous outbuildings, each with a special function. Near the big house were the kitchen, storehouse, smokehouse (for curing and preserving meat), and hen coop. More distant were the barns, toolsheds, artisans' workshops, and overseer's house. Large plantations sometimes had an infirmary and a chapel for slaves. Depending on the crop, there was also a tobacco shed, a rice mill, a sugar refinery, or a cotton gin house. Lavish or plain, plantations everywhere had an underlying similarity (Figure 13.2).

The plantation was the home of masters, mistresses, and slaves. Slavery shaped the lives of all the plantation's inhabitants, from work to leisure activities, but it affected each differently. A hierarchy of rigid roles and duties governed relationships. Presiding was the master, who ruled his wife, children, and slaves, none of whom had many legal rights and all of whom were designated by the state as dependents under his dominion and protection.

Paternalism and Male Honor

Whereas smaller planters supervised the labor of their slaves themselves, larger planters hired **overseers** who went to the fields with the slaves, leaving the planters free to concentrate on marketing, finance, and the general affairs of the plantation. Planters also found time to escape to town to discuss cotton prices, to the courthouse and legislature to debate politics, and to the woods to hunt and fish.

Increasingly, planters characterized their mastery in terms of what they called "Christian guardianship" and what historians have called **paternalism**. The concept of paternalism denied that the form of slavery practiced in the South was brutal and exploitative. Instead, paternalism claimed that plantations joined master and slave together in an enterprise that benefited all. In exchange for the slaves' labor and obedience, masters provided basic care and necessary guidance for a childlike, dependent people. In 1814, Thomas Jefferson captured the essence of the

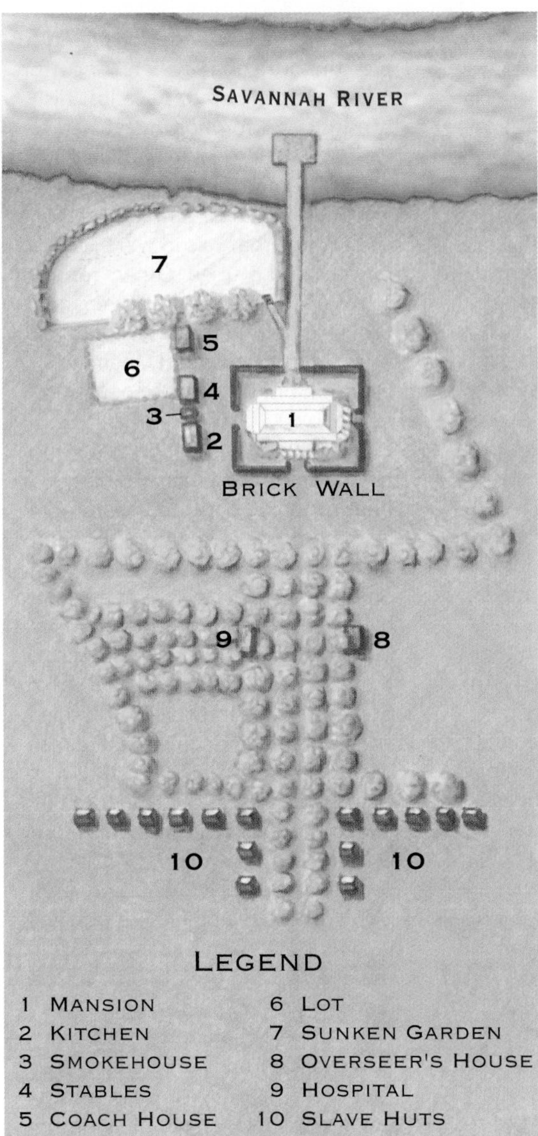

FIGURE 13.2 A Southern Plantation
Slavery determined how masters laid out their plantations, where they situated their "big houses" and slave quarters, and what kinds of buildings they constructed. This model of the Hermitage, the mansion built in 1830 for Henry McAlpin, a Georgia rice planter, shows the overseer's house poised in a grove of oak trees halfway between the owner's mansion and the slave huts. The placement of the mansion at the end of an extended road leading up from the river underscored McAlpin's affluence and authority. Adapted from *Back of the Big House: The Architecture of Plantation Slavery* by John Michael Vlach. Copyright © 1993 by the University of North Carolina Press. Reprinted with permission of the University of North Carolina Press. Original illustration property of the Historic American Buildings Survey, a division of the National Park Service.

advancing ideal: "We should endeavor, with those whom fortune has thrown on our hands, to feed & clothe them well, protect them from ill usage, require such reasonable labor only as is performed voluntarily by freemen, and be led by no repugnancies to abdicate them, and our duties to them." A South Carolina rice planter insisted, "I manage them as my children."

Paternalism was part propaganda and part self-delusion. But it was also economically shrewd. Masters increasingly recognized slaves as valuable assets, particularly after the nation closed its external slave trade in 1808 and the cotton boom simultaneously stimulated the demand for slaves. Planters realized that the expansion of the slave labor force could come only from natural reproduction. As one slave owner declared in 1849, "It behooves those who own them to make them last as long as possible." Another planter instructed his overseer to pay attention to "whatever tends to promote their health and render them prolific."

One consequence of this paternalism and economic self-interest was a small improvement in slaves' welfare. Diet improved, although nineteenth-century slaves still ate mainly fatty pork and cornmeal. Housing improved, although the cabins still had cracks large enough, slaves said, for cats to slip through. Clothing improved, although slaves seldom received much more than two crude outfits a year and perhaps a pair of cheap shoes. In the fields, workdays remained sunup to sundown, but planters often provided a rest period in the heat of the day. And most owners ceased the colonial practice of punishing slaves by branding and mutilation.

"I manage them as my children."
— A South Carolina rice planter, speaking of his slaves

Paternalism should not be mistaken for "Ol' Massa's" kindness and goodwill. It encouraged better treatment because it made economic sense to provide at least minimal care for valuable slaves. Nor did paternalism require that planters put aside their whips. They could whip and still claim that they were only fulfilling their responsibilities as guardians of their naturally lazy and at times insubordinate black dependents. State laws gave masters nearly "uncontrolled authority over the body" of the slave, according to one North Carolina judge. Paternalism offered slaves some informal protection against the most brutal

HISTORICAL QUESTION

How Often Were Slaves Whipped?

There is little doubt that the whipping of slaves was widespread and acceptable in the South. We know from white sources that whipping was the prescribed method of physical punishment on most antebellum plantations. Masters' instructions to overseers authorized whippings and often established the number of strokes an overseer could administer. Some planters allowed fifteen lashes, some fifty, and some one hundred. But slave owners' instructions, as revealing as they are, tell us more about the severity of beating than about their frequency.

Remembrances of former slaves confirm that whipping was widespread and frequent. In the 1930s, a government program gathered testimony from more than 2,300 elderly African Americans about their experiences as slaves. Their accounts offer grisly evidence of the cruelty of slavery. "You say how did our Master treat his slaves?" asked one woman. "Scandalous, they treated them just like dogs." She was herself whipped "till the blood dripped to the ground." Bert Strong never personally felt the sting of the lash, but he recalled hearing slaves on other farms "hollering when they get beat." He said, "They beat them till it a pity." Beatings occurred often, but how often?

The diary of Bennet H. Barrow, the master of Highland plantation in West Feliciana Parish, Louisiana, provides a rare picture of a master's punishment of his slaves. For a twenty-three-month period in 1840–1841, Barrow meticulously recorded every one of the 160 whippings he administered or ordered, which amounted to one whipping every four and a half days. Barrow's records establish that 60 of the 77 slaves who worked in his fields were whipped in this period, with 80 percent of the males and 70 percent of the females being whipped at least once. Most of the 17 field slaves who escaped being beaten were children and pregnant women.

In most instances, Barrow recorded not only the fact of a whipping but also his reasons for administering it. All sorts of "rascallity" made Barrow reach for his whip. The provocations included family quarrels in the slave quarter, impudence, running away, and failure to keep curfew. But nearly 80 percent of the reasons were related to poor work. Barrow gave beatings for picking "very trashy cotton," for "not picking as well as he can," and for failing to pick the prescribed weight of cotton. One slave claimed to have lost his eyesight and for months refused to work, until Barrow "gave him 25 cuts yesterday morning & ordered him to work Blind or not." Some planters used whips that raised welts, caused blisters, and bruised. Others resorted to rawhide and cowhide whips that broke the skin, caused scarring, and sometimes permanently maimed. Occasionally, slaves were beaten to death.

Whipping was not Barrow's only means of inflicting pain. His diary mentions confining slaves to a plantation jail, putting them in chains, shooting them, breaking a "sword cane" over one slave's head, having slaves mauled by dogs, placing them in stocks, "staking down" slaves for hours, holding their heads under water, and a variety of punishments intended to ridicule and to shame, including making men wear women's clothing and do "women's work," such as the laundry. Still, Barrow's preferred instrument of punishment was the whip.

On the Barrow plantation, as on many others, whipping was public. Victims were often tied to a stake in the quarter, and the other slaves were made to watch. In a real sense, the entire slave population on the plantation experienced a whipping every four and a half days, and all were familiar with its terror and agony.

Was whipping effective? Did it produce a hardworking, efficient, and conscientious labor force? Not

punishments, but whipping remained the planters' essential form of coercion. (See "Historical Question," above.)

Paternalism never won universal acceptance among planters, but by the nineteenth century it had become a kind of communal standard. With its notion that slavery imposed on masters a burden and a duty, paternalism provided slaveholders with a means of rationalizing their rule. But it also provided some slaves with leverage in controlling the conditions of their lives. Slaves learned to manipulate the slaveholder's need to see himself as a good master. To avoid a reputation as a cruel tyrant, planters sometimes negotiated with slaves, rather than just resorting to the whip. Masters sometimes granted slaves small garden plots in which they could work for themselves after working all day in the fields, or they gave slaves a few days off and a dance when they had gathered the last of the cotton.

Virginia statesman Edmund Randolph argued that slavery created in white southern men a "quick and acute sense of personal liberty" and a "disdain for every abridgement of personal independence." Indeed, prickly individualism and aggressive independence became crucial features according to Barrow's own record. No evidence indicates that whipping changed the slaves' behavior. What Barrow considered bad work continued. Unabated whipping is itself evidence of the failure of punishment to achieve the master's will. Slaves knew the rules, yet they continued to act "badly." And they continued to suffer.

Did Barrow whip as often as other planters whipped? We simply do not know. Still, the Barrow evidence allows us to speculate profitably on the frequency of whipping by large planters. We do know that Barrow did not consider himself a cruel man. He bitterly denounced his neighbor as "the most cruel Master i ever knew of" for castrating three of his slaves. Like most whites, he believed that the lash was essential to get the work done, and he used it no more than he believed absolutely necessary. Still, Barrow's whip fell on someone's back every few days.

Thinking about Beliefs and Attitudes

1. How could slaveholders, who increasingly saw themselves as "Christian guardians" to their slaves, have justified whipping them?
2. Why do you suppose masters relied on whipping as the preferred form of punishment?
3. Why do you suppose Barrow gave the overwhelming majority of whippings because of poor work?

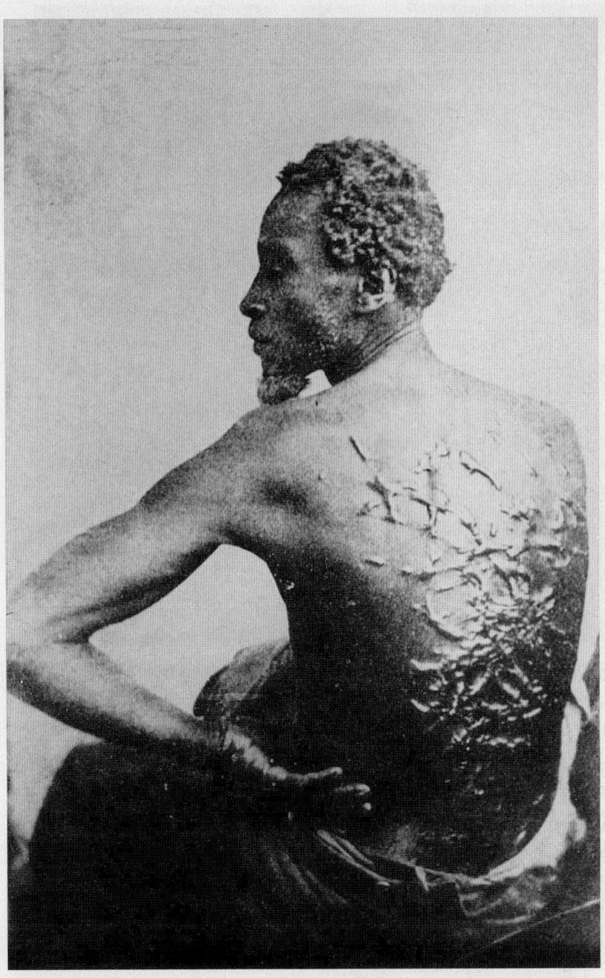

Gordon
This photograph of Gordon, a runaway slave from Baton Rouge, Louisiana, was taken on April 2, 1863. Frederick W. Mercer, an assistant surgeon with the Forty-seventh Massachusetts Regiment, examined four hundred other runaways and found many "to be as badly lacerated." Publication of Gordon's photograph in the popular *Harper's Weekly* made him a symbol of slavery's terrible brutality. Courtesy of the Massachusetts Historical Society.

of the southern concept of honor. Social standing, political advancement, and even self-esteem rested on an honorable reputation. Defending honor became a male passion. Andrew Jackson's mother reportedly told her son, "Never tell a lie, nor take what is not your own, nor sue anybody for slander or assault and battery. *Always settle them cases yourself.*" Among planters, such advice sometimes led to dueling, a ritual that had arrived from Europe in the eighteenth century. It died out in the North, but in the South, even after legislatures banned it, gentlemen continued to defend their honor with pistols at ten paces.

Southerners also expected an honorable gentleman to be a proper patriarch. Nowhere in America was masculine power more accentuated. Planters brooked no opposition from any of their dependents, black or white. The master's absolute dominion sometimes led to miscegenation. Laws prohibited interracial sex, but how many trips masters and their sons made to slave cabins is impossible to tell. As long as slavery gave white men extraordinary power, however, slave women were forced to submit to the sexual appetites of the men who owned them.

Southern Man with Children and Their Mammy
Obviously prosperous and looking like a man accustomed to giving orders and being obeyed, this patriarch poses around 1848 with his young daughters and their nurse. Why does the black woman appear in the daguerreotype? The absent mother may be dead, and her death might account for the inclusion of the African American woman in the family circle. In any case, her presence signals her importance in the household. Fathers left the raising of daughters to mothers and nurses. Collection of the J. Paul Getty Museum, Malibu, CA.

In time, as the children of one elite family married the children of another, ties of blood and kinship, as well as ideology and economic interest, linked planters to one another. Conscious of what they shared as slaveholders, planters worked together to defend their common interests. The values of the big house — slavery, honor, male domination — washed over the boundaries of plantations and flooded all of southern life.

The Southern Lady and Feminine Virtues

Like their northern counterparts, southern ladies were expected to possess the feminine virtues of piety, purity, chastity, and obedience within the context of marriage, motherhood, and domesticity. Countless toasts praised the southern lady as the perfect complement to her husband, the commanding patriarch. She was physically weak, "formed only for the less laborious occupations," and thus dependent on male protection. To gain this protection, she exhibited modesty and delicacy, possessed beauty and grace, and cultivated refinement and charm.

For women, this image of the southern lady was no blessing. **Chivalry** — the South's romantic ideal of male-female relationships — glorified the lady while it subordinated her. Chivalry's underlying assumptions about the weakness of women and the protective authority of men resembled the paternalistic defense of slavery.

Indeed, the most articulate spokesmen for slavery also vigorously defended the subordination of women. George Fitzhugh insisted that "a woman, like children, has but one right and that is the right to protection. The right to protection involves the obligation to obey. A husband, a lord and master, nature designed for every woman. . . . If she be obedient she stands little danger of maltreatment." Just as the slaveholder's mastery was written into law, so too were the paramount rights of husbands. Married women lost almost all their property rights to their husbands. Women throughout the nation found divorce difficult, but southern women found it almost impossible.

Daughters of planters confronted chivalry's demands at an early age. Their education aimed at fitting them to become southern ladies. At their private boarding schools, they read literature, learned languages, and studied the appropriate drawing-room arts. Elite women began courting at a young age and married early. Kate Carney exaggerated only slightly when she despaired in her diary: "Today, I am seventeen, getting quite old, and am not married." Yet marriage meant turning their fates over to their husbands and making enormous efforts to live up to their region's lofty ideal. One mother told her daughter: "A single life has fewer troubles; but then it is not the one for which our maker designed us."

Proslavery advocates claimed that slavery freed white women from drudgery. Surrounded "by her domestics," declared Thomas R. Dew, "she ceases to be a mere beast of burden" and "becomes the cheering and animating center of the family circle." In reality, however, having servants required the plantation mistress to work long hours. She managed the big house, directly supervising as many as a dozen slaves. But unlike her husband, the mistress had no overseer. All house servants answered directly to her. She assigned them tasks each morning, directed their work throughout the day, and punished them when she found fault. Southern ladies did not often lead lives of leisure.

Bird Store, 626 Royal Street, New Orleans
Most elite white women lived on plantations, but when they visited cities, they shopped. Here a wealthy mother and daughter shop for a pet in a New Orleans bird store. The attentive proprietor and attractive shop provide everything they need — birds, cages, food, even an inviting couch in case they want to rest before moving on. Elite white women were, in a way, like birds kept in golden cages. Could it be that they were attracted to the thought of owning birds of their own, something they could care for, train, and control? Historic New Orleans Collection.

Whereas masters used their status as slaveholders as a springboard into public affairs, mistresses' lives were circumscribed by the plantation. Masters left the plantation when they pleased, but mistresses needed chaperones to travel. When they could, they went to church, but women spent most days at home, where they often became lonely. In 1853, Mary Kendall wrote how much she enjoyed her sister's letter: "For about three weeks I did not have the pleasure of seeing one white female face, there being no white family except our own upon the plantation." Grand parties and balls occasionally broke the daily routine, but the burden of planning and supervising the preparation of the food and drink fell on the mistress.

As members of slaveholding families, mistresses lived privileged lives. But they also had significant grounds for discontent. No feature of plantation life generated more anguish among mistresses than miscegenation. Mary Boykin Chesnut of Camden, South Carolina, confided in her diary, "Ours is a monstrous system, a wrong and iniquity. Like the patriarchs of old, our men live all in one house with their wives and their concubines; and the mulattos one sees in every family partly resemble the white children. Any lady is ready to tell you who is the father of all the mulatto children in everybody's household but her own. Those, she seems to think drop from the clouds."

Most planters' wives, including Chesnut, accepted slavery. After all, the mistress's world

VISUAL ACTIVITY

The Price of Blood

This 1868 painting by T. S. Noble depicts a transaction between a slave trader and a rich planter. The trader nervously pretends to study the contract, while the planter waits impatiently for the completion of the sale. The planter's mulatto son, who is being sold, looks away. The children of white men and slave women were property and could be sold by the father/master. Morris Museum of Art, Augusta, GA.

READING THE IMAGE: Who is absent from the painting, and what does this suggest about the tragedy of miscegenation?

CONNECTIONS: The white, male planter represented the pinnacle of southern society. How did white women, black men, and black women fit into this strict hierarchy?

rested on slave labor, just as the master's did. By acknowledging the realities of male power, mistresses enjoyed the rewards of their class and race. But these rewards came at a price. Still, the heaviest burdens of slavery fell not on those who lived in the big house, but on those who toiled to support them.

REVIEW Why did the ideology of paternalism gain currency among planters in the nineteenth century?

▸ Slaves in the Quarter

On most plantations, only a few hundred yards separated the big house and the slave quarter. But the distance was great enough to provide slaves with some privacy. Out of eyesight and earshot of the big house, slaves drew together and built lives of their own. They created families, worshipped God, and developed an African American community and culture. Individually and collectively, slaves found subtle and not so subtle ways to resist their bondage.

Despite the rise of plantations, a substantial minority of slaves lived and worked elsewhere. Most labored on small farms, where they wielded a hoe alongside another slave or two and perhaps their master. But by 1860, almost half a million slaves (one in eight) did not work in agriculture at all. Some lived in towns and cities, where they worked in the homes and shops of their masters as domestics, day laborers, bakers, barbers, tailors, and more. Other slaves, far from urban centers, toiled as fishermen, lumbermen, railroad workers, and deckhands on riverboats. Slaves could also be found in most of the South's factories. Nevertheless, a majority of slaves (52 percent) counted plantations as their workplaces and homes.

Work

Ex-slave Albert Todd recalled, "Work was a religion that we were taught." Whites enslaved blacks for their labor, and all slaves who were capable of productive labor worked. Former slave Carrie Hudson recalled that children who were "knee high to a duck" were sent to the fields to carry water to thirsty workers or to protect ripening crops from hungry birds. Others helped in the slave nursery, caring for children even younger than themselves, or in the big house, where they swept floors or shooed flies in the dining room. When slave boys and girls reached the age of eleven or twelve, masters sent most of them to the fields, where they learned farmwork by laboring alongside their parents. After a lifetime of labor, old women left the fields to care for the small children and spin yarn, and old men moved on to mind livestock and clean stables.

The overwhelming majority of plantation slaves worked as field hands, and most grew cotton. Cotton had a long growing season, and work never stopped, from the clearing of the fields in January and February to the planting and cultivating in the spring and summer until the picking in the fall. Planters sometimes assigned men and women to separate gangs, the women working at lighter tasks and the men doing the heavy work of clearing and breaking the land. But women also did heavy work. "I had to work hard," Nancy Boudry remembered, and "plow and go and split wood just like a man." The backbreaking labor and the monotonous routines caused one ex-slave to observe that the "history of one day is the history of every day."

A few slaves (about one in ten) became house servants. Nearly all of those (nine out of ten) were women. They cooked, cleaned, babysat, washed clothes, and did the dozens of other tasks the master and mistress required. House servants enjoyed somewhat less physically demanding work than field hands, but they were constantly on call, with no time that was entirely their own. Since no servant could please constantly, most bore the brunt of white frustration and rage. Ex-slave Jacob Branch of Texas remembered, "My poor mama! Every washday old Missy give her a beating."

Even rarer than house servants were skilled artisans. In the cotton South, no more than one slave in twenty (almost all men) worked in a skilled trade. Most were blacksmiths and carpenters, but slaves also worked as masons, mechanics, millers, and shoemakers. Slave craftsmen took pride in their skills and often exhibited the independence of spirit that caused slaveholder James H. Hammond of South Carolina to declare in disgust that when a slave became a skilled artisan, "he is more than half freed." Skilled slave fathers took pride in teaching their crafts to their sons. "My pappy was one of the black smiths and worked in the shop," John Mathews remembered. "I had to help my pappy in the shop when I was a child and I learnt how to beat out the iron and make wagon tires, and make plows."

> **"My poor mama! Every washday old Missy give her a beating."**
> — Ex-slave JACOB BRANCH of Texas

Rarest of all slave occupations was that of **slave driver**. Probably no more than one male slave in a hundred worked in this capacity. These men were well named, for their primary task was driving other slaves to work harder in the fields. In some drivers' hands, the whip never rested. Ex-slave Jane Johnson of South Carolina called her driver the "meanest man, white or black, I ever see." But other drivers showed all the restraint they could. "Ole Gabe didn't like that whippin' business," West Turner of Virginia remembered. "When Marsa was there, he would lay it on 'cause he had to. But when old Marsa wasn't lookin', he never would beat them slaves."

Normally, slaves worked from what they called "can to can't," from "can see" in the morning to "can't see" at night. Even with a break at noon for a meal and rest, it made for a long day. For slaves, Lewis Young recalled, "work, work, work, 'twas all they do."

Family and Religion

From dawn to dusk, slaves worked for the master, but at night, when the labor was done, and all day Sunday and usually Saturday afternoon, slaves were left largely to themselves. Bone tired perhaps, they nonetheless used the time to develop

Isaac Jefferson
In this 1845 daguerreotype, seventy-year-old Isaac Jefferson proudly poses in the apron he wore while practicing his crafts as a tinsmith and nail maker. Slaves of Thomas Jefferson, Isaac, his wife, and their two children were deeded to Jefferson's daughter Mary when she married in 1797. Isaac worked at Jefferson's home, Monticello, until 1820, when he moved to Petersburg, Virginia. When work was slow on the home plantation, slave owners often would hire out their skilled artisans to neighbors who needed a carpenter, blacksmith, mason, or tinsmith. Special Collections Department, University of Virginia Library.

and enjoy what mattered most: family, religion, and community.

One of the most important consequences of slaves' limited autonomy was the preservation of the family. Though severely battered, the black family survived slavery. No laws recognized slave marriage, and therefore no master or slave was legally obligated to honor the bond. Nevertheless, plantation records show that slave marriages were often long-lasting. Young men and women in the quarter fell in love, married, and set up housekeeping in cabins of their own. The primary cause of the ending of slave marriages was death, just as it was in white families. But the second most frequent cause was the sale of the husband or wife, something no white family ever had to fear. Precise figures are unavailable, but during the massive deportation associated with the Second Middle Passage, sales destroyed hundreds of thousands of slave marriages.

In 1858, a South Carolina slave named Abream Scriven wrote a letter to his wife, who lived on a neighboring plantation. "My dear wife," he began, "I take the pleasure of writing you . . . with much regret to inform you I am Sold to man by the name of Peterson, a Treader and Stays in New Orleans." Scriven promised to send some things when he got to his new home in Louisiana, but he admitted that he was not sure how he would "get them to you and my children." He asked his wife to "give my love to my father and mother and tell them good Bye for me. And if we do not meet in this world I hope to meet in heaven. . . . My dear wife for you and my children my pen cannot express the griffe I feel to be parted from you all." He closed with words no master would have permitted in a slave's marriage vows: "I remain your truly husband until Death." The letter makes clear Scriven's love for his family; it also demonstrates slavery's massive assault on family life in the quarter.

Masters sometimes permitted slave families to work on their own. In the evenings and on Sundays, they tilled gardens, raised pigs and fowl, and chopped wood, selling the products in the market for a little pocket change. This "overwork," as it was called, allowed slaves to supplement their insufficient diets and even enjoy small luxuries. "Den each fam'ly have some chickens and sell dem and de eggs and maybe go huntin' and sell de hides and git some money," a former Alabama slave remembered. "Den us buy what am Sunday clothes with dat money, sech as hats and pants and shoes and dresses." Slave children remembered the extraordinary efforts their parents made to sustain their families. They held their parents in high esteem, grateful for the small bits of refuge from the rigors of slavery they provided.

Religion also provided slaves with a refuge and a reason for living. Evangelical Baptists and Methodists had great success in converting slaves from their African beliefs. By the mid-nineteenth century, perhaps as many as one-quarter of all slaves claimed church membership, and many of the rest would not have objected to being called Christians.

Planters promoted Christianity in the quarter because they believed that the slaves' salvation was part of the obligation of paternalism; they also hoped that religion would make slaves more obedient. South Carolina slaveholder

Slave Cabin, circa 1860
While slave dwellings varied from plantation to plantation, this crude cabin outside Savannah, Georgia, was typical. Constructed of logs, it was about fifteen feet square, with a dirt floor, shingled roof, and no glass. As one slave observed, "The wind and rain would come in and the smoke will not go out." While it has a substantial brick chimney, the cabin is also leaning and looks in danger of falling over. This photograph by an unknown photographer may have been taken on a Sunday, when the family is home and busy with domestic chores. Collection of the New-York Historical Society.

Charles Colcock Jones, the leading missionary to the slaves, published his *Catechism for Colored Persons* in 1834. It instructed slaves "to count their Masters 'worthy of all honour,' as those whom God has placed over them in this world." But slaves laughed up their sleeves at such messages. "That old white preacher just was telling us slaves to be good to our masters," one ex-slave said with a chuckle. "We ain't cared a bit about that stuff he was telling us 'cause we wanted to sing, pray, and serve God in our own way."

Meeting in their cabins or secretly in the woods, slaves created an African American Christianity that served their needs, not the masters'. Laws prohibited teaching slaves to read, but a few could read enough to struggle with the Bible. They interpreted the Christian message themselves. Rather than obedience, their faith emphasized justice. Slaves believed that God kept score and that the accounts of this world would be settled in the next. "The idea of a revolution in the conditions of the whites and blacks is the corner-stone" of the slaves' religion, recalled one ex-slave. But the slaves' faith also spoke to their experiences in this world. In the Old Testament, they discovered Moses, who delivered his people from slavery, and in the New Testament, they found Jesus, who offered salvation to all. Jesus' message of equality provided a potent antidote to the planters' claim that blacks were an inferior people whom God condemned to slavery.

Christianity did not entirely drive out traditional African beliefs. Even slaves who were Christians sometimes continued to believe that conjurers, witches, and spirits possessed the power to injure and protect. Moreover, slaves' Christian music, preaching, and rituals reflected the influence of Africa, as did many of their secular activities, such as wood carving, quilt making, dancing, and storytelling. But by the mid-nineteenth century, black Christianity had assumed a central place in slaves' quest for freedom. In the words of one spiritual, "O my Lord delivered Daniel / O why not deliver me too?"

Gourd Fiddle
Found in St. Marys County, Maryland, this slave-made gourd fiddle is an example of the musical instruments that African Americans crafted and played throughout the South. A hybrid of African and European elements, this fiddle offers material evidence of the cultural transformation of African slaves. Although Africans lost much in their forced journey to the Americas, they braided the traditions of Africa and the South to create something new — an African American culture. Music, a crucial component of that sustaining culture, provided slaves with a creative outlet and relief from the rigors of slavery. Smithsonian Institution/ photo by Aldo Tutino.

Resistance and Rebellion

Slaves did not suffer slavery passively. They were, as whites said, "troublesome property." Slaves understood that accommodation to what they could not change was the price of survival, but in a hundred ways they protested their bondage. Theoretically, the master was all-powerful and the slave powerless. But sustained by their families, religion, and community, slaves engaged in day-to-day resistance against their enslavers.

The spectrum of slave resistance ranged from mild to extreme. Telling a pointed story by the fireside in a slave cabin was probably the mildest form of protest. But when the weak got the better of the strong, as they did in tales of Br'er Rabbit and Br'er Fox (*Br'er* is a contraction of *Brother*), listeners could enjoy the thrill of a vicarious victory over their masters. Protest in the fields was riskier and included putting rocks in their cotton bags before having them weighed, feigning illness, and pretending to be so thick-headed that they could not understand the simplest instruction. Slaves broke so many hoes that owners outfitted the tools with oversized handles. Slaves so mistreated the work animals that masters switched from horses to mules, which could absorb more abuse. Although slaves worked hard in the master's fields, they also sabotaged his interests.

Running away was a common form of protest, but except along the borders with northern states and with Mexico, escape to freedom was almost impossible. Most runaways could hope only to escape for a few days. Seeking temporary respite from hard labor or avoiding punishment, they usually stayed close to their plantations, keeping to the deep woods or swamps and slipping back into the quarter at night to get food. "Lying out," as it was known, usually ended when the runaway, worn-out and ragged, gave up or was finally chased down by slave-hunting dogs.

Although resistance was common, outright rebellion — a violent assault on slavery by large numbers of slaves — was very rare. The scarcity of revolts in the South is not evidence of the slaves' contentedness, however. Rather, conditions gave rebels almost no chance of success. By 1860, whites in the South outnumbered blacks two to one and were heavily armed. Moreover, communication between plantations was difficult, and the South provided little protective wilderness into which rebels could retreat and defend themselves. Rebellion, as **Nat Turner**'s experience showed (see pages 393–394), was virtual suicide.

Despite steady resistance and occasional rebellion, slaves did not have the power to end their bondage. Slavery thwarted their hopes and

$50.00 Reward!!

Ran away from the Yard Corner of Jackson & Broad Streets, Augusta Ga. — on the evening of Tuesday 7th April 1863 a Woman "Dolly", whose likeness is here seen! — She is thirty years of age, light Complexion — hesitates somewhat when spoken to, and is not a very healthy woman — but rather good looking, with a fine set of teeth. Never changed her Owner, and has been a house Servant always. — It is thought she has been enticed off by some White Man, being herself a Stranger to this City, and belonging to a Charleston family. — For further particulars apply to Antoine Poullain Esqr Augusta Ga. —

Augusta Police Station

Louis Manigault Owner of Dolly

"$50.00 Reward!!"
Slave owners often used notices — reward posters like this one and newspaper advertisements — to recover runaway slaves. Typically, notices provided precise information about the runaway's physical appearance and clothing, since slaves often fled with only the clothes on their backs. Louis Manigault, a prominent rice planter, apparently could not accept that a trusted house servant like Dolly would flee on her own, and thus he suggests that "some white man" had enticed her away. What distinguishes this runaway notice from almost all others is Dolly's photograph. Manigault had apparently rewarded this favorite servant with a photograph, which he then used to track her down. Manigault Papers, Southern Historical Collection, North Carolina Collection, The Library of the University of North Carolina, Chapel Hill, collection #P484.

Freedom Paper
This legal document attests to the free status of the Reverend John F. Cook of Washington, D.C., his daughter Mary, and his son George. Cook was a free black man who kept his "freedom paper" in this watertight tin, which he probably carried with him at all times. Free blacks had to be prepared to prove their free status anytime a white man challenged them, for southern law presumed that a black person was a slave unless he or she could prove otherwise. Without such proof, free blacks risked enslavement. Moorland-Spingarn Research Center, Howard University, Washington, D.C.

aspirations. It broke some and crippled others. But slavery's destructive power had to contend with the resiliency of the human spirit. Slaves fought back physically, culturally, and spiritually. Not only did they survive bondage, but they also created in the quarter a vibrant African American culture that buoyed them up during long hours in the fields and brought them joy and hope in the few hours they had to themselves.

REVIEW What types of resistance did slaves participate in, and why did slave resistance rarely take the form of rebellion?

▸ The Plain Folk

Most whites in the South did not own slaves, not even one. In 1860, more than six million of the South's eight million whites lived in slaveless households. Some slaveless whites lived in cities and worked as artisans, mechanics, and traders. Others lived in the country and worked as storekeepers, parsons, and schoolteachers. But most "plain folk" were small farmers. Perhaps three out of four were **yeomen**, small farmers who owned their own land. As in the North, farm ownership provided a family with an economic foundation, social respectability, and political standing. Unlike their northern counterparts, however, southern yeomen lived in a region whose economy and society were increasingly dominated by unfree labor.

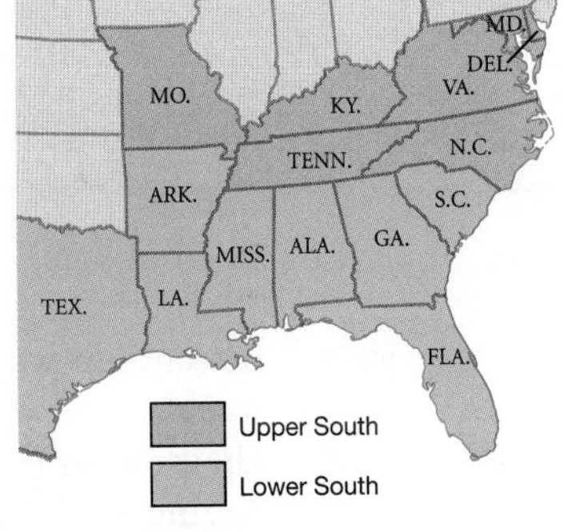

The Cotton Belt

In an important sense, the South had more than one white yeomanry. The huge southern landscape provided space enough for two yeoman societies, separated roughly along geographic lines. Yeomen throughout the South had much in common, but the life of a small farm family in the cotton belt — the flatlands that spread from South Carolina to east Texas — differed from the life of a family in the upcountry — the area of hills and mountains. And some rural slaveless whites were not yeomen; they owned no land at all and were sometimes desperately poor.

Plantation Belt Yeomen

Plantation belt yeomen lived within the orbit of the planter class. Small farms outnumbered plantations in the **plantation belt**, but they were dwarfed in importance. Small farmers grew mainly food crops, particularly corn, but they also devoted a portion of their land to cotton. With only family labor to draw on, they produced just a few 400-pound bales each year, whereas large planters measured their crop in hundreds of bales. The small farmers' cotton tied them to planters. Unable to afford cotton gins or baling presses of their own, they relied on slave owners to gin and bale their cotton. With no link to merchants in the port cities, plantation belt yeomen also turned to better-connected planters to ship and sell their cotton.

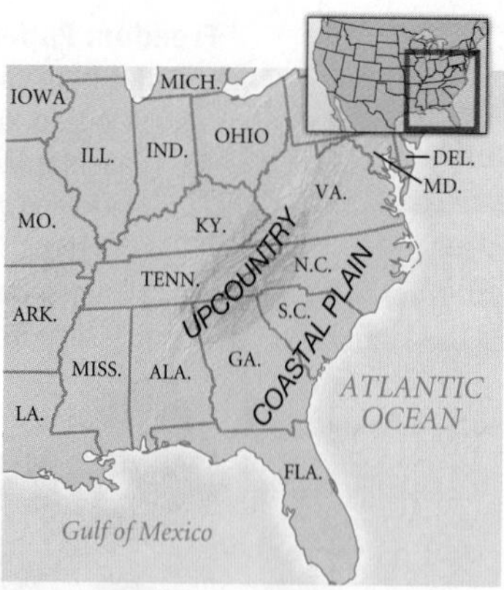

Upcountry of the South

A network of relationships laced small farmers and planters together. Planters hired out surplus slaves to ambitious yeomen who wanted to expand cotton production. They sometimes chose overseers from among the sons of local farm families. Plantation mistresses occasionally nursed ailing neighbors. Family ties could span class lines, making planter and yeoman kin as well as neighbors. Yeomen helped police slaves by riding in slave patrols, which nightly scoured country roads to make certain that no slaves were moving about without permission. On Sundays, plantation dwellers and plain folk came together in church to worship and afterward lingered to gossip and to transact small business.

Plantation belt yeomen may have envied, and at times even resented, wealthy slaveholders, but small farmers learned to accommodate. Planters made accommodation easier by going out of their way to behave as good neighbors and avoid direct exploitation of slaveless whites in their community. As a consequence, rather than raging at the oppression of the planter regime, the typical plantation belt yeoman sought entry into it. He dreamed of adding acreage to his farm, buying a few slaves of his own, and retiring from exhausting field work.

Upcountry Yeomen

By contrast, the hills and mountains of the South resisted the spread of slavery and plantations. In the western parts of Virginia, North Carolina, and South Carolina; in northern Georgia and Alabama; and in eastern Tennessee and Kentucky, the higher elevation, colder climate, rugged terrain, and poor transportation made it difficult for commercial agriculture to make headway. As a result, yeomen dominated these isolated areas, and planters and slaves were scarce.

At the core of this **upcountry** society was the independent farm family working its own patch of land; raising hogs, cattle, and sheep; and seeking self-sufficiency and independence. Toward that end, all members of the family worked, their tasks depending on their sex and age. Husbands labored in the fields, and with their sons they cleared, plowed, planted, and cultivated primarily food crops — corn, wheat, beans, sweet potatoes, and perhaps some fruit. Women and their daughters labored in and about the cabin most of the year. One upcountry farmer remembered that his mother "worked in the house cooking, spinning, weaving [and doing] patchwork." Women also tended the vegetable garden, kept a cow and some chickens, preserved food, cleaned their homes, fed their families, and cared for their children. Male and female tasks were equally crucial to the farm's success, but as in other white southern households, the domestic sphere was subordinated to the will of the male patriarch.

The typical upcountry yeoman also grew a little cotton or tobacco, but food production was more important than cash crops. Not much currency changed hands in the upcountry. Barter was common. A yeoman might trade his small cotton or tobacco crop to a country store owner for a little salt, bullets, needles, and nails, or swap extra sweet potatoes for a plow from a blacksmith or for leather from a tanner. Networks of exchange and mutual assistance tied individual homesteads to the larger community. Farm families joined together in logrolling, house and barn raising, and cornhusking.

Even the hills had some plantations and slaves, but the few upcountry folks who owned slaves usually had only two or three. As a result, slaveholders had much less social and economic power, and yeomen had more. But the upcountry did not oppose slavery. As long as upcountry plain folk were free to lead their own lives, they defended slavery and white supremacy just as staunchly as other white Southerners.

Poor Whites

The majority of slaveless white Southerners were hardworking, landholding small farmers, but Northerners held a different image of this group. They believed that slavery had condemned most whites to poverty and backwardness. One antislavery advocate charged that the South harbored

North Carolina Emigrants: Poor White Folks, 1845
James Henry Beard spent several years as a traveling portrait painter, counting among his sitters distinguished men like Henry Clay. But here his subject is a poor white family on the move. The wife clings to a child while perched on the back of a runty horse along with the family's entire belongings, which include a skillet and a pot. Two older children stand barefoot nearby, charged no doubt with looking after the family's cow and dog. The patriarch leans against a road sign, cradling his rifle. We don't know anything about the family's journey, but the painting suggests extreme poverty and desperation. Cincinnati Art Museum, Bridgeman Art Library.

three classes: "the slaves on whom devolves all the regular industry, the slaveholders who reap all the fruits, and an idle and lawless rabble who live dispersed over vast plains little removed from absolute barbarism." Critics called this third class a variety of derogatory names: hillbillies, crackers, rednecks, and poor white trash. According to critics, poor whites were not just whites who were poor. They were also supposedly ignorant, diseased, and degenerate. Even slaves were known to chant, "I'd rather be a nigger an' plow ol' Beck / Than a white hillbilly with a long red neck."

Contrary to northern opinion, only about one in four nonslaveholding rural white men was landless and very poor. Some worked as tenants, renting land and struggling to make a go of it. Others survived by herding pigs and cattle. And still others worked for meager wages, ditching, mining, logging, and laying track for railroads. A Georgian remembered that his "father worked by the day when ever he could get work."

Some poor white men earned reputations for mayhem and violence. One visitor claimed that a "bowie-knife was a universal, and a pistol a not at all unusual companion." Edward Isham, an illiterate roustabout, spent about as much time fighting as he did working. When he wasn't engaged in ear-biting, eye-gouging free-for-alls, he was fighting with sticks, shovels, rocks, axes, tomahawks, knives, and guns. Working at what he could find, he took up with and abandoned many women, gambled, drank, stole, had run-ins with the law, and in 1860 murdered a respected slaveholder, for which he was hanged.

Unlike Isham, most poor white men did not engage in ferocious behavior but instead lived responsible lives. Although they sat at the bottom of the white pecking order, they were ambitious people eager to climb into the yeomanry. The Lipscomb family illustrates the possibility of upward mobility. In 1845, Smith and Sally Lipscomb and their children abandoned their worn-out land in South Carolina for Benton County, Alabama. "Benton is a mountainous country but ther is a heep of good levil land to tend in it," Smith wrote back to his brother. Alabama, Smith said, "will be better for the rising generation if not for ourselves but I think it will be the best for us all that live any length of time." Indeed, primitive living conditions made life precarious. All of the Lipscombs fell ill, but all recovered, and the entire family went to work.

Because they had no money to buy land, they squatted on seven unoccupied acres. With the help of neighbors, they built a 22-by-24-foot cabin, a detached kitchen, and two stables. From daylight to dark, Smith and his sons worked the land, and the first year they produced several bales of cotton and enough food for the table. The women worked just as hard in the cabin, and Sally contributed to the family's income by selling homemade shirts and socks. In time, the Lipscombs bought land and joined the Baptist church, completing their transformation to respectable yeomen.

Many poor whites succeeded in climbing the economic ladder, but in the 1850s upward mobility slowed. The cotton boom of that decade caused planters to expand their operations, driving the price of land beyond the reach of poor families. Whether they gained their own land or not, however, poor whites shared common cultural traits with yeoman farmers.

The Culture of the Plain Folk

Situated on scattered farms and in tiny villages, rural plain folk lived isolated lives. Bad roads and a lack of newspapers meant that life revolved around family, a handful of neighbors, the local church, and perhaps a country store. Work occupied most hours, but plain folk still found time for pleasure. "Dancing they are all fond of," a visitor to North Carolina discovered, "especially when they can get a fiddle, or bagpipe." They also loved their tobacco. Men smoked and chewed (and spat), while women dipped snuff. But the most popular pastimes of men and boys were fishing and hunting. A traveler in Mississippi recalled that his host sent "two of his sons, little fellows that looked almost too small to shoulder a gun," for food. "One went off towards the river and the other struck into the forest, and in a few hours we were feasting on delicious venison, trout and turtle."

> "Education is not extended to the masses here as at the North."
> — A northern woman visiting the south in the 1850s

Plain folk did not usually associate "book learning" with the basic needs of life. A northern woman visiting the South in the 1850s observed, "Education is not extended to the masses here as at the North." Private academies charged fees that yeomen could not afford, and public schools were scarce. Although most people managed to pick up the "three R's," approximately one southern white man in five was illiterate in 1860, and the rate for white women was even higher. "People here prefer talking to reading," a Virginian remarked. Telling stories, reciting ballads, and singing hymns were important activities in yeoman culture.

Plain folk spent more hours in revival tents than in classrooms. Not all rural whites were religious, but many were, and the most characteristic feature of their evangelical Christian faith was the revival. Preachers spoke day and night to save souls. Revivalism crossed denominational lines, but Baptists and Methodists adopted it most readily and by midcentury had become the South's largest religious groups. By emphasizing free choice and individual worth, the plain folk's religion was hopeful and affirming. Hymns and spirituals provided guides to

Camp Meeting, mid-19th Century Camp meetings, or revivals, were a key feature of southern evangelical Christianity. Many preachers were itinerants who spoke wherever they could draw a crowd. Here an earnest clergyman preaches his message in an open field, with a tent in the background where coffee is being sold. The colorful individuals who surround the preacher include both the reverent and the not-so-reverent. Some of the audience is clearly skeptical, while others, like the two men sitting on the log, appear merely bemused. And still others have their backs to the preacher and pay no attention at all. Evangelical Christians, however, took their camp meetings, and their religion, seriously. Private Collection/Picture Research Consultants & Archives.

right and wrong — praising humility and steadfastness, condemning drunkenness and profanity. Above all, hymns spoke of the eventual release from worldly sorrows and the assurance of eternal salvation.

REVIEW Why did the lives of plantation belt yeomen and upcountry yeomen diverge?

▶ Black and Free: On the Middle Ground

All white Southerners — slaveholders and slaveless alike — considered themselves superior to all blacks, both slave and free. Not every black Southerner was a slave. In 1860, some 260,000 (approximately 6 percent) of the region's 4.1 million African Americans were free (see Figure 13.1, page 397). What is surprising is not that their numbers were small but that they existed at all. "**Free black**" seemed increasingly a contradiction to most white Southerners. According to the emerging racial thinking, blacks were supposed to be slaves; only whites were supposed to be free. Blacks who were free stood out, and whites made them more and more targets of oppression. Free blacks stood precariously between slavery and full freedom, on what a free black artisan in Charleston characterized in 1848 as "a middle ground." But they made the most of their freedom, and a few found success despite the restrictions placed on them by white Southerners.

Precarious Freedom

The population of free blacks swelled after the Revolutionary War, when the natural rights philosophy of the Declaration of Independence and the egalitarian message of evangelical Protestantism joined to challenge slavery. A brief flurry of emancipation — the act of freeing from slavery — visited the Upper South, where the ideological assault on slavery coincided with a deep depression in the tobacco economy. By 1810, free blacks in the South numbered more than 100,000, a fact that worried white Southerners, who, because of the cotton boom, wanted more slaves, not more free blacks.

In the 1820s and 1830s, state legislatures acted to stem the growth of the free black population and to shrink the liberty of those blacks who had gained their freedom. New laws denied masters the right to free their slaves. Other laws humiliated and restricted free blacks by subjecting them to special taxes, prohibiting them from interstate travel, denying them the right to have schools and to participate in politics, and requiring them to carry "freedom papers" to prove they were not slaves. Increasingly, whites subjected free blacks to the same laws as slaves. Free blacks could not testify under oath in a court of law or serve on juries. Like slaves, they were liable to whipping and the treadmill, a wooden wheel with steps on which victims were made to walk until they dropped. Free blacks were forbidden to strike whites, even to defend themselves. "Free negroes belong to a degraded caste of society," a South Carolina judge said in 1848. "They are in no respect on a perfect equality with the white man. . . . They ought, by law, to be compelled to demean themselves as inferiors."

"Free negroes belong to a degraded caste of society. They are in no respect on a perfect equality with the white man. . . . They ought, by law, to be compelled to demean themselves as inferiors."

— A South Carolina judge in 1848

Laws confined most free African Americans to a constricted life of poverty and dependence. Typically, free blacks were rural, uneducated, unskilled agricultural laborers and domestic servants who had to scramble to survive. Opportunities of any kind — for work, education, or community — were slim. Planters believed that free blacks set a bad example for slaves, subverting the racial subordination that was the essence of slavery.

Whites feared that free blacks might cherish their race more than their status as free people and that as a consequence they would lead slaves in rebellion. In 1822, whites in Charleston accused **Denmark Vesey**, a free black carpenter, of conspiring with plantation slaves to slaughter Charleston's white inhabitants. The authorities rounded up scores of suspects, who, prodded by torture and the threat of death, implicated others in the plot "to riot in blood, outrage, and rapine." Although the city fathers never found any weapons and Vesey and most of the accused steadfastly denied the charges of conspiracy, officials hanged thirty-five black men, including Vesey, and banished another thirty-seven blacks from the state.

Achievement despite Restrictions

Despite increasingly harsh laws and stepped-up persecution, free African Americans made the most of the advantages their status offered.

Unlike slaves, free blacks could legally marry. They could protect their families from arbitrary disruption and pass on their heritage of freedom to their children. Freedom also meant that they could choose occupations and own property. For most, however, these economic rights proved only theoretical, for a majority of the South's free blacks remained propertyless.

Still, some free blacks escaped the poverty and degradation whites thrust on them. Particularly in the cities of Charleston, Savannah, Mobile, and New Orleans, a small elite of free blacks emerged. Urban whites enforced restrictive laws only sporadically, allowing free blacks room to maneuver. The free black elite consisted overwhelmingly of light-skinned African Americans who worked at skilled trades, as tailors, carpenters, mechanics, and the like. The free black elite operated schools for their children and traveled in and out of their states, despite laws forbidding both activities. They worshipped with whites (in separate seating) in the finest churches and lived scattered about in white neighborhoods, not in ghettos. And like elite whites, some owned slaves. Blacks could own slaves because they had the right to own property, which in the South included human property. Of the 3,200 black slaveholders (barely 1 percent of the free black population), most owned only a few family members whom they could not legally free. Others owned slaves in large numbers and exploited them for labor.

One such free black slave owner was William Ellison of South Carolina. Born a slave in 1790, Ellison bought his freedom in 1816 and moved to a thriving plantation district about one hundred miles north of Charleston. He set up business as a cotton gin maker, a trade he had learned as a slave, and by 1835 he was prosperous enough to purchase the home of a former governor of the state. By the time of his death in 1861, he had become a cotton planter, with sixty-three slaves and an 800-acre plantation.

Most free blacks neither became slaveholders nor sought to raise a slave rebellion, as whites accused Denmark Vesey of doing. Rather, most free blacks simply tried to preserve their freedom, which was under increasing attack. Unlike blacks in the North whose freedom was secure, free blacks in the South clung to a precarious freedom by seeking to impress whites with their reliability, economic contributions, and good behavior.

REVIEW Why did many state legislatures pass laws restricting free blacks' rights in the 1820s and 1830s?

▸ The Politics of Slavery

By the mid-nineteenth century, all southern white men — planters and plain folk alike — and no southern black man, even those who were free, could vote. But even after the South's politics became democratic for the white male population, political power remained unevenly distributed. The nonslaveholding white majority wielded less political power than their numbers indicated. The slaveholding white minority wielded more. Self-conscious, cohesive, and with a well-developed sense of class interest, slaveholders busied themselves with party politics, campaigns, and officeholding and made demands of state governments. As a result, they received significant benefits. Nonslaveholding whites were concerned mainly with preserving their liberties and keeping their taxes low. Collectively, they asked government for little of an economic nature, and they received little.

Slaveholders sometimes worried about nonslaveholders' loyalty to slavery, but the majority of whites accepted the planters' argument that the existing social order served *all* Southerners' interests. Slavery rewarded every white man — no matter how poor — with membership in the South's white ruling race. It also provided the means by which nonslaveholders might someday advance into the ranks of the planters. White men in the South argued furiously about many things, but they agreed that they should take land from Indians, promote agriculture, uphold white supremacy and masculine privilege, and defend slavery from its enemies.

The Democratization of the Political Arena

The political reforms that swept the nation in the first half of the nineteenth century reached deeply into the South. Southern politics became democratic politics — for white men. Southerners eliminated the wealth and property requirements that had once restricted political participation. By the 1850s, every state had extended the right to vote to all adult white males. Most southern states also removed the property requirements for holding state offices. To be sure, undemocratic features lingered. Plantation districts still wielded disproportionate power in several state legislatures. Nevertheless, southern politics took place within an increasingly democratic political structure.

White male suffrage ushered in an era of vigorous electoral competition in the South. Eager voters rushed to the polls to exercise their new rights. High turnouts — often approaching 80 percent — became a hallmark of southern elections. Candidates crisscrossed their electoral districts, speaking to voters who demanded stirring oratory and also good entertainment — barbecues and bands, rum and races. In the South, it seemed, "everybody talked politics everywhere," even the "illiterate and shoeless."

As politics became aggressively democratic, it also grew fiercely partisan. From the 1830s to the 1850s, **Whigs** and **Democrats** battled for the electorate's favor. Both parties presented themselves as the plain white folk's best friend. All candidates declared their allegiance to republican equality and pledged themselves to defend the people's liberty. And each party sought to portray the other as a collection of rich, snobbish, selfish men who had antidemocratic designs up their silk sleeves.

The Whig and Democratic parties sought to serve the people differently, however. Southern Whigs tended, as Whigs did elsewhere in the nation, to favor government intervention in the economy, and Democrats tended to oppose it. Whigs backed state support of banks, railroads, and corporations, arguing that government aid would stimulate the economy, enlarge opportunity, and thus increase the general welfare. Democrats claimed that by granting favors to special economic interests, government intervention threatened individual liberty and restricted the common man's economic opportunity. Beginning with the panic of 1837 (see chapter 11), the parties clashed repeatedly on concrete economic and financial issues.

Planter Power

Whether Whig or Democrat, southern officeholders were likely to be slave owners. The power that slaveholders exerted over slaves did not translate directly into political authority over whites, however. In the nineteenth century, political power could be won only at the ballot box, and almost everywhere nonslaveholders were in the majority. Yet year after year, proud and noisily egalitarian common men elected wealthy slaveholders.

By 1860, the percentage of slave owners in state legislatures ranged from 41 percent in Missouri to nearly 86 percent in North Carolina (Table 13.1). Legislators not only tended to own slaves; they also often owned large numbers. The percentage of planters (individuals with twenty or more slaves) in southern legislatures in 1860 ranged from 5.3 percent in Missouri to 55.4 percent in South Carolina. Even in North Carolina, where only 3 percent of the state's white families belonged to the planter class, more than 36 percent of state legislators were planters. The democratization of politics in the nineteenth century meant that more ordinary citizens participated in elections, but yeomen did not throw the planters out of office.

Upper-class dominance of southern politics reflected the elite's success in persuading the yeoman majority that what was good for slaveholders was also good for plain folk. In reality, the South had, on the whole, done well by common white men. Most had farms of their own. They participated as equals in a democratic political system. They enjoyed an elevated social status, above all blacks and in theory equal to all other whites. They commanded patriarchal authority over their households. And as long as slavery existed, they could dream of joining the planter class. Slaveless white men found much to celebrate in the slave South.

Most slaveholders took pains to win the plain folk's trust and to nurture their respect. One South Carolinian told his wealthy neighbor that he had a bright political future because he never thought himself "too good to sit down & talk to a poor man." Mary Boykin Chesnut complained about the fawning attention her husband, U.S. senator from South Carolina, showed to poor men, including one who had "mud sticking up through his toes." Smart candidates found ways to convince wary plain folk of their democratic

TABLE 13.1 PERCENT OF SLAVEHOLDERS AND PLANTERS IN SOUTHERN LEGISLATURES, 1860

Legislature	Slaveholders	Planters*
North Carolina	85.8%	36.6%
South Carolina	81.7	55.4
Alabama	76.3	40.8
Mississippi	73.4	49.5
Georgia	71.6	29.0
Virginia	67.3	24.2
Tennessee	66.0	14.0
Louisiana	63.8	23.5
Kentucky	60.6	8.4
Florida	55.4	20.0
Texas	54.1	18.1
Maryland	53.4	19.3
Arkansas	42.0	13.0
Missouri	41.2	5.3

*Planters: Owned 20 or more slaves.

SOURCE: Adapted from Ralph A. Wooster, *The People in Power: Courthouse and Statehouse in the Lower South, 1850–1860*, page 40. Copyright © 1975 by Ralph A. Wooster. Courtesy of the University of Tennessee Press.

convictions and egalitarian sentiments, whether they were genuine or not.

In 1846 when Walter L. Steele ran for a seat in the North Carolina legislature, he commented sarcastically to a friend that he was "busily engaged in proving to the people, the soundness of my political faith, and the purity of my personal character & playing fool to a considerable extent, as you know, all candidates are obliged to do." He detested pandering to the crowd, but he had learned to speak with "candied tongue."

Georgia politics illustrate how well planters protected their interests in state legislatures. In 1850, about half of the state's revenues came from taxes on slaves, the characteristic form of planter wealth. However, the tax rate on slaves was trifling, only about one-fifth the rate on land. Moreover, planters benefited from public spending far more than other groups did. Financing railroads—which carried cotton to market — was the largest state expenditure. The legislature also established low tax rates on land, the characteristic form of yeoman wealth, which meant that the typical yeoman's annual tax bill was small. Still, relative to their wealth, large slaveholders paid less than did other whites. Relative to their numbers, they got more in return. Slaveholding legislators protected planters' interests while giving the impression of protecting the small farmers' interests as well.

The South's elite defended slavery in other ways. In the 1830s, whites decided that slavery was too important to debate. "So interwoven is [slavery] with our interest, our manners, our climate and our very being," one man declared ominously in 1833, "that no change can ever possibly be effected without a civil commotion from which the heart of a patriot must turn with horror." To end free speech on the slavery question, powerful whites dismissed slavery's critics from college faculties, drove them from pulpits, and hounded them from political life. Sometimes antislavery Southerners fell victim to vigilantes and mob violence. One could defend slavery; one could even delicately suggest mild reforms. But no Southerner could any longer safely call slavery evil or advocate its destruction.

"So interwoven is [slavery] with our interest, our manners, our climate and our very being that no change can ever possibly be effected without a civil commotion."

— A southern man in 1833

In the South, therefore, the rise of the common man occurred alongside the continuing, even growing, power of the planter class. Rather than pitting slaveholders against nonslaveholders, elections remained an effective means of binding the region's whites together. Elections affirmed the sovereignty of white men, whether planter or plain folk, and the subordination of African Americans. Those twin themes played well among white women as well. Though unable to vote, white women supported equality for whites and slavery for blacks. In the antebellum South, the politics of slavery helped knit together all of white society.

REVIEW How did planters benefit from their control of state legislatures?

▶ Conclusion: A Slave Society

By the early nineteenth century, northern states had either abolished slavery or put it on the road to extinction, while southern states were building the largest slave society in the New World. Regional differences increased over time, not merely because the South became more and more dominated by slavery, but also because developments in the North rapidly propelled it in a very different direction.

One-third of the South's population was enslaved by 1860. Bondage saddled blacks with enormous physical and spiritual burdens: hard labor, harsh treatment, broken families, and, most important, the denial of freedom itself. Although degraded and exploited, they were not defeated. Out of African memories and New World realities, blacks created a life-affirming African American culture that sustained and strengthened them. Their families, religion, and community provided defenses to white racism and power. Defined as property, they refused to be reduced to things. Perceived as inferior beings, they rejected the notion that they were natural slaves.

Slavery was crucial to the South's distinctiveness and to the loyalty and regional identification of its whites. The South was not merely a society with slaves; it had become a slave society. Slavery shaped the region's economy, culture, social structure, and politics. Whites south of the Mason-Dixon line believed that racial slavery was necessary and just. By making all blacks a pariah class, all whites gained a measure of equality and harmony.

Many features of white southern life helped to confine class tensions: the wide availability of land, rapid economic mobility, the democratic nature of political life, the patriarchal power among all white men, and, most of all, slavery. All stress along class lines was not erased, however, and anxious slaveholders continued to worry that yeomen would defect from the proslavery consensus. But during the 1850s, white Southerners' near universal acceptance of slavery would increasingly unite them in political opposition to their northern neighbors.

▶ Selected Bibliography

Slaveholders and the Economy

David L. Carlton and Peter A. Coclanis, *The South, the Nation, and the World: Perspectives on Southern Economic Development* (2003).

Steven Deyle, *Carry Me Back: The Domestic Slave Trade in American Life* (2005).

Richard Follett, *The Sugar Masters: Planters and Slaves in Louisiana's Cane World, 1820–1860* (2005).

Jonathan Martin, *Divided Mastery: Slave Hiring in the American South* (2004).

James David Miller, *South by Southwest: Planter Emigration and Identity in the Slave South* (2002).

Gavin Wright, *The Political Economy of the Cotton South: Households, Markets, and Wealth in the Nineteenth Century* (1978).

Slaves, Slavery, and Race Relations

Ira Berlin, *Generations of Captivity: A History of African-American Slaves* (2003).

Thomas C. Buchanan, *Black Life on the Mississippi: Slaves, Free Blacks, and the Western Steamboat World* (2004).

Erskine Clarke, *Dwelling Place: A Plantation Epic* (2005).

Eugene D. Genovese, *Roll, Jordan, Roll: The World the Slave Made* (1974).

Gwendolyn Midlo Hall, *Slavery and African Ethnicities in the Americas: Restoring the Links* (2005).

Anthony E. Kaye, *Joining Places: Slave Neighborhoods in the Old South* (2007).

Dylan C. Penningroth, *The Claims of Kinfolk: African American Property and Community in the Nineteenth-Century South* (2003).

Brenda E. Stevenson, *Life in Black and White: Family and Community in the Slave South* (1996).

Leonard Todd, *Carolina Clay: The Life and Legend of the Slave Potter Dave* (2008).

Society and Culture

Ira Berlin, *Slaves without Masters: The Free Negro in the Antebellum South* (1974).

Charles C. Bolton and Scott P. Culclasure, eds., *The Confessions of Edward Isham: A Poor White Life of the Old South* (1998).

Christine Jacobson Carter, *Southern Single Blessedness: Unmarried Women in the Urban South, 1800–1865* (2006).

Craig T. Friend and Lorri Glover, eds., *Southern Manhood: Perspectives on Masculinity in the Old South* (2004).

Steven Hahn, *The Roots of Southern Populism: Yeoman Farmers and the Transformation of the Georgia Upcountry, 1850–1890* (1983).

Christine Leigh Heyrman, *Southern Cross: The Beginnings of the Bible Belt* (1997).

Anya Jabour, *Scarlett's Sisters: Young Women in the Old South* (2007).

Michael P. Johnson and James L. Roark, *Black Masters: A Free Family of Color in the Old South* (1984).

Stephanie McCurry, *Masters of Small Worlds: Yeoman Households, Gender Relations, and the Political Culture of the Antebellum South* (1995).

Adam Rothman, *Slave Country: American Expansion and the Deep South* (2005).

Bertram Wyatt-Brown, *Southern Honor: Ethics and Behavior in the Old South* (1982).

Jeffrey Robert Young, *Domesticating Slavery: The Master Class in Georgia and South Carolina, 1670–1837* (1999).

Politics and Political Culture

Anthony Gene Carey, *Parties, Slavery, and the Union in Antebellum Georgia* (1997).

William J. Cooper Jr., *Liberty and Slavery: Southern Politics to 1860* (1983).

Lacy K. Ford Jr., *Deliver Us from Evil: The Slavery Question in the Old South* (2009).

Michael Perman, *Pursuit of Unity: A Political History of the American South* (2009).

Elizabeth R. Varon, *We Mean to Be Counted: White Women and Politics in Antebellum Virginia* (1998).

Peter Wallenstein, *From Slave South to New South: Public Policy in Nineteenth-Century Georgia* (1987).

▶ For more books about topics in this chapter, see the Online Bibliography at **bedfordstmartins.com/roark.**

▶ For additional primary sources from this period, see Michael Johnson, ed., *Reading the American Past*, Fifth Edition.

▶ For Web sites, images, and documents related to topics and places in this chapter, visit Make History at **bedfordstmartins.com/roark.**

Reviewing Chapter 13

KEY TERMS

Explain each term's significance.

The Growing Distinctiveness of the South

- Mason-Dixon line (p. 395)
- cotton kingdom (p. 395)
- slave codes (p. 397)
- miscegenation (p. 397)
- Thomas R. Dew (p. 399)
- John C. Calhoun (p. 400)
- planter (p. 401)
- plantation (p. 401)

Masters and Mistresses in the Big House

- overseer (p. 404)
- paternalism (p. 404)
- chivalry (p. 408)

Slaves in the Quarter

- slave driver (p. 411)
- Charles Colcock Jones (p. 413)
- Nat Turner (p. 414)

The Plain Folk

- yeomen (p. 415)
- plantation belt (p. 415)
- upcountry (p. 416)

Black and Free: On the Middle Ground

- free black (p. 419)
- Denmark Vesey (p. 419)

The Politics of Slavery

- Whigs (p. 421)
- Democrats (p. 421)

REVIEW QUESTIONS

Use key terms and dates to support your answer.

1. Why did the nineteenth-century southern economy remain primarily agricultural? (pp. 495–404)
2. Why did the ideology of paternalism gain currency among planters in the nineteenth century? (pp. 404–410)
3. What types of resistance did slaves participate in, and why did slave resistance rarely take the form of rebellion? (pp. 410–415)
4. Why did the lives of plantation belt yeomen and upcountry yeomen diverge? (pp. 415–419)
5. Why did many state legislatures pass laws restricting free blacks' rights in the 1820s and 1830s? (pp. 419–420)
6. How did planters benefit from their control of state legislatures? (pp. 420–422)

MAKING CONNECTIONS

Draw on key terms, the timeline, and review questions.

1. By the mid-nineteenth century, the South had become a "cotton kingdom." How did cotton's profitability shape the region's antebellum development? In your answer, discuss the region's distinctive demographic and economic features.
2. How did southern white legislators and intellectuals attempt to strengthen the institution of slavery in the 1820s? What prompted them to undertake this work? In your answer, be sure to explore regional and national influences.
3. Although bondage restricted slaves' autonomy and left slaves vulnerable to extreme abuse, they resisted slavery. Discuss the variety of ways in which slaves attempted to lessen the harshness of slavery. What were the short- and long-term effects of their efforts?
4. Despite vigorous political competition in the South, by 1860 legislative power was largely concentrated in the hands of a regional minority — slaveholders. Why were slaveholders politically dominant? In your answer, be sure to consider how the region's biracialism contributed to its politics.

LINKING TO THE PAST

Link events in this chapter to earlier events.

1. Compare and contrast Northerners' defense of free labor and white Southerners' defense of slave labor. (See chapter 12.)
2. How did President Andrew Jackson's Indian removal policies pave the way for the South's cotton empire? (See chapter 11.)

▶ **For practice quizzes and other study tools,** visit the Online Study Guide at **bedfordstmartins.com/roark.**

TIMELINE 1808–1860

1808	• External slave trade outlawed.
1810s–1850s	• Suffrage extended throughout South to all adult white males.
1813–1814	• Creek War opens Indian land to white settlement.
1820s–1830s	• Southern legislatures enact slave codes to strengthen slavery. • Southern legislatures enact laws to restrict growth of free black population. • Southern intellectuals fashion systematic defense of slavery.
1822	• Denmark Vesey executed for fomenting slave rebellion.
1829	• *Appeal . . . to the Coloured Citizens of the World* published.
1830	• Southern slaves number approximately two million.
1831	• Nat Turner's slave rebellion. • First issue of the *Liberator* published.
1834	• *Catechism for Colored Persons* published.
1836	• Arkansas admitted to Union as slave state.
1840	• Cotton accounts for more than 60 percent of nation's exports.
1845	• Texas and Florida admitted to Union as slave states.
1860	• Southern slaves number nearly four million, one-third of South's population.

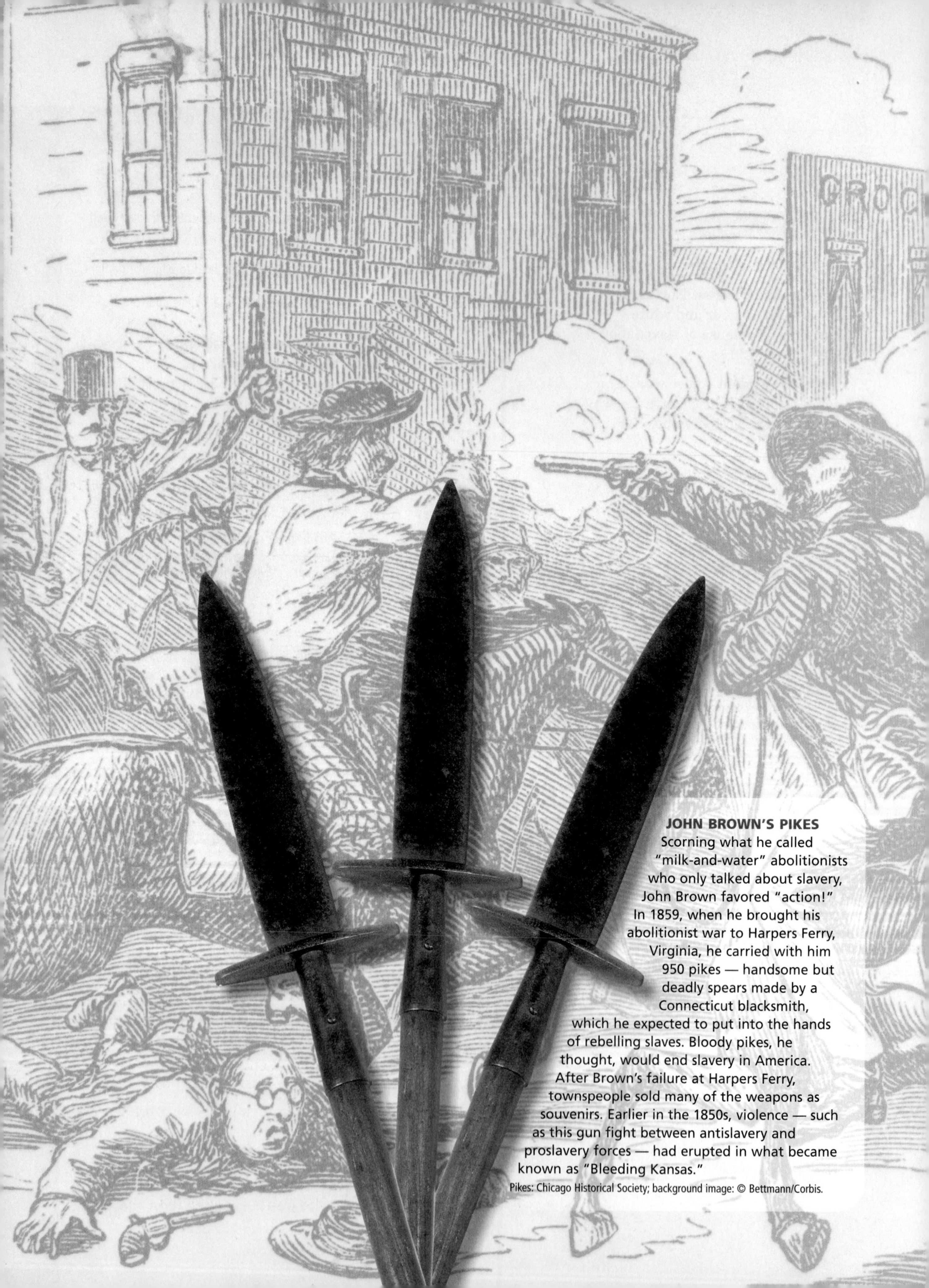

JOHN BROWN'S PIKES
Scorning what he called "milk-and-water" abolitionists who only talked about slavery, John Brown favored "action!" In 1859, when he brought his abolitionist war to Harpers Ferry, Virginia, he carried with him 950 pikes — handsome but deadly spears made by a Connecticut blacksmith, which he expected to put into the hands of rebelling slaves. Bloody pikes, he thought, would end slavery in America. After Brown's failure at Harpers Ferry, townspeople sold many of the weapons as souvenirs. Earlier in the 1850s, violence — such as this gun fight between antislavery and proslavery forces — had erupted in what became known as "Bleeding Kansas."

Pikes: Chicago Historical Society; background image: © Bettmann/Corbis.

14

The House Divided 1846–1861

OTHER THAN TWENTY CHILDREN, JOHN BROWN DID NOT HAVE MUCH to show for his life in 1859. Grizzled, gnarled, and fifty-nine years old, he had for decades lived like a nomad, hauling his large family back and forth across six states as he tried desperately to better himself. He turned his hand to farming, raising sheep, running a tannery, and selling wool, but failure dogged him. The world had given John Brown some hard licks — and yet it had not budged a conviction he had held since childhood: that slavery was wrong and ought to be destroyed. In the wake of the fighting that erupted over the future of slavery in Kansas in the 1850s, his beliefs turned violent. On May 24, 1856, he led an eight-man antislavery posse in the midnight slaughter of five allegedly proslavery men at Pottawatomie, Kansas. He told Mahala Doyle, whose husband and two oldest sons he killed, that if a man stood between him and what he thought right, he would take that man's life as calmly as he would eat breakfast.

After the killings, Brown slipped out of Kansas and reemerged in the East. More than ever, he was a man on fire for abolition. He spent thirty months begging money to support his vague plan for military operations against slavery. He captivated genteel easterners who were awed by his iron-willed determination and courage, but most could not accept violence. "These men are all talk," Brown declared. "What is needed is action — action!" But enough donated to the hypnotic-eyed Brown that he was able to gather a small band of antislavery warriors.

On the night of October 16, 1859, Brown took his war against slavery into the South. With only twenty-one men, including five African Americans, he invaded Harpers Ferry, Virginia. His band seized the town's armory and rifle works, but the invaders were immediately surrounded, first by local militia and then by Colonel Robert E. Lee, who commanded the U.S. troops in the area. When Brown refused to surrender, federal soldiers charged with bayonets. Although a few of Brown's raiders escaped, federal forces killed ten of his men (including two of his sons) and captured seven, among them Brown.

"When I strike, the bees will begin to swarm," Brown told Frederick Douglass a few months before the raid. As slaves rushed to Harpers Ferry, Brown said, he would arm them with the pikes he carried with him and with weapons stolen from the armory. They would then fight a war of liberation. Brown, however, neglected to inform the slaves when he had arrived in Harpers Ferry, and the few who knew of his arrival wanted nothing to do with his enterprise. "It was not a slave insurrection," Abraham Lincoln observed. "It was an attempt by white men to get up a revolt among slaves, in which the slaves refused to participate. In fact, it was so absurd that the slaves, with all their ignorance, saw plainly enough it could not succeed."

Although Brown's raid ended in utter defeat, white Southerners viewed it as proof of their growing suspicion that Northerners actively sought to incite slaves in bloody rebellion. For more than a decade, Northerners and Southerners had accused one another of hostile intentions, and by 1859 emotions were raw. Sectional tension was as old as the Constitution, but hostility had escalated with the outbreak of war with Mexico in May 1846 (see chapter 12). Only three months after the war began, national expansion and the slavery issue intersected when Representative David Wilmot introduced a bill to prohibit slavery in any territory that might be acquired as a result of the war. After that, the problem of slavery in the territories became the principal wedge that divided the nation.

"Mexico is to us the forbidden fruit," South Carolina senator John C. Calhoun declared at the war's outset. "The penalty of eating it [is] to subject our institutions to political death." For a decade and a half, the slavery issue intertwined with the fate of former Mexican land, poisoning the national political debate. Slavery proved powerful enough to transform party politics into sectional politics. Rather than Whigs and Democrats confronting one another across party lines, Northerners and Southerners eyed one another hostilely across the Mason-Dixon line. Sectional politics encouraged the South's separatist impulses. Southern separatism, a fitful tendency before the Mexican-American War, gained strength with each confrontation. As the nation lurched from crisis to crisis, southern disaffection and alienation mounted, and support for compromise and conciliation eroded. The era began with a crisis of union and ended with the Union in even graver peril. As Abraham Lincoln predicted in 1858, "A house divided against itself cannot stand."

John Brown
In this 1859 photograph, John Brown appears respectable, even statesmanlike, but contemporaries debated his mental state and moral character, and the debate still rages. Critics argue that he was a bloody terrorist, a religious fanatic who believed that he was touched by God for a great purpose, one for which he was willing to die. Admirers see a resolute and selfless hero, a rare white man who believed that black people were the equals of whites, and a shrewd political observer who recognized that only violence would end slavery in America. Library of Congress.

▸ The Bitter Fruits of War

Between 1846 and 1848, the nation grew by 1.2 million square miles, an incredible two-thirds. The gold rush of 1849 transformed the sleepy frontier of California into a booming, thriving economy (see chapter 12). The 1850s witnessed new "rushes," for gold in Colorado and silver in Nevada's Comstock Lode. People from around the world flocked to the West, where they produced a vibrant agriculture as well as tons of gold and silver. But it quickly became clear that Northerners and Southerners had very different visions of the West, particularly the place of slavery in its future.

History provided contradictory precedents for handling slavery in the territories. In 1787, the Northwest Ordinance banned slavery north of the Ohio River. In 1803, slavery was allowed to remain in the newly acquired Louisiana Territory. The Missouri Compromise of 1820 prohibited slavery in part of that territory but allowed it in the rest. In 1846, when the war with Mexico made likely the acquisition of new territory for the United States, politicians offered various plans. But when the war ended in 1848, Congress had made no headway in solving the issue of slavery in the land acquired from Mexico, called the Mexican cession. In 1850, Congress patched together a settlement, one that Americans hoped would be permanent.

The Wilmot Proviso and the Expansion of Slavery

In the years leading up to the Civil War, Americans focused not on slavery where it existed but on the possibility that slavery might expand into areas where it did not exist. Most Americans agreed that the Constitution left the issue of slavery to the individual states to decide. Northern states had done away with slavery, while southern states

"Guarding the Corn Fields," 1850

Neither proslavery southerners nor antislavery northerners were much concerned about the Native Americans who inhabited the western lands they coveted. But Seth Eastman, a young military officer posted to Indian Territory in Minnesota in the 1830s, had married the daughter of a chief, learned the Sioux language, and recorded sympathetically the lives he encountered. Women were responsible for agriculture, and when the corn began to ripen, they built scaffolds from which they could repel the flocks of blackbirds that preyed on the corn. Corn supplemented the game, fish, berries, and wild rice that formed the bulk of the Sioux diet.

W. Duncan and Nivin MacMillan Foundation. Photo courtesy Minneapolis Institute of Arts.

had retained it. But what about slavery in the nation's territories? The Constitution states that "Congress shall have power to . . . make all needful rules and regulations respecting the territory . . . belonging to the United States." The debate about slavery, then, turned toward Congress.

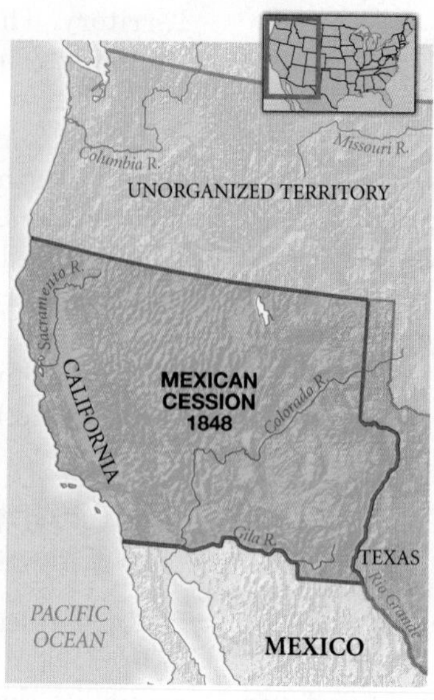

Mexican Cession, 1848

The spark for the national debate appeared in August 1846 when a Democratic representative from Pennsylvania, David Wilmot, proposed that Congress bar slavery from all lands acquired in the war with Mexico. The Mexicans had abolished slavery in their country, and Wilmot declared, "God forbid that we should be the means of planting this institution upon it."

Regardless of party affiliation, Northerners lined up behind the **Wilmot Proviso**. Many supported free soil, by which they meant territory in which slavery would be prohibited, because they wanted to preserve the West for **free labor**, for hardworking, self-reliant free men, not for slaveholders and slaves. But support also came from those who were simply anti-South. New slave territories would eventually mean new slave states, and Northerners opposed magnifying the political power of Southerners. Wilmot himself said his proposal would blunt "*the power* of slaveholders" in the national government.

Additional support for free soil came from Northerners who were hostile to blacks and wanted to reserve new land for whites. Wilmot himself blatantly encouraged racist support when he declared, "I would preserve for free white labor a fair country, a rich inheritance, where the sons of toil, of my own race and own color, can live without the disgrace which association with negro slavery brings upon free labor." It is no wonder that some called the Wilmot Proviso the "White Man's Proviso."

The thought that slavery might be excluded in the territories outraged white Southerners. Like Northerners, they regarded the West as a ladder for economic and social opportunity. They also believed that the exclusion of slavery was a slap in the face to veterans of the Mexican-American War, at least half of whom were Southerners. "When the war-worn soldier returns home," one Alabaman asked, "is he to be told that he cannot carry his property to the country won by his blood?"

Southern leaders also sought to maintain political parity with the North to protect the South's interests, especially slavery. The need seemed especially urgent in the 1840s, when the North's population and wealth were booming. James Henry Hammond of South Carolina predicted that ten new states would be carved from the acquired Mexican land. If free soil won, the North would "ride over us roughshod" in Congress, he claimed. "Our only safety is in *equality* of power."

The two sides squared off in the nation's capital. Because Northerners had a majority in the House, they easily passed the Wilmot Proviso. In the Senate, however, where slave states outnumbered free states fifteen to fourteen, Southerners defeated it in 1847. Senator **John C. Calhoun** of South Carolina boldly denied that Congress had the constitutional authority to exclude slavery from the nation's territories. He argued that because the territories were the "joint and common property" of all the states, Congress could not bar citizens of one state from migrating with their property (including slaves) to the territories. Whereas Wilmot demanded that Congress slam shut the door to slavery, Calhoun called on Congress to hold the door wide open.

In 1847, Senator **Lewis Cass** of Michigan offered a compromise through the doctrine of **popular sovereignty**, by which the people who settled the territories would decide for themselves slavery's fate. This solution, Cass argued, sat squarely in the American tradition of democracy and local self-government. It had the added attraction of removing the incendiary issue of the expansion of slavery from the nation's capital and lodging it in distant territorial legislatures, where it would excite fewer passions.

Popular sovereignty's most attractive feature was its ambiguity about the precise moment when settlers could determine slavery's fate. Northern advocates believed that the decision on slavery could be made as soon as the first territorial legislature assembled. With free-soil majorities likely because of the North's greater population, they would shut the door to slavery almost before the first slave arrived. Southern supporters believed that popular sovereignty guaranteed that slavery would be unrestricted throughout the entire territorial period. Only at

THE PROMISE OF TECHNOLOGY

Daguerreotypes

In the late 1830s, Frenchman Louis Daguerre improved on existing technology when he discovered how to keep photographic images from fading, a technique that arrived in New York City by 1839. The daguerreotype photographic process was cumbersome and complex and required several minutes of exposure, making candid shots impossible. Despite their shortcomings, daguerreotypes were an instant success, and by the 1850s Americans were buying millions of images each year.

No early American photographer was more important than Mathew Brady. In 1844, he opened his first gallery in New York City. Seeing himself as a historian of the nation, he shot portraits of distinguished citizens — presidents, congressmen, senators, and statesmen — as well as of everyday people who walked into his gallery. In 1850, Brady shot this image of a hollow-cheeked and dark-eyed John C. Calhoun, who had only months to live. Brady hoped that the new technology of photography would serve as a moral agent furthering political reconciliation and peace. By 1860, however, daguerreotypes had all but disappeared from American life, replaced by more efficient photographic processes, and the Union remained imperiled. Can you imagine why Mathew Brady believed that photographs could encourage "political reconciliation and peace"? National Portrait Gallery, Smithsonian Institution/Art Resource, NY.

the very end, when settlers in a territory drew up a constitution and applied for statehood, could they decide the issue of slavery. By then, slavery would have sunk deep roots. As long as the matter of timing remained vague, popular sovereignty gave hope to both sides.

When Congress ended its session in 1848, no plan had won a majority in both houses. Northerners who demanded no new slave territory anywhere, ever, and Southerners who demanded entry for their slave property into all territories, or else, staked out their extreme positions. Unresolved in Congress, the territorial question naturally became an issue in the presidential election of 1848.

The Election of 1848

When President Polk, worn-out and ailing, chose not to seek reelection, the Democratic convention nominated Lewis Cass of Michigan, the man most closely associated with popular sovereignty. The Whigs nominated a Mexican-American War hero, General **Zachary Taylor**. The Whigs declined to adopt a party platform, betting that the combination of a military hero and total silence on the slavery issue would unite their divided party. Taylor, who owned more than one hundred slaves on plantations in Mississippi and Louisiana, was hailed by Georgia politician Robert Toombs as a "Southern man, a slaveholder, a cotton planter."

Antislavery Whigs balked and looked for an alternative. Senator **Charles Sumner** called for a major political realignment, "one grand Northern party of Freedom." In the summer of 1848, antislavery Whigs and antislavery Democrats founded the **Free-Soil Party**, nominating a Democrat, Martin Van Buren, for president and a Whig, Charles Francis Adams, for vice president. The platform boldly proclaimed, "Free soil, free speech, free labor, and free men."

The November election dashed the hopes of the Free-Soilers. Although they succeeded in making slavery the campaign's central issue, they did not carry a single state. The major parties went through contortions to present their candidates favorably in both North and South, and their evasions succeeded. Taylor won the

General Taylor Cigar Case
This papier-mâché cigar case portrays General Zachary Taylor, Whig presidential candidate in 1848, in a colorful scene from the Mexican-American War. Shown here as a dashing, elegant officer, Taylor was in fact a short, thickset, and roughly dressed Indian fighter who had spent his career commanding small frontier garrisons. The inscription reminds voters that Taylor was a victor in the first four battles fought in the war and directs attention away from the fact that in politics he was a rank amateur. Collection of Janice L. and David J. Frent.

all-important electoral vote 163 to 127, carrying eight of the fifteen slave states and seven of the fifteen free states (Map 14.1). (Wisconsin had entered the Union earlier in 1848 as the fifteenth free state.) Northern voters were not yet ready for Sumner's "one grand Northern party of Freedom," but the struggle over slavery in the territories had shaken the major parties badly.

Debate and Compromise

Southern slaveholder Zachary Taylor entered the White House in March 1849 and almost immediately shocked the nation by championing a free-soil solution to the Mexican cession. Believing that he could avoid further sectional strife if California and New Mexico skipped the territorial stage, the new president encouraged the settlers to apply for admission to the Union as states. Predominantly antislavery, the settlers began writing free-state constitutions. "For the first time," Mississippian Jefferson Davis lamented, "we are about permanently to destroy the balance of power between the sections."

MAP 14.1
The Election of 1848

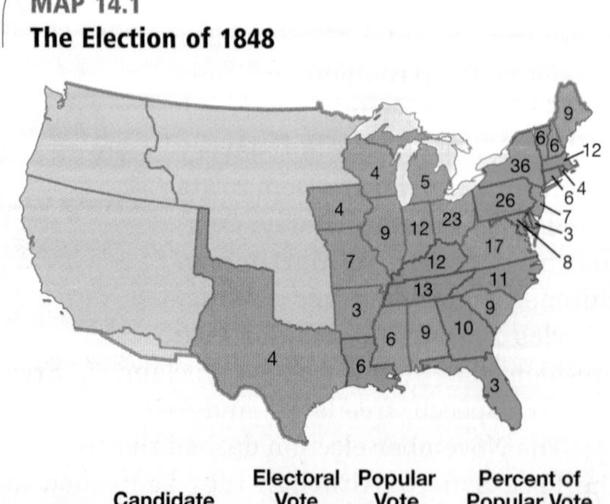

Candidate	Electoral Vote	Popular Vote	Percent of Popular Vote
Zachary Taylor (Whig)	163	1,360,099	47.4
Lewis Cass (Democrat)	127	1,220,544	42.5
Martin Van Buren (Free-Soil)	0	291,263	10.1

Congress convened in December 1849, beginning one of the most contentious and most significant sessions in its history. President Taylor urged Congress to admit California as a free state immediately and to admit New Mexico, which lagged behind a few months, as soon as it applied. Southerners exploded. A North Carolinian declared that Southerners who would "consent to be thus degraded and enslaved, ought to be whipped through their fields by their own negroes."

Into this rancorous scene stepped Senator Henry Clay of Kentucky, the architect of Union-saving compromises in the Missouri and nullification crises (see chapters 10 and 11). Clay offered a series of resolutions meant to answer and balance "all questions in controversy between the free and slave states, growing out of the subject of slavery." Admit California as a free state, he proposed, but organize the rest of the Southwest without restrictions on slavery. Require Texas to abandon its claim to parts of New Mexico, but compensate it by assuming its preannexation debt. Abolish the domestic slave trade in Washington, D.C., but confirm slavery itself in the nation's capital. Reassert Congress's lack of authority to interfere with the interstate slave trade, and enact a more effective fugitive slave law.

Both antislavery advocates and "fire-eaters" (as radical Southerners who urged secession from the Union were called) savaged Clay's plan. Senator Salmon P. Chase of Ohio ridiculed it as "sentiment for the North, substance for the South." Senator

Henry S. Foote of Mississippi denounced it as more offensive to the South than the speeches of abolitionists William Lloyd Garrison, Wendell Phillips, and Frederick Douglass combined. The most ominous response came from John C. Calhoun, who charged that unending northern agitation on the slavery question had "snapped" many of the "cords which bind these states together in one common union." He argued that the fragile political unity of North and South depended on continued equal representation in the Senate, which Clay's plan for a free California destroyed. "As things now stand," he said in February 1850, the South "cannot with safety remain in the Union."

After Clay and Calhoun had spoken, it was time for the third member of the "great triumvirate," Senator Daniel Webster of Massachusetts, to address the Senate. Like Clay, Webster defended compromise. He told Northerners that the South had legitimate complaints, but he told Southerners that secession from the Union would mean civil war. He appealed for an end to reckless proposals and, to the dismay of many Northerners, mentioned by name the Wilmot Proviso. A legal ban on slavery in the territories was unnecessary, he said, because the harsh climate effectively prohibited the expansion of cotton and slaves into the new American Southwest. "I would not take pains uselessly to reaffirm an ordinance of nature, nor to reenact the will of God," Webster declared.

Henry Clay Offering His California Compromise to the Senate on 5 February 1850

Pennsylvania-born artist Peter F. Rothermel, who specialized in dramatic historical paintings, captures the high intensity of the seventy-three-year-old Kentuckian's last significant political act. The citizens who packed the galleries of the U.S. Senate had come to hear "the lion of the day," and they were not disappointed. A renowned orator, Clay eloquently explained that his package of compromises required mutual concessions from both North and South but no sacrifice of "great principle" from either. Friends called his performance the "crowning grace to his public life." The Granger Collection, NY.

Free-soil forces recoiled from what they saw as Webster's desertion. Boston clergyman and abolitionist Theodore Parker could only conclude that "Southern men" must have offered Webster the presidency. Senator William H. Seward of New York responded that Webster's and Clay's compromise with slavery was "radically wrong and essentially vicious." He flatly rejected Calhoun's argument that Congress lacked the constitutional authority to exclude slavery from the territories. In any case, Seward said, in the most sensational moment in his address, there was a "higher law than the Constitution" — the law of God — to ensure freedom in all the public domain. Claiming that God was a Free-Soiler did nothing to cool the superheated political atmosphere.

"As things now stand, [the South] cannot with safety remain in the Union."
— HENRY CLAY

In May 1850, the Senate considered a bill that joined Clay's resolutions into a single comprehensive package, known as the Omnibus Bill because it was a vehicle on which "every sort of passenger" could ride. Clay bet that a majority of Congress wanted compromise and that the members would vote for the package, even though it might contain provisions they disliked. But the omnibus strategy backfired. Free-Soilers and proslavery Southerners voted down the comprehensive plan.

Fortunately for those who favored a settlement, Senator **Stephen A. Douglas**, a rising Democratic star from Illinois, broke the bill into its parts and skillfully ushered each through Congress. The agreement Douglas won in September 1850 was very much the one Clay had proposed in January. California entered the Union as a free state. New Mexico and Utah became territories where slavery would be decided by popular sovereignty. Texas accepted its boundary with New Mexico and received $10 million from the federal government. Congress ended the slave trade in the District of Columbia but

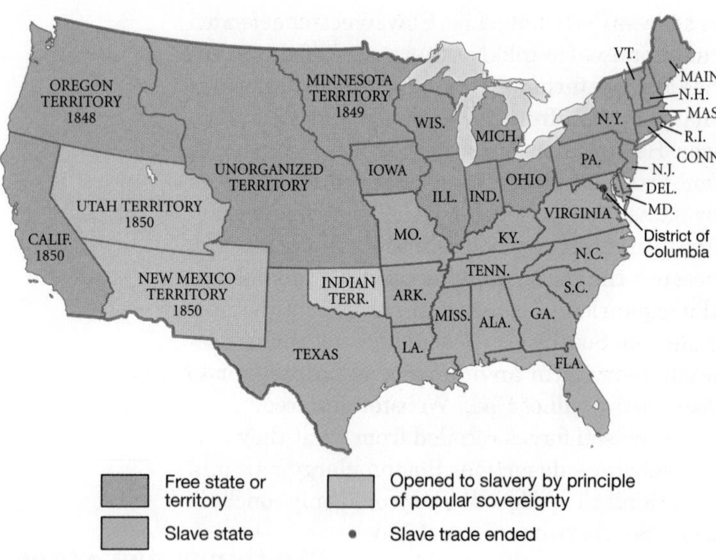

MAP 14.2
The Compromise of 1850
The patched-together sectional agreement was both clumsy and unstable. Few Americans — in either North or South — supported all five parts of the Compromise.

enacted a more stringent fugitive slave law. In September, Millard Fillmore, who had become president when Zachary Taylor died in July, signed into law each bill, collectively known as the **Compromise of 1850** (Map 14.2).

Actually, the Compromise of 1850 was not a true compromise at all. Douglas's parliamentary skill, not a spirit of conciliation, was responsible for the legislative success. Still, the nation breathed a sigh of relief, for the Compromise preserved the Union and peace for the moment. Some recognized, however, that the Compromise scarcely touched the deeper conflict over slavery. Free-Soiler Salmon Chase observed, "The question of slavery in the territories has been avoided. It has not been settled."

REVIEW Why did responses to the Wilmot Proviso split along sectional rather than party lines?

▸ The Sectional Balance Undone

The Compromise of 1850 began to come apart almost immediately. The thread that unraveled it was not slavery in the Southwest, the crux of the disagreement, but runaway slaves in New England, a part of the settlement that had previously received little attention. Instead of restoring calm, the Compromise brought the horrors of slavery into the North.

Millions of Northerners who had never seen a runaway slave confronted slavery in the early 1850s. Harriet Beecher Stowe's ***Uncle Tom's Cabin***, a novel that vividly depicts the brutality of the South's "peculiar institution," aroused passions so deep that many found goodwill toward white Southerners nearly impossible. But no groundswell of antislavery sentiment compelled Congress to reopen the slavery controversy. Politicians did it themselves. Four years after Congress stitched the sectional compromise together, it ripped the threads out. With the Kansas-Nebraska Act, it again posed the question of slavery in the territories, the deadliest of all sectional issues.

The Fugitive Slave Act

The issue of runaway slaves was as old as the Constitution, which contained a provision for the return of any "person held to service or labor in one state" who escaped to another. In 1793, a federal law gave muscle to the provision by authorizing slave owners to enter other states to recapture their slave property. Proclaiming the 1793 law a license to kidnap free blacks, northern states in the 1830s began passing "personal liberty laws" that provided fugitives with some protection.

Some northern communities also formed vigilance committees to help runaways. Each year, a few hundred slaves escaped into free states and found friendly northern "conductors" who put them aboard the **underground railroad**, which was not a railroad at all but a series of secret "stations" (hideouts) on the way to Canada. Harriet Tubman, an escaped slave from Maryland, returned to the South more than a dozen times and guided more than three hundred slaves to freedom in this way.

Furious about northern interference, Southerners in 1850 insisted on the stricter fugitive slave law that was passed as part of the Compromise. According to the **Fugitive Slave Act**, to seize an alleged slave, a slaveholder simply had to appear before a commissioner and swear that the runaway was his. The commissioner earned $10 for every individual returned to slavery but only $5 for those set free. Most galling to Northerners, the law stipulated that all citizens were expected to assist officials in apprehending runaways.

Abolitionist Theodore Parker denounced the law as "a hateful statute of kidnappers." In Boston in February 1851, an angry crowd overpowered federal marshals and snatched a runaway named Shadrach from a courtroom, put him on the underground railroad, and whisked him off to Canada. Three years later, when another Boston crowd rushed the courthouse in a failed attempt to rescue Anthony Burns, who had recently fled slavery in Richmond, a guard was shot dead. Martha Russell, a writer for the antislavery journal *National Era*, was among the angry crowd that watched Burns being escorted to the ship that would return him to Virginia. "Did you ever feel every drop of blood in you boiling and seething, throbbing and burning, until it seemed you should suffocate?" she asked. "I have felt all this today. I have seen that poor slave, Anthony Burns, carried back to slavery!"

To white Southerners, it seemed that fanatics of the "higher law" creed had whipped Northerners into a frenzy of massive resistance. Actually, the overwhelming majority of fugitives claimed by slaveholders were reenslaved peacefully. But brutal enforcement of the unpopular law had a radicalizing effect in the North, particularly in New England. To Southerners it seemed that Northerners had betrayed the Compromise. "The continued existence of the United States as one nation," warned the *Southern Literary Messenger*, "depends upon the full and faithful execution of the Fugitive Slave Bill."

"The continued existence of the United States as one nation depends upon the full and faithful execution of the Fugitive Slave Bill."
— Southern Literary Messenger

Ellen Craft in Disguise
In 1848, William and Ellen Craft, a slave couple from Macon, Georgia, executed a daring escape. Light-skinned, Ellen disguised herself as a sickly southern gentleman who was traveling to Philadelphia for medical treatment. She carried her right arm in a sling to explain why she couldn't sign travel documents. William acted as her personal servant as they anxiously made their way by train to Savannah, then on to Philadelphia by boat and train. The Crafts told their daring story throughout the North until the Fugitive Slave Law of 1850 drove them to Britain, where adoring crowds greeted them as celebrities. The Library of the University of North Carolina, Chapel Hill.

Uncle Tom's Cabin

The spectacle of shackled African Americans being herded south seared the conscience of every Northerner who witnessed such a scene. But even more Northerners were turned against slavery by a novel. **Harriet Beecher Stowe**, a white Northerner who had never set foot on a plantation, made the South's slaves into flesh-and-blood human beings almost more real than life.

A member of a famous clan of preachers, teachers, and reformers, Stowe despised the slave catchers and wrote to expose the sin of slavery. Published as a book in 1852, *Uncle Tom's Cabin, or Life among the Lowly* became a blockbuster hit, selling 300,000 copies in its first year and more than 2 million copies within ten years. Stowe's characters leaped from the page. Here was the gentle slave Uncle Tom, a Christian saint who forgave those who beat him to death; the courageous slave Eliza, who fled with her child across the frozen Ohio River; and the fiendish overseer Simon Legree, whose Louisiana plantation was a nightmare of torture and death.

***Uncle Tom's Cabin* Poster**
After Congress passed the Fugitive Slave Act in 1850, Harriet Beecher Stowe's outraged sister-in-law told her, "Now Hattie, if I could use a pen as you can, I would write something that will make this whole nation feel what an accursed thing slavery is." This poster advertising the novel Stowe wrote calls it "The Greatest Book of the Age." The novel's vivid characters gripped readers' imaginations and fueled the growing antislavery crusade. The Granger Collection, NY.

Mother of seven children, Stowe aimed her most powerful blows at slavery's destructive impact on the family. Her character Eliza succeeds in keeping her son from being sold away, but other mothers are not so fortunate. When told that her infant has been sold, Lucy drowns herself. Driven half mad by the sale of a son and daughter, Cassy decides "never again [to] let a child live to grow up!" She gives her third child an opiate and watches as "he slept to death."

Northerners shed tears and sang praises to *Uncle Tom's Cabin*. The poet Henry Wadsworth Longfellow judged it "one of the greatest triumphs recorded in literary history." What Northerners accepted as truth, Southerners denounced as slander. The Virginian George F. Holmes proclaimed Stowe a member of the "Woman's Rights" and "Higher Law" schools and dismissed the novel as a work of "intense fanaticism." Although it is impossible to measure precisely the impact of a novel on public opinion, *Uncle Tom's Cabin* clearly helped to crystallize northern sentiment against slavery and to confirm white Southerners' suspicion that they no longer received any sympathy in the free states.

Other writers — ex-slaves who knew life in slave cabins firsthand — also produced stinging indictments of slavery. Solomon Northup's compelling *Twelve Years a Slave* (1853) sold 27,000 copies in two years, and the powerful *Narrative of the Life of Frederick Douglass, as Told by Himself* (1845) eventually sold more than 30,000 copies. But no work touched the North's conscience as did the novel by a free white woman. A decade after its publication, when Stowe visited Abraham Lincoln at the White House, he reportedly said, "So you are the little woman who wrote the book that made this great war."

The Kansas-Nebraska Act

As the 1852 election approached, the Democrats and Whigs sought to close the sectional rifts that had opened within their parties. For their presidential nominee, the Democrats turned to Franklin Pierce of New Hampshire. Pierce's well-known sympathy with southern views on public issues caused his northern critics to include him among the "**doughfaces**," northern men malleable enough to champion southern causes. The Whigs were less successful in bridging differences. Adopting the formula that had worked in 1848, they chose another Mexican-American War hero, General Winfield Scott of Virginia. But the Whigs' northern and southern factions were hopelessly divided, and the party suffered a humiliating defeat. The Democrat Pierce carried twenty-seven states to Scott's four and won the electoral college vote 254 to 42 (see Map 14.4, page 442). In the afterglow of the Compromise of 1850, the Free-Soil Party lost almost half of the voters who had turned to it in the tumultuous political atmosphere of 1848.

Eager to leave the sectional controversy behind, the new president turned swiftly to foreign expansion. Manifest destiny remained robust. (See "Beyond America's Borders," page 440–441.) Pierce's major objective was Cuba, which was owned by Spain and in which slavery flourished, but antislavery Northerners blocked Cuba's acquisition to keep more slave territory from entering the Union.

Pierce's fortunes improved in Mexico. In 1853, diplomat James Gadsden negotiated a $10 million purchase of some 30,000 square miles of land in present-day Arizona and New Mexico. The **Gadsden Purchase** stemmed from the dream of a transcontinental railroad to California and Pierce's desire for a southern route through Mexican territory. The booming population of the Pacific coast made it obvious that the vast, loose-jointed Republic needed a railroad to bind it together. Talk of a railroad ignited rivalries in cities from New Orleans to Chicago as they maneuvered to become the eastern terminus. The desire for a transcontinental railroad evolved into a sectional contest, which by the 1850s inevitably involved slavery.

Illinois's Democratic senator Stephen A. Douglas badly wanted the transcontinental railroad for Chicago, and his chairmanship of the Senate Committee on Territories provided him with an opportunity. Any railroad that ran west from Chicago would pass through a region that Congress in 1830 had designated a "permanent" Indian reserve (see chapter 11). Douglas proposed giving this vast area between the Missouri River and the Rocky Mountains an Indian name, Nebraska, and then throwing the Indians out. Once the region achieved territorial status, whites could survey and sell the land, establish a civil government, and build a railroad.

Nebraska lay within the Louisiana Purchase and, according to the Missouri Compromise of 1820, was closed to slavery (see chapter 10). Since Douglas could not count on New England to back western economic development, he needed southern votes to pass his Nebraska legislation. But Southerners had no incentive to create another free territory or to help a northern city win the transcontinental railroad. Southerners, however, agreed to help if Congress organized Nebraska according to popular sovereignty. That meant giving slavery a chance in Nebraska Territory and reopening the dangerous issue of slavery expansion, which Douglas himself had helped to resolve only four years earlier.

In January 1854, Douglas introduced his bill to organize Nebraska Territory, leaving to the settlers themselves the decision about slavery. At southern insistence, and even though he knew it would "raise a hell of a storm," Douglas added an explicit repeal of the Missouri Compromise. Indeed, the Nebraska bill raised a storm of controversy. Free-Soilers branded Douglas's plan "a gross violation of a sacred pledge" and an "atrocious plot" to transform free land into a "dreary region of despotism, inhabited by masters and slaves."

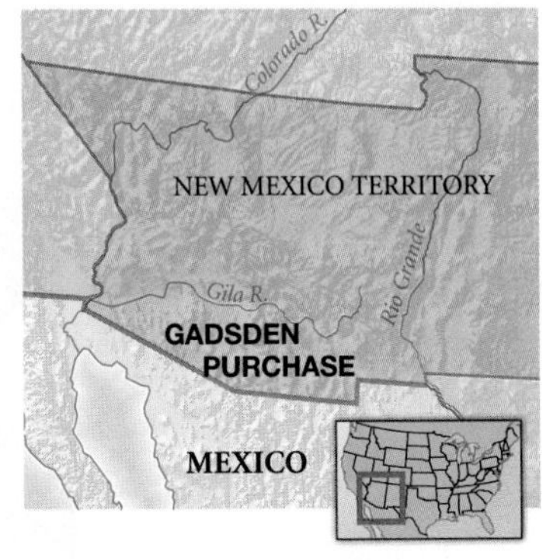

Gadsden Purchase, 1853

Undaunted, Douglas skillfully shepherded the explosive bill through Congress in May 1854. Nine-tenths of the southern members (Whigs and Democrats) and half of the northern Democrats cast votes in favor of the bill. Like Douglas, most northern supporters believed that popular sovereignty would make Nebraska free territory. Ominously, however, half of the northern Democrats broke with their party and opposed the bill. In its final form, the **Kansas-Nebraska Act** divided the huge territory in two: Nebraska and Kansas (Map 14.3). With this act, the government pushed the Plains Indians farther west, making way for farmers and railroads.

REVIEW Why did the Fugitive Slave Act provoke such strong opposition in the North?

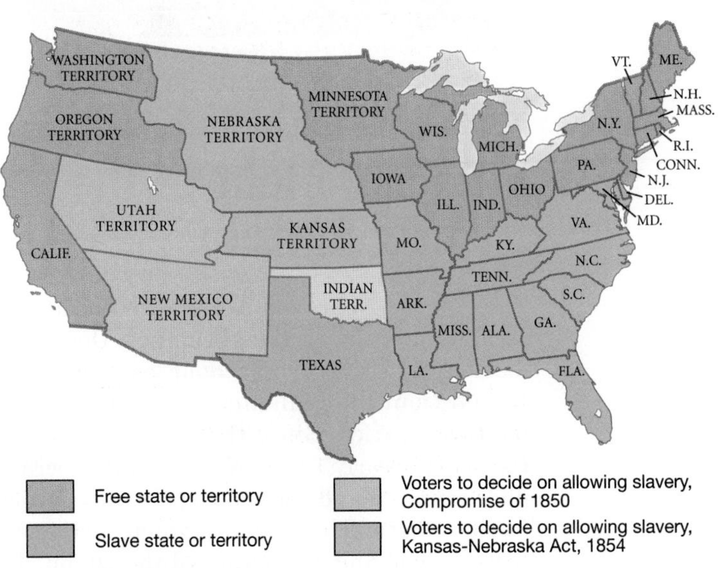

MAP ACTIVITY

MAP 14.3 The Kansas-Nebraska Act, 1854

Americans hardly thought twice about dispossessing the Indians of land guaranteed them by treaty, but many worried about the outcome of repealing the Missouri Compromise and opening up the region to slavery.

READING THE MAP: How many slave states and how many free states does the map show? Estimate the percentage of new territory likely to be settled by slaveholders.

CONNECTIONS: Who would be more likely to support changes in government legislation to discontinue the Missouri Compromise — slaveholders or free-soil advocates? Why?

Papago Indians
Major William Emory's Mexican boundary survey of the early 1850s provided Americans with glimpses of a little-known southwestern frontier. In this drawing, Papago Indian women in Arizona Territory use sticks to knock down cactus fruit. The Center for American History, The University of Texas at Austin.

▸ Realignment of the Party System

The Kansas-Nebraska Act marked a fateful escalation of the sectional conflict. Douglas's measure had several consequences, none more crucial than the realignment of the nation's political parties. Since the rise of the Whig Party in the early 1830s, Whigs and Democrats had organized and channeled political conflict in the nation. This party system dampened sectionalism and strengthened the Union. To achieve national political power, the Whigs and Democrats had to retain their strength in both North and South. Strong northern and southern wings required that each party compromise and find positions acceptable to both wings.

The Kansas-Nebraska controversy shattered this stabilizing political system. In place of two national parties with bisectional strength, the mid-1850s witnessed the development of one party heavily dominated by one section and another party entirely limited to the other section. Rather than "national" parties, the country had what one critic disdainfully called "geographic" parties. Parties now sharpened ideological and policy differences between the sections and no longer muffled moral issues such as slavery. The new party system also thwarted political compromise and instead promoted political polarization that further jeopardized the Union.

The Old Parties: Whigs and Democrats

As early as the Mexican-American War, members of the Whig Party had clashed over the future of slavery in annexed Mexican lands. By 1852, the Whig Party could please its proslavery southern wing or its antislavery northern wing but not both. The Whigs' miserable showing in the election of 1852 made a despairing New York Whig ask, "Was there ever such a deluge since Noah's time?" It was clear that the Whigs were no longer a strong national party. By 1856, after more than two decades of contesting the Democrats, they were hardly a party at all (Map 14.4).

The collapse of the Whig Party left the Democrats as the country's only national party. Although the Democrats were not immune to the disruptive pressures of the territorial question, they discovered in popular sovereignty a doctrine that many Democrats could support. Even so, popular sovereignty very nearly undid the party. When Stephen Douglas applied the doctrine to the part of the Louisiana Purchase where slavery had been barred, he divided northern Democrats and destroyed the dominance of the Democratic Party in the free states. After 1854, even though the Democrats were a southern-dominated party, they remained a national political organization. Gains in the South more than balanced Democratic losses in the North. During the 1850s, Democrats elected two presidents and won majorities in Congress in almost every election.

The breakup of the Whigs and the disaffection of significant numbers of northern

Democrats set many Americans politically adrift. As they searched for new political harbors, Americans found that the death of the old party system created a multitude of fresh political alternatives.

The New Parties: Know-Nothings and Republicans

Dozens of new political organizations vied for voters' attention. Out of the confusion, two emerged as true contenders. One grew out of the slavery controversy, a coalition of indignant antislavery Northerners. The other arose from an entirely different split in American society, between Roman Catholic immigrants and native Protestants.

The tidal wave of immigrants that broke over America from 1845 to 1855 produced a nasty backlash among Protestant Americans, who believed that the American Republic was about to drown in a sea of Roman Catholics from Ireland and Germany (see Figure 12.2, page 367). Most immigrants became Democrats because they perceived that party as more tolerant of newcomers than were the Whigs. But in the 1850s, they met sharp political opposition when nativists (individuals who were anti-immigrant) began to organize, first into secret fraternal societies and then in 1854 into a political party. Recruits swore never to vote for either foreign-born or Roman Catholic candidates and not to reveal any information about the organization. When questioned, they said, "I know nothing." Officially, they were the American Party, but most Americans called them **Know-Nothings**.

The Know-Nothings exploded onto the political stage in 1854 and 1855 with a series of dazzling successes. They captured state legislatures in the Northeast, West, and South and claimed dozens of seats in Congress. Their greatest triumph came in Massachusetts, a favorite destination for Irish immigrants. Know-Nothings elected the Massachusetts governor, all of the state senators, all but two of the state representatives, and all of the congressmen. Members of the Democratic and Whig parties described the phenomenal success of the Know-Nothings as a "tornado," a "hurricane," and "a freak of political insanity." By 1855, an observer might reasonably have concluded that the Know-Nothings had emerged as the successor to the Whigs.

The Know-Nothings were not the only new party making noise, however. One of the new

The Realignment of Political Parties

Whig Party

1848 Whig Party divides into two factions over slavery; Whigs adopt no platform and nominate war hero Zachary Taylor, who is elected president.

1852 Whigs nominate war hero General Winfield Scott for president; deep divisions in party result in humiliating loss.

1856 Shattered by sectionalism, Whig Party fields no presidential candidate.

Democratic Party

1848 President Polk declines to run again; Democratic Party nominates Lewis Cass, the man most closely associated with popular sovereignty, but avoids firm platform position on expansion of slavery.

1852 To bridge rift in party, Democrats nominate northern war veteran with southern views, Franklin Pierce, for president; he wins with 50.9 percent of popular vote.

1856 Democrat James Buchanan elected president on ambiguous platform; his prosouthern actions in office alienate northern branch of party.

1860 Democrats split into northern Democrats and southern Democrats; each group fields its own presidential candidate.

Free-Soil Party

1848 Breakaway antislavery Democrats and antislavery Whigs found Free-Soil Party; presidential candidate Martin Van Buren takes 10.1 percent of popular vote, mainly from Whigs.

1852 Support for Free-Soil Party ebbs in wake of Compromise of 1850; Free-Soil presidential candidate John P. Hale wins only 5 percent of popular vote.

American (Know-Nothing) Party

1851 Anti-immigrant American (Know-Nothing) Party formed.

1854–1855 American Party succeeds in state elections and attracts votes from northern and southern Whigs in congressional elections.

1856 Know-Nothing presidential candidate Millard Fillmore wins only Maryland; party subsequently disbands.

Republican Party

1854 Republican Party formed to oppose expansion of slavery in territories; attracts northern Whigs, northern Democrats, and Free-Soilers.

1856 Republican presidential candidate John C. Frémont wins all but five northern states, establishing Republicans as main challenger to Democrats.

1860 Republican Abraham Lincoln wins all northern states except New Jersey and is elected president in four-way race against divided Democrats and southern Constitutional Union Party.

BEYOND AMERICA'S BORDERS

Filibusters: The Underside of Manifest Destiny

Each year, the citizens of Caborca, a small town in the northern state of Sonora, Mexico, celebrate the defeat there in 1857 of an American army. The invaders did not wear the uniform of the U.S. Army, but instead marched as the private "Arizona Colonization Company." Their commander, Henry A. Crabb, a Mississippian who had followed the gold rush to California, saw fresh opportunity in the civil disorder that reigned south of the border. When the governor of Sonora faced an insurrection, he invited Crabb to help him repress his enemies in exchange for mineral rights and land.

Crabb marched his band of sixty-eight heavily armed ex-miners south from Los Angeles, but by the time the Americans arrived, the governor had put down the insurgency, and the Mexicans turned on the American invaders. Every American except one died either in battle or at the hands of Mexican firing squads. Crabb's head was preserved in alcohol and placed on display as a symbol of victory.

Henry Crabb was one of thousands of American adventurers, known as "filibusters" (from the Spanish *filibustero,* meaning "freebooter" or "pirate"), who in the mid-nineteenth century joined private armies that invaded foreign countries throughout the Western Hemisphere. Although these expeditions violated the U.S. Neutrality Act of 1818, private American armies attacked Canada, Mexico, Ecuador, Honduras, Cuba, and Nicaragua and planned invasions of places as far away as the Hawaiian kingdom. The federal government usually cracked down on filibusters, fearing that private invasions would jeopardize legitimate diplomatic efforts to promote trade and acquire territory.

Filibusters joined invading armies for reasons that ranged from personal gain to validating manhood. Many saw themselves as carrying on the work of manifest destiny, extending America's reach beyond Texas, California, and Oregon, the prizes of the 1830s and 1840s. In addition, during the 1840s and 1850s, when Northerners insisted on containing slavery's spread to the North and West, Southerners joined filibustering expeditions to expand slavery south beyond the U.S. border. A leading proslavery ideologue, George Fitzhugh, defended filibustering through historical comparison: "They who condemn the modern filibuster . . . must also condemn the discoverers and settlers of America, of the East Indies of Holland, and of the Indian and Pacific Oceans."

One of the most vigorous filibusters to appeal to southern interests was Narciso López, a Venezuelan-born Cuban who dedicated himself to the liberation of Cuba from Spanish rule. López claimed that Spain was planning to free Cuba's slaves, and he told Southerners that "self-preservation" demanded that they seize the island. In 1850, after gaining the support of Governor John Quitman of Mississippi, López and an army of 500 landed on the northwest coast of Cuba, but Spanish troops quickly drove them off. Two months later, he tried again. This time, the Spaniards crushed the invasion, killing 200 filibusters, shipping 160 prisoners to Spain, executing 50 invaders by firing squad, and publicly garroting López. John Quitman gathered another army of several thousand, but federal authorities seized one of his ships and ended the threat to Cuba.

The most successful of all filibusters was William Walker of Tennessee, a restless dreamer who longed for an empire of his own south of the border. In May 1855, Walker and an army of fifty-six men sailed from San Francisco to the west coast of Nicaragua. Two thousand reinforcements and a civil war in Nicaragua gave Walker his victory. He had himself proclaimed president, legalized slavery, and called on Southerners to come raise cotton, sugar, and coffee in "a magnificent country." Hundreds of Southerners took up land grants, but Walker's

antislavery organizations provoked by the Kansas-Nebraska Act called itself the **Republican Party**. The Republicans attempted to unite all those who opposed the extension of slavery into any territory of the United States, including Whigs, Free-Soilers, anti-Nebraska Democrats, and even Know-Nothings.

The Republican creed tapped into the basic beliefs and values of Northerners. Slavery, the Republicans believed, degraded the dignity of white labor by associating work with blacks and servility. As evidence, they pointed to the South, where, one Republican claimed, three-quarters of whites "retire to the outskirts of civilization, where they live a semi-savage life, sinking deeper and more hopelessly into barbarism with every succeeding generation." Republicans warned that the insatiable slaveholders of the South, whom antislavery Northerners called the "Slave Power," were conspiring through their control

Filibustering in Nicaragua
In this image of a pitched battle in Nicaragua in 1856, Costa Ricans on foot fight American filibusters on horseback. Costa Rican soldiers and their Central American allies defeated William Walker's filibusteros in 1857. Before then, the Pierce administration had extended diplomatic recognition to Walker's regime, and white Southerners had cheered Walker's attempt to "introduce civilization" in Nicaragua and to develop its rich resources "with slave labor." *London Illustrated Times*, May 24, 1856.

regime survived only until 1857, when a coalition of Central American countries sent Walker packing. Walker doggedly launched four other attacks on Nicaragua, but in 1860 Honduran forces captured and shot him.

Filibustering had lost steam by the time of the U.S. Civil War, but the Confederacy paid a diplomatic price for its association with filibustering. The Guatemalan minister Antonio José de Irisarri declared that there was "no foreign Nation which can have less cause for sympathy with the enemies of the American Union, than the Republics of Central America, because from the Southern States were set on foot those filibustering expeditions." No Central American nation recognized Confederate independence.

The peoples of Central America and the Caribbean, like the inhabitants of Sonora, still harbor bitter memories of filibusters' private wars of imperialism and honor those who fought off American advances. When U.S. Marines occupied Nicaragua in the 1920s, insurgents found inspiration in their country's defeat of William Walker's army of freebooters eighty years earlier. In 1951, on the centennial of López's invasion, Cubans erected a monument at the very spot where his ill-fated army came ashore. Costa Ricans celebrate Juan Santamaria as their national martyr for his courage in battling William Walker. Memories of the invasions by nineteenth-century filibusters set the stage for anti-American sentiment in Latin America that lingers to this day.

America in a Global Context

1. How did supporters of filibustering justify the practice?
2. What was the relationship between filibustering and sectional politics in the United States in the 1840s and 1850s?
3. Why would an expansionist-minded U.S. government frown on filibustering?

of the Democratic Party to expand slavery, subvert liberty, and undermine the Constitution.

Only if slavery was restricted to the South, Republicans believed, could the system of free labor flourish elsewhere. In the North, one Republican declared in 1854, "every man holds his fortune in his own right arm; and his position in society, in life, is to be tested by his own individual character" (see chapter 12). Without slavery, western territories would provide vast economic opportunity for free men. Powerful images of liberty and opportunity attracted a wide range of Northerners to the Republican cause.

Women as well as men rushed to the new Republican Party. Indeed, three women helped found the party in Ripon, Wisconsin, in 1854. Although they could not vote before the Civil War and suffered from a raft of other legal handicaps, women nevertheless participated in partisan politics by writing campaign literature,

1848

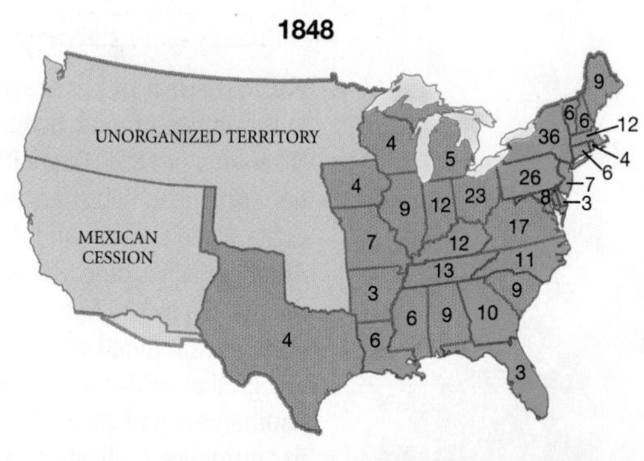

Candidate	Electoral Vote	Popular Vote	Percent of Popular Vote
Zachary Taylor (Whig)	163	1,360,099	47.4
Lewis Cass (Democrat)	127	1,220,544	42.5
Martin Van Buren (Free-Soil)	0	291,263	10.1

1852

Candidate	Electoral Vote	Popular Vote	Percent of Popular Vote
Franklin Pierce (Democrat)	254	1,601,274	50.9
Winfield Scott (Whig)	42	1,386,580	44.1
John P. Hale (Free-Soil)	5	155,825	5.0

1856

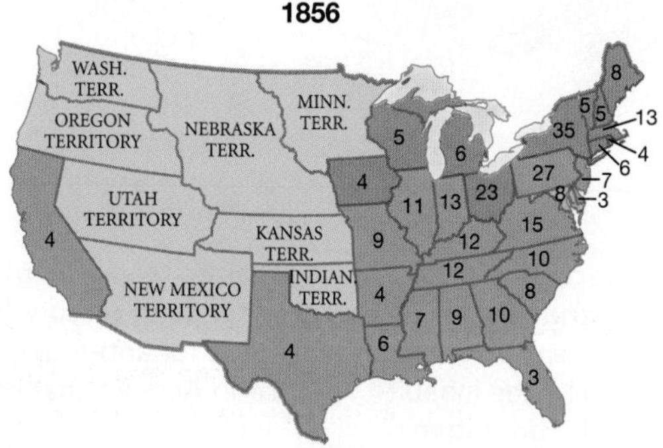

Candidate	Electoral Vote	Popular Vote	Percent of Popular Vote
James Buchanan (Democrat)	174	1,838,169	45.3
John C. Frémont (Republican)	114	1,341,264	33.1
Millard Fillmore (American)	8	874,534	21.6

1860

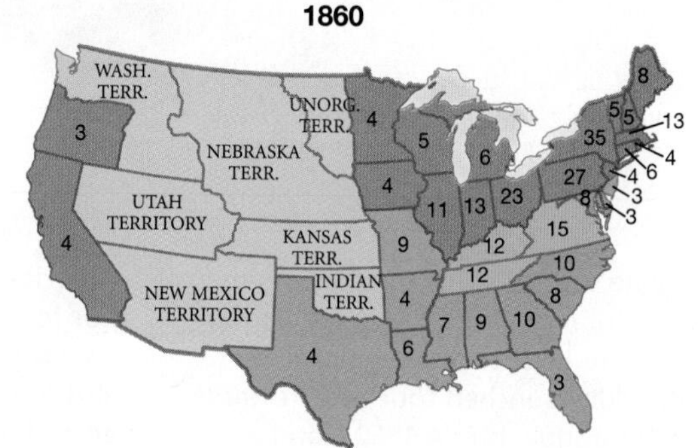

Candidate	Electoral Vote	Popular Vote	Percent of Popular Vote
Abraham Lincoln (Republican)	180	1,866,452	39.9
John C. Breckinridge (Southern Democrat)	72	847,953	18.1
Stephen A. Douglas (Northern Democrat)	12	1,375,157	29.4
John Bell (Constitutional Union)	39	590,631	12.6

MAP ACTIVITY

MAP 14.4 Political Realignment, 1848–1860

In 1848, slavery and sectionalism began taking their toll on the country's party system. The Whig Party was an early casualty. By 1860, national parties — those that contended for votes in both North and South — had been replaced by regional parties.

READING THE MAP: Which states did the Democrats pick up in 1852 compared to 1848? Which of these states did the Democrats lose in 1856? Compare the general geographic location of the states won by the Republicans in 1856 versus those won in 1860.

CONNECTIONS: In the 1860 election, which party benefited the most from the western and midwestern states added to the Union since 1848? Why do you think these states chose to back this party?

marching in parades, giving speeches, and lobbying voters. Women's antislavery fervor attracted them to the Republican Party, and participation in party politics in turn nurtured the woman's rights movement. Susan B. Anthony, who attended Republican meetings throughout the 1850s, found that her political activity made her disfranchisement all the more galling. She and other women

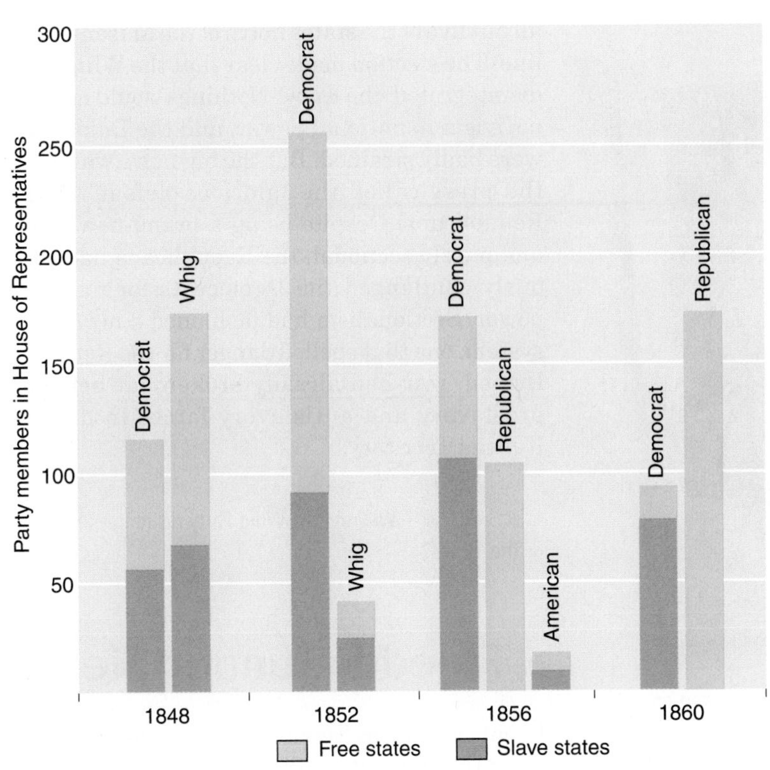

FIGURE 14.1 Changing Political Landscape, 1848–1860
The polarization of American politics between free states and slave states occurred in little more than a decade.

in the North worked on behalf of antislavery and to secure both woman suffrage and the right of married women to control their own property. (See "Seeking the American Promise," page 446.)

The Election of 1856

The election of 1856 revealed that the Republicans had become the Democrats' main challenger, and slavery in the territories, not nativism, was the election's principal issue. When the Know-Nothings insisted on a platform that endorsed the Kansas-Nebraska Act, most of the Northerners walked out, and the party came apart. The few Know-Nothings who remained nominated ex-president Millard Fillmore.

The Republicans adopted a platform that focused almost exclusively on "making every territory free." When they labeled slavery a "relic of barbarism," they signaled that they had written off the South. For president, they nominated the dashing soldier and California adventurer **John C. Frémont**, "Pathfinder of the West." Frémont lacked political credentials,

Know-Nothing Banner
Convinced that the incendiary issue of slavery had blinded Americans to the greater dangers of uncontrolled immigration and foreign influence, the Know-Nothings nominated Millard Fillmore for president in 1856. There is more than a little irony in this banner's appeal to "Native Americans" to stem the invasion from abroad. The Know-Nothings were referring to native-born Americans, but bona fide Native Americans — American Indians — also faced an invasion, and to them it made little difference whether the aggressors were fresh off the boat or born in the United States. Milwaukee County Historical Society.

John and Jessie Frémont Poster
The election of 1856 marked the first time a candidate's wife appeared on campaign items. In this poster, Jessie Benton Frémont rides a spirited horse alongside her husband, John C. Frémont, the Republican Party's presidential nominee. Jessie helped plan her husband's campaign, coauthored his election biography, and drew northern women into political activity as never before. "What a shame that women can't vote!" declared abolitionist Lydia Maria Child. "We'd carry 'our Jessie' into the White House on our shoulders, wouldn't we." Critics of Jessie's violation of women's traditional sphere ridiculed both Frémonts. A San Francisco man pronounced Jessie "the better man of the two." Museum of American Political Life.

but his wife, **Jessie Frémont**, the daughter of Senator Thomas Hart Benton of Missouri, knew the political map as well as her husband knew the western trails. Though careful to maintain a proper public image, the vivacious young mother and antislavery zealot helped attract voters and draw women into politics.

The Democrats, successful in 1852 in bridging sectional differences by nominating a northern man with southern principles, chose another "doughface," James Buchanan of Pennsylvania. They took refuge in the ambiguity of popular sovereignty and portrayed the Republicans as extremists ("Black Republican Abolitionists") whose support for the Wilmot Proviso risked pushing the South out of the Union.

The Democratic strategy carried the day for Buchanan, but Frémont did astonishingly well. Buchanan won 174 electoral votes against Frémont's 114 and Fillmore's 8 (see Map 14.4, page 442). Campaigning under the banner "Free soil, Free men, Frémont," the Republican carried all but five of the states north of the Mason-Dixon line. The election made clear that the Whigs had disintegrated, the Know-Nothings would not ride nativism to national power, and the Democrats were badly strained. But the big news was what the press called the "glorious defeat" of the Republicans. Despite being a brand-new party and purely sectional, the Republicans had seriously challenged the Democrats for national power. Sectionalism had fashioned a new party system, one that spelled danger for the Republic. Indeed, war had already broken out between proslavery and antislavery forces in distant Kansas Territory.

REVIEW Why did the Whig Party disintegrate in the 1850s?

▸ Freedom under Siege

Events in Kansas Territory in the mid-1850s provided the young Republican organization with an enormous boost and help explain its strong showing in the election of 1856. Republicans organized around the premise that the slaveholding South provided a profound threat to "free soil, free labor, and free men," and now Kansas reeled with violence that Republicans argued was southern in origin. Kansas, Republicans claimed, opened a window to southern values and intentions. Republicans also pointed to the brutal beating by a Southerner of a respected northern senator on the floor of Congress. Even the Supreme Court, in the Republicans' view, reflected the South's drive toward tyranny and minority rule. Then, in 1858, the issues dividing North and South received an extraordinary airing in a senatorial contest in Illinois, when the nation's foremost Democrat debated a resourceful Republican.

"Bleeding Kansas"

Three days after the House of Representatives approved the Kansas-Nebraska Act in 1854, Senator William H. Seward of New York boldly challenged the South. "Come on then, Gentlemen of the Slave States," he cried, "since there is no escaping your challenge, I accept it in behalf of the cause of freedom. We will engage in competition for the virgin soil of Kansas, and God give the victory to the side which is stronger in numbers as it is in right." Because of Stephen Douglas, popular sovereignty would determine whether Kansas became slave or free. No one really expected New Mexico and Utah, with their harsh landscapes, to become slave states when Congress instituted popular sovereignty there in 1850, but many believed that Kansas could go either way. Free-state and slave-state settlers each sought a majority at the ballot box, claimed God's blessing, and kept their rifles ready.

In both North and South, emigrant aid societies sprang up to promote settlement from free states or slave states. The most famous, the New England Emigrant Aid Company, sponsored some 1,240 settlers in 1854 and 1855. Tiny rural communities from Virginia to Texas raised money to support proslavery settlers.

Missourians, already bordered on the east by the free state of Illinois and on the north by the free state of Iowa, especially thought it important to secure Kansas for slavery. Thousands of rough frontiersmen, egged on by Missouri senator David Rice Atchison, invaded Kansas. "There are eleven hundred coming over from Platte County to vote," Atchison reported, "and if that ain't enough we can send five thousand — enough to kill every God-damned abolitionist in the Territory." Not surprisingly, proslavery candidates swept the territorial elections in November 1854. When Kansas's first territorial legislature met, it enacted a raft of proslavery laws. Antislavery men, for example, were barred from holding office or serving on juries. Ever-pliant President Pierce endorsed the work of the fraudulently elected legislature. Free-soil Kansans did not. They elected their own legislature, which promptly banned both slaves and free blacks from the territory. Organized into two rival governments and armed to the teeth, Kansans verged on civil war.

Fighting broke out on the morning of May 21, 1856, when several hundred proslavery men raided the town of Lawrence, the center of free-state settlement. Only one man died, but the "Sack of Lawrence," as free-soil forces called it, inflamed northern opinion. Elsewhere in Kansas, news of events in Lawrence provoked **John Brown**, a free-soil settler, to announce that "it was better that a score of bad men should die than that one man who came here to make Kansas a Free State should be driven out" and to lead the posse that massacred five allegedly proslavery settlers along Pottawatomie Creek (see pages 427–428). After that, guerrilla war engulfed the territory.

Just as **"Bleeding Kansas"** gave the fledgling Republican Party fresh ammunition for its battle against the Slave Power, so too did an event that occurred in the national capital. In May 1856, Senator Charles Sumner of Massachusetts delivered a speech titled "The Crime against Kansas," which included a scalding personal attack on South Carolina senator Andrew P. Butler. Sumner described Butler as a "Don Quixote" who had taken as his mistress "the harlot, slavery."

Preston Brooks, a young South Carolina member of the House and a kinsman of Butler's,

"Bleeding Kansas," 1850s

Armed Settlers Near Lawrence, Kansas
Armed with rifles, knives, swords, and pistols, these tough antislavery men gathered for a photograph near the free-soil town of Lawrence in 1856. Equally well-armed proslavery men attacked and briefly occupied Lawrence that same year. Kansas State Historical Society.

SEEKING THE AMERICAN PROMISE

"A Purse of Her Own": Petitioning for the Right to Own Property

In the early Republic, as today, having money and deciding how to spend it was a fundamental aspect of independent adulthood. Yet antebellum married women were denied this privilege, because of the laws of *coverture*, which placed wives under the full legal control of their husbands (see chapter 10). By law, husbands made all the financial decisions in a household. Even money that a wife earned or brought into a marriage from gifts or inheritance was not hers to control as long as she remained married. Ernestine Potowsky Rose of New York City thought that was wrong, and she became the first woman in the United States to take action to change the law.

Born in Poland in 1810, Ernestine Potowsky was the daughter of a rabbi, which meant that her destiny was fixed: an arranged marriage, many children, and a life strictly governed by religious law. Ernestine rejected this fate and left home for London. There, at age nineteen, she married William Rose, a like-minded socialist intellectual. The couple later emigrated to the United States and settled in New York City, where William, a jeweler, started a business.

Ernestine soon learned of a bill presented in 1837 in the New York assembly proposing that married women, "equally with males and unmarried females, possess the rights of *life*, *liberty*, and PROPERTY, and are equally entitled to be protected in all three." But opponents feared that it would undermine a central pillar of marriage: the assumption that husband and wife shared identical interests. How could a wife not trust her husband to control the money? Predictably, the bill failed to pass.

The devastating panics of 1837 and 1839 (see chapter 11), and the resulting bankruptcies, soon changed some traditionalists' minds about wives and property. Men in several state legislatures crafted laws that shielded a wife's inherited property from creditors collecting debts from her husband. Mississippi led the way in 1839, and by 1848 eighteen states had modified property laws in the name of family protection.

In New York, as support for such a law grew, Ernestine Rose mobilized a new constituency of women activists around the far more egalitarian argument that married women should be able to own and control property. She circulated petitions and spoke from public platforms, often joined by Elizabeth Cady Stanton, a young wife from western New York. In April 1848, three months before the Seneca Falls woman's rights convention (see chapter 12), the New York assembly finally awarded married women sole authority over property they brought to a marriage.

Rose welcomed the new law but recognized its key shortcoming: It made no provision for wages earned by a married woman. Nor did it alter inheritance laws that limited a widow's share of her husband's estate. Speaking at every national woman's rights convention from 1850 to 1860, Rose argued for women's economic independence. In 1853, she itemized the limited belongings allowed to a widow if her husband died without a will: "As to the personal property, after all debts and liabilities are discharged, the widow receives one-half of it; and, in addition, the law allows her, her own wearing apparel, her own ornaments, proper to her station, one bed, with appurtenances for the same, a stove, the Bible, family pictures, and all the school-books; also all spinning wheels and weaving looms, one table, six chairs, ten cups and saucers, one tea-pot, one sugar dish, and six spoons." While her audience laughed appreciatively, Rose questioned whether the spoons would be teaspoons, "since a widow might live on tea only." Spinning wheels, long gone in 1853, needed no elaboration from her to make the law sound pathetically out-of-date.

Of particular concern to Rose was the plight of poor wives. She and Susan B. Anthony traveled the state of New York and encountered women trapped in marriages with husbands who failed to support their dependents. Anthony, herself a life-

felt compelled to defend the honor of both his aged relative and his state. On May 22, Brooks entered the Senate, where he found Sumner working at his desk. He beat Sumner over the head with his cane until Sumner lay bleeding and unconscious on the floor. Brooks resigned his seat in the House, only to be promptly reelected. In the North, the southern hero became an archvillain. Like "Bleeding Kansas," "Bleeding Sumner" provided the Republican Party with a potent symbol of the South's "twisted and violent civilization."

The *Dred Scott* Decision

Political debate over slavery in the territories became so heated in part because the Constitution lacked precision on the issue. In 1857, in the long single woman, recalled that "as I passed from town to town I was made to feel the great evil of women's utter dependence on man. . . . Woman must have a purse of her own."

Rose's efforts paid off. In 1860, New York amended its law to include a wife's wages as her own, but only if she earned the money outside the household. Money earned selling eggs or caring for boarders still went directly into the husband's pocket. Perhaps the most significant beneficiaries of this law were women whose husbands were incompetent to support them or who had deserted them. These husbands now had no right to their wives' hard-gained earnings.

The revised New York law made other important changes to coverture. A wife could now sue (or be sued), make legal contracts of her own, and serve as joint guardian of her children, "with equal powers, rights and duties in regard to them." These changes, adopted in many states after 1860, began the long (and still ongoing) process of elevating married women to near equality with men.

Ernestine Rose
Ernestine Rose, in her mid-forties when this photograph was taken, managed to hold a smile for the several minutes required to capture her image on a photographic plate. Schlesinger Library, Radcliffe Institute for Advanced Study, Harvard University.

Questions for Consideration

1. What do the laws of coverture reveal about how married women were viewed in antebellum America?
2. Why did a woman need "a purse of her own"?
3. Why did men eventually agree to grant married women property rights?

case of *Dred Scott v. Sandford*, the Supreme Court announced its understanding of the meaning of the Constitution regarding slavery in the territories. The Court's decision demonstrated that it enjoyed no special immunity from the sectional and partisan passions that were convulsing the land.

In 1833, an army doctor bought the slave Dred Scott in St. Louis, Missouri, and took him as his personal servant to Fort Armstrong, Illinois, and then to Fort Snelling in Wisconsin Territory. Back in St. Louis in 1846, Scott, with the help of white friends, sued to prove that he and his family were legally entitled to their freedom. Scott based his claim on his travels and residences. He argued that living in Illinois, a free state, and Wisconsin, a free territory, had made his family free and that they remained free even after returning to Missouri, a slave state.

In 1857, the U.S. Supreme Court ruled in the case. Chief Justice **Roger B. Taney**, who hated Republicans and detested racial equality, wrote the Court's decision. First, the Court ruled in the ***Dred Scott* decision** that Scott could not legally claim violation of his constitutional rights because he was not a citizen of the United States. When the Constitution was written, Taney said, blacks "were regarded as beings of an inferior order . . . so far inferior, that they had no rights which the white man was bound to respect." Second, the laws of Dred Scott's home state, Missouri, determined his status, and thus his travels in free areas did not make him free. Third, Congress's power to make "all needful rules and regulations" for the territories did not include the right to prohibit slavery. The Court explicitly declared the Missouri Compromise unconstitutional, even though it had already been voided by the Kansas-Nebraska Act.

The Taney Court's extreme proslavery decision outraged Republicans. By denying the federal government the right to exclude slavery in the territories, it cut the legs out from under the Republican Party. Moreover, as the *New York Tribune* lamented, the decision cleared the way for "all our Territories . . . to be ripened into Slave States." Particularly frightening to African Americans in the North was the Court's declaration that free blacks were not citizens and had no rights.

The Republican rebuttal to the *Dred Scott* ruling relied heavily on the dissenting opinion of Justice Benjamin R. Curtis. Scott *was* a citizen of the United States, Curtis argued. At the time of the writing of the Constitution, free black men could vote in five states and participated in the ratification process. Scott *was* free. Because slavery was prohibited in Wisconsin, the "involuntary servitude of a slave, coming into the Territory with his master, should cease to exist." The Missouri Compromise *was* constitutional. The Founders had meant exactly what they said:

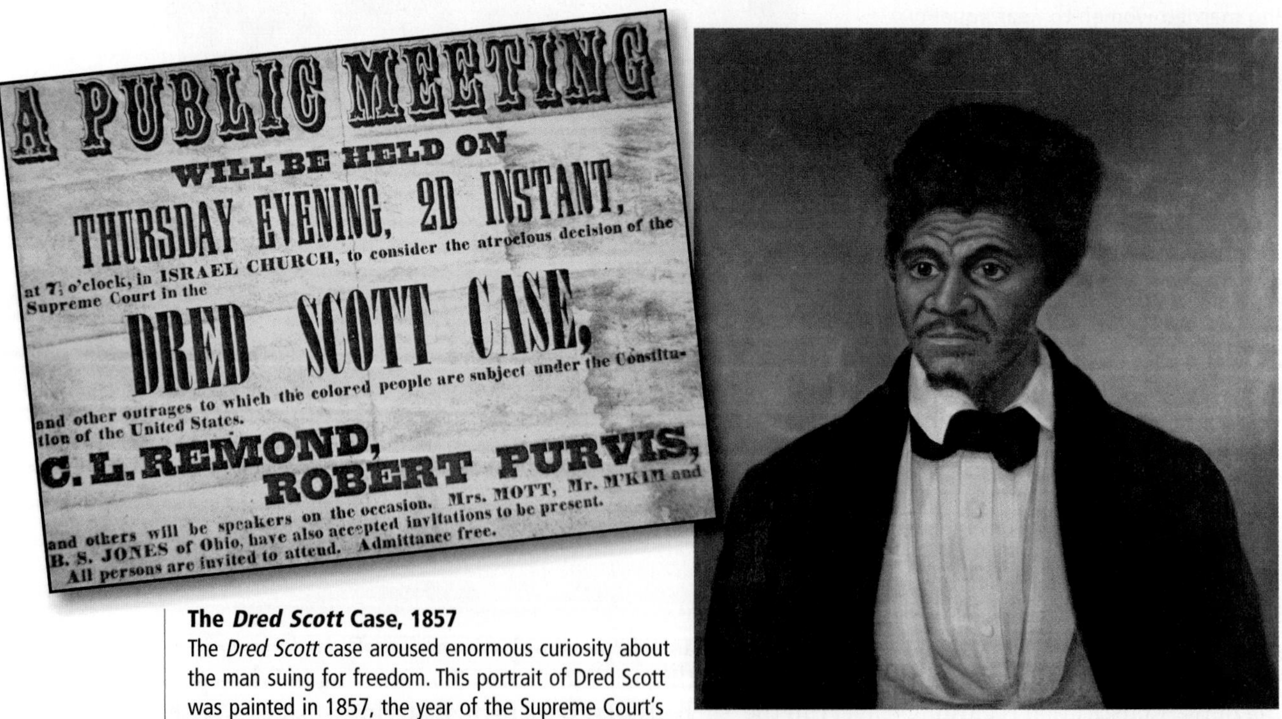

The *Dred Scott* Case, 1857

The *Dred Scott* case aroused enormous curiosity about the man suing for freedom. This portrait of Dred Scott was painted in 1857, the year of the Supreme Court's decision. African Americans in the North were particularly alarmed by the Court's ruling. The poster announces that two black leaders, Charles L. Remond and Robert Purvis, will speak at a public meeting about the "atrocious decision." Although the Court rejected his suit, he gained his freedom in May 1857 when a white man purchased and freed Scott and his family. Scott died of tuberculosis in September 1858. Poster: © Private Collection/Peter Newark American Pictures/The Bridgeman Art Library; Nationality/copyright status: American/out of copyright; Portrait: Collection of the New-York Historical Society.

Congress had the power to make "*all* needful rules and regulations" for the territories, including barring slavery.

In a seven-to-two decision, the Court rejected Curtis's arguments, thereby validating an extreme statement of the South's territorial rights. John C. Calhoun's claim that Congress had no authority to exclude slavery became the law of the land. White Southerners cheered, but the *Dred Scott* decision actually strengthened the young Republican Party. Indeed, that "outrageous" decision, one Republican argued, was "the best thing that could have happened," for it provided dramatic evidence of the Republicans' claim that a hostile "Slave Power" conspired against northern liberties.

Prairie Republican: Abraham Lincoln

By reigniting the sectional flames, the *Dred Scott* case provided Republican politicians with fresh challenges and fresh opportunities. **Abraham Lincoln** had long since put behind him his hardscrabble log-cabin beginnings in Kentucky and Indiana. He lived in a fine two-story house in Springfield, Illinois, and earned good money as a lawyer. The law provided Lincoln's living, but politics was his life. "His ambition was a little engine that knew no rest," observed his law partner William Herndon. Lincoln had served as a Whig in the Illinois state legislature and in the House of Representatives, but he had not held public office since 1849.

The disintegration of the Whig Party meant that Lincoln had no political home, but the Know-Nothings held no appeal. "How can anyone who abhors the oppression of negroes be in favor of degrading classes of white people?" he asked in 1855. "As a nation, we began by declaring that 'all men are created equal.' We now practically read it 'all men are created equal, except negroes.' When the Know-Nothings get control, it will read 'All men are created equal, except Negroes and foreigners and Catholics.'"

Convinced that slavery was a "monstrous injustice," a "great moral wrong," and an "unqualified evil to the negro, the white man, and the State," Lincoln gravitated toward the Republican Party. He condemned Douglas's Kansas-Nebraska Act of 1854 for giving slavery a new life and in 1856 joined the Republican Party. He accepted that the Constitution permitted slavery in those states where it existed, but he believed that Congress could contain its spread. Penned in, Lincoln believed, plantation slavery would wither, and in time Southerners would end slavery themselves.

Lincoln held what were, for his times, moderate racial views. Although he denounced slavery and defended black humanity, he also viewed black equality as impractical and unachievable. "Negroes have natural rights . . . as other men have," he said, "although they cannot enjoy them here." Insurmountable white prejudice made it impossible to extend full citizenship to blacks in America, he believed. Freeing blacks and allowing them to remain in this country would lead to a race war. In Lincoln's mind, social stability and black progress required that slavery end and that blacks leave the country.

Lincoln envisioned the western territories as "places for poor people to go to, and better their conditions." The "*free* labor system," he said, "opens the way for all — gives hope to all, and energy, and progress, and improvement of condition to all." But slavery's expansion threatened free men's basic right to succeed. The Kansas-Nebraska Act and the *Dred Scott* decision persuaded him that slaveholders were engaged in a dangerous conspiracy to nationalize slavery. The next step, Lincoln warned, would be "another Supreme Court decision, declaring that the Constitution of the United States does not permit a State to exclude slavery from its limits." Unless the citizens of Illinois woke up, he warned, the Supreme Court would make "Illinois a slave State."

In Lincoln's view, the nation could not "endure, permanently half slave and half free." Either opponents of slavery would arrest its spread and place it on the "course of ultimate extinction," or its advocates would see that it became legal in "*all* the States, *old* as well as *new* — *North* as well as *South*." Lincoln's convictions that slavery was wrong and that Congress must stop its spread formed the core of the Republican ideology. Lincoln so impressed his fellow Republicans in Illinois that in 1858 they chose him to challenge the nation's premier Democrat, who was seeking reelection to the U.S. Senate.

The Lincoln-Douglas Debates

When Stephen Douglas learned that the Republican Abraham Lincoln would be his opponent for the Senate, he observed: "He is the strong man of the party — full of wit, facts, dates — and the best stump speaker, with his droll ways and dry jokes, in the West. He is as honest as he is shrewd, and if I beat him my victory will be hardly won."

***The* Herald *in the Country*, by William Sidney Mount, 1853**
William Sidney Mount was the first American painter to achieve fame for his vivid depictions of everyday life. His motto was "Never paint for the few but for the many." Here, two men from the country keep up with the news by reading a copy of the *New York Herald.* Men like these increasingly accepted Abraham Lincoln's portrait of the Republican Party as the guardian of the common people's liberty and economic opportunity. When Lincoln claimed that southern slaveholders threatened free labor and democracy, northern men listened. The Long Island Museum of American Art, History and Carriages. Gift of Mr. and Mrs. Ward Melville, 1955.

Not only did Douglas have to contend with a formidable foe, but he also carried the weight of a burden not of his own making. The previous year, the nation's economy had experienced a sharp downturn. Prices had plummeted, thousands of businesses had failed, and many were unemployed. As a Democrat, Douglas had to go before the voters as a member of the party whose policies stood accused of causing the panic of 1857.

Douglas's response to another crisis in 1857, however, helped shore up his standing in Illinois. Proslavery forces in Kansas met in the town of Lecompton, drafted a proslavery constitution, and applied for statehood. Everyone knew that free-soilers outnumbered proslavery settlers, but President Buchanan instructed Congress to admit Kansas as the sixteenth slave state. Republicans denounced the "Lecompton swindle." Senator Douglas broke with the Democratic administration and denounced the **Lecompton constitution**; Congress killed the Lecompton bill. (When Kansans reconsidered the Lecompton constitution in an honest election, they rejected it six to one. Kansas entered the Union in 1861 as a free state.) By denouncing the fraudulent proslavery constitution, Douglas declared his independence from the South and, he hoped, made himself acceptable at home.

A relative unknown and a decided underdog in the Illinois election, Lincoln challenged Douglas to debate him face-to-face. The two met in seven communities for what would become a legendary series of debates. To the thousands who stood straining to see and hear, they must have seemed an odd pair. Douglas was five feet four inches tall, broad, and stocky; Lincoln was six feet four inches tall, angular, and lean. Douglas was in perpetual motion, darting across the platform, shouting, and jabbing the air; Lincoln stood still and spoke deliberately. Douglas wore the latest fashions and dazzled audiences with his flashy vests; Lincoln wore good suits but managed to look rumpled anyway.

The two men debated the crucial issues of the age — slavery and freedom. They showed the citizens of Illinois (and much of the nation because of widespread press coverage) the difference between an anti-Lecompton Democrat and a true Republican. Lincoln badgered Douglas with the question of whether he favored the spread of slavery. He tried to force Douglas into the damaging admission that the Supreme Court had repudiated Douglas's own territorial solution, popular sovereignty. At Freeport, Illinois, Douglas admitted that settlers could not now pass legislation barring slavery, but he argued that they could ban slavery just as effectively by not passing protective laws, such as those found in slave states. Southerners condemned Douglas's "Freeport Doctrine" and charged him with trying to steal the victory they had gained with the *Dred Scott* decision. Lincoln chastised his opponent for his "don't care" attitude about slavery, for "blowing out the moral lights around us."

Douglas worked the racial issue. He called Lincoln an abolitionist and an egalitarian enamored of "our colored brethren." Put on the defensive, Lincoln reaffirmed his faith in white rule: "I will say, then, that I am not, nor ever have been, in favor of bringing about in any way the social and political equality of the white and black race." But unlike Douglas, who told racist jokes, Lincoln was no negrophobe. He tried to steer the debate back to what he considered the true issue: the morality and future of slavery. "Slavery is wrong," Lincoln repeated, because "a man has the right to the fruits of his own labor."

As Douglas predicted, the election was hard-fought and closely contested. Until the adoption of the Seventeenth Amendment in 1911, citizens voted for state legislators, who in turn selected U.S. senators. Since Democrats won a slight majority in the Illinois legislature, the members returned Douglas to the Senate. But the **Lincoln-Douglas debates** thrust Lincoln, the prairie Republican, into the national spotlight.

REVIEW Why did the *Dred Scott* decision strengthen northern suspicions of a "Slave Power" conspiracy?

▸ The Union Collapses

Lincoln's thesis that the "slavocracy" conspired to make slavery a national institution now seems exaggerated. But from the northern perspective, the Kansas-Nebraska Act, the Brooks-Sumner affair, the *Dred Scott* decision, and the Lecompton constitution amounted to irrefutable evidence of the South's aggressiveness. White Southerners, of course, saw things differently. They were the ones who were under siege, they declared. Signs were everywhere that the North planned to use its numerical advantage to attack slavery, and not just in the territories. Republicans had made it clear that they were unwilling to accept the *Dred Scott* ruling as the last word on the issue of slavery expansion. And John Brown's attempt to incite a slave insurrection in Virginia in 1859 proved that Northerners were unwilling to be bound by Christian decency and reverence for life.

Threats of secession increasingly laced the sectional debate. Talk of leaving the Union had been heard for years, but until the final crisis, Southerners had used secession as a ploy to gain concessions within the Union, not to destroy it. Then the 1850s delivered powerful blows to Southerners' confidence that they could remain in the Union and protect slavery. When the Republican Party won the White House in 1860, many Southerners concluded that they would have to leave.

The Aftermath of John Brown's Raid

For his attack on Harpers Ferry, John Brown stood trial for treason, murder, and incitement of slave insurrection. "To hang a fanatic is to make a martyr of him and fledge another brood of the same sort," cautioned one newspaper, but on December 2, 1859, Virginia executed Brown. In life, he was a ne'er-do-well, but, as the poet Stephen Vincent Benét observed, "he knew how to die." Brown told his wife that he was "determined to make the utmost possible out of a defeat." He told the court: "If it is deemed necessary that I should forfeit my life for the furtherance of the ends of justice, and mingle my blood further with the blood of . . . millions in this slave country whose rights are disregarded by wicked, cruel, and unjust enactments, I say, let it be done."

After Brown's execution, Americans across the land contemplated the meaning of his life and death. Northern denunciation of Brown as a dangerous fanatic gave way to grudging respect. Some even celebrated his "splendid martyrdom." Ralph Waldo Emerson likened Brown to Christ when he declared that Brown made "the gallows as glorious as the cross." Some abolitionists explicitly endorsed Brown's resort to violence. William Lloyd Garrison, who usually professed pacifism, announced, "I am prepared to say 'success to every slave insurrection at the South and in every country.'"

Most Northerners did not advocate bloody rebellion, however. Like Lincoln, they concluded that Brown's noble antislavery ideals could not "excuse violence, bloodshed, and treason." Still, when northern churches marked John Brown's hanging with tolling bells, hymns, and prayer vigils, white Southerners contemplated what they had in common with people who "regard John Brown as a martyr and a Christian hero, rather than a murderer and robber." Georgia senator Robert Toombs announced solemnly that Southerners must "never permit this Federal government to pass into the traitorous hands of the black Republican party." At that moment, the presidential election was only months away.

Republican Victory in 1860

Events between Brown's hanging and the presidential election only heightened sectional hostility. Across the South, whites feverishly searched for other John Browns and whipped and sometimes lynched those they suspected. A southern business convention meeting in Nashville shocked

VISUAL ACTIVITY

***John Brown Going to His Hanging*, by Horace Pippin, 1942**

The grandparents of Horace Pippin, a Pennsylvania artist, were slaves. His grandmother witnessed the hanging of John Brown, and this painting recalls the scene she so often described to him. Pippin used a muted palette to establish the bleak setting and to tell the grim story, but he managed to convey a striking intensity nevertheless. Historically accurate, the painting depicts Brown tied and sitting erect on his coffin, passing resolutely before the silent, staring white men. The black woman in the lower right corner presumably is Pippin's grandmother. Romare Bearden, a leading twentieth-century African American artist, recalled the central place of John Brown in black memory: "Lincoln and John Brown were as much a part of the actuality of the Afro-American experience, as were the domino games and the hoe cakes for Sunday morning breakfast. I vividly recall the yearly commemorations for John Brown and see my grandfather reading Brown's last speech to the court, which was a regular part of the ceremony at Pittsburgh's Shiloh Baptist Church." Pennsylvania Academy of Fine Arts, Philadelphia. John Lambert Fund.

READING THE IMAGE: What was the artist trying to convey about the tone of John Brown's execution? According to the painting, what were the feelings of those gathered to witness the event?
CONNECTIONS: How did Brown's trial and execution contribute to the growing split between North and South?

the nation (including many Southerners) by calling for the reopening of the African slave trade, closed since 1808 and considered an abomination almost everywhere in the Western world. Chief Justice Taney provoked new indignation when he ruled northern personal liberty laws unconstitutional and reaffirmed the Fugitive Slave Act. Then, the normally routine business of electing a Speaker of the House threatened to turn bloody as Democrats and Republicans battled over control of the office. After two months of acrimonious debate, one congressman observed that the "only persons who do not have a revolver and a knife are those who have two revolvers." A last-minute compromise may have averted a shootout.

When the Democrats converged on Charleston for their convention in April 1860, fire-eating Southerners denounced Stephen Douglas and demanded a platform that featured a federal slave code for the territories, a goal of extreme proslavery Southerners for years. Not only was Congress powerless to block slavery's spread, they argued, but it was obligated to offer slavery all "needful protection." But northern Democrats knew that northern voters would not stomach a federal slave code. When the delegates approved a platform with popular sovereignty, representatives from the entire Lower South and Arkansas stomped out of the convention. The remaining Democrats adjourned to meet a few weeks later in Baltimore, where they nominated Douglas for president.

Bolting southern Democrats immediately reconvened in Richmond, where they approved a platform with a federal slave code and nominated their own candidate for president: John C. Breckinridge of Kentucky, who was serving as vice president under Buchanan. Southern moderates, however, refused to support Breckinridge. They formed the **Constitutional Union Party** to provide voters with a Unionist choice. Instead of adopting a platform and confronting the slavery question, the Constitutional Union Party merely approved a vague resolution pledging "to recognize no political principle other than *the Constitution . . . the Union . . . and the Enforcement of the Laws.*" For president, they nominated former senator John Bell of Tennessee.

The Republicans smelled victory, but they estimated that they needed to carry nearly all the free states to win. To make their party more appealing, they expanded their platform beyond antislavery. They hoped that free homesteads, a protective tariff, a transcontinental railroad, and a guarantee of immigrant political rights would provide an economic and social agenda broad enough to unify the North. While reasserting their commitment to stop the spread of slavery, they also denounced John Brown's raid as "among the gravest of crimes" and confirmed the security of slavery in the South.

Republicans cast about for a moderate candidate to go with their evenhanded platform. The foremost Republican, William H. Seward, had made enemies with his radical "higher law" doctrine, which claimed that there was a higher moral law than the Constitution, and with his "irrepressible conflict" speech, in which he declared that North and South were fated to collide. Lincoln, however, since bursting onto the national scene in 1858 had demonstrated his clear purpose, good judgment, and solid Republican credentials. That, and his residence in Illinois, a crucial state, made him attractive to the party. On the third ballot, the delegates chose Lincoln. Defeated by Douglas in a state contest less than two years earlier, Lincoln now stood ready to take him on for the presidency.

The election of 1860 was like none other in American politics. It took place in the midst of the nation's severest crisis. Four major candidates crowded the presidential field. Rather than a four-cornered contest, however, the election broke into two contests, each with two candidates. In the North, Lincoln faced Douglas;

Abraham Lincoln
Lincoln actively sought the Republican presidential nomination in 1860. While in New York City to give a political address, he had his photograph taken by Mathew Brady. "While I was there I was taken to one of the places where they get up such things," Lincoln explained, sounding more innocent than he was, "and I suppose they got my shadow, and can multiply copies indefinitely." Multiply they did. Later, Lincoln credited his victory to his New York speech and to this dignified photograph by Brady. The Lincoln Museum, Fort Wayne, Indiana, #0-17.

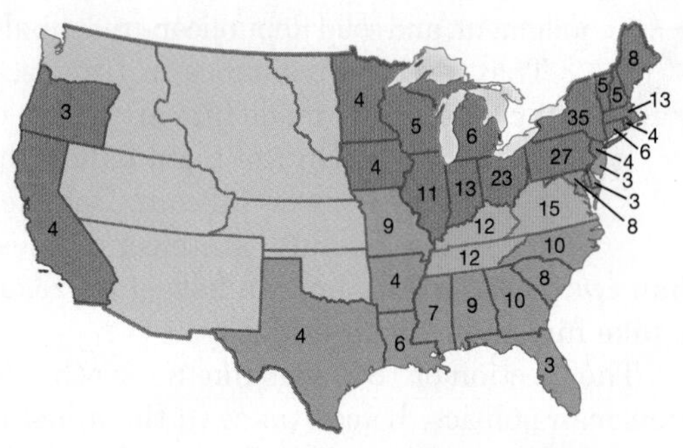

Candidate	Electoral Vote	Popular Vote	Percent of Popular Vote
Abraham Lincoln (Republican)	180	1,866,452	39.9
John C. Breckinridge (Southern Democrat)	72	847,953	18.1
Stephen A. Douglas (Northern Democrat)	12	1,375,157	29.4
John Bell (Constitutional Union)	39	590,631	12.6

MAP 14.5
The Election of 1860

in the South, Breckinridge confronted Bell. So outrageous did Southerners consider the Republican Party that they did not even permit Lincoln's name to appear on the ballot in ten of the fifteen slave states.

An unprecedented number of voters cast their ballots on November 6, 1860. Approximately 82 percent of eligible northern men and 70 percent of eligible southern men went to the polls. Lincoln swept all of the eighteen free states except New Jersey, which split its electoral votes between him and Douglas. Although Lincoln received only 39 percent of the popular vote, he won easily in the electoral college with 180 votes, 28 more than he needed for victory (Map 14.5). Lincoln did not win because his opposition was splintered. Even if the votes of his three opponents had been combined, Lincoln still would have won. He won because his votes were concentrated in the free states, which contained a majority of electoral votes. Ominously, however, Breckinridge, running on a southern-rights platform, won the entire Lower South, plus Delaware, Maryland, and North Carolina.

> **"Mr. Lincoln and his party assert that this doctrine of equality applies to the negro, and necessarily there can exist no such thing as property in our equals."**
>
> — Former Georgia governor HOWELL COBB

Secession Winter

Across the country, telegraphs tapped out the news of Lincoln's victory. Antislavery advocate Charles Francis Adams of Massachusetts could hardly believe the results: "There is now scarcely a shadow of a doubt that the great revolution has actually taken place, and that the country has once and for all thrown off the domination of the Slaveholders." What Adams celebrated as liberation, anxious white Southerners feared was the onset of Republican tyranny. Throughout the South, they began debating what to do. Although Breckinridge had carried the South, a vote for "southern rights" was not necessarily a vote for secession. Besides, slightly more than half of the Southerners who had voted had cast ballots for Douglas and Bell, two stout defenders of the Union.

Southern Unionists tried to calm the fears that Lincoln's election triggered. Let the dust settle, they pleaded. Former congressman Alexander Stephens of Georgia asked what Lincoln had done to justify something as extreme as secession. Had he not promised to respect slavery where it existed? In Stephens's judgment, the fire-eater cure would be worse than the Republican disease. Secession might lead to war, which would loosen the hinges of southern society and possibly even open the door to slave insurrection. "Revolutions are much easier started than controlled," he warned. "I consider slavery much more secure in the Union than out of it."

Secessionists emphasized the dangers of delay. "Mr. Lincoln and his party assert that this doctrine of equality applies to the negro," former Georgia governor Howell Cobb declared, "and necessarily there can exist no such thing as property in our equals." Lincoln's election without a single electoral vote from the South meant that Southerners were no longer able to defend themselves within the Union, Cobb argued. Why wait, he asked, for Lincoln to appoint abolitionist judges, marshals, customs collectors, and postmasters to federal posts throughout the South? As for war, there would be none. The Union was a voluntary compact, and Lincoln would not coerce patriotism. If Northerners did resist with force, secessionists argued, one southern woodsman could whip five of Lincoln's greasy mechanics.

For all their differences, southern whites agreed that they had to defend slavery. John Smith Preston of South Carolina spoke for the overwhelming majority when he declared, "The

"The Union Is Dissolved!"
On December 20, 1860, the *Charleston Mercury* put out this special edition of the paper to celebrate South Carolina's secession from the Union. Six weeks earlier, upon hearing the news that Lincoln had won the presidency, the *Mercury* had predicted as much, announcing, "The revolution of 1860 has been initiated." Chicago Historical Society.

CHARLESTON MERCURY

EXTRA:

Passed unanimously at 1.15 o'clock, P. M., December 20th, 1860.

AN ORDINANCE

To dissolve the Union between the State of South Carolina and other States united with her under the compact entitled "The Constitution of the United States of America."

We, the People of the State of South Carolina, in Convention assembled, do declare and ordain, and it is hereby declared and ordained,

That the Ordinance adopted by us in Convention, on the twenty-third day of May, in the year of our Lord one thousand seven hundred and eighty-eight, whereby the Constitution of the United States of America was ratified, and also, all Acts and parts of Acts of the General Assembly of this State, ratifying amendments of the said Constitution, are hereby repealed; and that the union now subsisting between South Carolina and other States, under the name of "The United States of America," is hereby dissolved.

THE UNION IS DISSOLVED!

South cannot exist without slavery." They disagreed about whether the mere presence of a Republican in the White House made it necessary to exercise what they considered a legitimate right to secede.

The debate about what to do was briefest in South Carolina; it seceded from the Union on December 20, 1860. By February 1861, the six other Lower South states marched in South Carolina's footsteps. In some states, the vote was close. In general, slaveholders spearheaded secession, while nonslaveholders in the Piedmont and mountain counties, where slaves were relatively few, displayed the greatest attachment to the Union. In February, representatives from South Carolina, Georgia, Florida, Alabama, Mississippi, Louisiana, and Texas met in Montgomery, Alabama, where they celebrated the birth of the **Confederate States of America**. Mississippi senator Jefferson Davis became president, and Alexander Stephens of Georgia, who had spoken so eloquently about the dangers of revolution, became vice president. In March 1861, Stephens declared that the Confederacy's "cornerstone" was "the great truth that the negro is not equal to the white man; that slavery, subordination to the superior race, is his natural and moral condition."

Lincoln's election had split the Union. Now secession split the South. Seven slave states seceded during the winter, but the eight slave states of the Upper South rejected secession, at least for the moment. The Upper South had a smaller stake in slavery. Barely half as many white families in the Upper South held slaves (21 percent) as in the Lower South (37 percent). Slaves represented twice as large a percentage of the population in the Lower South (48 percent) as in the Upper South (23 percent). Consequently, whites in the Upper South had fewer fears that Republican ascendancy meant economic catastrophe, social chaos, and racial war. Lincoln would need to do more than just be elected to provoke them into secession.

Secession of the Lower South, December 1860–February 1861

The nation had to wait until March 4, 1861, when Lincoln took office, to see what he would do. (Presidents-elect waited four months to take office until 1933, when the Twentieth Amendment to the Constitution shifted the inauguration to January 20.) After his election, Lincoln chose to stay in Springfield and to say nothing. "Lame-duck" president James Buchanan sat in Washington and did nothing. Buchanan demonstrated,

William H. Seward said mockingly, that "it is the President's duty to enforce the laws, unless somebody opposes him." In Congress, efforts at cobbling together a peace-saving compromise came to nothing.

Lincoln began his inaugural address with reassurances to the South. He had "no lawful right" to interfere with slavery where it existed, he declared again, adding for emphasis that he had "no inclination to do so." Conciliatory about slavery, Lincoln proved inflexible about the Union. The Union, he declared, was "perpetual." Secession was "anarchy" and "legally void." The Constitution required him to execute the law "in all the States." The decision for civil war or peace rested in the South's hands, Lincoln said: "You can have no conflict, without being yourselves the aggressors. *You* have no oath registered in Heaven to destroy the government, while I shall have the most solemn one to 'preserve, protect, and defend' it." What Confederates in Charleston held in their hands at that very moment were the cords for firing the cannons aimed at the federal garrison at Fort Sumter.

REVIEW Why did some southern states secede immediately after Lincoln's election?

▸ Conclusion: Slavery, Free Labor, and the Failure of Political Compromise

As their economies, societies, and cultures diverged in the nineteenth century, Northerners and Southerners expressed different concepts of the American promise and the place of slavery within it. Their differences crystallized into political form in 1846 when David Wilmot proposed banning slavery in any territory won in the Mexican-American War. "As if by magic," a Boston newspaper observed, "it brought to a head the great question that is about to divide the American people." Discovery of gold and other precious metals in the West added urgency to the controversy over slavery in the territories. Congress attempted to address the issue with the Compromise of 1850, but the Fugitive Slave Act and the publication of *Uncle Tom's Cabin* hardened northern sentiments against slavery and confirmed southern suspicions of northern ill will. The bloody violence that erupted in Kansas in 1856 and the incendiary *Dred Scott* decision in 1857 further eroded hope for a solution to this momentous question.

During the extended crisis of the Union that stretched from 1846 to 1861, the slavery question intertwined with national politics. The traditional Whig and Democratic parties struggled to hold together as new parties, most notably the Republican Party, emerged. Politicians fixed their attention on the expansion of slavery, but from the beginning the nation recognized that the controversy had less to do with slavery in the territories than with the future of slavery in America.

For more than seventy years, statesmen had found compromises that accepted slavery and preserved the Union. But as each section grew increasingly committed to its labor system and the promise it offered, Americans discovered that accommodation had limits. In 1859, John Brown's militant antislavery pushed white Southerners to the edge. In 1860, Lincoln's election convinced whites in the Lower South that slavery and the society they had built on it were at risk in the Union, and they seceded. In his inaugural address, Lincoln pleaded, "We are not enemies but friends. We must not be enemies." By then, however, seven southern states had ceased to sing what he called "the chorus of the Union." It remained to be seen whether disunion would mean war.

▸ Selected Bibliography

General Works

Don E. Fehrenbacher, *The Slaveholding Republic: An Account of the United States Government's Relations to Slavery* (2001).

Michael Holt, *Fate of Their Country: Politicians, Slavery Extension, and the Coming of the Civil War* (2004).

Bruce C. Levine, *Half Slave and Half Free: The Roots of the Civil War* (1992).

James M. McPherson, *Ordeal by Fire: The Civil War and Reconstruction* (1982).

Mark E. Neely, *Boundaries of American Political Culture in the Civil War Era* (2005).

Eric H. Walther, *The Shattering of the Union: America in the 1850s* (2004).

Sean Wilentz, *The Rise of American Democracy: Jefferson to Lincoln* (2005).

Northern Sectionalism

Tom Chaffin, *Pathfinder: John Charles Frémont and the Course of American Empire* (2002).

Rodney O. Davis and Douglas L. Wilson, eds., *The Lincoln-Douglas Debates* (2008).

Eric Foner, *Free Labor, Free Soil, Free Men: The Ideology of the Republican Party before the Civil War* (1970).

William E. Gienapp, *The Origins of the Republican Party, 1852–1856* (1987).

Susan-Mary Grant, *North over South: Northern Nationalism and American Identity in the Antebellum Era* (2000).

David Grimsted, *American Mobbing, 1828–1865: Toward Civil War* (1998).

Joan D. Hedrick, *Harriet Beecher Stowe: A Life* (1994).

Pamela Herr, *Jessie Benton Frémont: A Biography* (1987).

Nancy Isenberg, *Sex and Citizenship in Antebellum America* (1998).

David S. Reynolds, *John Brown, Abolitionist: The Man Who Killed Slavery, Sparked the Civil War, and Seeded Civil Rights* (2005).

James Brewer Stewart, *Wendell Phillips, Liberty's Hero* (1986).

Wendy Hamand Venet, *Neither Ballots nor Bullets: Women Abolitionists and the Civil War* (1991).

Douglas L. Wilson, *Honor's Voice: The Transformation of Abraham Lincoln* (1998).

Kenneth J. Winkle, *The Young Eagle: The Rise of Abraham Lincoln* (2001).

Southern Sectionalism

William J. Cooper Jr., *The South and the Politics of Slavery, 1828–1856* (1978).

John Patrick Daly, *When Slavery Was Called Freedom: Evangelicalism, Proslavery, and the Causes of the Civil War* (2002).

Lacy K. Ford Jr., *Origins of Southern Radicalism: The South Carolina Upcountry, 1800–1860* (1988).

William W. Freehling, *The Road to Disunion, vol. 1, Secessionists at Bay, 1776–1854* (1990).

William A. Link, *Roots of Secession: Slavery and Politics in Antebellum Virginia* (2002).

Robert E. May, *Manifest Destiny's Underworld: Filibustering in Antebellum America* (2002).

Christopher J. Olsen, *Political Culture and Secession in Mississippi: Masculinity, Honor, and the Antiparty Tradition, 1830–1860* (2002).

Manisha Sinha, *The Counterrevolution of Slavery: Politics and Ideology in Antebellum South Carolina* (2000).

Mitchell Snay, *Gospel of Disunion: Religion and Separatism in the Antebellum South* (1993).

Secession

Daniel Crofts, *Reluctant Confederates: Upper South Unionists in the Secession Crisis* (1989).

Charles B. Dew, *Apostles of Disunion: Southern Secession Commissioners and the Causes of the Civil War* (2001).

Michael P. Johnson, *Toward a Patriarchal Republic: The Secession of Georgia* (1977).

David M. Potter, *Lincoln and His Party in the Secession Crisis* (1942).

Lorman A. Ratner and Dwight L. Teeter Jr., *Fanatics and Fire-Eaters: Newspapers and the Coming of the Civil War* (2003).

▶ **For more books about topics in this chapter,** see the Online Bibliography at **bedfordstmartins.com/roark.**

▶ **For additional primary sources from this period,** see Michael Johnson, ed., *Reading the American Past*, Fifth Edition.

▶ **For Web sites, images, and documents related to topics and places in this chapter,** visit Make History at **bedfordstmartins.com/roark.**

Reviewing Chapter 14

KEY TERMS

Explain each term's significance.

The Bitter Fruits of War

- **Wilmot Proviso (p. 430)**
- **free labor (p. 430)**
- **John C. Calhoun (p. 430)**
- **Lewis Cass (p. 430)**
- **popular sovereignty (p. 430)**
- **Zachary Taylor (p. 431)**
- **Charles Sumner (p. 431)**
- **Free-Soil Party (p. 431)**
- **Stephen A. Douglas (p. 433)**
- **Compromise of 1850 (p. 434)**

The Sectional Balance Undone

- ***Uncle Tom's Cabin* (p. 434)**
- **underground railroad (p. 434)**
- **Fugitive Slave Act (p. 434)**
- **Harriet Beecher Stowe (p. 435)**
- **doughfaces (p. 436)**
- **Gadsden Purchase (p. 437)**
- **Kansas-Nebraska Act (p. 437)**

Realignment of the Party System

- **Know-Nothings (p. 439)**
- **Republican Party (p. 440)**
- **John C. Frémont (p. 443)**
- **Jessie Frémont (p. 444)**

Freedom under Siege

- **John Brown (p. 445)**
- **"Bleeding Kansas" (p. 445)**
- **Roger B. Taney (p. 448)**
- ***Dred Scott* decision (p. 448)**
- **Abraham Lincoln (p. 449)**
- **Lecompton constitution (p. 450)**
- **Lincoln-Douglas debates (p. 451)**

The Union Collapses

- **Constitutional Union Party (p. 453)**
- **southern Unionists (p. 454)**
- **secessionists (p. 454)**
- **Confederate States of America (p. 455)**

REVIEW QUESTIONS

Use key terms and dates to support your answer.

1. Why did responses to the Wilmot Proviso split along sectional rather than party lines? (pp. 429–434)
2. Why did the Fugitive Slave Act provoke such strong opposition in the North? (pp. 434–437)
3. Why did the Whig Party disintegrate in the 1850s? (pp. 438–444)
4. Why did the *Dred Scott* decision strengthen northern suspicions of a "Slave Power" conspiracy? (pp. 444–451)
5. Why did some southern states secede immediately after Lincoln's election? (pp. 451–456)

MAKING CONNECTIONS

Draw on key terms, the timeline, and review questions.

1. The process of compromise that had successfully contained tensions between slave and free states since the nation's founding collapsed with secession. Why did compromise fail at this moment? In your answer, address specific political conflicts and attempts to solve them between 1846 and 1861.
2. In the 1850s, many Americans supported popular sovereignty as the best solution to the explosive question of slavery in the western territories. Why was this solution so popular, and why did it ultimately prove inadequate? In your answer, be sure to address popular sovereignty's varied critics as well as its champions.
3. In the 1840s and 1850s, the United States witnessed the realignment of its long-standing two-party system. Why did the old system fall apart, what emerged to take its place, and how did this process contribute to the coming of the Civil War?
4. Abraham Lincoln believed that he had staked out a moderate position on the question of slavery, avoiding the extremes of immediate abolitionism and calls for the unlimited protection of slavery. Why, then, did some southern states determine that his election necessitated the radical act of secession?

LINKING TO THE PAST

Link events in this chapter to earlier events.

1. How did social and economic developments in the South during the first half of the nineteenth century influence the decisions that southern politicians made in the 1840s and 1850s? (See chapter 13.)
2. How did the policies of the Republican Party reflect the free-labor ideals of the North? (See chapter 12.)

▶ **FOR PRACTICE QUIZZES AND OTHER STUDY TOOLS**, visit the Online Study Guide at **bedfordstmartins.com/roark.**

TIMELINE 1820–1861

1820	• Missouri Compromise.
1846	• Wilmot Proviso introduced in Congress.
1847	• Wilmot Proviso defeated in Senate. • Compromise of "popular sovereignty" offered.
1848	• Free-Soil Party founded. • Whig Zachary Taylor elected president.
1849	• California gold rush.
1850	• Taylor dies; Vice President Millard Fillmore becomes president. • Compromise of 1850 becomes law.
1852	• *Uncle Tom's Cabin* published. • Democrat Franklin Pierce elected president.
1853	• Gadsden Purchase.
1854	• American (Know-Nothing) Party emerges. • Kansas-Nebraska Act. • Republican Party founded.
1856	• "Bleeding Kansas." • "Sack of Lawrence." • Preston Brooks canes Charles Sumner. • Pottawatomie massacre. • Democrat James Buchanan elected president.
1857	• *Dred Scott* decision. • Congress rejects Lecompton constitution. • Panic of 1857.
1858	• Abraham Lincoln and Stephen A. Douglas debate slavery; Douglas wins Senate seat.
1859	• John Brown raids Harpers Ferry, Virginia.
1860	• Republican Abraham Lincoln elected president. • South Carolina secedes from Union.
1861	• Six other Lower South states secede. • Confederate States of America formed. • Lincoln takes office.

UNION PARADE DRUM

This drum from Belfast, Maine, was made of wood cut into thin layers, then steamed and shaped into a round shell. The drum heads were made from calfskin that was stretched tight by ropes. The fierce eagle, flag, and motto announced the cause. Drums got soldiers up in the morning; signaled them to report for breakfast, roll call, and guard duty; and announced lights out. The most important use of drums was on the battlefield where they communicated orders from commanding officers to their troops. The life of a drummer seemed glorious, and boys as young as ten eagerly served in northern units.

Drum: photo courtesy Allan Katz Americana, Woodbridge, CT; background image: Library of Congress.

15 The Crucible of War 1861–1865

ON THE RAINY NIGHT OF SEPTEMBER 21, 1862, IN WILMINGTON, North Carolina, twenty-four-year-old William Gould and seven other runaway slaves crowded into a small boat on the Cape Fear River and quietly pushed away from the dock. They rowed hard throughout the night, reaching the Atlantic Ocean by dawn. They plunged into the swells and made for the Union navy patrolling offshore. At 10:30 that morning, the USS *Cambridge* took the men aboard.

Astonishingly, on the same day that Gould reached the federal ship, President Abraham Lincoln revealed his intention to issue a proclamation of emancipation freeing the slaves in the Confederate states. Because the proclamation would not take effect until January 1863, Gould was not legally free in the eyes of the U.S. government. But the U.S. Navy, suffering from a shortage of sailors, cared little about the formal status of runaway slaves. Within days, all eight runaways became sailors in the U.S. Navy.

William Gould could read and write, and he began making almost daily entries in his diary. In some ways, Gould's naval experience looked like that of a white sailor. He found duty on a ship in the blockading squadron both boring and exhilarating. Long days of tedious work were sometimes interrupted by a "period of daring exploit." When Gould's ship closed on a Confederate vessel, he declared that "we told them good morning in the shape of a shot." In a five-day period in 1862, the *Cambridge* helped capture four blockade runners and ran another aground.

But Gould's Civil War experience was shaped by his race. Like most black men in the Union military, he saw service as an opportunity to fight slavery. From the beginning, Gould linked union and freedom, which he called "the holiest of all causes." Gould witnessed a number of ugly racial incidents on federal ships, however. "There was A malee [melee] on Deck between the white and colard [colored] men," he observed. Later, when a black regiment came aboard, "they were treated verry rough by the crew," he said. The white sailors "refused to let them eat off the mess pans and called them all kinds of names[;] . . . in all they was treated shamefully."

Still, Gould was proud of his service in the navy and monitored the progress of racial equality during the war. On shore leave in 1863, he cheered the "20th Regmt of U.S. (collard) Volunteers . . . pronounce[d] by all to be A splendid Regement." In March 1865, he celebrated the "passage of an amendment of the Con[sti]tution prohibiting slavery througho[ut] the United States." And a month later, he thrilled to the "Glad Tidings that the Stars and Stripe[s] had been planted over the Capital of the D—nd

Confederacy by the invincible Grant." He added, we must not forget the "Mayrters to the cau[se] of Right and Equality."

Slaves like the eight runaways from Wilmington took the first steps toward making the war for union also a war for freedom. Early in the fighting, black abolitionist Frederick Douglass challenged the friends of freedom to "*be up and doing; — now is your time.*" But for the first eighteen months of the war, federal soldiers fought solely to uphold the Constitution and preserve the nation. With the Emancipation Proclamation, however, the northern war effort took on a dual purpose: to save the Union and to free the slaves.

Even if the Civil War had not touched slavery, the conflict still would have transformed America. As the world's first modern war, it mobilized the entire populations of North and South, harnessed the productive capacities of both economies, and produced battles that fielded 200,000 soldiers and created casualties in the tens of thousands. The carnage lasted four years and cost the nation an estimated 620,000 lives, nearly as many as in all of its other wars combined. The war helped mold the modern American nation-state, and the federal government emerged with new power and responsibility over national life. The war encouraged industrialization. It tore families apart and pushed women into new work and roles. But because the war for union also became a war against slavery, the northern victory had truly revolutionary meaning.

Recalling the Civil War years, Frederick Douglass said, "It is something to couple one's name with great occasions." It *was* something — for William Gould and millions of other Americans. Poet Walt Whitman believed that the war was the "very centre, circumference, umbilicus" of his life. Whether they fought for the Confederacy or the Union, whether they labored behind the lines to supply Yankee or rebel soldiers, whether they prayed for the safe return of Northerners or Southerners, all Americans endured the crucible of war. But the war affected no group more than the 4 million African Americans who saw its beginning as slaves and emerged as free people.

The Crew of the USS *Hunchback*
African Americans served as sailors in the federal military long before they were permitted to become soldiers. Blacks initially served only as coal heavers, cooks, and stewards, but within a year some black sailors joined their ships' gun crews. The *Hunchback* was one of the Union's innovative ironclad ships. Although ironclads made wooden navies obsolete, they were far from invincible. During the assault on Charleston in 1863, five of the nine federal ironclads were partially or wholly disabled. National Archives.

"And the War Came"

Abraham Lincoln faced the worst crisis in the history of the nation: disunion. He revealed his strategy on March 4, 1861, in his inaugural address, which was firm yet conciliatory. First, he sought to stop the contagion of secession by avoiding any act that would push the skittish Upper South (North Carolina, Virginia, Maryland, Delaware, Kentucky, Tennessee, Missouri, and Arkansas) out of the Union. Second, he sought to reassure the seceding Lower South (South Carolina, Georgia, Florida, Alabama, Mississippi, Louisiana, and Texas) that the Republicans would not abolish slavery. Lincoln believed that Unionists there would assert themselves and overturn the secession decision. Always, Lincoln denied the right of secession and upheld the Union.

His counterpart, **Jefferson Davis**, fully intended to establish the Confederate States of America as an independent republic. To achieve permanence, Davis had to sustain the secession fever that had carried the Lower South out of the Union. Even if the Lower South held firm, however, the Confederacy would remain weak without additional states. Davis watched for opportunities to add new stars to the Confederate flag.

Neither man sought war; both wanted to achieve their objectives peacefully. As Lincoln later observed, "Both parties deprecated war, but one of them would *make* war rather than let the nation survive, and the other would *accept* war rather than let it perish. And the war came."

Fort Sumter The Confederate bombardment that started the Civil War on April 12, 1861, lobbed more than 4,000 rounds at Fort Sumter, located on an artificial island inside the entrance to Charleston harbor. Cannonballs pulverized the outer walls, while hot shot ignited the wooden buildings inside. Shrapnel from thirty-three hours of cannon fire shredded this flag, which flew over the fort throughout the bombardment. When Union major Robert Anderson surrendered on April 13, he and his men marched out of the fort under this tattered banner. When Anderson returned to Fort Sumter in April 1865, he triumphantly raised this very flag. Photograph: Minnesota Historical Society; flag: Confederate Museum, United Daughters of the Confederacy.

Attack on Fort Sumter

Major Robert Anderson and some eighty U.S. soldiers occupied **Fort Sumter**, which was perched on a tiny island at the entrance to Charleston harbor in South Carolina. The fort with its American flag became a hated symbol of the nation that Southerners had abandoned, and they wanted federal troops out. Sumter was also a symbol to Northerners, a beacon affirming federal sovereignty in the seceded states.

Lincoln decided to hold Fort Sumter, but to do so, he had to provision it, for Anderson was running dangerously short of food. In the first week of April 1861, Lincoln authorized a peaceful expedition to bring supplies, but not military reinforcements, to the fort. The president understood that he risked war, but his plan honored his inaugural promises to defend federal property and to avoid using military force unless first attacked. Masterfully, Lincoln had shifted the fateful decision of war or peace to Jefferson Davis.

On April 9, Davis and his cabinet met to consider the situation in Charleston harbor. The territorial integrity of the Confederacy demanded the end of the federal presence, Davis argued. But his secretary of state, Robert Toombs of Georgia, pleaded against military action. "Mr. President," he declared, "at this time it is suicide, murder, and will lose us every friend at the North. You will wantonly strike a hornet's nest which extends from mountain to ocean, and legions now quiet will swarm out and sting us to death." But Davis sent word to Confederate troops in Charleston to take the fort before the relief expedition arrived. Thirty-three hours of bombardment on April 12 and 13 reduced the fort to rubble. Miraculously, not a single Union soldier died. On April 14, with the fort ablaze, Major Anderson offered his surrender and lowered the U.S. flag. The Confederates had Fort Sumter, but they also had war.

On April 15, when Lincoln called for 75,000 militiamen to serve for ninety days to put down the rebellion, several times that number rushed to defend the flag. Democrats responded as fervently as Republicans. Stephen A. Douglas, the recently defeated Democratic candidate for president, pledged his support. "There are only two sides to the question," he said. "Every man must be for the United States or against it. There can be no neutrals in this war, *only patriots — or traitors*." But the people of the Upper South found themselves torn.

"Every man must be for the United States or against it. There can be no neutrals in this war, *only patriots — or traitors.*"

— Senator STEPHEN A. DOUGLAS

The Upper South Chooses Sides

The Upper South faced a horrendous choice: either to fight against the Lower South or to fight against the Union. Many who only months earlier had rejected secession now embraced the Confederacy. To vote against southern independence was one thing, to fight fellow Southerners quite another. Thousands felt betrayed, believing that Lincoln had promised to achieve a peaceful reunion by waiting patiently for Unionists to retake power in the seceding states. It was a "politician's war," one man declared, but he conceded that "this is no time now to discuss the causes, but it is the duty of all who regard Southern institutions of value to side with the South, make common cause with the Confederate States and sink or swim with them."

One by one, the states of the Upper South jumped off the fence. Virginia, Arkansas, Tennessee, and North Carolina joined the Confederacy (Map 15.1). But in the border states of Delaware, Maryland, Kentucky, and Missouri, Unionism triumphed. Only in Delaware, where slaves accounted for less than 2 percent of the population, was the victory easy. In Maryland, Unionism needed a helping hand. Rather than allow the state to secede and make Washington, D.C., a federal island in a Confederate sea, Lincoln suspended the writ of habeas corpus, essentially setting aside constitutional guarantees that protect citizens from arbitrary arrest and detention, and he ordered U.S. troops into Baltimore. Maryland's legislature rejected secession.

The struggle turned violent in the West. In Missouri, Unionists won a narrow victory, but southern-sympathizing guerrilla bands roamed the state for the duration of the war, terrorizing civilians and soldiers alike. In Kentucky, Unionists also narrowly defeated secession, but the prosouthern minority claimed otherwise. The Confederacy, not especially careful about counting votes, eagerly made Missouri and Kentucky the twelfth and thirteenth stars on the Confederate flag.

Throughout the border states, but especially in Kentucky, the Civil War divided families. Seven of Senator Henry Clay's grandsons fought: four for the Confederacy and three for the Union. Lincoln understood that the border states — particularly Kentucky — contained indispensable resources, population, and wealth and also controlled major rivers and railroads. "I think to lose Kentucky is nearly the same as to lose the whole game," Lincoln said. "Kentucky gone, we can not hold Missouri, nor, as I think, Maryland. These all against us, . . . we would as well consent to separation at once."

In the end, only eleven of the fifteen slave states joined the Confederate States of America. Moreover, the four seceding Upper South states contained significant numbers of people who felt little affection for the Confederacy. Dissatisfaction was so rife in the western counties of Virginia

MAP 15.1
Secession, 1860–1861
After Lincoln's election, the fifteen slave states debated what to do. Seven states quickly left the Union, four left after the firing on Fort Sumter, and four remained loyal to the Union.

that in 1863 citizens there voted to create the separate state of West Virginia, loyal to the Union. Still, the acquisition of four new states greatly strengthened the Confederacy's drive for national independence.

REVIEW Why did both the Union and the Confederacy consider control of the border states crucial?

▸ The Combatants

Only slaveholders had a direct economic stake in preserving slavery (estimated at some $3 billion in 1860), but most whites in the Confederacy defended the institution, the way of life built on it, and the Confederate nation. The degraded and subjugated status of blacks elevated the status of the poorest whites. "It matters not whether slaves be actually owned by many or by few," one Southerner declared. "It is enough that one simply belongs to the superior and ruling race, to secure consideration and respect." Moreover, Yankee "aggression" was no longer a mere threat; it was real and at the South's door. Southern whites equated the secession of 1861 with the declaration of independence from tyrannical British rule in 1776. As one Georgia woman said, Southerners wanted "nothing from the North but — to *be let alone*."

For Northerners, rebel "treason" threatened to destroy the best government on earth. The South's failure to accept the democratic election of a president and its firing on the nation's flag challenged the rule of law, the authority of the Constitution, and the ability of the people to govern themselves. As an Indiana soldier told his wife, a "good government is the best thing on earth. Property is nothing without it, because it is not protected; a family is nothing without it, because they cannot be educated." Only a Union victory, Lincoln declared, would secure America's promise "to elevate the condition of man."

Northerners and Southerners rallied behind their separate flags, fully convinced that they were in the right and that God was on their side. But no one could argue that the Confederacy's resources and forces equaled the Union's. Yankees took heart from their superior power, but the rebels believed they had advantages that nullified every northern strength. Both sides mobilized swiftly in 1861, and each devised what it believed would be a winning military and diplomatic strategy.

How They Expected to Win

The balance sheet of northern and southern resources reveals enormous advantages for the Union (Figure 15.1). The twenty-three states remaining in the Union had a population of 22.3 million; the eleven Confederate states had a population of only 9.1 million, of whom 3.67 million (40 percent) were slaves. The North's economic advantages were even more overwhelming. Yet Southerners expected to win — for some good reasons — and they came very close to doing so.

"Britain could not conquer three million, the world cannot conquer the South."
— A Louisianan

Southerners knew they bucked the military odds, but hadn't the liberty-loving colonists in 1776 also done so? "Britain could not conquer three million," a Louisianan proclaimed, and "the world cannot conquer the South." How could anyone doubt the outcome of

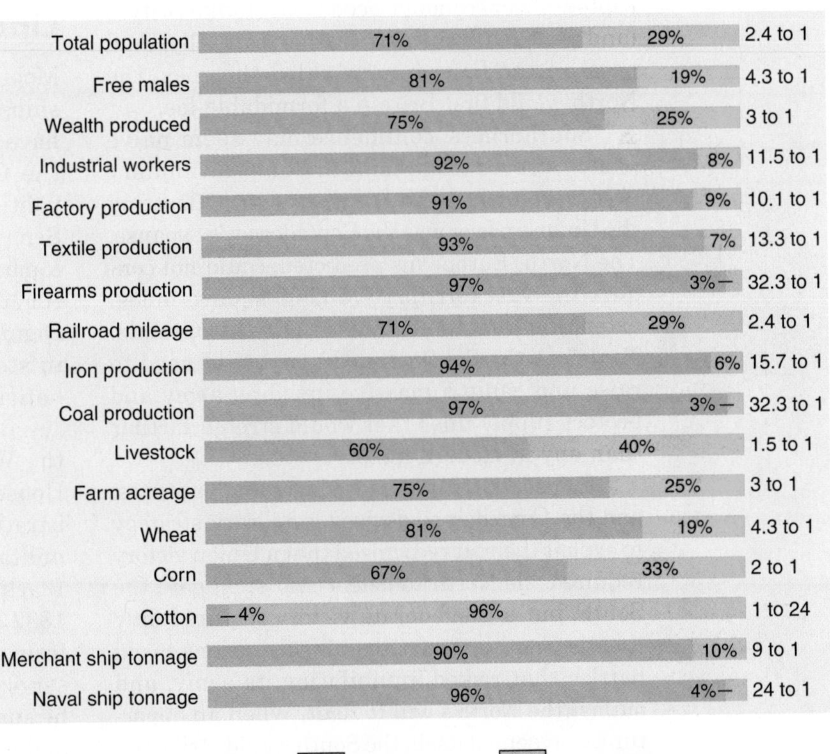

FIGURE 15.1 Resources of the Union and the Confederacy
The Union's enormous statistical advantages failed to convince Confederates that their cause was doomed.

a contest between lean, hard, country-born rebel warriors defending family, property, and liberty, and soft, flabby, citified Yankee mechanics waging an unconstitutional war?

The South's confidence also rested on its belief that northern prosperity depended on the South's cotton. Without cotton, New England textile mills would stand idle. Without planters purchasing northern manufactured goods, northern factories would drown in their own unsold surpluses. And without the foreign exchange earned by the overseas sales of cotton, the financial structure of the entire Yankee nation would collapse. A Virginian spoke for most Confederates when he declared that in the South's ability to "withhold the benefits of our trade, we hold a power over the North more powerful than a powerful army in the field."

King Cotton diplomacy would also make Europe a powerful ally of the Confederacy, Southerners reasoned. After all, they said, Britain's economy (and, to a lesser degree, France's) also depended on cotton. Of the 900 million pounds of cotton Britain imported annually, more than 700 million pounds came from the American South. If the supply was interrupted, sheer economic need would make Britain (and perhaps France) a Confederate ally. And because the British navy ruled the seas, the North would find Britain a formidable foe.

Southerners' confidence may seem naive today, but even tough-minded European military observers picked the South to win. Offsetting the Union's power was the Confederacy's expanse. The North, Europeans predicted, could not conquer the vast territory (750,000 square miles) extending from the Potomac to the Rio Grande. To defeat the South, the Union would need to raise and equip a massive invading army and protect supply lines that would stretch farther than any in modern history.

Indeed, the South enjoyed major advantages, and the Confederacy devised a military strategy to exploit them. It recognized that a Union victory required the North to defeat and subjugate the South, but a Confederate victory required only that the South stay at home, blunt invasions, avoid battles that risked annihilating its army, and outlast the North's will to fight. When an opportunity presented itself, the South would strike the invaders. Like the American colonists, the South could win independence by not losing the war.

If the North did nothing, the South would by default establish itself as a sovereign nation. The Lincoln administration, therefore, adopted an offensive strategy that applied pressure at many points. Lincoln declared a naval blockade of the Confederacy to deny it the ability to sell cotton abroad, giving the South far fewer dollars to pay for war goods. Even before the North could mount an effective blockade, however, Jefferson Davis decided voluntarily to cease exporting cotton. He wanted to create a cotton "famine" that would enfeeble the northern economy and precipitate European intervention. But the cotton famine Davis created devastated the South, not the North, and kept Europe on the diplomatic sidelines. Lincoln also ordered the Union army into Virginia, at the same time planning a march through the Mississippi valley that would cut the Confederacy in two. Dubbed the **Anaconda Plan**, this ambitious strategy took advantage of the Union's superior resources.

Neither side could foresee the magnitude and duration of the war. Americans thought of war in terms of the Mexican-American War of the 1840s, a conflict that had cost relatively few lives and had inflicted only light damage on the countryside. On the eve of the fighting, they could not know that four ghastly years of bloodletting lay ahead.

Lincoln and Davis Mobilize

Mobilization required effective political leadership, and at first glance the South appeared to have the advantage. Jefferson Davis brought to the Confederate presidency a distinguished political career, including experience in the U.S. Senate. He was also a West Point graduate, a combat veteran and authentic hero of the Mexican-American War, and a former secretary of war. Dignified and ramrod straight, with "a jaw sawed in steel," Davis appeared to be everything a nation could want in a wartime leader.

By contrast, Abraham Lincoln brought to the White House one lackluster term in the House of Representatives and almost no administrative experience. His sole brush with anything military was as a captain in the militia in the Black Hawk War, a brief struggle in Illinois in 1832 in which whites expelled the last Indians from the state. Lincoln later joked about his service in the Black Hawk War as the time when he survived bloody encounters with mosquitoes and led raids on wild onion patches. The lanky, disheveled Illinois lawyer-politician looked anything but military or presidential in his bearing.

In fact, the hardworking Davis proved to be less than he appeared. He had no gift for military strategy yet intervened often in military affairs. He was an even less able political leader. Quarrelsome and proud, he had an acid tongue that made enemies the Confederacy could ill afford. The Confederacy's intimidating problems might have defeated an even more talented leader, however. For example, state sovereignty, which was enshrined in the Confederate constitution, made Davis's task of organizing a new nation and fighting a war difficult in the extreme.

With Lincoln the North got far more than met the eye. He proved himself a master politician and a superb leader. When forming his cabinet, Lincoln appointed the ablest men, no matter that they were often his chief rivals and critics. He appointed Salmon P. Chase secretary of the treasury, knowing that Chase had presidential ambitions. As secretary of state, he chose his chief opponent for the Republican nomination in 1860, William H. Seward. Despite his civilian background, Lincoln displayed an innate understanding of military strategy. No one was more crucial in mapping the Union war plan. Moreover, Lincoln's eloquent letters and speeches helped galvanize the northern people in defense of the nation he called "the last best hope of earth."

Northern Volunteers, 1861
Lincoln called the Civil War a "People's Contest," a "struggle for maintaining in the world that form and substance of government, whose leading object is to elevate the condition of men — to lift artificial weights from all shoulders — clear the paths of laudable pursuit for all — to afford all an unfettered start, and a fair chance, in the race of life." Northerners shared Lincoln's vision, and in countless small towns from Iowa to Maine, when word arrived that soldiers were needed, scores of young men like these in Illinois rushed to volunteer. Private Collection/Picture Research Consultants & Archives.

Lincoln and Davis began gathering their armies. Confederates had to build almost everything from scratch, and Northerners had to channel their superior numbers and industrial resources to the purposes of war. On the eve of the war, the federal army numbered only 16,000 men, most of them scattered over the West subjugating Indians. One-third of the officers followed the example of the Virginian Robert E. Lee, resigning their commissions and heading south. The U.S. Navy was in better shape. Forty-two ships were in service, and a large merchant marine would in time provide more ships and sailors for the Union cause. Possessing a much weaker navy, the South pinned its hopes on its armies.

The Confederacy made prodigious efforts to build new factories to produce tents, blankets, shoes, and its gray uniforms, but many rebel soldiers slept in the open air without blankets and were sometimes without shoes. Even when factories managed to produce what the soldiers needed, southern railroads — captured, destroyed, or left in disrepair — often could not deliver the goods. Food production proved less of a problem, but food sometimes rotted before it reached the soldiers. The one bright spot was the Confederacy's Ordnance Bureau, headed by Josiah Gorgas, a near miracle worker when it came to manufacturing gunpowder, cannons, and rifles. In April 1864, Gorgas proudly observed: "Where three years ago we were not making a gun, a pistol nor a sabre, no shot nor shell . . . we now make all these in quantities to meet the demands of our large armies."

Recruiting and supplying huge armies required enormous

The Minié Ball
The Union army was one of the best-equipped armies in history, but none of its weaponry proved more vital than a French innovation by Captain Claude Minié. In 1848, Minié created an inch-long bullet that was rammed down a rifle barrel and would spin at great speed as it left the muzzle. The spin gave the bullet greater distance and accuracy than bullets fired from smoothbore weapons. When the war began, most soldiers carried smoothbore muskets, but by 1863 infantry on both sides fought with rifles. Bullets caused more than 90 percent of battle wounds, and minié balls proved extremely destructive to human bodies on impact. Picture Research Consultants & Archives.

new revenues. At first, the Union and the Confederacy sold war bonds, which essentially were loans from patriotic citizens. In addition, both sides turned to taxes. The North raised one-fifth of its wartime revenue from taxes; the South raised only one-twentieth. Eventually, both began printing paper money. Inflation soared, but the Confederacy suffered more because it financed a greater part of its wartime costs through the printing press. Prices in the Union rose by about 80 percent during the war, while inflation in the Confederacy topped 9,000 percent.

Within months of the bombardment of Fort Sumter, both sides found men to fight and ways to supply them. But the underlying strength of the northern economy gave the Union the decided advantage. With their military and industrial muscles beginning to ripple, Northerners became itchy for action that would smash the rebellion. Horace Greeley's *New York Tribune* began to chant: "Forward to Richmond! Forward to Richmond!"

REVIEW Why did the South believe it could win the war despite numerical disadvantages?

▸ Battling It Out, 1861–1862

During the first year and a half of the war, armies fought major campaigns in both East and West. Because the rival capitals — Richmond and Washington, D.C. — were only ninety miles apart and each was threatened more than once with capture, the eastern campaign was especially dramatic. But the battles in the West proved more decisive. As Yankee and rebel armies pounded each other on land, the navies fought on the seas and on the rivers of the South. In Europe, Confederate and U.S. diplomats competed for advantage in the corridors of power. All the while, casualty lists on both sides reached appalling lengths.

> **"If General McClellan does not want to use the army I would like to *borrow* it."**
> — ABRAHAM LINCOLN

Stalemate in the Eastern Theater

In the summer of 1861, Lincoln ordered the 35,000 Union troops assembling outside Washington to attack the 20,000 Confederates defending Manassas, a railroad junction in Virginia about thirty miles southwest of Washington. On July 21, the army forded Bull Run, a branch of the Potomac River, and engaged the southern forces (Map 15.2). But fast-moving southern reinforcements blunted the Union attack and then counterattacked. What began as an orderly Union retreat turned into a panicky stampede. Demoralized federal troops ran over shocked civilians as the soldiers raced back to Washington.

By Civil War standards, the casualties (wounded and dead) at the **battle of Bull Run** (or **Manassas**, as Southerners called the battle) were light, about 2,000 Confederates and 1,600 Federals. The significance of the battle lay in the lessons Northerners and Southerners drew from it. For Southerners, it confirmed the superiority of rebel fighting men and the inevitability of Confederate nationhood. Manassas was "*one of the decisive battles of the world*," a Georgian proclaimed. It "*has* secured our independence." While victory fed southern pride, defeat sobered Northerners. It was a major setback, admitted the *New York Tribune*, but "let us go to work, then, with a will." Bull Run taught Lincoln that victory would be neither quick nor easy. Within four days of the disaster, the president authorized the enlistment of 1 million men for three years.

Lincoln also found a new general, the young **George B. McClellan**, whom he appointed commander of the newly named Army of the Potomac. Having graduated from West Point second in his class, the thirty-four-year-old McClellan believed that he was a great soldier and that Lincoln was a dunce, the "original Gorilla." A superb administrator and organizer, McClellan energetically whipped his dispirited soldiers into shape, but he was reluctant to send them into battle. For all his energy, McClellan lacked decisiveness. Lincoln wanted a general who would advance, take risks, and fight, but McClellan went into winter quarters. "If General McClellan does not want to use the army I would like to *borrow* it," Lincoln declared in frustration.

Finally, in May 1862, McClellan launched his long-awaited offensive. He transported his highly polished army, now 130,000 strong, to the mouth of the James River and began slowly moving up the Yorktown peninsula toward Richmond. When he was within six miles of the Confederate capital, General Joseph Johnston hit him like a hammer. In the assault, Johnston was wounded and was replaced by **Robert E. Lee**, who would become the South's most celebrated general. Lee named his command the Army of Northern Virginia.

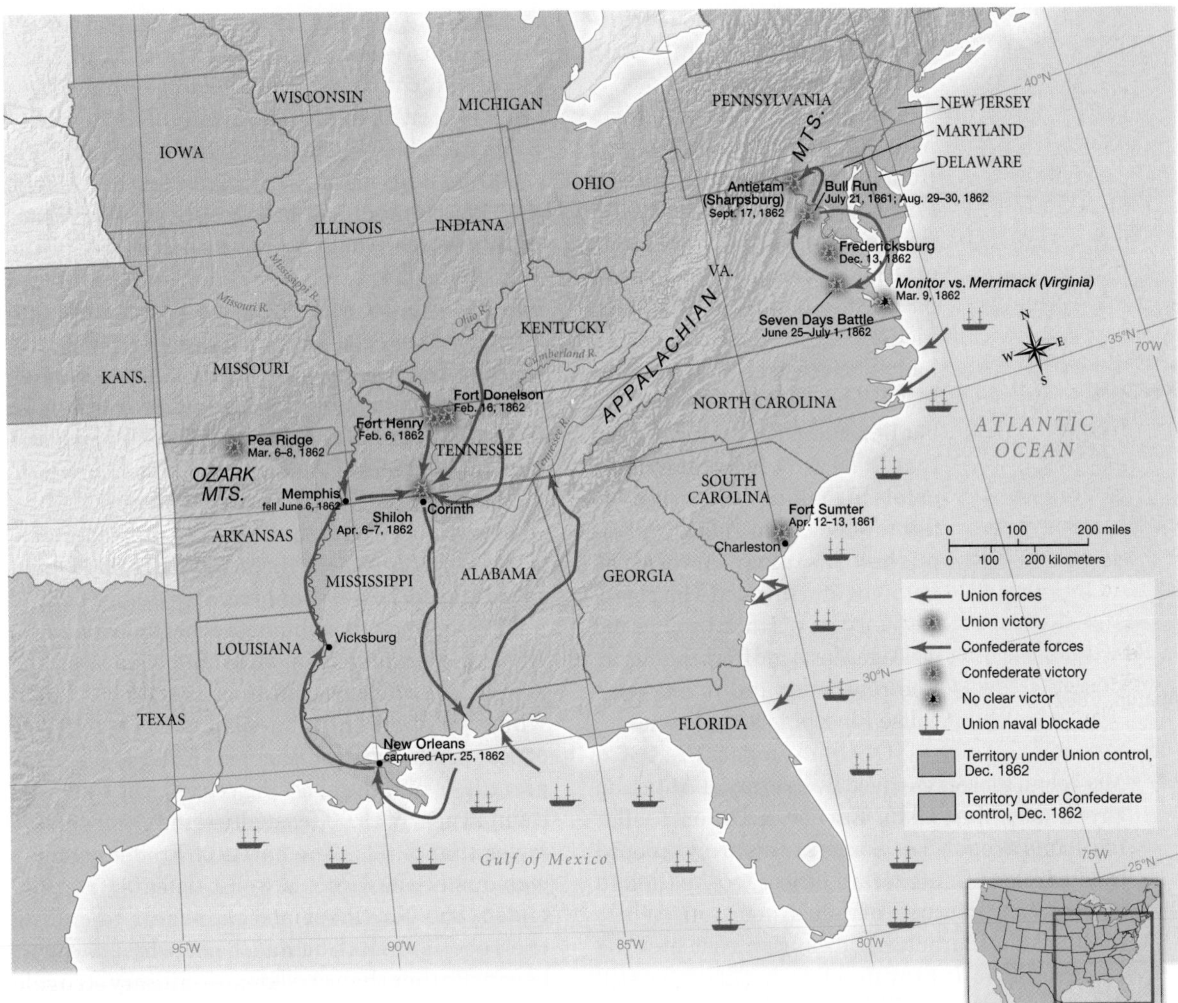

MAP ACTIVITY

Map 15.2 The Civil War, 1861–1862

While most eyes were focused on the eastern theater, especially the ninety-mile stretch of land between Washington, D.C., and the Confederate capital of Richmond, Virginia, Union troops were winning strategic victories in the West.

READING THE MAP: In which states did the Confederacy and the Union each win the most battles during this period? Which side used or followed water routes most for troop movements and attacks?

CONNECTIONS: Which major cities in the South and West fell to Union troops in 1862? Which strategic area did those Confederate losses place in Union hands? How did this outcome affect the later movement of troops and supplies?

The contrast between Lee and McClellan could hardly have been greater. McClellan brimmed with conceit and braggadocio; Lee was courteous and reserved. On the battlefield, McClellan grew timid and irresolute, and Lee became audaciously, even recklessly, aggressive. And Lee had at his side in the peninsula campaign military men of real talent: Thomas J. Jackson, nicknamed "Stonewall" for holding the line at Manassas, and James E. B. ("Jeb") Stuart, a dashing twenty-nine-year-old cavalry commander who rode circles around Yankee troops. Jackson ranks among the most brilliant commanders of the war, but in May 1863 he died at the battle of Chancellorsville.

Lee's assault initiated the Seven Days Battle (June 25–July 1) and began McClellan's march back down the peninsula. By the time McClellan reached safety, 30,000 men from both sides had died or been wounded. Although Southerners suffered twice the casualties of Northerners, Lee had saved Richmond. Lincoln wired McClellan

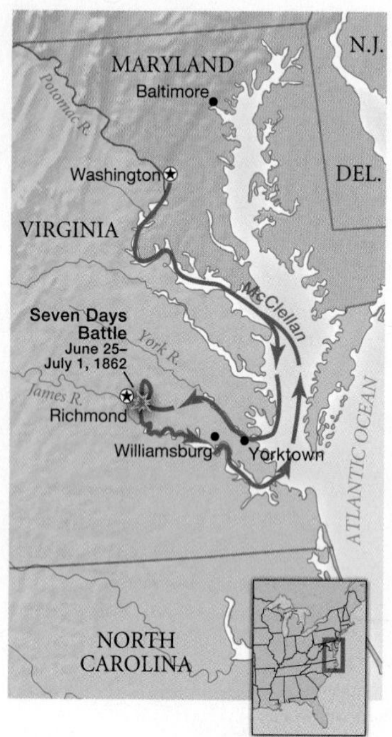

Peninsula Campaign, 1862

to abandon the peninsula campaign and replaced him with General John Pope.

In August, north of Richmond, at the second battle of Bull Run, Lee's smaller army battered Pope's forces and sent them scurrying back to Washington. Lincoln ordered Pope to Minnesota to pacify the Indians and restored McClellan to command. Lincoln had not changed his mind about McClellan's capacity as a warrior, but he reluctantly acknowledged that "if he can't fight himself, he excels in making others ready to fight." Lee could fight, and he pushed his army across the Potomac and invaded Maryland. A victory on northern soil would dislodge Maryland from the Union, Lee reasoned, and might even cause Lincoln to sue for peace.

On September 17, 1862, McClellan's forces engaged Lee's army at Antietam Creek (see Map 15.2). Earlier, a Union soldier had found a copy of Lee's orders to his army dropped by a careless Confederate officer, so McClellan had a clear picture of Lee's position. While McClellan's characteristic caution cost him the opportunity to destroy the opposing army, he still did severe damage. With "solid shot . . . cracking skulls like eggshells," according to one observer, the armies went after each other. At Miller's Cornfield, the firing was so intense that "every stalk of corn in the . . . field was cut as closely as could have been done with a knife." By nightfall, 6,000 men lay dead or dying on the battlefield, and 17,000 more had been wounded. **The battle of Antietam** would be the bloodiest day of the war. Instead of being the war-winning fight Lee had anticipated when he came north, Antietam sent the battered Army of Northern Virginia limping back home. McClellan claimed to have saved the North, but Lincoln again removed him from command of the Army of the Potomac and appointed General Ambrose Burnside.

Though bloodied, Lee found an opportunity in December to punish the enemy at Fredericksburg, Virginia, where Burnside's 122,000 Union troops faced 78,500 Confederates dug in behind a stone wall on the heights above the Rappahannock River. Half a mile of open ground separated the armies. "A chicken could not live on that field when we open on it," a Confederate artillery officer predicted. Yet Burnside ordered a frontal assault. When the shooting ceased, the Federals counted nearly 13,000 casualties, the Confederates fewer than 5,000. The battle of Fredericksburg was one of the Union's worst defeats. As 1862 ended, the North seemed no nearer to ending the rebellion than it had been when the war began. Rather than checkmate, military struggle in the East had reached stalemate.

***The Battle of Savage's Station,* by Robert Knox Sneden, 1862**
In 1862, thirty-year-old Robert Sneden joined the Fortieth New York Volunteers and soon found himself in Virginia, part of George McClellan's peninsula campaign. A gifted artist and an eloquent writer, Sneden captured an early Confederate assault in what became known as the Seven Days Battle. The "storm of lead was continuous and deadly on the approaching lines of the Rebels," Sneden observed. "They bravely rushed up, however, to within twenty feet of our artillery." Sneden produced hundreds of vivid drawings and thousands of pages of remembrances, providing one of the most complete accounts of a Union soldier's Civil War experience.

The Dead of Antietam

In October 1862, photographer Mathew Brady opened an exhibition at his New York gallery that shocked the nation. The exhibition consisted of ninety-five photographs that presented the battle of Antietam as the soldiers saw it. The image here is of Confederate soldiers killed near the Dunkard Church, photographed two days later by Alexander Gardner. A New York Times reporter observed, "Mr. Brady has done something to bring to us the terrible reality and earnestness of the war. If he has not brought bodies and laid them in our door-yards and along [our] streets, he had done something very like it." Library of Congress.

Union Victories in the Western Theater

While most eyes focused on events in the East, the decisive early encounters of the war were taking place between the Appalachian Mountains and the Ozarks (see Map 15.2). Confederates wanted Missouri and Kentucky, states they claimed but did not control. Federals wanted to split Arkansas, Louisiana, and Texas from the Confederacy by taking control of the Mississippi River and to occupy Tennessee, one of the Confederacy's main producers of food, mules, and iron — all vital resources.

Before Union forces could march on Tennessee, they needed to secure Missouri to the west. Union troops swept across Missouri to the border of Arkansas, where in March 1862 they encountered a 16,000-man Confederate army, which included three regiments of Indians from the so-called Five Civilized Tribes—the Choctaw, Chickasaw, Creek, Seminole, and Cherokee. Although Indians fought on both sides during the war, Native Americans who sided with the South hoped that the Confederacy would grant them more independence than had the United States. The Union victory at the battle of Pea Ridge left Missouri free of Confederate troops, but Missouri was not free of Confederate fighters. Guerrilla bands led by the notorious William Clarke Quantrill and "Bloody Bill" Anderson burned, tortured, scalped, and murdered Union civilians and soldiers until the final year of the war.

Even farther west, Confederate armies sought to fulfill Jefferson Davis's vision of a slaveholding empire stretching all the way to the Pacific. Both sides recognized the immense value of the gold and silver mines of California, Nevada, and Colorado. And both sides bolstered their armies in the Southwest with Mexican Americans, some 2,500 fighting for the Confederacy and 1,000 joining Union forces. A quick strike by Texas troops took Santa Fe, New Mexico, in the winter of 1861–62. Then in March 1862, a band of Colorado miners ambushed and crushed southern forces at Glorieta Pass, outside Santa Fe. Confederate military failures in the far West meant that there would be no Confederate empire beyond Texas.

The principal western battles took place in Tennessee, where General **Ulysses S. Grant** emerged as the key northern commander. Grant had graduated from West Point and served bravely in Mexico. When the Civil War began, he was a thirty-nine-year-old dry-goods clerk in Galena, Illinois. Gentle at home, he became pugnacious on the battlefield. "The art of war is simple," he said. "Find out where your enemy is, get at him as soon as you can and strike him as hard as you can, and keep moving on." Grant's philosophy of war as attrition would take a huge toll in human life, but it played to the North's superiority in manpower. In his private's uniform and slouch hat, Grant did not look much like a general. But Lincoln, who did not look much like a president, learned his worth. Later, to critics who wanted the president to sack Grant because of his drinking, Lincoln would say, "*I can't spare this man. He fights.*"

In February 1862, operating in tandem with U.S. Navy

Battle of Glorieta Pass, 1862

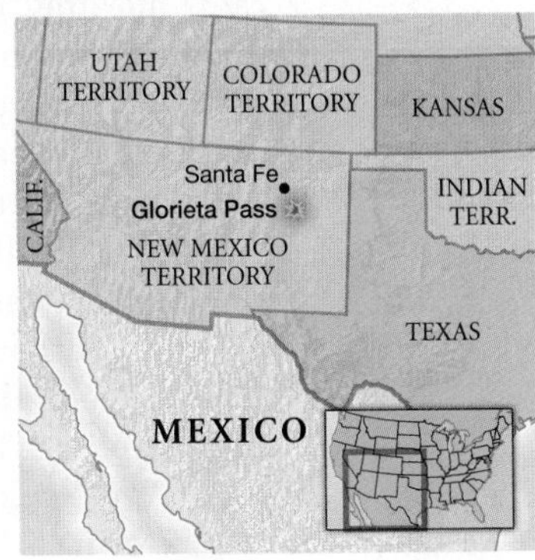

Native American Recruits
Both the Union and the Confederacy enrolled Indian soldiers. Here, a Union recruiter swears in two recruits. The Confederates promised to assume the financial obligations of the old treaties with the United States, guarantee slavery, respect tribal independence, and permit the tribes to send delegates to Richmond. Cherokee chief John Ross, who signed with the Confederacy, likened his difficult choice to that of a man in a flood who sees a log floating by: "By refusing [the log] he is a doomed man. By seizing hold of it he has a chance for his life." Approximately 20,000 Indians fought in the Civil War, sometimes against each other. Wisconsin Historical Society.

gunboats, Grant captured Fort Henry on the Tennessee River and Fort Donelson on the Cumberland (see Map 15.2). Defeat forced the Confederates to withdraw from all of Kentucky and most of Tennessee, but Grant followed.

On April 6, General Albert Sidney Johnston's army surprised Grant at Shiloh Church in Tennessee. Union troops were badly mauled the first day, but Grant remained cool and brought up reinforcements throughout the night. The next morning, the Union army counterattacked, driving the Confederates before it. The **battle of Shiloh** was terribly costly to both sides; there were 20,000 casualties, among them General Johnston. Grant later said that after Shiloh he "gave up all idea of saving the Union except by complete conquest."

Although no one knew it at the time, Shiloh ruined the Confederacy's bid to control the theater of operations in the West. The Yankees quickly captured the strategic town of Corinth, Mississippi; the river city of Memphis; and the South's largest city, New Orleans. By the end of 1862, the far West and most — but not all — of the Mississippi valley lay in Union hands. At the same time, the outcome of the struggle in another theater of war was also becoming clearer.

The Atlantic Theater

When the war began, the U.S. Navy's blockade fleet consisted of about three dozen ships to patrol more than 3,500 miles of southern coastline, and rebel merchant ships were able to slip in and out of southern ports nearly at will. Taking on cargoes in the Caribbean, sleek Confederate blockade runners brought in vital supplies — guns and medicine. But with the U.S. Navy commissioning a new blockader almost weekly, the naval fleet eventually numbered 150 ships on duty, and the Union navy dramatically improved its score.

Unable to build a conventional navy equal to the expanding U.S. fleet, the Confederates experimented with a radical new maritime design: the ironclad warship. At Norfolk, Virginia, the wooden hull of the frigate *Merrimack* was layered with two-inch-thick armor plate. Rechristened *Virginia*, the ship steamed out in March 1862 and sank two wooden federal ships, killing at least 240 Union sailors (see Map 15.2). When the *Virginia* returned to finish off the federal blockaders the next morning, it was challenged by the *Monitor*, a federal ironclad of even more

THE PROMISE OF TECHNOLOGY

The World's First Successful Submarine

As the federal blockade of southern ports gradually began to strangle Confederate shipping, Southerners were forced to innovate in naval technology: the ironclad, floating mines (called torpedoes), and, most spectacular of all, the submarine. Three years of trial and error, experimentation, and wartime innovation produced the CSS *H. L. Hunley.* A sleek, forty-foot, nine-man vessel, the *Hunley* was an engineering marvel that exhibited both sophisticated technology and primitive features. General P. G. T. Beauregard felt compelled to explain to men who were considering volunteering for its crew the "desperately hazardous nature of the service required." On the night of February 17, 1864, the *Hunley* sank the Union blockader USS *Housatonic* and then itself sank with its entire crew. No other submarine would sink an enemy ship until World War I, more than half a century later. The *Hunley* is shown here at Charleston in 1863 in a painting by Conrad Wise Chapman.

How does the *Hunley* confirm the adage "Necessity is the mother of invention"? Museum of the Confederacy.

radical design, topped with a revolving turret holding two eleven-inch guns. On March 9, the two ships hurled shells at each other for two hours, but when neither could penetrate the other's armor, the battle ended in a draw.

The Confederacy never found a way to break the **Union blockade** despite exploring many naval innovations, including a new underwater vessel — the submarine. Each month, the Union fleet tightened its noose. By 1863, the South had abandoned its embargo policy and desperately wanted to ship cotton to pay for imports of arms, shoes, and uniforms needed to fight the war. The growing effectiveness of the federal blockade, a southern naval officer observed, "shut the Confederacy out from the world, deprived it of supplies, weakened its military and naval strength." By 1865, the blockaders were intercepting about half of the southern ships attempting to break through. The Confederacy was sealed off, with devastating results.

International Diplomacy

What the Confederates could not achieve on the seas, they sought to achieve through international diplomacy. Confederates and Unionists both realized that the world was watching the struggle in North America. Nationalists everywhere understood that the American Civil War engaged issues central to their own nation-building efforts. The Confederates rested their claims to separate nationhood on the principles of self-determination and rightful rebellion against despotic power, and they desperately wanted Europe to intervene. The Lincoln

Major Battles of the Civil War, 1861–1862

April 12–13, 1861	Attack on Fort Sumter
July 21, 1861	First battle of Bull Run (Manassas)
February 6, 1862	Battle of Fort Henry
February 16, 1862	Battle of Fort Donelson
March 6–8, 1862	Battle of Pea Ridge
March 9, 1862	Battle of the *Merrimack* (the *Virginia*) and the *Monitor*
March 26, 1862	Battle of Glorieta Pass
April 6–7, 1862	Battle of Shiloh
May–July 1862	McClellan's peninsula campaign
June 6, 1862	Fall of Memphis
June 25–July 1, 1862	Seven Days Battle
August 29–30, 1862	Second battle of Bull Run (Manassas)
September 17, 1862	Battle of Antietam
December 13, 1862	Battle of Fredericksburg

FIGURE 15.2 GLOBAL COMPARISON: European Cotton Imports, 1860–1870
In 1860, the South enjoyed a near monopoly in supplying cotton to Europe's textile mills, but the Civil War almost entirely halted its exports. Figures for Europe's importation of cotton for 1861 to 1865 reveal one of the reasons the Confederacy's King Cotton diplomacy failed: Europeans found other sources of cotton. Which countries were most important in filling the void? When the war ended in 1865, cotton production resumed in the South, and exports to Europe again soared. Did the South regain its near monopoly? How would you characterize the United States' competitive position five years after the war?

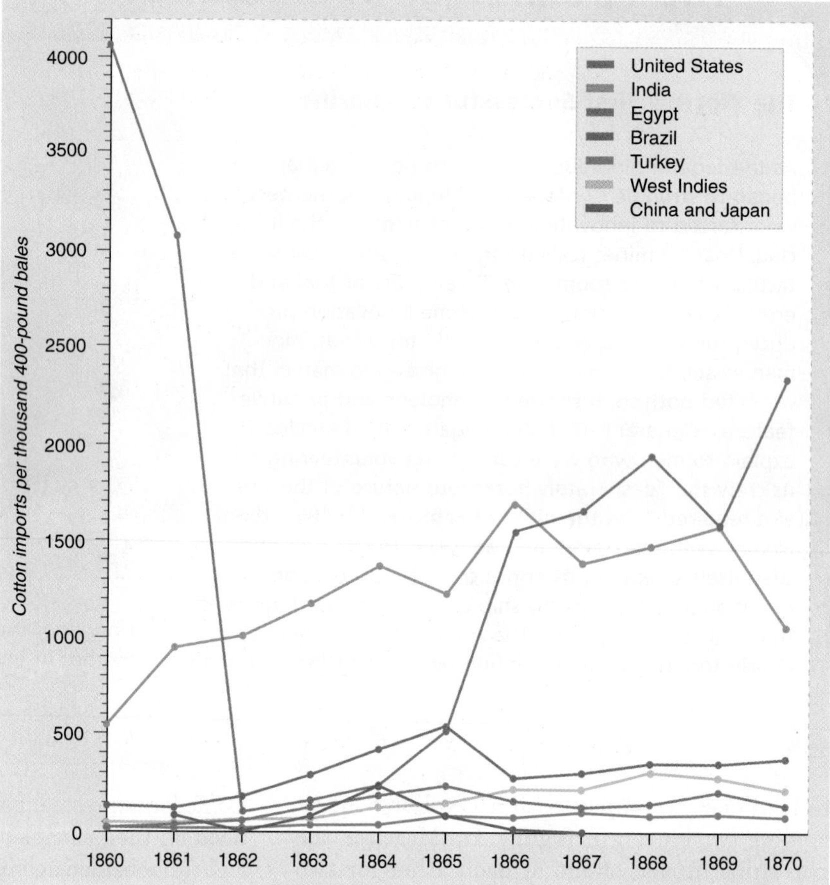

administration explained why the Union had to be preserved and why Europe had to remain neutral. "The question," Lincoln noted, is "whether a constitutional republic, or a democracy — a government of the people, by the same people — can or cannot, maintain its territorial integrity, against its own domestic foes."

More practically, the Confederates based their hope for European support on King Cotton. In theory, cotton-starved European nations would have no choice but to break the Union blockade and recognize the Confederacy. Southern hopes were not unreasonable, for at the height of the "cotton famine" in 1862, when 2 million British workers were unemployed, Britain tilted toward recognition. Along with several other European nations, Britain granted the Confederacy "belligerent" status, which enabled it to buy goods and build ships in European ports. The British-built Confederate cruiser *Alabama* sank or captured sixty-four Union merchant ships before the USS *Kearsarge* sank it off the coast of France in 1864. But no country challenged the Union blockade or recognized the Confederate States of America as a nation, a bold act that probably would have drawn that country into war.

King Cotton diplomacy failed for several reasons. A bumper cotton crop in 1860 meant that the warehouses of British textile manufacturers bulged with surplus cotton throughout 1861. In 1862, when a cotton shortage did occur, European manufacturers found new sources in India, Egypt, and elsewhere (Figure 15.2). In addition, the development of a brisk trade between the Union and Britain — British war materiel for American grain and flour — helped offset the decline in textiles and encouraged Britain to remain neutral.

Europe's temptation to intervene disappeared for good in 1862. Union military successes in the West made Britain and France think twice about linking their fates to the struggling Confederacy. Moreover, in September 1862, Lincoln announced a new policy that made an alliance with the Confederacy an alliance with slavery — a commitment the French and British, who had outlawed slavery in their empires and looked forward to its eradication worldwide, were not willing to make. After 1862, the South's cause was linked irrevocably with slavery and reaction, and the Union's cause was linked with freedom and democracy. The Union, not the Confederacy, had won the diplomatic stakes.

REVIEW Why did the Confederacy's bid for international support fail?

▸ Union *and* Freedom

For a year and a half, Lincoln insisted that the North fought strictly to save the Union and not to abolish slavery. Despite Lincoln's repeated pronouncements, however, the war for union became a war for African American freedom. Each month the conflict dragged on, it became clearer that the Confederate war machine depended heavily on slavery. Rebel armies used slaves to build fortifications, haul materiel, tend horses, and perform camp chores. On the home front, slaves labored in ironworks and shipyards, and they grew the food that fed both soldiers and civilians. Slavery undergirded the Confederacy as certainly as it had the Old South. As Frederick Douglass put it, slavery was "the stomach of this rebellion." Union military commanders and politicians alike gradually realized that to defeat the Confederacy, the North would have to destroy slavery. "I am a slow walker," Lincoln said, "but I never walk back."

From Slaves to Contraband

Lincoln detested human bondage, but as president he felt compelled to act prudently in the interests of the Union. He doubted his right under the Constitution to tamper with the "domestic institutions" of any state, even states in rebellion. An astute politician, Lincoln worked within the tight limits of public opinion. The issue of black freedom was particularly explosive in the loyal border states, where slaveholders threatened to jump into the arms of the Confederacy at even the hint of emancipation.

Black freedom also raised alarms in the free states. The Democratic Party gave notice that adding emancipation to the goal of union would make the war strictly a Republican affair. Moreover, many white Northerners were not about to risk their lives to satisfy what they considered abolitionist "fanaticism." "We Won't Fight to Free the Nigger," one popular banner read. They feared that emancipation would propel "two or three million semi-savages" northward, where they would crowd into white neighborhoods, compete for white jobs, and mix with white "sons and daughters." Thus, emancipation threatened to dislodge the loyal slave states from the Union, alienate the Democratic Party, deplete the armies, and perhaps even spark race warfare.

Yet proponents of emancipation pressed Lincoln as relentlessly as did the anti-emancipation forces. Abolitionists argued that by seceding, Southerners had forfeited their right to the protection of the Constitution and that Lincoln could — as the price of their treason — legally confiscate their property in slaves. When Lincoln refused, abolitionists scalded him. Frederick Douglass labeled him "the miserable tool of traitors and rebels."

The Republican-dominated Congress declined to leave slavery policy entirely in President Lincoln's hands. In August 1861, Congress approved the Confiscation Act, which allowed the seizure of any slave employed directly by the Confederate military. It also fulfilled the free-soil dream of prohibiting slavery in the territories and abolished slavery in Washington, D.C. Democrats and border-state representatives voted against even these mild measures, but Congress's attitude was clearly stiffening against slavery.

Slaves, not politicians, became the most insistent force for emancipation. By escaping their masters by the tens of thousands and running away to Union lines, they forced slavery on the North's wartime agenda. Runaways made Northerners answer a crucial question: Were the runaways now free, or were they still slaves who, according to the fugitive slave law, had to be returned to their masters? At first, Yankee military officers sent the fugitives back. But Union armies needed laborers. At Fort Monroe, Virginia, General Benjamin F. Butler refused to turn them over to their owners, calling them **contraband of war**, meaning "confiscated property," and put them to work. Congress made Butler's practice national policy in March 1862 when it forbade returning fugitive slaves to their masters. Slaves were still not legally free, but there was a tilt toward emancipation.

> **"The miserable tool of traitors and rebels."**
>
> — FREDERICK DOUGLASS, speaking of Lincoln, when he refused to confiscate the slaves of Southerners

Lincoln's policy of noninterference with slavery gradually crumbled. To calm Northerners' racial fears, Lincoln offered colonization, the deportation of African Americans from the United

Human Contraband
These refugees from slavery crossed the Rappahannock River in Virginia in August 1862 to seek sanctuary with a federal army. Most slaves fled with little more than the clothes on their backs, but not all escaped slavery empty-handed. The oxen, horse, wagon, and goods seen here could have been procured by a number of means — purchased during slavery, "borrowed" from the former master, or gathered during flight. Refugees who possessed draft animals and a wagon had much more economic opportunity than those who had only their labor to sell. Library of Congress.

States to Haiti, Panama, or elsewhere. In the summer of 1862, he told a delegation of black visitors that deep-seated racial prejudice among whites made it impossible for blacks to achieve equality in the United States. One African American responded, "This is our country as much as it is yours, and we will not leave." Congress voted a small amount of money to underwrite colonization, but after one miserable experiment on a small island in the Caribbean, practical limitations and stiff black opposition sank further efforts.

While Lincoln was developing his own antislavery initiatives, he snuffed out actions that he believed would jeopardize northern unity. He was particularly alert to Union commanders who tried to dictate slavery policy from the field. In August 1861, when John C. Frémont, former Republican presidential nominee and now commander of federal troops in Missouri, freed the slaves belonging to Missouri rebels, Lincoln forced the general to revoke his edict. The following May, when General David Hunter freed the slaves in Georgia, South Carolina, and Florida, Lincoln countermanded his order. Events moved so rapidly, however, that Lincoln found it impossible to control federal policy on slavery.

From Contraband to Free People

On August 22, 1862, Lincoln replied to an angry abolitionist who demanded that he attack slavery. "My paramount objective in this struggle *is* to save the Union," Lincoln said deliberately, "and is *not* either to save or destroy slavery. If I could save the Union without freeing *any* slave I would do it, and if I could save it by freeing *all* the slaves I would do it; and if I could save it by freeing some and leaving others alone I would also do that." Instead of simply restating his old position that union was the North's sole objective, Lincoln announced that slavery was no longer untouchable and that he would emancipate every slave if doing so would preserve the Union.

By the summer of 1862, events were tumbling rapidly toward emancipation. On July 17, Congress adopted the second Confiscation Act. The first had confiscated slaves employed by the Confederate military; the second declared all slaves of rebel masters "forever free of their servitude." In theory, this breathtaking measure freed most Confederate slaves, for slaveholders formed the backbone of the rebellion. Congress had traveled far since the war began.

Lincoln had, too. In July 1862, the president told two members of his cabinet that he had "about come to the conclusion that we must free the slaves or be ourselves subdued." A few days later, before the entire cabinet, he read a draft of a preliminary emancipation proclamation that promised to free *all* the slaves in the seceding states on January 1, 1863. Lincoln described emancipation as an "act of justice," but it was the lengthening casualty lists that finally brought him around. Emancipation, he declared, was "a military necessity, absolutely essential to the preservation of the Union." Only freeing the slaves would "strike at the heart of the rebellion." On September 22, Lincoln issued his preliminary **Emancipation Proclamation** promising freedom to slaves in areas still in rebellion on January 1, 1863.

The limitations of the proclamation — it exempted the loyal border states and the Union-occupied areas of the Confederacy — caused some to ridicule the act. The *Times* (London) observed cynically, "Where he has no power Mr. Lincoln will set the negroes free, where he retains power he will consider them as slaves." But Lincoln had no power to free slaves in loyal states, and invading Union armies would liberate slaves in the Confederacy as they advanced.

By presenting emancipation as a "military necessity," Lincoln hoped he had disarmed his conservative critics. Emancipation would deprive the Confederacy of valuable slave laborers, shorten the war, and thus save lives. Democrats, however, fumed that the "shrieking and howling abolitionist faction" had captured the White House and made it "a nigger war." Democrats made political hay out of Lincoln's action in the November 1862 elections, gaining thirty-four congressional seats. House Democrats quickly proposed a resolution branding emancipation "a high crime against the Constitution." The Republicans, who maintained narrow majorities in both houses of Congress, barely beat it back.

As promised, on New Year's Day 1863, Lincoln issued the final Emancipation Proclamation. Later in 1863 at Gettysburg, Pennsylvania, Lincoln famously confirmed the war's new purpose: "that this nation, under God, shall have a new birth of freedom — and that government of the people, by the people, for the people, shall not perish from the earth." In addition to freeing the slaves in the rebel states, the Emancipation Proclamation also committed the federal government to the fullest use of African Americans to defeat the Confederate enemy.

The War of Black Liberation

Even before Lincoln proclaimed emancipation a Union war aim, African Americans in the North had volunteered to fight. Military service, one black volunteer declared, would mean "the elevation of a downtrodden and despised race." But the War Department, doubtful of blacks' abilities and fearful of white reaction to serving side by side with them, refused to make black men soldiers. Instead, the army employed black men as manual laborers; black women sometimes found employment as laundresses and cooks. The navy, however, accepted blacks from the outset, including runaway slaves such as **William Gould** (see pages 461–62).

As Union casualty lists lengthened, Northerners gradually and reluctantly turned to African Americans to fill the army's blue uniforms. With

Black Men Working along the Wharf, 1860–1865
The black men seen here with picks and shovels working at the federal supply depot at City Point, Virginia, were likely fugitive slaves. Hundreds of thousands of able-bodied runaways cleared forests, built roads, erected bridges, constructed fortifications, and transported supplies for the U.S. army. They were overworked, paid irregularly, given inadequate food and clothing, and even physically assaulted, but they kept pouring into Union lines. Their labor became indispensable to the war effort, and as one Northerner remembered, "The truth was we never could get enough of them." Library of Congress.

SEEKING THE AMERICAN PROMISE

The Right to Fight: Black Soldiers in the Civil War

"A war undertaken and brazenly carried on for the perpetual enslavement of colored men, calls logically and loudly for colored men to help suppress it," black leader Frederick Douglass declared at the beginning of the war. But it was only in 1863 that the lengthening casualty lists finally convinced the Lincoln administration to begin aggressively recruiting black soldiers.

In February 1863, James Henry Gooding, a twenty-six-year-old seaman from New Bedford, enlisted in the 54th Massachusetts Colored Regiment. Like most black soldiers, Gooding viewed military service as an opportunity to strike blows against slavery and white prejudice. The destruction of slavery, he believed, "depends on the free black men of the North" because "those who are in bonds must have some one to open the door; when the slave sees the white soldier approach, he dares not trust him and why? Because he has heard that *some* have treated him worse than their owners in rebellion. But if the slave sees a black soldier, he knows he has got a friend." Fighting for the Union also offered a chance to attack white racism. In military service lay "the germs of the elevation of a downtrodden and despised race," Gooding believed, the chance for African Americans "to make themselves a people."

Fighting, Gooding said, offered blacks a chance to destroy the "foul aspersion that they were not men." According to the white commander of the 59th U.S. Colored Infantry, when an ex-slave put on a uniform of army blue, the change was dramatic: "Yesterday a filthy, repulsive 'nigger,' to-day a neatly-attired man; yesterday a slave, to-day a freeman; yesterday a civilian, to-day a soldier." Others noticed the same transformation: "Put a United States uniform on his back and the *chattel* is a man." Black veterans agreed. "This was the biggest thing that ever happened in my life," one ex-soldier remembered. "I felt like a man with a uniform and a gun in my hand." Another said, "I felt freedom in my bones."

Black courage under fire ended skepticism about the capabilities of African American troops. As one white officer observed after a battle, "They seemed like men who were fighting to vindicate their manhood and they did it well." The truth is, another remarked, "they have fought their way into the respect of all the army." After the 54th served courageously in South Carolina, Gooding reported: "It is not for us to blow our horn; but when a regiment of white men gave us three cheers as we were passing them, it shows that we did our duty as men should."

Yet discrimination within the Union army continued. When the government refused to pay blacks the same as whites, the 54th refused to accept unequal pay. Gooding wrote to President Lincoln himself to explain his regiment's decision: "Now the main question is, Are we Soldiers, or are we Labourers? . . . Now your Excellency, we have done a Soldier's Duty. Why Can't we have a Soldier's pay?" The 54th's principled stance helped reverse the government's position, and in June 1864 Congress equalized the pay of black and white soldiers.

As Union troops advanced deeper into the Confederacy, former slaves greeted black soldiers as heroes. In March 1865, the white officer of a black regiment in North Carolina reported that black soldiers "stepped like lords & conquerors. The frantic demonstrations of the negro population will never die out of my memory. Their cheers & heartfelt 'God bress ye's' & cries of 'De chains is broke; De chains is broke' mingled

the Militia Act of July 1862, Congress authorized enrolling blacks in "any military or naval service for which they may be found competent." After the Emancipation Proclamation, whites — like it or not — were fighting and dying for black freedom, and few insisted that blacks remain out of harm's way behind the lines. Indeed, whites insisted that blacks share the danger, especially after March 1863, when Congress resorted to the draft to fill the Union army.

The military was far from color-blind. The Union army established segregated black regiments, paid black soldiers $10 per month rather than the $13 it paid whites, refused blacks the opportunity to become commissioned officers, punished blacks as if they were slaves, and assigned blacks to labor battalions rather than to combat units. Still, when the war ended, 179,000 African American men had served in the Union army, approximately 10 percent of all soldiers. An astounding 71 percent of black men ages eighteen to forty-five in the free states wore Union blue, a participation rate that was substantially higher than that of white men. More than 130,000 black soldiers came from the slave states, perhaps 100,000 of them ex-slaves.

In time, whites allowed blacks to put down their shovels and to shoulder rifles. At the sublimely with the lusty shout of our brave soldiery." Hardened and disciplined by their military service, black soldiers drew tremendous strength from their participation in the Union effort. Despite their second-class status, they found army life a great counterweight to the degradation and dependency of slavery.

Eager to shoulder the rights, privileges, and responsibilities of freedom, black veterans often took the lead in the hard struggle for equality after the war. Blacks in the Union army that occupied the South after 1865 assumed a special obligation to protect former slaves. "The fact is," one black chaplain said, "when colored soldiers are about they [whites] are afraid to kick colored women and abuse colored people on the Streets, as they usually do." Black veterans believed that their military service entitled African Americans not only to freedom but also to civil and political rights. Sergeant Henry Maxwell announced: "We want two more boxes besides the cartridge box — the ballot and the jury box." Black men had demonstrated what they could do if permitted to become soldiers; they now demanded the chance to perform as citizens.

James Henry Gooding did not have a chance to participate in the postwar struggle for equal rights. Wounded and captured at the battle of Olustee in Florida, he was sent to the infamous Confederate prison Andersonville, where he died on July 19, 1864.

Company E, 4th U.S. Colored Infantry, Fort Lincoln, Virginia
The Lincoln administration was slow to accept black soldiers into the Union army, in part because of doubts about their fighting ability. But eventually, the battlefield valor of black troops eroded white skepticism. Colonel Thomas W. Higginson, the white commander of the Union's 1st South Carolina Infantry, made up of former slaves, celebrated the courage his men displayed in their first skirmish: "No officer in this regiment now doubts that the key to the successful prosecution of this war lies in the unlimited employment of black troops. . . . Instead of leaving their homes and families to fight they are fighting for their homes and families." Library of Congress.

Questions for Consideration

1. Why did the Union resist enrolling black troops?
2. Why was the right to fight so important to black men?
3. How did military service affect black men?

battles of Port Hudson and Milliken's Bend on the Mississippi River and at Fort Wagner in Charleston harbor, black courage under fire finally dispelled notions that African Americans could not fight. More than 38,000 black soldiers died in the Civil War, a mortality rate that was higher than that of white troops. Blacks played a crucial role in the triumph of the Union and the destruction of slavery in the South. (See "Seeking the American Promise," page 478.)

REVIEW Why did the Union change policy in 1863 to allow black men to serve in the army?

▸ The South at War

Most white Southerners shifted their allegiance from the Union to the Confederacy easily, convinced that their new nation embodied the principles of the American Revolution. But by seceding, Southerners brought on themselves a firestorm of unimaginable fury. Monstrous losses on the battlefield nearly bled the Confederacy to death. Southerners on the home front also suffered, even at the hands of their own government. Efforts by the Davis administration in Richmond to centralize power in

VISUAL ACTIVITY

Confederate Soldiers and Their Slaves

Soldiers of the Seventh Tennessee Cavalry pose with their slaves. Many slaveholders took "body servants" with them to war. These slaves cooked, washed, and cleaned for the white soldiers. In 1861, James H. Langhorne reported to his sister: "Peter . . . is charmed with being with me & 'being a soldier.' I gave him my old uniform overcoat & he says he is going to have his picture taken . . . to send to the servants." Do you think Peter was "puttin' on ol' massa" or just glad to be free of plantation labor? Daguerreotype courtesy of Tom Farish. Photographed by Michael Latil.

READING THE IMAGE: What can we glean from this image about a Confederate soldier's life in the military?

CONNECTIONS: This daguerreotype likely was not taken for any purpose other than to capture the camaraderie of four southern cavalrymen, yet the inclusion of the two slaves speaks volumes. What are the possible ramifications of slaveholders bringing "body servants" to war?

order to fight the war tested the loyalty of some men and women. Wartime economic changes hurt everyone, some more than others. By 1863, planters and yeomen who had stood together began to drift apart. Most disturbing of all, slaves became open participants in the destruction of slavery and the Confederacy.

Revolution from Above

As a Confederate general observed, Southerners were engaged in a total war "in which the whole population and the whole production . . . are to be put on a war footing, where every institution is to be made auxiliary to war." Jefferson Davis faced the task of building an army and navy from almost nothing, supplying them from factories that were scarce and anemic, and paying for it all from a treasury that did not exist. Finding eager soldiers proved easiest. Hundreds of officers defected from the U.S. Army, and hundreds of thousands of eager young rebels volunteered to follow them. Very quickly, the Confederacy developed formidable striking power.

The Confederacy's economy and finances proved tougher problems. Because of the Union blockade, the government had no choice but to build an industrial sector itself. Government-owned clothing and shoe factories, mines, arsenals, and powder works sprang up. The government also harnessed private companies, such as the huge Tredegar Iron Works in Richmond, to the war effort. Paying for the war became the most difficult task. A flood of paper money caused debilitating inflation. By 1863, people in Charleston paid ten times more for food than they had paid at the start of the war. By Christmas 1864, a Confederate soldier's monthly pay no longer bought a pair of socks. The Confederacy manufactured much more than most people imagined possible, but it never produced all that the South needed.

Richmond's war-making effort brought unprecedented government intrusion into the private lives of Confederate citizens. In April 1862, the Confederate Congress passed the first **conscription** (draft) law in American history. All able-bodied white males between the ages of eighteen and thirty-five (later seventeen and fifty) were liable to serve in the rebel army. The government adopted a policy of **impressment**, which allowed officials to confiscate food, horses, wagons, and whatever else they wanted from private citizens and to pay for them at below-market rates. After March 1863, the Confederacy legally impressed slaves, employing them as military laborers.

Richmond's centralizing efforts ran head-on into the South's traditional values of **states' rights** and unfettered individualism. Southerners lashed out at what Georgia governor Joseph E. Brown denounced as the "dangerous usurpation by Congress of the reserved right of the States." Richmond and the states struggled for control of money, supplies, and soldiers, with damaging

The Texas Brigade in Camp, 1861
Rebel soldiers who did not have slave servants to attend them spent much of their time doing chores. Standing in front of their winter quarters near Dumfries, Virginia, the Texans here are busy washing dishes, washing clothes, chopping firewood, and cooking. The soldier with the skillet displays the corn bread he has just cooked. Confederate troops ate salted meat and corn bread more than anything else, and soldiers grew very tired of the old standbys. "If any person offers me cornbread after this war comes to a close," a Louisianan declared just before Lee's surrender, "I shall probably tell him to — go to hell!" Photograph: Austin History Center, Austin Public Library; Skillet: Photograph Courtesy of the Concord Museum, Concord, MA; Sifter: Museum of the Confederacy/Southern Progress.

consequences for the war effort. Despite the strain, popular commitment to the new nation endured.

Hardship Below

Hardships on the home front fell most heavily on the poor. Flour, which cost three or four cents a pound in 1861, cost thirty-five cents in 1863. The draft stripped yeoman farms of men, leaving the women and children to grow what they ate. Government agents took 10 percent of harvests as a "tax-in-kind" on agriculture. Like inflation, shortages afflicted the entire population, but the rich lost luxuries while the poor lost necessities. In the spring of 1863, **bread riots** broke out in a dozen cities and villages across the South. In Richmond, a mob of nearly a thousand hungry women broke into shops and took what they needed.

"Men cannot be expected to fight for the Government that permits their wives & children to starve," one Southerner observed. Although a few wealthy individuals shared their bounty and the Confederate and state governments made efforts at social welfare, every attempt fell short. In late 1864, one desperate farmwife told her husband, "I have always been proud of you, and since your connection with the Confederate army, I have been prouder of you than ever before. I would not have you do anything wrong for the world, but before God, Edward, unless you come home, we must die." When the war ended, one-third of the soldiers had already gone home. A Mississippi deserter explained, "We are poor men and are willing to defend our country but our families [come] first."

"Men cannot be expected to fight for the Government that permits their wives & children to starve."
— A Southerner

Yeomen perceived a profound inequality of sacrifice. They called it "a rich man's war and a poor man's fight." The draft law permitted a man who had money to hire a substitute to take his place. Moreover, the "**twenty-Negro law**" exempted

Maria Isabella ("Belle") Boyd, Spy
Only seventeen when the war broke out, Belle Boyd became, in the words of a northern journalist, "insanely devoted to the rebel cause." Her first act for the Confederacy came on July 3, 1861, when she shot a drunken federal soldier who barged into her Virginia home and insulted her mother. Her relations with occupying northern troops improved, and soon this compelling young woman was eavesdropping on officers' conversations and slipping messages to Confederate armies. Boyd's information handed Stonewall Jackson an easy victory at Front Royal, Virginia, in May 1862. Imprisoned several times for spying, Boyd took up a theatrical career when the war ended. Courtesy Warren Rifles Confederate Museum, Front Royal, VA.

one white man on every plantation with twenty or more slaves. The government intended this law to provide protection for white women and to see that slaves tended the crops, but yeomen perceived it as rich men evading military service. A Mississippian complained that stay-at-home planters sent their slaves into the fields to grow cotton while in plain view "poor soldiers' wives are plowing with *their own* hands to make a subsistence for themselves and children — while their husbands are suffering, bleeding and dying for their country." In fact, most slaveholders went off to war, but the extreme suffering of common folk and the relative immunity of planters increased class friction.

The Richmond government hoped that the crucible of war would mold a region into a nation. Officials actively promoted Confederate nationalism to "excite in our citizens an ardent and enduring attachment to our Government and its institutions." Patriotic songwriters, poets, authors, and artists extolled southern culture. Clergymen assured their congregations that God had blessed slavery and the new nation. Jefferson Davis claimed that the Confederacy was part of a divine plan and asked citizens to observe national days of fasting and prayer. Although these efforts failed to win over thousands of die-hard Unionists and the animosity between yeomen and planters increased, the Confederacy succeeded in inspiring loyalty and pride among the majority of whites. Still, the war threatened to rip the southern social fabric along its racial seam.

The Disintegration of Slavery

The legal destruction of slavery was the product of presidential proclamation, congressional legislation, and eventually constitutional amendment, but the practical destruction of slavery was the product of war, what Lincoln called war's "friction and abrasion." Slaves took advantage of the upheaval to reach for freedom. Some half a million of the South's 4 million slaves ran away to Union military lines. More than 100,000 runaways took up arms as federal soldiers and sailors and attacked slavery directly. Other men and women stayed in the slave quarter, where they staked their claim to more freedom.

War disrupted slavery in a dozen ways. Almost immediately, it called the master away, leaving the mistress to assume responsibility for the plantation. But mistresses could not maintain traditional standards of slave discipline in wartime, and the balance of power shifted. Slaves got to the fields late, worked indifferently, and quit early. Some slaveholders responded violently; most saw no alternative but to strike bargains — offering gifts or part of the crop — to keep slaves at home and at work. An Alabama woman complained that she "begged . . . what little is done." Slaveholders had believed that they "knew" their slaves, but they learned that they did not. When the war began, a North Carolina woman praised her slaves as "diligent and respectful." When it ended, she said, "As to the idea of a *faithful servant, it is all a fiction*."

As military action sliced through the southern countryside, some slaveholders fled, leaving their slaves behind. Many more took their slaves with them, but flight meant additional chaos and offered slaves new opportunities to resist bondage. Whites' greatest fear — retaliatory violence — rarely occurred, however. Slaves who stayed home steadily undermined white mastery and expanded control over their own lives.

REVIEW How did wartime hardship in the South contribute to class friction?

Union Army Horse Artillery, 1860–1865
As the North successfully harnessed its enormous industrial capacity to meet the needs of war, cannon, shells, and carriages poured out of its factories. A fraction of that abundance is seen here in Virginia as a powerful battery of Union field artillery moves forward to assist infantry units. Each cannon required more than a dozen men and many horses to service it. Assignment to an artillery battery was dangerous for man and beast. Life expectancy for an artillery horse was less than eight months, and it is estimated that 1.5 million horses died in the war. © Bettmann/Corbis.

▶ The North at War

Although little fighting took place on northern soil, Northerners could not avoid being touched by the war. Almost every family had a son, husband, father, or brother in uniform. A New Hampshire man reported in 1863 that "there is mourning all over the land, for there is scarcely a place but what some one has lost a friend or an acquaintance either in battle or the Hospital." Moreover, total war blurred the distinction between home front and battlefield. Men marched off to fight, but preserving the country was also women's work. For civilians as well as soldiers, for women as well as men, war was transforming.

The need to build and fuel the Union war machine boosted the economy. The Union sent nearly 2 million men into the military and still increased production in almost every area. But because the rewards and burdens of patriotism were distributed unevenly, the North experienced sharp, even violent, divisions. Workers confronted employers, whites confronted blacks, and Democrats confronted Republicans. Still, Northerners on the home front remained fervently attached to the Union.

The Government and the Economy

When the war began, the United States had no national banking system, no national currency, and no federal income tax. But the secession of eleven slave states cut the Democrats' strength in Congress in half and destroyed their capacity to resist Republican economic programs. The Legal Tender Act of February 1862 created a national currency, paper money that Northerners called "greenbacks." With the passage of the National Banking Act in February 1863, Congress established a system of national banks that by the 1870s had largely replaced the antebellum system of decentralized state banks. Congress also enacted a series of sweeping tax laws. By revolutionizing the country's banking, monetary, and tax structures, the Republicans generated enormous economic power.

The Republicans' wartime legislation also aimed at integrating the West more thoroughly into the Union. In May 1862, Congress approved the Homestead Act, which offered 160 acres of public land to settlers who would live and labor on it. The Homestead Act bolstered western loyalty and in time resulted in more than a million new farms. The Pacific Railroad Act in July 1862 provided massive federal assistance for building a transcontinental railroad that ran from Omaha to San Francisco when completed in 1869. Congress further bound East and West by subsidizing the Pony Express mail service and a transcontinental telegraph.

Two additional initiatives had long-term economic consequences. Congress created the Department of Agriculture and passed the Land-Grant College Act (also known as the Morrill Act after its sponsor, Representative Justin Morrill of Vermont), which set aside public land to support universities that emphasized "agriculture and mechanical arts." The Lincoln administration immeasurably strengthened the North's effort to win the war, but its ideas also permanently changed the nation.

Women and Work at Home and at War

More than a million farm men were called to the military, so farm women added men's chores to their own. "I met more women driving teams on the road and saw more at work in the fields than men," a visitor to Iowa reported in the fall of 1862. Rising production testified to their success in plowing, planting, and harvesting. Rapid mechanization assisted farm women in their new roles. Cyrus McCormick sold 165,000 of his reapers during the war years. The combination of high prices for farm products and increased production ensured that war and prosperity joined hands in the rural North.

A few industries, such as textiles (which depended on southern cotton), declined during the war, but many more grew. Huge profits prompted one Pennsylvania ironmaster to remark, "I am in no hurry for peace." With orders pouring in and a million nonfarmworkers at war, unemployment declined and wages often rose. The boom proved friendlier to owners than to workers, however. Inflation and taxes cut so deeply into workers' paychecks that their standard of living actually fell.

In cities, women stepped into jobs vacated by men, particularly in manufacturing, and also into essentially new occupations such as government secretaries and clerks. The number of women working for wages rose 40 percent during the war. As more and more women entered the workforce, employers cut wages.

Women Doing Laundry for Federal Soldiers, ca. 1861

Northern women eagerly joined the Union war effort. Thousands aided in the work of the U.S. Christian Commission, the U.S. Sanitary Commission, and other philanthropic organizations to provide soldiers with Bibles, fresh food, and new socks. But some women were forced by their desperate financial circumstances to wash soldiers' dirty clothes to make a living. Army camps were difficult places for "respectable" women to work. One Union soldier discouraged his wife even from visiting, noting, "It is not a fit place for any woman, for there is all kinds of talk, songs and everything not good for them 2 hear."

In 1864, New York seamstresses working fourteen-hour days earned only $1.54 a week. Urban workers resorted increasingly to strikes to wrench decent salaries from their employers, but their protests rarely succeeded. Nevertheless, tough times failed to undermine the patriotism of most workers.

Most middle-class white women stayed home and contributed to the war effort in traditional ways. They sewed, wrapped bandages, and sold homemade goods at local fairs to raise money to aid the soldiers. Other women expressed their patriotism in an untraditional way — as wartime nurses. Thousands of women on both sides defied prejudices about female delicacy and volunteered to nurse the wounded. Many northern female volunteers worked through the **U.S. Sanitary Commission**, a huge civilian organization that coordinated the efforts of seven thousand local women's groups to buy and distribute clothing, food, and medicine; recruit doctors and nurses; and bury the dead.

Some volunteers went on to become paid military nurses. **Dorothea Dix**, well known for her efforts to reform insane asylums, was named superintendent of female nurses in April 1861. Dix appointed some 3,000 nurses by 1863, when the power to select nurses was taken from her and given to army surgeons. Most nurses worked in hospitals behind the battle lines, but some, like **Clara Barton**, who later founded the American Red Cross, worked in battlefield units. Women who served in the war went on to lead the postwar movement to establish training schools for female nurses.

Politics and Dissent

At first, the bustle of economic and military mobilization seemed to silence politics, but bipartisan unity did not last. Within a year, Democrats were labeling the Republican administration a "reign of terror" and denouncing Republican policies — expanding federal power, subsidizing private business, emancipating the slaves — as unconstitutional, arguing that the "Constitution is as binding in war as in peace." In turn, Republicans were calling Democrats the party of "Dixie, Davis, and the Devil."

When the Republican-dominated Congress enacted the draft law in March 1863, Democrats had another grievance. The law required that all men between the ages of twenty and forty-five enroll and make themselves available for a lottery that would decide who went to war. What poor men found particularly galling were provisions that allowed a draftee to hire a substitute or simply to pay a $300 fee and get out of his military obligation. As in the South, common folk could be heard chanting, "A rich man's war and a poor man's fight."

Linking the draft and emancipation, Democrats argued that Republicans employed an unconstitutional means (the draft) to achieve an unconstitutional end (emancipation). In the summer of 1863, antidraft, antiblack mobs went on rampages in northern cities. In July in New York City, Democratic Irish workingmen — crowded into filthy tenements, gouged by inflation, enraged by the draft, and dead set against fighting to free blacks — erupted in four days of rioting. The **New York City draft riots** killed at least 105 people, most of them black, and left the Colored Orphan Asylum a smoking ruin.

Lincoln called Democratic opposition to the war "the fire in the rear" and believed that it was even more threatening to national survival than were Confederate armies. The antiwar wing of the Democratic Party, the Peace Democrats — whom some called "Copperheads," after the poisonous snake — found their chief spokesman in Ohio congressman **Clement Vallandigham**. He argued that the Confederacy could never be conquered and that Lincoln's attempt had "made this country one of the worst despotisms on earth." Vallandigham demanded: "Stop fighting. Make an armistice. . . . Withdraw your army from the seceding States."

> **"A rich man's war and a poor man's fight."**
> — A chant of common folk

In September 1862, in an effort to stifle opposition to the war, Lincoln placed under military arrest any person who discouraged enlistments, resisted the draft, or engaged in "disloyal" practices. Before the war ended, his administration imprisoned nearly 14,000 individuals, most in the border states. The administration's heavy-handed tactics suppressed free speech, but the campaign fell short of a reign of terror, for the majority of the prisoners were not northern Democratic opponents but Confederates, blockade runners, and citizens of foreign countries, and most of those arrested gained quick release. Still, Lincoln's net did capture Vallandigham, who was arrested, convicted of treason, and eventually banished. In May 1863, Union soldiers escorted the Ohioan to Confederate lines in Tennessee.

REVIEW Why was the U.S. Congress able to pass such a bold legislative agenda during the war?

▶ Grinding Out Victory, 1863–1865

In the early months of 1863, the Union's prospects looked bleak, and the Confederate cause stood at high tide. Then, in July 1863, the tide began to turn. The military man most responsible for this shift was Ulysses S. Grant. Elevated to supreme command, Grant knit together a powerful war machine that integrated a sophisticated command structure, modern technology, and complex logistics and supply systems. But the arithmetic of this plain man remained unchanged: Killing more of the enemy than he kills of you equaled "the complete overthrow of the rebellion."

The North ground out the victory battle by bloody battle. The balance tipped in the Union's favor in 1863, but Southerners were not deterred. The fighting escalated in the last two years of the war. As national elections approached in the fall of 1864, Lincoln expected a war-weary North to reject him. Instead, northern voters declared their willingness to continue the war in the defense of the ideals of union and freedom.

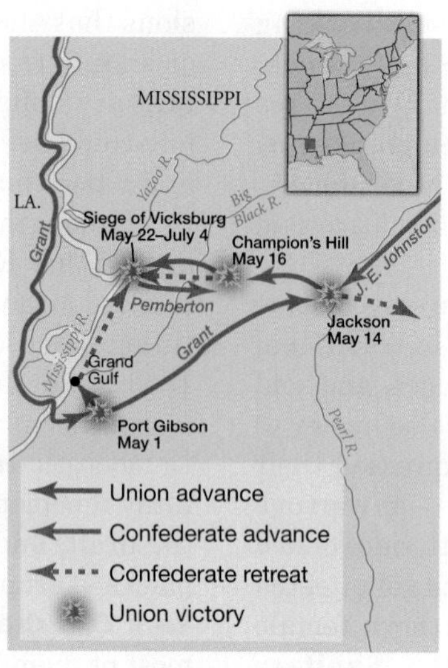

Vicksburg Campaign, 1863

Vicksburg and Gettysburg

Vicksburg, Mississippi, situated on the eastern bank of the Mississippi River, stood between Union forces and complete control of the river. In May 1863, Union forces under Grant laid siege to the city in an effort to starve out the enemy. Civilian residents moved into caves to escape the incessant Union bombardment, and as the **siege of Vicksburg** dragged on, they ate mules and rats to survive. After six weeks, on July 4, 1863, nearly 30,000 rebels marched out of Vicksburg, stacked their arms, and surrendered unconditionally. A Yankee captain wrote home to his wife: "The backbone of the Rebellion is this day broken. The Confederacy is divided. . . . Vicksburg is ours. The Mississippi River is opened, and Gen. Grant is to be our next President."

On the same Fourth of July, word arrived that Union forces had crushed General Lee at Gettysburg, Pennsylvania (Map 15.3). Emboldened by his victory at Chancellorsville in May, Lee and his 75,000-man army had invaded Pennsylvania. On June 28, Union forces under General George G. Meade intercepted the Confederates at the small town of Gettysburg, where Union soldiers occupied the high ground. Three days of furious fighting involving 165,000 troops could not dislodge the Federals from the hills. Lee ached for a decisive victory, and on July 3 he ordered a major assault against the Union center on Cemetery Ridge. The dug-in Yankees enjoyed three-quarters of a mile of clear vision, and they raked the line of Confederate soldiers under General George E. Pickett with cannon and rifle fire. The **battle of Gettysburg** cost Lee more than one-third of his army — 28,000 casualties. "It's all my fault," he lamented. On the night of July 4, 1863, he marched his battered army back to Virginia.

Battle of Gettysburg, July 1–3, 1863

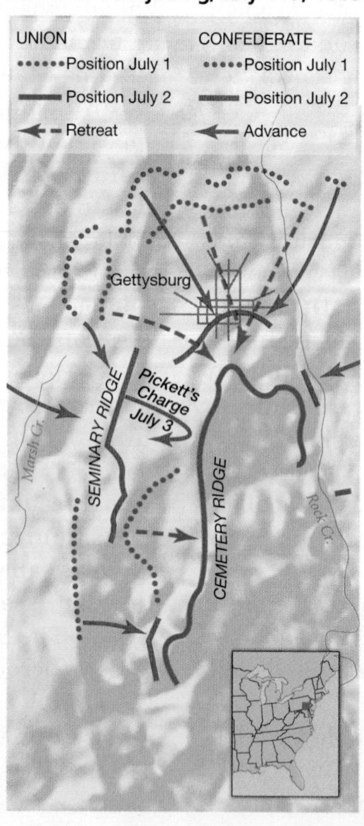

The twin disasters at Vicksburg and Gettysburg proved to be the turning point of the war. The Confederacy could not replace the nearly 60,000 soldiers who were captured, wounded, or killed. Lee never launched another major offensive north of the Mason-Dixon line. It is hindsight, however, that permits us to see the pair of battles as decisive. At the time, the Confederacy still controlled the heartland of the South, and Lee still had a vicious sting. War-weariness threatened to erode the North's will to win before Union armies could destroy the Confederacy's ability to go on.

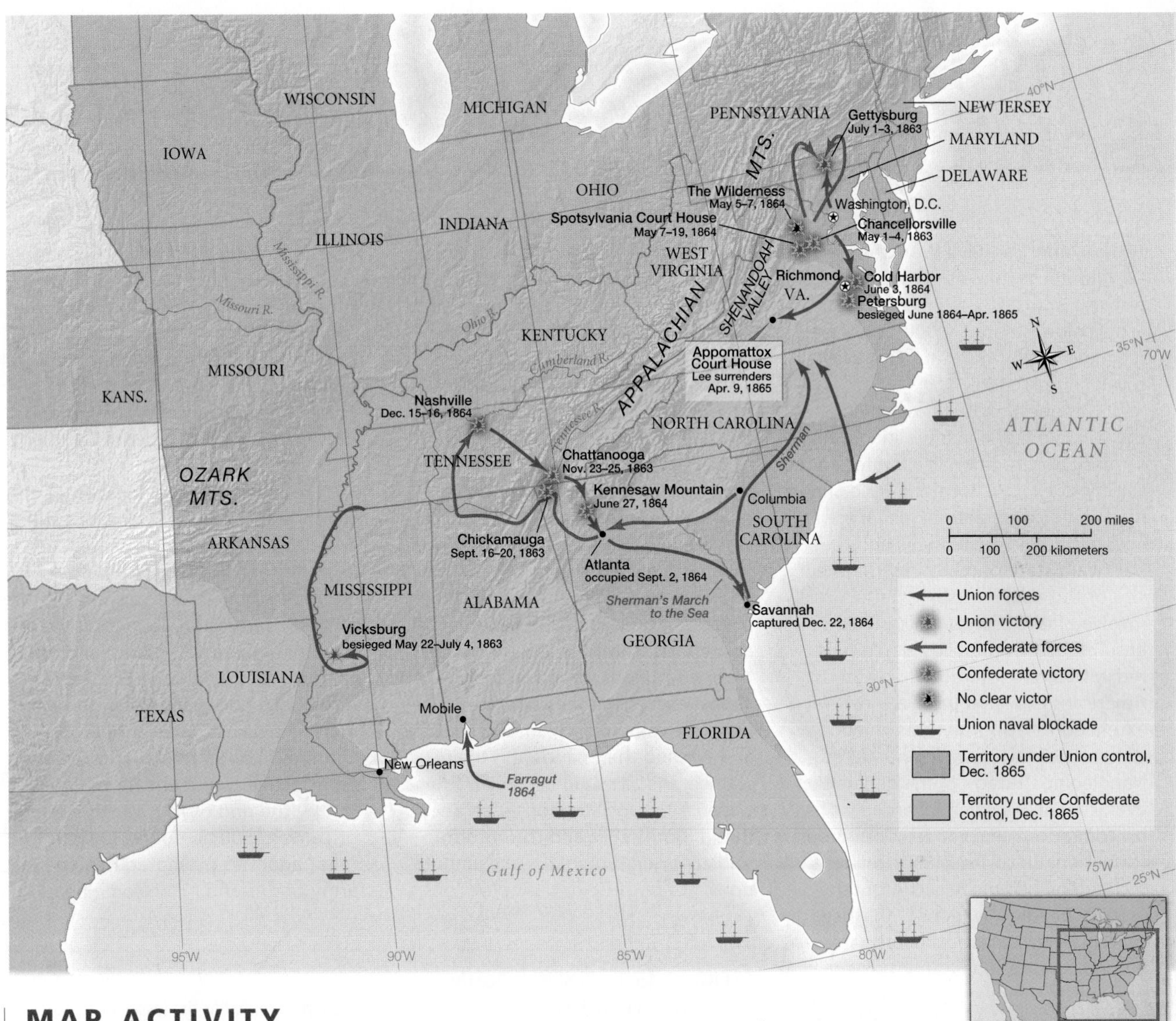

MAP ACTIVITY

Map 15.3 The Civil War, 1863–1865

Ulysses S. Grant's victory at Vicksburg divided the Confederacy at the Mississippi River. William Tecumseh Sherman's march from Chattanooga to Savannah divided it again. In northern Virginia, Robert E. Lee fought fiercely, but Grant's larger, better-supplied armies prevailed.

READING THE MAP: Describe the difference between Union and Confederate naval capacity. Were the battles shown on the map fought primarily in Union-controlled or in Confederate-controlled territory? (Look at the land areas on the map.)

CONNECTIONS: Did former slaves serve in the Civil War? If so, on which side(s), and what did they do?

Grant Takes Command

In September 1863, Union general William Rosecrans placed his army in a dangerous situation in Chattanooga, Tennessee, where he had retreated after defeat at the battle of Chickamauga (see Map 15.3). Rebels surrounded the disorganized bluecoats and threatened to starve them into submission. Grant, now commander of Union forces between the Mississippi River and the Appalachians, arrived in Chattanooga in October. Within weeks, he opened an effective supply line, broke the siege, and routed the Confederate army. The victory at Chattanooga on November 25 opened the door to Georgia. It also confirmed Lincoln's estimation of Grant. In March 1864, the president asked Grant to come east to become the general in chief of all Union armies.

HISTORICAL QUESTION

Why Did So Many Soldiers Die?

The American Civil War was the bloodiest conflict in American history (Figure 15.3). Some 260,000 rebel soldiers and 360,000 Union soldiers died. Why were the Civil War totals so horrendous?

This question is almost as old as the war itself, and in answering it historians have traditionally pointed to a variety of explanations: the scale and duration of the fighting; military strategy; battlefield technology; and the backward state of medicine. The sheer size of the armies — some battles involved more than 200,000 soldiers — ensured that battlefields would turn red with blood. Moreover, what most Americans expected to be a short war extended for four full years. In addition, armies fought with antiquated Napoleonic strategy. In the generals' eyes, the ideal soldier advanced with his comrades in a compact, close-order formation. But by the 1860s, military technology had made such frontal assaults deadly. Weapons with rifled barrels were replacing smoothbore muskets and cannons, and the new weapons' greater range and accuracy made sitting ducks of charging infantry units. As a result, battles took thousands of lives in a single day. On July 2, 1862, the morning after the battle at Malvern Hill in Virginia, a Union officer surveyed the scene: "Over 5,000 dead and wounded men were on the ground . . . enough were alive and moving to give to the field a singular crawling effect."

When the war began, Union and Confederate medical departments could not cope with skirmishes, much less large-scale battles. They had no ambulance corps to remove the wounded from the scene. They had no field hospitals. Wounded soldiers often lay on battlefields for hours, sometimes days. Only the shock of massive casualties compelled reform. Gradually, both North and South organized effective ambulance corps, built hospitals, and hired trained surgeons and nurses.

Soldiers did not always count speedy transportation to a hospital as a blessing, however. As one Union soldier said, "I had rather risk a battle than the Hospitals." Field doctors gained a reputation as butchers, but a wounded man's real enemy was medical ignorance. Physicians had almost no knowledge of the cause and transmission of disease or the benefits of antiseptics. Unaware of basic germ theory, surgeons spread infection almost every time they operated. They wore the same bloody smocks for days and washed their hands and their scalpels and saws in buckets of dirty water. Although surgeons used anesthesia (both ether and chloroform), soldiers often did not survive amputations, not because of the operations but because of the gangrene that inevitably followed. A Union doctor discovered in 1864 that bromine arrested gangrene, but the best that most amputees could hope for was maggots, which ate dead flesh on the stump and thus inhibited the spread of infection. The growing ranks of nurses, including Dorothea Dix and Clara Barton, improved wounded men's odds and alleviated their suffering. Still, during the Civil War, nearly one of every five wounded rebel soldiers died, and one of every six Yankees. A century later, in Vietnam, only one wounded American soldier in four hundred died.

Soldiers who avoided battlefield wounds and hospital infections still faced sickness. Deadly diseases such as dysentery and typhoid swept through crowded army camps, where latrines were often dangerously close to drinking-water supplies, and mosquitoes, flies, and body lice were more than nuisances. Pneumonia and malaria also cut down thousands. Quinine from South America proved an effective treatment for malaria, but by the end of the war the going price was $500 an ounce. Civilian relief agencies promoted hygiene in army camps and made some head-

FIGURE 15.3 Civil War Deaths
The loss of life in the Civil War — 620,000 — was almost equal to the losses in all other American wars through the Vietnam War combined.

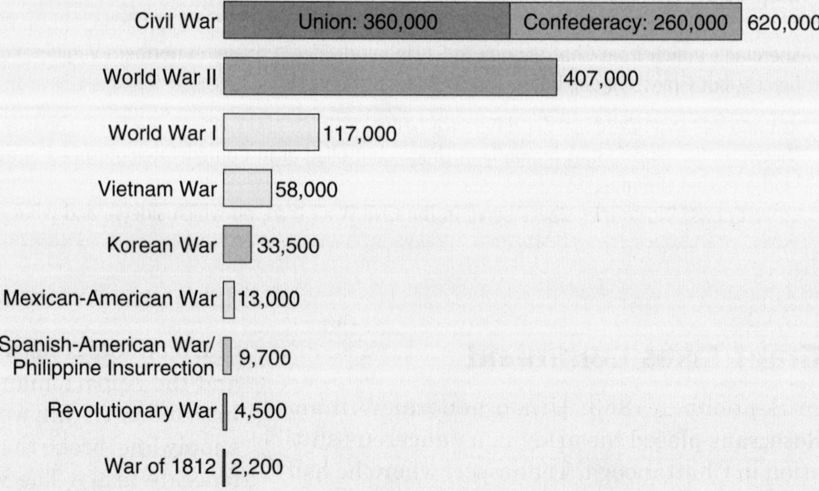

Wounded Men at Savage's Station
Misery did not end when the cannons ceased firing. Northern and southern surgeons performed approximately 60,000 amputations with simple instruments such as those included in this surgical kit. The wounded men shown here were but a fraction of those injured or killed during General George McClellan's peninsula campaign in 1862. Photo: Library of Congress; Surgical kit: Chicago Historical Society.

way. Nevertheless, disease killed nearly twice as many soldiers as did combat. Many who died of disease were prisoners of war. Approximately 30,000 Northerners died in Confederate prisons, and approximately 26,000 Southerners died in Union prisons.

Recently, historians have probed another explanation for the death toll, turning to soldiers' cultural attitudes and values to explain why they were willing to die in such great numbers. Some have explored how the nineteenth-century code of masculinity propelled valor on the battlefields, and how patriotism, for either the Union or the Confederacy, moved soldiers to risk everything. But scholars have focused most especially on how soldiers' religious beliefs about death made it easier for them to negotiate dying. The triumph of evangelical Protestantism in the early nineteenth century meant that Civil War soldiers faced death with calm resignation. They believed in a heaven that promised bodily resurrection and family reunion; the assurance of everlasting life, therefore, made it easier to face death. Culture, then, as well as the scope and length of the war, strategy, technology, and primitive medicine, helps explain the war's tremendous carnage.

Thinking about Cause and Effect

1. In what ways were Civil War strategists fighting the world's first "modern" war? In what ways were they still fighting a traditional-style war? How does this contrast account for the number of dead and wounded soldiers?
2. How did the high casualty rates lead to new opportunities for both women and blacks?

Major Battles of the Civil War, 1863–1865

May 1–4, 1863	Battle of Chancellorsville
July 1–3, 1863	Battle of Gettysburg
July 4, 1863	Fall of Vicksburg
September 16–20, 1863	Battle of Chickamauga
November 23–25, 1863	Battle of Chattanooga
May 5–7, 1864	Battle of the Wilderness
May 7–19, 1864	Battle of Spotsylvania Court House
June 3, 1864	Battle of Cold Harbor
June 27, 1864	Battle of Kennesaw Mountain
September 2, 1864	Fall of Atlanta
November–December 1864	Sheridan sacks Shenandoah Valley Sherman's "March to the Sea"
December 15–16, 1864	Battle of Nashville
December 22, 1864	Fall of Savannah
April 2–3, 1865	Fall of Petersburg and Richmond
April 9, 1865	Lee surrenders at Appomattox Court House

In Washington, General Grant implemented his grand strategy for a war of attrition. He ordered a series of simultaneous assaults from Virginia all the way to Louisiana. Two actions proved particularly significant. In one, General **William Tecumseh Sherman**, whom Grant appointed his successor to command the western armies, plunged southeast toward Atlanta. In the other, Grant, who took control of the Army of the Potomac, went head-to-head with Lee in Virginia for almost four straight weeks.

Grant and Lee met in the first week of May 1864 in a dense tangle of scrub oaks and small pines. Often unable to see more than ten paces, the armies pounded away at each other until approximately 18,000 Yankees and 11,000 rebels had fallen. The savagery of the **battle of the Wilderness** did not compare with that at Spotsylvania Court House a few days later. Frenzied men fought hand to hand for eighteen hours in the rain. One veteran remembered men "piled upon each other in some places four layers deep, exhibiting every ghastly phase of mutilation." (See "Historical Question," page 488.) Spotsylvania cost Grant another 18,000 casualties and Lee 10,000, but the Yankee bulldog would not let go. Grant kept moving and tangled with Lee again at Cold Harbor, where he suffered 13,000 additional casualties to Lee's 5,000.

Twice as many Union soldiers as rebel soldiers died in four weeks of fighting in Virginia in May and June, but because Lee had only half as many troops as Grant, his losses were equivalent to Grant's. Grant knew that the South could not replace the losses. Moreover, the campaign carried Grant to the outskirts of Petersburg, just south of Richmond, where he abandoned the costly tactic of the frontal assault and began a siege that immobilized both armies and dragged on for nine months.

Grant Planning the Attack at Cold Harbor
On June 2, 1864, General Ulysses S. Grant moved his headquarters to Bethesda Church, Maryland, carried the pews outdoors, and planned the attack he would make at Cold Harbor. Here, Grant leans over a pew to study a map. The next day, he ordered frontal assaults against entrenched Confederate forces, resulting in enormous Union losses. "I am disgusted with the generalship displayed," young Brigadier General Emory Upton observed. "Our men have, in many cases, been foolishly and wantonly slaughtered." Years later, Grant said that he regretted the assault at Cold Harbor, but in 1864 he kept pushing toward Richmond. Library of Congress.

***The Dead Line*, by Robert Sneden, Andersonville Prison, 1864**
The train carrying prisoner of war Robert Sneden arrived at Andersonville in February 1864 as the Confederates were completing the stockade surrounding their newest prison. Soon the sixteen and a half acres in southwestern Georgia were crammed with humanity and had to be expanded. Andersonville's 33,000 Union prisoners made it the fifth-largest city in the Confederacy. Sneden sketched this scene of a man being shot by a guard while trying to take part of a fence (the "dead line" that prisoners could not cross) for firewood. More than 13,000 prisoners perished at Andersonville. Smallpox, dysentery, scurvy, malnutrition, and infections proved far greater threats to them than bullets. © 1996, Lora Robbins Collection of Virginia Art, Virginia Historical Society.

Simultaneously, Sherman invaded Georgia. Grant instructed Sherman to "get into the interior of the enemy's country as far as you can, inflicting all the damage you can against their War resources." In May, Sherman moved 100,000 men south against 65,000 rebels. Skillful maneuvering, constant skirmishing, and one pitched battle, at Kennesaw Mountain, brought Sherman to Atlanta, which fell on September 2.

Intending to "make Georgia howl," Sherman marched out of Atlanta on November 15 with 62,000 battle-hardened veterans, heading for Savannah, 285 miles away on the Atlantic coast. One veteran remembered, "[We] destroyed all we could not eat, stole their niggers, burned their cotton & gins, spilled their sorghum, burned & twisted their R. Roads and raised Hell generally." **Sherman's March to the Sea** aimed at destroying the will of the southern people. A few weeks earlier, General **Philip H. Sheridan** had carried out his own scorched-earth campaign in the Shenandoah Valley, complying with Grant's order to turn the valley into "a barren waste . . . so that crows flying over it for the balance of this season will have to carry their provender [food] with them." When Sherman's troops entered an undefended Savannah in mid-December, the general telegraphed Lincoln that he had "a Christmas gift" for him. A month earlier, Union voters had bestowed on the president an even greater gift.

The Election of 1864

In the summer of 1864, with Sherman temporarily checked outside Atlanta and Grant bogged down in the siege of Petersburg, the Democratic Party smelled victory in the fall elections. Rankled by a seemingly never-ending war, inflation, the draft, the attack on civil liberties, and the commitment to blacks, Northerners appeared ready for a change. Lincoln himself concluded, "It seems exceedingly probable that this administration will not be re-elected."

The Democrats were badly divided, however. Peace Democrats insisted on an armistice, while "war" Democrats supported the conflict but opposed Republican means of fighting it. The party tried to paper over the chasm by nominating a war candidate, General George McClellan, but adopting a peace platform that demanded that "immediate efforts be made for a cessation of hostilities." Republicans denounced the peace plank as a cut-and-run plan that "virtually

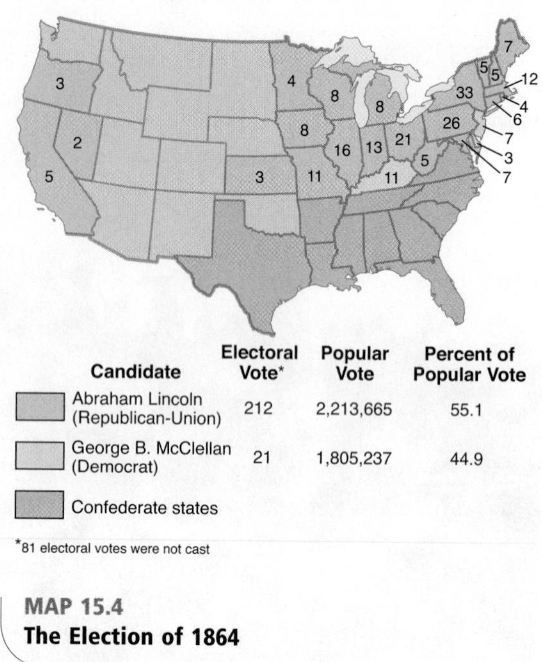

Candidate	Electoral Vote*	Popular Vote	Percent of Popular Vote
Abraham Lincoln (Republican-Union)	212	2,213,665	55.1
George B. McClellan (Democrat)	21	1,805,237	44.9
Confederate states			

*81 electoral votes were not cast

MAP 15.4
The Election of 1864

Robert E. Lee and Friends, by Mathew Brady, 1865
One week after his surrender at Appomattox Court House, Robert E. Lee sat for this portrait by Mathew Brady, the country's foremost photographer. Lee is joined by his eldest son, Major General George Washington Custis Lee (left), and a longtime aide, Lieutenant Colonel Walter H. Taylor (right). Lee's sober, weary expression reflects four hard years of war and his final defeat. Already a matchless hero among white Southerners, Lee was well on his way toward saintly immortality. In 1868, one woman described Lee as "bathed in the white light which falls directly upon him from the smile of an approving and sustaining God." Library of Congress.

proposed to surrender the country to the rebels in arms against us."

The capture of Atlanta in September turned the political tide in favor of the Republicans. Lincoln received 55 percent of the popular vote, but his electoral margin was a whopping 212 to McClellan's 21(Map 15.4). Lincoln's party won a resounding victory, one that gave him a mandate to continue the war until slavery and the Confederacy were dead.

The Confederacy Collapses

As 1865 dawned, military disaster littered the Confederate landscape. With the destruction of John B. Hood's army at Nashville in December 1864, the interior of the Confederacy lay in Yankee hands (see Map 15.3). Sherman's troops, resting momentarily in Savannah, eyed South Carolina hungrily. Farther north, Grant had Lee's army pinned down in Petersburg, a few miles from Richmond.

In the final days, some Confederates turned their backs on the rebellion. News from the battlefield made it difficult not to conclude that the Yankees had beaten them. Soldiers' wives begged their husbands to return home to keep their families from starving, and the stream of deserters grew dramatically. In most cases, when white Southerners lost the will to continue, it was not because they lost faith in independence but because they had been battered into submission. Despite the deep divisions within the Confederacy, white Southerners had demonstrated a remarkable endurance for their cause. Half of the 900,000 Confederate soldiers had been killed or wounded, and ragged, hungry women and children had sacrificed throughout one of the bloodiest wars then known to history.

The end came with a rush. On February 1, 1865, Sherman's troops stormed out of Savannah into South Carolina, the "cradle of the Confederacy." In Virginia, Lee abandoned Petersburg on April 2, and Richmond fell on April 3. Grant pursued Lee until he surrendered on April 9, 1865, at Appomattox Court House, Virginia. Grant offered generous peace terms. He allowed Lee's men to return home and to keep their horses to help "put in a crop to carry themselves and their families through the next winter." With Lee gone, the remaining Confederate armies lost hope and gave up within two weeks. After four years, the war was over.

No one was more relieved than Lincoln, but his celebration was restrained. He told his cabinet that his postwar burdens would weigh almost as heavily as those of wartime. Seeking a distraction, Lincoln attended Ford's Theatre on the evening of Good Friday, April 14, 1865. John Wilkes Booth, an actor with southern sympathies, slipped into the president's box and shot Lincoln in the head. He died at 7:22 the following morning. Vice President Andrew Johnson became president. The man who had led the nation through the war would not lead it during the postwar search for a just peace.

REVIEW Why were the siege of Vicksburg and the battle of Gettysburg crucial to the outcome of the war?

▶ Conclusion: The Second American Revolution

A transformed nation emerged from the crucible of war. Antebellum America was decentralized politically and loosely integrated economically. To bend the resources of the country to a Union victory, Congress enacted legislation that reshaped the nation's political and economic character. It created a national currency and banking system and turned to free land, a transcontinental railroad, and miles of telegraph lines to bind the West to the rest of the nation. Congress also established the sovereignty of the federal government and permanently increased its power. To most citizens before the war, Washington meant the post office and little more. During the war, the federal government drafted, taxed, and judged Americans in unprecedented ways. The massive changes brought about by the war — the creation of a national government, a national economy, and a national spirit — led one historian to call the American Civil War the "Second American Revolution."

The Civil War also had a profound effect on individual lives. When the war began in 1861, millions of men dropped their hoes, hammers, and pencils; put on blue or gray uniforms; and fought and suffered for what they passionately believed was right. The war disrupted families, leaving women at home with additional responsibilities and giving others wartime work in factories, offices, and hospitals. It offered blacks new and more effective ways to resist slavery and agitate for equality.

The war devastated the South. Three-fourths of southern white men of military age served in the Confederate army, and half of them were wounded or killed or died of disease. The war destroyed two-fifths of the South's livestock, wrecked half of the farm machinery, and blackened dozens of cities and towns. The immediate impact of the war on the North was more paradoxical. The struggle cost the North a heavy price: 360,000 lives. But rather than devastating the land, the war set the countryside and cities humming with business activity. The radical shift in power from South to North signaled a new direction in American development: the long decline of agriculture and the rise of industrial capitalism.

Most revolutionary of all, the war ended slavery. Ironically, the South's war to preserve slavery destroyed it. Nearly 200,000 black men, including ex-slave William Gould, dedicated their wartime service to its eradication. Because slavery was both a labor and a racial system, the institution was entangled in almost every aspect of southern life. Slavery's uprooting inevitably meant fundamental change. But the full meaning of abolition remained unclear in 1865. Determining the new economic, political, and social status of nearly 4 million ex-slaves would be the principal task of reconstruction.

▸ Selected Bibliography

General Works

Orville Vernon Burton, *The Age of Lincoln* (2007).
James M. McPherson, *The Battle Cry of Freedom: The Civil War Era* (1988).
Adam I. P. Smith, *The American Civil War* (2007).

Military History

Michael J. Bennett, *Union Jacks: Yankee Sailors in the Civil War* (2004).
Joseph T. Glatthaar, *General Lee's Army: From Victory to Collapse* (2008).
Mark Grimsley, *The Hard Hand of War: Union Military Policy toward Southern Civilians, 1861–1865* (1995).
Chandra Manning, *What This Cruel War Was Over: Soldiers, Slavery, and the Civil War* (2007).
James M. McPherson, *Tried by War: Abraham Lincoln as Commander in Chief* (2008).
Brooks D. Simpson, *Ulysses S. Grant: Triumph over Adversity, 1822–1865* (2000).
Russell F. Weigley, *A Great Civil War: A Military and Political History, 1861–1865* (2000).

The North and South at War

Stephen V. Ash, *When the Yankees Came: Conflict and Chaos in the Occupied South, 1861–1865* (1995).
Iver Bernstein, *The New York City Draft Riots: Their Significance for American Society and Politics in the Age of the Civil War* (1990).
William A. Blair, *Virginia's Private War: Feeding Body and Soul in the Confederacy, 1861–1865* (1998).
William J. Cooper, *Jefferson Davis, American* (2000).
Drew Gilpin Faust, *This Republic of Suffering: Death and the American Civil War* (2008).
William W. Freehling, *The South vs. the South: How Anti-Confederate Southerners Shaped the Course of the Civil War* (2001).
Gary W. Gallagher, *The Confederate War* (1997).
Judith Ann Giesberg, *Civil War Sisterhood: The U.S. Sanitary Commission and Women's Politics in Transition* (2000).
Mark E. Neely Jr., *The Fate of Liberty: Abraham Lincoln and Civil Liberties* (1991).
George C. Rable, *Civil Wars: Women and the Crisis of Southern Nationalism* (1989).
Heather Cox Richardson, *The Greatest Nation of the Earth: Republican Economic Policies during the Civil War* (1997).
James L. Roark, *Masters without Slaves: Southern Planters in the Civil War and Reconstruction* (1977).
Anne Sarah Rubin, *A Shattered Nation: The Rise and Fall of the Confederacy, 1861–1868* (2005).
Mark S. Schantz, *Awaiting the Heavenly Country: The Civil War and America's Culture of Death* (2008).
Nina Silber, *Daughters of the Union: Northern Women Fight the Civil War* (2006).
Margaret M. Storey, *Loyalty and Loss: Alabama's Unionists in the Civil War and Reconstruction* (2004).
Amy Murrell Taylor, *The Divided Family in Civil War America* (2005).
Jennifer L. Weber, *Copperheads: The Rise and Fall of Lincoln's Opponents in the North* (2008).

The Struggle for Freedom

Ira Berlin et al., eds., *Freedom: A Documentary History of Emancipation, 1861–1867*, 5 vols. (1982–2008).
Eric Foner, *The Fiery Trial: Abraham Lincoln and American Slavery* (2010).

Joseph T. Glatthaar, *Forged in Battle: The Civil War Alliance of Black Soldiers and White Officers* (1990).

William B. Gould IV, ed., *Diary of a Contraband: The Civil War Passage of a Black Sailor* (2002).

Michael P. Johnson, ed., *Abraham Lincoln, Slavery, and the Civil War: Selected Writings and Speeches* (2011).

Bruce Levine, *Confederate Emancipation: Southern Plans to Free and Arm Slaves during the Civil War* (2006).

James Oakes, *The Radical and the Republican: Frederick Douglass, Abraham Lincoln, and the Triumph of Antislavery Politics* (2007).

▶ **For more books about topics in this chapter,** see the Online Bibliography at **bedfordstmartins.com/roark.**

▶ **For additional primary sources from this period,** see Michael Johnson, ed., *Reading the American Past*, Fifth Edition.

▶ **For Web sites, images, and documents related to topics and places in this chapter,** visit Make History at **bedfordstmartins.com/roark.**

Reviewing Chapter 15

KEY TERMS

Explain each term's significance.

"And the War Came"

- Abraham Lincoln (p. 463)
- Jefferson Davis (p. 463)
- Fort Sumter (p. 463)

The Combatants

- King Cotton diplomacy (p. 466)
- Anaconda Plan (p. 466)

Battling It Out, 1861–1862

- battle of Bull Run/Manassas (p. 468)
- George B. McClellan (p. 468)
- Robert E. Lee (p. 468)
- battle of Antietam (p. 470)
- Ulysses S. Grant (p. 471)
- battle of Shiloh (p. 472)
- Union blockade (p. 473)

Union *and* Freedom

- contraband of war (p. 475)
- Emancipation Proclamation (p. 476)
- William Gould (p. 477)

The South at War

- conscription (p. 480)
- impressment (p. 480)
- states' rights (p. 480)
- bread riots (p. 481)
- twenty-Negro law (p. 481)

The North at War

- U.S. Sanitary Commission (p. 485)
- Dorothea Dix (p. 485)
- Clara Barton (p. 485)
- New York City draft riots (p. 485)
- Clement L. Vallandigham (p. 485)

Grinding Out Victory, 1863–1865

- siege of Vicksburg (p. 486)
- battle of Gettysburg (p. 486)
- William Tecumseh Sherman (p. 490)
- battle of the Wilderness (p. 490)
- Sherman's March to the Sea (p. 491)
- Philip H. Sheridan (p. 491)

REVIEW QUESTIONS

Use key terms and dates to support your answer.

1. Why did both the Union and the Confederacy consider control of the border states crucial? (pp. 463–465)
2. Why did the South believe it could win the war despite numerical disadvantages? (pp. 465–468)
3. Why did the Confederacy's bid for international support fail? (pp. 468–475)
4. Why did the Union change policy in 1863 to allow black men to serve in the army? (pp. 475–479)
5. How did wartime hardship in the South contribute to class friction? (pp. 483–485)
6. Why was the U.S. Congress able to pass such a bold legislative agenda during the war? (pp. 485–486)
7. Why were the siege of Vicksburg and the battle of Gettysburg crucial to the outcome of the war? (pp. 486–493)

MAKING CONNECTIONS

Draw on key terms, the timeline, and review questions.

1. Despite loathing slavery, Lincoln embraced emancipation as a war objective late and with great caution. Why? In your answer, trace the progression of Lincoln's position, considering how legal, political, military, and moral concerns influenced his policies.
2. The Emancipation Proclamation did not accomplish the destruction of slavery on its own. How did a war over union bring about the end of slavery? In your answer, consider the direct actions of slaves and Union policymakers as well as indirect factors within the Confederacy.
3. In addition to restoring the Union and destroying slavery, what other significant changes did the war produce on the home front and in the nation's capital? In your answer, discuss economic, governmental, and social developments, being attentive to regional variations.
4. Brilliant military strategy alone did not determine the outcome of the war; victory also depended on generating revenue, materiel mobilization, diplomacy, and politics. In light of these considerations, explain why the Confederacy believed it would succeed and why it ultimately failed.

LINKING TO THE PAST

Link events in this chapter to earlier events.

1. Why were white slaveholders surprised by the wartime behavior of slaves? (See chapter 13.)
2. In what ways did the Lincoln administration's wartime policies fulfill the prewar aspirations of Northerners? (See chapters 12 and 14.)

▶ **For practice quizzes and other study tools**, visit the Online Study Guide at **bedfordstmartins.com/roark.**

TIMELINE 1861–1865

1861
- **April** Attack on Fort Sumter.
- **April–May** Four Upper South states join Confederacy.
- **July** Union forces routed in first battle of Bull Run (Manassas).
- **August** First Confiscation Act.

1862
- **February** Grant captures Fort Henry and Fort Donelson.
- **March** Confederates defeated at battle of Glorieta Pass.
- **March** Union victory at battle of Pea Ridge.
- **April** Battle of Shiloh in Tennessee ends Confederate bid to control Mississippi valley.
- **April** Confederate Congress authorizes draft.
- **May** Homestead Act.
- **May–July** Union forces defeated during Virginia peninsula campaign.
- **July** Second Confiscation Act.
- **July** Militia Act.
- **September** Battle of Antietam stops Lee's advance into Maryland.

1863
- **January** Emancipation Proclamation becomes law.
- **February** National Banking Act.
- **March** Congress authorizes draft.
- **July** Fall of Vicksburg to Union forces.
- **July** Lee defeated at battle of Gettysburg.
- **July** New York City draft riots.

1864
- **March** Grant appointed Union general in chief.
- **May–June** Wilderness campaign.
- **September** Fall of Atlanta to Sherman.
- **November** Lincoln reelected.
- **December** Fall of Savannah to Sherman.

1865
- **April 2–3** Fall of Petersburg and Richmond.
- **April 9** Lee surrenders to Grant.
- **April 15** Lincoln dies from bullet wound; Vice President Andrew Johnson becomes president.

CARPETBAG
A carpetbag was a nineteenth-century suitcase made from carpet, often brightly colored. Applied first to wildcat bankers on the western frontier, the term "carpetbagger" was a derogatory name for rootless and penniless adventurers who could carry everything they owned in a single bag. Critics of Republican administrations in the South hurled the name "carpetbaggers" at white Northerners who moved South during Reconstruction and became active in politics. The background image of bombed-out Richmond provides a reminder that one of the central tasks of the Reconstruction governments was the rebuilding of the South's battered cities and devastated agricultural economy.
Carpetbag: Nancy Gewirz/Antique Textile Resource; background: Library of Congress.

16 Reconstruction

1863–1877

IN 1856, JOHN RAPIER, A FREE BLACK BARBER IN FLORENCE, ALABAMA, urged his four freeborn sons to flee the increasingly repressive and dangerous South. Searching for a color-blind society, the brothers scattered around the world. James T. Rapier chose Canada, where he went to live with his uncle in a largely black community and studied Greek and Latin in a log schoolhouse. After his conversion at a Methodist revival, James wrote to his father: "I have not thrown a card in 3 years[,] touched a woman in 2 years[,] smoked nor drunk any Liquor in going on 2 years." He vowed, "I will endeavor to do my part in solving the problems [of African Americans] in my native land."

The Union victory in the Civil War gave James Rapier the opportunity to redeem his pledge. In 1865, after more than eight years of exile, the twenty-seven-year-old Rapier returned to Alabama, where he presided over the first political gathering of former slaves in the state. Alabama freedmen produced a petition that called on the federal government to thoroughly reconstruct the South, to guarantee suffrage, free schools, and equal rights for all men, regardless of color.

Rapier soon discovered that Alabama's whites found it agonizingly difficult to accept defeat and black freedom. They responded to the revolutionary changes under the banner "White Man — Right or Wrong — Still the White Man!" In 1868, when Rapier and other Alabama blacks vigorously supported the Republican presidential candidate, former Union general Ulysses S. Grant, the recently organized Ku Klux Klan went on a bloody rampage of whipping, burning, and shooting. A mob of 150 outraged whites scoured Rapier's neighborhood seeking four black politicians they claimed were trying to "Africanize Alabama." They caught and hanged three, but the "nigger carpetbagger from Canada" escaped. Rapier considered fleeing the state, but he decided to stay and fight.

By the early 1870s, Rapier had emerged as Alabama's most prominent black leader. Demanding that the federal government end the violence against ex-slaves, guarantee their civil rights, and give them land, he won election in 1872 to the House of Representatives, where he joined six other black congressmen. Defeated for reelection in 1874 in a campaign marked by white violence and ballot-box stuffing, Rapier turned to cotton farming, generously giving thousands of dollars of his profits to black schools and churches.

But persistent black poverty and unrelenting racial violence convinced Rapier that blacks could never achieve equality and prosperity in the South. He purchased land in Kansas and urged Alabama's blacks to escape with

James T. Rapier
Black suffrage sent fourteen African American congressmen to Washington, D.C., during Reconstruction, among them James T. Rapier of Alabama. Temporarily at least, he and his black colleagues helped shape post-emancipation society. In 1874, when Rapier spoke on behalf of a civil rights bill, he described the humiliation of being denied service at inns all along his route from Montgomery to Washington. Elsewhere in the world, he said, class and religion were invoked to defend discrimination. In Europe, "they have princes, dukes, lords"; in India, "brahmans or priests, who rank above the sudras or laborers." But in America, "our distinction is color." Alabama Department of Archives and History.

him. In 1883, however, before he could leave Alabama, Rapier died of tuberculosis at the age of forty-five.

In 1865, Union general Carl Schurz had foreseen many of the troubles Rapier would encounter in the postwar South. Schurz concluded that the Civil War was "a revolution but half accomplished." Northern victory had freed the slaves, he observed, but it had not changed former slaveholders' minds about blacks' unfitness for freedom. Left to themselves, whites would "introduce some new system of forced labor, not perhaps exactly slavery in its old form but something similar to it." To defend their freedom, Schurz concluded, blacks would need federal protection, land of their own, and voting rights. Until whites "cut loose from the past, it will be a dangerous experiment to put Southern society upon its own legs."

As Schurz discovered, the end of the war did not mean peace. The United States was one of only two societies in the New World in which slavery ended in a bloody war. (The other was Haiti.) Not surprisingly, racial turmoil continued in the South after the armies quit fighting in 1865. The nation entered one of its most chaotic and conflicted eras — Reconstruction, a violent period that would define the defeated South's status within the Union and the meaning of freedom for ex-slaves.

The place of the South within the nation and the extent of black freedom were determined not only in Washington, D.C., where the federal government played an active role, but also in the state legislatures and county seats of the South, where blacks eagerly participated in the process. Moreover, on farms and plantations from Virginia to Texas, ex-slaves struggled to become free workers while ex-slaveholders clung to the Old South. A small band of white women joined in the struggle for racial equality, and soon their crusade broadened to include gender equality. Their attempts to secure voting rights for women were thwarted, however.

Reconstruction witnessed a gigantic struggle to determine the consequences of Confederate defeat and emancipation. In the end, white Southerners prevailed. Their New South was a different South from the one to which most whites wished to return but also vastly unlike the one of which James Rapier dreamed.

▸ Wartime Reconstruction

Reconstruction did not wait for the end of war. As the odds of a northern victory increased, thinking about reunification quickened. Immediately, a question arose: Who had authority to devise a plan for reconstructing the Union? President Abraham Lincoln firmly believed that reconstruction was a matter of executive responsibility. Congress just as firmly asserted its jurisdiction. Fueling the argument were significant differences about the terms of reconstruction. Lincoln's primary aim was the restoration of national unity, which he sought through a program of speedy, forgiving political reconciliation. Congress feared that the president's program meant restoring the old southern ruling class to power. It wanted assurances of white loyalty and guarantees of black rights.

In their eagerness to formulate a plan for political reunification, neither Lincoln nor Congress gave much attention to the South's land and labor problems. But as the war rapidly eroded slavery and traditional plantation agriculture, Yankee military commanders in the Union-occupied areas of the Confederacy had no choice but to oversee the emergence of a new labor system.

"To Bind Up the Nation's Wounds"

On March 4, 1865, in his second inaugural address, President Lincoln surveyed the history of the war and then looked ahead to peace. "With malice toward none; with charity for all; with firmness in the right, as God gives us to see the right," Lincoln said, "let us strive on to finish the work we are in; to bind up the nation's wounds . . . to do all which may achieve and cherish a just, and a lasting peace." Lincoln had contemplated reunion for nearly two years. While deep compassion for the enemy guided his thinking about peace, his plan for reconstruction aimed primarily at shortening the war and ending slavery.

Lincoln's Proclamation of Amnesty and Reconstruction in December 1863 set out his terms. He offered a full pardon, restoring property (except slaves) and political rights, to rebels willing to renounce secession and to accept emancipation. His offer excluded only high-ranking Confederate military and political officers and a few other groups. When 10 percent of a state's voting population had taken an oath of allegiance, the state could organize a new government and be readmitted into the Union. Lincoln's plan did not require ex-rebels to extend social or political rights to ex-slaves, nor did it anticipate a program of long-term federal assistance to freedmen. Clearly, the president looked forward to the rapid, forgiving restoration of the broken Union.

Lincoln's easy terms enraged abolitionists such as Wendell Phillips of Boston, who charged that the president "makes the negro's freedom a mere sham." He "is willing that the negro should be free but seeks nothing else for him." He compared Lincoln to the most passive of the Civil War generals: "What McClellan was on the battlefield — 'Do as little hurt as possible!' — Lincoln is in civil affairs — 'Make as little change as possible!'" Phillips and other northern radicals called instead for a thorough overhaul of southern society. Their ideas proved to be too drastic for most Republicans during the war years, but Congress agreed that Lincoln's plan was inadequate.

In July 1864, Congress put forward a plan of its own. Congressman Henry Winter Davis of Maryland and Senator Benjamin Wade of Ohio jointly sponsored a bill that demanded that at least half of the voters in a conquered rebel state take the oath of allegiance before reconstruction could begin. The **Wade-Davis bill** also banned all ex-Confederates from participating in the drafting of new state constitutions. Finally, the bill guaranteed the equality of freedmen before the law. Congress's reconstruction would be neither as quick nor as forgiving as Lincoln's. When Lincoln refused to sign the bill and let it die, Wade and Davis charged the president with usurpation of power. They warned Lincoln to confine himself to "his executive duties — to obey and execute, not make the laws — to suppress by arms armed rebellion, and leave political organization to Congress."

Undeterred, Lincoln continued to nurture the formation of loyal state governments under his own plan. Four states — Louisiana, Arkansas, Tennessee, and Virginia — fulfilled the president's requirements, but Congress refused to seat representatives from the "Lincoln states." In his last public address in April 1865, Lincoln defended his plan but for the first time expressed publicly his endorsement of suffrage for southern blacks, at least "the very intelligent, and . . . those who serve our cause as soldiers." The announcement demonstrated that Lincoln's thinking about reconstruction was still evolving. Four days later, he was dead.

Wartime Reconstruction

This cartoon from the presidential campaign of 1864 shows the "Rail Splitter" Abraham Lincoln leveraging the broken nation back together while his running mate, Andrew Johnson, who once was a tailor by trade, stitches the Confederate states securely back into the Union. Optimism that the task of reconstructing the nation after the war would be both quick and easy shines through the cartoon. The Granger Collection, NY.

Land and Labor

Of all the problems raised by the North's victory in the war, none proved more critical than the South's transition from slavery to free labor. As federal armies invaded and occupied the Confederacy, hundreds of thousands of slaves became free workers. In addition, Union armies controlled vast territories in the South where legal title to land had become unclear. The Confiscation Acts passed during the war punished "traitors" by taking away their property. The question of what to do with federally occupied land and how to organize labor on it engaged former slaves, former slaveholders, Union military commanders, and federal government officials long before the war ended.

"What's the use of being free if you don't own land enough to be buried in?

— A former slave

In the Mississippi valley, occupying federal troops announced a new labor code. It required slaveholders to sign contracts with ex-slaves and to pay wages. It obligated employers to provide food, housing, and medical care. It outlawed whipping, but it reserved to the army the right to discipline blacks who refused to work. The code required black laborers to enter into contracts, work diligently, and remain subordinate and obedient. Military leaders clearly had no intention of promoting a social or economic revolution. Instead, they sought to restore plantation agriculture with wage labor. The effort resulted in a hybrid system that one contemporary called "compulsory free labor," something that satisfied no one.

Planters complained because the new system fell short of slavery. Blacks could not be "transformed by proclamation," a Louisiana sugar planter declared. Yet under the new system, blacks "are expected to perform their new obligations without coercion, & without the fear of punishment which is essential to stimulate the idle and correct the vicious." Without the right to whip, he argued, the new labor system did not have a chance. Either Union soldiers must "*compel* the negroes to work," planters insisted, or the planters themselves must "be authorized and sustained in using force."

African Americans found the new regime too reminiscent of slavery to be called free labor. Its chief deficiency, they believed, was the failure to provide them with land of their own. Freedmen believed they had a moral right to land because they and their ancestors had worked it without compensation for more than two centuries. "What's the use of being free if you don't own land enough to be buried in?" one man asked. Several wartime developments led freedmen to believe that the federal government planned to undergird black freedom with landownership.

In January 1865, General William Tecumseh Sherman set aside part of the coast south of Charleston for black settlement. He devised the plan to relieve himself of the burden of thousands of impoverished blacks who trailed desperately behind his army. By June 1865, some 40,000 freedmen sat on 400,000 acres of "Sherman land." In addition, in March 1865, Congress passed a bill establishing the Bureau of Refugees, Freedmen, and Abandoned Lands. The **Freedmen's Bureau**, as it was called, distributed food and clothing to destitute Southerners and eased the transition of blacks from slaves to free persons. Congress also authorized the agency to divide abandoned and confiscated land into 40-acre plots, to rent them to freedmen, and eventually to sell them "with such title as the United States can convey." By June 1865, the bureau had situated nearly 10,000 black families on a half million acres abandoned by fleeing planters. Other ex-slaves eagerly anticipated farms of their own.

Despite the flurry of activity, wartime reconstruction failed to produce agreement about whether the president or Congress had the authority to devise policy or what proper policy should be.

The African American Quest for Autonomy

Ex-slaves never had any doubt about what they wanted from freedom. They had only to contemplate what they had been denied as slaves. (See "Documenting the American Promise," page 504.) Slaves had to remain on their plantations; freedom allowed blacks to see what was on the other side of the hill. Slaves had to be at work in the fields by dawn; freedom permitted blacks to sleep through a sunrise. Freedmen also tested the etiquette of racial subordination. "Lizzie's maid passed me today when I was coming from church *without speaking to me*," huffed one plantation mistress.

To whites, emancipation looked like pure anarchy. Blacks, they said, had reverted to their natural condition: lazy, irresponsible, and wild. Without the discipline of slavery, whites predicted, blacks would go the way of "the Indian and the buffalo." Actually, former slaves were experimenting with freedom, but they could not long afford to roam the countryside, neglect work, and casually provoke whites. Soon, most were back at work in whites' kitchens and fields.

But other items on ex-slaves' agenda of freedom endured. They continued to dream of land and economic independence. "The way we can best take care of ourselves is to have land," one former slave declared in 1865, "and turn it and till it by our own labor." Freedmen also wanted to learn to read and write. Many black soldiers had become literate in the Union army, and they understood the value of the pen and book. "I wishes the Childern all in School," one black veteran asserted. "It is beter for them then to be their Surveing a mistes [mistress]."

The restoration of broken families was another persistent black aspiration. Thousands of freedmen took to the roads in 1865 to look for kin who had been sold away or to free those who were being held illegally as slaves. A black soldier from Missouri wrote his daughters that he was coming for them. "I will have you if it cost me my life," he declared. "Your Miss Kitty said that I tried to steal you," he told them. "But I'll let her know that god never intended for a man to steal his own flesh and blood." And he swore that "if she meets me with ten thousand soldiers, she [will] meet her enemy."

Independent worship was another continuing aspiration. African Americans greeted freedom with a mass exodus from white churches, where they had been required to worship when slaves. Some joined the newly established southern branches of all-black northern churches, such as the African Methodist Episcopal Church. Others formed black versions of the major southern denominations, Baptists and Methodists. Freedmen interpreted the events of the Civil War and reconstruction as Christian people. One

DOCUMENTING THE AMERICAN PROMISE

The Meaning of Freedom

The Emancipation Proclamation states that "all persons held as slaves" within the states still in rebellion on January 1, 1863, "are, and henceforward shall be, free." Although the proclamation in and of itself did not free any slaves, it transformed the character of the war. Despite often intolerable conditions, black people focused on the possibilities of freedom.

DOCUMENT 1
Letter from John Q. A. Dennis to Edwin M. Stanton, July 26, 1864

John Q. A. Dennis, formerly a slave in Maryland, wrote to ask Secretary of War Edwin M. Stanton for help in reuniting his family.

BOSTON. Dear Sir I am Glad that I have the Honour to Write you a few line I have been in troble for about four yars my Dear wife was taken from me Nov 19th 1859 and left me with three Children and I being a Slave At the time Could Not do Anny thing for the poor little Children for my master it was took me Carry me some forty mile from them So I Could Not do for them and the man that they live with half feed them and half Cloth them & beat them like dogs & when I was admitted to go to see them it use to brake my heart & Now I say again I am Glad to have the honour to write to you to see if you Can Do Anny thing for me or for my poor little Children I was keap in Slavy untell last Novr 1863. then the Good lord sent the Cornel borne [federal colonel William Birney?] Down their in Marland in worsester Co So as I have been recently freed I have but letle to live on but I am Striveing Dear Sir but what I went too know of you Sir is it possible for me to go & take my Children from those men that keep them in Savery if it is possible will you pleas give me a permit from your hand then I think they would let them go. . . .

Hon sir will you please excuse my Miserable writeing & answer me as soon as you can I want get the little Children out of Slavery, I being Criple would like to know of you also if I Cant be permited to rase a Shool Down there & on what turm I Could be admited to Do so No more At present Dear Hon Sir

SOURCE: *Freedom: A Documentary History of Emancipation, 1861–1867*, ser. 1, vol. 1, *The Destruction of Slavery*, 386, edited by Ira Berlin, Joseph P. Reidy, and Leslie S. Rowland.

DOCUMENT 2
Report from Reverend A. B. Randall, February 28, 1865

A. B. Randall, the white chaplain of a black regiment stationed in Little Rock, Arkansas, affirmed the importance of legal marriage to freed slaves and emphasized their conviction that emancipation was only the first step toward full freedom.

Weddings, just now, are very popular, and abundant among the Colored People. They have just learned, of the Special Order No. 15. of Gen Thomas [Adjutant General Lorenzo Thomas] by which, they may not only be lawfully married, but have their Marriage Certificates, Recorded; in a book furnished by the Government. This is most desirable. . . . Those who were captured . . . at Ivy's Ford, on the 17th of January, by Col Brooks, had their Marriage Certificates, taken from them; and destroyed; and then were roundly cursed, for having such papers in their posession. I have married, during the month, at this Post; Twenty five couples; mostly, those, who have families; & have been living together for years. I try to dissuade single men, who are soldiers, from marrying, till their time of enlistment is out: as that course seems to me, to be most judicious. The Colord People here, generally consider, this war not only; their exodus, from bondage; but the road, to Responsibility; Competency; and an honorable Citizenship — God grant that their hopes and expectations may be fully realized.

SOURCE: *Freedom: A Documentary History of Emancipation, 1861–1867*, ser. 2, vol. 1, *The Black Military Experience*, 712, edited by Ira Berlin, Joseph P. Reidy, and Leslie S. Rowland.

DOCUMENT 3
Petition "to the Union Convention of Tennessee Assembled in the Capitol at Nashville," January 9, 1865

In January 1865, black Tennesseans petitioned a convention of white Unionists debating the reorganization of state government.

We the undersigned petitioners, American citizens of African descent, natives and residents of Tennessee, and devoted friends of the great National cause, do most respectfully ask a patient hearing of your honorable body in regard to matters deeply affecting the future condition of our unfortunate and long suffering race.

First of all, however, we would say that words are too weak to tell how profoundly grateful we are to the Federal Government for the good work of freedom which it is gradually carrying forward; and for the Emancipation Proclamation which has set free all the slaves in some of the rebellious States, as well as many of the slaves in Tennessee. . . .

We claim freedom, as our natural right, and ask that in harmony and co-operation with the nation at large, you should cut up by the roots the system of slavery, which is not only a wrong to us, but the source of all the evil which at present afflicts the State. For slavery, corrupt itself, corrupted nearly all, also, around it, so that it has influenced nearly all the slave States to rebel against the Federal Government, in order to set up a government of pirates under which slavery might be perpetrated.

In the contest between the nation and slavery, our unfortunate people have sided, by instinct, with the former. We have little fortune to devote to the national cause, for a hard fate has hitherto forced us to live in poverty, but we do devote to its success, our hopes, our toils, our whole heart, our sacred honor, and our lives. We will work, pray, live, and, if need be, die for the Union, as cheerfully as ever a white patriot died for his country. The color of our skin does not lessen in the least degree, our love either for God or for the land of our birth. . . .

We know the burdens of citizenship, and are ready to bear them. We know the duties of the good citizen, and are ready to perform them cheerfully, and would ask to be put in a position in which we can discharge them more effectually. . . .

This is a democracy — a government of the people. It should aim to make every man, without regard to the color of his skin, the amount of his wealth, or the character of his religious faith, feel personally interested in its welfare. Every man who lives under the Government should feel that it is his property, his treasure, the bulwark and defence of himself and his family. . . .

This is not a Democratic Government if a numerous, law-abiding, industrious, and useful class of citizens, born and bred on the soil, are to be treated as aliens and enemies, as an inferior degraded class, who must have no voice in the Government which they support, protect and defend, with all their heart, soul, mind, and body, both in peace and war. . . .

The possibility that the negro suffrage proposition may shock popular prejudice at first sight, is not a conclusive argument against its wisdom and policy. No proposition ever met with more furious or general opposition than the one to enlist colored soldiers in the United States army. The opponents of the measure exclaimed on all hands that the negro was a coward; that he would not fight; that one white man, with a whip in his hand could put to flight a regiment of them. . . . Yet the colored man has fought so well, on almost every occasion, that the rebel government is prevented, only by its fears and distrust of being able to force him to fight for slavery as well as he fights against it, from putting half a million of negroes into its ranks.

The Government has asked the colored man to fight for its preservation and gladly has he done it. It can afford to trust him with a vote as safely as it trusted him with a bayonet.

SOURCE: *Freedom: A Documentary History of Emancipation, 1861–1867*, ser. 2, vol. 1, *The Black Military Experience*, 811–16, edited by Ira Berlin, Joseph P. Reidy, and Leslie S. Rowland.

Questions for Analysis and Debate

1. How does John Q. A. Dennis interpret his responsibility as a father?
2. Why do you think ex-slaves wanted their marriages legalized?
3. Why, according to petitioners to the Union Convention of Tennessee, did blacks deserve voting rights?

SAML. DOVE wishes to know of the whereabouts of his mother, Areno, his sisters Maria, Neziah, and Peggy, and his brother Edmond, who were owned by Geo. Dove, of Rockingham county, Shenandoah Valley, Va. Sold in Richmond, after which Saml. and Edmond were taken to Nashville, Tenn., by Joe Mick; Areno was left at the Eagle Tavern, Richmond

Respectfully yours,
SAML. DOVE.

Utica, New York, Aug. 5, 1865–3m

U. S. CHRISTIAN COMMISSION, NASHVILLE, TENN., July 19, 1865.

Harry Stephens and Family, 1866, and Samuel Dove Ad, 1865
Dressed in their Sunday best, this Virginia family sits proudly for a photograph. Many black families were not as fortunate as the Stephens family. Separated by slavery or war, former slaves desperately sought news of missing family members through newspaper advertisements like the one posted by Samuel Dove in August 1865. We do not know whether he succeeded in locating his mother, brother, and sisters. Ad: Chicago Historical Society; Family: The Metropolitan Museum of Art, Gilman Collection, Purchase, The Horace W. Goldsmith Foundation Gift, 2005 (2005.100.277)/Art Resource, NY.

black woman thanked Lincoln for the Emancipation Proclamation, declaring, "When you are dead and in Heaven, in a thousand years that action of yours will make the Angels sing your praises I know it."

REVIEW Why did Congress object to Lincoln's wartime plan for reconstruction?

▸ Presidential Reconstruction

Abraham Lincoln died on April 15, 1865, just hours after John Wilkes Booth shot him at a Washington, D.C., theater. Chief Justice Salmon P. Chase immediately administered the oath of office to Vice President **Andrew Johnson** of Tennessee. Congress had adjourned in March and would not reconvene until December. Throughout the summer and fall, the "accidental president" made critical decisions about the future of the South without congressional advice. With dizzying speed, he drew up and executed a plan of reconstruction.

Congress returned to the capital in December to find that, as far as the president and former Confederates were concerned, reconstruction was completed. Most Republicans, however, thought Johnson's puny demands of ex-rebels made a mockery of the sacrifice of Union soldiers. Instead of honoring the dead by insisting on "a new birth of freedom," as Lincoln had promised in his 1863 speech at Gettysburg, Johnson had acted as midwife to the rebirth of the Old South and the stillbirth of black liberty. They proceeded to dismantle Johnson's program and substitute a program of their own.

***A Pastoral Visit,* 1881**
Freedom from bondage permitted blacks to flee white ministers and churches, to "come out from under the yoke," as one ex-slave put it. In *A Pastoral Visit,* Virginia-born artist Richard Norris Brooke portrays a dignified elderly black minister seated at a table with a family of his parishioners. In this sympathetic and respectful depiction, the poor family shares what it has. It is safe to say that no white minister had ever sat down for a meal in this humble northern Virginia cabin. In the Collection of the Corcoran Gallery of Art, Washington, D.C.

Johnson's Program of Reconciliation

Born in 1808 in Raleigh, North Carolina, Andrew Johnson was the son of illiterate parents. Self-educated and ambitious, Johnson moved to Tennessee, where he worked as a tailor, accumulated a fortune in land, acquired five slaves, and built a career in politics championing the South's common white people and assailing its "illegitimate, swaggering, bastard, scrub aristocracy." The only senator from a Confederate state to remain loyal to the Union, Johnson held the planter class responsible for secession. Less than two weeks before he became president, he announced what he would do to planters if he ever had the chance: "I would arrest them — I would try them — I would convict them and I would hang them."

Despite such statements, Johnson was no friend of the Republicans. A Democrat all his life, Johnson occupied the White House only because the Republican Party in 1864 had needed a vice presidential candidate who would appeal to loyal, Union-supporting Democrats. Johnson vigorously defended states' rights (but not secession) and opposed Republican efforts to expand the power of the federal government. A steadfast supporter of slavery, Johnson had owned slaves until 1862, when Tennessee rebels, angry at his Unionism, confiscated them. When he grudgingly accepted emancipation, it was more because he hated planters than sympathized with slaves. "Damn the negroes," he said. "I am fighting those traitorous aristocrats, their masters." At a time when the nation confronted the future of black Americans, the new president harbored unshakable racist convictions. Africans, Johnson said, were "inferior to the white man in point of intellect — better calculated in physical structure to undergo drudgery and hardship."

> **"Damn the negroes. I am fighting those traitorous aristocrats, their masters."**
> — President ANDREW JOHNSON

Like Lincoln, Johnson stressed the rapid restoration of civil government in the South. Like Lincoln, he promised to pardon most, but not all, ex-rebels. Johnson recognized the state governments created by Lincoln but set out his own requirements for restoring the other rebel states to the Union. All that the citizens of a state had to do was to renounce the right of secession, deny that the debts of the Confederacy were legal and binding, and ratify the Thirteenth Amendment abolishing slavery, which became part of the Constitution in December 1865.

Johnson's eagerness to restore relations with southern states and his lack of sympathy for blacks also led him to return to pardoned ex-Confederates all confiscated and abandoned land, even if it was in the hands of freedmen. Reformers were shocked. They had expected the president's hatred of planters to mean the permanent confiscation of the South's plantations and the distribution of the land to loyal freedmen. Instead, his instructions canceled the promising beginnings made by General Sherman and the Freedmen's Bureau to settle blacks on land of their own. As one freedman observed, "Things was hurt by Mr. Lincoln getting killed."

White Southern Resistance and Black Codes

In the summer of 1865, delegates across the South gathered to draw up the new state constitutions required by Johnson's plan of reconstruction. Rather than take their medicine, delegates choked on even the president's mild requirements. Refusing to renounce secession, the South Carolina and Georgia conventions merely "repudiated" their secession ordinances, preserving in principle their right to secede. South Carolina and Mississippi refused to disown their Confederate war debts. Mississippi rejected the Thirteenth Amendment outright, and Alabama rejected it in part. Despite these defiant acts, Johnson did nothing. White Southerners began to think that by standing up for themselves they — not victorious Northerners — would shape reconstruction.

In the fall of 1865, newly elected southern legislators across the South adopted a series of laws known as **black codes**, which made a travesty of black freedom. The codes sought to keep ex-slaves subordinate to whites by subjecting them to every sort of discrimination. Several states made it illegal for blacks to own a gun. Mississippi made insulting gestures and language by blacks a criminal offense. The codes barred blacks from jury duty. Not a single southern state granted any black the right to vote.

At the core of the black codes, however, lay the matter of labor. Faced with the death of slavery, legislators sought to hustle freedmen back to the plantations. Whites were almost universally opposed to black landownership. Whitelaw Reid, a northern visitor to the South, found that the "man who should sell small tracts to them would be in actual personal danger." South Carolina attempted to limit blacks to either farmwork or domestic service by requiring them to pay annual taxes of $10 to $100 to work in any other occupation. Mississippi declared that blacks who did not possess written evidence of employment could be declared vagrants and be subject to involuntary plantation labor. Under so-called apprenticeship laws, courts bound thousands of black children — orphans and others whose parents they deemed unable to support them — to work for planter "guardians."

Johnson refused to intervene. A staunch defender of states' rights, he believed that the citizens of every state should be free to write their own constitutions and laws. Moreover, Johnson was as eager as other white Southerners to restore white supremacy and black subordination. As he remarked in 1865, "White men alone must manage the South."

But Johnson also followed the path that he believed offered him the greatest political return. A conservative Tennessee Democrat at the head of a northern Republican Party, he began to look southward for political allies. Despite tough talk about punishing traitors, he personally pardoned fourteen thousand wealthy or high-ranking ex-Confederates. By pardoning powerful whites, by accepting governments even when they failed to satisfy his minimal demands, and by acquiescing in the black codes, he won useful southern friends.

In the fall elections of 1865, white Southerners dramatically expressed their mood. To represent them in Congress, they chose former Confederates. Of the eighty senators and representatives they sent to Washington, fifteen had served in the Confederate army, ten of them as generals. Another sixteen had served in civil and judicial posts in the Confederacy. Nine others had served in the Confederate Congress. One — Alexander Stephens — had been vice president of the Confederacy. As one Georgian remarked, "It looked as though Richmond had moved to Washington."

The Black Codes
Titled "Selling a Freeman to Pay His Fine at Monticello, Florida," this 1867 drawing from a northern magazine equates black codes with the reinstitution of slavery. The laws stopped short of reenslavement but sharply restricted blacks' freedom. In Florida, as in other southern states, certain acts, such as breaking a labor contract, were made criminal offenses, the penalty for which could be involuntary plantation labor for a year. The Granger Collection, NYC.

Expansion of Federal Authority and Black Rights

Southerners had blundered monumentally. They had assumed that what Andrew Johnson was willing to accept, Republicans would accept as well. But southern intransigence compelled even moderates to conclude that ex-rebels were a "generation of vipers," still untrustworthy and dangerous. So angry were Republicans with the rebels that the federal government refused to supply artificial limbs to disabled Southerners, as they did for Union veterans.

The black codes became a symbol of southern intentions to "restore all of slavery but its name." Northerners were hardly saints when it came to racial justice, but black freedom had become a hallowed war aim. "We tell the white men of Mississippi," the *Chicago Tribune* roared, "that the men of the North will convert the State of Mississippi into a frog pond before they will allow such laws to disgrace one foot of the soil in which the bones of our soldiers sleep and over which the flag of freedom waves."

The moderate majority of the Republican Party wanted only assurance that slavery and treason were dead. They did not champion black equality, the confiscation of plantations, or black voting, as did the radical minority within the party. But southern obstinacy had succeeded in forging unity (at least temporarily) among Republican factions. In December 1865, exercising

Congress's right to determine the qualifications of its members, Republicans refused to seat the southern representatives elected in the fall elections. Rather than accept Johnson's claim that the "work of restoration" was done, Congress challenged his executive power.

Republican senator Lyman Trumbull declared that the president's policy meant that an ex-slave would "be tyrannized over, abused, and virtually reenslaved without some legislation by the nation for his protection." Early in 1866, the moderates produced two bills that strengthened the federal shield. The first, the Freedmen's Bureau bill, prolonged the life of the agency established by the previous Congress. It had distributed food, supervised labor contracts, and sponsored schools for freedmen. Arguing that the Constitution never contemplated a "system for the support of indigent persons," President Andrew Johnson vetoed the bill. Congress failed by a narrow margin to override the president's veto.

The moderates designed their second measure, what would become the **Civil Rights Act of 1866**, to nullify the black codes by affirming African Americans' rights to "full and equal benefit of all laws and proceedings for the security of person and property as is enjoyed by white citizens." The act boldly required the end of racial discrimination in state laws and represented an extraordinary expansion of black rights and federal authority. The president argued that the civil rights bill amounted to "unconstitutional invasion of states' rights" and vetoed it. In essence, he denied that the federal government possessed the authority to protect the civil rights of blacks.

In April 1866, an incensed Republican Party again pushed the civil rights bill through Congress and overrode the presidential veto. In July, it passed another Freedmen's Bureau bill and overrode Johnson's veto. For the first time in American history, Congress had overridden presidential vetoes of major legislation. As a worried South Carolinian observed, Johnson had succeeded in uniting the Republicans and probably touched off "a fight this fall such as has never been seen."

REVIEW How did the North respond to the passage of black codes in the southern states?

Reconstruction Cartoon

Most white southerners had difficulty adjusting to defeat, but no one defied and damned the Yankees like white women. This 1865 cartoon pokes fun at two Richmond ladies as they pass by a Union officer on their way to receive free government rations. One says sourly to the other, "Don't you think that Yankee must feel like shrinking into his boots before such high-toned Southern ladies as we?" Just a step behind the white women is a smiling black woman, who obviously views the Yankee through different eyes. Miriam and Ira D. Wallach Division of Art, Prints and Photographs, The New York Public Library. Astor, Lenox and Tilden Foundations.

▶ Congressional Reconstruction

By the summer of 1866, President Andrew Johnson and Congress had dropped their gloves and stood toe-to-toe in a bare-knuckle contest unprecedented in American history. Johnson made it clear that he would not budge on either constitutional issues or policy. Moderate Republicans responded by amending the Constitution. But the obstinacy of Johnson and white Southerners pushed Republican moderates ever closer to the radicals and to acceptance of additional federal intervention in the South. Congress also voted to impeach the president for the first time since the nation was formed. In time, Congress debated whether to make voting rights color-blind, while women sought to make voting sex-blind as well.

The Fourteenth Amendment and Escalating Violence

In June 1866, Congress passed the **Fourteenth Amendment** to the Constitution, and two years later it gained the necessary ratification of three-fourths of the states. The most important provisions of this complex amendment made all native-born or naturalized persons American citizens and prohibited states from abridging the "privileges and immunities" of citizens, depriving them of "life, liberty, or property without due process of law," and denying them "equal protection of the laws." By making blacks national citizens, the amendment provided a national guarantee of equality before the law. In essence, it protected blacks against violation by southern state governments.

The Fourteenth Amendment also dealt with voting rights. It gave Congress the right to reduce the congressional representation of states that withheld suffrage from some of its adult male population. In other words, white Southerners could either allow black men to vote or see their representation in Washington slashed. Whatever happened, Republicans stood to benefit from the Fourteenth Amendment. If southern whites granted voting rights to freedmen, Republicans would gain valuable black votes. If whites refused, the representation of southern Democrats would plunge.

The Fourteenth Amendment's suffrage provisions ignored the small band of politicized women who had emerged from the war demanding "the ballot for the two disenfranchised classes, negroes and women." Founding the **American Equal Rights Association** in 1866, **Susan B. Anthony** and **Elizabeth Cady Stanton** lobbied for "a government by the people, and the whole people; for the people and the whole people." They felt betrayed when their old antislavery allies refused to work for their goals. "It was the Negro's hour," Frederick Douglass explained. Senator Charles Sumner suggested that woman suffrage could be "the great question of the future."

The Fourteenth Amendment provided for punishment of any state that excluded voters on the basis of race but not on the basis of sex. The amendment also introduced the word *male* into the Constitution when it referred to a citizen's right to vote. Stanton predicted that "if that word 'male' be inserted, it will take us a century at least to get it out."

Tennessee approved the Fourteenth Amendment in July, and Congress promptly welcomed the state's representatives and senators back. Had President Johnson counseled other southern states to ratify this relatively mild amendment and warned them that they faced the fury of an outraged Republican Party if they refused, they might have listened. Instead, Johnson advised Southerners to reject the Fourteenth Amendment and to rely on him to trounce the Republicans in the fall congressional elections.

Johnson had decided to make the Fourteenth Amendment the overriding issue of the 1866 elections and to gather its white opponents into a new conservative party, the National Union Party. The president's strategy suffered a setback when whites in several southern cities went on rampages against blacks. When a mob in New Orleans assaulted delegates to a black suffrage convention, thirty-four blacks died. In Memphis, white mobs killed at least forty-six people. The slaughter shocked Northerners and renewed skepticism about Johnson's claim that southern whites could be trusted. "Who doubts that the Freedmen's Bureau ought to be abolished forthwith," a New Yorker observed sarcastically, "and the blacks remitted to the paternal care of their old masters, who 'understand the nigger, you know, a great deal better than the Yankees can.'"

The 1866 elections resulted in an overwhelming Republican victory. Johnson had bet that Northerners would not support federal protection of black rights and that a racist backlash would blast the Republican Party. But the war was still fresh in northern minds, and as one Republican explained, southern whites "with all their intelligence were traitors, the blacks with all their ignorance were loyal."

Elizabeth Cady Stanton and Susan B. Anthony, 1870
Outspoken suffragists Elizabeth Cady Stanton (left) and Susan B. Anthony (right) were veteran reformers who advocated, among other things, better working conditions for labor, married women's property rights, liberalization of divorce laws, and women's admission into colleges and trade schools. Their passion for other causes led some conservatives to oppose women's political rights because they equated the suffragist cause with radicalism in general. Women could not easily overcome such views, and the long struggle for the vote eventually drew millions of women into public life. ©Bettmann/Corbis.

"If that word 'male' be inserted [in the Fourteenth Amendment], it will take us a century at least to get it out."
— ELIZABETH CADY STANTON

Memphis Riots, May 1866
On May 1, 1866, two carriages, one driven by a white man and the other by a black man, collided on a busy street in Memphis, Tennessee. This minor incident led to three days of bloody racial violence in which dozens of blacks and two whites died. South Memphis, pictured in this lithograph from *Harper's Weekly*, was a shantytown where the families of black soldiers stationed at nearby Fort Pickering lived. The army commander refused to send troops to protect soldiers' families and property, and white mobs ran wild. The Granger Collection, NYC.

Radical Reconstruction and Military Rule

When Johnson continued to urge Southerners to reject the Fourteenth Amendment, every southern state except Tennessee voted it down. "The last one of the sinful ten," thundered Representative James A. Garfield of Ohio, "has flung back into our teeth the magnanimous offer of a generous nation." After the South rejected the moderates' program, the radicals seized the initiative.

Reconstruction Military Districts, 1867

Each act of defiance by southern whites had boosted the standing of the radicals within the Republican Party. Except for freedmen themselves, no one did more to make freedom the "mighty moral question of the age." Radicals such as Massachusetts senator Charles Sumner and Pennsylvania representative Thaddeus Stevens did not speak with a single voice, but they united in demanding civil and political equality. Southern states were "like clay in the hands of the potter," Stevens declared in January 1867, and he called on Congress to begin reconstruction all over again.

In March 1867, Congress overturned the Johnson state governments and initiated military rule of the South. The **Military Reconstruction Act** (and three subsequent acts) divided the ten unreconstructed Confederate states into five military districts. Congress placed a Union general in charge of each district and instructed him to "suppress insurrection, disorder, and violence" and to begin political reform. After the military had completed voter registration, which would include black men, voters in each state would elect delegates to conventions that would draw up new state constitutions. Each constitution would guarantee black suffrage. When the voters of each state had approved the constitution and the state legislature had ratified the Fourteenth Amendment, the state could submit its work to Congress. If Congress approved, the state's senators and representatives could be seated, and political reunification would be accomplished.

Radicals proclaimed the provision for black suffrage "a prodigious triumph," for it extended far beyond the limited suffrage provisions of the Fourteenth Amendment. Republicans now believed that only the voting power of ex-slaves could bring about a permanent revolution in the South. When combined with the disfranchisement of thousands of ex-rebels, it promised to cripple any neo-Confederate resurgence and guarantee Republican state governments in the South.

Despite its bold suffrage provision, the Military Reconstruction Act of 1867 disappointed those who also advocated the confiscation of southern plantations and their redistribution to ex-slaves. Thaddeus Stevens agreed with the freedman who said, "Give us our own land and we take care of ourselves, but without land, the old masters can hire us or starve us, as they please." But most Republicans believed they had provided blacks with what they needed: equal legal rights and the ballot. If blacks were to get land, they would have to gain it themselves.

Declaring that he would rather sever his right arm than sign such a formula for "anarchy and chaos," Andrew Johnson vetoed the Military Reconstruction Act. Congress overrode his veto the very same day, dramatizing the shift in power from the executive to the legislative branch of government. With the passage of the Reconstruction Acts of 1867, congressional reconstruction was virtually completed. Congress left whites owning most of the South's land but, in a departure that justified the term "radical reconstruction," had given black men the ballot. In 1867, the nation began an unprecedented experiment in interracial democracy — at least in the South, for Congress's plan did not touch the North. But before the spotlight swung away from Washington to the South, the president and Congress had one more scene to play.

Impeaching a President

Despite his defeats, Andrew Johnson had no intention of yielding control of reconstruction. In a dozen ways, he sabotaged Congress's will and encouraged southern whites to resist. He issued a flood of pardons, waged war against the

Andrew Johnson Cartoon

Appearing in 1868 during President Andrew Johnson's impeachment trial, this cartoon includes captions that read: "This little boy would persist in handling books above his capacity" and "And this was the disastrous result." The cartoonist's portrait of Johnson being crushed by the Constitution refers to the president's flouting of the Tenure of Office Act, which caused Republicans to vote for his impeachment. The cartoon's celebration of Johnson's destruction proved premature, however. The Granger Collection, NYC.

THIS LITTLE BOY WOULD PERSIST IN HANDLING BOOKS ABOVE HIS CAPACITY.

AND THIS WAS THE DISASTROUS RESULT.

Freedmen's Bureau, and replaced Union generals eager to enforce Congress's Reconstruction Acts with conservative officers eager to defeat them. Johnson claimed that he was merely defending the "violated Constitution." At bottom, however, the president subverted congressional reconstruction to protect southern whites from what he considered the horrors of "Negro domination."

When Congress realized that overriding Johnson's vetoes did not ensure that it got its way, it looked for other ways to exert its will. According to the Constitution, the House of Representatives can impeach and the Senate can try any federal official for "treason, bribery, or other high crimes and misdemeanors." Radicals argued that Johnson's abuse of constitutional powers and his failure to fulfill constitutional obligations to enforce the law were impeachable offenses. But moderates interpreted the constitutional provision to mean violation of criminal statutes. As long as Johnson refrained from breaking the law, impeachment (the process of formal charges of wrongdoing against the president or other federal official) remained stalled.

Then, in August 1867, Johnson suspended Secretary of War Edwin M. Stanton from office. The Tenure of Office Act, which had been passed earlier in the year, demanded the approval of the Senate for the removal of any government official who had been appointed with Senate approval. As required by the act, the president requested the Senate to consent to Stanton's dismissal. When the Senate balked, Johnson removed Stanton anyway. "Is the President crazy, or only drunk?" asked a dumbfounded Republican moderate. "I'm afraid his doings will make us all favor impeachment."

News of Johnson's open defiance of the law convinced every Republican in the House to vote for a resolution impeaching the president. Supreme Court chief justice Salmon Chase presided over the Senate trial, which lasted from March until May 1868. Chase refused to allow Johnson's opponents to raise broad issues of misuse of power and forced them to argue their case exclusively on the narrow legal grounds of Johnson's removal of Stanton. Johnson's lawyers argued that the president had not committed a criminal offense, that the Tenure of Office Act was unconstitutional, and that in any case it did not apply to Stanton, who had been appointed by Lincoln. When the critical vote came, thirty-

Major Reconstruction Legislation, 1865–1875

1865	
Thirteenth Amendment (ratified 1865)	Abolishes slavery.
1865 and 1866	
Freedmen's Bureau Acts	Establish the Freedmen's Bureau to distribute food and clothing to destitute Southerners and help freedmen with labor contracts and schooling.
Civil Rights Act of 1866	Affirms the rights of blacks to enjoy "full and equal benefit of all laws and proceedings for the security of person and property as is enjoyed by white citizens" and effectively requires the end of legal discrimination in state laws.
Fourteenth Amendment (ratified 1868)	Makes native-born blacks citizens and guarantees all citizens "equal protection of the laws." Threatens to reduce representatives of a state that denies suffrage to any of its male inhabitants.
1867	
Military Reconstruction Acts	Impose military rule in the South, establish rules for readmission of ex-Confederate states to the Union, and require those states to guarantee the vote to black men.
1869	
Fifteenth Amendment (ratified 1870)	Prohibits racial discrimination in voting rights in all states in the nation.
1875	
Civil Rights Act of 1875	Outlaws racial discrimination in transportation, public accommodations, and juries.

five senators voted guilty and nineteen not guilty. The impeachment forces fell one vote short of the two-thirds needed to convict.

After his trial, Johnson called a truce, and for the remaining ten months of his term, congressional reconstruction proceeded unhindered by presidential interference. Without interference from Johnson, Congress revisited the suffrage issue.

The Fifteenth Amendment and Women's Demands

In February 1869, Republicans passed the **Fifteenth Amendment** to the Constitution, which prohibited states from depriving any citizen of the right to vote because of "race, color, or previous condition of servitude." The Reconstruction Acts of 1867 already required black suffrage in the South; the Fifteenth Amendment extended black voting nationwide. Partisan advantage played an important role in the amendment's passage. Gains by northern Democrats in the 1868 elections worried Republicans, and black voters now represented the balance of power in several northern states. By giving the ballot to northern blacks, Republicans could lessen their own political vulnerability. As one Republican congressman observed, "Party expediency and exact justice coincide for once."

Some Republicans, however, found the final wording of the Fifteenth Amendment "lame and halting." Rather than absolutely guaranteeing the right to vote, the amendment merely prohibited exclusion on grounds of race. The distinction would prove to be significant. In time, white Southerners would devise tests of literacy and property and other apparently nonracial measures that would effectively disfranchise blacks yet not violate the Fifteenth Amendment. But an amendment that fully guaranteed the right to vote courted defeat outside the South. Rising antiforeign sentiment—against the Chinese in California and European immigrants in the Northeast — caused states to resist giving up total control of suffrage requirements. In March 1870, after three-fourths of the states had ratified it, the Fifteenth Amendment became part of the Constitution. Republicans generally breathed a sigh of relief, confident that black suffrage was "the last great point that remained to be settled of the issues of the war."

Woman suffrage advocates, however, were sorely disappointed with the Fifteenth Amendment's failure to extend voting rights to women. The amendment denied states the right to forbid suffrage only on the basis of race. Elizabeth Cady Stanton and Susan B. Anthony condemned the Republicans' "negro first" strategy and pointed out that women remained "the only class of citizens wholly unrepresented in the government." Stanton wondered aloud why ignorant black men should legislate for educated and cultured white women. Increasingly, activist women concluded that woman "must not put her trust in man." The Fifteenth Amendment severed the early feminist movement from its abolitionist roots. Over the next several decades, feminists established an independent suffrage crusade that drew millions of women into political life.

Republicans took enough satisfaction in the Fifteenth Amendment to promptly scratch the "Negro question" from the agenda of national politics. Even that steadfast crusader for equality Wendell Phillips concluded that the black man now held "sufficient shield in his own hands. . . . Whatever he suffers will be largely now, and in future, his own fault." Northerners had no idea of the violent struggles that lay ahead.

REVIEW Why did Johnson urge the southern states to reject the Fourteenth Amendment?

▸ The Struggle in the South

Northerners believed they had discharged their responsibilities with the Reconstruction Acts and the amendments to the Constitution, but Southerners knew that the battle had just begun. Black suffrage established the foundation for the rise of the Republican Party in the South. Gathering together outsiders and outcasts, southern Republicans won elections, wrote new state constitutions, and formed new state governments.

Challenging the established class for political control was dangerous business. Equally dangerous were the confrontations that took place on southern farms and plantations, where blacks sought to give economic meaning to their newly won legal and political equality. Ex-masters had their own ideas about the labor system that should replace slavery. Freedom remained contested territory, and Southerners fought pitched battles with one another to determine the contours of their new world.

HISTORICAL QUESTION

What Did the Ku Klux Klan Really Want?

In 1866, six Confederate veterans in Pulaski, Tennessee, founded the Ku Klux Klan for fun and fellowship. But by 1868, when congressional reconstruction went into effect, the Klan had spread across the South, and members had shifted to more serious matters.

According to former Confederate general and Georgia Democratic politician John B. Gordon, the Klan owed its popularity to the "instinct of self-preservation . . . the sense of insecurity and danger, particularly in those neighborhoods where the Negro population largely predominated." Everywhere whites looked, he said, they saw "great crime." Republican politicians marched ignorant freedmen to the polls, where they blighted honest government. Ex-slaves drove overseers from plantations and claimed the land for themselves. Black rapists made white women cower behind barred doors. It was necessary, Gordon declared, "in order to protect our families from outrage and preserve our own lives, to have something that we could regard as a brotherhood — a combination of the best men of the country, to act purely in self-defense."

Behind the Klan's high-minded and self-justifying rhetoric, however, lay another agenda. It was revealed in their actions, not their words. Klansmen embarked on a campaign to reverse history. Garbed in robes and hoods, they engaged in guerrilla warfare against free labor, civil equality, and political democracy. They aimed to terrorize their enemies — ex-slaves and white Republicans — into submission. Changes in four particular areas of southern life proved flash points for Klan violence: racial etiquette, education, labor, and politics.

The Klan punished those blacks and whites who broke the Old South's racial code. The Klan considered "impudence" a punishable offense. Asked to define "impudence" before a congressional investigating committee, one white man responded: "Well, it is considered impudence for a negro not to be polite to a white man — not to pull off his hat and bow and scrape to a white man, as was done formerly." Klansmen whipped blacks for speaking disrespectfully, refusing to yield the sidewalk, and dressing well. Black women who "dress up and fix up like ladies" risked a midnight visit from the Klan. The Klan sought to restore racial subordination in every aspect of private and public life.

Klansmen also took aim at black education. White men found the sight of blacks in classrooms hard to stomach. Schools were easy targets, and scores of them went up in flames. Teachers, male and female, were flogged, or worse. Klansmen drove northern-born teacher Alonzo B. Corliss from North Carolina for "teaching niggers and making them like white men." In Cross Plains, Alabama, the Klan hanged an Irish-born teacher along with four black men. Planters wanted ex-slaves back in the fields, not at desks. In 1869, an Alabama newspaper announced that the burning of a black school should be "a warning for them to stick hereafter to 'de shovel and de hoe,' and let their dirty-backed primers go."

Planters turned to the Klan as part of their effort to preserve plantation agriculture. An Alabama white admitted that in his area the Klan was "intended principally for the negroes who failed to work." Hooded bands "punished Negroes whose landlords had complained of them." Sharecroppers who disputed their share at "settling up time" risked a visit from the night riders. It was dangerous for freedmen to consider changing employers. "If we got out looking for some other place to go," an ex-slave from Texas remembered, "them KKK they would tend to Mister negro good and plenty."

Above all, the Klan terrorized Republicans. Klansmen became the military arm of the Democratic Party. They drove blacks from the polls on election day and assaulted Republican officeholders. Klansmen gave Andrew Flowers, a black politician in Chattanooga, a brutal beating and told him that they "did not intend any nigger to hold office in the United States." Jack Dupree, president of the Republican Club in Monroe County, Mississippi, a man known to "speak his mind," had his throat cut and was disemboweled while his wife was forced to watch.

Political violence reached astounding levels. Arkansas experienced nearly three hundred political killings in the three months before the fall elections

Freedmen, Yankees, and Yeomen

African Americans made up the majority of southern Republicans. After gaining voting rights in 1867, nearly all eligible black men registered to vote as Republicans, grateful to the party that had freed them and granted them the franchise. "It is the hardest thing in the world to keep a negro away from the polls," observed an Alabama white man. Black women, like white women, remained disfranchised, but they mobilized along with black men. In the 1868 presidential election, they bravely wore buttons supporting the Republican candidate, Ulysses S. Grant. Southern blacks did not all have identical political priorities, but they

Ku Klux Klan Rider in Tennessee about 1868 and Klan Banner
The white robes that we associate with the Ku Klux Klan are a twentieth-century phenomenon. During Reconstruction, Klansmen wore robes of various designs and colors. Hooded horses added another element to the Klan's terror. The Klansman holds a flag that looks very much like the satanic dragon on the colorful Klan banner shown here, which contains a Latin motto from Saint Augustine's definition of Catholic truth: "that which [has been believed] always, everywhere, by all." Among Klansmen, this motto was likely to refer to the truth of white supremacy.
Rider: Tennessee State Museum Collection; banner: Chicago Historical Society.

in 1868. Louisiana was even bloodier, suffering more than one thousand killings in the same year. In Georgia, the Klan murdered three scalawag members of the legislature and drove ten others from their homes. As one Georgia Republican commented after a Klan attack: "We don't call them [D]emocrats, we call them southern murderers."

It proved hard to arrest Klansmen and harder still to convict them. "If a white man kills a colored man in any of the counties of this State," observed a Florida sheriff, "you cannot convict him." Federal intervention — in the Ku Klux Klan Acts of 1870 and 1871— signaled an end to much of the Klan's power but not to counterrevolutionary violence in the South. Other groups continued the terror in the cause of white supremacy.

Thinking about Beliefs and Attitudes

1. What changes during Reconstruction particularly provoked the Klan? Why do you think these issues were so important to Klansmen?
2. Why did Klansmen believe that their actions were justified? Why do you think they hid their identities?
3. What southern traditions did the Klan seek to perpetuate?

united in their desire for education and equal treatment before the law.

Northern whites who made the South their home after the war were a second element of the South's Republican Party. Conservative white Southerners called them **carpetbaggers**, men so poor that they could stuff all their earthly belongings in a single carpet-sided suitcase and swoop southward like buzzards to "fatten on our misfortunes." But most Northerners who moved south were young men who looked upon the South as they did the West — as a promising place to make a living. Northerners in the southern Republican Party consistently supported programs that encouraged vigorous economic development along the lines of the northern free-labor model.

A Southern Legislature in the Carpet-Bagger Days
This late-nineteenth-century wood engraving reveals the southern Democratic view of Republican state governments during Reconstruction. It drips with prejudice and misinformation. Contrary to fact, the legislators are depicted as overwhelmingly black. Rather than serious men, they are lazy, drunk, and disorderly. While some lie about on cushions, others have literally drunk themselves under the table, which is spread with food rather than legislative documents. The white man in the foreground who calmly observes the circus is probably meant to be a manipulative carpetbagger, while the white man in the rear with the hat, pipe, and rifle slung over his shoulder is probably a treasonous scalawag. The Granger Collection, NYC.

Southern whites made up the third element of the South's Republican Party. Approximately one out of four white Southerners voted Republican. The other three condemned the one who did as a traitor to his region and his race and called him a **scalawag**, a term for runty horses and low-down, good-for-nothing rascals. Yeoman farmers accounted for the majority of southern white Republicans. Some were Unionists who emerged from the war with bitter memories of Confederate persecution. Others were small farmers who wanted to end state governments' favoritism toward plantation owners. Yeomen supported initiatives for public schools and for expanding economic opportunity in the South.

The South's Republican Party, then, was made up of freedmen, Yankees, and yeomen — an improbable coalition. The mix of races, regions, and classes inevitably meant friction as each group maneuvered to define the party. But Reconstruction represents an extraordinary moment in American politics: Blacks and whites joined together in the Republican Party to pursue political change. Formally, of course, only men participated in politics — casting ballots and holding offices — but white and black women also played a part in the political struggle by joining in parades and rallies, attending stump speeches, and even campaigning.

Reconstruction politics was not for cowards. Most whites in the South condemned southern Republicans as illegitimate and felt justified in doing whatever they could to stamp them out. Violence against blacks — the "white terror" — took brutal institutional form in 1866 with the formation in Tennessee of the **Ku Klux Klan**, a social club of Confederate veterans that quickly developed into a paramilitary organization supporting Democrats. The Klan went on a rampage of whipping, hanging, shooting, burning, and throat-cutting to defeat Republicans and restore white supremacy. (See "Historical Question," page 516.) Rapid demobilization of the Union army after the war left only twenty thousand troops to patrol the entire South. Without effective military protection, southern Republicans had to take care of themselves.

Republican Rule

In the fall of 1867, southern states held elections for delegates to state constitutional conventions, as required by the Reconstruction Acts. About 40 percent of the white electorate stayed home because they had been disfranchised or because they had decided to boycott politics. Republicans won three-fourths of the seats. About 15 percent of the Republican delegates to the conventions were Northerners who had moved south, 25 percent were African Americans, and 60 percent were white Southerners. As a British visitor observed, the delegate elections reflected "the mighty revolution that had taken place in America." But Democrats described the state conventions as zoos of "baboons, monkeys, mules . . . and other jackasses." In fact, the conventions brought together serious, purposeful men who hammered out the legal framework for a new order.

The reconstruction constitutions introduced two broad categories of changes in the South: those that reduced aristocratic privilege and increased democratic equality and those that expanded the state's responsibility for the general welfare. In the first category, the constitutions adopted universal male suffrage, abolished property qualifications for holding office, and made more offices elective and fewer appointed. In the second category, they enacted prison reform; made the state responsible for caring for orphans, the insane, and the deaf and mute; and exempted debtors' homes from seizure.

To Democrats, however, the new state constitutions looked like wild revolution. They were blind to the fact that no constitution confiscated and redistributed land, as virtually every former slave wished, or disfranchised ex-rebels wholesale, as most southern Unionists advocated. And Democrats were convinced that the new constitutions initiated "Negro domination" in politics. In fact, although four out of five Republican voters were black men, more than four out of five Republican officeholders were white. Southerners sent fourteen black congressmen and two black senators to Washington, but only 6 percent of Southerners in Congress during Reconstruction were black (Figure 16.1). The sixteen black men in Congress included exceptional men, such as Representative **James T. Rapier** of Alabama (see pages 499–500) and Mississippi senator Blanche K. Bruce, who was born a slave in Virginia and became a local school superintendent in Mississippi, a position that paved his way to the Senate. No state legislature experienced "Negro rule," despite black majorities in the populations of some states.

FIGURE 16.1 Southern Congressional Delegations, 1865–1877
The statistics contradict the myth of black domination of congressional representation during Reconstruction.

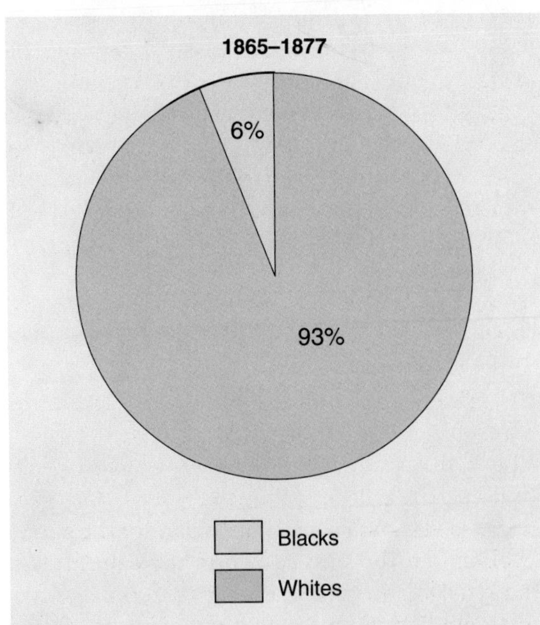

Southern voters ratified the new constitutions and swept Republicans into power. When the former Confederate states ratified the Fourteenth Amendment, Congress readmitted them. Southern Republicans then turned to a staggering array of problems. Wartime destruction — burned cities, shattered bridges, broken levees, devastated railroads — littered the landscape. The South's share of the nation's wealth had fallen from 30 percent to only 12 percent. Manufacturing, always a small contributor to the southern economy, limped along at a fraction of prewar levels, and once-powerful agricultural production remained anemic. Without the efforts of the Freedmen's Bureau, black and white Southerners would have starved. Making matters worse, racial harassment and reactionary violence dogged Southerners who sought reform. In this desperate context, Republicans struggled to breathe life into the region.

Activity focused on three areas — education, civil rights, and economic development. Every state inaugurated a system of public education. Before the Civil War, whites had deliberately kept slaves illiterate, and planter-dominated governments rarely spent tax money to educate the children of yeomen. By 1875, half of Mississippi's and South Carolina's eligible children (the majority of whom were black) were attending school. Although schools were underfunded, literacy rates rose sharply. Public schools were racially segregated, but education remained for many blacks a tangible, deeply satisfying benefit of freedom and Republican rule.

State legislatures also attacked racial discrimination and defended civil rights. Republicans especially resisted efforts to segregate blacks from whites in public transportation. Mississippi levied fines of up to $1,000 and three years in jail for owners of railroads and steamboats that pushed blacks into "smoking cars" or to lower decks. Well-off blacks took particular aim at hotels and theaters that denied "full and equal rights." But passing color-blind laws was one thing; enforcing them was another. A Mississippian complained: "Education amounts to nothing, good behavior counts for nothing, even money cannot buy for a colored man or woman decent treatment and the comforts that white people claim and can obtain." Despite the laws, segregation — later called Jim Crow — developed at white insistence and became a feature of southern life long before the end of the Reconstruction era.

Republican governments also launched ambitious programs of economic development. They envisioned a South of diversified agriculture, roaring factories, and booming towns. State legislatures chartered scores of banks and industrial companies, appropriated funds to fix ruined levees and drain swamps, and went on a railroad-building binge. These efforts fell far short of solving the South's economic troubles, however. In addition, Republican spending to stimulate economic growth meant rising taxes and enormous debt that siphoned funds from schools and other programs.

The southern Republicans' record, then, was mixed. To their credit, the biracial party adopted an ambitious agenda to change the South, even though money was scarce, the Democrats continued their harassment, and factionalism threatened the Republican Party from within. However, corruption infected Republican governments in the South. Public morality reached new lows everywhere in the nation after the Civil War, and the chaos of the postwar South proved fertile soil for bribery, fraud, and influence peddling. Despite shortcomings, however, the Republican Party made headway in its efforts to purge the South of aristocratic privilege and racist oppression. Republican governments had less success in overthrowing the long-established white oppression of black farm laborers in the rural South.

Students at a Freedmen's School in Virginia, ca. 1870s, and a One-Cent Primer
"The people are hungry and thirsty after knowledge," a former slave observed immediately after the Civil War. African American leader Booker T. Washington remembered "a whole race trying to go to school." The students at this Virginia school stand in front of their log-cabin classroom reading books, but more common were eight-page primers that cost a penny. These simple readers offered ex-slaves the elements of literacy. For people long forbidden to learn to read and write, literacy symbolized freedom. Literacy also allowed those who were deeply religious to experience the joy of reading the Bible for themselves and those who were merely practical to understand labor contracts and participate knowledgeably in politics. Primer: Gladstone Collection; students: Valentine Museum, Cook Collection.

Black Woman in Cotton Fields, Thomasville, Georgia Few images of everyday black women during the Reconstruction era survive. Taken in 1895, this photograph nevertheless goes to the heart of the labor struggle following the Civil War, when white landlords wanted emancipated slaves to continue working in the fields. Freedom allowed some women to escape field labor, but not this Georgian, who probably worked to survive. The photograph reveals a strong person with a clear sense of who she is. Though worn to protect her head and body from the fierce heat, her intricately wrapped headdress dramatically expresses her individuality. Her bare feet also reveal something about her life. Courtesy, Georgia Department of Archives and History, Atlanta, GA.

White Landlords, Black Sharecroppers

Ex-slaves who wished to escape slave labor and ex-masters who wanted to reinstitute old ways clashed repeatedly. Except for having to pay subsistence wages, planters had not been required to offer many concessions to emancipation. They continued to believe that African Americans would not work without coercion. Whites moved quickly to restore the antebellum (pre–Civil War) world of work gangs, white overseers, field labor for black women and children, clustered cabins, minimal personal freedom, and even whipping whenever they could get away with it.

Ex-slaves resisted every effort to turn back the clock. They argued that if any class could be described as "lazy," it was the planters, who, as one former slave noted, "lived in idleness all their lives on stolen labor." Ex-slaves believed that land of their own would anchor their economic independence and end planters' interference in their personal lives. They could then, for example, make their own decisions about whether women and children would labor in the fields. Indeed, within months after the war, perhaps one-third of black women abandoned field labor to work on chores in their own cabins just as poor white women did. Hundreds of thousands of black children enrolled in school. But without their own land, ex-slaves had little choice but to work on plantations, and they feared that their return to the planters' fields would undermine their independence.

Freedmen resisted efforts by ex-masters to restore slavelike conditions on plantations. Instead of working for wages, David Golightly Harris of South Carolina observed, "the negroes all seem disposed to rent land," which increased their independence from whites. By rejecting wage labor, by striking, and by abandoning the most reactionary employers, blacks sought to force concessions. Out of this tug-of-war between white landlords and black laborers emerged a new system of southern agriculture.

Sharecropping was a compromise that offered something to both ex-masters and ex-slaves but satisfied neither. Under the new system, planters divided their cotton plantations into small farms that freedmen rented, paying with a share of each year's crop, usually half. Sharecropping gave blacks more freedom than the system of wages and labor gangs and released them from day-to-day supervision by whites. Black families abandoned the old slave quarters and scattered over plantations, building separate cabins for themselves on the patches of land they rented (Map 16.1). Black families now decided who would work, for how long, and how hard. Black women negotiated with ex-mistresses about work the white women wanted done

A Post-Slavery Encounter

***A Visit from the Old Mistress*, 1876**

Winslow Homer, one of the nation's foremost painters, was widely recognized for his ability to convey drama and emotion on canvas. Homer typically sketched and painted ordinary people in their everyday lives. During the Civil War, Homer worked as an illustrator for *Harper's Weekly*, depicting scenes of the war for curious Northerners. In 1875, he traveled from his home in New York City to Virginia, where he observed firsthand the transformation of relationships between former slaves and their former owners.

A Visit from the Old Mistress captures the moment when a white woman arrives in the humble cabin of former slaves and encounters three black women, one of whom holds a toddler. Homer typically said little about his paintings, and there is much we don't know about the story being told in this work. Why has the old mistress come? We can imagine that she has come to talk about work she wants done in the big house. If so, she would have come asking, not commanding, for the end of slavery meant that ex-slaves had control over their own labor and negotiated what they would be paid and the conditions under which they would work.

Notice the way Homer has arranged the subjects of his painting, with the former slaves on one side of the room and the former mistress on the other. What does the generous space between them suggest? How do the two sides compare? Look particularly at the women's clothing and their stance. What does the white woman's posture suggest? How are the three black women positioned, and what does this say about their attitude toward the old mistress? What do you detect in the facial expressions of the people in this image?

The end of slavery required wrenching readjustments in the lives of Southerners, black and white. Do you think Homer's simple domestic scene reveals an opinion about what the artist witnessed, or does *A Visit from the Old Mistress* try merely to capture truthfully a complex moment? How might this painting have looked different if it had been created before emancipation?

SOURCE: Smithsonian American Art Museum, Washington, D.C./Art Resource, NY.

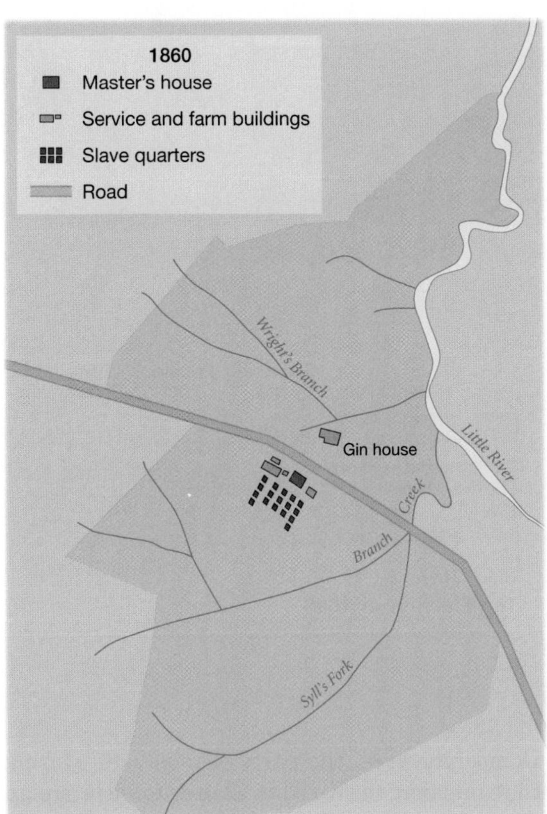

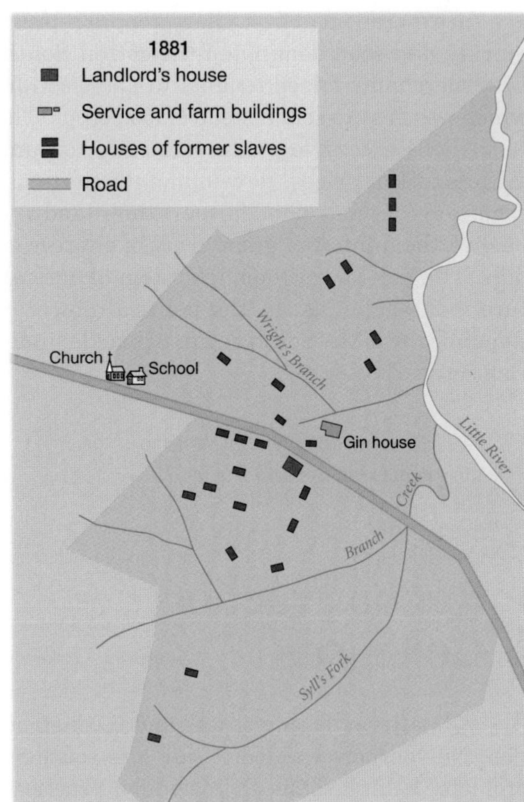

MAP ACTIVITY

Map 16.1 A Southern Plantation in 1860 and 1881

These maps of the Barrow plantation in Georgia illustrate some of the ways in which ex-slaves expressed their freedom. Freedmen and freedwomen deserted the clustered living quarters behind the master's house, scattered over the plantation, built family cabins, and farmed rented land. The former Barrow slaves also worked together to build a school and a church.

READING THE MAP: Compare the number and size of the slave quarters in 1860 with the homes of the former slaves in 1881. How do they differ? Which buildings were prominently located along the road in 1860, and which could be found along the road in 1881?

CONNECTIONS: How might the former master feel about the new configuration of buildings on the plantation in 1881? In what ways did the new system of sharecropping replicate the old system of plantation agriculture? In what ways was it different?

in the big house. (See "Visualizing History," page 522.) Still, most black families remained dependent on white landlords, who had the power to evict them at the end of each growing season. For planters, sharecropping offered a way to resume agricultural production, but it did not allow them to restore the old slave plantation.

Sharecropping introduced a new figure — the country merchant — into the agricultural equation. Landlords supplied sharecroppers with land, mules, seeds, and tools, but blacks also needed credit to obtain essential food and clothing before they harvested their crops. Thousands of small crossroads stores sprang up to offer credit. Under an arrangement called a **crop lien**, a merchant would advance goods to a sharecropper in exchange for a *lien*, or legal claim, on the farmer's future crop. Some merchants charged exorbitant rates of interest, as much as 60 percent, on the goods they sold. At the end of the growing season, after the landlord had taken half of the farmer's crop for rent, the merchant took most of the rest. Sometimes, the farmer's debt to the merchant exceeded the income he received from his remaining half of the crop, and the farmer would have no choice but to borrow more from the merchant and begin the cycle all over again.

An experiment at first, sharecropping spread quickly and soon dominated the cotton South. Lien merchants forced tenants to plant cotton, which was easy to sell, instead of food crops. The result was excessive production of cotton and falling cotton prices, developments that cost thousands of small white farmers their land and pushed them into the great army of sharecroppers. The new sharecropping system of agriculture took shape just as the political power of Republicans in the South began to buckle under Democratic pressure.

REVIEW What brought the elements of the South's Republican coalition together?

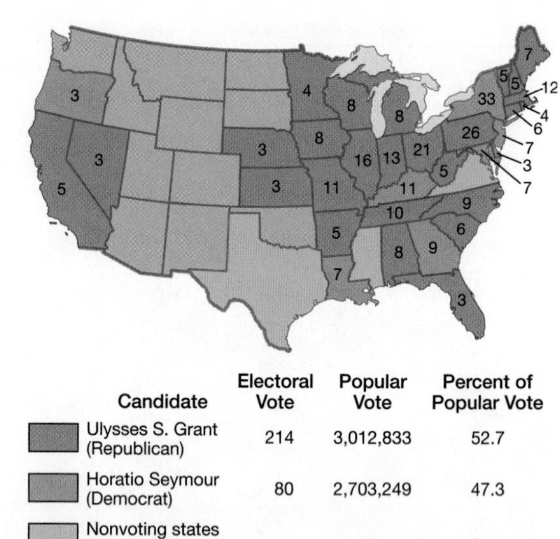

Candidate	Electoral Vote	Popular Vote	Percent of Popular Vote
Ulysses S. Grant (Republican)	214	3,012,833	52.7
Horatio Seymour (Democrat)	80	2,703,249	47.3
Nonvoting states (Reconstruction)			

MAP 16.2
The Election of 1868

▶ Reconstruction Collapses

By 1870, after a decade of war and reconstruction, Northerners wanted to put "the southern problem" behind them. Increasingly, practical, business-minded men came to the forefront of the Republican Party, replacing the band of reformers and idealists who had been prominent in the 1860s. While northern commitment to defend black freedom eroded, southern commitment to white supremacy intensified. Without northern protection, southern Republicans were no match for the Democrats' economic coercion, political fraud, and bloody violence. One by one, Republican state governments fell in the South. The election of 1876 both confirmed and completed the collapse of reconstruction.

"His imperturbability is amazing. I am in doubt whether to call it greatness or stupidity."
— Congressman JAMES A. GARFIELD, speaking of President Grant

Grant's Troubled Presidency

In 1868, the Republican Party's presidential nomination went to **Ulysses S. Grant**, the North's favorite general. Hero of the Civil War and a supporter of congressional reconstruction, Grant was the obvious choice. His Democratic opponent, Horatio Seymour of New York, ran on a platform that blasted congressional reconstruction as "a flagrant usurpation of power . . . unconstitutional, revolutionary, and void." The Republicans answered by **"waving the bloody shirt"** — that is, they reminded voters that the Democrats were "the party of rebellion." During the campaign, the Ku Klux Klan erupted in a reign of terror across the South, murdering hundreds of Republicans. Fear of violence cost Grant votes, but he gained a narrow 309,000-vote margin in the popular vote and a substantial victory (214 votes to 80) in the electoral college (Map 16.2).

Grant was not as good a president as he was a general. The talents he had demonstrated on the battlefield — decisiveness, clarity, and resolution — were less obvious in the White House. He hoped to forge a policy that secured both justice for blacks and sectional reconciliation, but he took office at a time when a majority of white Northerners had grown weary of the "Southern Question" and were increasingly willing to let southern whites manage their own affairs. Moreover, Grant surrounded himself with fumbling kinfolk and old friends from his army days. He made a string of dubious appointments that led to a series of damaging scandals. Charges of corruption tainted his vice president, Schuyler Colfax, and brought down two of his cabinet officers. Though never personally implicated in any scandal, Grant was aggravatingly naive and blind to the rot that filled his administration. Republican congressman James A. Garfield declared: "His imperturbability is amazing. I am in doubt whether to call it greatness or stupidity."

In 1872, anti-Grant Republicans bolted and launched the Liberal Party. To clean up the graft and corruption,

VISUAL ACTIVITY

Grant and Scandal

This anti-Grant cartoon by Thomas Nast, the nation's most celebrated political cartoonist, shows the president falling headfirst into the barrel of fraud and corruption that tainted his administration. During Grant's eight years in the White House, many members of his administration failed him. Sometimes duped, sometimes merely loyal, Grant stubbornly defended wrongdoers, even to the point of perjuring himself to keep an aide out of jail. Library of Congress.

READING THE IMAGE: How does Thomas Nast portray President Grant's role in corruption? According to this cartoon, what caused the problems?
CONNECTIONS: How responsible was President Grant for the corruption that plagued his administration?

Liberals proposed ending the spoils system, by which victorious parties rewarded loyal workers with public office, and replacing it with a nonpartisan civil service commission that would oversee competitive examinations for appointment to office (as discussed in chapter 18). Liberals also demanded that the federal government remove its troops from the South and restore "home rule" (southern white control). Democrats liked the Liberals' southern policy and endorsed the Liberal presidential candidate, Horace Greeley, the longtime editor of the *New York Tribune*. The nation, however, still felt enormous affection for the man who had saved the Union and reelected Grant with 56 percent of the popular vote.

Grant's ambitions for his administration extended beyond reconstruction, but not even foreign affairs could escape the problems of the South. Grant coveted Santo Domingo (present-day Dominican Republic) in the Caribbean and argued that the acquisition of this tropical land would permit the United States to expand its trade and would also provide a new home for the South's blacks, who were so desperately harassed by the Klan. Aggressive foreign policy had not originated with the Grant administration. Lincoln's and Johnson's secretary of state, William H. Seward, had thwarted French efforts to set up a puppet empire under Maximilian in Mexico, and his purchase of Alaska ("Seward's Ice Box") from Russia in 1867 for only $7 million fired Grant's imperialist ambition. But in the end, Grant could not convince Congress to approve the treaty annexing Santo Domingo. The South preoccupied Congress and undermined Grant's initiatives.

Northern Resolve Withers

Although Grant genuinely wanted to see blacks' civil and political rights protected, he understood that most Northerners had grown weary of reconstruction and were increasingly willing to let southern whites manage their own affairs. Citizens wanted to shift their attention to other issues, especially after the nation slipped into a devastating economic depression in 1873. More than eighteen thousand businesses collapsed, leaving more than a million workers on the streets. Northern businessmen wanted to invest in the South but believed that recurrent federal intrusion was itself a major cause of instability in the region. Republican leaders began to question the wisdom of their party's alliance with the South's lower classes — its small farmers and sharecroppers. One member of Grant's administration proposed allying with the "thinking and influential native southerners . . . the intelligent, well-to-do, and controlling class."

Congress, too, wanted to leave reconstruction behind, but southern Republicans made that

Grant's Proposed Annexation of Santo Domingo

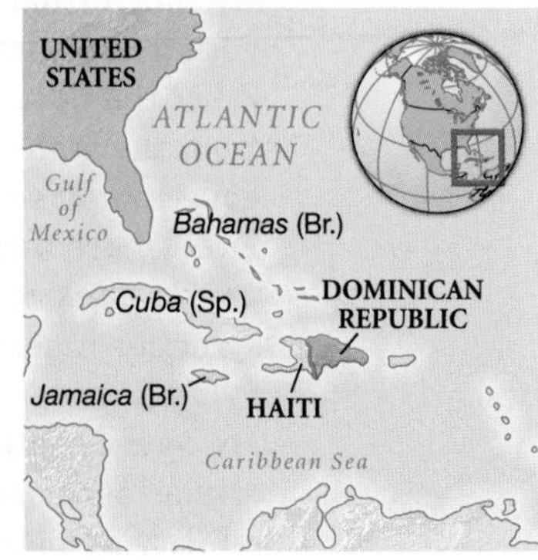

difficult. When the South's Republicans begged for federal protection from Klan violence, Congress enacted three laws in 1870 and 1871 that were intended to break the back of white terrorism. The severest of the three, the **Ku Klux Klan Act** (1871), made interference with voting rights a felony. Federal marshals arrested thousands of Klansmen and came close to destroying the Klan, but they did not end all terrorism against blacks. Congress also passed the **Civil Rights Act of 1875**, which boldly outlawed racial discrimination in transportation, public accommodations, and juries. But federal authorities never enforced the law aggressively, and segregated facilities remained the rule throughout the South.

By the early 1870s, the Republican Party had lost its leading champions of African American rights to death or defeat at the polls. Other Republicans concluded that the quest for black equality was mistaken or hopelessly naive. In May 1872, Congress restored the right of office-holding to all but three hundred ex-rebels. Many Republicans had come to believe that traditional white leaders offered the best hope for honesty, order, and prosperity in the South.

Underlying the North's abandonment of reconstruction was unyielding racial prejudice. Northerners had learned to accept black freedom during the war, but deep-seated prejudice prevented many from accepting black equality. Even the actions they took on behalf of blacks often served partisan political advantage. Northerners generally supported Indiana senator Thomas A. Hendricks's harsh declaration that "this is a white man's Government, made by the white man for the white man."

The U.S. Supreme Court also did its part to undermine reconstruction. The Court issued a series of decisions that significantly weakened the federal government's ability to protect black Southerners. In the ***Slaughterhouse* cases** (1873), the Court distinguished between national and state citizenship and ruled that the Fourteenth Amendment protected only those rights that stemmed from the federal government, such as voting in federal elections and interstate travel. Since the Court decided that most rights derived from the states, it sharply curtailed the federal government's authority to defend black citizens. Even more devastating, the ***United States v. Cruikshank*** ruling (1876) said that the reconstruction amendments gave Congress the power to legislate against discrimination only by states, not by individuals. The "suppression of ordinary crime," such as assault, remained a state responsibility. The Supreme Court did not declare reconstruction unconstitutional but eroded its legal foundation.

The mood of the North found political expression in the election of 1874, when for the first time in eighteen years the Democrats gained control of the House of Representatives. As one Republican observed, the people had grown tired of the "negro question, with all its complications, and the reconstruction of Southern States, with all its interminable embroilments." Reconstruction had come apart. The people were tired of it. Grant grew increasingly unwilling to enforce it. Congress gradually abandoned it. And the Supreme Court denied the constitutionality of significant parts of it. Rather than defend reconstruction from its southern enemies, Northerners steadily backed away from the challenge. By the early 1870s, southern Republicans faced the forces of reaction largely on their own.

White Supremacy Triumphs

Reconstruction was a massive humiliation to most white Southerners. Republican rule meant intolerable insults: Black militiamen patrolled town streets, black laborers negotiated contracts with former masters, black maids stood up to former mistresses, black voters cast ballots, and black legislators such as James T. Rapier enacted laws. Whites resisted the consequences of their defeat in the Civil War by making it clear that military failure did not discredit their "civilization." They expressed their devotion to all that was good in the South — racial hierarchy, honor, vigorous masculinity — by making an idol of Robert E. Lee, the embodiment of the southern gentleman. They celebrated the "great Confederate cause," or **Lost Cause**, by extolling the deeds of their soldiers, "the noblest band of men who ever fought or ever took pen to record." Southern women took the lead in erecting monuments to the Confederate dead and, with pageantry, oratory, and flowers, in keeping alive the memory of the Lost Cause throughout the old Confederacy.

But the most important way white Southerners responded to the humiliation of reconstruction was their assault on Republican governments in the South, which attracted more hatred than did any other political regimes in American history. The northern retreat from reconstruction permitted southern Democrats to harness white rage to politics. Taking the name **Redeemers**, Democrats in the South promised to replace "bayonet rule" (a few federal troops continued to be stationed in the South) with "home rule." They branded Republican governments a carnival of extravagance, waste, and fraud and promised that honest, thrifty Democrats would supplant the irresponsible tax-and-spend Republicans. Above all, Redeemers swore to save southern civilization from a descent into "African barbarism." As one man put it, "We must render this either a white man's government, or convert the land into a Negro man's cemetery."

Southern Democrats adopted a multipronged strategy to overthrow Republican governments. First, they sought to polarize the parties around color. They went about gathering all the South's white voters into the Democratic Party, leaving the Republicans to depend on blacks, who made up a minority of the population in almost every southern state. To dislodge whites from the Republican Party, Democrats fanned the flames of racial prejudice. A South Carolina Democrat crowed that his party appealed to the "proud Caucasian race, whose sovereignty on earth God has proclaimed." Local newspapers published the names of whites who kept company with blacks, and neighbors ostracized offenders. One victim proclaimed, "No white man can live in the South in the future and act with any other than the Democratic party unless he is willing and prepared to live a life of social isolation."

Democrats also exploited the severe economic plight of small white farmers by blaming it on Republican financial policy. Government spending soared during reconstruction, and small farmers saw their tax burden skyrocket. "This is tax time," a South Carolinian reported. "We are nearly all on our head about them. They are so high & so little money to pay with" that farmers were "selling every egg and chicken they can get." In 1871, Mississippi reported that one-seventh of the state's land — 3.3 million acres — had been forfeited for nonpayment of taxes. The small farmers' economic distress had a racial dimension. Because few freedmen succeeded in acquiring land, they rarely paid taxes. In Georgia in 1874, blacks made up 45 percent of the population but paid only 2 percent of the taxes. From the perspective of a small white farmer, Republican rule meant that he was paying more taxes and paying them to aid blacks.

"White Man's Country"
White supremacy emerged as a central tenet of the Democratic Party before the Civil War, and Democrats kept up a vicious racist attack on Republicans throughout Reconstruction. This silk ribbon from the 1868 presidential campaign between Republican Ulysses S. Grant and his Democratic opponent, New York governor Horatio Seymour, openly declares the Democrats' racial goal. During the campaign, Democratic vice presidential nominee Francis P. Blair Jr. promised that a Seymour victory would restore "white people" to power by declaring the reconstruction governments in the South "null and void." Collection of Janice L. and David J. Frent.

"Of Course He Wants to Vote the Democratic Ticket"
This Republican cartoon from the October 21, 1876, issue of *Harper's Weekly* comments sarcastically on the possibility of honest elections in the South. The caption reads: "You're free as air, ain't you? Say you are or I'll blow yer black head off." The cartoon demonstrates not only some Northerners' concern that violence would deliver the election to the Democrats but also the perception that white Southerners were crude, drunken, ignorant brutes. The Granger Collection, NY.

If racial pride, social isolation, and financial hardship proved insufficient to drive yeomen from the Republican Party, Democrats turned to terrorism. "Night riders" targeted white Republicans as well as blacks for murder and assassination. Whether white or black, a "dead Radical is very harmless," South Carolina Democratic leader Martin Gary told his followers.

But the primary victims of white violence were black Republicans, especially local leaders. Emanuel Fortune, whom the Klan drove from Jackson County, Florida, declared: "The object of it is to kill out the leading men of the republican party." But violence targeted all black voters, not just leaders. And it escalated to an unprecedented ferocity on Easter Sunday in 1873 in tiny Colfax, Louisiana. The black majority in the area had made Colfax a Republican stronghold until 1872, when Democrats turned to intimidation and fraud to win the local election. Republicans refused to accept the result and eventually occupied the courthouse in the middle of the town. After three weeks, 165 white men attacked. They overran the Republicans' defenses and set the courthouse on fire. When the blacks tried to surrender, the whites murdered them. At least 81 black men were slaughtered that day. Although the federal government indicted the attackers, the Supreme Court ruled that it did not have the right to prosecute. And since local whites would not prosecute neighbors who killed blacks, the defendants in the **Colfax massacre** went free.

Even before adopting the all-out white supremacist tactics of the 1870s, Democrats had taken control of the governments of Virginia, Tennessee, and North Carolina. The new campaign brought fresh gains. The Redeemers retook Georgia in 1871, Texas in 1873, and Arkansas and Alabama in 1874. Mississippi became a scene of open, unrelenting, and often savage intimidation of black voters and their few remaining white allies. As the state election approached in 1876, Governor Adelbert Ames appealed to Washington for federal troops to control the violence, only to hear from the attorney general that the "whole public are tired of these annual autumnal outbreaks in the South." Abandoned, Mississippi Republicans succumbed to the Democratic onslaught in the fall elections. By 1876, only three Republican state governments survived in the South (Map 16.3).

MAP ACTIVITY

Map 16.3 The Reconstruction of the South

Myth has it that Republican rule of the former Confederacy was not only harsh but long. In most states, however, conservative southern whites stormed back into power in months or just a few years. By the election of 1876, Republican governments could be found in only three states, and they soon fell.

READING THE MAP: List in chronological order the readmission of the former Confederate states to the Union. Which states reestablished conservative governments most quickly?

CONNECTIONS: What did the former Confederate states need to do in order to be readmitted to the Union? How did reestablished conservative governments react to reconstruction?

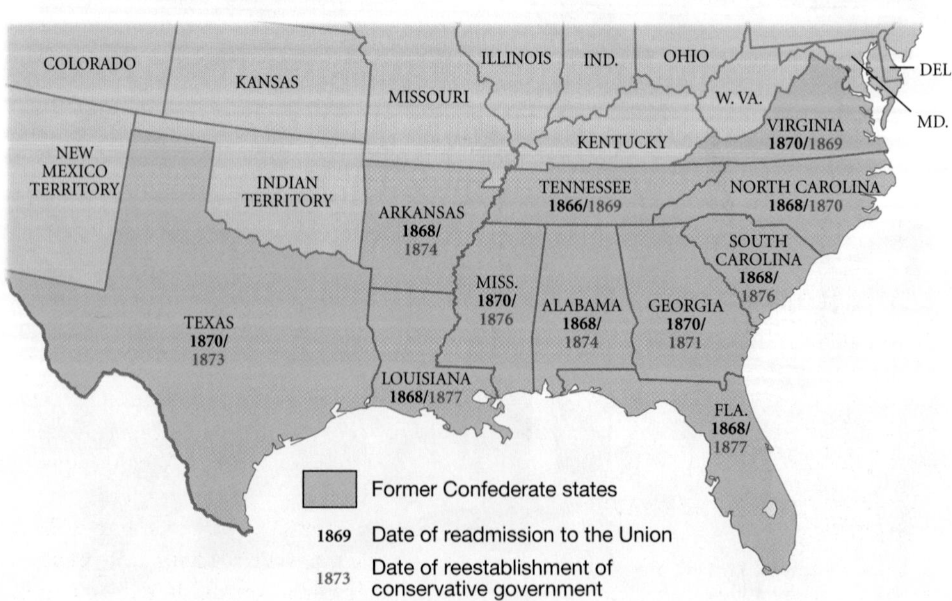

An Election and a Compromise

The centennial year of 1876 witnessed one of the most tumultuous elections in American history. Its chaos and confusion provided a fitting conclusion to the experiment known as reconstruction. The election took place in November, but not until March 2 of the following year did the nation know who would be inaugurated president on March 4. The Democrats nominated New York's governor, **Samuel J. Tilden**, who immediately targeted the corruption of the Grant administration and the "despotism" of Republican reconstruction. The Republicans put forward **Rutherford B. Hayes**, governor of Ohio. Privately, Hayes considered "bayonet rule" a mistake but concluded that waving the bloody shirt — reminding voters that the Democrats were the "party of rebellion" — remained the Republicans' best political strategy.

On election day, Tilden tallied 4,288,590 votes to Hayes's 4,036,000. But in the all-important electoral college, Tilden fell one vote short of the majority required for victory. The electoral votes of three states — South Carolina, Louisiana, and Florida, the only remaining Republican governments in the South — remained in doubt because both Republicans and Democrats in those states claimed victory. To win, Tilden needed only one of the nineteen contested votes. Hayes had to have all of them.

Congress had to decide who had actually won the elections in the three southern states and thus who would be president. The Constitution provided no guidance for this situation. Moreover, Democrats controlled the House, and Republicans controlled the Senate. Congress created a special electoral commission to arbitrate the disputed returns. All of the commissioners voted their party affiliation, giving every state to the Republican Hayes and putting him over the top in electoral votes (Map 16.4).

Some outraged Democrats vowed to resist Hayes's victory. Rumors flew of an impending coup and renewed civil war. But the impasse was broken when negotiations behind the scenes resulted in an informal understanding known as the **Compromise of 1877**. In exchange for a Democratic promise not to block Hayes's inauguration and to deal fairly with the freedmen, Hayes vowed to refrain from using the army to uphold the remaining Republican regimes in the South and to provide the South with substantial federal subsidies for railroads. Two days later, the nation celebrated Hayes's peaceful inauguration.

Stubborn Tilden supporters bemoaned the "stolen election" and damned "His Fraudulency," Rutherford B. Hayes. Old-guard radicals such as William Lloyd Garrison denounced Hayes's bargain as a "policy of compromise, of credulity, of weakness, of subserviency, of surrender." But the nation as a whole celebrated, for the country had weathered a grave crisis. The last three Republican state governments in the South fell quickly once Hayes abandoned them and withdrew the U.S. Army. Reconstruction came to an end.

REVIEW How did the Supreme Court undermine the Fourteenth and Fifteenth Amendments?

MAP 16.4
The Election of 1876

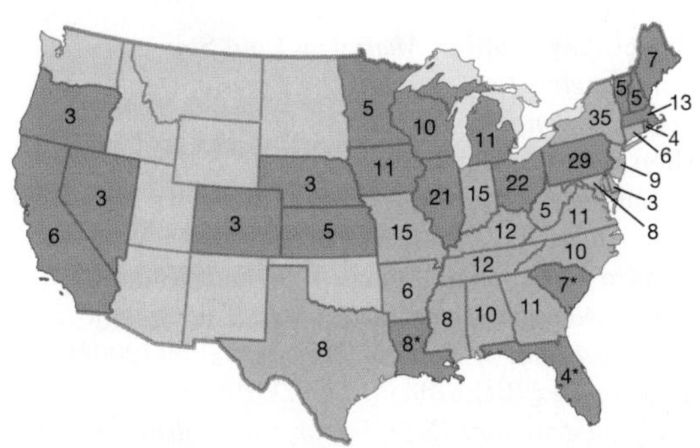

Candidate	Electoral Vote	Popular Vote	Percent of Popular Vote
Rutherford B. Hayes (Republican)	185*	4,036,298	47.9**
Samuel J. Tilden (Democrat)	184	4,288,590	51.0

*19 electoral votes were disputed.

**Percentages do not total 100 because some popular votes went to other parties.

▸ Conclusion: "A Revolution But Half Accomplished"

In 1865, when General Carl Schurz visited the South, he discovered "a revolution but half accomplished." White Southerners resisted the passage from slavery to free labor, from white racial despotism to equal justice, and from white political monopoly to biracial democracy. The old elite wanted to get "things back as near to slavery as possible," Schurz reported, while African Americans such as James T. Rapier and some whites were eager to exploit the revolutionary implications of defeat and emancipation.

The northern-dominated Republican Congress pushed the revolution along. Although it refused to provide for blacks' economic welfare, Congress employed constitutional amendments to require ex-Confederates to accept legal equality and share political power with black men. Congress was not willing to extend such power to women, however. Conservative southern whites fought ferociously to recover their power and privilege. When Democrats regained control of politics, whites used both state power and private violence to wipe out many of the gains of Reconstruction, leading one observer to conclude that the North had won the war but the South had won the peace.

The Redeemer counterrevolution, however, did not mean a return to slavery. Northern victory in the Civil War ensured that ex-slaves no longer faced the auction block and could send their children to school, worship in their own churches, and work independently on their own rented farms. Sharecropping, with all its hardships, provided more autonomy and economic welfare than bondage had. It was limited freedom, to be sure, but it was not slavery.

The Civil War and emancipation set in motion the most profound upheaval in the nation's history, and nothing reactionary whites did entirely erased its revolutionary impact. War destroyed the largest slave society in the New World. The world of masters and slaves succumbed to that of landlords and sharecroppers, a world in which white racial dominance continued, though with greater freedom for blacks. War also gave birth to a modern nation-state, and Washington increased its role in national affairs. When the South returned to the Union, it did so as a junior partner. The victorious North set the nation's compass toward the expansion of industrial capitalism and the final conquest of the West.

Despite massive changes, however, the Civil War remained only a "half accomplished" revolution. By not fulfilling the promises the nation seemed to hold out to black Americans at war's end, Reconstruction represents a tragedy of enormous proportions. The failure to protect blacks and guarantee their rights had enduring consequences. Almost a century after Reconstruction, the nation would embark on what one observer called a "second reconstruction." The solid achievements of the Thirteenth, Fourteenth, and Fifteenth Amendments to the Constitution would provide a legal foundation for the renewed commitment. It is worth remembering, though, that it was only the failure of the first reconstruction that made the modern civil rights movement necessary.

▶ Selected Bibliography

General Works

Michael W. Fitzgerald, *Splendid Failure: Postwar Reconstruction in the American South* (2007).

Eric Foner, *Reconstruction: America's Unfinished Revolution* (1988).

James M. McPherson, *Ordeal by Fire: The Civil War and Reconstruction* (3rd ed., 2000).

The Meaning of Freedom

Ira Berlin et al., eds., *Freedom: A Documentary History of Emancipation, 1861–1867,* 5 vols. to date (1982–).

John Hope Franklin and Loren Schweninger, *In Search of the Promised Land: A Slave Family in the Old South* (2006).

Thavolia Glymph, *Out of the House of Bondage: The Transformation of the Plantation Household* (2008).

Leon F. Litwack, *Been in the Storm So Long: The Aftermath of Slavery* (1979).

Susan Eva O'Donovan, *Becoming Free in the Cotton South* (2007).

Howard N. Rabinowitz, *Race Relations in the Urban South, 1865–1890* (1978).

Roger L. Ransom and Richard Sutch, *One Kind of Freedom: The Economic Consequences of Emancipation* (1977).

Loren Schweninger, *James T. Rapier and Reconstruction* (1978).

Clarence E. Walker, *A Rock in a Weary Land: The African Methodist Episcopal Church during the Civil War and Reconstruction* (1982).

The Politics of Reconstruction

Richard F. Bensel, *Yankee Leviathan: The Origins of Central State Authority in America, 1859–1877* (1990).

Philip Dray, *Capitol Men: The Epic Story of Reconstruction through the Lives of the First Black Congressmen* (2008).

Ellen Carol DuBois, *Feminism and Suffrage: The Emergence of an Independent Women's Movement in America, 1848–1869* (1978).

Richard L. Hume and Jerry B. Gough, *Blacks, Carpetbaggers, and Scalawags: The Constitutional Conventions of Radical Reconstruction* (2008).

Heather Cox Richardson, *The Death of Reconstruction: Race, Labor, and Politics in the Post–Civil War North, 1865–1901* (2001).

Leslie A. Schwalm, *Emancipation's Diaspora: Race and Reconstruction in the Upper Midwest* (2009).

Brooks D. Simpson, *The Reconstruction Presidents* (1998).

Mark Wahlgren Summers, *A Dangerous Stir: Fear, Paranoia, and the Making of Reconstruction* (2009).

C. Vann Woodward, *Reunion and Reaction: The Compromise of 1877 and the End of Reconstruction* (1951).

The Struggle in the South

James Alex Baggett, *The Scalawags: Southern Dissenters in the Civil War and Reconstruction* (2003).
Nancy D. Bercaw, *Gendered Freedoms: Race, Rights, and the Politics of Household in the Delta, 1861–1875* (2003).
Stephen Budiansky, *The Bloody Shirt: Terror after the Civil War* (2008).
Jane Turner Censer, *The Reconstruction of White Southern Womanhood, 1865–1895* (2003).
Paul A. Cimbala, *Under the Guardianship of the Nation: The Freedmen's Bureau and the Reconstruction of Georgia, 1865–1870* (1997).
Jane E. Dailey, *Before Jim Crow: The Politics of Race in Post-Emancipation Virginia* (2000).
Laura F. Edwards, *Gendered Strife and Confusion: The Political Culture of Reconstruction* (1997).
Sarah E. Gardner, *Blood and Irony: Southern White Women's Narratives of the Civil War, 1861–1937* (2004).
Stephen Kantrowitz, *Ben Tillman and the Reconstruction of White Supremacy* (2000).
Charles Lane, *The Day Freedom Died: The Colfax Massacre, the Supreme Court, and the Betrayal of Reconstruction* (2008).
George C. Rable, *But There Was No Peace: The Role of Violence in the Politics of Reconstruction* (1984).
James L. Roark, *Masters without Slaves: Southern Planters in the Civil War and Reconstruction* (1977).
Hyman Rubin III, *South Carolina Scalawags* (2006).
Peter Wallenstein, *From Slave South to New South: Public Policy in Nineteenth-Century Georgia* (1987).

▶ **FOR MORE BOOKS ABOUT TOPICS IN THIS CHAPTER,** see the Online Bibliography at **bedfordstmartins.com/roark.**

▶ **FOR ADDITIONAL PRIMARY SOURCES FROM THIS PERIOD,** see Michael Johnson, ed., *Reading the American Past*, Fifth Edition.

▶ **FOR WEB SITES, IMAGES, AND DOCUMENTS RELATED TO TOPICS AND PLACES IN THIS CHAPTER,** visit Make History at **bedfordstmartins.com/roark.**

Reviewing Chapter 16

KEY TERMS

Explain each term's significance.

Wartime Reconstruction

- Wade-Davis bill (p. 501)
- Freedmen's Bureau (p. 503)

Presidential Reconstruction

- Andrew Johnson (p. 506)
- black codes (p. 508)
- Civil Rights Act of 1866 (p. 510)

Congressional Reconstruction

- Fourteenth Amendment (p. 510)
- American Equal Rights Association (p. 511)
- Susan B. Anthony (p. 511)
- Elizabeth Cady Stanton (p. 511)
- Military Reconstruction Act (p. 512)
- Fifteenth Amendment (p. 515)

The Struggle in the South

- carpetbagger (p. 517)
- scalawag (p. 518)
- Ku Klux Klan (p. 518)
- James T. Rapier (p. 519)
- sharecropping (p. 521)
- crop lien (p. 523)

Reconstruction Collapses

- Ulysses S. Grant (p. 524)
- "waving the bloody shirt" (p. 524)
- Ku Klux Klan Act (p. 526)
- Civil Rights Act of 1875 (p. 526)
- *Slaughterhouse* cases (p. 526)
- *United States v. Cruikshank* (p. 526)
- Lost Cause (p. 526)
- Redeemers (p. 526)
- Colfax massacre (p. 528)
- Samuel J. Tilden (p. 529)
- Rutherford B. Hayes (p. 529)
- Compromise of 1877 (p. 529)

REVIEW QUESTIONS

Use key terms and dates to support your answer.

1. Why did Congress object to Lincoln's wartime plan for reconstruction? (pp. 501–506)
2. How did the North respond to the passage of black codes in the southern states? (pp. 506–510)
3. Why did Johnson urge the southern states to reject the Fourteenth Amendment? (pp. 510–515)
4. What brought the elements of the South's Republican coalition together? (pp. 515–524)
5. How did the Supreme Court undermine the Fourteenth and Fifteenth Amendments? (pp. 524–529)

MAKING CONNECTIONS

Draw on key terms, the timeline, and review questions.

1. Reconstruction succeeded in advancing black civil rights but failed to secure them over the long term. Why and how did the federal government retreat from defending African Americans' civil rights in the 1870s? In your answer, cite specific actions by Congress and the Supreme Court.
2. Why was distributing plantation land to former slaves such a controversial policy? In your answer, discuss why landownership was important to freedmen and why Congress rejected redistribution as a general policy.
3. At the end of the Civil War, it remained to be seen exactly how emancipation would transform the South. How did emancipation change political and labor organization in the region? In your answer, discuss how ex-slaves exercised their new freedoms and how white Southerners attempted to limit them.
4. The Republican Party shaped Reconstruction through its control of Congress and state legislatures in the South. How did the identification of the Republican Party with Reconstruction policy affect the party's political fortunes in the 1870s? In your answer, be sure to address developments on the federal and state levels.

LINKING TO THE PAST

Link events in this chapter to earlier events.

1. In what ways did the attitudes and actions of President Johnson increase northern resolve to reconstruct the South and the South's resolve to resist reconstruction?
2. White women, abolitionists, and blacks all had hopes for a brighter future that were in some ways dashed during the turmoil of reconstruction. What specific goals of these groups slipped away? What political allies abandoned their causes, and why?

▶ **FOR PRACTICE QUIZZES AND OTHER STUDY TOOLS,** see the Online Study Guide at **bedfordstmartins.com/roark.**

TIMELINE 1863–1877

1863	• Proclamation of Amnesty and Reconstruction.
1864	• Lincoln refuses to sign Wade-Davis bill.
1865	• Freedmen's Bureau established. • President Abraham Lincoln shot; dies on April 15; succeeded by Andrew Johnson. • Black codes enacted. • Thirteenth Amendment becomes part of Constitution.
1866	• Congress approves Fourteenth Amendment. • Civil Rights Act. • American Equal Rights Association founded. • Ku Klux Klan founded.
1867	• Military Reconstruction Act. • Tenure of Office Act.
1868	• Impeachment trial of President Johnson. • Republican Ulysses S. Grant elected president.
1869	• Congress approves Fifteenth Amendment.
1871	• Ku Klux Klan Act.
1872	• Liberal Party formed. • President Grant reelected.
1873	• Economic depression sets in for remainder of decade. • *Slaughterhouse* cases. • Colfax massacre.
1874	• Democrats win majority in House of Representatives.
1875	• Civil Rights Act.
1876	• *United States v. Cruikshank.*
1877	• Republican Rutherford B. Hayes assumes presidency; Reconstruction era ends.

LAKOTA VEST

This Lakota vest demonstrates how Native Americans adopted Euro-American articles of clothing and decorative motifs while employing materials that perpetuated native traditions. The vest belonged to Thomas American Horse, who had his initials worked into the beads at the neck. The American flag, as the vest demonstrates, figured frequently as a design in Indian art. The coming of the American flag, and with it the railroads and the slaughter of the buffalo pictured on the cover of *Leslie's Weekly* in 1871, points to the great changes that Indians faced in the struggle to control the vast land and resources of the American West.

Vest: Private Collection, photograph American Hurrah Archive, NYC; background: Library of Congress.

17

The Contested West
1865–1900

TO CELEBRATE THE FOUR HUNDREDTH ANNIVERSARY OF COLUMBUS'S voyage to the New World, Chicago hosted the World's Columbian Exposition in 1893. Architects and landscapers created a magical White City on the shores of Lake Michigan, complete with a Midway Plaisance where the first Ferris wheel awed and delighted the four million fairgoers.

Among the organizations vying to hold meetings in the White City was the American Historical Association, whose members — dedicated to the advancement of historical studies — gathered on a warm July evening to hear Frederick Jackson Turner deliver his landmark essay "The Significance of the Frontier in American History." Turner began by noting that the 1890 census could no longer discern a clear frontier line. His tone was elegiac: "The existence of an area of free land, its continuous recession, and the advance of settlement westward," he observed, "explained American development."

Of course, *west* has always been a comparative term in American history. Until the gold rush focused attention on California, the West for settlers lay beyond the Appalachians and east of the Mississippi in lands drained by the Ohio River, a part of the country now known as the Old Northwest. But by the second half of the nineteenth century, with the end of the Mexican-American War, the West now stretched from Canada to Mexico, from the Mississippi River to the Pacific Ocean.

Turner, who had originally studied the old frontier east of the Mississippi, viewed the West as a process as much as a place. The availability of land provided a "safety valve," releasing social tensions and providing opportunities for social mobility that worked to Americanize Americans. The West demanded strength and nerve, fostered invention and adaptation, and produced self-confident, individualistic Americans. Turner's theory underscored the exceptionalism of America's history, highlighting its difference from the rest of the world. His "frontier thesis" would earn him a professorship at Harvard and a permanent place in American history.

Yet the historians who applauded Turner in Chicago had short memories. That afternoon, they had crossed the midway to attend Buffalo Bill Cody's Wild West extravaganza, which featured exhibitions of riding, shooting, and roping and presented dramatic reenactments of great moments in western lore. Part circus, part theater, the show included 100 cowboys, 97 Indians,

180 horses, and 18 American bison. The troupe performed the "Attack on the Settler's Cabin" and their own version of "Custer's Last Stand," ending with Buffalo Bill galloping to the rescue through a cloud of dust only to mouth the words "Too late." The historians cheering in the stands that July afternoon no doubt dismissed Buffalo Bill's history as amateur, but he made a point that Turner's thesis ignored: The West was neither free nor open. The story of the country was a story of fierce and violent contest for land and resources.

In the decades following the Civil War, the United States pursued empire in the American West in Indian wars that lasted until 1890. Pushed off their land and onto reservations, Native Americans resisted as they faced waves of miners and settlers and the transformation of the environment by railroads, mines, barbed wire, and mechanized agriculture. The pastoral agrarianism Turner celebrated in his frontier thesis belied the urban, industrial West already emerging on the Comstock Lode in Nevada and in the commercial farms of California.

Buffalo Bill's mythic West, with its heroic cowboys and noble savages, obscured the complex reality of the West as a fiercely contested terrain. Competing groups of Anglos, Hispanics, former slaves, Chinese, and a host of others arrived seeking the promise of land and riches, while the Indians who inhabited the vast territory struggled to preserve their sovereignty and their cultural identity. And, with its emphasis on the rugged individualism of white men pioneering the frontier, Turner's vision of the West overlooked racial diversity and failed to acknowledge the role of women in community building.

Yet in the waning decade of the nineteenth century, as history blurred with nostalgia, Turner's evocation of the frontier as a crucible for American identity hit a nerve in a population facing rapid changes. A major depression started in May 1893, even before the Columbian Exposition opened its doors. Americans already worried about the economy, immigration, and urban industrialism found in Turner's message a new cause for concern. Would America continue to be America now that the frontier was closed? As they struggled with the question, it became clear that the West did not exist out of place and time. Nor was it particularly exceptional. The problems confronting the United States at the turn of the twentieth century — the exploitation of land and labor, the consolidation of capital, and vicious ethnic and racial rivalries — all played themselves out under western skies.

Buffalo Bill Poster Buffalo Bill Cody used colorful posters to publicize his Wild West show during the 1880s and 1890s. One of his most popular features was the reenactment of Custer's Last Stand, which he performed for Queen Victoria in London and at the World's Columbian Exposition in Chicago. Sitting Bull, who fought at the Battle of the Little Big Horn, toured with the company in 1885 and traveled to England with the show. Cody's romantic depictions of western history helped create the myth of the Old West. Buffalo Bill Historical Center, Cody, Wyoming.

▸ Conquest and Empire in the West

While the European powers expanded their authority and wealth through imperialism and colonialism, establishing far-flung empires in Asia, Africa, and South America, the United States focused its attention on the West. As posited by **Frederick Jackson Turner**, American exceptionalism stressed how the history of the United States differed from that of European nations, citing America's western frontier as a case in point. Yet recent historians have argued that the process by which the United States expanded its borders in the nineteenth century can best be understood in the global context of imperialism and colonialism — language applied to European powers in this period that makes explicit how expansion in the American West involved the conquest, displacement, and rule over native peoples. (See "Beyond America's Borders," page 542.)

The federal government, through chicanery and conquest, pushed the Indians off their lands (Map 17.1) and onto designated Indian territories or reservations. The Indian wars that followed the Civil War depleted the Native American population and handed the lion's share of Indian land over to white settlers. The decimation of the bison herds inevitably pushed the Plains Indians onto reservations, where they lived as wards of the state. Through the lens of colonialism, we can see how the United States, with its commitment to an imperialist, expansionist ideology, colonized the West.

Indian Removal and the Reservation System

Beginning in the early days of the Republic, the government advocated a policy of **Indian removal**. With plenty of land open in the West, the army removed eastern tribes — often against their will — to territory west of the Mississippi. In the 1830s, President Andrew Jackson pushed the Five Civilized Tribes — the Cherokee, Choctaw, Chickasaw, Creek, and Seminole peoples — off their land in the southern United States. Jackson's Indian removal forced thousands of men, women, and children to leave their homes in Georgia and Tennessee and walk hundreds of miles west. So many died of hunger, exhaustion, and disease along the way that the Cherokees called their path "the trail on which we cried." At the end of this trail of tears stood land set aside as Indian Territory (present-day Oklahoma). Here, the government promised, the Indians could remain "as long as grass shall grow." But hunger for western land soon negated that promise.

Manifest destiny — the belief that the United States had a "God-given" right to aggressively spread the values of white civilization and expand the nation from ocean to ocean — dictated U.S. policy. In the name of manifest destiny, Americans forced the removal of the Five Civilized Tribes to Oklahoma; colonized Texas and won its independence from Mexico in 1836; conquered California, Arizona, New Mexico, and parts of Utah and Colorado in the Mexican-American War of 1846–1848; and invaded Oregon in the mid-1840s.

By midcentury, western land no longer seemed inexhaustible, and instead of removing Indians to the west, the government sought to take control of Indian lands and promised in return to pay annuities and put the Indians on lands reserved for their use — **reservations**. In 1851, some ten thousand Plains Indians came together at Fort Laramie in Wyoming to negotiate a treaty that ceded a wide swath of their land to allow passage of wagon trains headed west. In return, the government promised that the rest of the Indian land would remain inviolate.

The Indians who "touched the pen" to the 1851 **Treaty of Fort Laramie** hoped to preserve their culture in the face of the white onslaught, which had already decimated their population and despoiled their environment. White invaders cut down trees, miners polluted streams, and hunters killed off bison and small game. Whites brought alcohol, guns, and something even more deadly — disease. Smallpox was the biggest killer of Native Americans in the West. Epidemics spread from Mexico up to Canada. Between 1780 and 1870, the population of the Plains tribes declined by half. Cholera, diphtheria, measles, scarlet fever, and other contagious diseases also took their toll. "If I could see this thing, if I knew where it came from, I would go there and fight it," a Cheyenne warrior anguished. Disease shifted the balance of power on the plains from Woodland agrarian tribes like the Mandan and Hidatsa (who died at the rate of 79 percent) to the Lakota (Western) Sioux, who fled the contagion of villages to take up life as equestrian (horse-riding) nomads on the western plains. As the Sioux pushed west, they displaced weaker tribes.

In the Southwest, the Navajo people, like the Cherokee, endured a forced march called the "Long Walk" from their homeland to the desolate Bosque Redondo Reservation in New Mexico in 1864. "This ground we were brought on, it is not productive," complained the Navajo leader Barboncito. "We plant but it does not yield. All the stock we brought here have nearly all died."

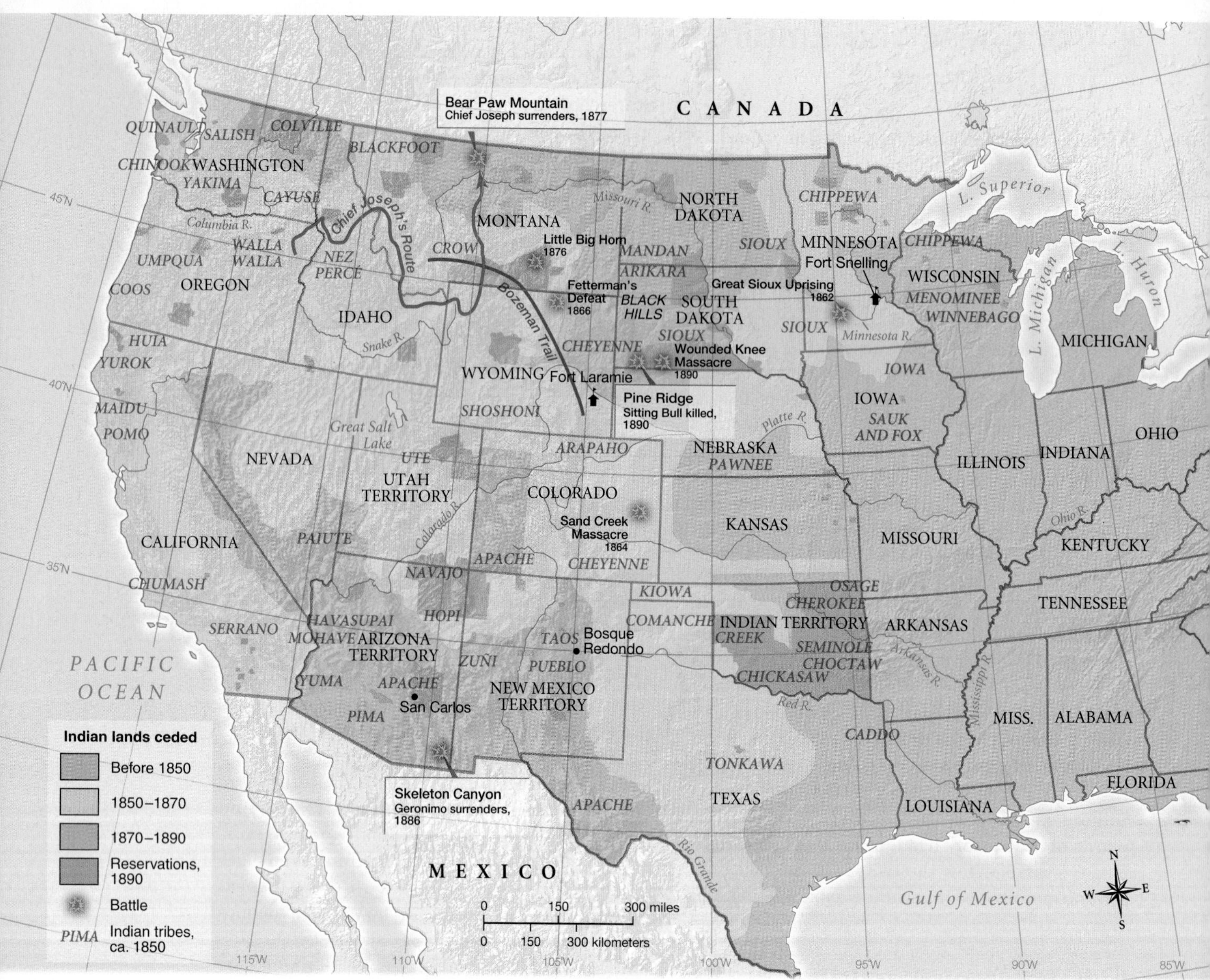

MAP ACTIVITY

Map 17.1 The Loss of Indian Lands, 1850–1890

By 1890, western Indians were isolated on small, scattered reservations. Native Americans had struggled to retain their land in major battles, from the Santee Uprising in Minnesota in 1862 to the massacre at Wounded Knee, South Dakota, in 1890.

READING THE MAP: Where was the largest reservation located in 1890? Which states on this map show no reservations in 1890? Compare this map to Map 17.3, Federal Land Grants to Railroads and the Development of the West.

CONNECTIONS: Why did the federal government force Native Americans onto reservations? What developments prompted these changes?

Poverty and starvation stalked the reservations. Confined by armed force, the Indians eked out an existence on stingy government rations. These once proud peoples found themselves dependent on government handouts and the assistance of Indian agents who, in the words of Paiute Sarah Winnemucca, did "nothing but fill their pockets." Winnemucca launched a lecture campaign in the United States and Europe denouncing the government's reservation policy.

Styled as stepping-stones on the road to "civilization," Indian reservations closely resembled

Waiting for Rations on the Reservation
Indians who agreed to give up land and go onto reservations received food and clothing rations from the local Indian agency. Here a group of Lakota Sioux gather to receive their goods at the Standing Rock Reservation in 1881. On the right is a ration card from the Rosebud reservation. Indian agencies were notorious for their paltry provisions. Often Indians outwitted the government by taking rations during the winter, when they were hungry, only to leave the reservation to resume their nomadic hunting life during the summer season. The decimation of the great bison herds drove them permanently onto the reservations in the 1880s. Photograph: National Anthropological Archives, Smithsonian Institution, Washington, D.C.; ration ticket: National Museum of the American Indian, Smithsonian Institution (239391), Washington, D.C. Photos by Photo Services.

colonial societies where native populations, ruled by outside bureaucrats, saw their culture assaulted, their religious practices outlawed, their children sent away to school, and their way of life attacked in the name of progress and civilization. Self-styled "friends of the Indians," many of them easterners with little experience in the West, maintained that reservations would provide a classroom of civilization where Indians could be taught to speak English, to worship a Christian god, to give up hunting for farming, and to reject tribal ways.

To Americans raised on theories of racial superiority, the Indians constituted, in the words of one Colorado militia major, "an obstacle to civilization . . . [and] should be exterminated." This attitude pervaded the military, and the cavalry annihilated entire villages with ruthless efficiency. In November 1864 at the Sand Creek massacre in Colorado Territory, Colonel John M. Chivington and his Colorado militia descended on a village of Cheyenne, mostly women and children. Their leader, Black Kettle, raised a white flag and an American flag to signal surrender, but the charging cavalry ignored his signal and butchered 270 Indians. Chivington watched as his men scalped and mutilated their victims and later justified the killing of Indian children with the terse remark, "Nits make lice." The city of Denver treated Chivington and his men as heroes, but a congressional inquiry castigated the soldiers for their "fiendish malignity" and condemned the "savage cruelty" of the massacre.

The Decimation of the Great Bison Herds

In the centuries following the arrival of the first European settlers, the great herds of buffalo (American bison), once numbering as many as thirty million, fell into serious decline. A host of environmental and human factors contributed to the destruction of the bison. The dynamic ecology of the Great Plains, with its droughts, fires, and blizzards, combined with the ecological imperialism of humans (Indian buffalo-robe traders as well as whites and their cattle), put increasing pressure on the bison. By the 1850s,

HARPER'S WEEKLY
A JOURNAL OF CIVILIZATION
Vol. XVIII.—No. 937.] NEW YORK, SATURDAY, DECEMBER 12, 1874.

VISUAL ACTIVITY

"Slaughtered for the Hide"

In 1874, *Harper's Weekly* featured this cover with its illustration of a buffalo hide hunter skinning a carcass on the southwestern plains. By 1872, the Santa Fe railroad reached Kansas, making Dodge City the center for the shipment of buffalo hides to the East, where they were made into leather belting used to run the nation's machinery. In a matter of months, hunters decimated the great southern bison herds. City father Colonel Richard Dodge wrote of the carnage, "The air was foul with sickening stench, and the vast plain which only a short twelve months before teemed with animal life, was a dead, solitary putrid desert." Dodge estimated that hunters slaughtered more than three million bison between 1872 and 1874. The grim reality of the trade makes the magazine's subtitle, "A Journal of Civilization," highly ironic. Library of Congress.

READING THE IMAGE: What virtues and stereotypes of the West does this magazine cover extol?

CONNECTIONS: How might the notion of "civilization" have differed according to the Native American perspective?

a combination of drought and commerce had driven the great herds onto the far western plains.

After the Civil War, the accelerating pace of industrial expansion brought about the near extinction of the bison. Industrial demand for heavy leather belting used in machinery and the development of larger, more accurate rifles combined to hasten the slaughter of the bison. At the same time, the nation's growing transcontinental rail system cut the range in two and divided the herds. For the Sioux and other nomadic tribes of the plains, the buffalo constituted a way of life —a source of food, fuel, and shelter and a central part of their religion and rituals. To the railroads, the bison were a nuisance, at best a cheap source of meat for their workers and a target for sport. "It will not be long before all the buffaloes are extinct near and between the railroads," Ohio senator John Sherman predicted in 1868.

In the end, the army took credit for the conquest of the Plains Indians, but victory came about largely as a result of the decimation of the great bison herds. General Philip Sheridan acknowledged as much when he applauded white hide hunters for "destroying the Indians' commissary." With their food supply gone, Indians had to choose between starvation and the reservation. "A cold wind blew across the prairie when the last buffalo fell," the great Sioux leader **Sitting Bull** lamented, "a death wind for my people."

On the southern plains in 1867, more than five thousand warring Comanches, Kiowas, and Southern Arapahos gathered at Medicine Lodge Creek in Kansas to negotiate a treaty. Satak, or Sitting Bear, a prominent Kiowa chief and medicine man, explained why the Indians sought peace: "In the far-distant past . . . the world seemed large enough for both the red man and the white man." But, he observed, "its broad plains seem now to contract, and the white man grows jealous of his red brother." To preserve their land from white encroachment, the Indians signed the Treaty of Medicine Lodge, agreeing to move to a reservation. Yet they continued to leave the reservation's confines to hunt during the summer months. After 1870, hide hunters poured into the region, and within a decade they had nearly exterminated the southern bison herds. Luther Standing Bear recounted the sight and stench: "I saw the bodies of hundreds of dead buffalo lying about, just wasting, and the odor was terrible. . . . They were letting our food lie on the plains to rot." With the buffalo gone, the Indians faced starvation and reluctantly moved to the reservations.

Indian Wars and the Collapse of Comanchería

The Indian wars in the West marked the last resistance of a Native American population devastated by disease and demoralized by the removal policy pursued by the federal government. More accurately called "settlers' wars" (since they began with "peaceful settlers," often miners, overrunning Native American land), the wars flared up again only a few years after the signing of the Fort Laramie treaty. The Dakota Sioux in Minnesota went to war in 1862. For years, under the leadership of Chief Little Crow, the Dakota, also known as the Santee, had pursued a policy of accommodation, ceding land in return for the promise of annuities. But with his people on the verge of starvation (the local Indian agent told the hungry Dakota, "Go and eat grass"), Little Crow reluctantly led his angry warriors in a desperate campaign against the intruders, killing more than 1,000 settlers. American troops quelled what was called the Great Sioux Uprising (also called the Santee Uprising) and marched 1,700 Sioux to Fort Snelling, where 400 Indians were put on trial for murder and 38 died in the largest mass execution in American history.

After the Civil War, President Ulysses S. Grant faced the prospect of protracted Indian war on the Great Plains. Reluctant to spend more money and sacrifice more lives in battle, Grant adopted a "peace policy" designed to segregate and control the Indians while opening up land to white settlers. This policy won the support of both friends of the Indians, who feared for their survival, and Indian haters, who coveted their land and wished to confine them to the least desirable areas in the West. General William Tecumseh Sherman summed up the new Indian policy succinctly: "Remove all to a safe place and then reduce them to a helpless condition." The army herded the Indians onto reservations (see Map 17.1), where the U.S. Bureau of Indian Affairs supposedly ministered to their needs. But peace in the West remained elusive.

The great Indian empire of **Comanchería**, which in the eighteenth century stretched from the Canadian plains to Mexico, by 1865 numbered fewer than five thousand Comanches, who ranged from west Texas north to Oklahoma. Through decades of dealings with the Spanish and French, the Comanches had built a complex empire based on trade in horses, hides, guns, and captives. Expert equestrians, the Comanches inaugurated the horse-centered way of life that eventually came to characterize the Plains Indians.

In 1871, Grant's peace policy in the West gave way to all-out warfare as the U.S. Army dispatched three thousand soldiers to wipe out the remains of the Comanche empire. Comanchería had been greatly reduced, but Comanche raiding parties took a toll in lives and livestock and virtually obliterated white settlements in west Texas. To defeat the Indians, the army adopted the tactics General William Sherman had used in his march through Confederate Georgia during the Civil War. At the decisive battle of Palo Duro Canyon in 1874, only three Comanche warriors died in battle, but U.S. soldiers took the Indians' camp, burning more than two hundred tepees, hundreds of robes and blankets, and thousands of pounds of winter supplies and shooting more than a thousand horses. Coupled with the decimation of the bison, the army's scorched-earth policy led to the final collapse of the Comanche people—more an economic than a military defeat. Crippled by poverty, malnutrition, and the loss of their trading-raiding economy, the surviving Indians of Comanchería, now numbering fewer than 1,500, reluctantly retreated to the reservation at Fort Sill.

The Fight for the Black Hills

On the northern plains, the fever for gold fueled the conflict between Indians and Euro-Americans. In 1866, the Cheyenne united with the Sioux in Wyoming to protect their hunting grounds in the Powder River valley, which were threatened by the construction of the Bozeman Trail connecting Fort Laramie with the goldfields in Montana. Captain William Fetterman, who had boasted that with eighty men he could ride through the Sioux nation, was killed along with all of his troops in an Indian attack. The Sioux's impressive victories led to the second **Treaty of Fort Laramie** in 1868, in which the United States agreed to abandon the Bozeman Trail and guaranteed the Indians control of the **Black Hills**, land sacred to the Lakota Sioux.

The second Treaty of Fort Laramie was full of contradictions — in one breath promising to preserve Indian land and in the next forcing the tribes to relinquish all territory outside their reservations. A controversial provision of the treaty guaranteed the Indians access to their traditional hunting grounds "so long as the buffalo may range thereon in such numbers as to justify the chase." With the bison facing extermination, the provision was ominous. Yet the government's fork-tongued promises induced some of the tribes to accept the treaty. The great Sioux chief Red Cloud led many of his people onto the reservation. Red Cloud soon

BEYOND AMERICA'S BORDERS

Imperialism, Colonialism, and the Treatment of the Sioux and the Zulu

Viewed through the lens of colonialism, the British war with the Zulu in South Africa offers a compelling contrast to the United States' war against the Lakota Sioux. The Zulu, like the Sioux, came to power as a result of devastating intertribal warfare. In the area that is today the KwaZulu-Natal province of the Republic of South Africa, the Zulu king Shaka united his empire by 1826 with an army of more than twenty thousand. And like the Sioux, the Zulu earned a formidable reputation as brave warriors who fought to protect their land from white encroachment.

In 1806, the British seized the Cape of Good Hope to secure shipping interests, leading to conflicts with Dutch-speaking settlers there known as the Boers, who had inhabited the southern tip of Africa since the seventeenth century. Clashes between Britons and Boers eventually resulted in the Great Trek, the migration of nearly twelve thousand Boers northeastward beginning in 1835. There they claimed land and established the South African Republic (the Transvaal) in 1853 and the Orange Free State in 1854, both independent of British rule. But the Great Trek brought the Boers into Zululand, where they met with bloody resistance.

The Zulu lived in a highly complex society, with all the young men organized into *amabutho*, regiments of warriors arranged by age and bound to local chiefs under the supreme command of the Zulu king, who demanded obedience and bravery. During his harsh reign, Shaka inspected his regiments after each battle, picking out cowards and putting them to death on the spot. Young men could not start their own households without the local chief's permission, thus ensuring an ample stock of warriors and making the Zulu army, in the words of one English observer, "a celibate, man-slaying machine." The Boer settlers repeatedly faced the wrath of the Zulu, who slaughtered the first trekkers to arrive in Zululand and raided Boer settlements to steal cattle.

The British entered the fray in 1879, sparking the Anglo-Zulu War, which a recent historian has condemned as being "as unnecessary as it was unjust." Sir Theophilus Shepstone, British secretary for native affairs, hinted at Britain's motive when he wrote in 1878, "Had [its] 30,000 warriors been in time changed to labourers working for wages, Zululand would have been a prosperous peaceful country instead of what it is now, a source of perpetual danger to itself and its neighbors."

With aims of both placating the Boers and securing a source of labor for British economic expansion — made paramount by the discovery of diamonds in the region — British troops under Lord Chelmsford invaded Zululand. Leading soldiers armed with the latest rifles and artillery, Chelmsford — with a confidence reminiscent of that of George Armstrong Custer — expected to subdue the Zulu easily. But in January 1879, at the battle of Isandhlwana, the Zulu army of

Zululand and Cape Colony, 1878

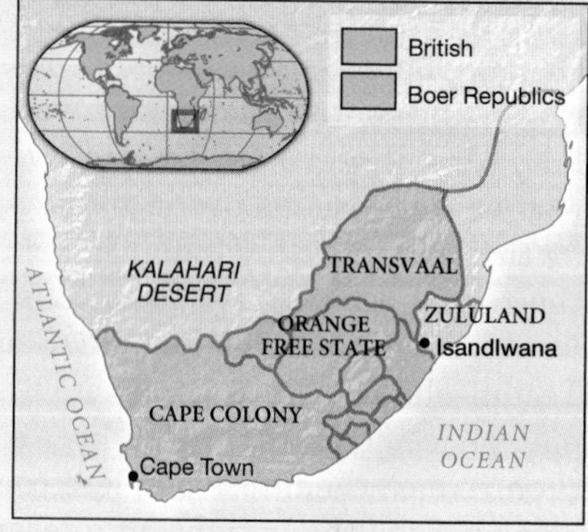

regretted his decision. "Think of it!" he told a visitor to the Pine Ridge Reservation. "I, who used to own . . . country so extensive that I could not ride through it in a week . . . must tell Washington when I am hungry. I must beg for that which I own." Several Sioux chiefs, among them **Crazy Horse** of the Oglala band and Sitting Bull of the Hunkpapa, refused to sign the treaty. Crazy Horse said that he wanted no part of the "piecemeal penning" of his people.

In 1874, the discovery of gold in the Black Hills of the Dakotas led the government to break its promise to Red Cloud. Miners began pouring into the region, and the Northern Pacific Railroad made plans to lay track. Lieutenant Colonel **George Armstrong Custer**, whose troopers found gold in the area, trumpeted news of the strike. At first, the government offered to purchase the Black Hills. But to the Lakota Sioux, the Black Hills were sacred — "the heart of everything that is." They refused to sell. The army responded by issuing an ultimatum ordering all Lakota Sioux and Northern Cheyenne bands onto the Pine Ridge Reservation and threatening to hunt down those who refused.

more than 25,000 surprised a British encampment. In less than two hours, more than 4,000 Zulu and British were killed. Only a handful of British soldiers managed to escape, and Chelmsford lost 1,300 officers and men.

When news of Isandhlwana reached London, commentators compared the massacre to Custer's defeat at the Little Big Horn three years earlier and noted that native forces armed with spears had defeated a modern army. The military disaster shocked and outraged the nation, damaging the British military's reputation of invincibility.

Vowing that the Zulu would "pay dearly for their triumph of a day," the British immediately launched unconditional war against the Zulu. In the ensuing battles, neither side took prisoners. The Zulu beat the British twice more, but after seven months the British finally routed the Zulu army and abandoned Zululand to its fate — partition, starvation, and civil war.

Zulu Warriors
Chief Ngoza (center) poses with Zulu men in full war dress. Their distinctive cowhide shields date to the reign of King Shaka. Each warrior also carried two or three throwing spears and an *ikwa*, or flat-bladed stabbing spear used in close combat. Zulu warriors marched at the double and could cover up to fifty miles a day. Campbell Collections of the University of KwaZulu-Natal.

Historians would later compare the British victory to the U.S. Army's defeat of the Sioux in the American West, but the Zulu and Sioux met different economic fates. As Shepstone hinted in 1878, the British goal had been to subdue the Zulu and turn them into cheap labor. Compared to the naked economic exploitation of the Zulu, the U.S. policy toward the Sioux, with its forced assimilation on reservations and its misguided attempts to turn the nomadic tribes into sedentary, God-fearing farmers, may seem less exploitative if no less ruthless in its cultural imperialism.

Both the Little Big Horn and Isandhlwana became legends that spawned a romantic image of the "noble savage": fierce in battle, honored in defeat. Describing this myth, historian James Gump, who has chronicled the subjugation of the Sioux and the Zulu, observed, "Each western culture simultaneously dehumanized and glamorized the Sioux and Zulu," and noted that the noble savage mythology was "a product of the racist ideologies of the late nineteenth century as well as the guilt and compassion associated with the bloody costs of empire building."

Imperial powers, both Britain and the United States defeated indigenous rivals and came to dominate their lands (and, in the case of the Zulu, their labor) in the global expansion that marked the nineteenth century.

America in a Global Context

1. How was the British war with the Zulu similar to and different from the American war with the Sioux?
2. Compare the fate of the defeated Zulu with that of the Sioux.

In the summer of 1876, the army launched a three-pronged attack led by Custer, General **George Crook**, and Colonel John Gibbon. Crazy Horse stopped Crook at the Battle of the Rosebud. Custer, leading the second prong of the army's offensive, divided his troops and ordered an attack. On June 25, he spotted signs of the Indians' camp. Crying "Hurrah Boys, we've got them," he led 265 men of the Seventh Cavalry into the largest Indian camp ever assembled on the Great Plains, more than 8,000 Indians. Nomadic bands of Sioux, Cheyenne, and Arapaho had come together for a summer buffalo hunt and camped along the banks of the Greasy Grass River (whites called it the Little Big Horn). Indian warriors led by Sitting Bull and Crazy Horse set upon Custer and his men and quickly annihilated them. "It took us about as long as a hungry man to eat his dinner," the Cheyenne chief Two Moons recalled. Gibbon arrived two days later to discover the carnage.

"Custer's Last Stand," as the **Battle of the Little Big Horn** was styled in myth, turned out to be the last stand for the Sioux. The Indians'

Crazy Horse at the Little Big Horn
This pictograph by Amos Bad Heart Bull, an Oglala Sioux from the Pine Ridge Reservation, pictures Crazy Horse at the center of the battle of the Little Big Horn. Although the artist was only seven years old in 1876, he based his pictures on the recollections of his uncle and other Oglala elders. Crazy Horse ritually prepared for battle by painting hail stones on his body, wearing a small stone tied behind one ear, and placing a single eagle feather in his hair. According to one of the Arapaho warriors who fought beside him against Custer, Crazy Horse "was the bravest man he ever saw." The Granger Collection, New York.

nomadic way of life meant they could not remain a combined force for long. The bands that had massed at the Little Big Horn scattered, and the army hunted them down. "Wherever we went," wrote the Oglala holy man Black Elk, "the soldiers came to kill us." In 1877, Crazy Horse was captured and killed. Four years later, in 1881, Sitting Bull surrendered. The government took the Black Hills and confined the Lakota to the Great Sioux Reservation. The Sioux never accepted the loss of the Black Hills. In 1923, they filed suit, demanding the return of the land illegally taken from them. After a protracted court battle lasting nearly sixty years, the U.S. Supreme Court ruled in 1980 that the government had illegally abrogated the Treaty of Fort Laramie and upheld an award of $122.5 million in compensation to the tribes. The Sioux refused the settlement and continue to press for the return of the Black Hills.

REVIEW How did the slaughter of the bison contribute to the Plains Indians' removal to reservations?

▸ Forced Assimilation and Resistance Strategies

More than two hundred years of contact with whites utterly transformed Native American societies. The indigenous peoples Christopher Columbus had mistakenly dubbed "Indians" included more than five hundred distinct tribal entities with different languages, myths, religions, and physical appearance. According to the census of 1900, the Indian population in the continental United States stood at 250,000 (admittedly an undercount), down from estimates as high as 15 million at the time of first contact with Europeans. Not only had the population been decimated by war, disease, and the obliteration of the bison, but Indian lands had shrunk so much that by 1890 Euro-Americans controlled 97.5 percent of the territory formerly occupied by Native Americans.

Imperialistic attitudes of whites toward Indians continued to evolve in the late nineteenth century. To "civilize" the Indians, the U.S. government sought to force assimilation on their children. Reservations, once designed as steppingstones to civilization, became increasingly unpopular among whites who coveted Indian land. A new policy of allotment gained favor. It promised to put Indians on parcels of land, forcing them into farming, and then to redistribute the rest of the land to settlers. In the face of this ongoing assault on their way of life, Indians actively resisted, contested, and adapted to colonial rule.

Indian Schools and the War against Indian Culture

Indian schools constituted the cultural battleground of the Indian wars in the West, their avowed purpose being "to destroy the Indian in him and save the man." In 1877, Congress appropriated funds for Indian education, reasoning that "it was less expensive to educate Indians than to kill them." Virginia's Hampton Institute, created in 1868 to school newly freed slaves, accepted its first Indian students in 1878. Although many Indian schools operated on the reservations, authorities much preferred boarding facilities that isolated students from the "contamination" of tribal values.

Many Native American parents resisted sending their children away. When all else failed, the military kidnapped the children and sent them off to school. An agent at the Mescalero Apache Agency in Arizona Territory reported in 1886 that "it became necessary to visit the camps unexpectedly with a detachment of police, and seize such children as were proper and take them away to school, willing or unwilling." The parents put up a struggle. "Some hurried their children off to the mountains or hid them away in camp, and the police had to chase and capture them like so many wild rabbits," the agent observed. "This unusual proceeding created quite an outcry. The men were sullen and muttering, the women loud in their lamentations and the children almost out of their wits with fright." Once at school, the children were stripped and scrubbed, their clothing and belongings were confiscated, and their hair was hacked off and doused with kerosene to kill lice. Issued stiff new uniforms, shoes, and what one boy recalled as the "torture" of woolen long underwear, the children often lost not only their possessions but also their names: Hehakaavita (Yellow Elk) became Thomas Goodwood; Polingaysi Qoyawayma became Elizabeth White.

Hampton Pageant, 1892
The Indian students in this picture are dressed for Columbia's Roll Call, a pageant at Hampton Institute honoring the nation's heroes on Indian Citizen Day, 1892. Among others portrayed are Christopher Columbus, Pocahontas, George Washington, and, in the center, a student dressed as Columbia, symbol of the Republic, draped in the American flag. There was no mention of Crazy Horse, Sitting Bull, or Geronimo, all Indians who resisted white encroachment and appropriation of their land in the West. Courtesy of Hampton University Archives.

The curriculum featured agricultural and manual arts for boys and domestic skills for girls, training designed to make Indians "willing workers" who would no longer be a burden to the government. The **Carlisle Indian School** in Pennsylvania, founded in 1879, became the model for later institutions. To encourage assimilation, Carlisle pioneered the "outing system" — sending students to live with white families during summer vacations. The policy reflected the school's slogan: "To civilize the Indian, get him into civilization. To keep him civilized, let him stay."

Merrill Gates, a member of the Board of Indian Commissioners, summed up the goal of Indian education: "To get the Indian out of the blanket and into trousers, — and trousers with a pocket in them, *and with a pocket that aches to be filled with dollars*!" Gates's faith in the "civilizing" power of the dollar reflected the unabashed materialism of the Gilded Age. But the cultural annihilation that Gates cheerfully predicted did not prove so easy.

The Dawes Act and Indian Land Allotment

In the 1880s, the practice of rounding up Indians and herding them onto reservations lost momentum in favor of allotment — a new policy designed to encourage assimilation through farming and the ownership of private property. Americans vowing to avenge Custer urged the government to get tough with the Indians. Reservations, they argued, took up too much good land that white settlers could put to better use. At the same time, people sympathetic to the Indians were appalled at the desperate poverty on the reservations and feared for the Indians' survival. Helen Hunt Jackson, in her classic work *A Century of Dishonor* (1881), convinced many readers that the Indians had been treated unfairly. "Our Indian policy," the *New York Times* concluded, "is usually spoliation behind the mask of benevolence."

"Our Indian policy is usually spoliation behind the mask of benevolence"
— The *New York Times*

The Indian Rights Association, a group of mainly white easterners formed in 1882, campaigned for the dismantling of the reservations, now viewed as obstacles to progress. To "cease to treat the Indian as a red man and treat him as a man" meant putting an end to tribal communalism and fostering individualism. "Selfishness," declared Senator Henry Dawes of Massachusetts, "is at the bottom of civilization." Dawes called for "allotment in severalty" — the institution of private property.

In 1887, Congress passed the **Dawes Allotment Act**, dividing up reservations and allotting parcels of land to individual Indians as private property. Each unmarried Indian man and woman as well as married men and children (married women were excluded) became eligible to receive 160 acres of land from reservation property. Indians who took allotments earned U.S. citizenship. To protect Indians from land speculators, the government held most of the allotted land in trust, and the Indians could not sell it for twenty-five years. Since Indian land far surpassed the acreage needed for allotments, the government reserved the right to sell the "surplus" to white settlers.

The Dawes Act effectively reduced Indian land from 138 million acres to a scant 48 million. The legislation, in the words of one critic, worked "to despoil the Indians of their lands and to make them vagabonds on the face of the earth." The Dawes Act completed the dispossession of the western Indian peoples and dealt a crippling blow to traditional tribal culture. Amended in 1891 and again in 1906, it remained in effect until 1934, when the United States restored the right of Native Americans to own land communally (as discussed in chapter 24).

Indian Resistance and Survival

Faced with the extinction of their entire way of life, different groups of Indians responded in different ways in the waning decades of the nineteenth century. In the 1870s, Comanche and Kiowa raiding parties frustrated the U.S. Army by using the reservation at Fort Sill as an asylum, knowing that troops could not pursue them onto reservation land. They brazenly used the reservations as a seasonal supply base during the winter months, taking the meager annuities doled out by the Indian agents, only to resume their nomadic ways when spring came. Soon other tribes followed their lead.

Some tribes, including the Crow, Arikara, Pawnee, and Shoshoni, chose to fight alongside the army against their old enemies, the Sioux. The Crow chief Plenty Coups explained why he allied with the United States: "Not because we loved the white man . . . or because we hated the Sioux . . . but because we plainly saw that this course was the only one which might save our beautiful country for us." The Crow and Shoshoni got to stay in their homelands and avoided the fate of other tribes shipped to reservations far away.

Indians who refused to stay on reservations risked being hunted down — a clear indication that reservations were intended to keep Indians in, not to keep whites out, as the friends of the Indians had intended. The Nez Percé war of 1877 is perhaps the most harrowing example of the army's policy. In 1863, the government dictated a treaty drastically reducing Nez Percé land. Most of the chiefs refused to sign the treaty and did not move to the reservation. In 1877, the army issued an ultimatum — come in to the reservation or be hunted down. Some eight hundred Nez Percé people, many of them women and children, fled across the mountains of Idaho, Wyoming, and Montana, heading for the safety of Canada. At the end of their 1,300-mile trek, 50 miles from freedom, they stopped to rest in the snow. The army's Indian scouts spotted their tepees, and the soldiers attacked. Yellow Wolf recalled their plight: "Children crying with cold. No fire. There could be no light. Everywhere the crying, the death wail." After a five-day siege, the Nez Percé leader, **Chief Joseph**, surrendered.

Chief Joseph
Chief Joseph came to symbolize the heroic resistance of the Nez Percé. General Nelson Miles promised the Nez Percé that they could return to their homeland if they surrendered. But he betrayed them, as he would betray the Apache people seven years later. The Nez Percé were shipped off to Indian Territory (Oklahoma). In 1879, Chief Joseph traveled to Washington, D.C., to speak for his people. "Let me be a free man," he pleaded, "free to choose my own teachers, free to follow the religion of my fathers, free to think and talk and act for myself — and I will obey every law." National Anthropological Archives, Smithsonian Institution, Washington, D.C. (#2906).

His speech, reported by a white soldier, would become famous. "I am tired of fighting," he said as he surrendered his rifle. "Our chiefs are killed. It is cold and we have no blankets. The little children are freezing to death. . . . I am tired. My heart is sick and sad. From where the sun now stands, I will fight no more forever."

In the Southwest, the Apaches resorted to armed resistance. They roamed the Sonoran Desert of southern Arizona and northern Mexico, perfecting a hit-and-run guerrilla warfare that terrorized white settlers and bedeviled the army in the 1870s and 1880s. General George Crook combined a policy of dogged pursuit with judicious diplomacy. Crook relied on Indian scouts to track the raiding parties, recruiting nearly two hundred, including Apaches, Navajos, and Paiutes. By 1882, Crook had succeeded in persuading most of the Apaches to settle on the San Carlos Reservation in Arizona Territory. A desolate piece of desert inhabited by scorpions and rattlesnakes, San Carlos, in the words of one Apache, was "the worst place in all the great territory stolen from the Apaches."

Geronimo, a respected shaman (medicine man) of the Chiricahua Apache, refused to stay at San Carlos and repeatedly led raiding parties in the early 1880s. His warriors attacked ranches to obtain ammunition and horses. Among Geronimo's band was **Lozen**, a woman who rode with the warriors, armed with a rifle and a cartridge belt. The sister of a great chief who described her as being as "strong as a man, braver than most, and cunning in strategy," Lozen never married and remained a warrior in Geronimo's band even after her brother's death. In the spring of 1885, Geronimo and his followers, including Lozen, went on a ten-month offensive, moving from the Apache sanctuary in the Sierra Madre to raid and burn ranches and towns on both sides of the Mexican border. General Crook caught up with Geronimo in the fall and persuaded him to return to San Carlos, only to have him slip away on the way back to the reservation. Chagrined, Crook resigned his post. General **Nelson Miles**, Crook's replacement, adopted a policy of hunt and destroy.

Geronimo's band of thirty-three Apaches, including women and children, managed to elude Miles's troops for more than five months. In the end, this small band fought two thousand soldiers to a stalemate. After months of pursuit, Lieutenant Leonard Wood, a member of Miles's spit-and-polish cavalry, discarded his horse and most of his clothes until he was reduced to wearing nothing "but a pair of canton flannel drawers, and an old blue blouse, a pair of moccasins and a hat without a crown."

Eventually, Miles's scouts cornered Geronimo in 1886 at Skeleton Canyon. Caught between Mexican regulars and the U.S. Army, Geronimo agreed to march north with the soldiers and negotiate a settlement. "We have not slept for six months," he admitted, "and we are worn out." Although fewer than three dozen Apaches had been considered "hostile," when General Miles induced them to surrender, the government rounded up nearly five hundred Apaches, including the scouts who had helped track Geronimo, and sent them as prisoners to Florida. By 1889, more than a quarter of them had died, some as a result of illnesses contracted in the damp lowland climate and some by suicide. Their plight roused public opinion, and in 1892 they were moved to Fort Sill in Oklahoma and later to New Mexico.

Geronimo lived to become something of a celebrity. He appeared at the St. Louis Exposition in 1904, and he rode in President Theodore Roosevelt's inaugural parade in 1905. In a newspaper interview, he confessed, "I want to go to my old home before I die. . . . Want to go back to the mountains again. I asked the Great White Father to allow me to go back, but he said no." None of the Apaches were permitted to return to Arizona; when Geronimo died in 1909, he was buried in Oklahoma.

On the plains, many tribes turned to a nonviolent form of resistance — a compelling new religion called the **Ghost Dance**. The Paiute shaman Wovoka, drawing on a cult that had developed in the 1870s, combined elements of Christianity and traditional Indian religion to found the Ghost Dance religion in 1889. Wovoka claimed that he had received a vision in which the Great Spirit spoke through him to all Indians, prophesying that if they would unite in the Ghost Dance ritual, whites would be destroyed in an apocalypse. The shaman promised that Indian warriors slain in battle would return to life and that buffalo once again would roam the land unimpeded. This religion, born of despair and with a message of hope, spread like wildfire over the plains. The Ghost Dance was performed in Idaho, Montana, Utah, Wyoming, Colorado, Nebraska, Kansas, the Dakotas, and Indian Territory by tribes as diverse as the Sioux, Arapaho, Cheyenne, Pawnee, and Shoshoni. Dancers often went into hypnotic trances, dancing until they dropped from exhaustion.

The Ghost Dance was nonviolent, but it frightened whites, especially when the Sioux taught that wearing a white ghost shirt made Indians immune to soldiers' bullets. Soon whites began to fear an uprising. "Indians are dancing in the snow and are wild and crazy," wrote the Bureau of Indian Affairs agent at the Pine Ridge Reservation in South Dakota. Frantic, he pleaded for reinforcements. "We are at the mercy of these dancers. We need protection, and we need it now." President Benjamin Harrison dispatched several thousand federal troops to Sioux country to handle any outbreak.

Ghost Dancers
Arapaho women at the Darlington Agency in Indian Territory (Oklahoma) participate in the Ghost Dance. Different tribes performed variations of the dance, but generally dancers formed a circle and danced until they reached the trance-like state shown here. The ceremonial drum (right) features a drawing of a thunderbird. Whites feared the dancers and demanded that the army dispatch troops to subdue them. The result was the killing of Sitting Bull and the massacre at Wounded Knee.
Ghost Dance: National Anthropological Archives, Smithsonian Institution, Washington, D.C. (#81-9626); Drum: Collection of Charles Stoneroad, Courtesy of the Oakland Museum of California.

In December 1890, when Sitting Bull joined the Ghost Dance, he was killed by Indian police as they tried to arrest him at his cabin on the Standing Rock Reservation. His people, fleeing the scene, joined with a larger group of Miniconjou Sioux, who were apprehended by the Seventh Cavalry, Custer's old regiment, near Wounded Knee Creek, South Dakota. As the Indians laid down their arms, a soldier attempted to take a rifle from a deaf Miniconjou man, and the gun went off. The soldiers opened fire. In the ensuing melee, Indian men, women, and children were mowed down in minutes by the army's brutally efficient Hotchkiss rapid-fire guns. Caught in the crossfire, one Indian recounted, "I saw my friends sinking about me, and heard the whine of many bullets." In a matter of minutes, eighty-three Indian men lay dead. The cavalry then hunted down women and children attempting to flee into the bluffs and canyons. The next day, more than two hundred Sioux lay dead or dying in the snow.

Settler Jules Sandoz surveyed the scene the day after the massacre at **Wounded Knee**. "Here in ten minutes an entire community was as the buffalo that bleached on the plains," he wrote. "There was something loose in the world that hated joy and happiness as it hated brightness and color, reducing everything to drab agony and gray." It had taken Euro-Americans 250 years to wrest control of the eastern half of the United States from the Indians. It took them less than 40 years to take the western half. The subjugation of the American Indians marked the first chapter in a national mission of empire that would presage overseas imperialistic adventures in Asia, Latin America, the Caribbean, and the Pacific islands.

REVIEW In what ways did different Indian groups defy and resist colonial rule?

▸ Gold Fever and the Mining West

Mining stood at the center of the United States' quest for empire in the West. The California gold rush of 1849 touched off the frenzy. The four decades following witnessed equally frenetic rushes for gold and other metals, most notably on the **Comstock Lode** in Nevada and later in New Mexico, Colorado, the Dakotas, Montana, Idaho, Arizona, and Utah. Each rush built on the last, producing new mining technologies and innovations in financing as hordes of miners, eager to strike it rich, moved from one boomtown to the next. Mining in the West, however, was a story not only of boom and bust but also of community building and the development of territories into states (Map 17.2).

At first glance, the mining West may seem much different from the East, but by the 1870s the term *urban industrialism* described Virginia City, Nevada, as accurately as it did Pittsburgh or Cleveland. A close look at mining on the Comstock Lode indicates some of the patterns and paradoxes of western mining. The diversity of peoples drawn to the West by the promise of mining riches and land made the region the most cosmopolitan in the nation, as well as the most contested. And a look at territorial government uncovers striking parallels with the corruption and cupidity in politics east of the Mississippi.

Mining on the Comstock Lode

By 1859, refugees from California's played-out goldfields flocked to the Washoe basin in Nevada. There prospectors found the gold they sought mired in blackish sand they called "that blasted blue stuff." Eventually, an enterprising miner had the stuff assayed, and it turned out that the Washoe miners had stumbled on the richest vein of silver ore on the continent — the legendary Comstock Lode, named for prospector Henry Comstock.

To exploit even potentially valuable silver claims required capital and expensive technology well beyond the means of the prospector. An active San Francisco stock market sprang up to finance operations on the Comstock. Shrewd businessmen soon recognized that the easiest way to get rich was not to mine at all but to sell their claims or to form mining companies and sell shares of stock. The most unscrupulous mined the wallets of gullible investors by selling shares in bogus mines. Speculation, misrepresentation, and outright thievery ran rampant. In twenty years, more than $300 million poured from the earth in Nevada alone. A little stayed in Virginia City, but a great deal more went to speculators in California, some of whom got rich without ever leaving San Francisco.

The promise of gold and silver drew thousands to the mines of the West, the honest as well as the unprincipled. As author Mark Twain observed in Virginia City's *Territorial Enterprise*, "All the peoples of the earth had representative adventures in the Silverland." Irish, Chinese, Germans, English, Scots, Welsh, Canadians, Mexicans, Italians, Scandinavians, French, Swiss,

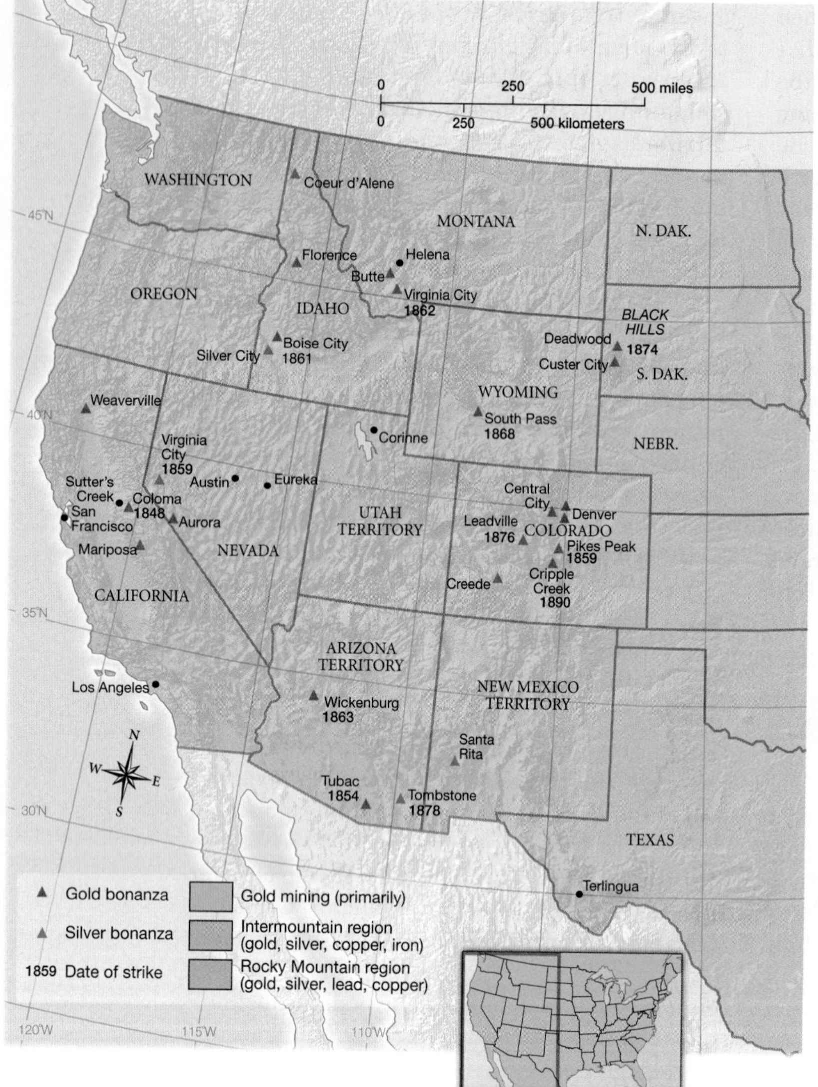

MAP 17.2
Western Mining, 1848–1890
Rich deposits of gold, silver, copper, lead, and iron larded the mountains of the West, from the Sierra Nevada of California to the Rockies of Colorado and the Black Hills of South Dakota. Beginning with the gold strike on Sutter's Creek in California in 1848 and continuing through the rush for gold in Cripple Creek, Colorado, in 1890, miners from all over the world flocked to the West. Few struck it rich, but many stayed on as paid workers in the increasingly mechanized corporate mines.

Chileans, and other South and Central Americans came to share in the bonanza. With them came a sprinkling of Russians, Poles, Greeks, Japanese, Spaniards, Hungarians, Portuguese, Turks, Pacific Islanders, and Moroccans, as well as other North Americans, African Americans, and American Indians. This polyglot population, typical of mining boomtowns, made Virginia City in the 1870s more cosmopolitan than New York or Boston. In the part of Utah Territory that eventually became Nevada, as many as 30 percent of the people came from outside the United States, compared to 25 percent in New York and 21 percent in Massachusetts.

Irish immigrants formed the largest ethnic group in the mining district. In Virginia City, fully one-third of the population claimed at least one parent from Ireland. Irish and Irish American women constituted the largest group of women on the Comstock. As servants, boardinghouse owners, and washerwomen, they made up a significant part of the workforce. By contrast, the Chinese community, numbering 642 in 1870, remained overwhelmingly male. Virulent anti-Chinese sentiment barred the men from work in the mines, but despite the violent anti-Asian rhetoric, the mining community came to depend on Chinese labor. Many boardinghouses and affluent homes employed a Chinese cook or servant along with an Irish parlor maid.

As was so often the case in the West, where Euro-American ambitions clashed with Native American ways, the discovery of precious metals on the Comstock spelled disaster for the Indians. No sooner had the miners struck pay dirt than they demanded that army troops "hunt Indians" and establish forts to protect transportation to and from the diggings. This sudden and dramatic intrusion left Nevada's native tribes — the Northern Paiute and Bannock Shoshoni — exiles in their own land. At first they resisted, but over time they made peace with the invaders and developed resourceful strategies to adapt and preserve their culture and identity despite the havoc wreaked by western mining and settlement.

In 1873, Comstock miners uncovered a new vein of ore, a veritable cavern of gold and silver. This "Big Bonanza" speeded the transition from small-scale industry to corporate oligopoly, creating a radically new social and economic environment. The Comstock became a laboratory for new mining technology. Huge stamping mills pulverized rock with pistonlike hammers driven by steam engines. Enormous Cornish pumps sucked water from the mine shafts, and huge ventilators circulated air in the underground chambers. No backwoods mining camp, Virginia City was an industrial center with more than 1,200 stamping mills working on average a ton of ore every day. Almost 400 men worked in milling, nearly 300 labored in manufacturing industries, and roughly 3,000 toiled in the mines. The Gould and Curry mine covered sixty acres. Most of the miners who came to the Comstock ended up as laborers for the big companies.

New technology eliminated some of the dangers of mining but often created new ones. In the hard-rock mines of the West, accidents in the 1870s disabled one out of every thirty miners and killed one in eighty. Ross Moudy, who worked as a miner in Cripple Creek, Colorado, recalled how a stockholder visiting the mine nearly fell to his death. The terrified visitor told the miner next to him that "instead of being paid $3 a day, they ought to have all the gold they could take out." Moudy's biggest worry was carbon dioxide, which often filled the tunnels because of poor ventilation. "Many times," he confessed, "I have been carried out unconscious." Those who avoided accidents still breathed air so dangerous that respiratory diseases eventually disabled them. After a year on the job, Moudy joined a labor union "because I saw it would help me to keep in work and for protection in case of accident or sickness." The union provided good sick benefits and hired nurses, "so if one is alone and sick he is sure to be taken care of." On the Comstock Lode, because of the difficulty of obtaining skilled labor, the richness of the ore, and the need for a stable workforce, labor unions formed early and held considerable bargaining power. Comstock miners commanded $4 a day, the highest wage in the mining West.

The mining towns of the "Wild West" are often portrayed as lawless outposts, filled with saloons and rough gambling dens and populated almost exclusively by men, except for the occasional dance-hall floozy. The truth is more complex, as Virginia City's development attests. An established urban community built to serve an industrial giant, Virginia City in its first decade boasted

"Mining on the Comstock"
This illustration, made at Gold Hill, Nevada, in 1876, shows a sectional view of a mine, highlighting the square-set timber method, an innovation in mining that assembled prefabricated timbers into cubes stacked on cubes that could support virtually any underground chasm. Note also the tunnels, incline, cooling-off room, blower, and air shaft, along with a collection of miner's tools. Mines like the one pictured here honeycombed the hills of Gold City and neighboring Virginia City on the Comstock Lode in Nevada. University of California at Berkeley, Bancroft Library.

churches, schools, theaters, an opera house, and hundreds of families. By 1870, women composed 30 percent of the population, and 75 percent of the women listed their occupation in the census as housekeeper. Mary McNair Mathews, a widow from Buffalo, New York, who lived on the Comstock in the 1870s, worked as a teacher, nurse, seamstress, laundress, and lodging-house operator. She later published a book on her adventures.

By 1875, Virginia City boasted a population of 25,000 people, making it one of the largest cities between St. Louis and San Francisco. A must-see stop on the way west, the "Queen of the Comstock" hosted American presidents as well as legions of lesser dignitaries. No rough outpost of the Wild West, Virginia City represented, in the words of a recent chronicler, "the distilled essence of America's newly established course — urban, industrial, acquisitive, and materialistic, on the move, 'a living polyglot' of cultures that collided and converged."

The Diverse Peoples of the West

The West of the late nineteenth century was indeed a polyglot place, as much so as the big cities of the East. The sheer number of peoples who mingled in the West produced a complex blend of racism and prejudice. One historian has noted, not entirely facetiously, that there were at least eight oppressed "races" in the West — Indians, Latinos, Chinese, Japanese, blacks, Mormons, strikers, and radicals.

African Americans who ventured out to the territories faced hostile settlers determined to keep the West "for whites only." In response, they formed all-black communities such as Nicodemas, Kansas. That settlement, founded by thirty black Kentuckians in 1877, grew to a community of seven hundred by 1880. Isolated and often separated by great distances, small black settlements grew up throughout the West, in Nevada, Utah, and the Pacific Northwest, as well as in Kansas. Black soldiers who served in the West during the Indian wars often stayed on as settlers. Called **buffalo soldiers** because Native Americans thought their hair resembled that of the bison, these black troops numbered up to 25,000. In the face of discrimination, poor treatment, and harsh conditions, the buffalo soldiers served with distinction and boasted the lowest desertion rate in the army.

Hispanic peoples had lived in Texas and the Southwest since Juan de Oñate led pioneer settlers up the Rio Grande in 1598. Hispanics had occupied the Pacific coast since San Diego was founded in 1769. Overnight, they were reduced to a "minority" after the United States annexed Texas in 1845 and took land stretching to California after the Mexican-American War ended in 1848. At first, the Hispanic owners of large *ranchos* in California, New Mexico, and Texas greeted conquest as an economic opportunity — new markets for their livestock and buyers for their lands. But racial prejudice soon ended their optimism. Californios (Mexican residents of California), who had been granted American citizenship by the Treaty of Guadalupe Hidalgo (1848), faced discrimination by Anglos who sought to keep them out of California's mines and commerce. Whites illegally squatted on *rancho* land while protracted litigation over Spanish and Mexican land grants forced the Californios into court. Although the U.S. Supreme Court eventually validated most of their claims, it took so long — seventeen years on average — that many Californios sold their property to pay taxes and legal bills. The city of Oakland, California, sits on what was once a 19,000-acre ranch owned by the Peralta family, who lost the land to Anglos.

Swindles, chicanery, and intimidation dispossessed scores of Californios. Many ended up segregated in urban barrios (neighborhoods) in their own homeland. Their percentage of California's population declined from 82 percent in 1850 to 19 percent in 1880 as Anglos migrated to the state. In New Mexico and Texas, Mexicans remained a majority of the population but became increasingly impoverished as Anglos dominated business and took the best jobs. Skirmishes between Hispanics and whites in northern New Mexico over the fencing of the open range lasted for decades. Groups of Hispanics with names such as *Las Manos Negras* (the Black Hands) cut fences and burned barns. In Texas, violence along the Rio Grande pitted Tejanos (Mexican residents of Texas) against the Texas Rangers, who saw their role as "keeping Mexicans in their place."

Even more than the Mexicans, the Chinese suffered brutal treatment at the hands of employers and other laborers. Drawn by the promise of gold, more than 20,000 Chinese had joined the rush to California by 1852. Miners determined to keep "California for Americans" succeeded in passing prohibitive foreign license laws to keep the Chinese out of the mines. But Chinese immigration continued. In the 1860s, when white workers moved on to find riches in the bonanza mines of Nevada, Chinese laborers took jobs abandoned by the whites. Railroad magnate Charles Crocker hired Chinese gangs to work on the Central Pacific, reasoning that "the race that built the Great Wall" could lay tracks across the treacherous Sierra Nevada. Some 12,000

Buffalo Soldiers to the Rescue in Colorado
In this painting, artist Frederic Remington portrays the bravery of African American "buffalo soldiers." In 1879 the Ute went on the warpath in Colorado when an Indian agent threatened to destroy their ponies to force them into farming. The Ute killed the whites, and the soldiers pursuing them soon found themselves pinned down and under siege. Captain Francis Dodge and his troop of thirty-five buffalo soldiers rode twenty-three hours to the rescue. Remington's picture is imagined — painted well after the fact. Although Remington spent a stint tracking Geronimo in Arizona for *Harper's Magazine*, he returned to the East and there gained renown for his depictions of the mythic Old West. The Granger Collection, New York.

Chinese, representing 90 percent of Crocker's workforce, completed America's first transcontinental railroad in 1869.

By 1870, more than 63,000 Chinese immigrants lived in America, 77 percent of them in California. A 1790 federal statute that limited naturalization to "white persons" was modified after the Civil War to extend naturalization to blacks ("persons of African descent"). But the Chinese and other Asians continued to be denied access to citizenship. As perpetual aliens, they constituted a reserve army of transnational laborers that many saw as a threat to American labor. For the most part, the Chinese did not displace white workers but instead found work as railroad laborers, cooks, servants, and farmhands while white workers sought out more lucrative fields. In the 1870s, when California and the rest of the nation weathered a major economic depression, the Chinese became easy scapegoats. California workingmen rioted and fought to keep Chinese workers out of the state, claiming they were "coolie labor"— involuntary contract laborers recruited by business interests determined to keep wages at rock bottom.

In 1876, the Workingmen's Party formed to fight for Chinese exclusion. Racial and cultural animosities stood at the heart of anti-Chinese agitation. Denis Kearney, the fiery San Francisco leader of the movement, made clear this racist bent when he urged legislation to "expel every one of the moon-eyed lepers." Nor was California alone in its anti-immigrant nativism. As the country confronted growing ethnic and racial diversity with the rising tide of global immigration in the decades following the Civil War, many questioned the principle of racial equality at the same time they argued against the assimilation of "nonwhite" groups. In this climate, Congress passed the **Chinese Exclusion Act** in 1882, effectively barring Chinese immigration and setting a precedent for further immigration restrictions.

"Expel every one of the moon-eyed lepers."
— San Francisco leader DENIS KEARNEY, speaking of Chinese immigrants

Chinese Workers
Chinese section hands, wearing their distinctive conical hats, are shown here in 1898 shoveling dirt for the North Pacific Coast Railroad in Corte Madera, California. Charles Crocker was the first railroad executive to hire Chinese laborers to work on the Central Pacific railroad in the 1860s, reasoning that the race that built the Great Wall could build tracks through the Sierra Nevada. California Historical Society, FN-25345.

The Chinese Exclusion Act led to a sharp drop in the Chinese population — from 105,465 in 1880 to 89,863 in 1900 — because Chinese immigrants, overwhelmingly male, did not have families to sustain their population. Eventually, Japanese immigrants, including women as well as men, replaced the Chinese, particularly in agriculture. As "nonwhite" immigrants, they could not become naturalized citizens, but their children born in the United States claimed the rights of citizenship. Japanese parents, seeking to own land, purchased it in their children's names. Although anti-Asian prejudice remained strong in California and elsewhere in the West, Asian immigrants formed an important part of the economic fabric of the western United States.

The Mormons, who had fled west to Utah Territory in 1844 to avoid religious persecution, established Salt Lake City, a thriving metropolis of more than 150,000 residents by 1882. To counter criticism of the Mormon practice of polygamy (church leader Brigham Young had twenty-seven wives), the Utah territorial legislature gave women the right to vote in 1870, the first universal woman suffrage act in the nation. (Wyoming had granted suffrage to white women in 1869.) Although woman's rights advocates argued that the newly enfranchised women would "do away with the horrible institution of polygamy," it remained in force. Not until 1890 did the church hierarchy yield to pressure and renounce polygamy. The fierce controversy over polygamy postponed statehood for Utah until 1896.

Territorial Government

The federal government practiced a policy of benign neglect when it came to territorial government in the West. The president appointed a governor, a secretary, and two to four judges, along with an attorney and a marshal. In Nevada Territory, that meant that a handful of officials governed an area the size of New England. Originally a part of the larger Utah Territory, Nevada, propelled by mining interests, moved on the fast track to statehood, entering the Union in 1864, long before its population or its development merited statehood.

More typical were the territories extant in 1870 — New Mexico, Utah, Washington, Colorado, Dakota, Arizona, Idaho, Montana, and Wyoming. These areas remained territories for inordinately long periods ranging from twenty-three to sixty-two years. While awaiting statehood, they were subject to territorial governors who were underpaid, often unqualified, and largely ignored in Washington. Most territorial governors won their posts because of party loyalty and had little knowledge of the areas they served, little notions of their duties, and limited ability to perform them.

In theory, territorial governors received adequate salaries, as high as $3,500 in an era when the average workingman earned less than $500 a year. In practice, the funds rarely arrived in a timely fashion, and more than one governor found that he had to pay government expenses out of his own pocket. As one cynic observed, "Only the rich or those having 'no visible means of support,' can afford to accept office." John C. Frémont, the governor of Arizona Territory, complained he was so poor that he could not inspect the Grand Canyon because he didn't have money to keep a horse.

Territorial governors with fewer scruples accepted money from special interests — mine owners and big ranchers. Nearly all territorial appointees tried to make ends meet by maintaining business connections with the East or by taking advantage of investment opportunities in the West. Distance and the lack of funds made it difficult to summon officers from Washington to investigate charges of corruption. Officials who ventured west to look into such charges often felt intimidated by gun-packing westerners. One judge sent to New Mexico Territory in 1871 reported that he "stayed three days, made up his mind that it would be dangerous to do any investigating, . . . and returned to his home without any action." Underfunded and overlooked, victims of political cronyism, and prey to special interests, territorial governments were rife with conflicts of interest and corruption, mirroring the self-serving political and economic values of the country as a whole in the rush for riches that followed the Civil War.

REVIEW How did industrial technology change mining in Nevada?

Admission of States in the Trans-Mississippi West

Year	State	Year	State
1821	Missouri	1889	North Dakota
1836	Arkansas	1889	South Dakota
1845	Texas	1889	Montana
1846	Iowa	1889	Washington
1850	California	1890	Idaho
1858	Minnesota	1890	Wyoming
1859	Oregon	1896	Utah
1861	Kansas	1907	Oklahoma
1864	Nevada	1912	New Mexico
1867	Nebraska	1912	Arizona
1876	Colorado		

▸ Land Fever

In the three decades following 1870, more land was settled than in all the previous history of the country. Americans by the hundreds of thousands packed up and moved west, goaded if not by the hope of striking gold, then by the promise of owning land. The agrarian West shared with the mining West a persistent restlessness, an equally pervasive addiction to speculation, and a penchant for exploiting natural resources and labor.

Two factors stimulated the land rush in the trans-Mississippi West. The **Homestead Act of 1862** promised 160 acres free to any citizen or prospective citizen, male or female, who settled on the land for five years. Even more important, **transcontinental railroads** opened up new areas and actively recruited settlers. After the completion of the first transcontinental railroad in 1869, homesteaders abandoned the covered wagon, and by the 1880s they could choose from four competing rail lines and make the trip west in a matter of days.

Although the country was rich in land and resources, not all who wanted to own land achieved their goal. During the transition from the family farm to large commercial farming, small farms gave way to vast spreads worked by migrant labor or paid farmworkers. Just as industry corporatized and consolidated in the East, the period from 1870 to 1900 witnessed corporate consolidation in mining, ranching, and agriculture.

Moving West: Homesteaders and Speculators

A Missouri homesteader remembered packing as her family pulled up stakes and headed west to Oklahoma in 1890. "We were going to God's Country," she wrote. "You had to work hard on that rocky country in Missouri. I was glad to be leaving it. . . . We were going to a new land and get rich."

Norwegian Immigrant and Sod House Norwegian immigrant Beret Olesdater sits in front of her sod house in Lac qui Parle, Minnesota, in 1896. On the plains, where trees were scarce and lumber was often prohibitively expensive, settlers built with the materials at hand. The dugout was the most primitive dwelling, carved into a hillside. Huts cut from blocks of sod, like the one pictured here, marked a step up. Life for women on the plains proved especially lonely and hard. © Minnesota Historical Society/Corbis.

People who ventured west searching for "God's Country" faced hardship, loneliness, and deprivation. To carve a farm from the raw prairie of Iowa, the plains of Nebraska, or the forests of the Pacific Northwest took more than fortitude and backbreaking toil. It took luck. Blizzards, tornadoes, grasshoppers, hailstorms, drought, prairie fires, accidental death, and disease were only a few of the catastrophes that could befall even the best farmer. Homesteaders on free land still needed as much as $1,000 for a house, a team of farm animals, a well, fencing, and seed. Poor farmers called "sodbusters" did without even these basics, living in dugouts carved into hillsides and using muscle instead of machinery.

Midwestern Settlement before 1862

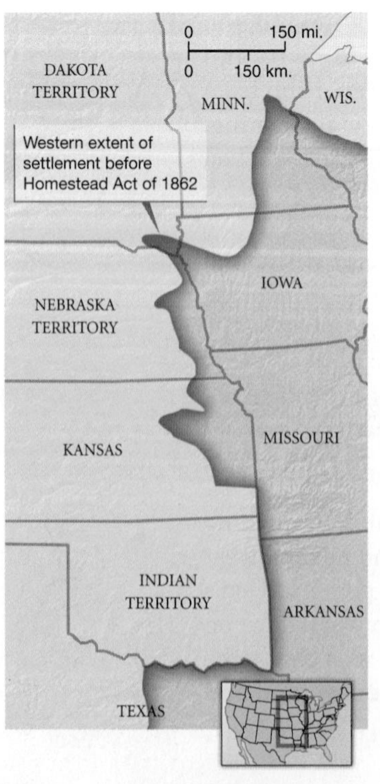

"Father made a dugout and covered it with willows and grass," one Kansas girl recounted. When it rained, the dugout flooded, and "we carried the water out in buckets, then waded around in the mud until it dried." Rain wasn't the only problem. "Sometimes the bull snakes would get in the roof and now and then one would lose his hold and fall down on the bed. . . . Mother would grab the hoe . . . and after the fight was over Mr. Bull Snake was dragged outside." The sod house, a step up from the dugout, had walls cut from blocks of sod and a roof of sod, lumber, or tin. (See "Documenting the American Promise," page 558.)

For women on the frontier, obtaining simple daily necessities such as water and fuel meant backbreaking labor. Out on the plains, where water was scarce, women often had to trudge to the nearest creek or spring. "A yoke was made to place across [Mother's] shoulders, so as to carry at each end a bucket of water," one daughter recollected, "and then water was brought a half mile from spring to house." Gathering fuel was another heavy chore. Without ready sources of coal or firewood, settlers on the plains turned to what substitutes they could scavenge — twigs, tufts of grass, corncobs, sunflower stalks. But by far the most prevalent fuel was "chips" — chunks of dried cattle and buffalo dung, found in abundance on the plains.

Despite the hardships, some homesteaders succeeded in building comfortable lives. The sod hut made way for a more substantial house; the log cabin yielded to a white clapboard home with a porch and a rocking chair. For others, the promise of the West failed to materialize. Already by the 1870s, much of the best land had been taken. Too often, homesteaders found that only the least desirable tracts were left — poor land, far from markets, transportation, and society. "There is plenty of land for sale in California," one migrant complained in 1870, but "the majority of the available lands are held by speculators, at prices far beyond the reach of a poor man." The railroads, flush from land grants provided by the state and federal governments, owned huge swaths of land in the West and actively recruited settlers. Altogether, the land grants totaled approximately 180 million acres — an area almost one-tenth the size of the United States (Map 17.3). Of the 2.5 million farms established between 1860 and 1900,

Railroad Locomotive
In the years following the Civil War, the locomotive replaced the covered wagon, enabling settlers to travel from Chicago or St. Louis to the West Coast in two days. By the 1890s, more than 72,000 miles of track stretched west of the Mississippi River. The first transcontinental railroad, completed in 1869, soon led to the creation of competing systems, so that by the 1880s travelers going west could choose from four railroad lines. In this photograph, men and women perched on a locomotive celebrate the completion of a section of track.
Library of Congress.

homesteading accounted for only one in five; the vast majority of farmland sold for a profit.

As land grew scarce on the prairie in the 1870s, farmers began to push farther west, moving into western Kansas, Nebraska, and eastern Colorado—the region called the **Great American Desert** by settlers who had passed over it on their way to California and Oregon. Many agricultural experts warned that the semiarid land (where less than twenty inches of rain fell annually) would not support a farm on the 160 acres allotted to homesteaders. But their words of caution were drowned out by the extravagant claims of western promoters, many employed by the railroads to sell off their land grants. "Rain follows the plow" became the slogan of western boosters, who insisted that cultivation would alter the climate of the region and bring more rainfall. Instead, drought followed the plow. Droughts were a cyclical fact of life on the Great Plains. Plowed up, the dry topsoil blew away in the wind. A period of relatively good rainfall in the early 1880s encouraged farming; then a protracted drought in the late 1880s and early 1890s sent starving farmers reeling back from the plains. Thousands left, some in wagons carrying the slogan "In God we trusted, in Kansas we busted."

Fever for fertile land set off a series of spectacular land runs in Oklahoma. When two million acres of land in former Indian Territory opened for settlement in 1889, thousands of homesteaders massed on the border. At the opening pistol shot, "with a shout and a yell the swift riders shot out, then followed the light buggies or wagons," a reporter wrote. "Above all, a great cloud of dust hover[ed] like smoke over a battlefield." By nightfall, Oklahoma boasted two tent cities with more than ten thousand residents. In the last frenzied land rush on Oklahoma's Cherokee strip in 1893, several settlers were killed in the stampede, and nervous men guarded their claims with rifles. As public land grew scarce, the hunger for land grew fiercer for both farmers and ranchers.

Ranchers and Cowboys

Cattle ranchers followed the railroads onto the plains, establishing a cattle kingdom from Texas to Wyoming between 1865 and 1885. Cowboys drove huge herds, as many as three thousand head of cattle that grazed on public lands as they followed cattle tracks like the Chisholm Trail from Texas to railheads in Kansas. More than 1.5 million Texas longhorns went to market before the range began to close in the 1880s.

Cattle Trails, 1860–1890

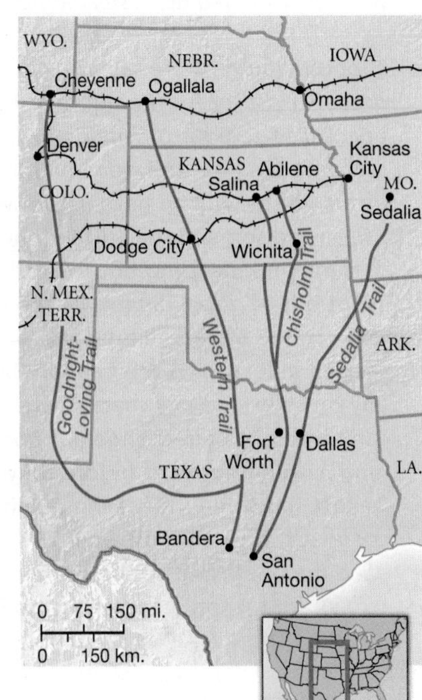

Barbed wire revolutionized the cattle business and sounded the death knell for the open range. In 1874, Joseph F. Glidden, an Illinois sheriff, invented and patented barbed wire. Gambler and promoter John "Bet a Million" Gates made his fortune by corralling a herd of Texas longhorns in downtown San Antonio, proving the merit of the flimsy-looking wire he went on to market profitably. As the largest ranches in Texas began to fence, nasty fights broke out between big ranchers and "fence cutters," who resented the end of the free

Young Women Homesteaders and the Promise of the West

"Young men! Poor men! Widows! Resolve to have a home of your own!" urged New York editor Horace Greeley. "If you are able to buy and pay for one in the East, very well; if not, make one in the broad and fertile West!" In his exhortation to go west, Greeley did not speak to men alone. Many women, and not just widows, heeded the call. The Homestead Act of 1862 allowed unmarried women and female heads of households to claim free land. Many did. The number of women establishing homesteads in the West ranged from 5 percent of homesteaders in the early settlements to more than 20 percent after 1900.

Among the women homesteaders were Clara and Mary Troska and their two cousins Helen and Christine Sonnek, who headed to North Dakota. "Mary, Helen, Christine and I packed our suitcases," Clara wrote. "I took my mandolin, Christine took hers and her rifle. . . . We were on our way to Minot." Young women like Clara between the ages of twenty-one and twenty-five constituted the largest percentage of women (53 percent) taking up claims in the Dakotas.

Like Christine Sonnek, who took her mandolin along with her rifle, homesteading women prepared to enjoy their new environment despite its challenges. Their letters, diaries, and reminiscences reveal not only the hardships they faced but also the sense of promise that lured them west. Adventurous, resourceful, and exuberant, many of these young homesteading women seemed to relish their experiences.

DOCUMENT 1
The Varied Activities of a Woman Homesteader

Dakota homesteader Bess Cobb's letter to a friend reveals the optimism and high spirits that energized the young women who filed homesteading claims.

Suppose you girls are saying "poor Bess" and feeling dreadfully sorry for me out here in the wild and wooly uncivilized regions of America. But really time just seems to fly. I haven't done half I had planned and I am afraid winter will be here before we are ready for it. I've sewed some, done a little fancy-work and lots of darning and mending but most of my time has been spent out of doors digging in the garden and riding. . . . You can see a team miles away — up one valley we can see ten miles, up to the Cannon Ball river — so when any one starts to our shack, if we see them in time we can comb our hair, change our gowns and get a good meal in running order before they arrive. You see Dakota has some redeeming qualities. Wish you could come out, but I suppose you think I am too far away. I have the neatest little shack I've ever seen and "my crops" are tip top. I know you would enjoy our camp life for a short time.

SOURCE: "Excerpts from a letter written by Bess Cobb, Guide to Manuscripts 1364, State Historical Society, North Dakota Heritage Center, Bismarck," from pages 140–41 in *Land in Her Own Name: Women as Homesteaders in North Dakota* by H. Elaine Lindgren. Copyright © 1996. Reprinted with permission of University of Oklahoma Press.

DOCUMENT 2
A Hard Winter

Lucy Goldthorpe, a young schoolteacher, came from Iowa to Dakota in 1905. Here she describes to a reporter her survival during the winter and contrasts her childhood fantasies with homestead reality.

There were many long, cold days and nights in my little homestead shack that winter! The walls were only single board thickness, covered with tar paper on the outside. I'd spent money sparingly, because I didn't have much, but I had worked hard all during summer and fall in an effort to winterize the structure. Following the pattern used by many of the settlers, I covered the interior walls with a blue building paper. Everything was covered, including the ceiling, and the floor. To help seal out the cold I'd added layers of gunny sacks over the paper on the floor and then the homemade wool rugs I'd shipped from home.

Regardless of what I did the cold crept in through the thin walls. With no storm entry at the door and only single windows my little two-lid laundry stove with oven attached to the pipe had a real struggle to keep the place livable. . . .

A neighbor family returning to their claim "from the outside" brought me fresh vegetables. They were such a prized addition to my meals that I put the bag in bed with me at night to keep them from freezing. Night after night I stored food and my little alarm clock in the stove pipe oven; that was the only way I could keep the clock running and be sure of a non-frozen breakfast.

Each day brought new, unexpected challenges and at times I wondered if I would be able to stay with it until the land was mine. Could any land be worth the lonely hours and hardships? The howling wind and driving snow, the mournful wail of coyotes searching the tormented land for food did nothing to make the winter any more pleasant. . . .

As a child I had enjoyed hearing my father tell of the hardships of the early days. They seemed so exciting to me as I listened in the warmth and security of our well built, fully winterized Iowa home. Like most youngsters I'd wished for the thrill of those other days. Little did I think that an opportunity for just that would come through homesteading alone, far out in the windswept, unsettled land. Believe me, it wasn't nearly as glamorous as the imagination would have it!

SOURCE: Roberta M. Starry, "Petticoat Pioneer." Excerpt from page 48 in *The West* 7, no. 5, October 1967. Copyright © 1967. Reprinted with permission.

DOCUMENT 3
Socializing and Entertainment

Homesteading wasn't all hard times. Young, single homesteaders found time for fun. Here Effie Vivian Smith describes a "shack party" during the winter of 1906 on her Dakota claim.

I never enjoyed myself better in my life than I have this winter. We go some place or some one is here from 1 to 4 times a week. A week ago last Fri. a load of 7 drove out to my claim. Cliff, Clara, David, and I had gone out the Wed. before and such a time as we had. My shack is 10 feet 3 inches by 16 feet and I have only 2 chairs and a long bench for seats, a table large enough for 6, a single bed, and only 3 knives so 2 of them ate with paring knives & 1 with the butcher knife. We had two of them sit on the bed and moved the table up to them. . . . We played all the games we could think of both quiet and noisy and once all but Clara went out & snowballed. They brought a bu[shel] of apples, & a lot of nuts, candy, & gum & we ate all night. . . .

We have just started a literary society in our neighborhood. Had our first debate last Fri. The question was Resolved that city life is better than country life. All the judges decided in the negative. . . . Tomorrow our crowd is going to a literary [society] 6 or 7 miles from here, and the next night to a dance at the home of one of our bachelor boys. We always all go in our sleigh. I am learning to dance this winter but don't attend any except the ones we get up ourselves and they are just as nice & just as respectable as the parties we used to have at Ruthven [Iowa]. I just love to dance. . . .

SOURCE: H. Elaine Lindgren, "Letter to her cousin, written on January 9, 1906." From pages 177–78 in *Land in Her Own Name: Women as Homesteaders in North Dakota*. Copyright © 1996 University of Oklahoma Press. Reprinted with permission.

DOCUMENT 4
Homesteading Pays Off

Homesteading proved rewarding for many women, not only economically but also because of the sense of accomplishment they experienced. Here Theona Carkin tells how the sale of her Dakota homestead helped finance her university degree.

Life in general was dotted with hardships but there were many good times also. I have always felt that my efforts on my homestead were very worthwhile and very rewarding, and I have always been proud of myself for doing it all.

By teaching off and on . . . and upon selling the homestead, I was able to pay all my own college expenses.

SOURCE: "99-Year-Old U Graduate Recalls Early Childhood." From page 5 in *Alumni Review*, June 1985. Published by the University of North Dakota, Grand Forks.

Questions for Analysis and Debate

1. What sorts of hardships did the young women homesteaders encounter in the Dakotas?
2. How did their youth affect how they reacted to hardship?
3. What did the young women find particularly appealing about their experiences as homesteaders?
4. What did they wish to convey about their experiences?
5. How did homesteading benefit women who chose not to remain on the land?

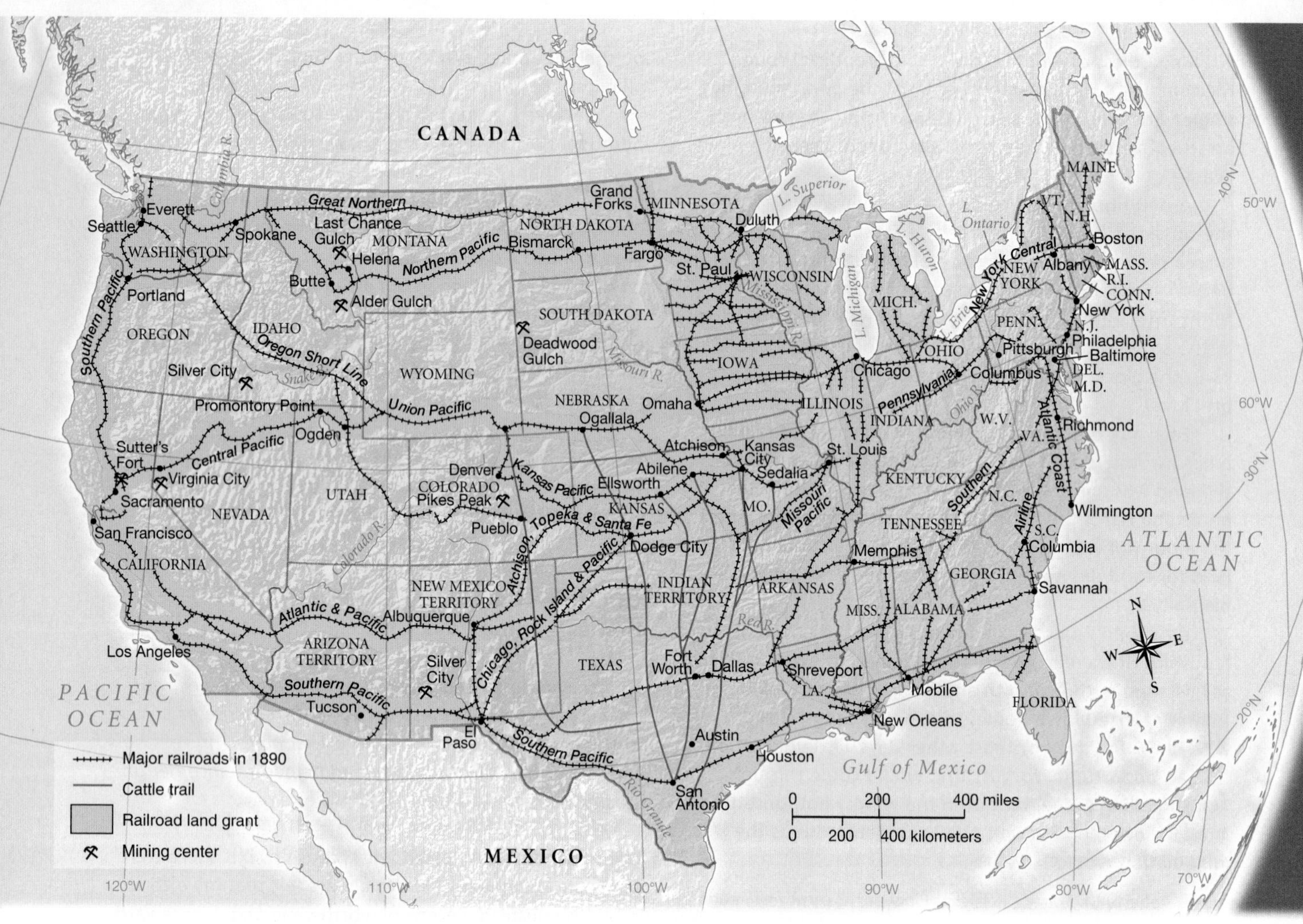

MAP ACTIVITY

Map 17.3 Federal Land Grants to Railroads and the Development of the West, 1850–1900
Generous federal land grants meant that railroads could sell the desirable land next to the track at a profit or hold it for speculation. Railroads received more than 180 million acres, an area as large as Texas. Built well ahead of demand, the western railroads courted settlers, often onto land not fit for farming.

READING THE MAP: Which mining cities and towns were located directly on a railroad line? Which towns were located at the junction of more than one line or railroad branch?

CONNECTIONS: In what ways did the growth of the railroads affect the population of the West? What western goods and products did the railroads help bring east and to ports for shipping around the world?

range. One old-timer observed, "Those persons, Mexicans and Americans, without land but who had cattle were put out of business by fencing."

Fencing forced small-time ranchers who owned land but could not afford to buy barbed wire or sink wells to sell out for the best price they could get. The displaced ranchers, many of them Mexicans, ended up as wageworkers on the huge spreads owned by Anglos or by European syndicates.

On the range, the cowboy gave way to the cattle king and, like the miner, became a wage laborer. Many cowboys were African Americans (as many as five thousand in Texas alone). Writers of western literature chose to ignore the presence of black cowboys like Deadwood Dick (Nat Love), who was portrayed as a white man in the dime novels of the era.

By 1886, cattle overcrowded the range. Severe blizzards during the winter of 1886–87 decimated the herds. "A whole generation of cowmen," wrote

THE PROMISE OF TECHNOLOGY

Barbed Wire

The original working model of Joseph Glidden's barbing machine, patented in 1874, consisted of an old-fashioned coffee mill with its casing cut away and its grinder altered to cut and coil small lengths of wire. The barbs were strung by hand between strands of plain wire. Despite its flimsiness, barbed wire could contain cattle, as master promoter John "Bet a Million" Gates demonstrated by corralling a herd of Texas longhorns in downtown San Antonio in 1879. How did barbed wire transform cattle ranching in the West? Ellwood House Museum, De Kalb, IL.

one chronicler, "went dead broke." Fencing worsened the situation. During blizzards, cattle stayed alive by keeping on the move. But when they ran up against barbed wire fences, they froze to death. In the aftermath of the "Great Die Up," new labor-intensive forms of cattle ranching replaced the open-range model.

Tenants, Sharecroppers, and Migrants

In the post–Civil War period, as agriculture became a big business tied by the railroads to national and global markets, an increasing number of laborers worked land that they would never own. In the southern United States, farmers labored under particularly heavy burdens. The Civil War wiped out much of the region's capital, which had been invested in slaves, and crippled the plantation economy. Newly freed slaves rarely obtained land of their own and often ended up as farm laborers. "The colored folks stayed with the old boss man and farmed and worked on the plantations," a black Alabama sharecropper observed bitterly. "They were still slaves, but they were free slaves." Some freedpeople did manage to pull together enough resources to go west. In 1879, more than fifteen thousand black **Exodusters** moved from Mississippi and Louisiana to take up land in Kansas.

California's Mexican cowboys, or *vaqueros*, commanded decent wages throughout the Southwest. Skilled horsemen, the vaqueros boasted that five of them could do the work of thirty Anglo cowboys. The vocabulary of ranching, with words such as *rodeo*, *lasso*, and *lariat*, testified to the centrality of the vaqueros' place in the cattle industry. But by 1880, as the coming of the railroads ended the long cattle drives and as large feedlots began to replace the open range, the value of their skills declined. Many vaqueros ended up as migrant laborers, often on land their families had once owned. Similarly, in Texas, Tejanos found themselves displaced. After the heyday of cattle ranching ended in the late 1880s, cotton production rose in the southeastern regions of the state. Ranchers turned their pastures into sharecroppers' plots and hired displaced cowboys, most of them Mexicans, as seasonal laborers for as little as seventy-five cents a day, thereby creating a growing army of agricultural wageworkers.

Land monopoly and large-scale farming fostered tenancy and migratory labor on the West Coast. By the 1870s, less than 1 percent of California's population owned half the state's available agricultural land. The rigid economics of large-scale commercial agriculture and the seasonal nature of the crops spawned a ragged army of migratory agricultural laborers. Derisively labeled "blanket men" or "bindle stiffs," these transients worked the fields in the growing season and wintered in the flophouses of San Francisco. Most farm laborers were Chinese immigrants. After passage of the Chinese Exclusion Act of 1882, Mexicans, Filipinos, and Japanese immigrants filled the demand for migratory workers.

A Vaquero
Rafael "Chappo" Remudas is pictured here in Burns, Oregon, around 1890. He came as a vaquero to the high desert in 1872 and became boss of the P Ranch, handing down his skills to a new generation of white "buckaroos," who replaced the vaqueros. Chappo proudly sits his horse, surrounded by the tools of his trade: his lasso wound tightly around his saddle horn, his kerchief tied at his neck, *tapederos* (covered stirrups to protect his feet), heavy leggings, a flat-crowned sombrero, and his silver-mounted bridle.
Photo courtesy of the Harney County Historical Society, Burns, OR.

Commercial Farming and Industrial Cowboys

In the late nineteenth century, the population of the United States remained overwhelmingly rural. The 1870 census showed that nearly 80 percent of the nation's people lived on farms and in villages of fewer than 8,000 inhabitants. By 1900, the figure had dropped to 66 percent (Figure 17.1). At the same time, the number of farms rose. Rapid growth in the West increased the number of the nation's farms from 2 million in 1860 to more than 5.7 million in 1900.

Despite the hardships individual farmers experienced, new technology and farming techniques revolutionized American farm life. Mechanized farm machinery halved the time and labor cost of production and made it possible to cultivate vast tracts of land. Meanwhile, urbanization provided farmers with expanding markets for their produce, and railroads carried crops to markets thousands of miles away. Even before the start of the twentieth century, American agriculture had entered the era of what would come to be called agribusiness — farming as a big business — with the advent of huge commercial farms.

As farming moved onto the prairies and plains, mechanization took command. Steel plows, reapers, mowers, harrows, seed drills, combines, and threshers replaced human muscle. Horse-drawn implements gave way to steam-powered machinery. By 1880, a single combine could do the work of twenty men, vastly increasing the acreage a farmer could cultivate. Mechanization spurred the growth of bonanza wheat farms, some more than 100,000 acres, in California and

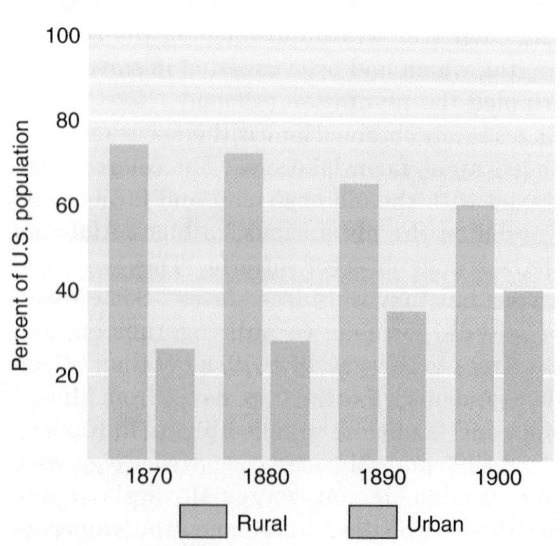

FIGURE 17.1 Changes in Rural and Urban Populations, 1870–1900
Between 1870 and 1900, both the number of urban dwellers and the number of farms increased, even as the number of rural inhabitants fell. Mechanization made it possible to farm with fewer hands, fueling the exodus from farm to city throughout the second half of the nineteenth century.

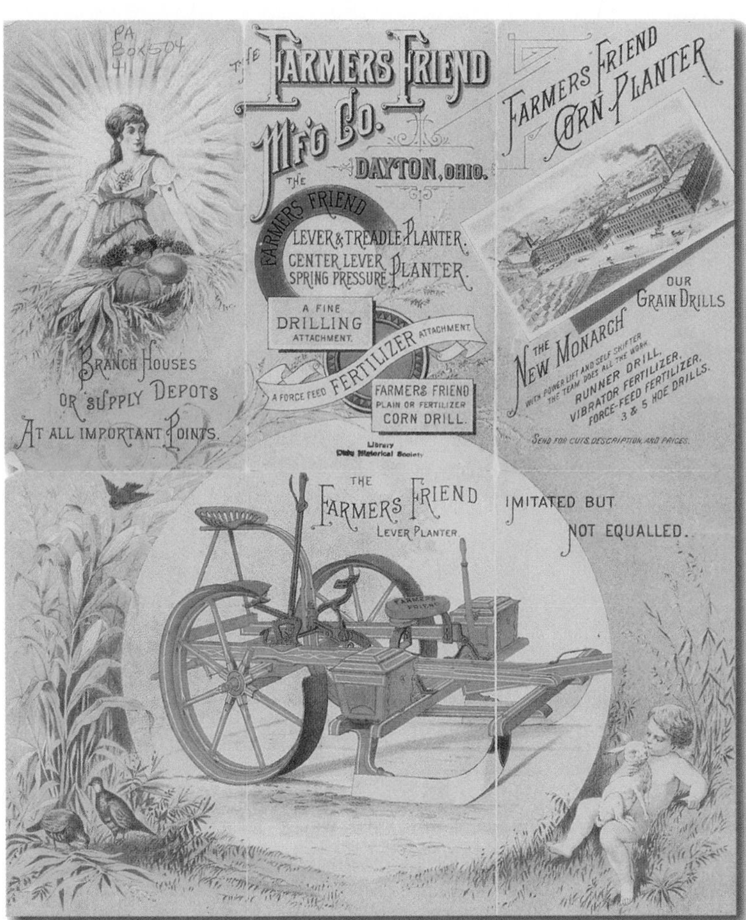

Mechanical Corn Planter
Mechanical planters came into use in the 1860s. The Farmers Friend Manufacturing Company of Dayton, Ohio, advertised its lever and treadle corn planter in the early 1880s. Although this planter, which featured attachments for grain drilling and fertilizing, appears to have been designed to be drawn by farm animals, steam-powered farm implements would soon replace animal power. Notice how the female figure on the left, symbolizing the bucolic farm life, is offset by the company's impressive factory in Dayton on the right.
Ohio Historical Society.

the Red River Valley of North Dakota and Minnesota. This agricultural revolution meant that Americans raised more than four times the corn, five times the hay, and seven times the wheat and oats they had before the Civil War.

Like cotton farmers in the South, western grain and livestock farmers increasingly depended on foreign markets for their livelihood. A fall in global market prices meant that a farmer's entire harvest went to pay off debts. In the depression that followed the panic of 1893, many heavily mortgaged farmers lost their land to creditors. As a Texas cotton farmer complained, "By the time the World Gets their Liveing out of the Farmer as we have to Feed the World, we the Farmer has nothing Left but a Bear Hard Liveing." Commercial farming, along with mining, represented another way in which the West developed its own brand of industrialism. The far West's industrial economy sprang initially from California gold and the vast territory that came under American control following the Mexican-American War. In the ensuing rush on land and resources, environmental factors interacted with economic and social forces to produce enterprises as vast in scale and scope as anything found in the East.

Two Alsatian immigrants, Henry Miller and Charles Lux, pioneered the West's mix of agriculture and industrialism. Beginning as meat wholesalers, Miller and Lux quickly expanded their business to encompass cattle, land, and land reclamation projects such as dams and irrigation systems. With a labor force of migrant workers, a highly coordinated corporate system, and large sums of investment capital, the firm of **Miller & Lux** became one of America's industrial behemoths. Eventually, these "industrial cowboys" grazed a herd of 100,000 cattle on 1.25 million acres of company land in California, Oregon, and Nevada and employed more than 1,200 migrant laborers on their corporate ranches. Miller & Lux dealt with the labor problem by offering free meals to migratory workers, thus keeping wages low while winning goodwill among an army of unemployed who competed for the work. When the company's Chinese cooks rebelled at washing the dishes resulting from the free meals, the migrant laborers were forced to eat

Loggers in Washington, 1890
Loggers pose on and beside one huge felled tree. The loggers worked in all-male crews with a "faller" cutting down the tree, "buckers" cutting it into manageable pieces, and "whistle punks" relaying information. By 1890, loggers using only axes and handsaws had harvested over one billion board feet of timber in the state of Washington alone. The massive deforestation continued and picked up speed as steam power replaced brawn and horse-power. Loggers lived a hard, dirty life in remote migratory camps, working long hours and sometimes wearing the same clothes for months on end. ©Bettmann/Corbis.

after the ranch hands and use their dirty plates. By the 1890s, more than eight hundred migrants a year followed what came to be known as the "Dirty Plate Route" on Miller & Lux ranches throughout California.

Since the days of Thomas Jefferson, agrarian life had been linked with the highest ideals of a democratic society. Now agrarianism itself had been transformed. The farmer was no longer a self-sufficient yeoman but often a businessman or a wage laborer tied to a global market. And even as farm production soared, industrialization outstripped it. More and more farmers left the fields for urban factories or found work in the "factories in the fields" of the new industrialized agribusiness. Now that the future seemed to lie not with the small farmer but with industrial enterprises, was democracy itself at risk? This question would ignite a farmers' revolt in the 1880s and dominate political debate in the 1890s.

REVIEW Why did many homesteaders find it difficult to acquire good land in the West?

▶ Conclusion: The West in the Gilded Age

In 1871, author Mark Twain published *Roughing It*, a chronicle of his days spent in mining towns in California and Nevada. There he found corrupt politics, vulgar display, and mania for speculation, the same cupidity he later skewered in *The Gilded Age* (1873), his biting satire of greed and corruption in the nation's capital. Far from being an antidote to the meretricious values of the East — an innocent idyll out of place and time — the American West, with its get-rich-quick ethos and its addiction to gambling and speculation, helped set the tone for the Gilded Age.

Twain's view countered that of Frederick Jackson Turner and perhaps better suited a West that witnessed the overbuilding of railroads, the consolidation of business in mining and ranching; the rise of commercial farming; corruption and a penchant for government handouts; racial animosity, whether in the form of Indian wars or Chinese exclusion; the exploitation of labor and natural resources, which led to the decimation of the great bison herds, the pollution of rivers with mining wastes, and the overgrazing of the plains; and the beginnings of an imperial policy that would provide a template for U.S. adventures abroad. Turner, intent on promoting what was unique about the frontier, failed to note that the same issues that came to dominate debate east of the Mississippi — the growing power of big business, the exploitation of land and labor, corruption in politics, and ethnic and racial tensions exacerbated by colonial expansion and unparalleled immigration — took center stage in the West at the end of the nineteenth century.

▶ Selected Bibliography

General

Najia Aarin-Heriot, *Chinese Immigrants, African Americans, and Racial Anxiety in the United States, 1848–1882* (2003).
Robert V. Hine and John Mack Faragher, *The American West: A New Interpretive History* (2000).
Patricia Nelson Limerick, *Something in the Soil: Legacies and Reckonings in the New West* (2000).
Valerie Matsumoto and Blake Allmendinger, eds., *Over the Edge: Remapping the American West* (1999).
Louis S. Warren, *Buffalo Bill's America: William Cody and the Wild West Show* (2005).
Richard White, *"It's Your Misfortune and None of My Own": A New History of the American West* (1991).
Richard White, *Railroaded: The Transcontinentals and the Making of Modern America* (2011).
David M. Wrobel, *Promised Lands: Promotion, Memory, and the Creation of the American West* (2002).

Indians

David Wallace Adams, *Education for Extinction: American Indians and the Boarding School Experience, 1875–1928* (1995).
Gary Clayton Anderson, *The Conquest of Texas: Ethnic Cleansing in the Promised Land, 1820–1875* (2005).
Stuart Banner, *How the Indians Lost Their Land: Law and Power on the Frontier* (2005).
Ned Blackhawk, *Violence over the Land: Indian Empires in the Early American West* (2006).
Colin Calloway, *First Peoples: A Documentary Survey of American Indian History* (3rd ed., 2008).
James O. Gump, *The Dust Rose like Smoke: The Subjugation of the Zulu and the Sioux* (1994).
Pekka Hamalainen, *The Comanche Empire* (2008).
Andrew C. Isenberg, *The Destruction of the Bison: An Environmental History, 1730–1920* (2000).
Edward Lazarus, *Black Hills, White Justice: The Sioux Nation versus the United States, 1775 to the Present* (1991).
Jeffrey Ostler, *The Plains Sioux and U.S. Colonialism from Lewis and Clark to Wounded Knee* (2004).
Nathaniel Philbrick, *The Last Stand: Custer, Sitting Bull, and the Battle of the Little Bighorn* (2010).
Francis Paul Prucha, *The Great Father: The United States Government and the American Indian* (1986).
Charles M. Robinson III, *A Good Year to Die: The Story of the Great Sioux War* (1995).
Alan Trachtenberg, *Shades of Hiawatha: Staging Indians, Making Americans, 1880–1930* (2004).

Mining, Ranching, and Farming

Suchen Chan, *This Bittersweet Soil: The Chinese in American Agriculture, 1860–1919* (1986).
Suchen Chan, Douglas Henry Daniels, Mario T. Garcia, and Terry P. Wilson, *Peoples of Color in the American West* (1994).
Roger Daniels, *Asian American: Chinese and Japanese in the United States since 1850* (1997).
Deborah Fitzgerald, *Every Farm a Factory: The Industrial Ideal in American Agriculture* (2003).
Manuel G. Gonzales, *Mexicanos: A History of Mexicans in the United States* (1999).
J. S. Holliday, *Rush for Riches: Gold Fever and the Making of California* (1999).
David Igler, *Industrial Cowboys: Miller & Lux and the Transformation of the Far West, 1850–1920* (2001).
Andrew C. Isenberg, *Mining California: An Ecological History* (2005).
Ronald M. James, *The Roar and the Silence: The History of Virginia City and the Comstock Lode* (1998).
William Loren Katz, *Black West: A Documentary and Pictorial History of the African American Role in the Westward Expansion of the United States* (2005).
Karen R. Merrill, *Public Lands and Political Meaning: Ranchers, the Government, and the Property between Them* (2002).
Rodman Wilson Paul, *Mining Frontiers of the Far West, 1848–1880* (rev. ed., 2001).
William G. Robbins, *Colony and Empire: The Capitalist Transformation of the American West* (1994).
Steven Stoll, *Larding the Lean Earth: Soil and Society in Nineteenth-Century America* (2002).

For more books about topics in this chapter, see the Online Bibliography at **bedfordstmartins.com/roark.**

For additional primary sources from this period, see Michael Johnson, ed., *Reading the American Past,* Fifth Edition.

For Web sites, images, and documents related to topics and places in this chapter, visit Make History at **bedfordstmartins.com/roark.**

Reviewing Chapter 17

KEY TERMS

Explain each term's significance.

Conquest and Empire in the West
- Frederick Jackson Turner (p. 537)
- Indian removal (p. 537)
- reservations (p. 537)
- Treaty of Fort Laramie (1851) (p. 537)
- Sitting Bull (p. 540)
- Comanchería (p. 541)
- Treaty of Fort Laramie (1868) (p. 541)
- Black Hills (p. 541)
- Crazy Horse (p. 542)
- George Armstrong Custer (p. 542)
- George Crook (p. 543)
- Battle of the Little Big Horn (p. 543)

Forced Assimilation and Resistance Strategies
- Carlisle Indian School (p. 545)
- Dawes Allotment Act (p. 546)
- Chief Joseph (p. 546)
- Geronimo (p. 547)
- Lozen (p. 547)
- Nelson Miles (p. 547)
- Ghost Dance (p. 548)
- Wounded Knee (p. 549)

Gold Fever and the Mining West
- Comstock Lode (p. 549)
- buffalo soldiers (p. 552)
- Chinese Exclusion Act (p. 553)

Land Fever
- Homestead Act of 1862 (p. 555)
- transcontinental railroad (p. 555)
- Great American Desert (p. 557)
- Exodusters (p. 561)
- Miller & Lux (p. 563)

REVIEW QUESTIONS

Use key terms and dates to support your answer.

1. How did the slaughter of the bison contribute to the Plains Indians' removal to reservations? (pp. 537–544)
2. In what ways did different Indian groups defy and resist colonial rule? (pp. 544–559)
3. How did industrial technology change mining in Nevada? (pp. 549–555)
4. Why did many homesteaders find it difficult to acquire good land in the West? (pp. 555–564)

MAKING CONNECTIONS

Draw on key terms, the timeline, and review questions.

1. Westward migration brought settlers into conflict with Native Americans. What was the U.S. government's policy toward Indians in the West, and how did it evolve over time? How did the Indians resist and survive white encroachment? In your answer, discuss the cultural and military features of the conflict.
2. The economic and industrial developments characteristic of the East after the Civil War also made their mark on the West. How did innovations in business and technology transform mining and agriculture in the West? In your answer, be sure to consider effects on production and the consequences for the lives of miners and agricultural laborers.
3. Settlers from all over the world came to the American West seeking their fortunes but found that opportunity was not equally available to all. In competition for work and land, why did Anglo-American settlers usually have the upper hand? How did legal developments contribute to this circumstance?
4. Railroads had a profound impact on the development of the western United States. What role did railroads play in western settlement, industrialization, and agriculture? How did railroads affect Indian populations in the West?

LINKING TO THE PAST

Link events in this chapter to earlier events.

1. In what ways were the goals of migrants to the West similar to those of the northerners who moved to the South after the Civil War? How did they differ? (See chapter 16.)
2. How did the racism of the West compare with the racist attitudes against African Americans in the Reconstruction South? (See chapter 16.)

▶ FOR PRACTICE QUIZZES AND OTHER STUDY TOOLS, visit the Online Study Guide at **bedfordstmartins.com/roark**.

TIMELINE 1851–1900

1851	• First Treaty of Fort Laramie.
1862	• Homestead Act. • Great Sioux Uprising (Santee Uprising).
1864	• Sand Creek massacre.
1867	• Treaty of Medicine Lodge.
1868	• Second Treaty of Fort Laramie.
1869	• First transcontinental railroad completed.
1870	• Hunters begin to decimate bison herds.
1873	• "Big Bonanza" discovered on Comstock Lode.
1874	• Discovery of gold in Black Hills.
1876	• Battle of the Little Big Horn.
1877	• Chief Joseph surrenders. • Crazy Horse arrested and killed.
1878	• Indian students enroll at Hampton Institute in Virginia.
1879	• Carlisle Indian School opens in Pennsylvania. • More than fifteen thousand Exodusters move to Kansas.
1881	• Sitting Bull surrenders.
1882	• Chinese Exclusion Act. • Indian Rights Association formed.
1886	• Geronimo surrenders.
1886–1888	• Severe blizzards decimate cattle herds.
1887	• Dawes Allotment Act.
1889	• Rise of Ghost Dance. • Two million acres in Oklahoma opened for settlement.
1890	• Sitting Bull killed. • Massacre at Wounded Knee, South Dakota.
1893	• Last land rush takes place in Oklahoma Territory. • Frederick Jackson Turner presents "frontier thesis."
1900	• Census finds 66 percent of population lives in rural areas, compared to 80 percent in 1870.

CAMPAIGN PINS

These gilt campaign pins depicting James G. Blaine thumbing his nose at rival Grover Cleveland proved ironic—the Democrat Cleveland won the presidency in 1884 by campaigning for honest government. Public concern about the lucrative partnership of government and business made Thomas Kepler's 1889 cartoon, "The Bosses of the Senate," a defining symbol of the Gilded Age. The trusts are caricatured as bloated moneybags who dominate the Senate chambers. The motto "This is a Senate of the Monopolists, by the Monopolists, and for the Monopolists" hangs prominently on the wall.

Pins: Collection of Janice L. and David J. Frent; background: Library of Congress.

18 Business and Politics in the Gilded Age 1865–1900

ONE NIGHT OVER DINNER, AUTHORS MARK TWAIN AND CHARLES Dudley Warner teased their wives about the sentimental novels they read. When the two women challenged them to write something better, they set to work. Warner supplied the melodrama, while Twain "hurled in the facts." The result was a runaway best seller, a savage satire of the "get-rich-quick" era that would forever carry the book's title, *The Gilded Age* (1873).

Twain left no one unscathed in the novel — political hacks, Washington lobbyists, Wall Street financiers, small-town boosters, and the "great putty-hearted public" that tolerated the plunder. Underneath the glitter of the Gilded Age lurked vulgarity, crass materialism, and political corruption. Twain had witnessed the crooked partnership of business and politics in the administration of Ulysses S. Grant. Here he describes how a lobbyist finagled to get a bill through Congress:

> Why the matter is simple enough. A Congressional appropriation costs money. . . . A majority of the House Committee, say $10,000 apiece — $40,000; a majority of the Senate Committee, the same each — say $40,000; a little extra to one or two chairmen of one or two such committees, say $10,000 each — $20,000; and there's $100,000 of the money gone, to begin with. Then, seven male lobbyists, at $3,000 each — $21,000; one female lobbyist, $3,000; a high moral Congressman or Senator here and there — the high moral ones cost more, because they give tone to a measure — say ten of these at $3,000 each, is $30,000; then a lot of small fry country members who won't vote for anything whatever without pay — say twenty at $500 apiece, is $10,000 altogether; lot of jimcracks for Congressmen's wives and children — those go a long way — you can't spend too much money in that line — well, those things cost in a lump, say $10,000 — along there somewhere; — and then comes your printed documents. . . . [W]ell, never mind the details, the total in clean numbers foots up $118,254.42 thus far!

In Twain's satire, Congress is for sale to the highest bidder. The corrupt interplay of business and politics raised serious questions about the health of American democracy.

The Gilded Age seemed to tarnish all who touched it. No one would learn that better than Twain, who, even as he attacked it as an "era of incredible rottenness," fell prey to its enticements. Born Samuel Langhorne Clemens, he grew up in a rough Mississippi River town, where he became a

Mark Twain and *The Gilded Age*
Popular author Mark Twain (Samuel Langhorne Clemens) wrote acerbically about the excesses of the Gilded Age in his novel of that name written with Charles Dudley Warner and published in 1873. No one knew the meretricious lure of the era better than Twain, who succumbed to a get-rich-quick scheme that led him to the brink of bankruptcy. Photo: Beinecke Rare Book and Manuscript Library, Yale University; book: Newberry Library.

riverboat pilot. Taking the pen name Mark Twain, he gained fame chronicling western mining booms. In 1866, he came east to launch a career as an author, public speaker, and itinerant humorist. Twain played to packed houses, but his work was judged too vulgar for the genteel tastes of the time because he wrote about common people using common language. His masterpiece, *The Adventures of Huckleberry Finn*, was banned in Boston when it appeared in 1884.

Huck Finn's creator eventually stormed the citadels of polite society, hobnobbing with the wealthy and living in increasingly lavish style. Succumbing to the money fever of his age, Twain plunged into a scheme in the hope of making millions. By the 1890s, he faced bankruptcy and began a dogged climb out of debt.

Twain's tale was common in an age when the promise of wealth led as many to ruin as to riches. In the Gilded Age, fortunes were made and lost with dizzying frequency. Those who pursued riches, whether in the mines of the West or in the stock market, found many rocks in their path. Wall Street panics in 1873 and 1893 periodically interrupted the boom times and plunged the country into economic depression. But with railroad overbuilding and industry expanding on every level, the mood of the country remained buoyant.

The rise of industrialism in the United States and the interplay of business and politics strike the key themes in the Gilded Age. From 1870 to 1890, the transition from a rural, agricultural economy to urban industrialism, global in its reach, transformed American society. The growth of old industries and the creation of new ones, along with the rise of big business, signaled the coming of age of industrial capitalism. Economic issues increasingly shaped party politics, although old divisions engendered by sectionalism and slavery by no means disappeared. Meanwhile, new concerns over lynchings, temperance, and suffrage propelled women into more active roles in society.

Perhaps nowhere were the hopes and fears that industrialism inspired more evident than in the public's attitude toward the business moguls of the day. Men like Andrew Carnegie, John D. Rockefeller, and J. P. Morgan sparked the popular imagination as the heroes and villains in the high drama of industrialization. And as concern grew over the power of big business and the growing chasm between rich and poor, many Americans looked to the government for solutions.

▶ Old Industries Transformed, New Industries Born

In the years following the Civil War, the American economy underwent a transformation. Where once wealth had been measured in tangible assets — property, livestock, buildings — the economy now ran on money and the new devices of business — paper currency, securities, and anonymous corporate entities. Wall Street, the heart of the country's financial system, increasingly affected Main Street. The scale and scope of American industry expanded dramatically. Old industries like iron transformed into modern industries typified by the behemoth U.S. Steel. Discovery and invention stimulated new industries, from oil refining to electric light and power. The expansion of the nation's rail system in the decades after the Civil War played the key role in the transformation of the American economy.

Jay Gould, Andrew Carnegie, John D. Rockefeller, and other business leaders pioneered new strategies to seize markets and consolidate power in the rising railroad, steel, and oil industries. Always with an eye to the main chance, these business tycoons set the tone in the get-rich-quick era of freewheeling capitalism that came to be called the **Gilded Age**.

Railroads: America's First Big Business

The military conquest of America's inland empire and the dispossession of Native Americans (see chapter 17) relied on an elaborate new railroad system, which allowed businesses to expand on a nationwide scale. The first transcontinental railroad, completed in 1869, linked new markets in the West to the nation's eastern and midwestern farms and cities. Between 1870 and 1880, overbuilding doubled the amount of track in the country and it nearly doubled again in the following decade. By 1900, the nation boasted more than 193,000 miles of railroad track — more than in all of Europe and Russia combined (Map 18.1). The railroads had become America's first big business. Privately owned but publicly financed by enormous land grants from the federal government and the states, the railroads epitomized the insidious nexus of business and politics in the Gilded Age.

To understand how the railroads came to dominate American life, there is no better place to start than with the career of **Jay Gould**, who pioneered the expansion of America's railway system and became the era's most notorious speculator. Jason "Jay" Gould bought his first railroad before he turned twenty-five. It was only sixty-two miles long, in bad repair, and on the brink of failure, but within two years he sold it at a profit of $130,000.

Gould, by his own admission, knew little about railroads and cared less about their operation. The secretive Gould operated in the stock market like a shark, looking for vulnerable railroads, buying enough stock to take control, and threatening to undercut his competitors until they bought him out at a high profit. The railroads that fell into his hands fared badly and often went bankrupt. Gould's genius lay not in providing transportation, but in cleverly buying and selling railroad stock on Wall Street, the nerve center of the new economy.

"The most hated man in America."
— Railroad tycoon JAY GOULD, speaking of himself

Jay Gould as a Spider
In this 1885 political cartoon titled "Justice in the Web," artist Fredrick Burr Opper portrays Jay Gould as a hideous spider whose web, formed by Western Union telegraph lines, has entrapped "justice" through its monopoly of the telegraph industry. The telegraph, by transmitting coded messages across electric wire, formed the nervous system of the new industrial order. Gould, who controlled Western Union as well as the Erie and the Union Pacific Railroads, made his fortune by stock speculation. Images like this one fueled the public's distaste for Gould and made him, in his own words, "the most hated man in America." Granger Collection.

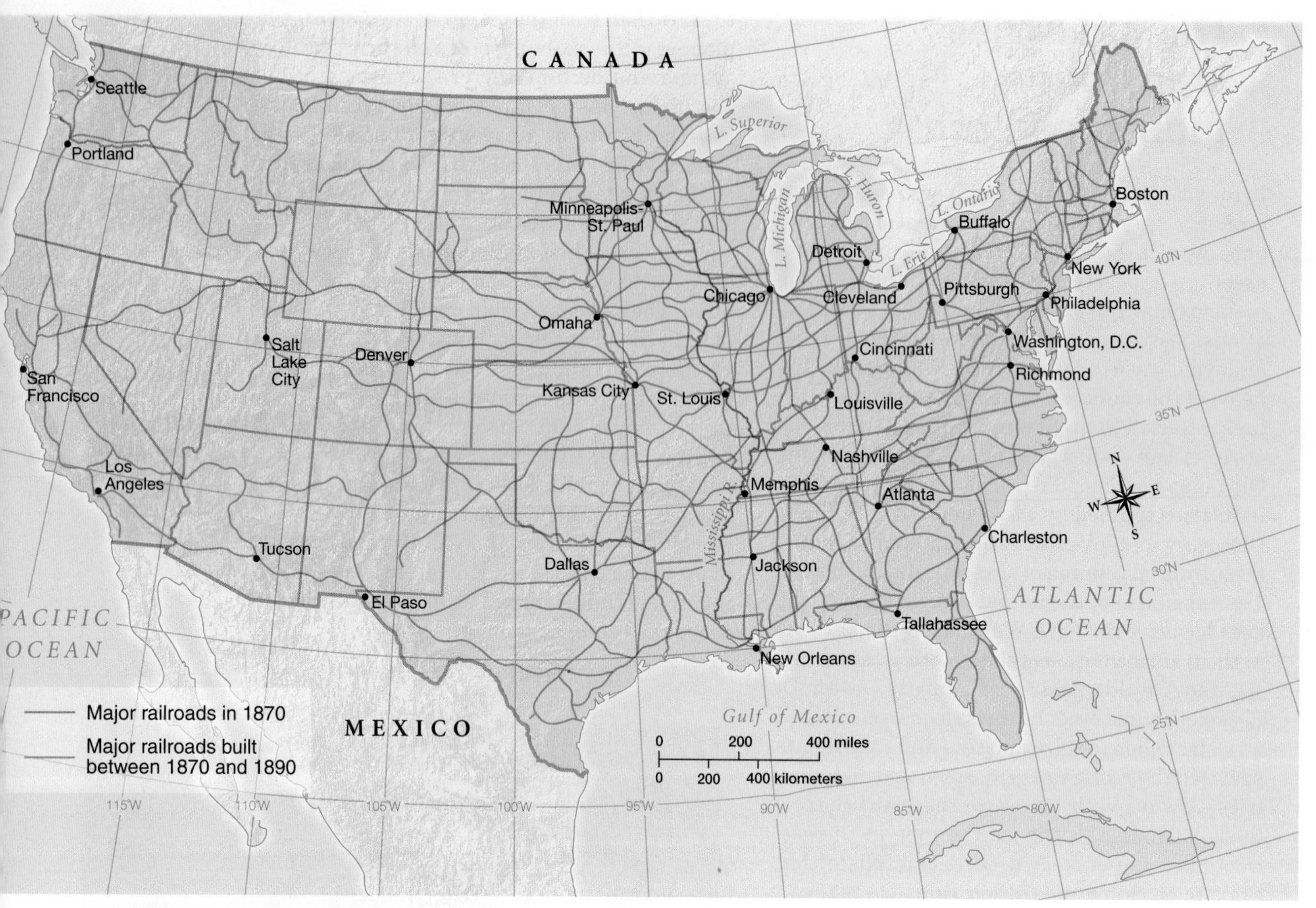

MAP ACTIVITY

MAP 18.1 Railroad Expansion, 1870–1890

Railroad mileage nearly quadrupled between 1870 and 1890, with the greatest growth occurring in the trans-Mississippi West. The western railroads — the Great Northern, Northern Pacific, Southern Pacific, and Atlantic and Pacific — were completed in the 1880s. Fueled by speculation and built ahead of demand, the western railroads made fortunes for individual speculators. But they rarely paid for themselves and often left disaster in their wake. At the same time, they fed a culture of insider dealing and political corruption.

READING THE MAP: Where were most of the railroad lines located in 1870? By 1890, how many railroads reached the west coast? What was the end point of the only western route?

CONNECTIONS: Why were so many rails laid between 1870 and 1890? How did the railroads affect the nation's economy?

The New York Stock Exchange, dating back to 1792, expanded as the volume of stock increased sixfold between 1869 and 1901. Where on one sleepy day in 1830 only thirty-one stocks traded, by 1886 more than a million shares a day changed hands. As the scale and complexity of the financial system increased, the line between investment and speculation blurred, causing many Americans to question if the concern with paper profits fueled the boom and bust cycles that led to panic and depression, putting hardworking Americans out of jobs. Yet however crass their motives, millionaire speculators like Jay Gould built America's rail system. In the 1880s, Gould moved to put together a second transcontinental railroad. His competitors had little choice but to adopt his strategy of expansion and consolidation, which in turn encouraged overbuilding and stimulated a national market.

The dramatic growth of the railroads created the country's first big business. Before the Civil War, even the largest textile mill in New England employed no more than 800 workers. By contrast, the Pennsylvania Railroad by the 1870s boasted a payroll of more than 55,000 workers. Capitalized at more than $400 million, the Pennsylvania Railroad constituted the largest private enterprise in the world.

The big business of railroads bestowed enormous riches on a handful of tycoons. Both Gould and his competitor "Commodore" Cornelius Vanderbilt amassed fortunes estimated at $100 million. Such staggering wealth eclipsed that of upper-class Americans from previous generations and left a legacy of lavish spending for an elite crop of ultrarich heirs. (See "Visualizing History," page 574.)

The Republican Party, firmly entrenched in Washington, worked closely with business interests, subsidizing the transcontinental railroad system with land grants of a staggering 100 million acres of public land and $64 million in tax incentives and direct aid. States and local communities joined the railroad boom, knowing that only those towns and villages along the tracks would grow and flourish. The combined federal and state land giveaway amounted to more than 180 million acres, an area larger than Texas.

A revolution in communication accompanied and supported the growth of the railroads. The telegraph, developed by Samuel F. B. Morse, marched across the continent alongside the railroad. By transmitting coded messages along electrical wire, the telegraph formed the "nervous system" of the new industrial order. Telegraph service quickly replaced Pony Express mail carriers in the West and transformed business by providing instantaneous communication. Again Jay Gould took the lead. In 1879, through stock manipulation, he seized control of Western Union, the company that monopolized the telegraph industry. By the end of the century, the telegraph carried 63 million messages a year and made it possible to move money around the world. Financiers in London and New York could follow the markets on ticker tape and transfer funds by wire.

The railroads soon fell on hard times. Already by the 1870s, lack of planning led to overbuilding. Across the nation, railroads competed fiercely for business. A manufacturer in an area served by competing railroads could get substantially reduced shipping rates in return for promises of steady business. Because railroad owners lost money through this kind of competition, they tried to set up agreements, or "pools," to end cutthroat competition by dividing up territory and setting rates. But these informal gentlemen's agreements invariably failed because men like Jay Gould, intent on undercutting all competitors, refused to play by the rules.

Novelist Charles Dudley Warner described how the rail speculators operated:

> [They fasten upon] some railway that is prosperous, pays dividends, pays a liberal interest on its bonds, and has a surplus. They contrive to buy, no matter at what the cost, a controlling interest in it. . . . Then they absorb its surplus; let it run down so that it pays no dividends and by-and-by cannot even pay its interest; then they squeeze the bondholders, who may be glad to accept anything that is offered out of the wreck, and perhaps then they throw the property into the hands of a receiver, or consolidate it with some other road at a value enormously greater than it cost them in stealing it. Having in one way or another sucked it dry, they look around for another road.

The public's alarm at the control wielded by the new railroad magnates and the tactics they employed provided a barometer of attitudes toward big business itself. When Gould died in 1892, the press described him as "the world's richest man." Rival Cornelius Vanderbilt judged Gould "the smartest man in America." But to the public, he was, as he himself admitted shortly before his death, "the most hated man in America."

Andrew Carnegie, Steel, and Vertical Integration

If Jay Gould was the man Americans loved to hate, **Andrew Carnegie** became one of America's heroes. Unlike Gould, for whom speculation was the game and wealth the goal, Carnegie turned his back on speculation and worked to build something enduring — Carnegie Steel, the biggest steel business in the world during the Gilded Age.

The growth of the steel industry proceeded directly from railroad building. The first railroads ran on iron rails, which cracked and broke with alarming frequency. Steel, both stronger and more flexible than iron, remained too expensive for use in rails until Englishman Henry Bessemer developed a way to make steel more cheaply from pig iron. Andrew Carnegie, among the first to champion the new "King Steel," came to dominate the emerging industry.

VISUALIZING HISTORY

The Vanderbilts and the Gilded Age

Nothing represented the Gilded Age better than the Gold Room of Marble House, the "cottage" Alva Vanderbilt opened in Newport, Rhode Island, in 1892. William K. Vanderbilt, Alva's husband, was the grandson of Cornelius Vanderbilt, the founder of the New York Central Railway and the richest man of his era. His sons doubled his wealth, and his grandsons spent it lavishly. Alva, who enjoyed building houses, judged Marble House her triumph and liked to describe it as "Versailles improved." Modeled after Marie Antoinette's château, the Petit Trianon, on the grounds of Versailles, the mansion suited Alva's ambition to bring French culture to America. Designed by Richard Morris Hunt, the architect of the plutocracy, Marble House replicated the glory of the seventeenth-century French royal palaces Alva had admired when she visited France in her youth. Why might Alva have chosen to model her Newport home after a French queen's château?

The Gold Room, Alva's miniature version of Versailles's Hall of Mirrors, is a riot of neoclassical exuberance, with panels of Greek gods and goddesses adorning the walls. Above the striated black-and-white marble mantelpiece, bronze figures bear a vast candelabra, while cupids cavort and cherubs blow

Marble House: The Vanderbilt Mansion in Newport, Rhode Island

The Gold Room in Marble House

Carnegie, a Scottish immigrant, landed in New York in 1848 at the age of twelve. He rose from a job cleaning bobbins in a textile factory to become one of the richest men in America. Before he died, he gave away more than $300 million, most notably to public libraries. His generosity, combined with his own rise from poverty, burnished his public image.

When Carnegie was a teenager, his skill as a telegraph operator caught the attention of Tom Scott, superintendent of the Pennsylvania Railroad. Scott hired Carnegie, soon promoted him, and lent him the money for his first foray into Wall Street investment. As a result of this crony capitalism, Carnegie became a millionaire before his thirtieth birthday. At that point, Carnegie turned trumpets on the walls and ceilings. Why do you think the Vanderbilts chose classical figures for their decoration? The enormous chandeliers and wood panels painted in red, green, and gold are multiplied in their dazzling magnificence by vast mirrors hung over the four doors, above the mantelpiece, and on the south wall. Critics charged that Marble House, with its Gold Room, was "a symbol of the heartless, glittering emptiness of the Gilded Age." What did they mean by this criticism?

The Vanderbilts' wealth and their lavish spending made it hard for old-money New Yorkers, living in their staid brownstones, to compete. Alva and William's Fifth Avenue mansion in New York City had a ballroom that could accommodate 1,600 guests. At their legendary costume ball in 1883, the Vanderbilts released live doves to astound their guests.

Alva Vanderbilt Releasing the Doves

Alva Vanderbilt, pictured right at her famous costume ball dressed as a Venetian princess, flouted convention by divorcing William in 1895. Her indomitable will, her quest for recognition, and her fearless defiance of convention led her to the women's rights cause. She would become a principal supporter of the National Woman's Party and serve as its president.

In 1909, Alva organized two highly successful suffrage meetings at Marble House and prevailed upon her old friends to give to the cause. Many bought tickets to the meetings just to have the opportunity to tour the mansion. Crowds of more than five hundred thronged the grounds. In 1932, shortly before she died, Alva sold Marble House with the assurance that it would be kept as she had designed it. In the 1960s, the Preservation Society of Newport County took over the house, and today it is a National Historic Landmark open to the public. Alva Vanderbilt no doubt felt a deep pride in her creation, once describing it as "like a fourth child," and she had no trouble opening it to raise funds for the suffragist cause. How might she feel about paying visitors wandering the rooms of Marble House today?

SOURCE: Marble House: © Dave G. Houser/Corbis; Gold Room: © Kelly-Mooney Photography/Corbis; Alva Vanderbilt: photo courtesy of The Preservation Society of Newport County.

away from speculation and struck out on his own to reshape the iron and steel industry. "My preference was always manufacturing," he wrote. "I wished to make something tangible." By applying the lessons of cost accounting and efficiency that he had learned from twelve years with the Pennsylvania Railroad, Carnegie turned steel into the nation's first manufacturing big business.

In 1872, Andrew Carnegie acquired one hundred acres in Braddock, Pennsylvania, on the outskirts of Pittsburgh, convenient to two railroad lines and fronted by the Monongahela River, a natural highway to Pittsburgh and the Ohio River and to the coal and iron mines farther north. There Carnegie built the largest, most up-to-date Bessemer steel plant in the world. At

Andrew Carnegie in 1894
"The man who dies rich . . . dies disgraced," asserted Andrew Carnegie. A classic rags-to-riches hero, Carnegie gave away more than $300 million before he died in 1919. Public libraries were among his favorite philanthropies; he contributed to the building of more than 2,500. But Carnegie was not so benign to his workers, whom he drove mercilessly, demanding a twelve-hour day, six days a week.
©Bettmann/Corbis.

that time, steelmakers produced about 70 tons a week. Within two decades, Carnegie's blast furnaces poured out an incredible 10,000 tons a week. He soon cut the cost of making rails by more than half, from $58 to $25 a ton. His formula for success was simple: "Cut the prices, scoop the market, run the mills full; watch the costs and profits will take care of themselves."

To guarantee the lowest costs and the maximum output, Carnegie pioneered a system of business organization called **vertical integration**. All aspects of the business were under Carnegie's control — from the mining of iron ore, to its transport on the Great Lakes, to the production of steel. Vertical integration, in the words of one observer, meant that "from the moment these crude stuffs were dug out of the earth until they flowed in a stream of liquid steel in the ladles, there was never a price, profit, or royalty paid to any outsider."

Always Carnegie kept his eyes on the account books, looking for ways to cut costs. The great productivity Carnegie encouraged came at a high price. He deliberately pitted his managers against one another, firing the losers and rewarding the winners with a share in the company. Workers achieved the output Carnegie demanded by enduring low wages, dangerous working conditions, and twelve-hour days six days a week. One worker, commenting on the contradiction between Carnegie's generous philanthropy in endowing public libraries and his tightfisted labor policy, observed, "After working twelve hours, how can a man go to a library?"

By 1900, Andrew Carnegie had become the best-known manufacturer in the nation, and

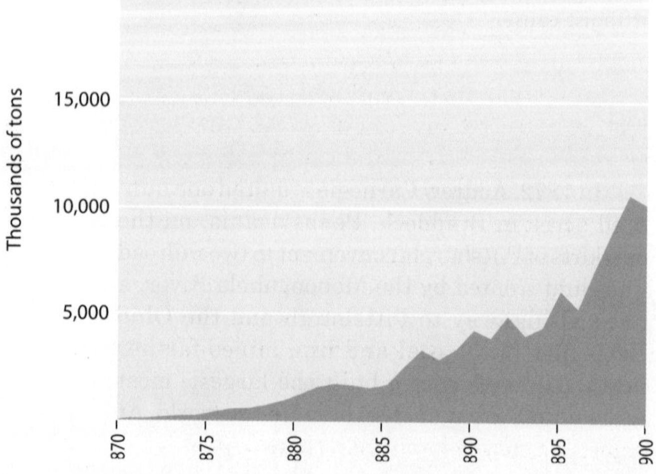

FIGURE 18.1 Iron and Steel Production, 1870–1900
Iron and steel production in the United States grew from nearly none in 1870 to 10 million tons a year by 1900. The secrets to the great increase in steel production were the use of the Bessemer process and vertical integration, pioneered by Andrew Carnegie. By 1900, Carnegie's mills alone produced more steel than all of Great Britain. With corporate consolidation after 1900, the rate of growth in steel proved even more spectacular.

the age of iron had yielded to an age of steel. Steel from Carnegie's mills supported the elevated trains in New York and Chicago, formed the skeleton of the Washington Monument, supported the first steel bridge to span the Mississippi, and girded America's first skyscrapers. Carnegie steel armored the naval fleet that helped make the United States a world military power. As a captain of industry, Carnegie's only rival was the titan of the oil industry, John D. Rockefeller.

John D. Rockefeller, Standard Oil, and the Trust

Edwin Drake's discovery of oil in Pennsylvania in 1859 sent thousands rushing to the oil fields in search of "black gold." In the days before the automobile and gasoline, crude oil was refined into lubricating oil for machinery and kerosene for lamps, the major source of lighting in nineteenth-century houses before the invention of gas lamps and electric lighting. The amount of capital needed to buy or build an oil refinery in the 1860s and 1870s remained relatively low—less than $25,000, or roughly what it cost to lay one mile of railroad track. With start-up costs so low, the new petroleum industry experienced riotous competition among many small refineries. Ultimately, **John D. Rockefeller** and his Standard Oil Company succeeded in controlling nine-tenths of the oil-refining business.

Rockefeller grew up the son of a shrewd Yankee who peddled quack cures for cancer. Under his father's rough tutelage, he learned how to drive a hard bargain. "I trade with the boys and skin 'em and just beat 'em every time I can," "Big Bill" Rockefeller boasted. "I want to make 'em sharp." John D. learned his lessons well. In 1865, at the age of twenty-five, he controlled the largest oil refinery in Cleveland. Like a growing number of business owners, Rockefeller abandoned partnership or single proprietorship to embrace the corporation as the business structure best suited to maximize profit and minimize personal liability. In 1870, he incorporated his oil business, founding the Standard Oil Company, a behemoth so huge that it served as the precursor not only of today's ExxonMobil but also of Amoco, Chevron, Sunoco, and ConocoPhillips.

As the largest refiner in Cleveland, Rockefeller demanded secret rebates from the railroads in exchange for his steady business. Rebates enabled Rockefeller to drive out his competitors through predatory pricing. The railroads, facing the pressures of cutthroat competition, needed Rockefeller's business so badly that they gave him a share of the rates that his competitors paid. A Pennsylvania Railroad official later confessed that Rockefeller extracted such huge rebates that the railroad, which could not risk losing his business, sometimes ended up paying him to transport Standard's oil. Secret deals, predatory pricing, and rebates enabled Rockefeller to undercut his competitors and pressure competing refiners to sell out or face ruin.

To gain legal standing for Standard Oil's secret deals, Rockefeller in 1882 pioneered a new form of corporate structure — the **trust**. The trust differed markedly from Carnegie's vertical approach in steel. Instead of attempting to control all aspects of the oil business, from the well to the consumer, Rockefeller used horizontal integration to control the refining process. Several trustees held stock in various refinery companies "in trust" for Standard's stockholders. This elaborate stock swap allowed the trustees to coordinate policy among the refineries, giving Rockefeller a virtual monopoly on the oil-refining business. The Standard Oil trust, valued at more than $70 million, paved the way for trusts in sugar, whiskey, matches, and many other products.

When the federal government responded to public pressure to outlaw the trust as a violation of free trade, Standard Oil changed tactics and reorganized as a holding company. Instead of stockholders in competing companies acting through trustees to set prices and determine territories, the holding company simply brought competing companies under one central administration. No longer technically separate businesses, they could act in concert without violating antitrust laws that forbade companies from forming "combinations in restraint of trade." As Standard Oil's empire grew, Rockefeller ended the independence of the refinery operators and closed inefficient plants. Next he moved to control sources of crude oil and took charge of the transportation and marketing of petroleum products. By the 1890s, Standard Oil ruled more than 90 percent of the oil business, employed 100,000 people, and was the biggest, richest, most feared, and most admired business organization in the world.

John D. Rockefeller enjoyed enormous success in business, but he was not well liked by the public. Before he died in 1937 at the age of ninety-eight, Rockefeller had become the country's first billionaire. But despite his modest habits, his pious Baptist

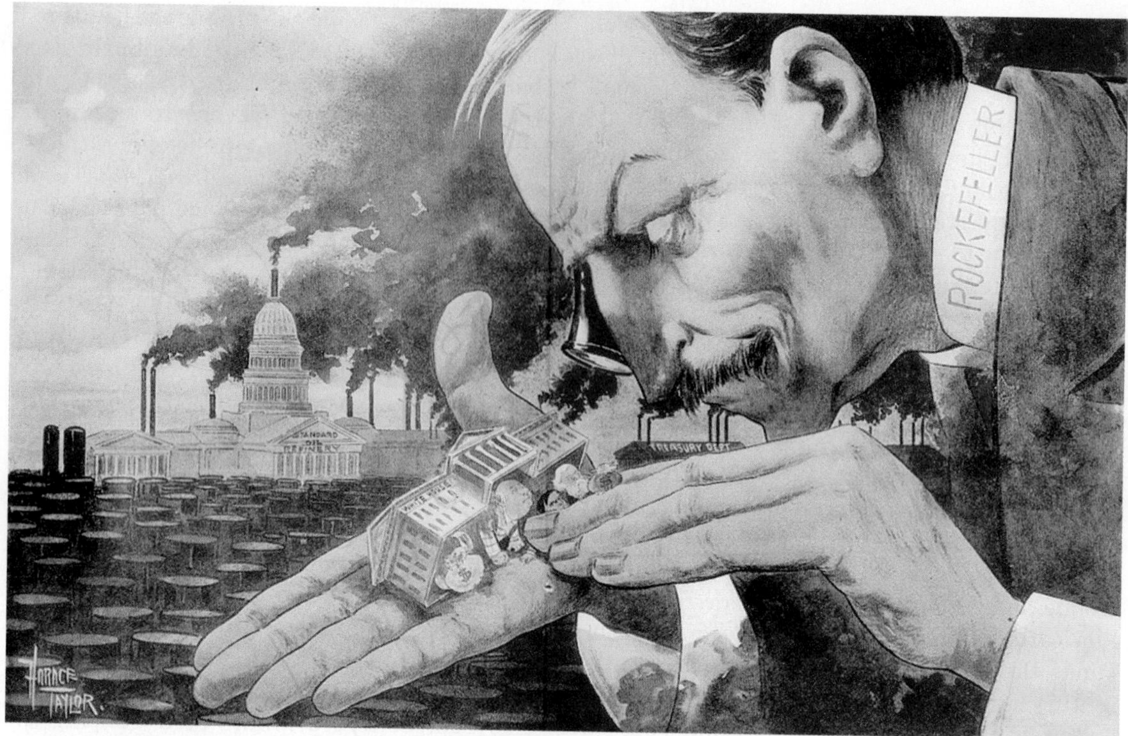

VISUAL ACTIVITY

"What a Funny Little Government"

The power wielded by John D. Rockefeller and the Standard Oil Company is captured in this political cartoon by Horace Taylor, which appeared in the January 22, 1900, issue of the *Verdict*. Rockefeller is pictured holding the White House and the Treasury Department in the palm of his hand, while in the background the U.S. Capitol has been converted into an oil refinery. Rockefeller and the company he ran held so much power that many feared democracy itself was threatened in the Gilded Age. Collection of the New-York Historical Society.

READING THE IMAGE: According to Horace Taylor, what kind of relationship did John D. Rockefeller have with the federal government? What benefits did he accrue from it?

CONNECTIONS: How much influence did industrialists such as Rockefeller exert over the national government in the late nineteenth century?

faith, and his many charitable gifts, he never shared in the public affection that Carnegie enjoyed. Editor and journalist Ida M. Tarbell's "History of the Standard Oil Company," which ran for three years (1902–1905) in serial form in *McClure's Magazine*, largely shaped the public's harsh view of Rockefeller.

Ida M. Tarbell had grown up in the Pennsylvania oil region, and her father had owned one of the small refineries gobbled up by Standard Oil. Her devastatingly thorough history chronicled the methods Rockefeller had used to take over the oil industry. Publicly, Rockefeller refused to respond to her allegations, although in private he dubbed her "Miss Tarbarrel." "If I step on that worm I will call attention to it," he explained. "If I ignore it, it will disappear." Yet by the time Tarbell finished publishing her story, Rockefeller slept with a loaded revolver by his bed in fear of would-be assassins. Standard Oil and the man who created it had become the symbol of heartless monopoly.

New Inventions: The Telephone and Electricity

The second half of the nineteenth century was an age of invention. Men like Thomas Alva Edison and Alexander Graham Bell became folk heroes. But no matter how dramatic the inventors or the inventions, the new electric and telephone industries pioneered by Edison and Bell soon eclipsed their inventors and fell under the control of bankers and industrialists.

Ida M. Tarbell, Scourge of Standard Oil
Inquisitive and determined to have a career as a writer, Ida M. Tarbell became one of America's first investigative reporters. Pictured here shortly before she became an editor at *McClure's Magazine*, Tarbell would earn her reputation from a scathing inquiry into "The History of the Standard Oil Company," which first ran as a series of nineteen articles (see inset) and came out in book form in 1904. Tarbell grew up in Pennsylvania's oil region, where her family suffered from the underhanded practices that John D. Rockefeller used to seize control of the refining business. She was particularly focused on the illegal rebates he wrung from railroads. Tarbell: Library of Congress; magazine: Special Collections, The Ida Tarbell Collection, Pelletier Library, Allegheny College.

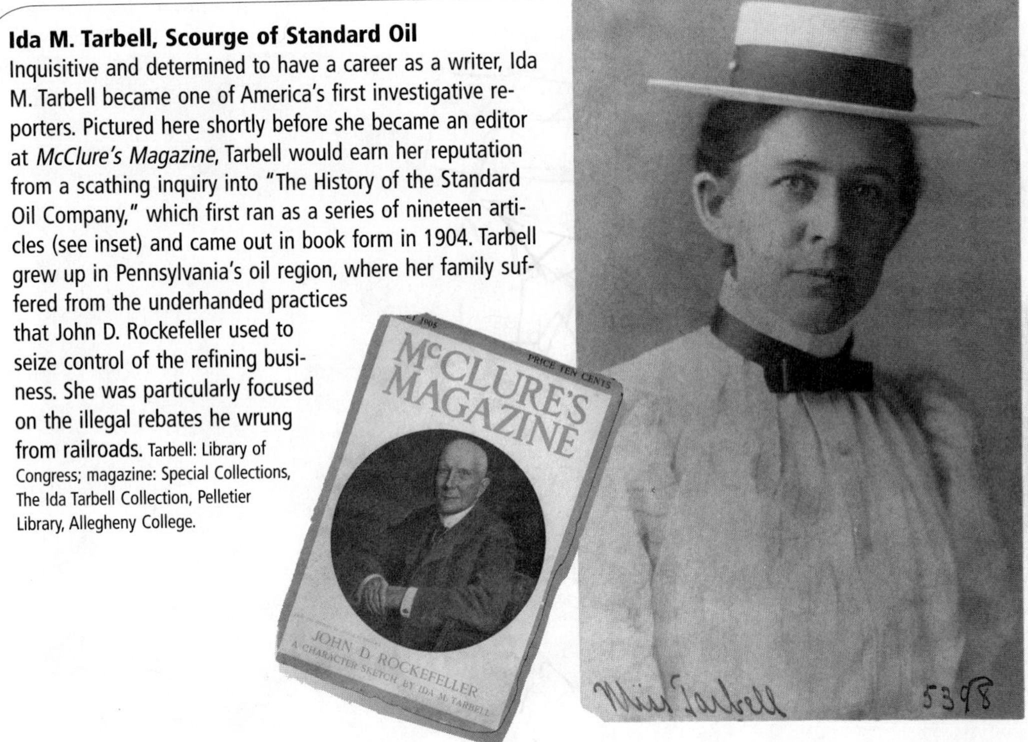

Alexander Graham Bell came to America from Scotland at the age of twenty-four with a passion to find a way to teach the deaf to speak (his wife and mother were deaf). Instead, he developed a way to transmit voice over wire — the telephone. Bell's invention astounded the world when he demonstrated it at the Philadelphia Centennial Exposition in 1876. Dumbfounded by the display, the emperor of Brazil cried out, "My God, it talks!"

In 1880, Bell's company, American Bell, pioneered "long lines" (long-distance telephone service), creating American Telephone and Telegraph (AT&T) as a subsidiary. In 1900, AT&T became the parent company of the system as a whole, controlling Western Electric, which manufactured and installed the equipment, and coordinating the Bell regional divisions. This complicated organizational structure meant that Americans could communicate not only locally but also across the country. And unlike a telegraph message, which had to be written out and taken to a telegraph station, sent over the wire, and then delivered by hand to the recipient, the telephone connected both parties immediately and privately. Bell's invention proved a boon to business, contributing to speed and efficiency. The number of telephones soared, reaching 310,000 in 1895 and more than 1.5 million in 1900.

Notable American Inventions 1865–1899

1865	Railroad sleeping car
1867	Typewriter
1868	Railroad refrigerator car
1870	Stock ticker
1874	Barbed wire
1876	Telephone
1877	Phonograph
1879	Incandescent lightbulb
1882	Electric fan
1885	Adding machine
1886	Coca-Cola
1888	Kodak camera
1890	Electric chair
1891	Zipper
1895	Safety razor
1896	Electric stove
1899	Tape recorder

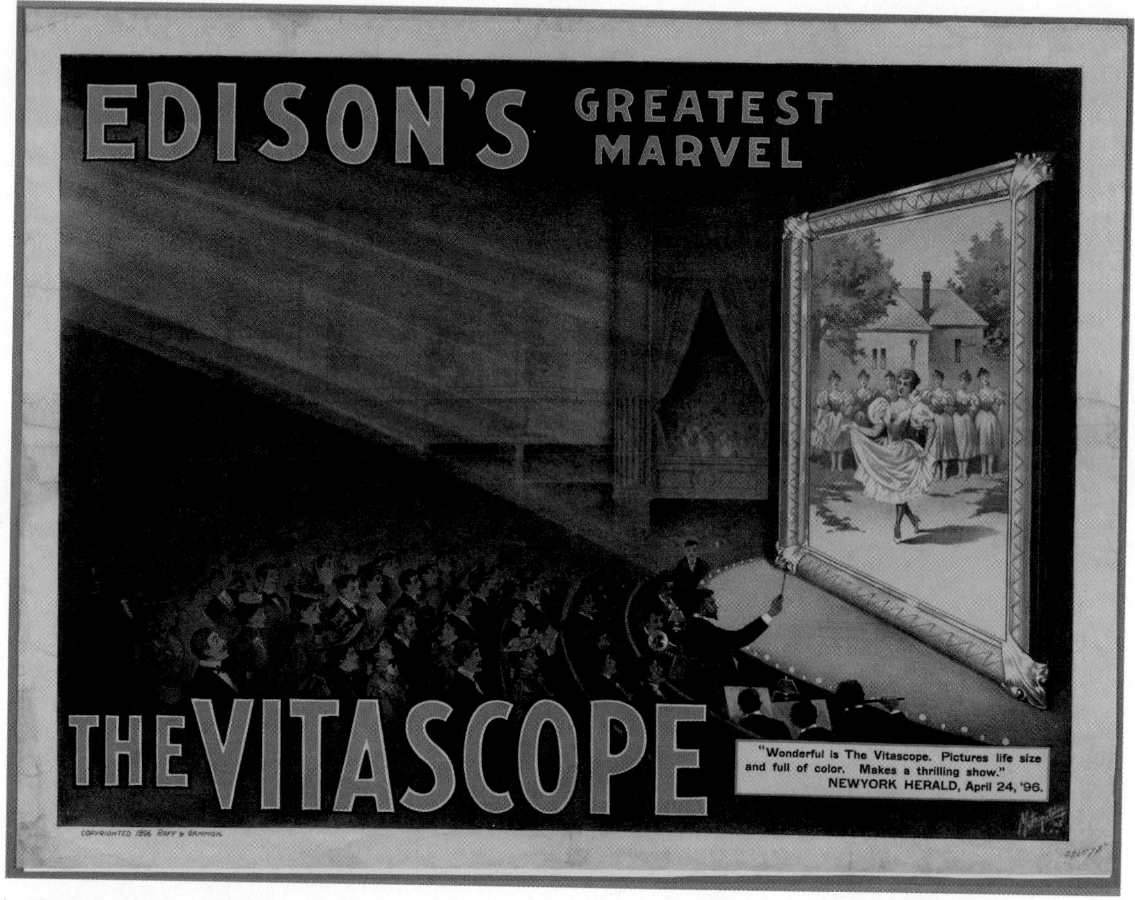

Thomas Edison and Moving Pictures
Edison's "greatest marvel," the Vitascope, was actually not his own invention. Edison was slow to develop a projection system, but the market for a machine that would project films for large audiences led him to acquire the Vitascope, pictured here in a postcard, from Thomas Armat and C. Francis Jenkins. The first theatrical exhibition took place in New York City in 1896. The Vitascope became a popular attraction in variety and vaudeville theaters, where rapt audiences like the one pictured here dressed up and enjoyed moving pictures accompanied by a live orchestra. Library of Congress.

Even more than Alexander Graham Bell, inventor **Thomas Alva Edison** embodied the old-fashioned virtues of Yankee ingenuity and rugged individualism that Americans most admired. A self-educated dynamo, he worked twenty hours a day in his laboratory in Menlo Park, New Jersey, vowing to turn out "a minor invention every ten days and a big thing every six months or so." He almost made good on his promise. At the height of his career, he averaged a patent every eleven days and invented such "big things" as the phonograph, the motion picture camera, and the filament for the incandescent lightbulb.

Edison, in competition with George W. Westinghouse, pioneered the use of electricity as an energy source. By the late nineteenth century, electricity had become a part of American urban life. It powered trolley cars and lighted factories, homes, and office buildings. Indeed, electricity became so prevalent in urban life that it symbolized the city, whose bright lights contrasted with rural America, left largely in the dark because private enterprise judged it not profitable enough to run electric lines to outlying farms and ranches.

While Americans thrilled to the new electric cities and the changes wrought by inventors, the day of the inventor quietly yielded to the heyday of the corporation. In 1892, the electric industry consolidated. Reflecting a nationwide trend in business, Edison General Electric dropped the name of its inventor, becoming simply General Electric (GE). For years, an embittered Edison

THE PROMISE OF TECHNOLOGY

Electrifying America

This 1889 cartoon was part of a campaign Thomas Edison waged against George Westinghouse in what came to be known as the "war of the currents." With the system of how best to provide electric current to the nation at stake, Edison launched a massive public relations campaign to discredit the high-voltage alternating current (AC) favored by Westinghouse. In the cartoon, innocent pedestrians are electrocuted by the wires as a policeman runs for help. The skull in the wires attached to the electric lightbulb warns that this new technology can be deadly. Although the direct current (DC) Edison championed was less dangerous to handle, it could reach only a one-mile radius from a power station. Despite his campaign to discredit Westinghouse, Edison lost the war of the currents. Cities that wanted electric lighting found Westinghouse's alternating current, despite the dangers of high voltage, less expensive and better suited to their needs. Was Edison taking a risk in trying to discredit alternating current? Granger Collection.

refused to set foot inside a GE building. General Electric could afford to overlook the slight. A prime example of the trend toward business consolidation taking place in the 1890s, GE soon dominated the market.

REVIEW What devices did John D. Rockefeller use to gain control of 90 percent of the oil-refining business by 1890?

▸ From Competition to Consolidation

Even as Rockefeller and Carnegie built their empires, the era of the "robber barons," as they were dubbed by their detractors, was drawing to a close. Increasingly, businesses replaced partnerships and sole proprietorships with the anonymous corporate structure that would come to dominate the twentieth century. At the same time, mergers led to the creation of huge new corporations.

Banks and financiers played a key role in this consolidation, so much so that the decades at the turn of the twentieth century can be characterized as a period of **finance capitalism** — investment sponsored by banks and bankers. When the depression that followed the panic of 1893 bankrupted many businesses, bankers stepped in to bring order and to reorganize major industries. During these years, a new social philosophy based on the theories of naturalist Charles Darwin helped to justify consolidation and to inhibit state or federal regulation of business. A conservative Supreme Court further frustrated attempts to control business by consistently declaring unconstitutional legislation designed to regulate railroads or to outlaw trusts and monopolies.

J. P. Morgan and Finance Capitalism

John Pierpont Morgan, the preeminent finance capitalist of the late nineteenth century, loathed competition and sought whenever possible to eliminate it by substituting consolidation and

J. P. Morgan, Photograph by Edward Steichen
Few photographs of J. P. Morgan exist. Morgan, who suffered from a skin condition that left him with a misshapen strawberry of a nose, rarely allowed his picture to be taken. But it was his eyes that people remembered — eyes so piercing that Edward Steichen, who took this photograph, observed that "meeting his gaze was a little like confronting the headlights of an express train." George Eastman House. Reprinted with permission of Joanna T. Steichen.

central control. Morgan's passion for order made him the architect of business mergers. The son of a prominent banker, **J. P. Morgan** inherited along with his wealth the stern business code of the old-fashioned merchant bankers, men who valued character and reputation. Aloof and silent, Morgan looked down on the climbers and the speculators with a haughtiness that led his rivals to call him "Jupiter," after the ruler of the Roman gods. At the turn of the twentieth century, he dominated American banking, exerting an influence so powerful that his critics charged he controlled a vast "money trust" even more insidious than Rockefeller's Standard Oil.

Morgan acted as a power broker in the reorganization of the railroads and the creation of industrial giants such as General Electric and U.S. Steel. When the railroads fell on hard times in the 1890s, he used his access to capital to rescue embattled, wrecked, and ruined companies. Morgan quickly took over the struggling railroads and moved to eliminate competition by creating what he called "a community of interest" among the managers he handpicked. By the time he finished "Morganizing" the railroads, a handful of directors controlled two-thirds of the nation's track.

Banker control of the railroads helped to coordinate the industry. But reorganization came at a high price. To keep investors happy and to guarantee huge profits from the sale of stock, Morgan heavily "watered" the stock of the railroads, issuing more shares than the assets of the company warranted. J. P. Morgan & Co. made millions of dollars from commissions and from blocks of stock acquired through reorganization. The flagrant overcapitalization created by the watered stock hurt the railroads in the long run, saddling them with enormous debt. Equally harmful was the management style of the Morgan directors. Bankers, not railroad men, they aimed at short-term profit and discouraged the continued technological and organizational innovation needed to run the railroads effectively.

In 1898, Morgan moved into the steel industry, directly challenging Andrew Carnegie. Morgan supervised the mergers of several smaller steel companies, which soon expanded from the manufacture of finished goods to compete head-to-head with Carnegie in steel production. The pugnacious Carnegie cabled his partners in the summer of 1900: "Action essential: crisis has arrived . . . have no fear as to the result; victory certain." The press trumpeted news of the impending fight between the feisty Scot and the haughty Wall Street banker, but what the papers called the "battle of the giants" in the end proved little more than the wily maneuvering of two businessmen so adept that even today it is difficult to say who won. For all his belligerence, the sixty-six-year-old Carnegie yearned to retire to Skibo Castle, his home in Scotland. He may well have welcomed Morgan's bid for power. Morgan, who disdained haggling, agreed to pay Carnegie's asking price, $480 million (the equivalent of about $10 billion in today's currency). According to legend, when Carnegie later teased Morgan, saying that he should have asked $100 million more, Morgan replied, "You would have got it if you had."

Morgan's acquisition of Carnegie Steel signaled the passing of the old entrepreneurial order personified by Andrew Carnegie and the arrival of a new, anonymous corporate world. The banker quickly moved to pull together Carnegie's chief competitors to form a huge new

Homestead Steelworks
The Homestead steelworks, outside Pittsburgh, is pictured shortly after J. P. Morgan bought out Andrew Carnegie and created U.S. Steel, the precursor of today's USX. Try to count the smokestacks in the picture. Air pollution on this scale posed a threat to the health of citizens and made for a dismal landscape. Workers complained that trees would not grow in Homestead. Hagley Museum & Library.

corporation, United States Steel, known today as USX. Created in 1901 and capitalized at $1.4 billion, U.S. Steel was the largest corporation in the world. Yet for all its size, it did not hold a monopoly in the steel industry. Significant small competitors, such as Bethlehem Steel, remained independent, creating a competitive system called an oligopoly, in which several companies control production. The smaller manufacturers simply followed the lead of U.S. Steel in setting prices and dividing the market so that each company held a comfortable share. Although oligopoly did not entirely eliminate competition, it did effectively blunt it.

When J. P. Morgan died in 1913, his estate totaled $68 million, not counting an estimated $50 million in art treasures. Andrew Carnegie, who gave away more than $300 million before his death six years later, is said to have quipped, "And to think he was not a rich man!" But Carnegie's gibe missed the mark. The quest for power, not wealth, had motivated J. P. Morgan, and his power could best be measured not in the millions he owned but in the billions he controlled. Even more than Carnegie or Rockefeller, Morgan left his stamp on the twentieth century and formed the model for corporate consolidation that economists and social scientists soon justified with a new social theory known as social Darwinism.

Social Darwinism, Laissez-Faire, and the Supreme Court

John D. Rockefeller Jr., the son of the founder of Standard Oil, once remarked to his Baptist Bible class that the Standard Oil Company, like the American Beauty rose, resulted from "pruning the early buds that grew up around it." The elimination of smaller, inefficient units, he said, was "merely the working out of a law of nature and a law of God." The comparison of the business world to the natural world gave rise to a theory of society paralleling the relatively new notion of evolution formulated by the British naturalist Charles Darwin. In his monumental work *On the Origin of Species* (1859), Darwin theorized that in the struggle for survival, adaptation to the environment triggered among species a natural selection process that led to

"The drunkard in the gutter is just where he ought to be, according to the fitness and tendency of things. . . . Millionaires are the product of natural selection."
— Social Darwinist
WILLIAM GRAHAM SUMNER

HISTORICAL QUESTION

Social Darwinism: Did Wealthy Industrialists Practice What They Preached?

Darwinism, with its emphasis on tooth-and-claw competition, seemed ideally suited to the get-rich-quick mentality of the Gilded Age. By placing the theory of evolution in an economic context, social Darwinism argued against government intervention in business while at the same time insisting that reforms to ameliorate the evils of urban industrialism would only slow evolutionary progress. Most of the wealthy industrialists of the day probably never read Charles Darwin or the exponents of social Darwinism. Nevertheless, the catchphrases of social Darwinism larded the rhetoric of business in the Gilded Age.

Andrew Carnegie, alone among the American business moguls, not only championed social Darwinism but also avidly read the works of its primary exponent, the British social philosopher Herbert Spencer. Significantly, Spencer, not Darwin, coined the catchphrase "survival of the fittest." Carnegie spoke of his indebtedness to Spencer in terms usually reserved for religious conversion: "Before Spencer, all for me had been darkness, after him, all had become light — and right." In his autobiography, Carnegie wrote, "I had found the truth of evolution. 'All is well since all grows better' became my motto, my true source of comfort."

Not content to worship Spencer from afar, Carnegie assiduously worked to make his acquaintance and then would not rest until he had convinced the reluctant Spencer to come to America. In Pittsburgh, Carnegie promised, Spencer could best view his evolutionary theories at work in the world of industry. Clearly, Carnegie viewed his steelworks as the apex of America's new industrial order, a testimony to the playing out of evolutionary theory in the economic world.

In 1882, Spencer undertook an American tour. Carnegie personally invited him to Pittsburgh, squiring him through the Braddock steel mills. But Spencer failed to appreciate Carnegie's achievement. The heat, noise, and pollution of Pittsburgh reduced Spencer to near collapse, and he could only choke out, "Six months' residence here would justify suicide." Carnegie must have been devastated.

How well Carnegie actually understood the principles of social Darwinism is debatable. In his 1900 essay "Popular Illusions about Trusts," Carnegie spoke of the "law of evolution that moves from the heterogeneous to the homogeneous," citing Spencer as his source. Spencer, however, had written of the movement "from an indefinite incoherent homogeneity to a definite coherent heterogeneity." Instead of acknowledging that the history of human evolution moved from the simple to the more complex, Carnegie seemed to insist that evolution moved from the complex to the simple. This confusion of the most basic evolutionary theory calls into question Carnegie's grasp of Spencer's ideas or indeed of Darwin's. Other business leaders too busy making money to read no doubt understood even less about the working of evolutionary theory and social Darwinism, which they so often claimed as their own.

evolution. Herbert Spencer in Britain and William Graham Sumner in the United States developed the theory of **social Darwinism**. The social Darwinists concluded that societal progress came about as a result of relentless competition in which the strong survived and the weak died out.

In social terms, the idea of the "survival of the fittest," coined by Herbert Spencer, had profound significance, as Sumner, a professor of political economy at Yale University, made clear in his book *What Social Classes Owe to Each Other* (1883). "The drunkard in the gutter is just where he ought to be, according to the fitness and tendency of things," Sumner insisted. Conversely, "millionaires are the product of natural selection," and although "they get high wages and live in luxury," Sumner claimed, "the bargain is a good one for society."

Social Darwinists equated wealth and power with "fitness" and believed that the unfit should be allowed to die off to advance the progress of humanity. Any efforts by the rich to aid the poor would only tamper with the rigid laws of nature and slow down evolution. Social Darwinism acted to curb social reform while at the same time glorifying great wealth. In an age when Rockefeller and Carnegie amassed hundreds of millions of dollars (billions in today's currency) and the average worker earned $500 a year, social Darwinism justified economic inequality (See "Historical Question," above.)

The distance between preachment and practice is boldly evident in the example of William Graham Sumner, America's foremost social Darwinist. Ironically, Sumner, who often sounded like an apologist for the rich, aroused the wrath of the very group he championed. The problem was that strict social Darwinists like Sumner insisted absolutely that the government ought not to meddle in the economy. The purity of Sumner's commitment to laissez-faire led him to adamantly oppose the protective tariffs the pro-business Republicans enacted to inflate the prices of manufactured goods produced abroad so that U.S. businesses could compete against foreign rivals. Sumner outspokenly attacked the tariff and firmly advocated free trade from his chair in political economy at Yale University. In 1890, the same year Congress passed the McKinley tariff, Sumner's fulminations against this highest tariff in the nation's history so outraged Yale's wealthy alumni that they mounted a campaign (unsuccessful) to have him fired.

Inconsistency never seemed to trouble Andrew Carnegie, who did not acknowledge a contradiction between his worship of Spencer and his strong support for the tariff. The comparison of Carnegie's position and Sumner's underscores the reality that although in theory laissez-faire constrained the government from playing an active role in business affairs, in practice industrialists fought for government favors — whether tariffs, land grants, or subsidies — that worked to their benefit. Only when legislatures proposed taxes or regulation did business leaders cry foul and invoke the "natural laws" of social Darwinism and its corollary, laissez-faire.

Herbert Spencer
The British writer and philosopher Herbert Spencer became a hero to industrialist Andrew Carnegie, who orchestrated Spencer's trip to America in 1882. The sage of social Darwinism proved a great disappointment to Carnegie. A cautious hypochondriac, Spencer guarded himself zealously against any painful contact with that teeming competitive world that he extolled. Once on American soil, Spencer spurned Carnegie's offer of hospitality during his visit to Pittsburgh and insisted on staying in a hotel. And when Carnegie eagerly demonstrated the wonders of the world's most modern steel mill to his guest, the tour reduced Spencer to a state of near collapse. Hulton Archives/Getty Images.

Thinking about Beliefs and Attitudes

1. In what ways did American business moguls think that the notion of evolution applied to them?
2. Why were most industrialists inconsistent in invoking the principles of social Darwinism?

Andrew Carnegie softened some of the harshness of social Darwinism in his essay "The Gospel of Wealth," published in 1889. The millionaire, Carnegie wrote, acted as a "mere trustee and agent for his poorer brethren, bringing to their service his superior wisdom, experience, and ability to administer, doing for them better than they could or would do for themselves." Carnegie preached philanthropy and urged the rich to "live unostentatious lives" and "administer surplus wealth for the good of the people." His **gospel of wealth** earned much praise but won few converts. Most millionaires followed the lead of J. P. Morgan, who contributed to charity but hoarded private treasures in his marble library.

Social Darwinism nicely suited an age in which the gross inequalities accompanying industrialization seemed to cry out for action. Assuaging the nation's conscience, social Darwinism justified neglect of the poor in the name of "race progress." With so many of the poor coming from different races and ethnicities, social Darwinism fueled racism. A new "scientific racism" purported to prove "Anglo-Saxons" superior to all other groups. Social Darwinism buttressed the status quo and reassured comfortable, white Americans that all was as it should be. Even the gospel of wealth, which mitigated the harshest dictates of social Darwinism, insisted that Americans lived in the best of all possible worlds and that the rich were the natural rulers.

With its emphasis on the free play of competition and the survival of the fittest, social Darwinism encouraged the economic theory of **laissez-faire** (French for "let it alone"). Business argued that government should not meddle in economic affairs, except to protect private property. A conservative Supreme Court agreed. During the 1880s and 1890s, the Court increasingly reinterpreted the Constitution to protect business from taxation, regulation, labor organization, and antitrust legislation.

In a series of landmark decisions, the Court used the Fourteenth Amendment, originally intended to protect freed slaves from state laws violating their rights, to protect corporations. Defining corporations as "persons," the Court reiterated the amendment's language, that no state can "deprive any person of life, liberty, or property, without due process of law." In 1886 in *Santa Clara County v. Southern Pacific Railroad*, the Court reasoned that legislation designed to regulate the railroad deprived the corporation of "due process." Using the same reasoning, the Court struck down state laws regulating railroad rates, declared income tax unconstitutional, and judged labor unions a "conspiracy in restraint of trade." The Court's elevation of the rights of property over other rights stemmed from the conservatism of its justices. According to Justice Stephen J. Field, the Constitution "allows no impediments to the acquisition of property." Field, born into a wealthy New England family, spoke with the bias of the privileged class to whom property rights were sacrosanct. Imbued with this ideology, the Court refused to impede corporate consolidation and did nothing to curb the excesses of big business or promote the humane treatment of workers. Only in the arena of politics did Americans tackle the issues raised by corporate capitalism.

REVIEW Why did the ideas of social Darwinism appeal to many Americans in the late nineteenth century?

▸ Politics and Culture

For many Americans, politics provided a source of identity, a means of livelihood, and a ready form of entertainment. No wonder voter turnout averaged a hefty 77 percent (compared to 57 percent in the 2008 presidential election). A variety of factors contributed to the complicated interplay of politics and culture. Patronage provided an economic incentive for voter participation, but ethnicity, religion, sectional loyalty, race, and gender all influenced the political life of the period.

Political Participation and Party Loyalty

Patronage proved a strong motivation for party loyalty among many voters. Political parties in power doled out federal, state, and local government jobs to their loyal supporters. With hundreds of thousands of jobs to be filled, the choice of party affiliation could mean the difference between a paycheck and an empty pocket. Money greased the wheels of this system of patronage, dubbed the **spoils system** from the adage "to the victor go the spoils." With their livelihoods tied to their party identity, government employees in particular had an incentive to vote in great numbers.

Political affiliation provided a powerful sense of group identity for many voters proud of their loyalty to the Democrats or the Republicans.

Hayes Campaign Lantern, 1876
Republicans carried this lantern in the presidential campaign of 1876. Designed for nighttime rallies, the lantern featured paper transparencies that allowed light to shine through the stars and illuminate the portrait of the candidate, Rutherford B. Hayes. Marching men with lighted lanterns held aloft must have been a dramatic sight in small towns across the country, where politics constituted a major form of entertainment in the nineteenth century.
Collection of Janice L. and David J. Frent.

Democrats, who traced the party's roots back to Thomas Jefferson, called theirs "the party of the fathers." The Republican Party, founded in the 1850s, still claimed strong loyalties in the North as a result of its alignment with the Union during the Civil War. Republicans proved particularly adept at evoking Civil War loyalty, using a tactic called "waving the bloody shirt" — reminding voters which side they had fought for in the Civil War. Noting the power of old sectional loyalties, one of the party faithful observed, "Iowa will go Democratic when Hell goes Methodist."

Religion and ethnicity also played a significant role in politics. In the North, Protestants from the old-line denominations, particularly Presbyterians and Methodists, flocked to the Republican Party, which championed a series of moral reforms, including local laws requiring businesses to close in observance of the Sabbath. In the burgeoning cities, the Democratic Party courted immigrants and working-class Catholic and Jewish voters, charging, rightly, that Republican moral crusades often masked attacks on immigrant culture.

Sectionalism and the New South

After the end of Reconstruction, most white voters in the former Confederate states remained loyal Democrats, voting for Democratic candidates in every presidential election for the next seventy years. Labeling the Republican Party the agent of "Negro rule," Democrats urged white southerners to "vote the way you shot." Yet the so-called solid South proved far from solid on the state and local levels. The economic plight of the South led to shifting political alliances and to third-party movements that challenged Democratic attempts to define politics along race lines and maintain the Democratic Party as the white man's party.

The South's economy, devastated by the war, foundered at the same time the North experienced an unprecedented industrial boom. Soon an influential group of southerners called for a **New South** modeled on the industrial North. Henry Grady, the ebullient young editor of the *Atlanta Constitution*, used his paper's influence (it boasted the largest circulation of any weekly in the country) to extol the virtues of a new industrial South. Part bully, part booster, Grady exhorted the South to use its natural advantages — cheap labor and abundant natural resources — to go head-to-head in competition with northern industry.

Grady's message fell on receptive ears. Many southerners, men and women, black and white, joined the national migration from farm to city, leaving the old plantations to molder and decay. With the end of military rule in 1877, southern Democrats took back state governments, calling themselves "Redeemers." Yet rather than restore the economy of the old planter class, they embraced northern promoters who promised prosperity and profits.

"Iowa will go Democratic when Hell goes Methodist."
— A Northern Republican

The railroads came first, opening up the region for industrial development. Southern railroad mileage grew fourfold from 1865 to 1890. The number of cotton spindles also soared as textile mill owners abandoned New England in search of the cheap labor and proximity to raw materials promised in the South. By 1900, the South had become the nation's leading producer of cloth, and more than 100,000 southerners, many of them women and children, worked in the region's textile mills.

The New South prided itself most on its iron and steel industry, which grew up in the area surrounding Birmingham, Alabama. During this period, the smokestack replaced the white-pillared plantation as the symbol of the New South. Andrew Carnegie toured the region in 1889 and observed, "The South is Pennsylvania's most formidable industrial enemy." But southern industry remained controlled by northern investors, who had no intention of letting the South beat the North at its own game. Elaborate mechanisms rigged the price of southern steel, inflating it, as one northern insider confessed, "for the purpose of protecting the Pittsburgh mills and in turn the Pittsburgh steel users." Similarly, in the lumber and mining industries, investors in the North and abroad, not southerners, reaped the lion's share of the profits.

In only one industry did the South truly dominate — tobacco. Capitalizing on the invention of a machine for rolling cigarettes, the American Tobacco Company, founded by the Duke family of North Carolina, eventually dominated the industry. As cigarettes replaced chewing tobacco in popularity at the turn of the twentieth century, a booming market developed for Duke's "ready mades." Soon the company sold 400,000 cigarettes a day.

In practical terms, the industrialized New South proved an illusion. Much of the South remained agricultural, caught in the grip of the insidious crop lien system (see chapter 16). White southern farmers, desperate to get out of debt, sometimes joined with African Americans to pursue their goals politically. Between 1865 and 1900, voters in every state south of the Mason-Dixon line experimented with political alliances that crossed the color line and threatened the status quo.

Gender, Race, and Politics

Gender — society's notion of what constitutes acceptable masculine or feminine behavior — influenced politics throughout the nineteenth century. From the early days of the Republic, citizenship had been defined in male terms. Citizenship and its prerogatives (voting and officeholding) served as a badge of manliness and rested on its corollary, patriarchy — the power and authority men exerted over their wives and families. With the advent of universal (white) male suffrage in the early nineteenth century, gender eclipsed class as the defining feature of citizenship; men's dominance over women provided the common thread that knit all white men together politically. The concept of **separate spheres** dictated political participation for men only. Once the public sphere of political participation became equated with manhood, women found themselves increasingly restricted to the private sphere of home and hearth.

Women were not alone in their limited access to the public sphere. Though Reconstruction legislation had guaranteed their freedom, blacks continued to face discrimination, especially in the New South. Segregation, commonly practiced under the rubric of **Jim Crow** laws (as discussed in chapter 21), prevented ex-slaves from riding in the same train cars as whites, from eating in the same restaurants, or from using the same toilet facilities.

Amid the turmoil of the post-Reconstruction South, some groups struck cross-racial alliances in search of political might. In Virginia, the "Readjusters," a coalition of blacks and whites determined to "readjust" (lower) the state debt and spend more money on public education, captured state offices from 1879 to 1883. Groups like the Readjusters rested on the belief that universal political rights (voting, officeholding, patronage) could be extended to black males in the public sphere while maintaining racial segregation in the private sphere. Democrats, for their part, fought back by trying to convince voters that black voting would inevitably lead to miscegenation (racial mixing). Black male political power and sexual power, they warned, went hand in hand. Ultimately, their arguments prevailed, and many whites returned to the Democratic fold to protect "white womanhood" and with it white supremacy.

The notion that black men threatened white southern womanhood reached its most vicious form in the practice of lynching — the killing and mutilation of black men by white mobs. By 1892, the practice had become so prevalent that a courageous black editor, **Ida B. Wells**, launched an antilynching movement. That year, a white mob lynched a friend of Wells's whose grocery store competed too successfully with a white-owned store. Wells shrewdly concluded that lynching served "as an excuse to get rid of Negroes who were acquiring wealth and property and thus keep the race terrorized." She began to collect data on lynching and discovered that in the decade between 1882 and 1892 lynching rose in the South by an overwhelming 200 percent, with more than 241 black people killed. The vast increase in lynching testified to the retreat of the federal government following Reconstruction and to white southerners' determination to maintain supremacy through terrorism and intimidation.

In the face of this carnage, Wells struck back. As the first salvo in her attack, she put to rest the "old threadbare lie that Negro men assault white women." As she pointed out, violations of black women by white men, which were much more frequent than black attacks on white women, went unnoticed and unpunished. Wells articulated lynching as a problem of race and gender. She insisted that the myth of black attacks on white southern women masked the reality that mob violence had more to do with economics and the shifting social structure of the South than with rape. She demonstrated in a sophisticated way how the southern patriarchal system, having lost its control over blacks with the end of slavery, used its control over white women to circumscribe the liberty of black men.

Wells's strong stance immediately resulted in reprisal. While she was traveling in the North, vandals ransacked her office in Tennessee and destroyed her printing equipment. Yet the warning that she would be killed on sight if she ever returned to Memphis only stiffened her resolve. As she wrote in her autobiography, *Crusade for Justice* (1928), "Having lost my paper, had a price put on my life and been made an exile . . . , I felt that I owed it to myself and to my race to

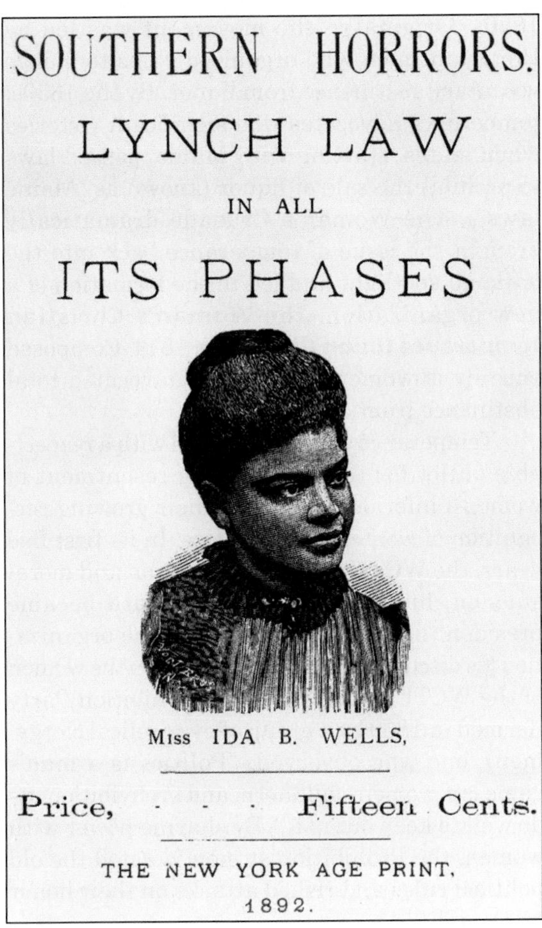
SOUTHERN HORRORS.

LYNCH LAW

IN ALL

ITS PHASES

Miss IDA B. WELLS,

Price, . . . Fifteen Cents.

THE NEW YORK AGE PRINT,
1892.

Ida B. Wells

Ida B. Wells began her antilynching campaign in 1892 after a friend's murder led her to examine the problem of lynching in the South. She spread her message in lectures and pamphlets like this one, distributed for fifteen cents. Wells brought the horror of lynching to a national and international audience and mobilized other African American women to undertake social action under the auspices of the National Association of Colored Women. She later became a founding member of the National Association for the Advancement of Colored People (NAACP). Manuscript, Archives and Rare Books Division, Schomburg Center for Research in Black Culture, The New York Public Library, Astor, Lenox, and Tilden Foundations.

tell the whole truth now that I was where I could do so freely." As a reporter, first for the *New York Age* and later for the *Chicago Inter-Ocean*, she used every opportunity to hammer home her message. Beginning in 1894 and continuing for decades, antilynching bills were introduced in Congress, only to be defeated by southern opposition.

Lynching did not end during Ida B. Wells's lifetime, but Wells's forceful voice brought the issue to national and international prominence. At her funeral in 1931, black leader W. E. B. Du Bois eulogized Wells as the woman who "began the awakening of the conscience of the nation." Wells's determined campaign against lynching provided just one example of women's political activism during the Gilded Age. The suffrage and temperance movements, along with the growing popularity of women's clubs, dramatized how women refused to be relegated to a separate sphere that kept them out of politics.

Women's Activism

No one better recognized the potency of the gendered notion of political rights than Elizabeth Cady Stanton, who lamented the introduction of the word *male* into the Fourteenth Amendment (see chapter 16). The explicit linking of manhood with citizenship and voting rights in the Constitution marked a major setback for reformers who supported the vote for women. In 1869, Stanton along with Susan B. Anthony formed the National Woman Suffrage Association, the first independent woman's rights organization in the United States (discussed in chapter 20). Women found ways to act politically long before they voted and cleverly used their moral authority as wives and mothers to move from the domestic sphere into the realm of politics.

The extraordinary activity of women's clubs in the period following the Civil War provides just one example. Women's clubs proliferated from the 1860s to the 1890s, often in response to the exclusionary policies of men's organizations. In 1868, newspaper reporter Jane Cunningham Croly (pen name Jennie June) founded the Sorosis Club in New York City after the New York Press Club denied entry to women journalists wishing to attend a banquet honoring the British author Charles Dickens. In 1890, Croly brought state and local clubs together under the umbrella of the **General Federation of Women's Clubs** (GFWC). Not wanting to alienate southern women, the GFWC barred black women's clubs from joining, despite their vehement objections. Women's clubs soon abandoned literary pursuits to devote themselves to "civic usefulness," endorsing an end to child labor, supporting the eight-hour workday, and helping pass pure food and drug legislation.

The temperance movement (the movement to end drunkenness) attracted by far the largest number of organized women in the late nineteenth century. By the late 1860s and the

"Woman's Holy War"
This political cartoon from 1874 styles the temperance campaign as "Woman's Holy War" and shows a woman knight in armor (demurely seated sidesaddle on her charger), wielding a battle-ax and trampling on barrels of liquor. The image of temperance women as ax-wielding Amazons proved a popular satiric image. The temperance movement experienced a resurgence in the 1870s after Bible-toting women marched to shut down saloons from New York to Michigan. Their activism led to the creation of the Woman's Christian Temperance Union in 1874.
Picture Research Consultants & Archives.

1870s, the liquor business was flourishing, with about one saloon for every fifty males over the age of fifteen. During the winter of 1873–74, temperance women adopted a radical new tactic. Armed with Bibles and singing hymns, they marched on taverns and saloons and refused to leave until the proprietors signed a pledge to quit selling liquor. Known as the Woman's Crusade, the movement spread like a prairie fire through small towns in Ohio, Indiana, Michigan, and Illinois and soon moved east into New York, New England, and Pennsylvania. Before it was over, more than 100,000 women had marched in more than 450 cities and towns.

The women's tactics may have been new, but the temperance movement dated back to the 1820s. Originally, the movement was led by Protestant men who organized clubs to pledge voluntary abstinence from liquor. By the 1850s, temperance advocates won significant victories when states, starting with Maine, passed laws to prohibit the sale of liquor (known as "Maine laws"). The Woman's Crusade dramatically brought the issue of temperance back into the national spotlight and led to the formation of a new organization, the **Woman's Christian Temperance Union** (WCTU) in 1874. Composed entirely of women, the WCTU advocated total abstinence from alcohol.

Temperance provided women with a respectable outlet for their increasing resentment of women's inferior status and their growing recognition of women's capabilities. In its first five years, the WCTU relied on education and moral suasion, but when Frances Willard became president in 1879, she politicized the organization (as discussed in chapter 20). When the women of the WCTU joined with the Prohibition Party (formed in 1869 by a group of evangelical clergymen), one wag observed, "Politics is a man's game, an' women, childhern, and prohyibitionists do well to keep out iv it." By sharing power with women, the Prohibitionist men violated the old political rules and risked attacks on their honor and manhood.

Even though they could not yet vote, women found ways to affect the political process. Like men, they displayed strong party loyalties and rallied around traditional Republican and Democratic candidates. Third parties courted women, recognizing that their volunteer labor and support could be key assets in party building. Nevertheless, despite growing political awareness among women, politics, particularly presidential politics, remained an exclusively male prerogative.

REVIEW How did race and gender influence politics?

▸ Presidential Politics

The presidents of the Gilded Age, from Rutherford B. Hayes (1877–1881) to William McKinley (1897–1901), are largely forgotten men, primarily because so little was expected of them. In wartime, Lincoln had expanded the power of the presidency, but following the war, even as the nation addressed western expansion, economic transformation, and nascent urban industrialism, the power of the presidency waned. The dominant creed of laissez-faire, coupled with the dictates of social Darwinism, warned the president and the government to leave business alone. Still, presidents in the Gilded Age grappled with corruption and party strife and struggled toward the creation of new political ethics designed to replace patronage with a civil service system that promised to award jobs on the basis of merit, not party loyalty.

Corruption and Party Strife

The political corruption and party factionalism that characterized the administration of Ulysses S. Grant (1869–1877) (see chapter 16) continued to trouble the nation in the 1880s. The spoils system — awarding jobs for political purposes — remained the driving force in party politics at all levels of government in the Gilded Age. Pro-business Republicans generally held a firm grip on the White House, while Democrats had better luck in Congress. Both parties relied on patronage to cement party loyalty. Corruption was rampant, with senators and representatives, and sometimes members of the executive branch, on the payrolls of business interests. The notion of "conflict of interest" did not exist; nor did a standard of accepted ethical behavior. Reformers eager to end corruption and the replace the spoils system with a merit-based civil service system faced an uphill battle.

A small but determined group of reformers championed a new ethics that would preclude politicians from getting rich from public office. The selection of U.S. senators particularly concerned them. Under the Constitution, senators were selected by state legislatures, not directly elected by the voters. Powerful business interests often contrived to control state legislatures and through them U.S. senators. As journalist Henry Demarest Lloyd quipped, Standard Oil "had done everything to the Pennsylvania legislature except to refine it." Nothing prevented a senator from collecting a paycheck from any of the great corporations. So many did so that political cartoonists often portrayed senators as huge money bags labeled with the names of the corporations they served. In this climate, a constitutional amendment calling for the direct election of senators faced stiff opposition from entrenched interests.

Republican president **Rutherford B. Hayes**, whose disputed election in 1876 signaled the end of Reconstruction in the South, tried to steer a middle course between spoilsmen and reformers. Although the Democratic press ridiculed him as "Rutherfraud" because he had not been popularly elected (see chapter 16), Hayes proved a hardworking, well-informed executive who wanted peace, prosperity, and an end to party strife. Yet the Republican Party remained divided into factions led by strong party bosses who boasted that they could make or break any president.

"[Standard Oil] had done everything to the Pennsylvania legislature except to refine it."
— Journalist
HENRY DEMAREST LLOYD

Foremost among the Republican bosses in the Senate stood Roscoe Conkling of New York, a master spoilsman who ridiculed civil service as "snivel service." He and his followers, called the "Stalwarts," represented the Grant faction of the party. Conkling's archrival, Senator James G. Blaine of Maine, led the "Half Breeds." Not as openly corrupt as the Grant wing of the party, the Half Breeds and their champion were nevertheless tainted with charges of corruption. A third group, called the "Mugwumps," consisted primarily of reform-minded Republicans from Massachusetts and New York who deplored the spoils system and advocated **civil service reform**. The name "Mugwump" came from the Algonquian word for "chief," but critics used the term derisively, punning that the Mugwumps straddled the fence on issues of party loyalty, "with their mug on one side and wump on the other."

President Hayes's middle course pleased no one, and he soon managed to alienate all factions of his party. No one was surprised when he announced that he would not seek reelection in 1880. To avoid choosing among its factions, the Republican Party in 1880 nominated a dark-horse candidate, Representative **James A. Garfield** of Ohio. To foster party unity, they picked Stalwart Chester A. Arthur as the vice presidential candidate. The Democrats made an attempt to overcome sectionalism and establish a national party by selecting as their presidential standard-bearer an old Union general, Winfield Scott Hancock. But as one observer noted, "It is a peculiarly constituted party that sends rebel brigadiers to Congress because of their rebellion, and then nominates a Union General as its candidate for president because of his loyalty." Hancock garnered only lukewarm support, receiving just 155 electoral votes to Garfield's 214, although the popular vote was less lopsided.

Garfield's Assassination and Civil Service Reform

"My God," Garfield swore after only a few months in office, "what is there in this place that a man should ever want to get into it?" Garfield, like Hayes, faced the difficult task of remaining independent while pacifying the party bosses and placating the reformers. As the federal bureaucracy grew to nearly 150,000 jobs, thousands of office seekers swarmed to the nation's capital, each clamoring for a position. In the days before Secret Service protection, the White House door stood open to all comers. Garfield took a fatalistic view. "Assassination," he told a friend, "can no more be guarded against than death by lightning, and it is best not to worry about either."

On July 2, 1881, less than four months after taking office, Garfield was shot. His assailant, Charles Guiteau, though clearly insane, turned out to be a disappointed office seeker who claimed to be motivated by political partisanship. He told the police officer who arrested him, "I did it; I will go to jail for it; Arthur is president, and I am a Stalwart." Throughout the hot summer, the country kept a deathwatch as Garfield lingered. When he died in September, Chester A. Arthur became president. The press almost universally condemned Republican factionalism for creating the political climate that produced Guiteau and led to the second political assassination in a generation.

Stalwart Roscoe Conkling saw his hopes for the White House dashed. Attacks on the spoils system increased, and the public joined the chorus calling for reform. Both parties claimed credit for passage of the Pendleton Civil Service Act of 1883, which established a permanent Civil Service Commission consisting of three members appointed by the president. Some fourteen thousand jobs came under a merit system that required examinations for office and made it impossible to remove jobholders for political reasons. The new law also prohibited federal jobholders from contributing to political campaigns, thus drying up the major source of the party bosses' revenue. Soon, business interests stepped in to replace officeholders as the nation's chief political contributors. Ironically, civil service reform thus gave business an even greater influence in political life.

Civil Service Exams
In this 1890s photograph, prospective police officers in Chicago take the written civil service exam. Civil service meant that politicians and party bosses could no longer use jobs in the government to reward the party faithful. Many people worried that merit examinations would favor the educated elite at the expense of immigrant groups such as the Irish, who had made a place for themselves in the political system by the late nineteenth century. Chicago Historical Society.

Reform and Scandal: The Campaign of 1884

With Conkling's downfall, James G. Blaine assumed leadership of the Republican Party and at long last captured the presidential nomination in 1884. A magnetic Irish American, Blaine inspired such devotion that his supporters called themselves Blainiacs. But Mugwumps like editor Carl Schurz insisted that Blaine "wallowed in spoils like a rhinoceros in an African pool." They bolted the party and embraced the Democrats' presidential nominee, the stolid **Grover Cleveland**, reform governor of New York. The burly, beer-drinking Cleveland distinguished himself from an entire generation of politicians by the simple motto "A public office is a public trust." First as mayor of Buffalo and later as governor of New York, he built a reputation for honesty, economy, and administrative efficiency. The Democrats, who had not won the presidency since 1856, had high hopes for his candidacy,

"Another Voice for Cleveland"
This political cartoon ran in the magazine *Judge* in the fall of 1884 during the presidential campaign. Grover Cleveland, the Democratic candidate, is pictured cringing from the cries of a babe in arms — an allusion to his admission that he had fathered an illegitimate child. Despite the lurid publicity, Cleveland won the election. Library of Congress.

especially after the Mugwumps threw their support to Cleveland. As the Mugwumps insisted, "The paramount issue this year is moral rather than political."

The Mugwumps soon regretted their words. The 1884 contest degenerated so far into scandal and nasty mudslinging that one disgusted journalist styled it "the vilest campaign ever waged." In July, Cleveland's hometown paper, the *Buffalo Telegraph*, dropped the bombshell that the candidate had fathered an illegitimate child in an affair with a local widow. Cleveland, a bachelor, stoically accepted responsibility for the child. Crushed by the scandal, the Mugwumps lost much of their enthusiasm. At public rallies, Blaine's partisans taunted Cleveland, chanting, "Ma, Ma, where's my Pa?" Silent but fuming, Cleveland waged his campaign in the traditional fashion by staying home.

Blaine set a new campaign style by launching a whirlwind national tour. On a last-minute stop in New York City, the exhausted candidate committed a misstep that may have cost him the election. He overlooked a remark by a supporter, a local clergyman who cast a slur on Catholic voters by styling the Democrats as the party of "Rum, Romanism, and Rebellion." Linking drinking (rum) and Catholicism (Romanism) offended Irish Catholic voters, whom Blaine had counted on to desert the Democratic Party and support him because of his Irish background.

With less than a week to go until the election, Blaine had no chance to recover from the negative publicity. He lost New York State by fewer than 1,200 votes and with it the election. In the final tally, Cleveland defeated Blaine by a scant 23,005 votes nationwide but won with

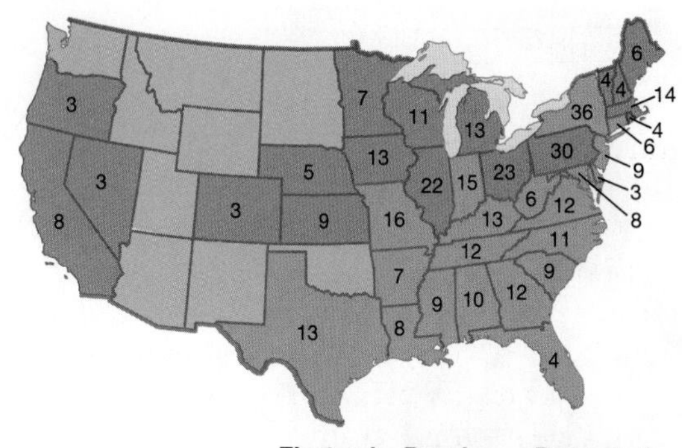

Candidate	Electoral Vote	Popular Vote	Percent of Popular Vote
Grover Cleveland (Democrat)	219	4,874,986	48.5*
James G. Blaine (Republican)	182	4,851,981	48.3

*Percentages do not total 100 because some popular votes went to other parties.

MAP 18.2
The Election of 1884

219 electoral votes to Blaine's 182 (Map 18.2), ending twenty-four years of Republican control of the presidency. Cleveland's followers had the last word. To the chorus of "Ma, Ma, where's my Pa?" they retorted, "Going to the White House, ha, ha, ha."

REVIEW How did the question of civil service reform contribute to divisions within the Republican Party?

▸ Economic Issues and Party Realignment

Four years later, in the election of 1888, fickle voters turned Cleveland out, electing Republican Benjamin Harrison, the grandson of President William Henry Harrison. Then, in the only instance in American history when a president once defeated at the polls returned to office, the voters brought Cleveland back in the election of 1892. What factors account for such a surprising turnaround? The 1880s witnessed a remarkable political realignment as a set of economic concerns replaced appeals to Civil War sectional loyalties. The tariff, federal regulation of the railroads and trusts, and the campaign for free silver restructured American politics. A Wall Street panic in 1893 set off a major depression that further fed political unrest.

The Tariff and the Politics of Protection

The tariff became a potent political issue in the 1880s. The concept of a protective tariff to raise the price of imported goods and stimulate American industry dated back to Alexander Hamilton in the founding days of the Republic. The Republicans turned the tariff to political ends in 1861 by enacting a measure that both raised revenues for the Civil War and rewarded their industrial supporters, who wanted protection from foreign competition. After the war, the pro-business Republicans continued to revise and enlarge the tariff. Manufactured goods such as steel and textiles, and some agricultural products, including sugar and wool, benefited from protection. Most farm products, notably wheat and cotton, did not. By the 1880s, the tariff produced more than $2.1 billion in revenue. Not only did the high tariff pay off the nation's Civil War debt and fund pensions for Union soldiers, but it also created a huge surplus that sat idly in the Treasury's vaults while the government argued about how (or even whether) to spend it.

To many Americans, particularly southern and midwestern farmers who sold their crops in a world market but had to buy goods priced artificially high because of the protective tariff, the answer was simple: Reduce the tariff. Advocates of free trade and moderates agitated for tariff reform. But those who benefited from the tariff—industrialists insisting that America's "infant industries" needed protection and some westerners producing protected raw materials such as wool, hides, and lumber—firmly opposed lowering the tariff. Many argued that workers, too, benefited from high tariffs that protected American wages by giving American products an edge over imported goods.

The Republican Party seized on the tariff question to forge a new national coalition. "Fold up the bloody shirt and lay it away," Blaine advised a colleague in 1880. "It's of no use to us. You want to shift the main issue to protection." By encouraging an alliance among industrialists, labor, and western producers of raw materials—groups seen to benefit from the tariff—Blaine hoped to solidify the North, Midwest, and West against the solidly Democratic South. Although the tactic failed for Blaine in the presidential election of 1884, it worked for the Republicans four years later.

Cleveland, who had straddled the tariff issue in the election of 1884, startled the nation in 1887 by calling for tariff reform. Cleveland attacked the tariff as a tax levied on American consumers by powerful industries. And he pointed out that high tariffs impeded the expansion of American markets abroad at a time when American industries needed to expand if they were to keep growing. The Republicans countered by arguing that "tariff tinkering" would only unsettle prosperous industries, drive down wages, and shrink the farmers' home market. Republican Benjamin Harrison, who supported the high tariff, ousted Cleveland from the White House in 1888, carrying all the western and northern states except Connecticut and New Jersey.

Back in power, the Republicans brazenly passed the highest tariff in the nation's history in 1890. The new tariff, sponsored by Republican representative William McKinley of Ohio and signed into law by Harrison, stirred up a hornet's nest of protest across the United States. The American people had elected Harrison to preserve protection but not to enact a higher tariff. Democrats condemned the **McKinley tariff** and labeled the Republican Congress that passed it the "Billion Dollar Congress" for its carnival of spending, which depleted the nation's surplus by enacting a series of pork barrel programs shamelessly designed to bring federal money to congressmen's own constituents. In the congressional election of 1890, angry voters swept the hapless Republicans, including tariff sponsor McKinley, out of office. Two years later, Harrison himself was defeated. Grover Cleveland, whose call for tariff revision had cost him the election in 1888, triumphantly returned to the White House vowing to lower the tariff. Such were the changes in the political winds whipped up by the tariff issue.

Controversy over the tariff masked deeper divisions in American society. Conflict between workers and farmers on the one side and bankers and corporate giants on the other erupted throughout the 1880s and came to a head in the 1890s. Both sides in the tariff debate spoke to concern over class conflict when they insisted that their respective plans, whether McKinley's high tariff or Cleveland's tariff reform, would bring prosperity and harmony. For their part, many working people shared the sentiment voiced by one labor leader that the tariff was "only a scheme devised by the old parties to throw dust in the eyes of laboring men."

Railroads, Trusts, and the Federal Government

American voters may have divided on the tariff, but increasingly they agreed on the need for federal regulation of the railroads and federal legislation to curb the power of the "trusts" (a term loosely applied to all large business combinations). As early as the 1870s, angry farmers in the Midwest who suffered from the unfair shipping practices of the railroads organized to fight for railroad regulation. The Patrons of Husbandry, or the Grange, founded in 1867 as a social and educational organization for farmers, soon became an independent political movement. By electing Grangers to state office, farmers made it possible for several midwestern states to pass laws in the 1870s and 1880s regulating the railroads. At first, the Supreme Court ruled in favor of state regulation (*Munn v. Illinois*, 1877). But in 1886, the Court reversed itself, ruling that because railroads crossed state boundaries, they fell outside state jurisdiction (*Wabash v. Illinois*). With more than three-fourths of railroads crossing state lines, the Supreme Court's decision effectively quashed the states' attempts at railroad regulation.

"[The tariff is] only a scheme devised by the old parties to throw dust in the eyes of laboring men."

— A labor leader

Anger at the *Wabash* decision finally led to the first federal law regulating the railroads, the Interstate Commerce Act, passed in 1887 during Cleveland's first administration. The act established the nation's first federal regulatory agency, the **Interstate Commerce Commission (ICC)**, to oversee the railroad industry. In its early years, the ICC was never strong enough to pose a serious threat to the railroads. For example, it could not end rebates to big shippers. In its early decades, the ICC proved more important as a precedent than effective as a watchdog.

Concern over the growing power of the trusts led Congress to pass the **Sherman Antitrust Act** in 1890. The act outlawed pools and trusts, ruling that businesses could no longer enter into agreements to restrict competition. It did nothing to restrict huge holding companies such as Standard Oil, however, and proved to be a weak sword against the trusts. In the following decade, the government successfully struck down only six trusts but used the law four times against labor by outlawing unions as a "conspiracy in restraint of trade." In 1895, the conservative Supreme Court dealt the antitrust law a crippling blow in *United States v. E. C. Knight Company*. In its decision, the Court ruled that "manufacture" did not constitute "trade." This semantic quibble drastically narrowed the law, in this case allowing the American Sugar Refining Company, which had bought out a number of other sugar companies (including E. C. Knight) and controlled 98 percent of the production of sugar, to continue its virtual monopoly.

Both the ICC and the Sherman Antitrust Act testified to the nation's concern about corporate abuses of power and to a growing willingness to use federal measures to intervene on behalf of the public interest. As corporate capitalism became more and more powerful, public pressure toward government intervention grew. Yet not until the twentieth century would more active presidents sharpen and use these weapons effectively against the large corporations.

The Fight for Free Silver

While the tariff and regulation of the trusts gained many backers, the silver issue stirred passions like no other issue of the day. On one side stood those who believed that gold constituted the only honest money. Although other forms of currency circulated, notably paper money such as banknotes and greenbacks, the government's support of the gold standard meant that anyone could redeem paper money for gold. Many who supported the gold standard were eastern creditors who did not wish to be paid in devalued dollars. On the opposite side stood a coalition of western silver barons and poor farmers from the West and South who called for **free silver**. The mining interests, who had seen the silver bonanza in the West drive down the price of the precious metal, wanted the government to buy silver and mint silver dollars. Farmers from the West and South who had suffered from deflation during the 1870s and 1880s hoped that increasing the money supply with silver dollars, thus causing inflation, would give them some debt relief by enabling them to pay off their creditors with cheaper dollars.

During the depression following the panic of 1873, critics of hard money organized the Greenback Labor Party, an alliance of farmers and urban wage laborers. The Greenbackers favored issuing paper currency not tied to the gold supply, citing the precedent of the greenbacks issued during the Civil War. The government had the right to define what constituted legal tender, the Greenbackers reasoned: "Paper is equally money, when . . . issued according to law." They proposed that the nation's currency be based on its wealth — land, labor, and capital — and not simply on its reserves of gold. The Greenback Labor Party captured more than a million votes and elected fourteen members to Congress in 1878. Although conservatives considered the Greenbackers dangerous cranks, their views eventually prevailed in the 1930s, when the country abandoned the gold standard.

After the Greenback Labor Party collapsed, proponents of free silver came to dominate the monetary debate in the 1890s. Advocates of free silver pointed out that until 1873 the country had enjoyed a system of bimetallism — the minting of both silver and gold into coins. In that year, at the behest of those who favored gold, the Republican Congress had voted to stop buying and minting silver, an act silver supporters denounced as the "crime of '73." By sharply contracting the money supply at a time when the nation's economy was burgeoning, the Republicans had enriched bankers and investors at the expense of cotton and wheat farmers and industrial wageworkers. In 1878 and again in 1890, with the Sherman Silver Purchase Act, Congress took steps to ease the tight money policy and appease advocates of silver by passing legislation requiring the government to buy silver and issue silver certificates. Though good for the mining interests, the laws did little to promote the inflation desired by farmers. Soon monetary reformers began to call for "the free and unlimited coinage of silver," a plan whereby nearly all the silver mined in the West would be minted into coins circulated at the rate of sixteen ounces of silver — equal in value to one ounce of gold.

By the 1890s, the silver issue crossed party lines. The Democrats hoped to use it to achieve a union between western and southern voters. Unfortunately for them, Democratic president Grover Cleveland remained a staunch conservative in money matters and supported the gold standard as vehemently as any Republican. After a panic on Wall Street in the spring of 1893, Cleveland called a special session of Congress and bullied the legislature into repealing the Silver Purchase Act because he believed it threatened economic confidence. Repeal proved disastrous for Cleveland, not only economically but also politically. It did nothing to bring prosperity and dangerously divided the country. Angry farmers, furious at the president's harsh monetary policy, warned Cleveland not to travel west of the Mississippi River if he valued his life.

U.S. Currency
Gold remained the nation's standard currency, but silver supporters, including farmers and western mining interests, demanded the minting of silver dollars and the issuance of silver certificates like the one above. On the left is a dollar gold piece. The American Numismatic Association; Picture Research Consultants & Archives.

Panic and Depression

President Cleveland had scarcely begun his second term in office in 1893 when the country faced the worst depression it had yet seen. In the face of economic disaster, Cleveland clung to the economic orthodoxy of the gold standard. In the winter of 1894–95, the president walked the floor of the White House, sleepless over the prospect that the United States might go bankrupt. Individuals and investors, rushing to trade in their banknotes for gold, strained the country's monetary system. The Treasury's gold reserves dipped so low that unless they could be buttressed, the unthinkable might happen: The U.S. Treasury might not be able to meet its obligations.

At this juncture, J. P. Morgan stepped in and suggested a plan. A group of bankers would purchase $65 million in U.S. government bonds, paying in gold. Cleveland knew that such a scheme would unleash a thunder of protest, yet to save the gold standard, the president had no choice but to accept Morgan's help. A storm of controversy erupted over the deal. The press claimed that Cleveland had lined his own pockets and rumored that Morgan had made $8.9 million. Neither allegation was true. Cleveland had not profited a penny, and Morgan made far less than the millions his critics claimed.

But if President Cleveland's action managed to salvage the gold standard, it did not save the country from hardship. The winter of 1894–95 was one of the worst times in American history. People faced unemployment, cold, and hunger. A firm believer in limited government, Cleveland insisted that nothing could be done to help: "I do not believe that the power and duty of the General Government ought to be extended to the relief of individual suffering which is in no manner properly related to the public service or benefit." Nor did it occur to Cleveland that his great faith in the gold standard prolonged the depression, favored creditors over debtors, and caused immense hardship for millions of Americans.

REVIEW Why were Americans split on the question of the tariff and currency?

▸ Conclusion: Business Dominates an Era

The gold deal between J. P. Morgan and Grover Cleveland underscored a dangerous reality: The federal government was so weak that its solvency depended on a private banker. This lopsided power relationship signaled the dominance of business in the era Mark Twain satirically but accurately characterized as the Gilded Age. Perhaps no other era in American history spawned greed, corruption, and vulgarity on so grand a scale — an era when speculators like Jay Gould not only built but wrecked railroads to turn paper profits; an era when the get-rich-quick ethic of the western prospector infused the whole continent; and an era when business boasted openly of buying politicians, who in turn lined their pockets at the public's expense.

Nevertheless, the Gilded Age was not without its share of solid achievements, many inextricably linked to its empire in the West (see chapter 17). Where dusty roads and cattle trails once sprawled across the continent, steel rails now bound the country together, creating a national market that enabled America to make the leap into the industrial age. Factories and refineries poured out American steel and oil at unprecedented rates. Businessmen like Carnegie, Rockefeller, and Morgan developed new strategies to consolidate American industry. New inventions, including the telephone and electric light and power, changed Americans' everyday lives. By the end of the nineteenth century, the country had achieved industrial maturity. It boasted the largest, most innovative, most productive economy in the world. No other era in the nation's history witnessed such a transformation.

Yet the changes that came with these developments worried many Americans and gave rise to the era's political turmoil. Race and gender profoundly influenced American politics, leading to new political alliances. Fearless activist Ida B. Wells fought racism in its most brutal form — lynching. Women's organizations championed causes, notably suffrage and temperance, and challenged prevailing views of woman's proper sphere. Reformers fought corruption by instituting civil service. And new issues — the tariff, the regulation of the trusts, and currency reform — restructured the nation's politics.

The Gilded Age witnessed a nation transformed. Fueled by expanding industry, cities grew exponentially, not only with new inhabitants from around the globe but also with new bridges, subways, and skyscrapers. The frenzied growth of urban America brought wealth and opportunity, but also the exploitation of labor, racism toward newcomers, and social upheaval that lent a new urgency to calls for social reform.

▸ Selected Bibliography

General Works

Charles W. Calhoun, ed., *The Gilded Age: Essays on the Origins of Modern America* (1996).

Sean Dennis Cashman, *America in the Gilded Age: From the Death of Lincoln to the Rise of Theodore Roosevelt* (1993).

Rebecca Edwards, *New Spirits: Americans in the Gilded Age, 1865–1905* (2006).

Jackson Lears, *Rebirth of a Nation: The Making of Modern America, 1877–1920* (2009).

Richard While, *Railroaded: The Transcontinentals and the Making of Modern America* (2011).

Business

Kathleen Brady, *Ida Tarbell: Portrait of a Muckraker* (1984).

Edward Chancellor, *Devil Take the Hindmost: A History of Financial Speculation* (1999).

Ron Chernow, *Titan: The Life of John D. Rockefeller, Sr.* (1998).

Steve Fraser, *Every Man a Speculator: A Cultural History of Wall Street in America* (2005).

Morton J. Horowitz, *The Transformation of American Law, 1870–1960* (1992).

Walter Licht, *Industrializing America* (1995).

David Nasaw, *Andrew Carnegie* (2006).

T. J. Stiles, *The First Tycoon: The Epic Life of Cornelius Vanderbilt* (2009).

Jean Strouse, *Morgan: American Financier* (1999).

Viviana A. Zelizer, *The Social Meaning of Money* (1994).

Politics

Paula Baker, *The Moral Framework of Public Life* (1991).

Richard F. Bensel, *The Political Economy of American Industrialization, 1877–1900* (2000).

Ruth Bordin, *Women and Temperance: The Quest for Power and Liberty, 1873–1900* (1990).

Alyn Brodsky, *Grover Cleveland: A Study in Character* (2000).

Robert W. Cherny, *American Politics in the Gilded Age, 1868–1900* (1997).

Jane Dailey, Glenda Elizabeth Gilmore, and Bryant Simon, eds., *Jumpin' Jim Crow: Southern Politics from the Civil War to Civil Rights* (2000).

Rebecca Edwards, *Angels in the Machinery: Gender in American Party Politics from the Civil War to the Progressive Era* (1997).
Dana Frank, *Buy American: The Untold Story of Economic Nationalism* (1999).
Paula Giddings, *Ida, a Sword among Lions: Ida B. Wells and the Campaign against Lynching* (2008).
Steven Hahn, *A Nation under Our Feet: Black Political Struggles in the Rural South from Slavery to the Great Migration* (2003).
Darlene Clark Hine and Kathleen Thompson, *A Shining Thread of Hope: The History of Black Women in America* (1998).
Ari Hoogenboom, *Rutherford B. Hayes: Warrior and President* (1995).
H. Paul Jeffers, *An Honest President: The Life and Presidencies of Grover Cleveland* (2000).
Ross Evans Paulson, *Liberty, Equality, and Justice: Civil Rights, Women's Rights, and the Regulation of Business, 1865–1932* (1997).
Dorothy Salem, *To Better Our World: Black Women in Organized Reform, 1890–1920* (1990).
Ian Tyrell, *Woman's World, Woman's Empire: The Woman's Christian Temperance Union in International Perspective, 1880–1930* (1991).
LeeAnn Whites, *Gender Matters: Civil War, Reconstruction, and the Making of the New South* (2005).

Culture

Judy Arlene Hilkey, *Character Is Capital: Success Manuals and Manhood in Gilded Age America* (1997).
Jane H. Hunter, *How Young Ladies Became Girls: The Victorian Origins of American Girlhood* (2002).
Paulette D. Kilmer, *The Fear of Sinking: The American Success Formula in the Gilded Age* (1996).
Alan Trachtenberg, *The Incorporation of America: Culture and Society in the Gilded Age* (anniversary edition, 2009).

For more books about topics in this chapter, see the Online Bibliography at **bedfordstmartins.com/roark**.

For additional primary sources from this period, see Michael Johnson, ed., *Reading the American Past*, Fifth Edition.

For Web sites, images, and documents related to topics and places in this chapter, visit Make History at **bedfordstmartins.com/roark**.

Reviewing Chapter 18

KEY TERMS

Explain each term's significance.

Old Industries Transformed, New Industries Born

Gilded Age (p. 571)
Jay Gould (p. 571)
Andrew Carnegie (p. 573)
vertical integration (p. 576)
John D. Rockefeller (p. 577)
trust (p. 577)
Ida M. Tarbell (p. 578)
Thomas Alva Edison (p. 580)

From Competition to Consolidation

finance capitalism (p. 581)
J. P. Morgan (p. 582)
social Darwinism (p. 584)
gospel of wealth (p. 585)
laissez-faire (p. 586)

Politics and Culture

spoils system (p. 586)
New South (p. 587)
separate spheres (p. 588)
Jim Crow (p. 588)
Ida B. Wells (p. 588)
General Federation of Women's Clubs (GFWC) (p. 589)
Woman's Christian Temperance Union (WCTU) (p. 590)

Presidential Politics

Rutherford B. Hayes (p. 591)
civil service reform (p. 591)
James A. Garfield (p. 591)
Grover Cleveland (p. 592)

Economic Issues and Party Realignment

McKinley tariff (p. 595)
Interstate Commerce Commission (ICC) (p. 595)
Sherman Antitrust Act (p. 595)
free silver (p. 596)

REVIEW QUESTIONS

Use key terms and dates to support your answer.

1. What devices did John D. Rockefeller use to gain control of 90 percent of the oil-refining business by 1890? (pp. 571–581)
2. Why did the ideas of social Darwinism appeal to many Americans in the late nineteenth century? (pp. 581–586)
3. How did race and gender influence politics? (pp. 586–590)
4. How did the question of civil service reform contribute to divisions within the Republican Party? (pp. 590–594)
5. Why were Americans split on the question of the tariff and currency? (pp. 594–597)

MAKING CONNECTIONS

Draw on key terms, the timeline, and review questions.

1. How did the railroads contribute to the growth of American industry? In your answer, discuss the drawbacks and benefits of these developments.
2. Late-nineteenth-century industrialization depended on developments in technology and business strategy. What were some of the key innovations in both arenas? How did they facilitate the maturation of American industry?
3. By the 1870s, several new concerns had displaced slavery as the defining question of American politics. What were these new issues, and how did they shape new regional, economic, and racial alliances and rivalries? In your answer, consider the part that political parties played in this process.
4. Energetic political activity characterized Gilded Age America, both within and beyond formal party politics. How did the activism of women denied the vote contribute to the era's electoral politics? In your answer, be sure to cite specific examples of political action.
5. The U.S. Congress and the Supreme Court facilitated the concentration of power in the hands of private business concerns during the Gilded Age. Citing specific policies and court decisions, discuss how government helped augment the power of big business in the late nineteenth century.

LINKING TO THE PAST

Link events in this chapter to earlier events.

1. In what ways did the military conquest of the trans-Mississippi West, with its dislocation of Native Americans, play a significant role in the industrial boom of the Gilded Age? (See chapter 17.)
2. In what ways did the rampant get-rich-quick mentality of western miners and land speculators help set the tone for the Gilded Age? Is the West the herald of the Gilded Age, or must we look to New York and Washington? (See chapter 17.)

▶ **For practice quizzes and other study tools**, visit the Online Study Guide at **bedfordstmartins.com/roark.**

TIMELINE 1869–1901

1869	• First transcontinental railroad completed. • National Woman Suffrage Association founded.
1870	• John D. Rockefeller incorporates Standard Oil Company.
1872	• Andrew Carnegie builds the largest, most up-to-date Bessemer steel plant in the world.
1873	• Wall Street panic leads to major economic depression.
1874	• Woman's Christian Temperance Union (WCTU) founded.
1876	• Alexander Graham Bell demonstrates telephone.
1877	• Republican Rutherford B. Hayes sworn in as president. • "Redeemers" come to power in South. • *Munn v. Illinois.*
1880	• Republican James A. Garfield elected president.
1881	• Garfield assassinated; Vice President Chester A. Arthur becomes president.
1882	• John D. Rockefeller develops the trust.
1883	• Pendleton Civil Service Act.
1884	• Democrat Grover Cleveland elected president.
1886	• *Wabash v. Illinois.*
1887	• Interstate Commerce Act.
1888	• Republican Benjamin Harrison elected president.
1890	• McKinley tariff. • General Federation of Women's Clubs (GFWC) founded. • Sherman Antitrust Act.
1892	• Ida B. Wells launches antilynching campaign.
1893	• Wall Street panic touches off national depression.
1895	• J. P. Morgan bails out U.S. Treasury.
1901	• U.S. Steel incorporated and capitalized at $1.4 billion.

BROOKLYN BRIDGE FAN
Advertisers used images of the Brooklyn Bridge to sell everything from patent medicine to soap. The front side of this colorful commemorative fan celebrates the opening of the bridge on May 24, 1883; the reverse side promotes a furniture company. The background photograph shows the wooden platforms that connected the gothic towers as the huge cables went into place high over the East River. It took fourteen years and cost the lives of twenty-seven men to complete the bridge.
Fan: Museum of the City of New York; background: ©Bettmann/Corbis.

19 The City and its Workers 1870–1900

"A TOWN THAT CRAWLED NOW STANDS ERECT, AND WE WHOSE BACKS were bent above the hearths know how it got its spine," boasted a steelworker surveying New York City. Where once wooden buildings stood rooted in the mire of unpaved streets, cities of stone and steel sprang up in the last decades of the nineteenth century. The labor of millions of workers, many of them immigrants, laid the foundations for urban America.

No symbol better represented the new urban landscape than the Brooklyn Bridge, opened in May 1883. The great bridge soared over the East River in a single mile-long span. Begun in 1869, the bridge was the dream of builder John Roebling, who died in a freak accident almost as soon as construction began.

Building the Brooklyn Bridge took fourteen years and cost the lives of twenty-seven men. Nearly three hundred workers labored around the clock in three shifts, six days a week, most for $2 a day. To sink the foundation deep into the riverbed, common laborers tunneled down through mud and debris, working in reinforced wooden boxes called caissons, which were open at the bottom and pressurized to keep the water from flooding in. Before long, the workers experienced a mysterious malady they called "bends" because it left them doubled over in pain after they came to the surface. Scientists later discovered that nitrogen bubbles trapped in the bloodstream caused the condition and that it could be prevented if the men came up slowly to allow for decompression.

The first death occurred when the caissons reached a depth of seventy-one feet. On April 22, 1872, a heavyset German immigrant named John Meyers complained that he did not feel well and headed home to his boardinghouse. Before he could reach his bed, he collapsed and died. Eight days later, another man dropped dead, and the entire workforce in the caissons went out on strike. Conditions had become so hazardous and terrifying that the workers demanded a higher wage for fewer hours of work.

One worker, Frank Harris, remembered the men's fear of working in the caissons. As a scrawny sixteen-year-old from Ireland, Harris started to work a few days after landing in America. He described his experience:

> The six of us were working naked to the waist in the small iron chamber with the temperature of about 80 degrees Fahrenheit: In five minutes the

sweat was pouring from us, and all the while we were standing in icy water that was only kept from rising by the terrific pressure. No wonder the headaches were blinding.

By the fifth day, Harris experienced terrible shooting pains in his ears, and fearing he might go deaf, he quit. Like Harris, many immigrant workers walked off the job, often as many as a hundred a week. But a ready supply of immigrants meant that the work never slowed or stopped; new workers eagerly entered the caissons, where they could earn in a day more than they made in a week in Ireland or Italy.

Washington Roebling, who took over as chief engineer after his father's death, routinely worked twelve to fourteen hours six days a week. Soon he, too, fell victim to the bends and ended up an invalid, directing the completion of the bridge through a telescope from his window in Brooklyn Heights. His wife, Emily Warren Roebling, acted as site superintendent and general engineer of the project. At the dedication of the bridge, Roebling turned to his wife and said, "I want the world to know that you, too, are one of the Builders of the Bridge."

At the end of the nineteenth century, the Brooklyn Bridge stood as a symbol of many things: the industrial might of the United States; the labor of the nation's immigrants; the ingenuity and genius of its engineers and inventors; the rise of iron and steel; and, most of all, the ascendancy of urban America. Poised on the brink of the twentieth century, the nation was shifting inexorably from a rural, agricultural society to an urban, industrial nation. In the burgeoning cities, tensions would erupt into conflict as workers squared off to fight for their rights to organize into labor unions and to demand safer working conditions, shorter hours, and better pay. And the explosive growth of the cities would foster political corruption as unscrupulous bosses and entrepreneurs cashed in on the building boom. Immigrants, political bosses, middle-class managers, poor laborers, and the very rich populated the nation's cities, crowding the streets, laboring in the stores and factories, and taking their leisure at the new ballparks, amusement parks, dance halls, and municipal parks that dotted the urban landscape. As the new century dawned, the city and its workers moved to center stage in American life.

Workers in the Caissons

In 1870 *Frank Leslie's Illustrated Weekly* ran an article on the construction of the Brooklyn Bridge. Illustrations show the workers inside the caissons below the East River. Crews entered through a cylindrical airlock that took them down more than seventy feet. There in the wooden caissons they worked with pick and shovel to break up the big boulders and haul the rock away. "What with the flaming lights, the deep shadows, the confusing noise of hammer, drills, and chains, the half-naked forms flitting about," wrote one reporter, the scene resembled hell. The hot, dangerous work fell primarily to Irish immigrant workers. Library of Congress.

▸ The Rise of the City

"We cannot all live in cities, yet nearly all seem determined to do so," New York editor Horace Greeley complained. The last three decades of the nineteenth century witnessed an urban explosion. Cities and towns grew more than twice as rapidly as the total population. Among the fastest-growing cities, Chicago expanded at a meteoric rate, doubling its population each decade. The number of cities with more than 100,000 inhabitants jumped from eighteen in 1870 to thirty-eight in 1900. Most of the nation's largest cities were east of the Mississippi, although St. Louis and San Francisco both ranked among the top ten urban areas. By 1900, the United States boasted three cities with more than a million inhabitants—New York, Chicago, and Philadelphia.

Patterns of **global migration** contributed to the rise of the city. In the port cities of the East Coast, more than fourteen million people arrived, many from southern and eastern Europe, and huddled together in dense urban ghettos. The word *slum* entered the American vocabulary along with a growing concern over the rising tide of newcomers. In the city, the widening gap between rich and poor became more visible, exacerbated by changes in the city landscape brought about by advances in transportation and technology.

The Urban Explosion: A Global Migration

The United States grew up in the country and moved to the city, or so it seemed by the end of the nineteenth century. Between 1870 and 1900, eleven million people moved into cities. Burgeoning industrial centers such as Pittsburgh, Chicago, New York, and Cleveland acted as giant magnets, attracting workers from the countryside. But rural Americans were by no means the only ones migrating to cities. Worldwide in scope, the movement from rural areas to urban industrial centers attracted millions of immigrants to American shores in the waning decades of the nineteenth century.

By the 1870s, the world could be conceptualized as three interconnected geographic regions (Map 19.1). At the center stood an industrial core bounded by Chicago and St. Louis in the west; Toronto, Glasgow, and Berlin in the north; Warsaw in the east; and Milan, Barcelona, Richmond, and Louisville in the south. Surrounding this industrial core lay a vast agricultural domain encompassing Canada, much of Scandinavia, Russia and Poland, Hungary, Greece, Italy and Sicily, southern Spain, the South and the western plains of America, central and northern Mexico, the hinterlands of northern China, and the southern islands of Japan. Capitalist development in the late nineteenth century shattered traditional patterns of economic activity in this rural periphery. As old patterns broke down, these rural areas exported, along with other raw materials, new recruits for the industrial labor force.

"We cannot all live in cities, yet nearly all seem determined to do so."
— New York editor HORACE GREELEY

Beyond this second circle lay an even larger third world including the Caribbean, Central and South America, the Middle East, Africa, India, and most of Asia. Ties between this part of the world and the industrial core strengthened in the late nineteenth century, but most of the people living there stayed put. They worked on plantations and railroads, and in mines and ports, as part of a huge export network managed by foreign powers that staked out spheres of influence and colonies in this vast region.

In the 1870s, railroad expansion and low steamship fares gave the world's peoples a newfound mobility, enabling industrialists to draw on a global population for cheap labor. When Andrew Carnegie opened his first steel mill in 1872, his superintendent hired workers he called "buckwheats" — young American boys just off the farm. By the 1890s, however, Carnegie's workforce was liberally sprinkled with other rural boys, Hungarians and Slavs who had migrated to the United States, willing to work for low wages.

Altogether, more than 25 million immigrants came to the United States between 1850 and 1920. They came from all directions: east from Asia, south from Canada, north from Latin America, and west from Europe (Map 19.2). Part of a worldwide migration, immigrants traveled to South America and Australia as well as to the United States. Yet more than 70 percent of all European immigrants chose North America as their destination.

The largest number of immigrants to the United States came from the British Isles and from German-speaking lands (Figure 19.1). The vast majority of immigrants were white; Asians accounted for fewer than one million immigrants, and other people of color numbered even fewer. Yet ingrained racial prejudices

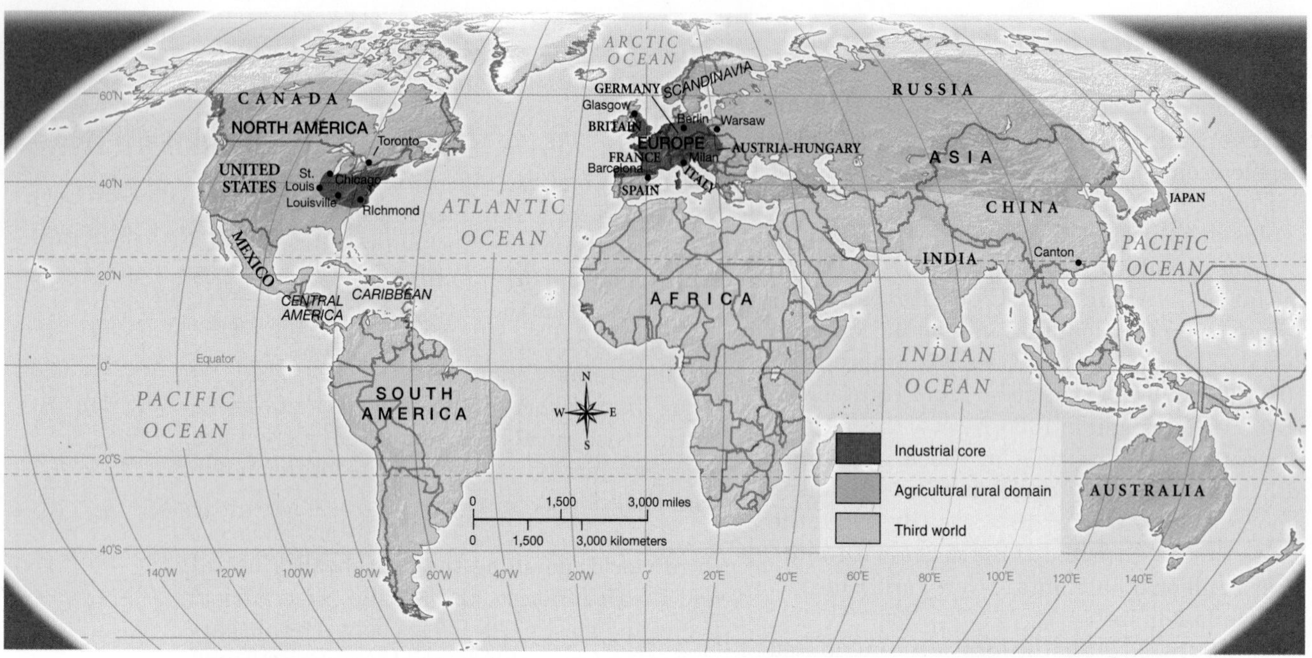

MAP ACTIVITY

Map 19.1 Economic Regions of the World, 1890s
The global nature of the world economy at the turn of the twentieth century is indicated by three interconnected geographic regions. At the center stands the industrial core — western Europe and the northeastern United States. The second region — the agricultural periphery — supplied immigrant laborers to the industries in the core. Beyond these two regions lay a vast area tied economically to the industrial core by colonialism.

READING THE MAP: What types of economic regions were contained in the United States in this period? Which continents held most of the industrial core? Which held most of the agricultural rural domain? Which held the greatest portion of the third world?
CONNECTIONS: Which of these three regions provided the bulk of immigrant workers to the United States? What major changes prompted the global migration at the end of the nineteenth century?

increasingly influenced the country's perception of immigration patterns. One of the classic formulations of the history of European immigration divided immigrants into two distinct waves that have been called the "old" and the "new" immigration. According to this theory, before 1880 the majority of immigrants came from northern and western Europe, with Germans, Irish, English, and Scandinavians making up approximately 85 percent of the newcomers. After 1880, the pattern shifted, with more and more ships carrying passengers from southern and eastern Europe. Italians, Hungarians, eastern European Jews, Turks, Armenians, Poles, Russians, and other Slavic peoples accounted for more than 80 percent of all immigrants by 1896 (Figure 19.2). Implicit in the distinction was an invidious comparison between "old" pioneer settlers and "new" unskilled laborers. Yet this sweeping generalization spoke more to perception than to reality. In fact, many of the earlier immigrants from Ireland, Germany, and Scandinavia came not as settlers or farmers, but as wageworkers, and they were met with much the same disdain as the Italians and Slavs who followed them.

The "new" immigration resulted from a number of factors. Improved economic conditions in western Europe coupled with increased immigration to Australia and Canada slowed the flow of immigrants coming into the United States from northern and western Europe. At the same time, economic depression in southern Italy, the persecution of Jews in eastern Europe, and a general desire to avoid conscription into the Russian army led many people from southern and eastern Europe to move to the United States. The need of America's industries for cheap, unskilled labor during prosperous years also stimulated immigration.

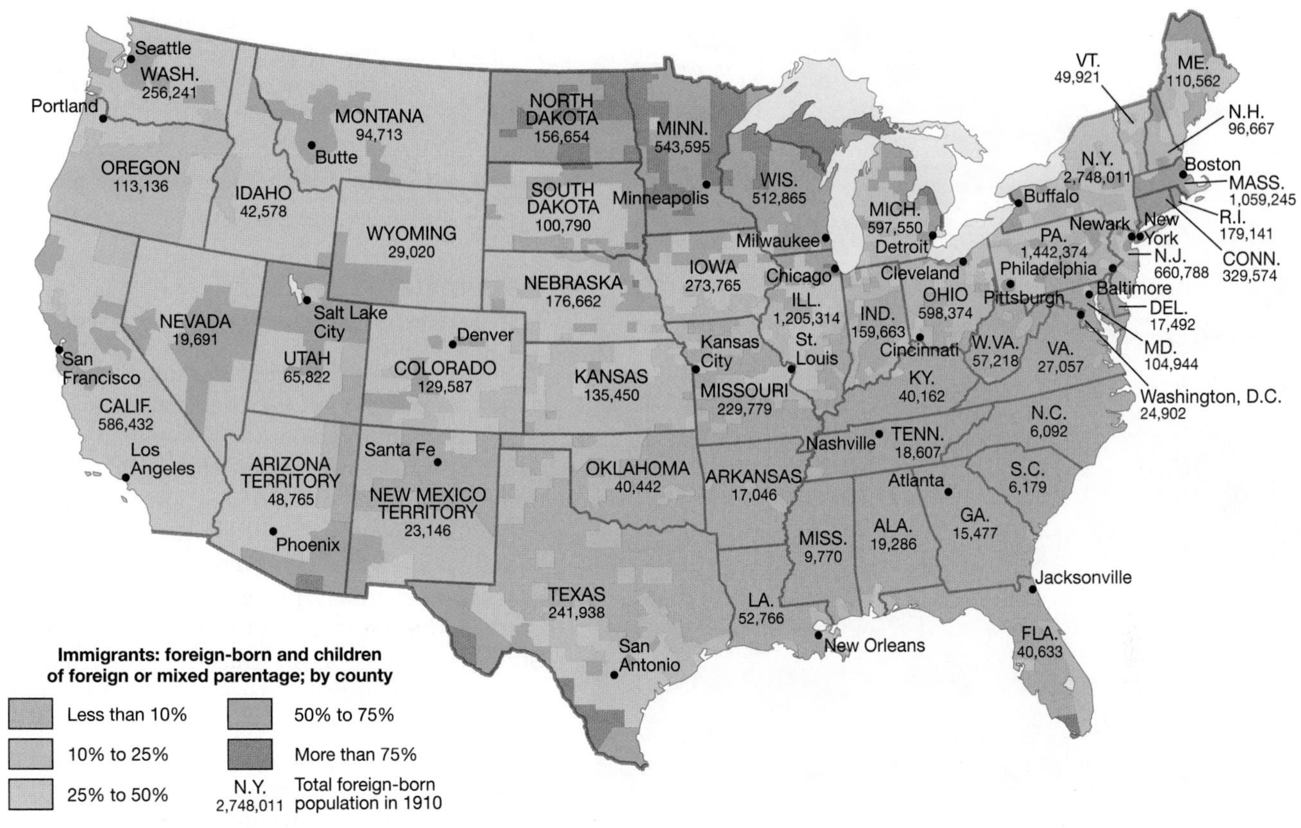

MAP ACTIVITY

Map 19.2 The Impact of Immigration, to 1910

Immigration flowed in all directions — south from Canada, north from Mexico and Latin America, east from Asia, and west from Europe.

READING THE MAP: Which states had high percentages of immigrants? Which cities attracted the most immigrants? Which cities attracted the fewest?

CONNECTIONS: Why did most immigrants gravitate toward the cities? Why do you think the South drew such a low percentage of immigrants?

Steamship companies courted immigrants — a highly profitable, self-loading cargo. By the 1880s, the price of a ticket from Liverpool had dropped to less than $25. Would-be immigrants eager for information about the United States relied on letters from friends and relatives, advertisements, and word of mouth — sources that were not always dependable or truthful. Even photographs proved deceptive: Workers dressed in their Sunday best looked more prosperous than they actually were to relatives in the old country, where only the very wealthy wore white collars or silk dresses. No wonder people left for the United States believing, as one Italian immigrant observed, "that if they were ever fortunate enough to reach America, they would fall into a pile of manure and get up brushing the diamonds out of their hair."

Most of the newcomers stayed in the nation's cities. By 1900, almost two-thirds of the country's immigrant population resided in cities, many of the immigrants too poor to move on. (The average laborer immigrating to the United States carried only about $21.50.) Although the foreign-born population rarely outnumbered the native-born population, taken together immigrants and their American-born children did constitute a majority in some areas, particularly in the nation's largest cities: Philadelphia, 55 percent; Boston, 66 percent; Chicago, 75 percent; and New York City, an amazing 80 percent in 1900.

Not all the newcomers came to stay. Perhaps eight million European immigrants — most of them young men — worked for a year or a season and then returned to their homelands. Immigration officers called these immigrants,

Russian Immigrant Family
A Russian immigrant family is shown leaving Ellis Island in 1900. Notice the white slips of paper pinned to their coats indicating that they have been processed. The family is well dressed, but the paucity of their possessions testifies to the struggles they face. She carries her belongings in a white cloth sack, and he has a suitcase in one hand and bedding draped over his arm. An immigration official in uniform stands on the left. Keystone-Mast Collection, UCR/California Museum of Photography, University of California, Riverside.

many of them Italians, "birds of passage" because they followed a regular pattern of migration to and from the United States. By 1900, almost 75 percent of the new immigrants were young, single men.

Women generally had less access to funds for travel and faced tighter family control. Because the traditional sexual division of labor relied on women's unpaid domestic labor and care of the very young and the very old, women most often came to the United States as wives, mothers, or daughters, not as single wage laborers. Only among the Irish did women immigrants outnumber men by a small margin from 1871 to 1891.

Jews from eastern Europe most often came with their families and came to stay. Beginning in the 1880s, a wave of violent **pogroms**, or persecutions, in Russia and Poland prompted the departure of more than a million Jews in the next two decades. (See "Seeking the American Promise," page 610.) Most of the Jewish immigrants settled in the port cities of the East, creating distinct ethnic enclaves, like Hester Street in the heart of New York City's Lower East Side, which rang with the calls of pushcart peddlers and vendors hawking their wares, from pickles to feather beds.

Racism and the Cry for Immigration Restriction

Ethnic diversity and racism played a role in dividing skilled workers (those with a craft or specialized ability) from the globe-hopping proletariat of unskilled workers (those who supplied muscle or tended machines). As industrialists mechanized to replace skilled workers with lower-paid unskilled labor, they drew on recent immigrants, particularly those from southern and eastern Europe, who had come to the United States in the hope of bettering their lives. Skilled workers, frequently members of older immigrant groups, criticized the newcomers. One Irish worker complained, "There should be a law . . . to keep all the Italians from comin' in and takin' the bread out of the mouths of honest people."

The Irish worker's resentment brings into focus the impact of racism on America's immigrant laborers. Throughout the nineteenth century and into the twentieth, members of the educated elite as well as the uneducated viewed ethnic and even religious differences as racial characteristics, referring to the Polish or the Jewish "race." Americans judged "new" immigrants of southern and eastern European "races" as inferior. Each wave of newcomers was deemed somehow inferior to the established residents. The Irish who criticized the Italians so harshly had themselves been stigmatized as a lesser "race" a generation earlier.

Immigrants not only brought their own religious and racial prejudices to the United States but also absorbed the popular prejudices of American culture. Social Darwinism, with its strongly racist overtones, decreed that whites stood at the top of the evolutionary ladder. But who was "white"? Skin color supposedly served as a marker for the "new" immigrants — "swarthy" Italians; dark-haired, olive-skinned Jews. But even blond, blue-eyed Poles were not considered white. The social construction of "race" is nowhere more apparent than in the testimony of an Irish dockworker who boasted that he hired only "white men," a category that he insisted excluded "Poles and Italians." For the new immigrants, Americanization and assimilation would prove inextricably part of becoming "white."

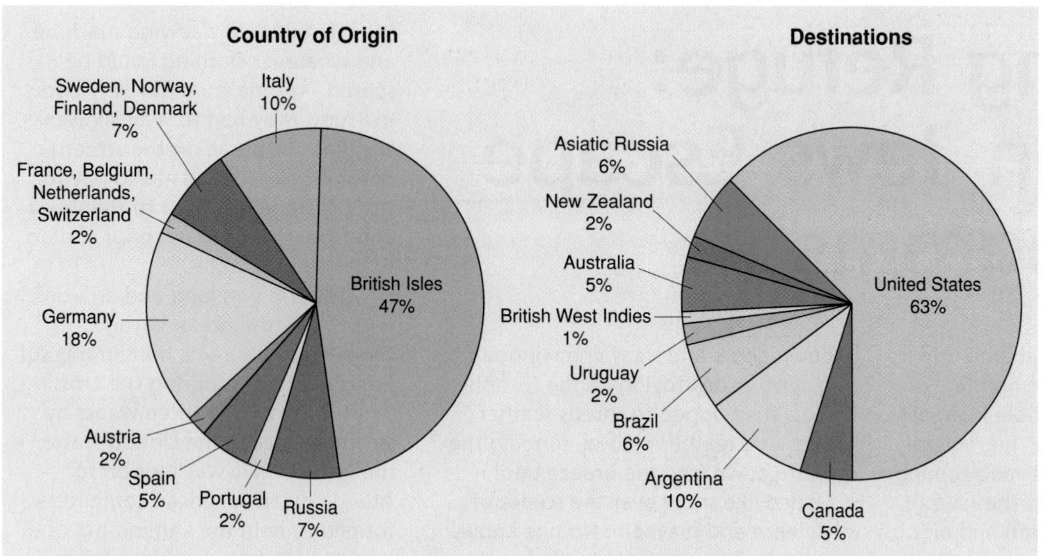

FIGURE 19.1 GLOBAL COMPARISON: European Emigration, 1870–1890
A look at European emigration between 1870 and 1890 shows that emigrants from Germany, Austria, and the British Isles (including England, Ireland, Scotland, and Wales) formed the largest group of out-migrants during those decades. After 1890, the origin of European emigrants tilted south and east, with Italians and eastern Europeans growing in number (see Figure 19.2). The United States, by far the most popular destination for global emigrants in this period, took in nearly two-thirds of the Europeans who left their homelands. What factors might account for the United States being the most popular destination for European emigrants?

For African Americans, the cities of the North promised not just economic opportunity but an escape from institutionalized segregation and persecution. Throughout the South, Jim Crow laws — restrictions that segregated blacks — became common in the decades following Reconstruction. Intimidation and lynching terrorized blacks. "To die from the bite of frost is far more glorious than

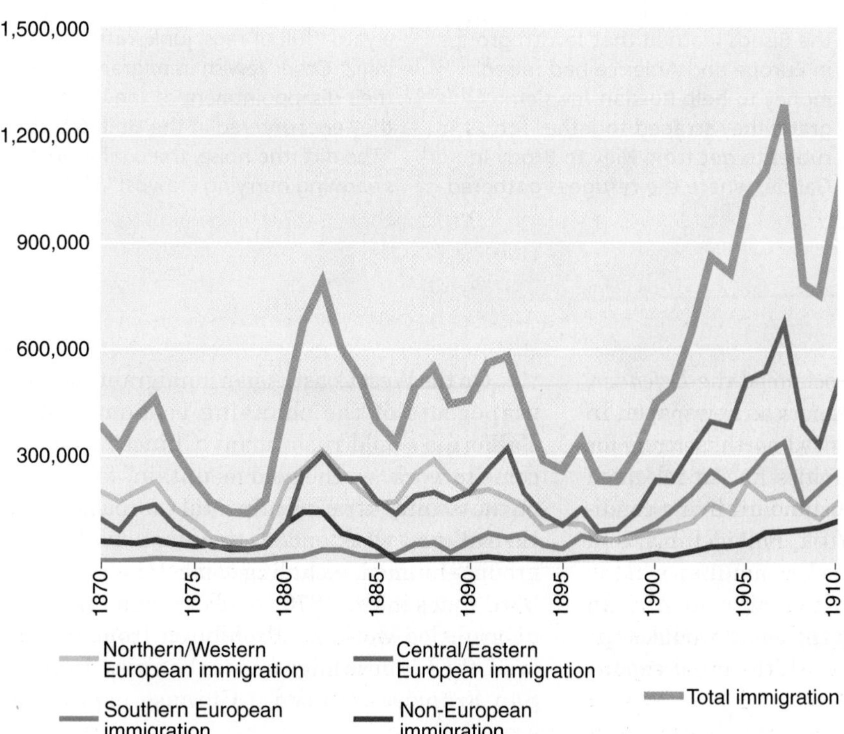

FIGURE 19.2 European Immigration, 1870–1910
Before 1880, more than 85 percent of U.S. immigrants came from northern and western Europe—Germany, Ireland, England, and the Scandinavian countries. After 1880, 80 percent of the "new" immigrants came from Italy, Turkey, Hungary, Armenia, Poland, Russia, and other Slavic countries.

SEEKING THE AMERICAN PROMISE

Seeking Refuge: Russian Jews Escape the Pogroms

Fifteen-year-old Abraham Bisno recalled running for his life. "I hid myself in a clay hole in an old brickyard on a hillside," he remembered. "I witnessed the mob coming down the hill to assault the Jewish settlement. I saw children and old people beaten — buildings burned — I heard women screaming."

Violent pogroms — deadly riots against Jews — erupted in Russia in 1881 in the wake of the assassination of Czar Alexander II, sparked by rumors that he had been murdered by Jews. Kiev, where Abraham Bisno lived with his parents, became the scene of a pogrom in late April. "For days on end," Bisno wrote, "entire neighborhoods were looted and largely destroyed by crowds estimated at over four thousand." Fanatical priests fed anti-Semitism (hatred of Jews) by denouncing the Jews as heartless "Christ-killers" who used the blood of Christian children in their rituals. The government failed to move quickly to put down the violence, even after only one of the ten who plotted the czar's assassination turned out to be Jewish.

Bands of Russians swarmed through the Jewish quarters, breaking down doors and smashing windows, looting or destroying all the furnishings. They ripped to shreds feather beds and feather pillows, sending the white down into the breeze until it settled like snow over the scenes of violence and mayhem. No one knows precisely how many Jews died at the hands of the mob, but estimates range as high as five hundred. "The building we lived in and the place we worked in were assaulted at the same time," Bisno recalled. "Mother ran for her life while we struggled for ours; we were all separated by the mob — the shop was destroyed, the goods carried away."

These and subsequent pogroms and persecutions prompted a great wave of Jewish migration. Between 1880 and 1914, more than 2.7 million Jews sought refuge from religious persecution, the vast majority of them heading to the United States. Among the first to emigrate were Abraham Bisno and his family. When the Bisnos learned that Jewish groups in Europe and America had raised money to help Russian Jews emigrate, they scraped together forty rubles to get from Kiev to Brody in Galicia, where the refugees gathered. "Our family sold a sewing machine and whatever clothing could be spared — some from our very backs." In Brody, they had to wait six weeks, begging for bread on the streets, before they received aid to pay for their passage overland to Hamburg and from there to Liverpool and on to the United States.

The trip was long and arduous, particularly the ocean voyage. Crowded in steerage, immigrants suffered seasickness during the crossing, which took two to three weeks by steamer. Once in the United States, the Bisno family was sent on to Atlanta by an American committee formed to help the immigrants. The men quickly found work as tailors. Bisno struck out on his own, moving to Chattanooga, where he apprenticed to an English-speaking tailor and quickly picked up the language by reading signs and advertisements. But the Bisnos were unhappy in the South. Abraham's mother complained that she could not find a butcher who sold kosher meat, and his father fretted that there was no Orthodox synagogue in the neighborhood. So after nine months, the family moved to a larger Jewish community in Chicago.

The slums of the nation's big cities, where many of the Jewish immigrants ended up, were far from a "promised land." The Bisnos lived in a dilapidated shack above a stable with a yard "full of rags, junk, rats, and vermin." Other Jewish immigrants voiced their disappointment at the conditions they encountered in the United States. "The dirt, the noise, the confusion, the swarming hurrying crowds!" Goldie

at the hands of a mob," proclaimed the *Defender*, Chicago's largest African American newspaper. In the 1890s, many blacks moved north, settling for the most part in the growing cities. Racism relegated them to poor jobs and substandard living conditions, but by 1900 New York, Philadelphia, and Chicago had the largest black communities in the nation. Although the most significant African American migration out of the South would occur during and after World War I, the great exodus was already under way.

On the West Coast, Asian immigrants became scapegoats of the changing economy. After California's gold rush, many Chinese who had come to work "on the gold mountain" found jobs on the country's transcontinental railroads. When the railroad work ended, they took work other groups shunned, including domestic service. But hard times in the 1870s made them a target for disgruntled workers. Prohibited from owning land, the Chinese migrated to the cities. In 1870, San Francisco housed a Chinese population

Stone exclaimed. "My heart sank. This was all so different from what I had expected or dreamed."

Bad as conditions were, the immigrant Jews appreciated the safe haven the United States afforded. And although the sweatshops where Bisno and other Jewish immigrants labored were dark and bleak, for most Jews the slums proved a temporary prison. The United States provided not only a refuge but also a chance to start over and prosper. Bisno watched as many of his friends and relatives, after saving or borrowing a little money, opened small businesses of their own. "All had to begin in a very small way," he recalled. "With a hundred or two hundred dollars they were able to start grocery stores, markets, cigar stores." Bisno quickly moved up in his trade, becoming a contractor in a sweatshop by the time he reached the age of sixteen. But then his life took a different course. Moved by the Haymarket martyrs, he converted to socialism in 1886, joined the Knights of Labor, and went on to become a labor organizer. The first president of the Chicago Cloak Makers' Union, he worked until his death in 1929 to improve the lot of garment workers.

Jewish Refugees from the Pogroms
In this colorful depiction, Liberty, dressed in the Stars and Stripes, opens the gates of the country to a Jewish immigrant couple and their children fleeing the pogroms in Russia. Abraham Bisno and his family were among the first group of immigrants to flee Kiev after the pogroms of 1881 and to seek refuge in the United States. Yivo Institute for Jewish Research.

Questions for Consideration

1. Compare the Jewish immigrants from Russia with other immigrant groups discussed in this chapter. What attracted each group to America? What were their expectations? How did each group fare?
2. What aspects of Bisno's life in America led him to join the labor movement? How may his childhood in Russia have influenced him in this direction?

estimated at 12,022, and it continued to grow until passage of the Chinese Exclusion Act in 1882 (see chapter 17). For the first time in the nation's history, U.S. law excluded an immigrant group on the basis of race.

Huang Zunxian came to San Francisco in 1882 as Chinese consul general. Disillusioned with the anti-Chinese violence he saw all around him, he wrote a series of angry poems that took Americans to task for their hypocrisy. One of them read:

> They have sealed the gates tightly
> Door after door with guards beating alarms.
> Anyone with a yellow-colored face
> Is beaten even if guiltless.
> The American eagle strides the heavens soaring
> With half of the globe clutched in his claw.
> Although the Chinese arrived later,
> Couldn't you leave them a little space?

Despite the Chinese Exclusion Act, some Chinese managed to come to America using a loophole that allowed relatives to join their

Rags to Riches
The formulaic novels of popular author Horatio Alger feature fatherless young men who, through the right combination of "pluck and luck," move ahead in the world. Alger's message of rags to riches fueled the dreams of countless young people in the late nineteenth century. Yet despite the myth, few Americans rose from rags to riches. Even Alger's heroes, such as his popular character Ragged Dick, pictured here, more often traded their rags for respectability, not for great wealth.
Picture Research Consultants & Archives.

families. By contrast, the nation's small Japanese community of about 3,000 expanded rapidly after 1890, until pressures to keep out all Asians led in 1910 to the creation of an immigration station at Angel Island in San Francisco Bay. Asian immigrants were detained there, sometimes for months, and many were deported as "undesirable." Their sad stories can be read in the graffiti on the barracks walls.

On the East Coast, the volume of immigration from Europe in the last two decades of the century proved unprecedented. In 1888 alone, more than half a million Europeans landed in America, 75 percent of them in New York City. The Statue of Liberty, a gift from the people of France erected in 1886, stood sentinel in the harbor. The verse inscribed at Liberty's base was penned by a young Jewish woman named Emma Lazarus:

> Give me your tired, your poor,
> Your huddled masses yearning to breathe free,
> The wretched refuse of your teeming shore,
> Send these, the homeless, tempest-tost to me,
> I lift my lamp beside the golden door!

The tide of immigrants to New York City soon swamped the immigration office at Castle Garden in lower Manhattan. After the federal government took over immigration in 1890, it built a facility on **Ellis Island** in New York harbor, opened in 1892. After a fire gutted the wooden building, an imposing new brick edifice replaced it in 1900. Its overcrowded halls became the gateway to the United States for millions.

To many Americans, the "new" immigrants seemed uneducated, backward, and uncouth — impossible to assimilate. "These people are not Americans," editorialized the popular journal *Public Opinion*, "they are the very scum and offal of Europe." Terence V. Powderly, head of the broadly inclusive Knights of Labor, complained that the newcomers "herded together like animals and lived like beasts." Blue-blooded Yankees led by Senator Henry Cabot Lodge of Massachusetts formed an unlikely alliance with leaders of organized labor — who feared that immigrants would drive down wages — to press for immigration restrictions. Lodge and his supporters championed a literacy test as a requirement for immigration, knowing that the vast majority of Italian and Slavic peasants could neither read nor write. In 1896, Congress approved a literacy test for immigrants, but President Grover Cleveland promptly vetoed it. "It is said," the president reminded Congress, "that the quality of recent immigration is undesirable. The time is quite within recent memory when the same thing was said of immigrants, who, with their descendants, are now numbered among our best citizens." Cleveland's veto forestalled immigration restriction but did not stop anti-immigrant forces from seeking to close the gates. They would continue to press for restrictions until they achieved their goal in the 1920s (as discussed in chapter 23).

The Social Geography of the City

During the Gilded Age, cities experienced demographic and technological changes that greatly altered the social geography of the city. Cleveland, Ohio, provides a good example. In the 1870s, Cleveland was a small city in both population and area. Oil magnate John D. Rockefeller could, and often did, walk from his large brick house on Euclid Avenue to his office downtown. On his

Knife and Scissors Sharpener Pushcart
Joseph Antonucci, an Italian immigrant, used this knife and scissors sharpener cart on Chicago's West Side in 1900. After a day's work, Antonucci usually parked the cart in a fire station or a customer's stable and then took the train home. Sometimes he pushed his cart for miles to ply his trade beyond the city limits in towns such as Hammond, Indiana. For poor immigrants who could not afford rent, pushcarts provided a cheap and portable means of livelihood. The cries of street peddlers, vendors, and scissors sharpeners like Antonucci added to the cacophony of the urban streets. Chicago Historical Society.

way, he passed the small homes of his clerks and other middle-class families. Behind these homes ran miles of alleys crowded with the dwellings of Cleveland's working class. Farther out, on the shores of Lake Erie, close to the factories and foundries, clustered the shanties of the city's poorest laborers.

Within two decades, the Cleveland that Rockefeller knew no longer existed. The coming of mass transit transformed the walking city. In its place emerged a central business district surrounded by concentric rings of residences organized by ethnicity and income. First the horse car in the 1870s and then the electric streetcar in the 1880s made it possible for those who could afford the five-cent fare to work downtown and flee after work to the "cool green rim" of the city, with its single-family homes, lawns, gardens, and trees. Social segregation — the separation of rich and poor, and of ethnic and old-stock Americans — was one of the major social changes engendered by the rise of the industrial metropolis, evident not only in Cleveland but in cities across the nation.

Race and ethnicity affected the way cities evolved. Newcomers to the nation's cities faced hostility and not surprisingly sought out their kin and country folk as they struggled to survive. Distinct ethnic neighborhoods often formed around a synagogue or church. African Americans typically experienced the greatest residential segregation, but every large city had its ethnic enclaves — Little Italy, Chinatown, Bohemia Flats, Germantown — where English was rarely spoken.

Poverty, crowding, dirt, and disease constituted the daily reality of New York City's immigrant poor — a plight documented by photojournalist **Jacob Riis** in his best-selling book *How the Other Half Lives* (1890). By taking his camera into the hovels of the poor, Riis opened the nation's eyes to conditions in the city's slums (see chapter 21, "Visualizing History," page 688). Riis invited his readers into a Bottle Street tenement:

> One, two, three beds are there, if the old boxes and heaps of foul straw can be called by that name; a broken stove with a crazy pipe from which the smoke leaks at every joint; a table of rough boards propped up on boxes, piles of rubbish in the corner. The closeness and smell are appalling.

While Riis's audience shivered at his revelations about the "other half," many middle-class Americans worried equally about the excesses of the wealthy. They feared the class antagonism fueled by the growing chasm between rich and poor so visible in the nation's cities, and shared Riis's view that "the real danger to society comes not only from the tenements, but from the ill-spent wealth which reared them."

The excesses of the Gilded Age's newly minted millionaires were nowhere more visible than in the lifestyle of the Vanderbilts. "Commodore"

The Electric Streetcar
This colorful electric streetcar ran in Washington, D.C., from 1888 to 1913, replacing horse-drawn vehicles. By 1900 over 200 miles of track ran through the nation's capital. The electric cars revolutionized the social geography of the city. The token shown gave riders the opportunity to travel from the city center to the suburbs for just a few cents. Streetcar: National Museum of American History, Smithsonian Institution, Behring Center; token: Picture Research Consultants & Archives.

Cornelius Vanderbilt, an uncouth ferryman who built the New York Central Railroad, died in 1877, leaving his son $90 million. William Vanderbilt doubled that sum, and his two sons proceeded to spend lavishly on Fifth Avenue mansions and "cottages" in Newport, Rhode Island, that sought to rival the palaces of Europe (see chapter 18, "Visualizing History," page 574). In 1883, Alva (Mrs. William) Vanderbilt launched herself into New York society by throwing a costume party so opulent that not even old New York society, which turned up its nose at the nouveau riche, could resist an invitation. Dressed as a Venetian princess, the hostess greeted her twelve hundred guests. But her sister-in-law Alice Vanderbilt stole the show by appearing as that miraculous new invention, the electric light, resplendent in a white satin evening dress studded with diamonds. The *New York World* speculated that Alva Vanderbilt's party cost more than a quarter of a million dollars (more than $4 million today).

Such ostentatious displays of wealth became especially alarming when they were coupled with disdain for the well-being of ordinary people. When a reporter in 1882 asked William Vanderbilt whether he considered the public good when running his railroads, he shot back, "The public be damned." The fear that America had become a plutocracy — a society ruled by the rich — gained credence from the fact that the wealthiest 1 percent of the population owned more than half the real and personal property in the country. As the new century dawned, reformers would form a progressive movement to address the problems of urban industrialism and the substandard living and working conditions it produced.

REVIEW Why did American cities experience explosive growth in the late nineteenth century?

▸ At Work in Industrial America

The number of industrial wageworkers in the United States exploded in the second half of the nineteenth century, more than tripling from 5.3 million in 1860 to 17.4 million in 1900. More than half of the country's men, women, and children made up the laboring class that performed manual work for wages. These workers toiled in a variety of settings. Many skilled workers and artisans still earned a living in small workshops. But with the rise of corporate capitalism, large factories, mills, and mines increasingly dotted the landscape. Sweatshops and outwork — the contracting of piecework, including finishing garments by hand, to be performed in the home — provided work experiences different from those of factory operatives and industrial workers. Pick-and-shovel labor, whether on the railroads or in the building trades, constituted yet another kind of work. Managers, as well as women "typewriters" and salesclerks, formed a new white-collar segment of America's workforce.

America's Diverse Workers

Common laborers formed the backbone of the American labor force. They built the railroads and subways, tunneled under New York's East River to anchor the Brooklyn Bridge, and helped lay the foundation of industrial America. These "human machines" stood at the bottom of the country's economic ladder and generally came from the most recent immigrant groups. Initially, the Irish wielded the picks and shovels that built American cities, but by the turn of the century, as the Irish bettered their lot, Slavs and Italians took up their tools.

At the opposite end of labor's hierarchy stood skilled craftsmen like iron puddler James J. Davis, a Welsh immigrant who worked in the Pennsylvania mills. Using brains along with brawn, puddlers took up the melted pig iron in the heat of the furnace and, with long, heavy "spoons" (poles), formed the cooling metal into 200-pound balls, relying on eye and intuition to make each ball uniform. Davis likened his work to baking bread: "I am like some frantic baker in the inferno. . . . My spoon weighs twenty-five pounds, my porridge is pasty iron, and the heat of my kitchen is so great that if my body was not hardened to it the ordeal would drop me in my tracks."

Possessing such a skill meant earning good wages. Davis made up to $7 a day, when there was work. But most industry and manufacturing work in the nineteenth century remained seasonal; few workers could count on year-round pay. In addition, two major depressions only twenty years apart, beginning in 1873 and 1893, spelled unemployment and hardship. In an era before unemployment insurance, workers' compensation, or old-age pensions, even the best worker could not guarantee security for his family. "The fear of ending in the poor-house is one of the terrors that dog a man through life," Davis confessed.

Skilled workers like Davis wielded power on the shop floor. Employers attempted to limit workers' control by replacing people with machines, breaking down skilled work into ever-smaller tasks that could be performed by unskilled factory operatives. New England's textile mills provide a classic example of the effects of mechanized factory labor in the nineteenth century. Mary, a weaver at the mills in Fall River, Massachusetts, went to work in the 1880s at the age of twelve. By then, mechanization of the looms had reduced the job of the weaver to watching for breaks in the thread. "At first the noise is fierce, and you have to breathe the cotton all the time, but you get used to it," Mary told a reporter from *Independent* magazine. "When the bobbin flies out and a girl gets hurt, you can't hear her shout — not if she just screams, you can't. She's got to wait, 'till you see her. . . . Lots of us is deaf."

Sweatshop Worker
Sweatshop workers endured crowded and often dangerous conditions. Most were young women, like the one shown here sewing pants in New York City. Young working women earned little money but prided themselves on their independence. Notice the young woman's stylish hairdo, white shirtwaist, and necklace (an indication that she did not turn over all the money in her pay envelope to her father, as was often the case). George Eastman House.

During the 1880s, the number of foreign-born mill workers almost doubled. At Fall River, Mary and her Scots-Irish family resented the new immigrants. "The Polaks learn weavin' quick," she remarked, using a common derogatory term to identify a rival group. "They just as soon live on nothin' and work like that. But it won't do 'em much good for all they'll make out of it." Employers encouraged racial and ethnic antagonism because it inhibited labor organization.

The majority of factory operatives in the textile mills were young, unmarried women like Mary. They worked from six in the morning to six at night six days a week, and they took home about $1 a day. The seasonal nature of the work also drove wages down. "Like as not your mill will 'shut down' three months," and "some weeks you only get two or three days' work," Mary recounted. After twenty years of working in the mill, Mary's family had not been able to scrape together enough money to buy a house: "We saved some, but something always comes."

Mechanization transformed the garment industry as well. With the introduction of the foot-pedaled sewing machine in the 1850s and the use of mechanical cloth-cutting knives in the 1870s, independent tailors were replaced with workers hired by contractors to sew pieces of cloth into suits and dresses. Working in **sweatshops**, small rooms hired for the season or even in the contractor's own tenement, women and children formed an important segment of garment workers. Discriminated against in the marketplace, where they earned less than men, women generally worked for wages for only eight to ten years, until they married.

Sadie Frowne, a sixteen-year-old Polish Jew, went to work in a Brooklyn sweatshop in the 1890s. Frowne sewed for eleven hours a day in a 20-by-14-foot room containing fourteen machines. "The machines go like mad all day, because the faster you work the more money you get," she recalled. Paid by the piece, she earned about $4.50 a week and, by rigid economy, tried to save $2. Young and single, Frowne typified the woman wage earner in the late nineteenth century. In 1890, the average workingwoman was twenty-two and had been working since the age of fifteen, laboring twelve hours a day six days a week and earning less than $6 a week. Only marriage delivered women from dead-end jobs. No wonder single working women scrimped to buy ribbons and finery to make themselves attractive to young men.

Bootblacks
The faces and hands of the two bootblacks shown here with a third boy on a New York City street in 1896 testify to their grimy trade. Boys as young as six years old found work on city streets as bootblacks and newsboys. Often they worked for contractors who took a cut of their meager earnings. When families could no longer afford to feed their children, boys often headed out on their own at a young age. For these child workers, even free education was a luxury they could not afford. Alice Austin photo, Staten Island Historical Society.

The Family Economy: Women and Children

In 1900, the typical male worker in manufacturing earned $435 a year, about $12,000 in today's dollars. Many working-class families, whether native-born or immigrant, lived in or near poverty, their economic survival dependent on the contributions of all family members, regardless of sex or age. "Father," asked one young immigrant girl, "does everybody in America live like this? Go to work early, come home late, eat and go to Sleep? And the next day again work, eat, and sleep?" Most workers did. The **family economy** meant that everyone needed to contribute to maintain even the most meager household. Children dutifully turned over their wages to their fathers and kept only a tiny portion for themselves. One statistician estimated that in 1900 as many as 64 percent of working-class families relied on income other than the husband's wages to make ends meet. The paid and unpaid work of women and children proved essential for family survival, let alone economic advancement.

In the cities, boys as young as six years old plied their trades as bootblacks and newsboys. Often working under an adult contractor, these children earned as little as fifty cents a day. Many of them were homeless — orphaned or

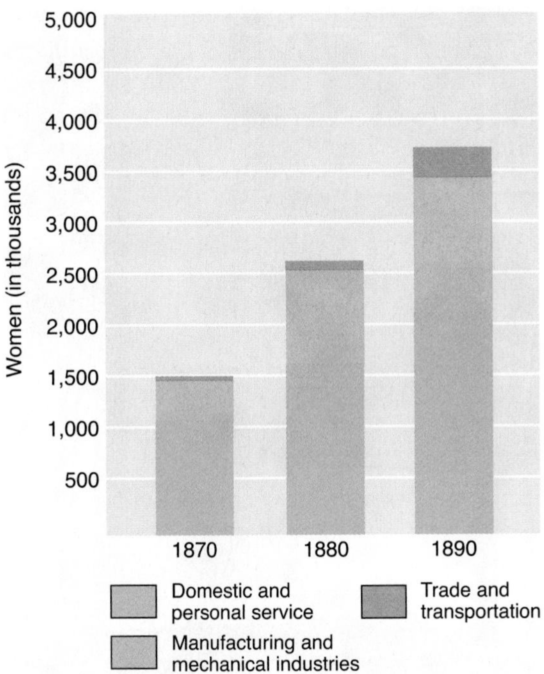

FIGURE 19.3 Women and Work, 1870–1890
In 1870, close to 1.5 million women worked in nonagricultural occupations. By 1890, that number had more than doubled to 3.7 million. More and more women sought work in manufacturing and mechanical industries, although domestic service still constituted the largest employment arena for women.

cast off by their families. "We wuz six, and we ain't got no father," a child of twelve told reporter Jacob Riis. "Some of us had to go."

Child labor increased decade by decade after 1870. The percentage of children under fifteen engaged in paid labor did not drop until after World War I. The 1900 census estimated that 1,750,178 children ages ten to fifteen were employed, an increase of more than a million over thirty years. Children in this age range constituted more than 18 percent of the industrial labor force. Many younger children not counted by the census worked beside their older siblings in mills, in factories, and on the streets.

In the late nineteenth century, the number of women workers also rose sharply, with their most common occupations changing slowly from domestic service to factory work and then to office work. In 1870, the census listed 1.5 million women working for wages in nonagricultural occupations. By 1890, the number had more than doubled, with 3.7 million women working for pay (Figure 19.3). Women's working patterns varied considerably according to race and ethnicity. White married women, even among the working class, rarely worked for wages outside the home. In 1890, only 3 percent were employed. Nevertheless, working-class married women found ways to contribute to the family economy. In many Italian families, for example, piecework such as making artificial flowers allowed married women to contribute to the family economy without leaving their homes. Black women, married and unmarried, worked for wages in much greater numbers. The 1890 census showed that 25 percent of married African American women were employed, often as domestics in the houses of white families.

"Father, does everybody in America live like this? Go to work early, come home late, eat and go to Sleep? And the next day again work, eat, and sleep?"
— A young immigrant girl

White-Collar Workers: Managers, "Typewriters," and Salesclerks

In the late nineteenth century, business expansion and consolidation led to a managerial revolution, creating a new class of white-collar workers who worked in offices and stores. As skilled workers saw their crafts replaced by mechanization, some moved into management positions. "The middle class is becoming a salaried class," a writer for the *Independent* magazine observed, "and is rapidly losing the economic and moral independence of former days." As large business organizations consolidated, corporate development separated management from ownership, and the job of directing the firm became the province of salaried executives and managers, the majority of whom were white men drawn from the 8 percent of Americans who held high school diplomas.

Until late in the century, when engineering schools began to supply recruits, many skilled workers moved from the shop floor to positions of considerable responsibility. William "Billy" Jones, the son of a Welsh immigrant, was one such worker. Beginning as an apprentice at the age of ten, Jones rose through the ranks to become plant superintendent at Andrew Carnegie's Pittsburgh steelworks in 1872. By all accounts, Jones was the best steel man in the industry, and Carnegie rewarded him with a "hell of a big salary," \$25,000 — the same salary as the president of the United States. Most middle managers averaged far less, \$1,100 a year being counted as a good salary. Senior executives, generally recruited from the college-educated elite, took home \$4,000 or more, and a company's general manager could earn as much as $15,000 a year, approximately 30 times what the average worker earned. (Today's top CEOs on average earn 550 times more than the average worker receives.) At the top of the economic pyramid, the great industrialists amassed fortunes that rank John D. Rockefeller, Andrew Carnegie, and Cornelius Vanderbilt among the top ten richest men in American history, easily outpacing today's billionaires.

The new white-collar workforce also included women **"typewriters"** and salesclerks. In the decades after the Civil War, as businesses became larger and more far-flung, the need for more elaborate and exact records, as well as the greater volume of correspondence, led to the hiring of more office workers. Mechanization transformed business as it had industry and manufacturing. The adding machine, the cash register, and the typewriter came into general use in the 1880s. Employers seeking literate workers soon turned to nimble-fingered women. Educated men had many other career choices, but for middle-class white women, secretarial work constituted one of the very few areas where they could put their literacy to use for wages.

Sylvie Thygeson was typical of the young women who went to work as secretaries. Thygeson grew up in an Illinois prairie town and went to work as a country schoolteacher after graduating high school in 1884. Realizing that teaching school did not pay a living wage, she mastered typing and stenography and found work as a secretary to help support her family. According to her account, she made "a fabulous sum of money" (possibly $25 a month). Nevertheless, she gave up her job after a few years when she met and married her husband.

Called "typewriters," women workers like Thygeson were seen as indistinguishable from the machines they operated. Far from viewing their jobs as dehumanizing, women typewriters took pride in their work and relished the economic independence it afforded them. But the entry of women into the workplace challenged traditional gender roles. Society distinguished between "ladies" (who stayed at home) and "working girls" (by definition lower-class women and a term often used for prostitutes). When white middle-class women entered offices as court reporters, typewriters, and stenographers, issues of class and gender clashed. Could a "lady" work? And if she did, did her economic independence threaten men and marriage? Some of this ambivalence can be seen in a poem published in 1896 in the Boston *Courier*. The poet waxes eloquent on his attraction to the "typewriter":

Clerical Worker
A stenographer takes dictation in an 1890s office. Notice that the apron, a symbol of feminine domesticity, has accompanied women into the workplace. In the 1880s, with the invention of the typewriter, many women put their literacy skills to use in the nation's offices. Brown Brothers.

The click of the keys, as her fingers fly,
  And the ring of the silvery bell,
I hardly hear, though I sit quite near,
  Enchained by her magic spell.

After several verses, however, he ruefully abandons his ardor in the face of her modesty and professional manner. And, more telling, he acknowledges that the independent working woman may not need him at all.

> So, to her of my love I shall never speak,
> Twould be vain I can clearly see.
> Why, she gets sixteen dollars a week.
> And what does she want of me?

As Sylvie Thygeson's story shows, most women chose marriage and the home over the office, despite concerns to the contrary. But by the 1890s, secretarial work was the overwhelming choice of native-born, single white women, who constituted more than 90 percent of the female clerical force. Not only considered more genteel than factory work or domestic labor, office work also meant more money for shorter hours. In 1883, Boston's clerical workers on average made more than $6 a week, compared with less than $5 for women working in manufacturing.

As a new consumer culture came to dominate American urban life in the late nineteenth century, department stores offered another employment opportunity for women in the cities. Boasting ornate facades, large plate-glass display windows, and marble and brass fixtures, stores such as Macy's in New York, Wanamaker's in Philadelphia, and Marshall Field in Chicago stood as monuments to the material promise of the era. Within these palaces of consumption, cash girls, stock clerks, and wrappers earned as little as $3 a week, while at the top of the scale, buyers like Belle Cushman of the fancy goods department at Macy's earned $25 a week, an unusually high salary for a woman in the 1870s. Salesclerks counted themselves a cut above factory workers. Their work was neither dirty nor dangerous, and even when they earned less than factory workers, they felt a sense of superiority.

REVIEW How did business expansion and consolidation change workers' occupations in the late nineteenth century?

▸ Workers Organize

By the late nineteenth century, industrial workers were losing ground in the workplace. In the fierce competition to reduce prices and cut costs, industrialists, led by Andrew Carnegie, invested heavily in new machinery that replaced skilled workers with unskilled labor. The erosion of skills and the redefinition of labor as mere "machine tending" left the worker with a growing sense of individual helplessness that served as a spur to collective action. In 1877, in the midst of a depression that left many workers destitute, labor flexed its muscle in the Great Railroad Strike and showed the power of collective action. This and other strikes underscored the tensions produced by rapid industrialization.

In the 1870s and 1880s, labor organizations grew, and the Knights of Labor and the American Federation of Labor attracted workers. Convinced of the inequity of the wage-labor system, labor organizers spoke eloquently of abolishing class privileges and monopoly. Their rhetoric as well as the violence often associated with strikes frightened many middle-class Americans and caused them to equate the labor movement with the specter of class war and anarchism.

The Great Railroad Strike of 1877

Economic depression following the panic of 1873 threw as many as three million people out of work. Those who were lucky enough to keep their jobs watched as pay cuts eroded their wages until they could no longer feed their families. In the summer of 1877, the Baltimore and Ohio (B&O) Railroad announced a 10 percent wage cut at the same time it declared a 10 percent dividend to its stockholders. Angry brakemen in West Virginia, whose wages had already fallen from $70 to $30 a month, walked out on strike. One B&O worker described the hardship that drove him to take such desperate action: "We eat our hard bread and tainted meat two days old on the sooty cars up the road, and when we come home, find our wives complaining that they cannot even buy hominy and molasses for food."

The West Virginia brakemen's strike touched off the **Great Railroad Strike** of 1877, a nationwide uprising that spread rapidly to Pittsburgh and Chicago, St. Louis and San Francisco (Map 19.3). Within a few days, nearly 100,000 railroad workers walked off the job. The spark of rebellion soon led an estimated 500,000 laborers to join the train workers. In Reading, Pennsylvania, militiamen refused to fire on the strikers, saying, "We may be militiamen, but we are workmen first." Rail traffic ground to a halt; the nation lay paralyzed.

Violence erupted as the strike spread. In Pittsburgh, strikers clashed with militia brought in from Philadelphia, who arrogantly boasted

MAP 19.3
The Great Railroad Strike of 1877
Starting in West Virginia and Pennsylvania, the strike spread as far north as Albany, New York, and as far west as San Francisco, bringing rail traffic to a standstill. Called the Great Uprising, the strike heralded the beginning of a new era of working-class protest and trade union organization.

they would clean up "the workingmen's town." Charging with bayonets leveled, the troops opened fire on the crowds, killing twenty people. Angry workers retaliated by reducing an area two miles long beside the tracks to smoldering rubble. Before the day ended, twenty more workers had been shot, and the railroad had sustained millions of dollars' worth of property damage. Nothing like the Pittsburgh riots had ever happened in American history. Armed workers had chased the Philadelphia militia out of town. Now business pressured the federal government to step in.

> **"The railroad strikers, as a rule, are good men, sober, intelligent, and industrious."**
> — President RUTHERFORD B. HAYES

Within eight days, the governors of nine states, acting at the prompting of the railroad owners and managers, defined the strike as an "insurrection" and called for federal troops. President Rutherford B. Hayes, after hesitating briefly, called out the army. By the time the troops arrived, the violence had run its course. Federal troops did not shoot a single striker in 1877. But they struck a blow against labor by acting as strikebreakers — opening rail traffic, protecting nonstriking train crews (known by the derogatory term "scabs"), and maintaining peace along the line. In three weeks, the strike was over.

Although many middle-class Americans initially sympathized with the conditions that led to the strike, they condemned the strikers for the violence and property damage that occurred. The *New York Times* editorialized about the "dangerous classes," and the *Independent* magazine offered the following advice on how to deal with "rioters": "If the club of a policeman, knocking out the brains of the rioter, will answer then well and good; but if it does not promptly meet the exigency, then bullets and bayonets . . . constitutes [*sic*] the one remedy and one duty of the hour."

"The strikes have been put down by force," President Hayes noted in his diary on August 5. "But now for the real remedy. Can't something be done by education of the strikers, by judicious control of the capitalists, by wise general policy

Destruction from the Great Railroad Strike of 1877
Pictures of the devastation caused in Pittsburgh during the strike shocked many Americans. When militiamen fired on striking workers, killing more than twenty strikers, the mob retaliated by destroying a two-mile area along the track, reducing it to a smoldering rubble. Property damage totaled $2 million. Curious pedestrians came out to view the destruction. Carnegie Library of Pittsburgh.

to end or diminish the evil? The railroad strikers, as a rule, are good men, sober, intelligent, and industrious." While Hayes acknowledged the workers' grievances, most businessmen and industrialists did not and fought the idea of labor unions, arguing that workers and employers entered into contracts as individuals and denying the right of unions to bargain collectively for their workers. For their part, workers quickly recognized that they held little power individually and flocked to join unions. As labor leader Samuel Gompers noted, the nation's first national strike dramatized the frustration and unity of the workers and served as an alarm bell to labor "that sounded a ringing message of hope to us all."

The Knights of Labor and the American Federation of Labor

The **Knights of Labor**, the first mass organization of America's working class, proved the chief beneficiary of labor's newfound consciousness. The Noble and Holy Order of the Knights of Labor had been founded in 1869 by Uriah Stephens, a Philadelphia garment cutter. A secret society of workers, the Knights envisioned a "universal brotherhood" of all workers, from common laborers to master craftsmen. The organization's secrecy and ritual served to bind Knights together at the same time that it discouraged company spies and protected members from reprisals.

Although the Knights played no active role in the 1877 railroad strike, membership swelled as a result of the growing interest in labor organizing that followed the strike. In 1878, the Knights abandoned secrecy and launched an ambitious campaign to organize workers, attempting to bridge the boundaries of ethnicity, gender, ideology, race, and occupation in a badly fragmented society. **Leonora Barry** served as general investigator for women's work from 1886 to 1890, helping the Knights recruit teachers, waitresses, housewives, and domestics along with factory and sweatshop workers. Women composed perhaps 20 percent of the membership. The Knights also made good on its vow to include African Americans, organizing more than 95,000 black workers. That the Knights of Labor often fell short of its goals to unify the working class proved less surprising than the scope of its efforts.

Under the direction of Grand Master Workman **Terence V. Powderly**, the Knights became the dominant force in labor during the 1880s. The organization advocated a kind of workers' democracy that embraced reforms including public ownership of the railroads, an income tax, equal pay for women workers, and the abolition of child labor. A loose mix of ideology, unionism, culture, fraternalism, and mysticism, the Knights called for one big union to create a cooperative commonwealth that would supplant the wage system and remove class distinctions. Only the "parasitic" members of society — gamblers, stockbrokers, lawyers, bankers, and liquor dealers — were denied membership.

In theory, the Knights of Labor opposed strikes. Powderly championed arbitration and preferred to use boycotts. But in practice, much of the organization's appeal came from the Knights' sweeping victory against railroad tycoon Jay Gould in the Great Southwest Strike of 1885. Despite the reservations of its leadership, the Knights became a militant labor organization that won passionate support from working people with the slogan "An injury to one is the concern of all."

The Knights of Labor was not without rivals. Many skilled workers belonged to craft unions organized by trade. Among the largest and richest of these unions stood the Amalgamated Association of Iron and Steel Workers, founded in 1876 and counting twenty thousand skilled workers as members. Trade unionists spurned the broad reform goals of the Knights and focused on workplace issues. **Samuel Gompers**, a cigar maker born in London of Dutch Jewish ancestry, promoted what he called "pure and simple" unionism. Gompers founded the Organized Trades and Labor Unions in 1881 and reorganized it in 1886 into the **American Federation of Labor** (AFL), which coordinated the activities of craft unions throughout the United States. His plan was simple: organize skilled workers such as machinists and locomotive engineers — those with the most bargaining power — and use strikes to gain immediate objectives such as higher pay and better working conditions. Gompers at first drew few converts. The AFL had only 138,000 members in 1886, compared with 730,000 for the Knights of Labor. But events soon brought down the Knights, and Gompers's brand of unionism came to prevail.

Haymarket and the Specter of Labor Radicalism

While the AFL and the Knights of Labor competed for members, more radical labor groups, including socialists and anarchists, believed that reform was futile and called instead for social revolution. Both the socialists and the anarchists, sensitive to criticism that they preferred revolution in theory to improvements here and now, rallied around the popular issue of the eight-hour day.

Since the 1840s, labor had sought to end the twelve-hour workday, which was standard in industry and manufacturing. By the mid-1880s, it seemed clear to many workers that labor shared too little in the new prosperity of the decade, and pressure mounted for the eight-hour day. Labor championed the popular issue and launched major rallies in cities across the nation. Supporters of the movement set May 1, 1886, as the date for a nationwide general strike in support of the eight-hour workday.

All factions of the nascent labor movement came together in Chicago on May Day for what was billed as the largest demonstration to date. A group of labor radicals led by anarchist Albert Parsons, a *Mayflower* descendant, and August Spies, a German socialist, spearheaded the eight-hour movement in Chicago. Chicago's Knights of Labor rallied to the cause even though Terence Powderly and the union's national leadership, worried about the increasing activism of the rank and file, refused to endorse the movement for shorter hours. Samuel Gompers was on hand, too, to lead the city's trade unionists, although he privately urged the AFL assemblies not to participate in the general strike.

Gompers's skilled workers were labor's elite. Many still worked in small shops where negotiations between workers and employers took place in an environment tempered by personal relationships. Well dressed in their frock coats and starched

VISUAL ACTIVITY

"The Chicago Riot"
Inflammatory pamphlets like this one, published in the wake of the Haymarket bombing, presented a one-sided view of the incident and stirred public passion. In this charged atmosphere, the anarchist speakers at the rally were tried and convicted for the bombing even though witnesses testified that none of them had thrown the bomb. The identity of the bomb thrower remains uncertain. Chicago Historical Society.

READING THE IMAGE: What does the cover suggest about the views of the author of the pamphlet?

CONNECTIONS: In what ways does this pamphlet reflect the public climate following the Haymarket bombing?

shirts, the AFL's skilled workers stood in sharp contrast to the dispossessed workers out on strike across town at Chicago's huge McCormick reaper works. There strikers watched helplessly as the company brought in strikebreakers to take their jobs and marched the "scabs" to work under the protection of the Chicago police and security guards supplied by the Pinkerton Detective Agency. Cyrus McCormick Jr., son of the inventor of the mechanical reaper, viewed labor organization as a threat to his power as well as to his profits; he was determined to smash the union.

During the May Day rally, 45,000 workers paraded peacefully down Michigan Avenue in support of the eight-hour day, many singing the song that had become the movement's anthem:

> We want to feel the sunshine;
> We want to smell the flowers,
> We're sure that God has willed it,
> And we mean to have eight hours.
> Eight hours for work, eight hours for rest,
> eight hours for what we will!

Trouble came two days later, when strikers attacked strikebreakers outside the McCormick works and police opened fire, killing or wounding six men. Angry radicals rushed out a circular urging workers to "arm yourselves and appear in full force" at a rally in Haymarket Square.

On the evening of May 4, the turnout at Haymarket was disappointing. No more than two or three thousand gathered in the drizzle to hear Spies, Parsons, and the other speakers. Mayor Carter Harrison, known as a friend of labor, mingled conspicuously in the crowd, pronounced the meeting peaceable, and went home to bed. Sometime later, police captain John "Blackjack" Bonfield, who had made his reputation cracking skulls, marched his men into the crowd, by now fewer than three hundred people, and demanded that it disperse. Suddenly, someone threw a bomb into the police ranks. After a moment of stunned silence, the police drew their revolvers. "Fire and kill all you can," shouted a police lieutenant. When the melee ended, seven policemen and an unknown number of other people lay dead. An additional sixty policemen and thirty or forty civilians suffered injuries.

News of the "Haymarket riot" provoked a nationwide convulsion of fear, followed by blind rage directed at anarchists, labor unions, strikers, immigrants, and the working class in general. Eight men, including Parsons and Spies, went on trial in Chicago, although witnesses testified that none of them had thrown the bomb. "Convict these men," thundered the state's attorney, Julius S. Grinnell, "make examples of them, hang them, and you save our institutions." Although the state could not link any of the defendants to the **Haymarket bombing**, the jury nevertheless found them all guilty. Four were executed, one committed suicide, and three received prison sentences. On the gallows, Spies spoke for the Haymarket martyrs: "The time will come when our silence will be more powerful than the voices you throttle today."

The bomb blast at Haymarket had lasting repercussions. To commemorate the death of the Haymarket martyrs, labor made May 1 an annual international celebration of the worker. But the Haymarket bomb, in the eyes of one observer, proved "a godsend to all enemies of the labor movement." It effectively scotched the eight-hour-day movement and dealt a blow to the Knights of Labor, already wracked by internal divisions. With the labor movement everywhere under attack, many skilled workers turned to the American Federation of Labor. Gompers's narrow economic strategy made sense at the time and enabled one segment of the workforce — the skilled — to organize effectively and achieve tangible gains. But the nation's unskilled workers remained untouched by the AFL's brand of trade unionism. The vast majority of America's workers would have to wait another forty years before a mainstream labor union, the Congress of Industrial Organizations (CIO), moved to organize the unskilled (as discussed in chapter 24).

REVIEW Why did the fortunes of the Knights of Labor rise in the late 1870s and decline in the 1890s?

Maids and Domestics
These Swedish immigrant women were working as maids in the Merchant's Hotel in Black River Falls, Wisconsin, when they posed for this picture in 1890. Each carries a tool of her trade—broom and dustpan, iron, potato peeler, dishcloth, pie plate, serving tray. The women, young and well dressed, have similar collars, but no clear uniform. Domestic work could be hard and lonely. Only the largest private house would have so many women employed.
Wisconsin Historical Society (WHi (V22d) 1386).

▸ At Home and at Play

The growth of urban industrialism not only dramatically altered the workplace but also transformed home and family life and gave rise to new forms of commercialized leisure. Industrialization redefined the very concepts of work and home. Increasingly, men went out to work for wages, while most white married women stayed home, either working in the home without pay — cleaning, cooking, and rearing children — or supervising paid domestic servants who did the housework.

Domesticity and "Domestics"

The separation of the workplace and the home that marked the shift to industrial society redefined the home as a "haven in the heartless world," presided over by a wife and mother who made the household her separate sphere. The growing separation of workplace and home led to a new ideology, one that sentimentalized the home and women's role in it. The cultural ideology that dictated woman's place in the home began to develop in the early 1800s and has been called the **cult of domesticity**, a phrase used to prescribe an ideal of middle-class, white womanhood that dominated the period from 1820 to the end of the nineteenth century.

The cult of domesticity and the elaboration of the middle-class home led to a major change in patterns of hiring household help. The live-in servants, or **domestics**, became a fixture in the North, replacing the hired girl of the previous century. In American cities by 1870, 15 to 30 percent of all households included live-in domestic servants, more than 90 percent of them women. Earlier in the mid-nineteenth century, native-born women increasingly took up other work and left domestic service to immigrants. In the East, the maid was so often Irish that "Bridget" became a generic term for female domestics. (The South continued to rely on black female labor, first slave and later free.)

Servants by all accounts resented the long hours and lack of privacy. "She is liable to be rung up at all hours," one study of domestics reported. "Her very meals are not secure from interruption, and even her sleep is not sacred." No wonder tension between domestic servants and their female employers proved endemic. Domestic service became the occupation of last resort, a "hard and lonely life" in the words of one female servant.

For women of the white middle class, domestics were a boon, freeing them from household drudgery and giving them more time to spend with their children or to pursue club work or reform. Thus, while domestic service supported the cult of domesticity, it created for those women who could afford it opportunities that expanded their horizons outside the home in areas such as women's clubs and the temperance and suffrage movements.

Such benefits of middle-class respectability contrasted sharply with the austerity of the working-class home. Reformer Margaret Byington recounted her visit with the family of a Slavic worker in Homestead, the Carnegie mill town outside Pittsburgh. The family lived in a two-room dwelling, and Byington found the young mother doing the family laundry in a big washtub set on a chair in the middle of the downstairs room, struggling to keep her two babies from tumbling into the scalding water. Further describing the congested home, Byington noted the room's single large bed and "the inevitable cook stove upon which in the place of honor was simmering the evening's soup. Upstairs in a second room, a boarder and the man of the house were asleep. Soon they would get up and turn their beds over to two more boarders, who were out at work." In the eyes of Byington and many middle-class reformers, the Slavs' crowded tenement, with its lack of privacy, scarcely qualified as a "home."

Cheap Amusements

Growing class divisions manifested themselves in patterns of leisure as well as in work and home life. The poor and working class took their leisure, when they had any, not in the crowded tenements that housed their families, but increasingly in the cities' new dance halls, music houses, ballparks, and amusement arcades, which by the 1890s formed a familiar part of the urban landscape.

The growing anonymity of urban industrial society posed a challenge to traditional rituals of courtship. Young workingwomen no longer

Beach Scene at Coney Island

Coney Island became a symbol of commercialized leisure and mechanical excitement at the turn of the twentieth century. This fanciful rendering captures the frenetic goings-on. Men and women, along with costumed clowns, frolic in the waves. Notice the woolen bathing outfits, with their leggings, modest skirts and blouses, and bathing hats. Men box and play ball, a woman flies on a parachute, while a uniformed policeman wades into the fray, brandishing his billy club. On the shore are the rides — with the Ferris wheel dominating the skyline — and the famous hotel in the shape of an elephant. Sunday crowds on the island reportedly reached 100,000. Beach scene: Library of Congress; Sand pail: Private Collection.

met prospective husbands only through their families. Fleeing crowded tenements, the young sought each other's company in dance halls and other commercial retreats. Scorning proper introductions, working-class youths "picked up" partners at dance halls, where drinking was part of the evening's entertainment. Young workingwomen, who rarely could afford more than trolley fare when they went out, counted on being "treated" by men, a transaction that often implied sexual payback. Young women's need to negotiate sexual encounters if they wished to participate in commercial amusements blurred the line between respectability and promiscuity and made the dance halls a favorite target of reformers who feared they lured teenaged girls into prostitution.

For men, baseball became a national pastime in the 1870s — then, as now, one force in urban life capable of uniting a city across class lines. Cincinnati mounted the first entirely paid team, the Red Stockings, in 1869. Soon professional teams proliferated in cities across the nation, and Mark Twain hailed baseball as "the very symbol, the outward and visible expression, of the drive and push and rush and struggle of the raging, tearing, booming nineteenth century."

The increasing commercialization of entertainment in the late-nineteenth-century city was best seen at **Coney Island**. A two-mile stretch of sand nine miles from Manhattan by trolley or steamship, Coney Island in the 1870s and 1880s attracted visitors to its beaches, dance pavilions, and penny arcades, where they consumed treats ranging from oysters to saltwater taffy. In the 1890s, Coney Island was transformed into the site of some of the largest and most elaborate amusement parks in the country. Promoter George Tilyou built Steeplechase Park in 1897, advertising "10 hours of fun for 10 cents." With its mechanical thrills and fun-house laughs, the amusement park encouraged behavior that one schoolteacher aptly described as "everyone with the brakes off." By 1900, as many as a million New Yorkers flocked to Coney Island on any given weekend, making the amusement park the unofficial capital of a new mass culture.

"Everyone with the brakes off."

— A schoolteacher's description of behavior at Coney Island's Steeplechase Amusement park

REVIEW How did urban industrialism shape the world of leisure?

City Growth and City Government

Private enterprise, not planners, built the cities of the United States. Boosters, builders, businessmen, and politicians all had a hand in creating the modern metropolis. With a few notable exceptions, such as Washington, D.C., and Savannah, Georgia, there was no such thing as a comprehensive city plan. Cities simply mushroomed, formed by the dictates of profit and the exigencies of local politics. With the rise of the city came the need for public facilities, transportation, and services that would tax the imaginations of America's architects and engineers and set the scene for the rough-and-tumble of big-city government, politics, and politicians.

Building Cities of Stone and Steel

Skyscrapers and mighty bridges dominated the imagination and the urban landscape. Less imposing but no less significant were the paved streets, the parks and public libraries, and the subways and sewers. In the late nineteenth century, Americans rushed to embrace new technology of all kinds, making their cities the most modern in the world.

Structural steel made enormous advances in building possible. A decade after the completion of the **Brooklyn Bridge** (see pages 603–604), engineers used the new technology to construct the Williamsburg Bridge just to the north. More prosaic and utilitarian than its neighbor, the new bridge was never as acclaimed, but it was longer by four feet and completed in half the time. It became the model for future building as the age of steel supplanted the age of stone and iron.

Chicago, not New York, gave birth to the modern skyscraper. Rising from the ashes of the Great Fire of 1871, which destroyed three square miles and left eighteen thousand people homeless, Chicago offered a generation of skilled architects and engineers the chance to experiment. Commercial architecture became an art form at the hands of a skilled group of architects who together constituted the "Chicago school." Men of genius such as Louis Sullivan gave Chicago some of the world's finest commercial buildings. Employing the dictum "Form follows

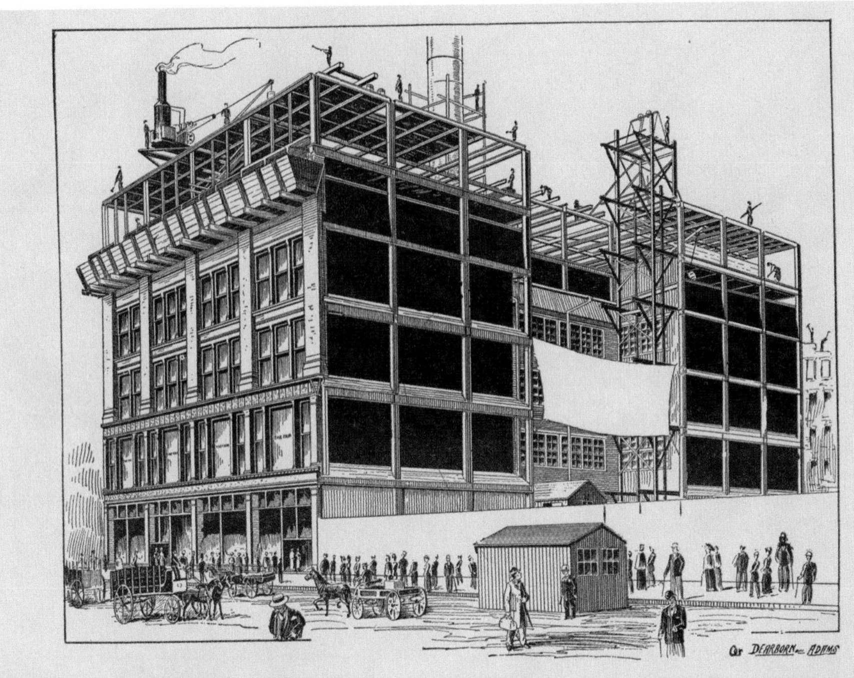

Chicago Skyscraper Going Up With the advent of structural steel, skyscrapers like this one in progress in Chicago in 1891 became prominent features of the American urban landscape. This architect's rendering of the Fair Building, a department store designed by William Le Baron Jenney, shows a modern skyscraper whose foundations supported the structural steel skeleton so that the walls could simply "hang" on the outside of the building, because they no longer had to support the structure. Newberry Library (*Inland Architect*, Nov. 1891).

function," they built startlingly modern structures. A fitting symbol of modern America, the skyscraper expressed the domination of corporate power.

Alongside the skyscrapers rose new residential apartments for the rich and the middle class. The "French flat" — apartments with the latest plumbing and electricity — gained popularity in the 1880s as affluent city dwellers overcame their distaste for multifamily housing (which carried the stigma of the tenement) and gave in to "flat fever." "Housekeeping isn't fun," cried one New York woman. "Give us flats!" In 1883 alone, more than one thousand new apartments went up in Chicago.

Across the United States, municipal governments undertook public works on a scale never before seen. They paved streets, built sewers and water mains, replaced gas lamps with electric lights, ran trolley tracks on the old horsecar lines, and dug underground to build subways, tearing down the unsightly elevated tracks that had clogged city streets. In San Francisco, Andrew Smith Hallidie mastered the city's hills, building a system of cable cars in 1873. Boston completed the nation's first subway system in 1897, and New York and Philadelphia soon followed.

Cities became more beautiful with the creation of urban public parks to complement the new buildings that quickly filled city lots. Much of the credit for America's greatest parks goes to one man — landscape architect **Frederick Law Olmsted**. The indefatigable Olmsted designed parks in Atlanta, Boston, Brooklyn, Hartford, Detroit, Chicago, and Louisville, as well as the grounds for the U.S. Capitol. But he is best remembered for the creation of New York City's Central Park. Completed in 1873, it became the first landscaped public park in the United States. Olmsted and his partner, Calvert Vaux, directed the planting of more than five million trees, shrubs, and vines to transform the eight hundred acres between 59th and 110th streets into an oasis for urban dwellers. "We want a place," he wrote, where people "may stroll for an hour, seeing, hearing, and feeling nothing of the bustle and jar of the streets."

American cities did not overlook the mind in their efforts at improvement. They created a comprehensive free public school system that educated everyone from the children of the middle class to the sons and daughters of immigrant workers. Yet the exploding urban population strained the system and led to crowded

The Boston Public Library
When the first public library in the country moved to its new site in Boston's Copley Square in 1895, the best artists and architects of the day lent their talents to build "a palace for the people." Architect Charles F. McKim designed the library around a cloistered courtyard in the style of a Renaissance palazzo. Sculptor Augustus Saint-Gaudens modeled the Sienna marble lions that guard the grand stairway. French muralist Puvis de Chavannes contributed the allegorical mural representing literature and learning. A frolicking nude Bacchante by Frederick MacMonnies graced the courtyard fountain for a few days until scandalized Bostonians demanded its removal. Today it has been restored to its place.
Library photograph: ©Richard Cheek for the Boston Public Library; statue: image copyright ©The Metropolitan Museum of Art/Art Resource, NY.

and inadequate facilities. In 1899, more than 544,000 pupils attended school in New York's five boroughs. Municipalities across the United States provided free secondary school education for all who wished to attend, even though only 8 percent of Americans completed high school.

To educate those who couldn't go to school, American cities created the most extensive free public library system in the world. In 1895, the Boston Public Library opened its bronze doors under the inscription "Free to All." Designed in the style of a Renaissance palazzo, with more than 700,000 books on the shelves ready to be checked out, the library earned the description "a palace of the people."

Despite the Boston Public Library's legend "Free to All," the poor did not share equally in the advantages of city life. The parks, the libraries, and even the subways and sewers benefited some city dwellers more than others. Few library cards were held by Boston's laborers, who worked six days a week and found the library closed on Sunday. And in the 1890s, there was nothing central about New York's Central Park. It was a four-mile walk from the tenements of Hester Street to the park's entrance at 59th Street and Fifth Avenue. Then, as now, the comfortable majority, not the indigent minority, reaped a disproportionate share of the benefits in the nation's big cities.

Any story of the American city, it seems, must be a tale of two cities — or, given the cities' great diversity, a tale of many cities within each metropolis. At the turn of the twentieth century, a central paradox emerged: The enduring monuments of America's cities — the bridges, skyscrapers, parks, and libraries — stood as the undeniable achievements of the same system of municipal government that reformers dismissed as boss-ridden, criminal, and corrupt.

Tammany Bank
This cast-iron bank, a campaign novelty, bears the name of the New York City Democratic machine. It conveys its political reform message graphically: When you put a penny in the politician's hand, he puts it in his pocket. Tammany Hall dominated city politics for more than a century, dispensing contracts and franchises worth millions of dollars. Some of those dollars invariably found their way into the pockets of Tammany politicians.
Collection of Janice L. and David J. Frent.

City Government and the "Bosses"

The physical growth of the cities required the expansion of public services and the creation of entirely new facilities: streets, subways, elevated trains, bridges, docks, sewers, and public utilities. There was work to be done and money to be made. The professional politician — the colorful big-city boss — became a phenomenon of urban growth and **bossism** a national phenomenon. Though corrupt and often criminal, the boss saw to the building of the city and provided needed social services for the new residents. Yet not even the big-city boss could be said to rule the unruly city. The governing of America's cities resembled more a tug-of-war than boss rule.

The most notorious of all the city bosses was **William Marcy "Boss" Tweed** of New York. At midcentury, Boss Tweed's Democratic Party "machine" held sway. A machine was really no more than a political party organized at the grassroots level. Its purpose was to win elections and reward its followers, often with jobs on the city's payroll. New York's citywide Democratic machine, **Tammany Hall**, commanded an army of party functionaries. At the bottom were district captains. In return for votes, they provided services for their constituents, everything from a scuttle of coal in the winter to housing for an evicted family. At the top were powerful ward bosses who distributed lucrative franchises for subways and streetcars. They formed a shadow government more powerful than the city's elected officials.

As chairman of the Tammany general committee, Tweed kept the Democratic Party together and ran the city through the use of bribery and graft. "As long as I count the votes," he shamelessly boasted, "what are you going to do about it?" The excesses of the Tweed ring soon led to a clamor for reform and cries of "Throw the rascals out." Cartoonist Thomas Nast pilloried Tweed in the pages of *Harper's Weekly*. His cartoons, easily understood even by those who could not read, did the boss more harm than hundreds of outraged editorials. Tweed's rule ended in 1871. Eventually, he was tried and convicted and later died in jail.

New York was not the only city to experience bossism and corruption. The British visitor James Bryce concluded in 1888, "There is no denying that the government of cities is the one conspicuous failure of the United States." More than 80 percent of the nation's thirty largest cities experienced some form of boss rule in the decades around the turn of the twentieth century. However, infighting among powerful ward bosses often meant that no single boss enjoyed exclusive power in the big cities.

"As long as I count the votes, what are you going to do about it?"
— New York's BOSS TWEED

Urban reformers and proponents of good government (derisively called "goo goos" by their rivals) challenged machine rule and sometimes succeeded in electing reform mayors. But the reformers rarely managed to stay in office for long. Their detractors called them "mornin' glories," observing that they "looked lovely in the mornin' and withered up in a short time." The bosses enjoyed continued success largely because the urban political machine helped the cities' immigrants and poor, who remained the bosses' staunchest allies. "What tells in holding your district," a Tammany ward boss observed, "is to go right down among the poor and help them in the different ways they need help. It's philanthropy, but it's politics, too — mighty good politics." Saloons were the epicenter of ward politics. They played a crucial role in workers' lives and often served informally as political headquarters, as well as employment agencies and union halls.

A few reform mayors managed to achieve success and longevity by following the bosses' model. **Hazen S. Pingree** of Detroit exemplified the successful reform mayor. A businessman who went into politics in the 1890s, Pingree, like most good-government candidates, promised to root out dishonesty and inefficiency. But when the depression of 1893 struck, Pingree emerged as a champion of the working class and the poor. He hired the unemployed to build schools, parks, and public baths. By providing jobs and needed services, he built a powerful political organization based on working-class support. Detroit's

Chicago's White City

This painting by H. D. Nichols captures the monumental architecture of the White City built for the World's Columbian Exposition in 1893. In the foreground, the central Court of Honor features a Frederick MacMonnies fountain, with Christopher Columbus at the prow of his ship. In the distance is Daniel Chester French's sixty-foot gilded statue *Republic*. Monumental, harmonious, and pristine, the White City was designed by Daniel Burnham and Frederick Law Olmsted to awe and overwhelm fairgoers. And so it did, drawing millions of visitors from America and abroad, who eagerly snapped up souvenirs, such as the playing cards pictured here, to commemorate their visit. Painting: Chicago Historical Society; Cards: Compliments of Columbus Antique Mall & Museum.

voters kept him in the mayor's office for four terms and then helped elect him governor twice.

The big-city boss, through the skillful orchestration of rewards, exerted powerful leverage and lined up support for his party from a broad range of constituents, from the urban poor to wealthy industrialists. In 1902, when journalist **Lincoln Steffens** began "The Shame of the Cities," a series of articles exposing city corruption, he found that business leaders who fastidiously refused to mingle socially with the bosses nevertheless struck deals with them. "He is a self-righteous fraud, this big businessman," Steffens concluded. "I found him buying boodlers [bribers] in St. Louis, defending grafters in Minneapolis, originating corruption in Pittsburgh, sharing with bosses in Philadelphia, deploring reform in Chicago, and beating good government with corruption funds in New York."

The complexity of big-city government, apparent in the many levels of corruption that Steffens uncovered, pointed to one conclusion: For all the color and flamboyance of the big-city boss, he was simply one of many actors in the drama of municipal government. Old-stock aristocrats, new professionals, saloonkeepers, pushcart peddlers, and politicians all fought for their interests in the hurly-burly of city government. They didn't much like each other, and they sometimes fought savagely. But they learned to live with one another. Compromise and accommodation — not boss rule — best characterized big-city government by the turn of the twentieth century, although the cities' reputation for corruption left an indelible mark on the consciousness of the American public.

White City or City of Sin?

Americans have always been of two minds about the city. They like to boast of its skyscrapers and bridges, its culture and sophistication, and they pride themselves on its bigness and bustle. At the same time, they fear it as the city of sin, the home of immigrant slums, the center of vice and crime. Nowhere did the divided view of the American city take form more graphically than in Chicago in 1893. In that year, Chicago hosted the **World's Columbian Exposition**, the grandest world's fair in the nation's history. (See "Beyond America's Borders," page 632.) The fairground on Lake Michigan offered a lesson in what Americans on the eve of the twentieth century imagined a city might be. Only five miles down the shore from downtown Chicago, the White City, as the fairground became known, seemed light-years away from Chicago, with its stockyards, slums, and bustling terminals. Frederick Law Olmsted and architect Daniel Burnham supervised the transformation of a swampy wasteland into a pristine paradise of lagoons, fountains, wooded islands, gardens, and imposing buildings.

"Sell the cookstove if necessaray and come," novelist Hamlin Garland wrote to his parents on the farm. And come they did, in spite of the panic and depression that broke out only weeks after the fair opened in May 1893. In six months, fairgoers purchased more than 27 million tickets, turning a profit of nearly a half million dollars for promoters. Visitors from home and abroad strolled the elaborate grounds and visited the exhibits — everything from a model of the Brooklyn Bridge carved in soap to the latest goods and inventions. Half carnival, half culture, the great fair offered something for everyone. On the Midway Plaisance, crowds thrilled to the massive wheel built by Mr. Ferris and watched agog as Little Egypt danced the hootchy-kootchy.

In October, the fair closed its doors in the midst of the worst depression the country had yet seen. During the winter of 1894, Chicago's unemployed and homeless took over the grounds, vandalized the buildings, and frightened the city's comfortable citizens out of their wits. When reporters asked Daniel Burnham what should be done with the moldering remains of the White City, he responded, "It should be torched." And it was. In July 1894, in a clash between federal troops and striking railway workers, incendiaries set fires that leveled the fairgrounds.

In the end, the White City remained what it had always been, a dreamscape. Buildings that looked like marble were actually constructed of staff, a plaster substance that began to crumble even before fire destroyed the fairgrounds. Perhaps it was not so strange, after all, that the legacy of the White City could be found on Coney Island, where two new amusement parks, Luna and Dreamland, sought to combine, albeit in a more tawdry form, the beauty of the White City and the thrill of the Midway Plaisance. More enduring than the White City itself was what it represented: the emergent industrial might of the United States, at home and abroad, with its inventions, manufactured goods, and growing consumer culture.

REVIEW How did municipal governments respond to the challenges of urban expansion?

BEYOND AMERICA'S BORDERS

The World's Columbian Exposition and Nineteenth-Century World's Fairs

The 1893 World's Columbian Exposition in Chicago and the other great world's fairs of the nineteenth century represented a unique phenomenon of industrial capitalism and a testament to the expanding global market economy. The Chicago fair, named to celebrate the four hundredth anniversary of Columbus's arrival in the New World, offered a cornucopia of international exhibits testifying to growing international influences ranging from cultural to technological exchange.

Great cities vied to host world's fairs, as much to promote commercial growth as to demonstrate their cultural refinement. Each successive fair sought to outdo its predecessor. Chicago's fair followed on the great success of the 1889 Universal Exposition in Paris. The Paris Exposition featured as its crowning glory the 900-foot steel tower constructed by Alexandre-Gustav Eiffel. How could Chicago, a prairie upstart, top that?

The answer was the creation of the White City, with its monumental architecture, landscaped grounds, and first Ferris wheel. The White City celebrated the classicism of the French Beaux Arts school, which borrowed heavily from the massive geometric styling and elaborate detailing of Greek and Renaissance architecture. Beneath its Renaissance facade, the White City acted as an enormous emporium dedicated to the unabashed materialism of the Gilded Age. Fairgoers could view virtually every kind of manufactured product in the world inside the imposing Manufactures and Liberal Arts Building, including Swiss glassware and clocks, Japanese lacquerware and bamboo, British woolen products, and French perfumes and linens. The German pavilion displayed fine wooden furniture as well as tapestries, porcelain, and jewelry belonging to the ruling family.

As suited an industrial age, manufactured products and heavy machinery drew the largest crowds. Displays introduced visitors to the latest mechanical and technological innovations, many the result of international influences. For five cents, fairgoers could put two hard rubber tubes into their ears and listen for the first time to a Gramophone playing the popular tune "The Cat Came Back." The Gramophone, which signaled the beginning of the recorded music industry, was itself the work of a German immigrant, Emile Berliner (Thomas Edison later claimed credit for a similar invention, calling it the phonograph).

Such international influences were evident throughout the Columbian Exposition. At the Tiffany pavilion, one of the most popular venues at the fair, visitors oohed and aahed over the display of lamps, ornamental metalwork, and fine jewelry that Louis Comfort Tiffany credited to the influence of Japanese art forms. Juxtaposed with Tiffany's finery stood a display of firearms in the Colt gallery. An American company since 1836, Colt had opened a factory in England in 1851, and its revolvers enjoyed an international reputation — the best-known firearms not only in America but also in Canada, Mexico, and many European countries. Colt's new automatic weapon, the machine gun, would soon play a major role on the world stage in both the Boxer uprising in China and the Spanish-American War.

All manner of foodstuffs — teas from India, Irish whiskey, and pastries and other confectionery from Germany and France — tempted fairgoers. American food products such as Shredded Wheat, Aunt Jemima syrup, and Juicy Fruit gum debuted at the fair, where they competed for ribbons. Winners such as Pabst "Blue Ribbon" Beer used the award in advertisements. And the fair introduced two new foods — carbonated soda and the hamburger — destined to become America's best-known contributions to international cuisine.

The Columbian Exposition also served as a testimony to American technological achievement and progress. By displaying technology in action, the White City tamed it and made it accessible to American and world consumers. The fair helped promote new technologies, particularly electric light and power. With 90,000 electric lights, 5,100 arc lamps, electric fountains, an electric elevated railroad, and electric launches plying the lagoons, the White City provided a glowing advertisement for electricity. In the Electricity Building, fairgoers visited the Bell Telephone Company exhibit,

"All Nations Are Welcome"
Uncle Sam, flanked by the city of Chicago, welcomes representatives carrying the flags of many nations to the World's Columbian Exposition in 1893. In the background are the fairgrounds on the shores of Lake Michigan. More than one hundred nations participated in the fair by sending exhibits and mounting pavilions to showcase their cultures and products. Chicago Historical Society.

marveled at General Electric's huge dynamo (electric generator), and gazed into the future at the all-electric home and model demonstration kitchen.

Consumer culture received its first major expression and celebration at the Columbian Exposition. Not only did this world's fair anticipate the mass marketing, packaging, and advertising of the twentieth century, but the vast array of products on display also cultivated the urge to consume. Thousands of concessionaires with products for sale sent a message that tied enjoyment inextricably to spending money and purchasing goods, both domestic and foreign. The Columbian Exposition set a pattern for the twentieth-century world's fairs that followed, making a powerful statement about the possibilities of urban life in an industrial age and encouraging the rise of a new middle-class consumer culture. As G. Brown Goode, head of the Smithsonian Institution observed, the Columbian Exposition was in many ways "an illustrated encyclopedia of civilization."

America in a Global Context

1. Would you describe the Columbian Exposition as a commercial venture, a cultural display, or an entertainment? Why?
2. What role did the fair play in popularizing new technologies?
3. What was meant by the observation that the fair was "an illustrated encyclopedia of civilization"?
4. How did the international flavor of the White City compare with the reality of global migration into America's fast-growing cities?

▸ Conclusion: Who Built the Cities?

As much as the great industrialists and financiers, as much as eminent engineers like John and Washington Roebling, common workers, most of them immigrants, built the nation's cities. The unprecedented growth of urban, industrial America resulted from the labor of millions of men, women, and children who toiled in workshops and factories, in sweatshops and mines, on railroads and construction sites across America.

America's cities in the late nineteenth century teemed with life. Immigrants and blue bloods, poor laborers and millionaires, middle-class managers and corporate moguls, secretaries, salesgirls, sweatshop laborers, and society matrons lived in the cities and contributed to their growth. Town houses and tenements jostled for space with skyscrapers and great department stores, while parks, ball fields, amusement arcades, and public libraries provided the city masses with recreation and entertainment.

Municipal governments, straining to build the new cities, experienced the rough-and-tumble of machine politics as bosses and their constituents looked to profit from city growth. Reformers deplored the graft and corruption that accompanied the rise of the cities. But they were rarely able to oust the party bosses for long because they failed to understand the services the political machines provided for their largely immigrant and poor constituents; nor did reformers account for the ties between city politicians and wealthy businessmen who sought to benefit from franchises and contracts.

For America's workers, urban industrialism along with the rise of big business and corporate consolidation drastically changed the workplace. Industrialists replaced skilled workers with new machines that could be operated by cheaper unskilled labor. And during hard times, employers did not hesitate to cut workers' already meager wages. As the Great Railroad Strike of 1877 demonstrated, when labor united, it could bring the nation to attention. Organization held out the best hope for the workers; first the Knights of Labor and later the American Federation of Labor won converts among the nation's working class.

The rise of urban industrialism challenged the American promise, which for decades had been dominated by Jeffersonian agrarian ideals. Could such a promise exist in the changing world of cities, tenements, immigrants, and huge corporations? In the great depression that came in the 1890s, mounting anger and frustration would lead farmers and workers to join forces and create a grassroots movement to fight for change under the banner of a new People's Party.

▸ Selected Bibliography

Immigration

John Bodnar, *The Transplanted: A History of Immigration in Urban America* (1985).

Vincent J. Cannato, *American Passage: The History of Ellis Island* (2010).

Roger Daniels, *Guarding the Golden Door: American Immigration Policy and Immigrants since 1882* (2004).

Martha Gardner, *The Qualities of a Citizen: Women, Immigration, and Citizenship, 1870–1965* (2005).

Dirk Hoerder, *Cultures in Contact: World Migrations in the Second Millennium* (2002).

Matthew Frye Jacobson, *Whiteness of a Different Color: European Immigrants and the Alchemy of Race* (1998).

David M. Reimers, *Unwelcome Strangers* (1998).

David R. Roediger, *Working toward Whiteness: How America's Immigrants Became White* (2005).

Ronald Takaki, *Strangers from a Different Shore: A History of Asian Americans* (1998).

Workers and Unions

Susan Porter Benson, *Counter Cultures: Saleswomen, Managers, and Customers in American Department Stores, 1890–1940* (1986).

Ileen A. DeVault, *United Apart: Gender and the Rise of Craft Unionism* (2004).

Hasia Diner, *Lower East Side Memories: A Jewish Place in America* (2000).

Leon Fink, *Workingman's Democracy: The Knights of Labor and American Politics* (1983).

James Green, *Death in the Haymarket: A Story of Chicago, the First Labor Movement, and the Bombing That Divided Gilded Age America* (2006).

Hamilton Hold, ed., *The Life Stories of Undistinguished Americans as Told by Themselves* (2000).

Jacqueline Jones, *American Work: Four Centuries of Black and White Labor* (1998).

Jackson Lears, *Rebirth of a Nation: The Making of Modern America, 1877–1920* (2009).

Susan Levine, *Labor's True Women: Carpet Weavers, Industrialization, and Labor Reform in the Gilded Age* (1984).

David Montgomery, *The Fall of the House of Labor: The Workplace, the State, and American Labor Activism, 1865–1925* (1987).

Roy Rosenzweig, *Eight Hours for What We Will: Workers and Leisure in an Industrial City, 1870–1920* (1983).

Timothy Spears, *Chicago Dreaming: Midwesterners and the City, 1871–1919* (2005).

Carole Srole, *Transcribing Class and Gender: Masculinity and Femininity in Nineteenth Century Courts and Offices* (2009).

Sharon Hartman Strom, *Beyond the Typewriter: Gender, Class, and the Origins of Modern American Office Work, 1900–1930* (1992).

Robert E. Weir, *Knights Unhorsed: Internal Conflict in a Gilded Age Social Movement* (2000).

The City and Its Amusements

LeRoy Ashby, *With Amusement for All: A History of American Popular Culture since 1830* (2006).

Sven Beckert, *The Monied Metropolis: New York City and the Consolidation of the American Bourgeoisie, 1850–1896* (2001).

Gary S. Cross and John K. Walton, *The Playful Crowd: Pleasure Places in the Twentieth Century* (2005).

Sarah Deutsch, *Women and the City: Gender, Space, and Power in Boston, 1870–1940* (2000).

Nan Enstad, *Ladies of Labor, Girls of Adventure: Working Women, Popular Culture, and Labor Politics at the Turn of the Twentieth Century* (1999).

Margaret Garb, *City of American Dreams: A History of Home Ownership and Housing Reform in Chicago, 1871–1919* (2005).

Richard Haw, *The Brooklyn Bridge: A Cultural History* (2005).

Elizabeth Hawes, *New York, New York: How the Apartment House Transformed Life in the City, 1869–1930* (1993).

Kathy Peiss, *Cheap Amusements: Working Women and Leisure in Turn-of-the-Century New York* (1986).

Roy Rosenzweig and Elizabeth Blackmar, *The Park and the People: A History of Central Park* (1992).

Witold Rybczynski, *A Clearing in the Distance: Frederick Law Olmsted and America in the Nineteenth Century* (1999).

Jules Tygiel, *Past Time: Baseball as History* (2000).

▶ **For more books about topics in this chapter,** see the Online Bibliography at **bedfordstmartins.com/roark.**

▶ **For additional primary sources from this period,** see Michael Johnson, ed., *Reading the American Past*, Fifth Edition.

▶ **For Web sites, images, and documents related to topics and places in this chapter,** visit Make History at **bedfordstmartins.com/roark.**

Reviewing Chapter 19

KEY TERMS

Explain each term's significance.

The Rise of the City

- global migration (p. 605)
- pogroms (p. 608)
- Ellis Island (p. 612)
- Jacob Riis (p. 613)

At Work in Industrial America

- sweatshops (p. 616)
- family economy (p. 616)
- "typewriters" (p. 618)

Workers Organize

- Great Railroad Strike (p. 619)
- Knights of Labor (p. 621)
- Leonora Barry (p. 622)
- Terence V. Powderly (p. 622)
- Samuel Gompers (p. 622)
- American Federation of Labor (p. 622)
- Haymarket bombing (p. 623)

At Home and at Play

- cult of domesticity (p. 624)
- domestics (p. 624)
- Coney Island (p. 626)

City Growth and City Government

- Brooklyn Bridge (p. 626)
- Frederick Law Olmsted (p. 627)
- bossism (p. 629)
- William Marcy "Boss" Tweed (p. 629)
- Tammany Hall (p. 629)
- Hazen S. Pingree (p. 630)
- Lincoln Steffens (p. 631)
- World's Columbian Exposition (p. 631)

REVIEW QUESTIONS

Use key terms and dates to support your answer.

1. Why did American cities experience explosive growth in the late nineteenth century? (pp. 605–614)
2. How did business expansion and consolidation change workers' occupations in the late nineteenth century? (pp. 614–619)
3. Why did the fortunes of the Knights of Labor rise in the late 1870s and decline in the 1890s? (pp. 619–624)
4. How did urban industrialism shape the world of leisure? (pp. 624–626)
5. How did municipal governments respond to the challenges of urban expansion? (pp. 626–633)

MAKING CONNECTIONS

Draw on key terms, the timeline, and review questions.

1. Americans expressed both wonder and concern at the nation's mushrooming cities. Why did cities provoke such divergent responses? In your answer, discuss the dramatic demographic, environmental, and political developments associated with urbanization.
2. Why did patterns of immigration to the United States in the late nineteenth century change? How did Americans respond to the immigrants who arrived late in the century? In your answer, consider how industrial capitalism, nationally and globally, contributed to these developments.
3. How did urban industrialization affect Americans' lives outside of work? Describe the impact of late-nineteenth-century economic developments on home life and leisure. In your answer, consider how class, race, gender, and ethnicity contributed to diverse urban experiences.
4. When workers began to embrace organization in the late 1870s, what did they hope to accomplish? Were they successful? Why or why not? In your answer, discuss both general conditions and specific events that shaped these developments.

LINKING TO THE PAST

Link events in this chapter to earlier events.

1. Compare the lives of migrant workers and industrial cowboys in the West to workers in the nation's cities. What are the major similarities? (See chapter 17.)
2. You have already looked at the development of America's industries in the nineteenth century from the vantage point of moguls such as Andrew Carnegie and John D. Rockefeller. How does your view of industrialism change when the focus is shifted to the nation's workers? (See chapter 18.)

▶ **For practice quizzes and other study tools,** visit the Online Study Guide at **bedfordstmartins.com/roark.**

TIMELINE 1869–1897

1869	• Knights of Labor founded. • Cincinnati mounts first paid baseball team, the Red Stockings.
1871	• Boss Tweed's rule in New York ends. • Chicago's Great Fire.
1873	• Panic on Wall Street touches off depression. • San Francisco's cable car system opens.
1877	• Great Railroad Strike.
1880s	• Immigration from southern and eastern Europe rises.
1882	• Chinese Exclusion Act.
1883	• Brooklyn Bridge opens.
1886	• American Federation of Labor (AFL) founded. • Haymarket bombing.
1890s	• African American migration from the South begins.
1890	• Jacob Riis publishes *How the Other Half Lives.*
1892	• Ellis Island opens in New York harbor to process immigrants.
1893	• World's Columbian Exposition. • Panic on Wall Street touches off major economic depression.
1895	• Boston Public Library opens.
1896	• President Grover Cleveland vetoes immigrant literacy test.
1897	• Steeplechase Park opens on Coney Island. • Nation's first subway system opens in Boston.

PEOPLE'S PARTY BANNER

This buffalo banner from the 1892 Populist convention declares "In the Old Parties We Trusted until Financially we are Busted" and promises to elect "Honest Men." In the background some of those men stand, along with women and children, on the steps of the capitol in Topeka in 1893, after being elected to the Kansas House of Representatives. Perhaps taking the buffalo as a mascot was a poor choice for the new party, for just as the great herds on the western plains had been decimated in the 1880s, the People's (or Populist) Party would go down to defeat in 1896.

Banner: Nebraska State Historical Society; background: Kansas State Historical Society.

20 Dissent, Depression, and War 1890–1900

FRANCES WILLARD TRAVELED TO ST. LOUIS IN FEBRUARY 1892 WITH high hopes. Political change was in the air, and Willard was there to help fashion a new reform party, one that she hoped would embrace her two passions — temperance and woman suffrage. As head of the Woman's Christian Temperance Union, an organization with members in every state and territory in the nation, Willard wielded considerable clout. At her invitation, twenty-eight of the country's leading reformers had already met in Chicago to draft a set of principles to bring to St. Louis. Always expedient, Willard had settled for a statement condemning the saloon rather than an endorsement for a stronger measure to prohibit the sale of alcohol. But at the convention, she hoped to press the case for woman suffrage and prohibition. Willard knew it would not be easy, but in the heady atmosphere of 1892 she determined to try. No American woman before her had played such a central role in a political movement. At the height of her political power, Willard took her place among the leaders on the podium in St. Louis.

Exposition Music Hall presented a colorful spectacle. "The banners of the different states rose above the delegates throughout the hall, fluttering like the flags over an army encamped," wrote one reporter. The fiery orator Ignatius Donnelly attacked the money kings of Wall Street. Mary Elizabeth Lease, a veteran campaigner from Kansas known for exhorting farmers to "raise less corn and more hell," added her powerful voice to the cause. Terence V. Powderly, head of the Knights of Labor, called on workers to join hands with farmers against the "nonproducing classes." Frances Willard urged the crowd to outlaw the liquor traffic and give the vote to women. Between speeches, the crowd sang labor songs like "Hurrah for the Toiler" and "All Hail the Power of Laboring Men."

Over the next few days, delegates hammered out a series of demands, breathtaking in their scope. They tackled the tough questions of the day — the regulation of business, the need for banking and currency reform, the right of labor to organize and bargain collectively, and the role of the federal government in regulating business, curbing monopoly, and guaranteeing democracy. But the new party determined to stick to economic issues and

Frances Willard
Frances Willard, the forward-thinking leader of the Woman's Christian Temperance Union, learned to ride a bicycle at age fifty-three. The bicycle became hugely popular in the 1890s, even though traditionalists fulminated that it was unladylike for women to straddle a bike and immodest for them to wear the divided skirts that allowed them to pedal. Shown here in 1895, Willard declared bicycling a "harmless pleasure" that encouraged "clear heads and steady hands." Willard brought her progressive ideas to the People's Party 1892 convention, where she shared a place on the platform with the new party's leaders. Photo: Courtesy of the Frances E. Willard Memorial Library and Archives (WCTU).

resisted endorsing either temperance or woman suffrage. As a member of the platform committee, Willard fought for both and complained of the "crooked methods . . . employed to scuttle these planks." Outmaneuvered in committee, she brought the issues to the floor of the convention, only to go down to defeat by a vote of 352 to 238.

Despite Willard's disappointment, the convention ended its work amid a chorus of cheers. According to one eyewitness, "Hats, paper, handkerchiefs, etc., were thrown into the air; . . . cheer after cheer thundered and reverberated through the vast hall reaching the outside of the building where thousands who had been waiting the outcome joined in the applause till for blocks in every direction the exultation made the din indescribable."

What was all the shouting about? The cheering crowd was celebrating the birth of a new political party, officially named the People's Party. Fed up with the Democrats and Republicans, a broad coalition of groups came together in St. Louis to fight for change. They resolved to reconvene in Omaha in July to nominate candidates for the upcoming presidential election. Defeated but not willing to abandon the new party, Willard resolved to work for the nomination of a presidential candidate committed to temperance and suffrage.

The St. Louis gathering marked an early milestone in one of the most turbulent decades in U.S. history. Unrest, agitation, agrarian revolt, labor strikes, a severe financial panic and depression, and a war of expansion shook the 1890s. As the decade opened, Americans dissatisfied with the two major political parties were already flocking to organizations including the Farmers' Alliance, the American Federation of Labor, and the Woman's Christian Temperance Union, and they worked together to create the political alliance that gave birth to the People's (or Populist) Party. In a decade of unrest and uncertainty, the People's Party countered laissez-faire economics by insisting that the federal government play a more active role to ensure greater economic equity in industrial America.

This challenge to the status quo culminated in 1896 in one of the most hotly contested presidential elections in the nation's history. At the close of the tumultuous decade, the Spanish-American War helped to bring the country together, with Americans rallying to support the troops. But disagreement over American imperialism and overseas expansion raised questions about the nation's role on the world stage as the United States stood poised to enter the twentieth century.

▸ The Farmers' Revolt

Hard times in the 1880s and 1890s created a groundswell of agrarian revolt. A bitter farmer wrote from Minnesota, "I settled on this Land in good Faith Built House and Barn. Broken up Part of the Land. Spent years of hard Labor in grubbing fencing and Improving." About to lose his farm to foreclosure, he lamented, "Are they going to drive us out like trespassers . . . and give us away to the Corporations?"

Crop prices for the nation's six million farmers fell decade after decade, even as their share of the world market grew (Figure 20.1). In parts of Kansas, wheat sold for so little that angry farmers burned their crops for fuel rather than take them to market. At the same time, consumer prices soared (Figure 20.2). Farmers couldn't make ends meet. In Kansas alone, almost half the farms had fallen into the hands of the banks by 1894 through foreclosure.

The Farmers' Alliance

At the heart of the farmers' problems stood a banking system dominated by eastern commercial banks committed to the gold standard, a railroad rate system that was capricious and unfair, and rampant speculation that drove up the price of land. In the West, farmers rankled under a system that allowed railroads to charge them exorbitant freight rates while granting rebates to large shippers (see chapter 18). In the South, lack of currency and credit drove farmers to the stopgap credit system of the crop lien, turning the entire region into "a vast pawn shop." Determined to do something, farmers banded together to fight for change.

Farm protest was not new. In the 1870s, farmers had supported the Grange and the Greenback Labor Party. As the farmers' situation grew more desperate, they organized, forming regional alliances. The first **Farmers' Alliance** came together in Lampasas County, Texas, to fight "landsharks and horse thieves." During the 1880s, the movement spread rapidly. In frontier farmhouses in Texas, in log cabins in the backwoods of Arkansas, and in the rural parishes of Louisiana, separate groups of farmers formed similar alliances for self-help.

As the movement grew, farmers' groups consolidated into two regional alliances: the Northwestern Farmers' Alliance, active in Kansas, Nebraska, and other midwestern Granger states; and the more radical Southern Farmers' Alliance. In the 1880s, traveling lecturers preached the Alliance message. Worn-out men and careworn women did not need to be convinced that something was wrong. By 1887, the Southern Farmers' Alliance had grown to more than 200,000 members, and by 1890 it counted more than 3 million members.

"We are going to get out of debt and be free and independent people once more."

— A Georgia farmer, on the effects of the Alliance movement

Kansas Farm Family Forced Off Their Farm

Hard times in the 1880s sent farmers reeling back from the plains. In 1894, almost half the farmers in Kansas lost their land because they could not make mortgage payments. The Owens family of Greeley County, pictured here, were among the defeated, forced to pack up their belongings and head east. The simple writing on their wagon tells the chronology of their retreat. Kansas State Historical Society.

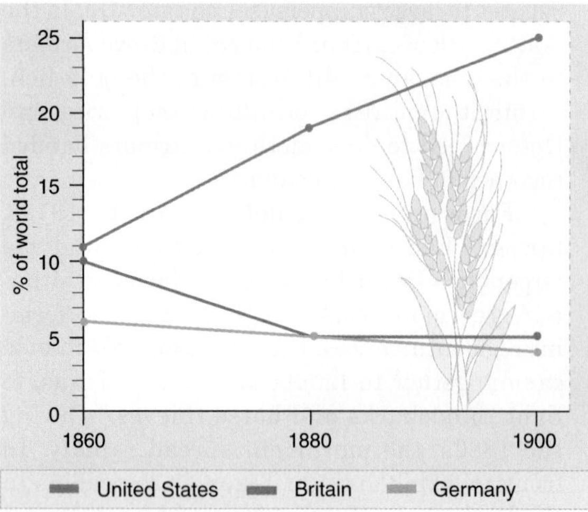

FIGURE 20.1 GLOBAL COMPARISON: Share of the World Wheat Market, 1860–1900
Although many countries produced wheat for home use, Britain, Germany, and the United States were among the largest wheat exporters. Exporting wheat worldwide became viable in the United States only after the completion of the transcontinental railroad in 1869. The resulting growth of the railroads, coupled with the development of improved mechanical reapers throughout the second half of the century, led to the mechanization of U.S. agriculture, allowing wheat farmers to harvest ever-larger crops. From 1860 to 1900, the United States' percentage of world wheat production more than doubled, while Germany's declined and Britain's was cut in half as a result of its growing emphasis on industrialization. What was the impact of entering a world market for U.S. wheat farmers?

Radical in its inclusiveness, the Southern Alliance reached out to African Americans, women, and industrial workers. Through cooperation with the **Colored Farmers' Alliance**, an African American group founded in Texas in the 1880s, blacks and whites attempted to make common cause. As Georgia's Tom Watson, a Southern Alliance stalwart, pointed out, "The colored tenant is in the same boat as the white tenant, . . . and . . . the accident of color can make no difference in the interests of farmers, croppers, and laborers."

The political culture of the Alliance encouraged the inclusion of women and children and used the family as its defining symbol. Women rallied to the Alliance banner along with their menfolk, drawn to meetings that combined picnic, parade, revival, country fair, and political convention. "I am going to work for prohibition, the Alliance, and for Jesus as long as I live," swore one woman.

In wagon trains, men and women in the thousands thronged to Alliance meetings to listen to speeches and to debate and discuss the issues of the day. The Alliance leaders aimed to do more than exhort their followers; they aimed to educate them. The Farmers' Alliance produced and distributed "a perfect avalanche of literature" — speeches, newspapers, books, and tracts — full of damning details about the political collusion between business and politics, along with detailed analyses of the securities and commodities markets, the tariff and international trade, and credit and currency. Alliance lecturers reached out to the illiterate, often speaking for hours under the broiling sun to educate their rapt audiences on the fine points of economics and politics.

At the heart of the Alliance movement stood a series of farmers' cooperatives. By "bulking" their cotton —

FIGURE 20.2 Consumer Prices and Farm Income, 1865–1910
Around 1870, consumer prices and farm income were about equal. During the 1880s and 1890s, however, farmers suffered great hardships as prices for their crops steadily declined and the cost of consumer goods continued to rise.

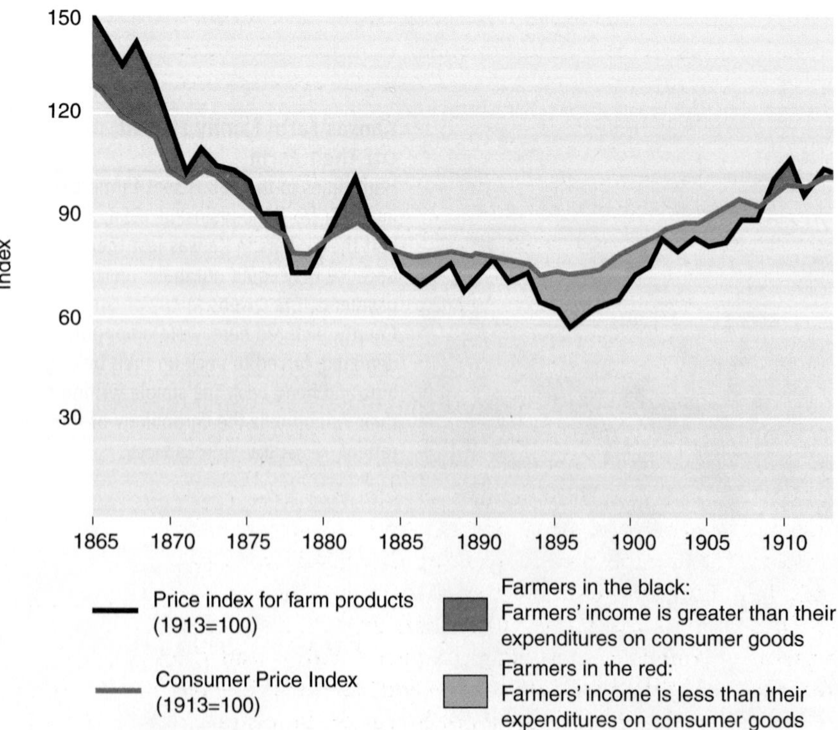

that is, selling it together — farmers could negotiate a better price. And by setting up trade stores and exchanges, they sought to escape the grasp of the merchant/creditor. Through the cooperatives, the Farmers' Alliance promised to change the way farmers lived. "We are going to get out of debt and be free and independent people once more," exulted one Georgia farmer.

Cooperatives sprang up throughout the South and West. But the Alliance faced insurmountable difficulties in running successful cooperatives. Opposition by merchants, bankers, wholesalers, and manufacturers made it impossible for the cooperatives to get credit. As the cooperative movement died, the Farmers' Alliance moved toward direct political action. Confounded by the failure of the Democrats and Republicans to break with commercial interests and support the farmers, Alliance leaders moved, often reluctantly, toward the formation of a third party.

Mary Elizabeth Lease
This painting of Lease, taken in 1895 at the height of her political activities in Kansas, shows a well-dressed, mild-eyed woman — belying her reputation as a hell-raiser who supposedly exhorted Kansas farmers to "raise less corn and more hell." Lease's admirers styled her "The People's Joan of Arc." But in the eyes of her detractors, who attacked not only her speeches but also the propriety of a woman who dared to pursue a career as a public speaker, she was "a lantern-jawed, google-eyed nightmare" and "a petticoated smut-mill." Kansas State Historical Society.

The Populist Movement

In the earliest days of the Alliance movement, a leader of the Southern Farmers' Alliance insisted, "The Alliance is a strictly white man's nonpolitical, secret business association." But by 1892, it was none of those things. Advocates of a third party carried the day at the convention of laborers, farmers, and common folk in 1892 in St. Louis, where the Farmers' Alliance gave birth to the **People's Party** and launched the Populist movement. "There is something at the back of all this turmoil more than the failure of crops or the scarcity of ready cash," a journalist observed in 1892.

The same spirit of religious revival that animated the Farmers' Alliance infused the People's Party. The Populists built on the work of the Alliance to mount a critique of industrial society and a call for action. Convinced that the money and banking systems worked to the advantage of the wealthy few, they demanded economic democracy. To help farmers get the credit they needed at reasonable rates, southern farmers hit on the ingenious idea of a **subtreasury** — a plan that would allow farmers to store their nonperishable crops until prices rose and to receive commodity credit from the federal government to obtain needed supplies. The subtreasury promised to get rid of the crop lien system once and for all. Although the idea would be enacted piecemeal in progressive and New Deal legislation in the twentieth century, conservatives in the 1890s dismissed it as far-fetched "corn tassel communism."

To the western farmer, the Populists promised land reform, championing a plan that would claim excessive land granted to railroads or sold to foreign investors. The Populists' boldest proposal called for government ownership of the railroads and the telegraph system to put an end to discriminatory rates. Citing examples of how the powerful railroads had corrupted the political system, the Populists did not shrink from advocating what their opponents branded state socialism.

The Populists also demanded currency reform. Farmers in all sections rallied to the cry for cheaper currency, calling for free silver and greenbacks — attempts to increase the nation's tight money supply and thus make credit easier to obtain. And to empower the common people, the Populist platform called for the direct election of senators (then chosen by state legislatures) and for other electoral reforms, including the secret ballot and the right to initiate legislation, to recall elected officials, and to submit issues to the people by means of a referendum. Because the Populists shared common cause with labor against corporate interests, they also supported the eight-hour workday and an end to contract labor.

The sweeping array of Populist reforms enacted in the Populist platform changed the agenda of politics for decades to come. More than just a response to hard times, Populism presented an alternative vision of American economic democracy.

REVIEW Why did American farmers organize alliances in the late nineteenth century?

▸ The Labor Wars

While farmers united to fight for change, industrial laborers fought their own battles in a series of bloody strikes so fiercely waged on both sides that historians have called them the "labor wars." Industrial workers felt increasingly threatened as businesses combined into huge corporations, and in the 1890s labor took a stand. At issue was the right of workers to organize and to speak through unions to bargain collectively and fight for better working conditions, higher wages, shorter hours, and greater worker control in the face of increased mechanization.

Three major conflicts of the period — the lockout of steelworkers in Homestead, Pennsylvania, in 1892; the miners' strike in Cripple Creek, Colorado, in 1894; and the Pullman strike in Illinois that same year — raised fundamental questions about the rights of labor and the sanctity of private property.

The Homestead Lockout

In 1892, steelworkers in Pennsylvania squared off against Andrew Carnegie in a decisive struggle over the right to organize in the Homestead steel mills. Carnegie was unusual among industrialists as a self-styled friend of labor. In 1886, he had written, "The right of the workingmen to combine and to form trade unions is no less sacred than the right of the manufacturer to enter into associations and conferences with his fellows."

"If we undertake to resist the seizure of our jobs, we will be shot down like dogs."
— A Homestead striker

Yet as much as he cherished his liberal beliefs, Carnegie cherished his profits more. In 1892, Carnegie resolved to crush the Amalgamated Iron and Steel Workers, one of the largest and richest craft unions in the American Federation of Labor (AFL). When the Amalgamated attempted to renew its contract at Carnegie's Homestead mill, its leaders were told that since "the vast majority of our employees are Non union, the Firm has decided that the minority must give place to the majority." While it was true that only 800 skilled workers belonged to the elite Amalgamated, the union had long enjoyed the support of the plant's 3,000 non-union workers. Slavs, who did much of the unskilled work, made common cause with the Welsh, Scottish, and Irish skilled workers who belonged to the union. Never before had the Amalgamated been denied a contract.

Carnegie preferred not to be directly involved in the union busting that lay on the horizon, so that spring he sailed to Scotland and left **Henry Clay Frick**, the toughest antilabor man in the industry, in charge of the Homestead plant. By summer, a strike looked inevitable. Frick prepared by erecting a fifteen-foot fence around the plant and topping it with barbed wire. Workers aptly dubbed it "Fort Frick." To defend his fort and protect strikebreakers, Frick hired 316 mercenaries from the Pinkerton National Detective Agency at the rate of $5 per day, more than double the wage of the average Homestead worker.

The Pinkerton Agency, founded before the Civil War, came into its own in the 1880s as a private security force for hire. Pinkerton agents were a motley crew, recruited from all levels of society, from urban thugs to college boys. The "Pinks" earned the hatred of workers by protecting strikebreakers and acting as company spies.

On June 28, the **Homestead lockout** began when Frick locked the workers out of the mills and prepared to bring in strikebreakers, whom the workers derogatorily referred to as "scabs." Hugh O'Donnell, the young Irishman who led the union, vowed to prevent scabs from entering the plant. On July 6 at 4 a.m., a lookout spotted two barges moving up the Monongahela River in the fog. Frick was attempting to smuggle Pinkertons into Homestead.

Workers sounded the alarm, and within minutes a crowd of more than a thousand, hastily armed with rifles, hoes, and fence posts, rushed to the riverbank to meet the enemy. When the Pinkertons attempted to come ashore, gunfire broke out, and more than a dozen Pinkertons and some thirty strikers fell, killed or wounded. The Pinkertons retreated to the barges. For twelve hours, the workers, joined by their family members, threw everything they had at the barges, from fireworks to dynamite. Finally, the

Pinkertons hoisted a white flag and arranged with O'Donnell to surrender. With three workers dead and scores wounded, the crowd, numbering perhaps ten thousand, was in no mood for conciliation. As the hated "Pinks" came up the hill, they were forced to run a gantlet of screaming, cursing men, women, and children. When a young guard dropped to his knees, weeping for mercy, a woman used her umbrella to poke out his eye. One Pinkerton had been killed in the siege on the barges. In the grim rout that followed their surrender, not one avoided injury.

The "battle of Fort Frick" ended in a dubious victory for the workers. They took control of the plant and elected a council to run the community. At first, public opinion favored their cause. Newspapers urged Frick to negotiate or submit to arbitration. A congressman castigated Carnegie for "skulking in his castle in Scotland." Populists, meeting in St. Louis, condemned the use of "hireling armies."

The action of the Homestead workers struck at the heart of the capitalist system, pitting the workers' right to their jobs against the rights of private property. The workers' insistence that "we are not destroying the property of the company — merely protecting our rights" did not prove as compelling to the courts and the state as the property rights of the mill owners. Four days after the confrontation, Pennsylvania's governor, who sympathized with the workers, nonetheless yielded to pressure from Frick and ordered eight thousand National Guard troops into Homestead to protect Carnegie's property. The strikers, thinking they had nothing to fear from the militia, welcomed the troops with a brass band. But they soon understood the reality. The troops' ninety-five-day occupation not only protected Carnegie's property but also enabled Frick to reopen the mills and bring in strikebreakers. "We have been deceived," one worker complained bitterly. "We have stood idly by and let the town be occupied by soldiers who come here, not as our protectors, but as the protectors of non-union men. . . . If we undertake to resist the seizure of our jobs, we will be shot down like dogs."

FRANK LESLIE'S ILLUSTRATED WEEKLY

HOMESTEAD TROUBLES.

NEW YORK, JULY 14, 1892.

Homestead Workers Attack the Pinkertons

The nation's attention was riveted on labor strife at the Homestead steel mill in the summer of 1892. *Frank Leslie's Illustrated Weekly* ran a cover story on the violence that Pinkerton agents faced from a crowd of men, women, and children armed with clubs, guns, and ax handles.

The workers, who had been locked out by Henry Clay Frick, were enraged that Frick had hired the Pinkertons to bring in strikebreakers. Overwhelmed by the strikers, the Pinkertons surrendered. Although the mob was armed (note the boy with a gun in the foreground), not one of the Pinkertons was shot as they ran the gantlet. All, however, were beaten. The New York Society Library.

Then, in a misguided effort to ignite a general uprising, **Alexander Berkman**, a Russian immigrant and anarchist, attempted to assassinate Frick. Berkman bungled his attempt. Shot twice and stabbed with a dagger, Frick survived and showed considerable courage, allowing a doctor to remove the bullets but refusing to leave his desk until the day's work was completed. "I do not think that I shall die," Frick remarked coolly, "but whether I do or not, the Company will pursue the same policy and it will win." After the assassination attempt, public opinion turned against the workers.

Berkman was quickly tried and sentenced to prison. Although the Amalgamated and the AFL denounced his action, the incident linked anarchism and unionism, already associated in the public mind as a result of the Haymarket bombing in 1886 (see chapter 19). Hugh O'Donnell later wrote, "The bullet from Berkman's pistol, failing in its foul intent, went straight through the heart of the Homestead strike."

In the end, the workers capitulated. The Homestead mill reopened in November, and the men returned to work, except for the union leaders, now blacklisted in every steel mill in the country. With the owners firmly in charge, the company slashed wages, reinstated the twelve-hour day, and eliminated five hundred jobs.

In the drama of events at Homestead, the significance of what occurred often remained obscured: The workers at Homestead had been taught a lesson. They would never again, in the words of the National Guard commander, "believe the works are their's [*sic*] quite as much as Carnegie's." Another forty-five years would pass before steelworkers, unskilled as well as skilled, successfully unionized. In the meantime, Carnegie's production tripled, even in the midst of a depression. "Ashamed to tell you profits these days," Carnegie wrote a friend in 1899. And no wonder: Carnegie's profits had grown from $4 million in 1892 to $40 million in 1900.

The Cripple Creek Miners' Strike of 1894

Less than a year after the Homestead lockout, a panic on Wall Street in the spring of 1893 touched off a bitter economic depression. In the West, silver mines fell on hard times, leading to the **Cripple Creek miners' strike of 1894**. When mine owners moved to lengthen the workday from eight to ten hours, the newly formed Western Federation of Miners (WFM) vowed to hold the line in Cripple Creek, Colorado. In February 1894, the WFM threatened to strike all mines working more than eight-hour shifts. The mine owners divided: Some quickly settled with the WFM; others continued to demand ten hours, provoking a strike.

The striking miners received help from many quarters. Working miners paid $15 a month to a strike fund, and miners in neighboring districts sent substantial contributions. The miners enjoyed the support and assistance of local businesses and grocers, who provided credit to the strikers. With these advantages, the Cripple Creek strikers could afford to hold out for their demands.

Even more significant, Governor Davis H. Waite, a Populist elected in 1892, had strong ties to the miners and refused to use the power of the state against the strikers. Governor Waite asked the strikers to lay down their arms and demanded that the mine owners disperse their hired deputies. The miners agreed to arbitration and selected Waite as their sole arbitrator. By May, the recalcitrant mine owners capitulated, and the union won an eight-hour day.

Governor Waite's intervention demonstrated the pivotal power of the state in the nation's labor wars. Having a Populist in power made a difference. A decade later, in 1904, with Waite out of office, mine owners relied on state troops to take back control of the mines, defeating the WFM and blacklisting all of its members. In retrospect, the Cripple Creek miners' strike of 1894 proved the exception to the rule of state intervention on the side of private property. More typical was the outcome of another strike in 1894 in Pullman, Illinois.

Eugene V. Debs and the Pullman Strike

The economic depression that began in 1893 swelled the ranks of the unemployed to three million, almost half of the working population. "A fearful crisis is upon us," wrote a labor publication. Nowhere were workers more demoralized than in the model town of Pullman, on the outskirts of Chicago.

In the wake of the Great Railroad Strike of 1877, **George M. Pullman**, the builder of Pullman railroad cars, had moved his plant and workers away from the "snares of the great city." In 1880, he purchased 4,300 acres nine miles south of Chicago and built a model town. The town of Pullman boasted parks, fountains, playgrounds, an auditorium, a library, a hotel, shops, and markets, along with 1,800 units of housing. Noticeably absent was a saloon.

The housing in Pullman was clearly superior to that in neighboring areas, but workers paid a high price to live in the model town. George M. Pullman expected a 6 percent return on his investment. As a result, Pullman's rents ran 10 to 20 percent higher than housing costs in nearby communities. And a family in Pullman could never own its own home. George Pullman refused to "sell an acre under any circumstances." As long as he controlled the town absolutely, he held the powerful whip of eviction over his employees and could quickly get rid of "troublemakers." Although observers at first praised the beauty and orderliness of the town, critics by the 1890s compared Pullman's model town to a "gilded cage" for workers.

The depression brought hard times to Pullman. Workers saw their wages slashed five times between May and December 1893, with cuts totaling at least 28 percent. At the same time, Pullman refused to lower the rents in his model town, insisting that "the renting of the dwellings and the employment of workmen at Pullman are in no way tied together." When workers went to the bank to cash their paychecks, they found that the rent had been taken out. One worker discovered only forty-seven cents in his pay envelope for two weeks' work. When the bank teller asked him whether he wanted to apply it to his back rent, he retorted, "If Mr. Pullman needs that forty-seven cents worse than I do, let him have it." At the same time, Pullman continued to pay his stockholders an 8 percent dividend, and the company accumulated a $25 million surplus.

At the heart of the labor problems at Pullman lay not only economic inequity but also the company's attempt to control the work process, substituting piecework for day wages and undermining skilled craftsworkers. The Pullman workers rebelled. During the spring of 1894, Pullman's desperate workers, seeking help, flocked to the ranks of the **American Railway Union** (ARU), led by the charismatic **Eugene V. Debs**. The ARU, unlike the skilled craft unions of the AFL, pledged to organize all railway workers — from engineers to engine wipers. "It has been my life's desire," wrote Debs, "to unify railroad employees and to eliminate the aristocracy of labor, which unfortunately exists, and organize them so all will be on an equality." The ARU's belief in industrial democracy, however, was not matched by a commitment to racial equality; by a narrow margin, union members voted to exclude African American workers.

George Pullman responded to union organization at his plant by firing three of the union's leaders the day after they led a delegation to protest wage cuts. Angry men and women walked off the job in disgust. What began as a spontaneous protest in May 1894 quickly blossomed into a strike that involved more than 90 percent of Pullman's 3,300 workers. "We do not know what the outcome will be, and in fact we do not much care," one worker confessed. "We do know that we are working for less wages than will maintain ourselves and families in the necessaries of life, and on that proposition we refuse to work any longer." Pullman countered by shutting down the plant.

A Pullman Craftsworker

Pullman Palace cars were known for their luxurious details. Here, a painter working in the 1890s applies elaborate decoration to the exterior of a Pullman car. In the foreground is an intricately carved door, an example of fine hand-detailing. The Pullman workers' strike in 1894 stemmed in part from the company's efforts to undermine the status of craftsworkers by reducing them to low-paid piecework. Control of the workplace, as much as issues related to wages and hours, fueled the labor wars of the 1890s. Chicago Historical Society.

In June, the Pullman strikers appealed to the ARU to come to their aid. Debs hesitated to commit his fledgling union to a major strike in the midst of a depression. He pleaded with the workers to find

The Press and the Pullman Strike: Framing Class Conflict

Press coverage of the 1894 Pullman strike and the subsequent American Railway Union boycott was extensive and usually partisan. How newspapers covered the Pullman strike provides a window into the way the press framed class conflict in the United States in the 1890s. The *Chicago Times*, for example, clearly supported the ARU, as was evident in its coverage of events. By contrast, the *Chicago Tribune* and most other Chicago newspapers sided with George M. Pullman and the General Managers Association. Nellie Bly, the era's most colorful investigative reporter, wrote a personal account of her experience with ARU members for the *New York World*.

DOCUMENT 1
***Chicago Tribune*, May 12, 1894**

PULLMAN MEN OUT
Discharges the Cause

Two thousand employees in the Pullman car works struck yesterday, leaving 800 others at their posts. This was not enough to keep the works going, so a notice was posted on the big gates at 6 o'clock . . . saying: "These shops closed until further notice."

Mr. Pullman said last night he could not tell when work would be resumed. The American Railway Union, which has been proselytizing for a week among the workmen, announces that it will support the strikers . . . [intimating] that the trainmen on the railways on which are organized branches of the union might refuse to handle any of the Pullman rolling stock.

DOCUMENT 2
***Chicago Times*, May 12, 1894**

PULLMAN MEN OUT
Firing Three Men Starts It

Almost the entire force of men employed in the Pullman shops went on strike yesterday. Out of the 4,800 men and women employed in the various departments there were probably not over 800 at work at 6 o'clock last evening. The immediate cause of the strike was the discharge or laying off of three men in the iron machine shop. The real but remote cause is the question of wages over which the men have long been dissatisfied and on account of which they had practically resolved to strike a month ago. . . .

The position of the company is that no increase in wages is possible. . . . President George M. Pullman told the committee that the company was doing business at a loss even at the reduced wages paid the men and offered to show his books in support of his assertion.

DOCUMENT 3
***Chicago Times*, May 15, 1894**

SKIMS OFF THE FAT
Pullman Company Declares a Dividend Today

Full Pockets Swallow $600,000 While Honest Labor Is Starving

Today the Pullman Company will declare a quarterly dividend of 2 per cent on its capital stock of $30,000,000 and President George M. Pullman is authority for the statement that his company owes no man a cent. This despite the assertion of Mr. Pullman that the works have been run at a loss for eight months. Six hundred thousand dollars to shareholders, while starvation threatens the workmen.

DOCUMENT 4
***Chicago Tribune*, July 1, 1894**

MOBS BENT ON RUIN
Men Who Attempt to Work Are Terrorized and Beaten

Continued and menacing lawlessness marked the progress yesterday of Dictator Debs and those who obey his orders in their efforts at coercing the railroads of the country into obeying the mandates of the American Railway Union. The Rock Island was the chief sufferer from the mob spirit which broke loose the moment its men struck. . . . At 10 o'clock the officials threw up their hands and discontinued service for the night. At Blue Island, anarchy reigned. The Mayor and police force of that town could do nothing to repress the riotous strikers and they did their own sweet will. . . .

On the Illinois Central it was the same old story of destruction of the company's property without interference from the police. . . . Dictator Debs was as blatant as ever yesterday. He asserted . . . that the fight against Pullman was now a thing of the past. He is waging his warfare against the General Managers, who had committed the sin of combining against him.

DOCUMENT 5
Chicago Tribune, July 7, 1894

YARDS FIRE SWEPT
Rioters Prevent Firemen from Saving the Property

From Brighton Park to Sixty-First Street the yards of the Pan-Handle road were last night put to the torch by the rioters. Between 600 and 700 freight cars have been destroyed, many of them loaded. Miles and miles of costly track are in a snarled tangle of heat-twisted rails. Not less than $750,000 — possibly a whole $1,000,000 of property — has been sacrificed to the caprice of a mob of drunken Anarchists and rebels. That is the record of the night's work by the Debs strikers in the Stock-Yards District.

DOCUMENT 6
Chicago Times, July 7, 1894

MEN NOT AWED BY SOLDIERS
Railway Union Is Confident of Winning against Armed Capital

Despite the presence of United States troops and the mobilization of five regiments of state militia, despite threats of martial law and total extermination of the strikers by bullet and bayonet, the great strike inaugurated by the American Railway Union holds three-fourths of the roads running out of Chicago in its strong fetters, and last night traffic was more fully paralyzed than at any time since the inception of the tie-up. . . . With the exception of an occasional car or two moved by the aid of the military, not a wheel is turning. . . .

If the soldiers are sent to this district, bloodshed and perhaps death will follow today, for this is the most lawless element in the city, as is shown by their riotous work yesterday. . . . But the perpetrators are not American Railway Union men. The people engaged in this outrageous work of destruction are not strikers, most of them are not even grown men. The persons who set the fires yesterday on the authority of the firemen and police are young hoodlums. . . . The setting fire to the cars yesterday was done openly where anyone could see it and when the slightest effort would have resulted in the apprehension of the guilty ones, but no such effort was made. The firemen were overwhelmed with the work of attending to a dozen different fires and could not, and the police on the scene apparently didn't care to or would not make arrests.

DOCUMENT 7
New York World, July 14, 1894

CHEERS FOR NELLIE BLY
Nellie Bly Covers the Strike

I found in my mail this morning an earnest request from the Pullman A. R. U. for me to be present at a meeting which was to be held in the Turner Hall, Kensington. . . .

Several of the workmen made speeches this afternoon trying to cheer the spirits of their hungry and disheartened brothers. I was introduced and asked to say a few words to the men. . . .

So I took my nerves in hand and my place before the table near where the speakers sat. I don't intend to repeat what I said, but I told them several truths. They were especially amused when I told them that I had come to Chicago very bitterly set against the strikers; that so far as I understood the question, I thought the inhabitants of the model town of Pullman hadn't a reason on earth to complain. With this belief I visited the town, intending in my articles to denounce the riotous and bloodthirsty strikers. Before I had been half a day in Pullman I was the most bitter striker in the town.

That is true. I've [flip]flopped, as they call it, and I am brave enough to confess it. If ever men and women had cause to strike, those men and women are in Pullman. I also said to these men, sitting so quietly and peaceably before me, hungry for a word of sympathy or a word of hope, that if any of them wished to make any statements to me I would be glad to have them do so. After the meeting I was besieged. If I attempted to tell half the tales of wrong I've listened to I could fill an entire copy of *The World*.

Questions for Analysis and Debate

1. How do the *Tribune* and *Times* articles differ in their portrayal of events and actors in the strike?
2. Which version of the strike do you think most middle-class readers, who tended to be sympathetic to the strikers but fearful of violence, would find most compelling?
3. Which version of the strike do you think was favored by business owners, who provided advertising revenue to the newspapers?
4. Do you think readers found Nellie Bly's article persuasive? Why or why not?

another solution. But when George Pullman adamantly refused arbitration, the ARU membership voted to boycott all Pullman cars. Beginning on June 29, switchmen across the United States refused to handle any train that carried Pullman cars.

The conflict escalated quickly. The General Managers Association (GMA), an organization of managers from twenty-four different railroads, acted in concert to quash the **Pullman boycott**. Determined to kill the ARU, they recruited strikebreakers and fired all the protesting switchmen. Their tactics set off a chain reaction. Entire train crews walked off the job in a show of solidarity with the Pullman workers. In a matter of days, the boycott/strike spread to more than fifteen railroads and affected twenty-seven states and territories. By July 2, rail lines from New York to California lay paralyzed. Even the GMA was forced to concede that the railroads had been "fought to a standstill."

The boycott remained surprisingly peaceful. In contrast to the Great Railroad Strike of 1877, no major riots broke out, and no serious property damage occurred. Debs, in a whirlwind of activity, fired off telegrams to all parts of the country advising his followers to avoid violence and respect law and order. But the nation's newspapers, fed press releases by the GMA, distorted the issues and misrepresented the strike. Across the country, papers ran headlines like "Wild Riot in Chicago" and "Mob Is in Control." (See "Documenting the American Promise," page 648.)

In Washington, Attorney General Richard B. Olney, a lawyer with strong ties to the railroads, determined to put down the strike. In his way stood the governor of Illinois, John Peter Altgeld, who, observing that the boycott remained peaceful, refused to call out troops. To get around Altgeld, Olney convinced President Grover Cleveland that federal troops had to intervene to protect the mails. To further cripple the boycott, two conservative Chicago judges issued an injunction so sweeping that it prohibited Debs from speaking in public. By issuing the injunction, the court made the boycott a crime punishable by a jail sentence for contempt of court, a civil process that did not require a jury trial. Even the conservative *Chicago Tribune* judged the injunction "a menace to liberty . . . a weapon ever ready for the capitalist." Furious, Debs risked jail by refusing to honor it.

Olney's strategy worked. President Grover Cleveland called out the army. On July 5, nearly 8,000 troops marched into Chicago. The GMA was jubilant. "It has now become a fight between the United States Government and the American Railway Union," a spokesman observed, "and we shall leave them to fight it out." Violence immediately erupted. In one day, troops killed 25 workers and wounded more than 60. In the face of bullets and bayonets, the strikers held firm. "Troops cannot move trains," Debs reminded his followers, a fact that was borne out as the railroads remained paralyzed despite the military intervention. But if the army could not put down the boycott, the injunction could and did. Debs was arrested and imprisoned for contempt of court. With its leader in jail, its headquarters raided and ransacked, and its members demoralized, the ARU was defeated along with

Nellie Bly in Her Traveling Clothes, 1890
The journalist Elizabeth Jane Cochran took the pen name Nellie Bly (from a popular song by composer Stephen Foster) when she began her career writing for the *Pittsburg Dispatch* in 1880. Best known for her vow to travel around the world in fewer than 80 days, she is shown here in her travel costume. Her dispatches to the *New York World* documenting her trip made her an international celebrity. But some of her best writing involved gritty stories about society's poor and outcast. In 1894 she interviewed striking workers at the Pullman Palace Car company. In direct defiance of her editor, Joseph Pulitzer, Bly declared her allegiance with the strikers. Library of Congress.

National Guard Occupying Pullman, Illinois
After President Grover Cleveland called out the troops to put down the Pullman strike in 1894, the National Guard occupied the town of Pullman to protect George M. Pullman's property. Here, guardsmen ring the Arcade building, the town shopping center, while curious men and women look on. The intervention of troops at Homestead and Pullman enabled the owners to bring in strikebreakers and defeat the unions. In Cripple Creek, Colorado, where a Populist governor used the militia to keep the peace and not fight the strikers, the miners won the day in 1894. Chicago Historical Society.

the boycott. Pullman reopened his factory, hiring new workers to replace many of the strikers and leaving 1,600 workers without jobs.

In the aftermath of the strike, a special commission investigated the events at Pullman, taking testimony from 107 witnesses, from the lowliest workers to George M. Pullman himself. Stubborn and self-righteous, Pullman spoke for the business orthodoxy of his era, steadfastly affirming the right of business to safeguard its interests through confederacies such as the GMA and at the same time denying labor's right to organize. "If we were to receive these men as representatives of the union," he stated, "they could probably force us to pay any wages which they saw fit."

From his jail cell, Eugene Debs reviewed the events of the Pullman strike. With the courts and the government ready to side with industrialists in the interest of defending private property, Debs realized that labor had little recourse. Strikes seemed futile, and unions remained helpless; workers would have to take control of the state itself. Debs went into jail a trade unionist and came out six months later a socialist. At first, he turned to the Populist Party, but after its demise he formed the Socialist Party in 1900 and ran for president on its ticket five times. Debs's dissatisfaction with the status quo was shared by another group even more alienated from the political process — women.

REVIEW What tactics led to the defeat of the strikers in the 1890s? Where were they able to succeed and why?

▸ Women's Activism

"Do everything," **Frances Willard** urged her followers in 1881 (see pages 639–40). The new president of the Woman's Christian Temperance Union (WCTU) meant what she said. The WCTU followed a trajectory that was common for women in the late nineteenth century. As women organized to deal with issues that touched their homes and families, they moved into politics, lending new urgency to the cause of woman suffrage. Urban industrialism dislocated women's lives no less than men's. Like men, women sought political change and organized to promote issues central to their lives, campaigning for temperance and woman suffrage.

Woman's Christian Temperance Union Postcards
The Woman's Christian Temperance Union distributed postcards like these to attack the liquor trade. These cards are typical in their portrayal of saloon backers as traitors to the nation. In the top card, notice the man trampling on the American flag as he casts his ballot—a sly allusion to the need for woman suffrage. The second card shows a saloon keeper recruiting an "army of drunkards." Collection of Joyce M. Tice.

Frances Willard and the Woman's Christian Temperance Union

A visionary leader, Frances Willard spoke for a group left almost entirely out of the U.S. electoral process. In 1890, only one state, Wyoming, allowed women to vote in national elections. But lack of the franchise did not mean that women were apolitical. The WCTU demonstrated the breadth of women's political activity in the late nineteenth century.

Women supported the temperance movement because they felt particularly vulnerable to the effects of drunkenness. Dependent on men's wages, women and children suffered when money went for drink. The drunken, abusive husband epitomized the evils of a nation in which women remained second-class citizens. The WCTU, composed entirely of women, viewed all women's interests as essentially the same and therefore did not hesitate to use the singular *woman* to emphasize gender solidarity. Although mostly white and middle-class, WCTU members resolved to speak for their entire sex.

"All this work has tended more toward the liberation of women than it has toward the extinction of the saloon."
— FRANCES WILLARD, on the activities of the WCTU

When Frances Willard became president in 1879, she radically changed the direction of the organization. Social action replaced prayer as women's answer to the threat of drunkenness. Viewing alcoholism as a disease rather than a sin and poverty as a cause rather than a result of drink, the WCTU became involved in labor issues, joining with the Knights of Labor to press for better working conditions for women workers. Describing workers in a textile mill, a WCTU member wrote in the organization's *Union Signal* magazine, "It is dreadful to see these girls, stripped almost to the skin . . . and running like racehorses from the beginning to the end of the day." She concluded, "The hard slavish work is drawing the girls into the saloon."

Willard capitalized on the cult of domesticity as a shrewd political tactic to move women into public life and gain power to ameliorate social problems. Using "home protection" as her watchword, she argued as early as 1884 that women needed the vote to protect home and family. By the 1890s, the WCTU's grassroots network of local unions had spread to all but the most isolated rural areas of the country. Strong and rich, with more than 200,000 dues-paying members, the WCTU was a formidable group.

Willard worked to create a broad reform coalition in the 1890s, embracing the Knights of Labor, the People's Party, and the Prohibition Party. Until her death in 1898, she led, if not a woman's rights movement, then the first organized mass movement of women united around a women's issue. By 1900, thanks largely to the WCTU, women could claim a generation of experience in political action — speaking, lobbying, organizing, drafting legislation, and running private charitable institutions. As Willard observed, "All this work has tended more toward the liberation of women than it has toward the extinction of the saloon."

Elizabeth Cady Stanton, Susan B. Anthony, and the Movement for Woman Suffrage

Unlike the WCTU, the organized movement for woman suffrage remained small and relatively weak in the late nineteenth century. The U.S. woman's rights movement was begun by **Elizabeth Cady Stanton** at the first woman's rights convention in the United States, at Seneca Falls, New York, in 1848. Women's rights advocates split in 1867 over whether the Fourteenth and Fifteenth Amendments, which granted voting rights to African American males, should have extended the vote to women as well. Stanton and her ally, **Susan B. Anthony**, launched the National Woman Suffrage Association in 1869, demanding the vote for women (see chapter 18). A more conservative group, the American Woman Suffrage Association (AWSA), formed the same year. Composed of men as well as women, the AWSA believed that women should vote in local but not national elections.

By 1890, the split had healed, and the newly united **National American Woman Suffrage Association** (NAWSA) launched campaigns on the state level to gain the vote for women. Twenty years had made a great change. Woman suffrage, though not yet generally supported, was no longer considered a crackpot idea. Thanks to the WCTU's support of the "home protection" ballot, suffrage had become accepted as a means to an end even when it was not embraced as a woman's natural right. The NAWSA honored Elizabeth Cady Stanton by electing her its first president, but Susan B. Anthony, who took the helm in 1892, emerged as the leading figure in the new united organization.

Stanton and Anthony, both in their seventies, were coming to the end of their public careers. Since the days of the Seneca Falls

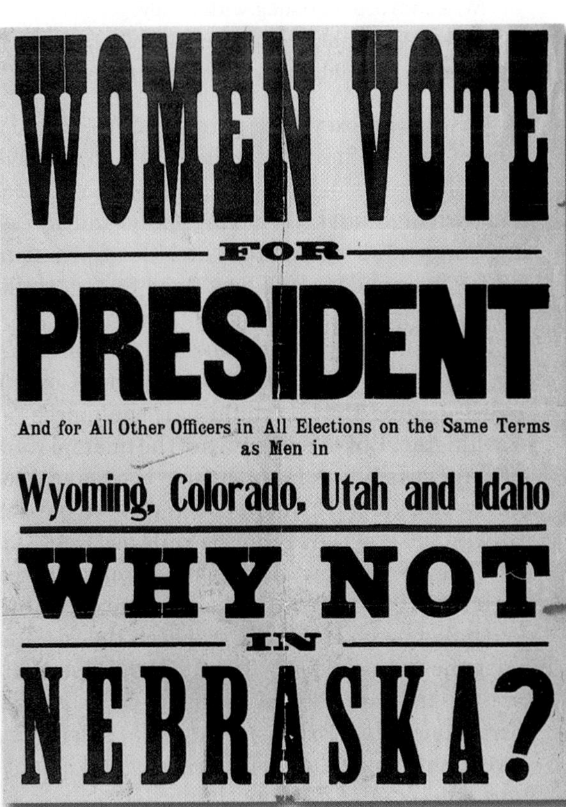

Campaigning for Woman Suffrage
In 1896, women voted in only four states — Wyoming, Colorado, Idaho, and Utah. The West led the way in the campaign for woman suffrage, with Wyoming Territory granting women the vote as early as 1869. Sparse population meant that only sixteen votes were needed in the state's territorial legislature to obtain passage of woman suffrage. The poster calls on Nebraska to join the suffrage column, while the flag illustrates the number of states in which women could vote. Poster: Nebraska State Historical Society; Flag: Smithsonian Institution, Washington, D.C.

woman's rights convention, they had worked for reforms for their sex, including property rights, custody rights, and the right to education and gainful employment. But the prize of woman suffrage still eluded them. Suffragists won victories in Colorado in 1893 and Idaho in 1896. One more state joined the suffrage column in 1896 when Utah entered the Union. But women suffered a bitter defeat in a California referendum on woman suffrage that same year. Never losing faith, Susan B. Anthony remarked in her last public appearance, in 1906, "Failure is impossible." It would take until 1920 for all women to gain the vote with the ratification of the Nineteenth Amendment, but the unification of the two woman suffrage groups in 1890 signaled a new era in women's fight for the vote, just as Frances Willard's place on the platform in 1892 in St. Louis symbolized women's growing role in politics and reform.

REVIEW How did women's temperance activism contribute to the cause of woman suffrage?

▸ Depression Politics

The depression that began in the spring of 1893 and lasted for more than four years put nearly half of the labor force out of work, a higher percentage than during the Great Depression of the 1930s (as discussed in chapters 23 and 24). The human cost of the depression was staggering. "I Take my pen in hand to let you know that we are Starving to death," a Kansas farm woman wrote to the governor in 1894. "Last cent gone," wrote a young widow in her diary. "Children went to work without their breakfasts." The burden of feeding and sheltering the unemployed and their families fell to private charity, city government, and some of the stronger trade unions. Following the harsh dictates of social Darwinism and laissez-faire, the majority of America's elected officials believed that it was inappropriate for the government to intervene. But the scope of the depression made it impossible for local agencies to supply sufficient relief, and increasingly Americans called on the federal government to take action. Armies of the unemployed marched on Washington to demand relief, and the Populist Party experienced a surge of support as the election of 1896 approached.

> **"I Take my pen in hand to let you know that we are Starving to death."**
> —A Kansas farm woman in 1894

Coxey's Army

Masses of unemployed Americans marched to Washington, D.C., in the spring of 1894 to call attention to their plight and to urge Congress to enact a public works program to end unemployment. Jacob S. Coxey of Massilon, Ohio, led the most publicized contingent. Convinced that men could be put to work building badly needed roads for the nation, Coxey proposed a scheme to finance public works through non-interest-bearing bonds. "What I am after," he maintained, "is to try to put this country in a condition so that no man who wants work shall be obliged to remain idle." His plan won support from the AFL and the Populists.

Starting out from Ohio with one hundred men, **Coxey's army**, as it was dubbed, swelled as it marched east through the spring snows of the Alleghenies. In Pennsylvania, Coxey recruited several hundred from the ranks of those left unemployed by the Homestead lockout. Called by Coxey the Commonweal of Christ, the army advanced to the tune of "Marching through Georgia":

> We are not tramps nor vagabonds,
> that's shirking honest toil,
> But miners, clerks, skilled artisans,
> and tillers of the soil
> Now forced to beg our brother worms
> to give us leave to toil,
> While we are marching with Coxey.
> Hurrah! hurrah! for the unemployed's appeal
> Hurrah! hurrah! for the marching commonweal!

On May 1, Coxey's army arrived in Washington. When Coxey defiantly marched his men onto the Capitol grounds, police set upon the demonstrators with nightsticks, cracking skulls and arresting Coxey and his lieutenants. Coxey went to jail for twenty days and was fined $5 for "walking on the grass."

Those who had trembled for the safety of the Republic heaved a sigh of relief after Coxey's arrest, hoping that it would halt the march on Washington. But other armies of the unemployed, totaling possibly as many as five thousand people, were still on their way. Too poor to pay for railway tickets, they rode the rails as "freeloaders." The more daring contingents commandeered entire trains, stirring fears of revolution. Journalists who covered the march did little to quiet the nation's fears. They delighted in military terminology, describing themselves as "war correspondents." To boost newspaper sales, they gave to the episode a tone of urgency and heightened the sense of a nation imperiled.

Coxey's Army
A contingent of Coxey's army stops to rest on its way to Washington, D.C. A "petition in boots," Coxey's followers were well dressed, as evidenced by the men in this photo wearing white shirts, vests, neckties, and bowler hats. Music was an important component of the march, including the anthem "Marching with Coxey," sung to the tune of "Marching through Georgia." Band members are pictured on the right with their instruments. Despite their peaceful pose, the marchers stirred the fears of many conservative Americans, who predicted an uprising of the unemployed. Instead, Coxey and a contingent of his marchers were arrested and jailed for "walking on the grass" when they reached the nation's capital. Ohio Historical Society.

By August, the leaderless, tattered armies dissolved. Although the "On to Washington" movement proved ineffective in forcing federal relief legislation, Coxey's army dramatized the plight of the unemployed and acted, in the words of one participant, as a "living, moving object lesson." Like the Populists, Coxey's army called into question the underlying values of the new industrial order and demonstrated how ordinary citizens turned to means outside the regular party system to influence politics in the 1890s.

The People's Party and the Election of 1896

Even before the depression of 1893 gave added impetus to their cause, the Populists had railed against the status quo. "We meet in the midst of a nation brought to the verge of moral, political, and material ruin," Ignatius Donnelly had declared in his keynote address at the creation of the People's Party in St. Louis in 1892. "The fruits of the toil of millions are boldly stolen to build up colossal fortunes for a few. . . . From the same prolific womb of governmental injustice we breed the two great classes — tramps and millionaires."

The fiery rhetoric frightened many who saw in the People's Party a call not to reform but to revolution. Throughout the country, the press denounced the Populists as "cranks, lunatics, and idiots." When one self-righteous editor dismissed them as "calamity howlers," Populist governor Lorenzo Lewelling of Kansas shot back, "If that is so I want to continue to howl until those conditions are improved."

The People's Party captured more than a million votes in the presidential election of 1892, a respectable showing for a new party (Map 20.1). But increasingly, sectional and racial animosities threatened its unity. In the South, the Populists' willingness to form common cause with black farmers made them anathema. Realizing that race prejudice obscured the common economic interests of black and white farmers, **Tom Watson** of Georgia openly courted African Americans, appearing on platforms with black speakers and promising "to wipe out the color line." When angry Georgia whites threatened to

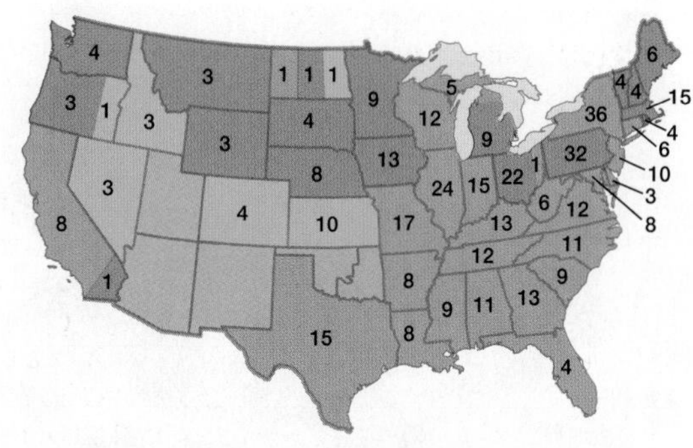

Candidate	Electoral Vote	Popular Vote	Percent of Popular Vote
Grover Cleveland (Democrat)	277	5,555,426	46.1
Benjamin Harrison (Republican)	145	5,182,690	43.0
James B. Weaver (People's)	22	1,029,846	8.5

MAP 20.1
The Election of 1892

lynch a black Populist preacher, Watson rallied two thousand gun-toting Populists to the man's defense. Although many Populists remained racist in their attitudes toward African Americans, the spectacle of white Georgians riding through the night to protect a black man from lynching was symbolic of the enormous changes the Populist Party promised in the South.

As the presidential election of 1896 approached, the depression intensified cries for reform not only from the Populists but also throughout the electorate. Depression worsened the tight money problem caused by the deflationary pressures of the gold standard. Once again, proponents of free silver stirred rebellion in the ranks of both the Democratic and the Republican parties. When the Republicans nominated Ohio governor **William McKinley** on a platform pledging the preservation of the gold standard, western advocates of free silver representing miners and farmers walked out of the convention. Open rebellion also split the Democratic Party as vast segments in the West and South repudiated President Grover Cleveland because of his support for gold. In South Carolina, Benjamin Tillman won his race for Congress by promising, "Send me to Washington and I'll stick my pitchfork into [Cleveland's] old ribs!"

The spirit of revolt animated the Democratic National Convention in Chicago in the summer of 1896. **William Jennings Bryan** of Nebraska, the thirty-six-year-old "boy orator from the Platte," whipped the convention into a frenzy with his passionate call for free silver. In his speech in favor of the silver plank in the party's platform, Bryan masterfully cataloged the grievances of farmers and laborers, closing his dramatic speech with a ringing exhortation: "Do not crucify mankind upon a cross of gold." Pandemonium broke loose as delegates stampeded to nominate Bryan, the youngest candidate ever to run for the presidency.

The juggernaut of free silver rolled out of Chicago and on to St. Louis, where the People's Party met a week after the Democrats adjourned. Smelling victory, many western Populists urged the party to ally with the Democrats and endorse Bryan. A major obstacle in the path of fusion, however, was Bryan's running mate, Arthur M. Sewall. A Maine railway director and bank president, Sewall, who had been placed on the ticket to appease conservative Democrats, embodied everything the Populists detested.

Populism's regional constituencies remained as divided over tactics as they were uniform in their call for change. Western Populists, including a strong coalition of farmers and miners in states such as Idaho and Colorado, championed free silver. In these largely Republican states, Populists had joined forces with Democrats in previous elections and saw no problem with becoming "Popocrats" once Bryan led the Democratic ticket on a free silver platform. Similarly in the Midwest, a Republican stronghold, Populists who had used fusion with the Democrats as a tactic to win elections had little trouble backing Bryan. But in the South, where Democrats had resorted to fraud and violence to steal elections from the Populists in 1892 and 1894, support for a Democratic ticket proved especially hard to swallow. Die-hard southern Populists wanted no part of fusion.

All of these tactical differences emerged as the Populists met in St. Louis in 1896 to nominate a candidate for president. To show that they remained true to their principles, delegates first voted to support all the planks of the 1892 platform, added to it a call for public works projects for the unemployed, and only narrowly defeated a plank for woman suffrage. To deal with the problem of fusion, the convention selected the vice presidential candidate first. The nomination of Tom Watson undercut opposition to Bryan's candidacy. And although Bryan quickly sent a telegram to protest that he would not drop Sewall as his running mate, mysteriously his message never reached the convention floor. Fusion triumphed. Watson's vice presidential nomination

Gold Elephant Campaign Button and Silver Ribbon from St. Louis, 1896
Mechanical elephant badges that opened to show portraits of William McKinley and his running mate, Garret Hobart, were popular campaign novelties in the election of 1896. The elephant, the mascot of the Republican Party, is gilded to indicate the party's support of the gold standard. By contrast, the delegate ribbon from the St. Louis National Silver Convention in 1896 features a silver eagle and fringe testifying to the power of free silver as a campaign issue. The Democrats nominated William Jennings Bryan on a free-silver platform, and the Populists put him on their ticket as well. Elephant: Collection of Janice L. and David J. Frent; ribbon: Nebraska State Historical Society.

paved the way for the selection of Bryan by a lopsided vote. The Populists did not know it, but their cheers for Bryan signaled not a chorus of victory but the death knell for the People's Party.

Few contests in the nation's history have been as fiercely fought and as full of emotion as the presidential election of 1896. On one side stood Republican William McKinley, backed by the wealthy industrialist and party boss Mark Hanna. Hanna played on the business community's fears of Populism to raise a Republican war chest more than double the amount of any previous campaign. On the other side, William Jennings Bryan, with few assets beyond his silver tongue, struggled to make up in energy and eloquence what his party lacked in campaign funds, crisscrossing the country in a whirlwind tour, traveling more than eighteen thousand miles and delivering more than six hundred speeches in three months. According to his own reckoning, he visited twenty-seven states and spoke to more than five million Americans.

As election day approached, the silver states of the Rocky Mountains lined up solidly for Bryan. The Northeast stood solidly for McKinley. Much of the South, with the exception of the border states, abandoned the Populists and returned to the Democratic "party of the fathers," leaving Tom Watson to lament that "[Populists] play Jonah while [Democrats] play the whale." The Midwest hung in the balance. Bryan intensified his campaign in Illinois, Michigan, Ohio, and Indiana. But midwestern farmers proved less receptive than western voters to the blandishments of free silver.

In the cities, Democrats charged the Republicans with mass intimidation. "Men, vote as you please," the head of New York's Steinway Piano Company reportedly announced to his workers on the eve of the election, "but if Bryan is elected tomorrow the whistle will not blow

"Swallowed!"
This political cartoon from 1900 shows William Jennings Bryan as a python swallowing the Democratic Party's donkey mascot. Bryan, who ran unsuccessfully in 1896, won the Democratic nomination again in 1900 and in 1908. Ironically, it was not the Democratic party so much as the Populist party that Bryan swallowed. By nominating the Democrat Bryan on their ticket in 1896, the Populist Party lost its identity. The Granger Collection, New York.

Wednesday morning." Intimidation alone did not explain the failure of urban labor to rally to Bryan. Republicans repeatedly warned workers that if the Democrats won, the inflated silver dollar would be worth only fifty cents. However much farmers and laborers might insist that they were united as producers against the non-producing bosses, it was equally true that inflation did not offer the boon to urban laborers that it did to western farmers.

On election day, four out of five voters went to the polls in an unprecedented turnout. In the critical midwestern states, as many as 95 percent of the eligible voters cast their ballots. In the end, the election hinged on between 100 and 1,000 votes in several key states, including Wisconsin, Iowa, and Minnesota. Although McKinley won twenty-three states to Bryan's twenty-two, the electoral vote showed a lopsided 271 to 176 in McKinley's favor (Map 20.2).

The biggest losers in 1896 turned out to be the Populists. On the national level, they polled fewer than 300,000 votes, a million less than in 1894. In the clamor to support Bryan, Populists in the South, determined to beat McKinley at any cost, swallowed their differences and drifted back to the Democratic Party. The People's Party was crushed, and with it the agrarian revolt.

But if Populism proved unsuccessful at the polls, it nevertheless set the domestic political agenda for the United States in the next decades, highlighting issues such as railroad regulation, banking and currency reform, electoral reforms, and an enlarged role for the federal government in the economy. Meanwhile, as the decade ended, the bugle call to arms turned America's attention to foreign affairs and effectively drowned out the trumpet of reform. The struggle for social justice gave way to a war for empire as the United States asserted its power on the world stage.

MAP 20.2
The Election of 1896

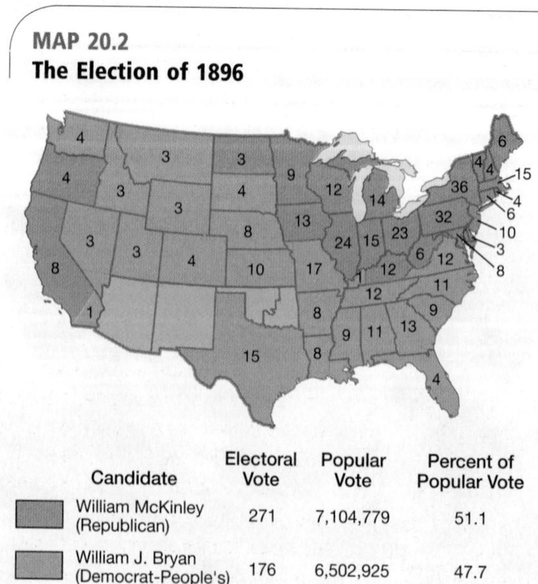

Candidate	Electoral Vote	Popular Vote	Percent of Popular Vote
William McKinley (Republican)	271	7,104,779	51.1
William J. Bryan (Democrat-People's)	176	6,502,925	47.7

REVIEW Why was the People's Party unable to translate national support into victory in the 1896 election?

▶ The United States and the World

Throughout much of the second half of the nineteenth century, U.S. interest in foreign policy took a backseat to territorial expansion in the American West. The United States stood aloof while Great Britain, France, Germany, Spain, Belgium, and an increasingly powerful Japan competed for empires in Asia, Africa, Latin America, and the Pacific. Between 1870 and 1900, European nations colonized more than 20 percent of the world's landmass and 10 percent of the world's population.

At the turn of the twentieth century, the United States pursued a foreign policy consisting of two currents—isolationism and expansionism. Although the determination to remain detached from European politics had been a hallmark of U.S. foreign policy since the nation's founding, Americans simultaneously believed in manifest destiny—the "obvious" right to expand the nation from ocean to ocean. With its own inland empire secured, the United States looked outward. Determined to protect its sphere of influence in the Western Hemisphere and to expand its trading in Asia, the nation moved away from isolationism and toward a more active role on the world stage. The push for commercial expansion joined with a sense of Christian mission and led both to the strengthening of the Monroe Doctrine in the Western Hemisphere and to a more assertive policy in Asia. All of these trends were in evidence during the Spanish-American War and the debates that followed.

Markets and Missionaries

The depression of the 1890s provided a powerful impetus to American commercial expansion. As markets weakened at home, American businesses looked abroad for profits. As early as 1890, Captain Alfred Thayer Mahan, leader of a growing group of American expansionists, prophesied, "Whether

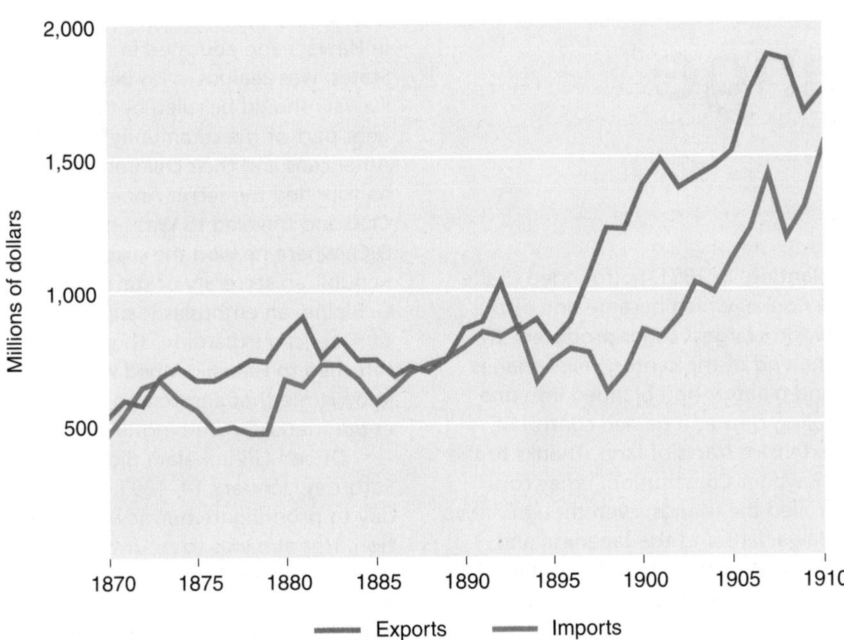

FIGURE 20.3 Expansion in U.S. Trade, 1870–1910
Between 1870 and 1910, American exports more than tripled. Imports generally rose, but they were held in check by the high protective tariffs championed by Republican presidents from Ulysses S. Grant to William Howard Taft. A decline in imports is particularly noticeable after the passage of the prohibitive McKinley tariff in 1890.

they will or not, Americans must now begin to look outward. The growing production of the country requires it." As the depression deepened, one diplomat warned that Americans "must turn [their] eyes abroad, or they will soon look inward upon discontent."

Exports constituted a small but significant percentage of the profits of American business in the 1890s (Figure 20.3). And where American interests led, businessmen expected the government's power and influence to follow to protect their investments. Companies like Standard Oil actively sought to use the U.S. government as their agent, often putting foreign service employees on the payroll. "Our ambassadors and ministers and consuls," wrote John D. Rockefeller appreciatively, "have aided to push our way into new markets and to the utmost corners of the world." Whether "our" referred to the United States or to Standard Oil remained ambiguous; in practice, the distinction was of little importance in late-nineteenth-century foreign policy.

America's foreign policy often appeared little more than a sidelight to business development. In Hawai'i (first called the Sandwich Islands), American sugar interests fomented a rebellion in 1893, toppling the increasingly independent Queen Lili'uokalani. (See "Beyond America's Borders," page 660.) They pushed Congress to annex the islands, which would allow planters to avoid the high McKinley tariff on sugar. When President Cleveland learned that Hawai'ians opposed annexation, he withdrew the proposal from Congress. But expansionists still coveted the islands and continued to look for an excuse to push through annexation.

However compelling the economic arguments about overseas markets proved, business interests alone did not account for the new expansionism that seized the nation during the 1890s. As Mahan confessed, "Even when material interests are the original exciting cause, it is the sentiment to which they give rise, the moral tone which emotion takes that constitutes the greater

Mei Foo Lamp
The Standard Oil Company sold more than a million Mei Foo ("beautiful companion") lamps in China during the 1890s to promote the sale of kerosene in the China market. The first oil tankers were square-rigged kerosene clipper ships that plied the Pacific beginning in 1892 as the petroleum industry rushed to capture the China trade. Standard Oil ads admonished, "If a person wishes to have luck, longevity, health and peace, he or she must live in a world of light." Courtesy of ExxonMobil Corporation.

BEYOND AMERICA'S BORDERS

Regime Change in Hawai'i

Queen Lili'uokalani came to the throne in Hawai'i in 1891 determined to take back power for her monarchy and her people. As a member of Hawai'i's native royalty, or *ali'i*, she had received a first-rate education in missionary school. As a young woman, she converted to Christianity, adopted the English name Lydia, and married the white (*haole*) governor of Maui. Yet she maintained a reverence for traditional Hawai'ian ways and resented the treatment of her people by the white minority. Her brother, King Kalakaua, had proven a weak leader, coerced by the white elite into signing the "Bayonet Constitution," which put the government squarely in the hands of the whites. Determined to rule, not simply to reign, Lili'uokalani moved ahead with plans to wrest power from the minority she referred to as Hawai'i's "guests."

American missionaries first came to Hawai'i in 1820. Some intermarried with their Christian converts, creating a group of *hapa haole* (half whites), as well as a growing number of children born in Hawai'i to white parents. The temptations of wealth led many missionaries, like Amos Starr Cooke, to acquire land and take up sugar planting. In 1851, he founded Castle & Cooke, which became one of the world's largest sugar producers. By the end of the century, missionaries and planters had blended into one ruling class and gained control of extensive tracts of land. Thanks to the "Bayonet Constitution," they controlled the islands, even though native Hawai'ians and the Japanese and Chinese "coolie" laborers imported to work on the sugar plantations outnumbered them ten to one.

Sugar became a booming business in Hawai'i as a result of favorable reciprocity treaties with the United States. But hard times came to the islands with the passage of the McKinley tariff in 1890. The tariff wiped out the advantage Hawai'ian sugar had enjoyed in the American market, with devastating results. Within two years, the value of Hawai'ian sugar exports plummeted from $13 million to $8 million.

One way to avoid the tariff was by incorporating Hawai'i into the United States through annexation. Foremost among those who championed this scheme was Lorrin Thurston, the thirty-five-year-old grandson of American missionaries. Thurston, born in Hawai'i and educated in the United States, was zealous in his belief that Hawai'i should be ruled by "the intelligent part of the community" — white Americans and their children. In 1892, he founded the secret Annexation Club and traveled to Washington, D.C., where he won the support of Republican secretary of state James G. Blaine, an enthusiastic supporter of American expansion. Thurston returned to Hawai'i armed with the knowledge that annexation had influential friends in Washington.

Queen Lili'uokalani picked Saturday, January 14, 1893, as the day to promulgate her new constitution. Her aim was to return Hawai'i to Hawai'ians by allowing only those with native ancestry the right to vote. Learning of her intentions, Thurston quickly hatched a plot to overthrow the monarchy. Thurston's daring plan could work only with the cooperation of the United States. So late that night, he called on John L. Stevens, the American minister to Hawai'i. Laying out his plan, he urged Stevens, a staunch annexationist, to support the overthrow of the queen and to pledge U.S. support for Thurston's actions. Without hesitating, Stevens promised to land Marines from the USS *Boston* "to protect American lives and property."

Two days later, 162 American Marines and sailors marched into Honolulu armed with carbines, howitzers (small cannons), and Gatling guns. The next day, Thurston and 17

force." Much of that moral tone was set by American missionaries intent on spreading the gospel of Christianity to the "heathen." No area on the globe constituted a greater challenge than China.

An 1858 agreement, the Tianjin (Tientsin) treaty admitted foreign missionaries to China. Although Christians converted only 100,000 in a population of 400 million, the Chinese nevertheless resented the interference of missionaries in village life. Opposition to foreign missionaries took the form of antiforeign secret societies, most notably the Boxers, whose Chinese name translated to "Righteous Harmonious Fist." No simple boxing club, the Boxers in 1899 began to hunt down and kill Chinese Christians and missionaries in northwestern Shandong (Shan-tung) Province. With the tacit support of China's Dowager Empress, the Boxers became bolder. Under the slogan "Uphold the Ch'ing Dynasty, Exterminate the Foreigners," they marched on the cities. Their rampage eventually led to the massacre of some 30,000 Chinese converts and 250 foreign nuns, priests, and missionaries along with their families. In August 1900, 2,500 U.S. troops joined an international of his confederates seized control of a government building and proclaimed themselves a "provisional government." Minister Stevens promptly recognized the revolutionaries as the legitimate government of Hawai'i.

To avoid bloodshed, Queen Lili'uokalani agreed to step aside. But in a masterstroke, she composed a letter addressed not to her enemies in the provisional government, but to the U.S. government. Protesting her overthrow, she yielded her authority "until such time as the Government of the United States, shall, upon the facts being presented to it, undo the action of its representatives and reinstate me in the authority which I claim as the constitutional sovereign of the Hawai'ian Islands." The action now shifted to Washington, where Grover Cleveland, a Democrat skeptical of America's adventures abroad, quickly squelched plans for annexation and supported the Hawai'ian queen. The provisional government, however, enjoyed the support of Republicans in Congress and refused to step down, biding its time, waiting for the Republicans to take back the White House.

In 1898, as the taste for empire swept the United States in the wake of the Spanish-American War, President William McKinley quietly signed a treaty annexing Hawai'i. His action pleased not only Hawai'i's sugar growers but also American expansionists, who judged Hawai'i strategically important in expanding U.S. trade with China.

"Hawai'i is ours," Grover Cleveland wrote sadly. "As I look back upon the first steps in this miserable business, and as I contemplate the means used to complete the outrage, I am ashamed of the whole affair."

Queen Lili'uokalani (1838–1917)
An accomplished woman who straddled two cultures, Lydia Kamakaeha Dominis, or Queen Lili'uokalani, spoke English as easily as her native Hawai'ian and was fluent in French and German as well. She traveled widely in Europe and the United States. Despite President Cleveland's belief that the monarchy should be restored, Lili'uokalani never regained her throne. In 1898, she published *Hawai'i's Story by Hawai'i's Queen*, outlining her version of the events that had led to her downfall. In 1993, on the one hundredth anniversary of the revolution that deposed her, Congress passed and President Bill Clinton signed a resolution offering an apology to native Hawai'ians for the overthrow of their queen. Courtesy of the Lili'uokalani Trust.

America in a Global Context

1. How did economic issues on the mainland affect the status of Hawai'i?
2. What role did party politics play in the annexation of Hawai'i?

force sent to rescue the foreigners and put down the uprising in the Chinese capital of Beijing (Peking). The European powers imposed the humiliating Boxer Protocol in 1901, giving themselves the right to maintain military forces in Beijing and requiring the Chinese government to pay an exorbitant indemnity of $333 million for the loss of life and property resulting from the **Boxer uprising**.

In the aftermath of the uprising, missionaries voiced no concern at the paradox of bringing Christianity to China at gunpoint. "It is worth any cost in money, worth any cost in bloodshed," argued one bishop, "if we can make millions of Chinese true and intelligent Christians." Merchants and missionaries alike shared such moralistic reasoning. Indeed, they worked hand in hand; trade and Christianity marched into Asia together. "Missionaries," admitted the American clergyman Charles Denby, "are the pioneers of trade and commerce. . . . The missionary, inspired by holy zeal, goes everywhere and by degrees foreign commerce and trade follow."

VISUAL ACTIVITY

The Open Door

The trade advantage gained by the United States through the Open Door policy, enunciated by Secretary of State John Hay in 1900, is portrayed graphically in this political cartoon. Uncle Sam stands prominently in the "open door," while representatives of the other great powers seek admittance to the "Flowery Kingdom" of China. Uncle Sam holds the golden key of "American diplomacy," while the Chinese man on the other side of the door beams with pleasure. In fact, the Open Door policy promised equal access for all powers to the China trade, not U.S. preeminence as the cartoon implies. Culver Pictures.

READING THE IMAGE: How does the cartoon portray the United States' role in international diplomacy?
CONNECTIONS: In what ways does this image misrepresent the reality of American and European involvement in China and of the Open Door policy?

The Monroe Doctrine and the Open Door Policy

The emergence of the United States as a world power pitted the nation against other colonial powers, particularly Germany and Japan, which posed a threat to the twin pillars of America's expansionist foreign policy — one dating back to President James Monroe in the 1820s, the other formalized in 1900 under President William McKinley. The first, the **Monroe Doctrine**, came to be interpreted as establishing the Western Hemisphere as an American "sphere of influence" and warned European powers to stay away or risk war. The second, the Open Door, dealt with maintaining market access to China.

American diplomacy actively worked to buttress the Monroe Doctrine, with its assertion of American hegemony (domination) in the Western Hemisphere. In the 1880s, Republican secretary of state James G. Blaine promoted hemispheric peace and trade through Pan-American cooperation but at the same time used American troops to intervene in Latin American border disputes. In 1895, President Cleveland risked war with Great Britain to enforce the Monroe Doctrine when a conflict developed between Venezuela and British Guiana. After American saber rattling, the British backed down and accepted U.S. mediation in the area despite their territorial claims in Guiana.

In Central America, American business triumphed in a bloodless takeover that saw French and British interests routed by behemoths such as the United Fruit Company of Boston. United Fruit virtually dominated the Central American nations of Costa Rica and Guatemala, while an importer from New Orleans turned Honduras into a "banana republic" (a country run by U.S. business interests). Thus, by 1895, the United States, through business as well as diplomacy, had successfully achieved hegemony in Latin America and the Caribbean, forcing even the British to concur with the secretary of state that "the infinite resources [of the United States] combined with its isolated position render it master of the situation and practically invulnerable as against any or all other powers."

At the same time that American foreign policy warned European powers to stay out of the Western Hemisphere, the United States competed for trade in the Eastern Hemisphere. As American interests in China grew, the United States became more aggressive in defending its presence in Asia and the Pacific. The United States risked war with Germany in 1889 to guarantee the U.S. Navy access to Pago Pago in the Samoan Islands, a port for refueling on the way to Asia. Germany, seeking dominance over the islands, challenged the United States by sending warships to the region. But before fighting broke out, a great typhoon destroyed the German and American ships. Acceding to the will of nature, the potential combatants later divided the islands amicably in the 1899 Treaty of Berlin.

The biggest prize in Asia remained the China market. In the 1890s, China, weakened by years of internal warfare, was beginning to be partitioned into spheres of influence by Britain, Japan, Germany, France, and Russia. Concerned about the integrity of China and no less about American trade, Secretary of State John Hay in 1899–1900 wrote a series of notes calling for an "open door" policy that would ensure trade access to all and maintain Chinese sovereignty. The notes — sent to Britain, Germany, and Russia and later to France, Japan, and Italy — were greeted by the major powers with polite evasion. Nevertheless, Hay skillfully managed to maneuver the major powers into doing his bidding, and in 1900 he boldly announced the Open Door as international policy. The United States, by insisting on the **Open Door policy**, managed to secure access to Chinese markets, expanding its economic power while avoiding the problems of maintaining a far-flung colonial empire on the Asian mainland. But as the Spanish-American War soon demonstrated, Americans found it hard to resist the temptations of overseas empire.

The Samoan Islands, 1889

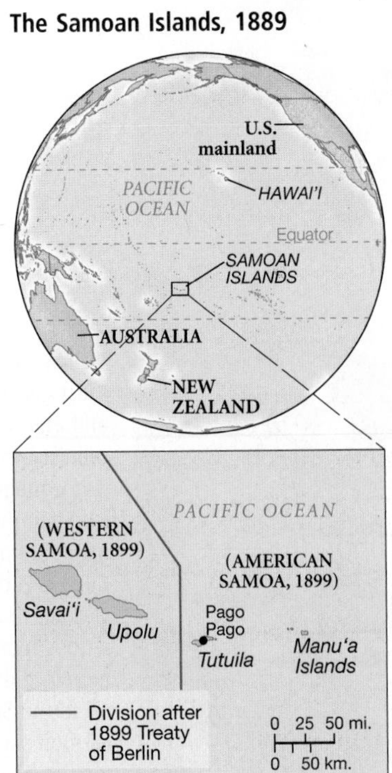

"A Splendid Little War"

The **Spanish-American War** began as a humanitarian effort to free Cuba from Spain's colonial grasp and ended with the United States itself acquiring territory overseas and fighting a dirty guerrilla war with Filipino nationalists who, like the Cubans, sought independence. Behind the contradiction stood the twin pillars of American foreign policy: The Monroe Doctrine made Spain's presence in Cuba unacceptable, and U.S. determination to keep open the door to Asia made the Philippines attractive as a stepping-stone to China. Precedent for the nation's imperial adventures also came from the recent Indian wars in the American West, which provided a template for the subjugation of native peoples in the name of civilization.

Looking back on the Spanish-American War of 1898, Secretary of State John Hay judged it "a splendid little war; begun with the highest motives, carried on with magnificent intelligence and spirit, favored by that fortune which loves the brave." At the close of a decade marred by bitter depression, social unrest, and political upheaval, the war offered Americans a chance to wave the flag and march in unison. War fever proved as infectious as the tune of a John Philip Sousa march. Few argued the merits of the conflict until it was over and the time came to divide the spoils.

The war began with moral outrage over the treatment of Cuban revolutionaries, who had launched a fight for independence against the Spanish colonial regime in 1895. In an attempt to isolate the guerrillas, the Spanish general Valeriano Weyler herded Cubans into crowded and unsanitary concentration camps, where thousands died of hunger, disease, and exposure. Starvation soon spread to the cities. Tens of thousands of Cubans died, and countless others were left without food, clothing, or shelter. By 1898, fully a quarter of the island's population had perished in the Cuban revolution.

> **"You furnish the pictures and I'll furnish the war."**
> — Newspaper owner, WILLIAM RANDOLPH HEARST

As the Cuban rebellion dragged on, pressure for American intervention mounted. American newspapers fueled public outrage at Spain. A fierce circulation war raged in New York City between William Randolph Hearst's *Journal* and Joseph Pulitzer's *World*. Their competition provoked what came to be called **yellow journalism**, named for the colored ink used in a popular comic strip. Practitioners of yellow journalism pandered to the public's appetite for sensationalism. The Cuban war provided a wealth of dramatic copy. Newspapers fed the American people a daily diet of "Butcher" Weyler and Spanish atrocities. Hearst sent artist Frederic Remington to document the horror, and when Remington wired home, "There is no trouble here. There will be no war," Hearst shot back, "You furnish the pictures and I'll furnish the war."

American interests in Cuba were, in the words of the U.S. minister to Spain, more than "merely theoretical or sentimental." American business had more than $50 million invested in Cuban sugar, and American trade with Cuba, a brisk $100 million a year before the rebellion, had dropped to near zero. Nevertheless, the business community balked, wary of a war with Spain. When industrialist Mark Hanna, the Republican kingmaker and senator from Ohio, urged restraint, a hotheaded **Theodore Roosevelt** exploded, "We will have this war for the freedom of Cuba, Senator Hanna, in spite of the timidity of commercial interests."

To expansionists like Roosevelt, more than Cuban independence was at stake. War with

Yellow Journalism
Most cartoonists followed the lead of Hearst and Pulitzer in promoting war with Spain. Cartoonist Grant Hamilton drew this cartoon for *Judge* magazine in March 1898. It shows a brutish Spain (the "Devil's Deputy") with bloody hands trampling on a sailor from the *Maine*. Cuba is prostrate, and a pile of skulls represents civilians "starved to death by Spain." Such vicious representations of Spain became common in the American press in the weeks leading up to the Spanish-American War. What does the cartoon say about American attitudes toward race? Collection of the New-York Historical Society.

Spain opened up the prospect of expansion into Asia as well, since Spain controlled not only Cuba and Puerto Rico but also Guam and the Philippine Islands. Appointed assistant secretary of the navy in April 1897, Roosevelt took the helm in the absence of his boss and audaciously ordered the U.S. fleet to Manila in the Philippines. In the event of conflict with Spain, Roosevelt would have the navy in a position to capture the islands and gain an entry point to China.

President McKinley slowly moved toward intervention. In a show of American force, he dispatched the battleship *Maine* to Cuba. On the night of February 15, 1898, a mysterious explosion destroyed the *Maine*, killing 267 crew members. The source of the explosion remained unclear, but inflammatory stories in the press enraged Americans, who immediately blamed the Spanish government. (See "Historical Question," page 666.) Rallying to the cry "Remember the *Maine*," Congress declared war on Spain in April. In a surge of patriotism, more than a million men rushed to enlist. War brought with it a unity of purpose and national harmony that ended a decade of political dissent and strife. "In April, everywhere over this good fair land, flags were flying," wrote Kansas editor William Allen White. "At the stations, crowds gathered to hurrah for the soldiers, and to throw hats into the air, and to unfurl flags."

Soon they had something to cheer about. Five days after McKinley signed the war resolution, a U.S. Navy squadron commanded by Admiral George Dewey destroyed the Spanish fleet in Manila Bay (Map 20.3). Dewey's stunning victory caught the United States by surprise. Although naval strategists including Theodore Roosevelt had been orchestrating the move for some time,

MAP ACTIVITY

Map 20.3 The Spanish-American War, 1898

The Spanish-American War was fought in two theaters, the Philippine Islands and Cuba. Five days after President William McKinley called for a declaration of war, Admiral George Dewey captured Manila without the loss of a single American sailor. The war lasted only eight months. Troops landed in Cuba in mid-June and by mid-July had taken Santiago and Havana and destroyed the Spanish fleet.

READING THE MAP: Which countries held imperial control over countries and territories immediately surrounding the Philippine Islands and Cuba?

CONNECTIONS: What role did American newspapers play in the start of the war? How did the results of the war serve American aims in both Asia and the Western Hemisphere?

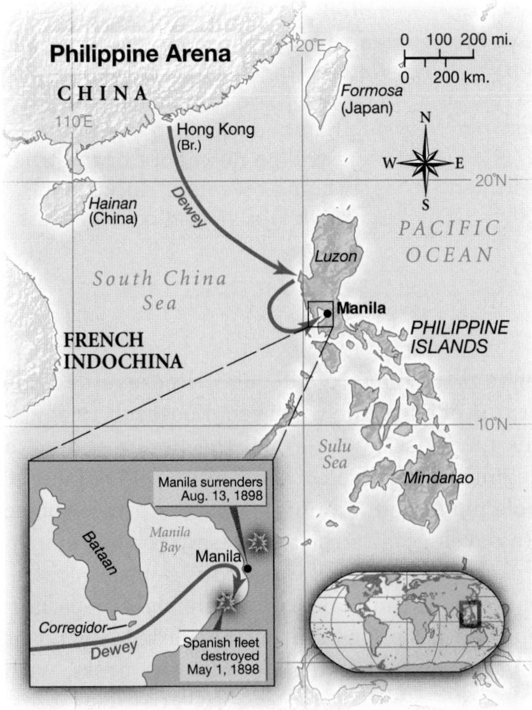

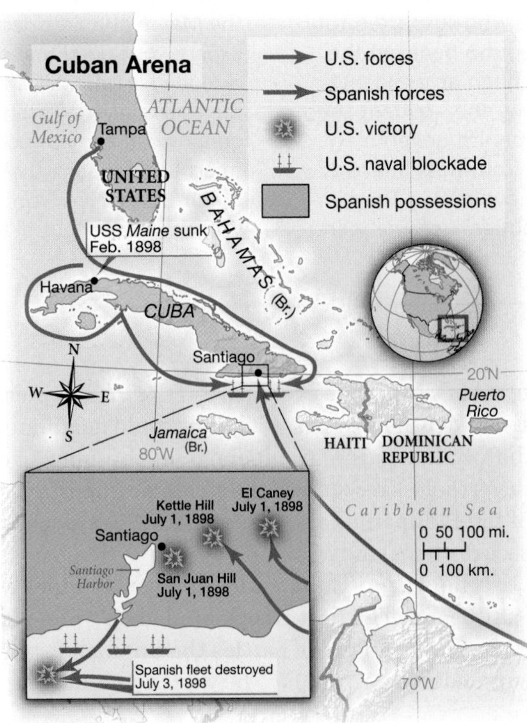

HISTORICAL QUESTION

Did Terrorists Sink the *Maine*?

At 9:40 p.m. on the evening of February 15, 1898, the U.S. battleship *Maine* blew up in Havana harbor. "The shock threw us backward," reported one eyewitness. "From the deck forward of amidships shot a streak of fire as high as the tall buildings on Broadway. Then the glare of light widened out like a funnel at the top, and down through this bright circle fell showers of wreckage and mangled sailors." In all, 267 sailors drowned or burned to death in one of the worst naval catastrophes to occur during peacetime.

Captain Charles Dwight Sigsbee, the last man to leave the burning ship, filed a terse report saying that the *Maine* had blown up and "urging [that] public opinion should be suspended until further report." But the yellow press, led by William Randolph Hearst's *New York Journal*, ran banner headlines proclaiming, "The War Ship *Maine* Was Split in Two by an Enemy's Secret Infernal Machine!"

Public opinion quickly divided between those who suspected foul play and those who believed the explosion had been an accident. Foremost among the accident theorists was the Spanish government, along with U.S. business interests who hoped to avoid war. The "jingoes," as proponents of war were called, rushed to blame Spain. Even before the details were known, Assistant Secretary of the Navy Theodore Roosevelt wrote, "The *Maine* was sunk by an act of dirty treachery on the part of the Spaniards I believe; though we shall never find out definitely, and officially it will go down as an accident."

In less than a week, the navy formed a court of inquiry, and divers inspected the wreckage. The panel reported on March 25, 1898, that a mine had exploded under the bottom of the ship, igniting gunpowder in the forward magazine. The panel could not determine whether the mine had been planted by the Spanish government or by recalcitrant followers of Valeriano Weyler. The infamous Weyler had been ousted after the American press dubbed him "the Butcher" for his harsh treatment of the Cubans.

As time passed, however, more people came to view the explosion of the *Maine* as an accident. European experts concluded that the *Maine* had exploded accidentally, from a fire in the coal bunker adjacent to the reserve gunpowder. Perhaps poor design, not treachery, had sunk the *Maine*.

In 1910, New York congressman William Sultzer put it succinctly: "The day after the ship was sunk, you could hardly find an American who did not believe that she had been foully done to death by a treacherous enemy. Today you can hardly find an American who believes Spain had anything to do with it." The *Maine* still lay in the mud of Havana harbor, a sunken tomb containing the remains of many sailors. The Cuban government asked for the removal of the wreck, and veterans demanded a decent burial for the sailors. So in March 1910, Congress voted to raise the *Maine* and reinvestigate.

The "Final Report on Removing the Wreck of Battleship *Maine* from the Harbor of Habana, Cuba" appeared in April 1913. This report confirmed that the original naval inquiry was in error, but it ruled out the accident theory by concluding that the nature of the initial explosion indicated a homemade bomb — once again casting suspicion on Weyler's fanatic followers. Following the investigation and removal of human remains, the wreckage of the *Maine* was towed out to sea and, with full funeral honors, sunk in six hundred fathoms of water.

Controversy over the *Maine* proved harder to sink. In the Vietnam era, when faith in the "military establishment" plummeted, Admiral Hyman Rickover launched yet another investigation. Viewing the 1913 "Final Report" as a cover-up, he complained that the ship had been sunk so deep "that there will be no chance of the true facts being revealed." Rickover, a maverick who held the naval brass

few Americans had ever heard of the Philippines. Even McKinley confessed that he could not immediately locate the archipelago on the map. He nevertheless recognized the strategic importance of the Philippines and dispatched U.S. troops to secure the islands.

The war in Cuba ended almost as quickly as it began. The first troops landed on June 22, and after a handful of battles the Spanish forces surrendered on July 17. The war lasted just long enough to elevate Theodore Roosevelt to the status of bona fide war hero. Roosevelt resigned his navy post and formed the Rough Riders, a regiment composed of a sprinkling of Ivy League polo players and a number of western cowboys. Roosevelt admired horsemanship and had gained the cowboys' respect during his stint as a cattle rancher in the Dakotas. While the troops languished in Tampa awaiting their orders, Roosevelt and his men staged rodeos for the press, with in low esteem, blamed "the warlike atmosphere in Congress and the press, and the natural tendency to look for reasons for the loss that did not reflect on the Navy." Judging the sinking an accident, Rickover warned, "We must make sure that those in 'high places' do not without more careful consideration of the consequences, exert our prestige and might."

Two decades later, the pendulum swung back. A 1995 study of the *Maine* published by the Smithsonian Institution concluded that zealot followers of General Weyler sank the battleship: "They had the opportunity, the means, and the motivation, and they blew up the *Maine* with a small low-strength mine they made themselves." According to this theory, the terrorists' homemade bomb burst the *Maine*'s hull, triggering a massive explosion. And in 1998 *National Geographic* employed computer models to show that an external explosion (bomb) was capable of sinking the *Maine*.

863,956 WORLDS CIRCULATED YESTERDAY

The World.

"Circulation Books Open to All."

VOL. XXXVIII. NO. 13,339. — NEW YORK, THURSDAY, FEBRUARY 17, 1898.

AINE EXPLOSION CAUSED BY BOMB OR TORPEDO

Capt. Sigsbee and Consul-General Lee Are in Doubt---The World Has Sent a Special Tug, With Submarine Divers, to Havana to Find Out---Lee Asks for an Immediate Court of Inquiry---260 Men Dead.

A SUPPRESSED DESPATCH TO THE STATE DEPARTMENT, THE CAPTAIN SAYS THE ACCIDENT WAS MADE POSSIBLE BY AN ENEMY.

E. C. Pendleton, Just Arrived from Havana, Says He Overheard Talk There of a Plot to Blow Up the Ship---Capt. Zalinski, the Dynamite Expert, and Other Experts Report to The World that the Wreck Was Not Accidental---Washington Officials Ready for Vigorous Action if Spanish Responsibility Can Be Shown---Divers to Be Sent Down to Make Careful Examinations.

THE WHOLE STORY OF THE DISASTER TOLD IN A FEW WORDS.

"Maine Explosion Caused by Bomb or Torpedo"
The yellow press wasted no time claiming foul play in the explosion of the *Maine*. The front page of the New York *World* on February 17, 1898, two days after the blast, trumpeted the news and graphically portrayed the destruction of the ship. The text hinted at a plot to blow up the *Maine* and insisted that the explosion was not accidental, although there was no evidence to back up the assertion. The extent of the destruction and the deaths of 267 sailors fueled war fever.

Thinking about Evidence

1. How have explanations for the sinking of the *Maine* changed over time? Has the evidence changed, or have interpretations of the evidence shifted?
2. What does the word *terrorism* suggest about how our understanding of the event may have changed in the twenty-first century?

the likes of New York socialite William Tiffany busting broncos in competition with Dakota cowboy Jim "Dead Shot" Simpson. When the Rough Riders shipped out to Cuba, journalists fought for a berth with the colorful regiment. The Rough Riders' charge up Kettle Hill and Roosevelt's role in the decisive battle of San Juan Hill made front-page news. Overnight, Roosevelt became the most famous man in America. By the time he sailed home from Cuba, a coalition of independent Republicans was already plotting his political future.

The Debate over American Imperialism

After a few brief campaigns in Cuba and Puerto Rico brought the Spanish-American War to an end, the American people woke up in possession of an empire that stretched halfway around the globe. As part of the spoils of war, the United States acquired Cuba, Puerto Rico, Guam, and the Philippines. Yielding to pressure from American sugar growers, President McKinley expanded the empire further, annexing Hawai'i in July 1898.

Contemptuous of the Cubans, whom General William Shafter declared "no more fit for self-government than gun-powder is for hell," the U.S. government directed the writing of a new Cuban constitution in 1900 and refused to give up military control of the island until the Cubans accepted the so-called Platt Amendment — a series of provisions that granted the United States the right to intervene to protect Cuba's "independence," as well as the power to oversee Cuban debt so that European creditors would not find an excuse for intervention. For good measure, the United States gave itself a ninety-nine-year lease on a naval base at Guantánamo. In return, McKinley promised to implement an extensive sanitation program to clean up the island, making it more attractive to American investors.

MAP ACTIVITY

Map 20.4 U.S. Overseas Expansion through 1900

The United States extended its interests abroad with a series of territorial acquisitions. Although Cuba was granted independence, the Platt Amendment kept the new nation firmly under U.S. control. In the wake of the Spanish-American War, the United States woke up to find that it held an empire extending halfway around the globe.

READING THE MAP: Does the map indicate that more territory was acquired by purchase or by war, occupation, or unilateral decision? How many purchases of land outside the continental United States did the government make?
CONNECTIONS: What foreign policy developments occurred in the 1890s? How did American political leaders react to them? Where was U.S. expansion headed and why?

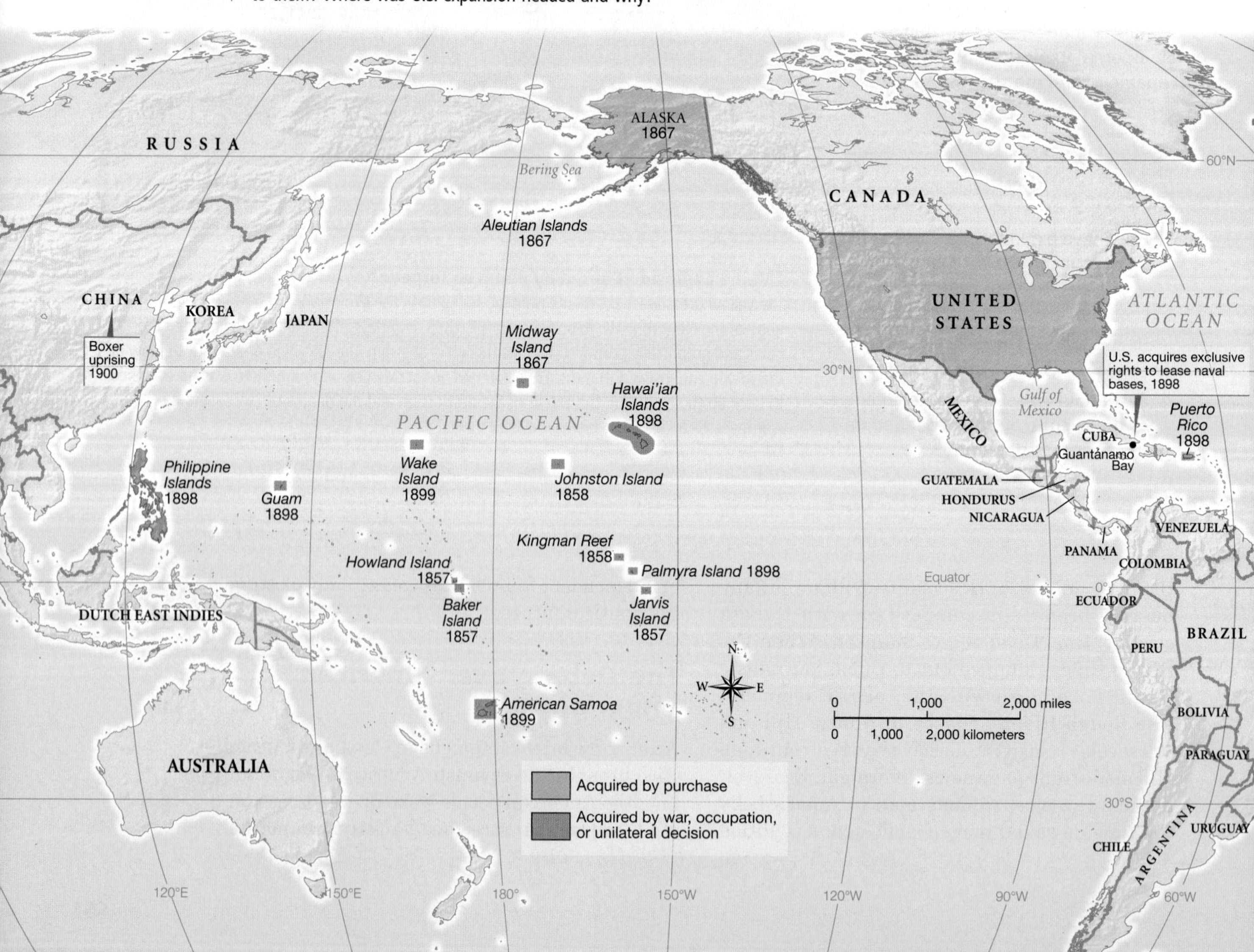

Columbia's Easter Bonnet
The United States, symbolized by the female figure of Columbia, tries on "World Power" in this cartoon from *Puck* that appeared in 1901 after the Spanish-American War left the United States in control of Spain's former colonies in Guam, the Philippines, and Puerto Rico. The bonnet, in the shape of an American battleship, indicates the key role the U.S. Navy played in the conflict. "Expansion," spelled out in the smoke from the ship's smokestack, points to a new overseas direction for American foreign policy at the turn of the twentieth century. Library of Congress.

In the formal Treaty of Paris (1898), Spain ceded the Philippines to the United States along with the former Spanish colonies of Puerto Rico and Guam (Map 20.4). Empire did not come cheap. When Spain initially balked at these terms, the United States agreed to pay an indemnity of $20 million for the islands. Nor was the cost measured in money alone. Filipino revolutionaries under **Emilio Aguinaldo**, who had greeted U.S. troops as liberators, bitterly fought the new masters. It would take seven years and 4,000 American dead — almost ten times the number killed in Cuba — not to mention an estimated 20,000 Filipino casualties, to defeat Aguinaldo and secure American control of the Philippines, America's coveted stepping-stone to China.

At home, a vocal minority, mostly Democrats and former Populists, resisted the country's foray into overseas empire, judging it unwise, immoral, and unconstitutional. William Jennings Bryan, who enlisted in the army but never saw action, concluded that American expansionism only distracted the nation from problems at home. Pointing to the central paradox of the war, Representative Bourke Cockran of New York admonished, "We who have been the destroyers of oppression are asked now to become its agents." Mark Twain, lending his bitter eloquence to the cause of anti-imperialism, lamented that the United States had become "yet another Civilized Power, with its banner of the Prince of Peace in one hand and its loot-basket and its butcher-knife in the other."

The anti-imperialists were soon drowned out by cries for empire. As Senator Knute Nelson of Minnesota assured his colleagues, "We come as ministering angels, not as despots." Fresh from the conquest of Native Americans in the West, the nation largely embraced the heady mixture of racism and missionary zeal that fueled American adventurism abroad. The *Washington Post* trumpeted, "The taste of empire is in the mouth of the people," thrilled at the prospect of "an imperial policy, the Republic renascent, taking her place with the armed nations."

REVIEW Why did the United States largely abandon its isolationist foreign policy in the 1890s?

▶ Conclusion: Rallying around the Flag

A decade of domestic strife ended amid the blare of martial music and the waving of flags. The Spanish-American War drowned out the calls for social reform that had fueled the Populist politics of the 1890s. During that decade, angry farmers facing hard times looked to the Farmers' Alliance to fight for their vision of economic democracy, workers staged bloody battles across the country to assert their rights, and women attacked drunkenness and the conditions that fostered it and mounted a suffrage movement to secure their basic political rights. In St. Louis in 1892, Frances Willard joined with other disaffected Americans to form a new People's Party to fight for change.

The bitter depression that began in 1893 led to increased labor strife. The Pullman boycott brutally dramatized the power of property and the conservatism of the laissez-faire state. Even the miners' victory in Cripple Creek,

Colorado, in 1894 proved short-lived. But workers' willingness to confront capitalism on the streets of Chicago, Homestead, Cripple Creek, and a host of other sites across America eloquently testified to labor's growing determination, unity, and strength.

As the depression deepened, the sight of Coxey's army of unemployed marching on Washington to demand federal intervention in the economy signaled a growing shift in the public mind against the stand-pat politics of laissez-faire personified by President William McKinley. The call for the government to take action to better the lives of workers, farmers, and the dispossessed manifested itself in the fiercely fought presidential campaign of William Jennings Bryan in 1896. With the outbreak of the Spanish-American War in 1898, the decade ended on a harmonious note with patriotic Americans rallying around the flag. Few questioned America's foray into overseas empire. The United States took its place on the world stage, buttressing its hemispheric domination with the Monroe Doctrine and employing the Open Door policy, which promised access to the riches of China. But even though Americans basked in patriotism and contemplated empire, old grievances had not been laid to rest. The People's Party had been beaten, but the Populist spirit lived on in the demands for greater government involvement in the economy, expanded opportunities for direct democracy, and a more equitable balance of profits and power between the people and the big corporations. This reform agenda would be taken up by a new generation of progressive reformers in the first decades of the twentieth century.

▸ Selected Bibliography

The Farmers Alliance, the Labor Wars, and Women's Activism

Peter H. Argersinger, *The Limits of Agrarian Radicalism: Western Populism and American Politics* (1995).

Jean H. Baker, *Sisters: The Lives of America's Suffragists* (2005).

Ruth Bordin, *Frances Willard: A Biography* (1986).

Ellen Carol DuBois, *Woman Suffrage and Women's Rights* (1998).

Michel Lewis Goldberg, *An Army of Women: Gender and Politics in Gilded Age Kansas* (1997).

Steven Hahn, *A Nation under Our Feet: Black Political Struggles in the Rural South from Slavery to the Great Migration* (2003).

Elizabeth Jameson, *All That Glitters: Class, Conflict, and Community in Cripple Creek* (1998).

Michael Kazin, *The Populist Persuasion: An American History* (rev. ed., 1998).

Paul Krause, *The Battle for Homestead, 1880–1892* (1992).

Jackson Lears, *The Rebirth of a Nation: The Making of Modern America, 1877–1920* (2009).

Connie L. Lester, *Up from the Mudsills of Hell: The Farmers' Alliance, Populism, and Progressive Agriculture in Tennessee, 1870–1915* (2006).

Michael McGerr, *A Fierce Discontent: The Rise and Fall of the Progressive Movement in America* (2005).

David Nasaw, *Andrew Carnegie* (2006).

Charles Postel, *The Populist Vision (2007).*

Nick Salvatore, *Eugene V. Debs: Citizen and Socialist* (1982).

Depression and the Election of 1896

Steve Fraser, *Every Man a Speculator: A Cultural History of Wall Street in America* (2005).

Stephen Kantrowitz, *Ben Tillman and the Reconstruction of White Supremacy* (2000).

Michael Kazin, *A Godly Hero: The Life of William Jennings Bryan* (2006).

Kenneth L. Kusmer, *Down and Out, on the Road: The Homeless in American History* (2002).

Gretchen Ritter, *Goldbugs and Greenbacks: The Antimonopoly Tradition in the Politics of Finance in America* (1997).

Troy Rondinone, *The Great Industrial War: Framing Class Conflict in the Media, 1865–1950* (2010).

Carol A. Schwantes, *Coxey's Army: An American Odyssey* (1985).

Douglas Steeples and David O. Whitten, *Democracy in Desperation: The Depression of 1893* (1998).

U.S. Foreign Policy and the Spanish-American War

Fred Anderson and Andrew Cayton, *The Domination of War: Empire and Liberty in North America, 1500–2000* (2005).

Kristin Hoganson, *Fighting for American Manhood: How Gender Politics Provoked the Spanish-American and Philippine-American Wars* (1998).

Matthew Frye Jacobson, *Barbarian Virtues: The United States Encounters Foreign Peoples at Home and Abroad, 1876–1917* (2000).

Amy Kaplan, *The Anarchy of Empire in the Making of U.S. Culture* (2002).

Stephen Kinzer, *Overthrow: America's Century of Regime Change from Hawaii to Iraq* (2006).

Walter LaFeber, *The American Search for Opportunity, 1865–1913* (1994).
Brian Linn, *The Philippine War, 1899–1902* (2000).
Paul T. McCartney, *Power and Progress: American National Identity, the War of 1898, and the Rise of American Imperialism* (2006).
Ivan Musicant, *Empire by Default: The Spanish American War and the Dawn of the American Century* (1998).
Diana Preston, *Besieged in Peking: The Story of the 1900 Boxer Uprising* (1999).
Margaret Strobel, *Gender, Sex, and Empire* (1993).
Evan Thomas, *The War Lovers: Roosevelt, Lodge, Hearst, and the Rush to Empire, 1898* (2010).

▶ **For more books about topics in this chapter,** see the Online Bibliography at **bedfordstmartins.com/roark.**

▶ **For additional primary sources from this period,** see Michael Johnson, ed., *Reading the American Past*, Fifth Edition.

▶ **For Web sites, images, and documents related to topics and places in this chapter,** visit Make History at **bedfordstmartins.com/roark.**

Reviewing Chapter 20

KEY TERMS

Explain each term's significance.

The Farmers' Revolt

Farmers' Alliance (p. 641)
Colored Farmers' Alliance (p. 642)
People's Party (Populist Party) (p. 643)
subtreasury (p. 643)

The Labor Wars

Henry Clay Frick (p. 644)
Homestead lockout (p. 644)
Alexander Berkman (p. 645)
Cripple Creek miners' strike of 1894 (p. 646)
George M. Pullman (p. 646)
American Railway Union (ARU) (p. 647)
Eugene V. Debs (p. 647)
Pullman boycott (p. 650)

Women's Activism

Frances Willard (p. 651)
Elizabeth Cady Stanton (p. 653)
Susan B. Anthony (p. 653)
National American Woman Suffrage Association (NAWSA) (p. 653)

Depression Politics

Coxey's army (p. 654)
Tom Watson (p. 655)
William McKinley (p. 656)
William Jennings Bryan (p. 656)

The United States and the World

Boxer uprising (p. 661)
Monroe Doctrine (p. 662)
Open Door policy (p. 663)
Spanish-American War (p. 663)
yellow journalism (p. 664)
Theodore Roosevelt (p. 664)
Emilio Aguinaldo (p. 669)

REVIEW QUESTIONS

Use key terms and dates to support your answer.

1. Why did American farmers organize alliances in the late nineteenth century? (pp. 641–644)
2. What tactics led to the defeat of the strikers in the 1890s? Where were they able to succeed and why? (pp. 644–651)
3. How did women's temperance activism contribute to the cause of woman suffrage? (pp. 651–654)
4. Why was the People's Party unable to translate national support into victory in the 1896 election? (pp. 654–658)
5. Why did the United States largely abandon its isolationist foreign policy in the 1890s? (pp. 658–669)

MAKING CONNECTIONS

Draw on key terms, the timeline, and review questions.

1. In the late nineteenth century, Americans clashed over the disparity of power brought about by industrial capitalism. Why did many farmers and urban workers look to the government to help advance their vision of economic justice? In your answer, discuss specific reforms working-class Americans pursued and the strategies they employed.
2. In the 1890s, workers mounted labor protests and strikes. What circumstances gave rise to these actions? How did they differ from earlier strikes, such as the Great Railroad Strike of 1877? In your answer, discuss specific actions, being sure to consider how local and national circumstances contributed to their ultimate resolution.
3. How did women's activism in the late nineteenth century help advance the cause of woman suffrage? In your answer, discuss specific gains made in the late nineteenth century, as well as shifts in reformers' strategies.
4. Given the farmers' unrest in the 1890s, why did the Populist Party fail to defeat Republican William McKinley in the election of 1896? What coalitions failed to come together?

LINKING TO THE PAST

Link events in this chapter to earlier events.

1. How did the conquest of Native Americans in the West foreshadow U.S. expansion abroad? In what ways did the assumptions of racial superiority evident in U.S. Indian policy affect the treatment of Cubans and Filipinos? (See chapter 17.)
2. Why in the midst of burgeoning growth did the United States experience a major depression in the 1890s? Draw on your knowledge of the development of U.S. industries such as the railroads. (See chapter 18.)

▶ **FOR PRACTICE QUIZZES AND OTHER STUDY TOOLS,** visit the Online Study Guide at **bedfordstmartins.com/roark.**

TIMELINE 1884–1901

1884	• Frances Willard, head of Woman's Christian Temperance Union, calls for woman suffrage.
1890	• National American Woman Suffrage Association (NAWSA) formed. • Wyoming only state allowing women to vote in national elections. • Southern Farmers' Alliance numbers three million members.
1892	• People's (Populist) Party founded. • Homestead lockout.
1893	• Stock market crash touches off severe economic depression. • President Grover Cleveland nixes attempt to annex Hawai'i.
1894	• Miners' strike in Cripple Creek, Colorado. • Coxey's army marches to Washington, D.C. • Federal troops and court injunction crush Pullman boycott.
1895	• President Grover Cleveland enforces Monroe Doctrine in border dispute between British Guiana and Venezuela.
1896	• Democrats and Populists support William Jennings Bryan for president. • Republican William McKinley elected president.
1898	• U.S. battleship *Maine* explodes in Havana harbor. • Congress declares war on Spain. • Admiral George Dewey destroys Spanish fleet in Manila Bay, the Philippines. • U.S. troops defeat Spanish forces in Cuba. • Treaty of Paris ends war with Spain and cedes Philippines, Puerto Rico, and Guam to the United States. • United States annexes Hawai'i.
1899–1900	• Secretary of State John Hay enunciates Open Door policy in China. • Boxer uprising in China.
1901	• Boxer Protocol imposed on Chinese government.

Appendix Directory

APPENDIX I.

Documents

APPENDIX II.

Facts and Figures: Government, Economy, and Demographics

APPENDIX I. Documents

THE DECLARATION OF INDEPENDENCE

In Congress, July 4, 1776,

THE UNANIMOUS DECLARATION OF THE THIRTEEN UNITED STATES OF AMERICA

When in the course of human events, it becomes necessary for one people to dissolve the political bands which have connected them with another, and to assume, among the powers of the earth, the separate and equal station to which the laws of nature and of nature's God entitle them, a decent respect to the opinions of mankind requires that they should declare the causes which impel them to the separation.

We hold these truths to be self-evident, that all men are created equal; that they are endowed by their Creator with certain unalienable rights; that among these, are life, liberty, and the pursuit of happiness. That, to secure these rights, governments are instituted among men, deriving their just powers from the consent of the governed; that, whenever any form of government becomes destructive of these ends, it is the right of the people to alter or to abolish it, and to institute a new government, laying its foundation on such principles, and organizing its powers in such form, as to them shall seem most likely to effect their safety and happiness. Prudence, indeed, will dictate that governments long established, should not be changed for light and transient causes; and, accordingly, all experience hath shown, that mankind are more disposed to suffer, while evils are sufferable, than to right themselves by abolishing the forms to which they are accustomed. But, when a long train of abuses and usurpations, pursuing invariably the same object, evinces a design to reduce them under absolute despotism, it is their right, it is their duty, to throw off such government and to provide new guards for their future security. Such has been the patient sufferance of these colonies, and such is now the necessity which constrains them to alter their former systems of government. The history of the present King of Great Britain is a history of repeated injuries and usurpations, all having, in direct object, the establishment of an absolute tyranny over these States. To prove this, let facts be submitted to a candid world: He has refused his assent to laws the most wholesome and necessary for the public good.

He has forbidden his governors to pass laws of immediate and pressing importance, unless suspended in their operation till his assent should be obtained; and, when so suspended, he has utterly neglected to attend to them.

He has refused to pass other laws for the accommodation of large districts of people, unless those people would relinquish the right of representation in the legislature; a right inestimable to them, and formidable to tyrants only.

He has called together legislative bodies at places unusual, uncomfortable, and distant from the depository of their public records, for the sole purpose of fatiguing them into compliance with his measures.

He has dissolved representative houses repeatedly for opposing, with manly firmness, his invasions on the rights of the people.

He has refused, for a long time after such dissolutions, to cause others to be elected; whereby the legislative powers, incapable of annihilation, have returned to the people at large for their exercise; the state remaining in the mean-time exposed to all the danger of invasion from without, and convulsions within.

He has endeavoured to prevent the population of these States; for that purpose, obstructing the laws for naturalization of foreigners, refusing to pass others to encourage their migration hither, and raising the conditions of new appropriations of lands.

He has obstructed the administration of justice, by refusing his assent to laws for establishing judiciary powers.

He has made judges dependent on his will alone, for the tenure of their offices, and the amount and payment of their salaries.

He has erected a multitude of new offices, and sent hither swarms of officers to harass our people, and eat out their substance.

He has kept among us, in times of peace, standing armies, without the consent of our legislature.

He has affected to render the military independent of, and superior to, the civil power.

He has combined, with others, to subject us to a jurisdiction foreign to our Constitution, and unacknowledged by our laws; giving his assent to their acts of pretended legislation:

For quartering large bodies of armed troops among us:

For protecting them by a mock trial, from punishment, for any murders which they should commit on the inhabitants of these States:

For cutting off our trade with all parts of the world:

For imposing taxes on us without our consent:

For depriving us, in many cases, of the benefit of trial by jury:

For transporting us beyond seas to be tried for pretended offences:

For abolishing the free system of English laws in a neighboring province, establishing therein an arbitrary government, and enlarging its boundaries, so as to render it at once an example and fit instrument for introducing the same absolute rule into these colonies:

For taking away our charters, abolishing our most valuable laws, and altering, fundamentally, the powers of our governments:

For suspending our own legislatures, and declaring themselves invested with power to legislate for us in all cases whatsoever.

He has abdicated government here, by declaring us out of his protection, and waging war against us.

He has plundered our seas, ravaged our coasts, burnt our towns, and destroyed the lives of our people.

He is, at this time, transporting large armies of foreign mercenaries to complete the works of death, desolation, and tyranny, already begun, with circumstances of cruelty and perfidy scarcely paralleled in the most barbarous ages, and totally unworthy the head of a civilized nation.

He has constrained our fellow citizens, taken captive on the high seas, to bear arms against their country, to become the executioners of their friends, and brethren, or to fall themselves by their hands.

He has excited domestic insurrections amongst us, and has endeavored to bring on the inhabitants of our frontiers, the merciless Indian savages, whose known rule of warfare is an undistinguished destruction of all ages, sexes, and conditions.

In every stage of these oppressions, we have petitioned for redress; in the most humble terms; our repeated petitions have been answered only by repeated injury. A prince, whose character is thus marked by every act which may define a tyrant, is unfit to be the ruler of a free people.

Nor have we been wanting in attention to our British brethren. We have warned them, from time to time, of attempts made by their legislature to extend an unwarrantable jurisdiction over us. We have reminded them of the circumstances of our emigration and settlement here. We have appealed to their native justice and magnanimity, and we have conjured them, by the ties of our common kindred, to disavow these usurpations, which would inevitably interrupt our connections and correspondence. They, too, have been deaf to the voice of justice and consanguinity. We must, therefore, acquiesce in the necessity which denounces our separation, and hold them as we hold the rest of mankind, enemies in war, in peace, friends.

We, therefore, the representatives of the United States of America, in general Congress assembled, appealing to the Supreme Judge of the world for the rectitude of our intentions, do, in the name, and by authority of the good people of these colonies, solemnly publish and declare, that these united colonies are, and of right ought to be, free and independent states: that they are absolved from all allegiance to the British Crown, and that all political connection between them and the state of Great Britain is, and ought to be, totally dissolved; and that, as free and independent states, they have full power to levy war, conclude peace, contract alliances, establish commerce, and to do all other acts and things which independent states may of right do. And, for the support of this declaration, with a firm reliance on the protection of Divine Providence, we mutually pledge to each other our lives, our fortunes, and our sacred honor.

The foregoing Declaration was, by order of Congress, engrossed, and signed by the following members:

JOHN HANCOCK

New Hampshire
Josiah Bartlett
William Whipple
Matthew Thornton

Massachusetts Bay
Samuel Adams
John Adams
Robert Treat Paine
Elbridge Gerry

Rhode Island
Stephen Hopkins
William Ellery

Connecticut
Roger Sherman
Samuel Huntington
William Williams
Oliver Wolcott

New York
William Floyd
Phillip Livingston
Francis Lewis
Lewis Morris

New Jersey
Richard Stockton
John Witherspoon
Francis Hopkinson
John Hart
Abraham Clark

Pennsylvania
Robert Morris
Benjamin Rush
Benjamin Franklin
John Morton
George Clymer
James Smith
George Taylor
James Wilson
George Ross
Caesar Rodney
George Read
Thomas M'Kean

Maryland
Samuel Chase
William Paca
Thomas Stone
Charles Carroll, of Carrollton

North Carolina
William Hooper
Joseph Hewes
John Penn

South Carolina
Edward Rutledge
Thomas Heyward, Jr.
Thomas Lynch, Jr.
Arthur Middleton

Virginia
George Wythe
Richard Henry Lee
Thomas Jefferson
Benjamin Harrison
Thomas Nelson, Jr.
Francis Lightfoot Lee
Carter Braxton

Georgia
Button Gwinnett
Lyman Hall
George Walton

Resolved, That copies of the Declaration be sent to the several assemblies, conventions, and committees, or councils of safety, and to the several commanding officers of the continental troops; that it be proclaimed in each of the United States, at the head of the army.

THE ARTICLES OF CONFEDERATION AND PERPETUAL UNION

Agreed to in Congress, November 15, 1777.
Ratified March 1781.

BETWEEN THE STATES OF NEW HAMPSHIRE, MASSACHUSETTS BAY, RHODE ISLAND AND PROVIDENCE PLANTATIONS, CONNECTICUT, NEW YORK, NEW JERSEY, PENNSYLVANIA, DELAWARE, MARYLAND, VIRGINIA, NORTH CAROLINA, SOUTH CAROLINA, GEORGIA.*

Article 1

The stile of this confederacy shall be "The United States of America."

Article 2

Each State retains its sovereignty, freedom and independence, and every power, jurisdiction, and right, which is not by this confederation expressly delegated to the United States, in Congress assembled.

Article 3

The said states hereby severally enter into a firm league of friendship with each other for their common defence, the security of their liberties and their mutual and general welfare; binding themselves to assist each other against all force offered to, or attacks made upon them, or any of them, on account of religion, sovereignty, trade, or any other pretence whatever.

Article 4

The better to secure and perpetuate mutual friendship and intercourse among the people of the different states in this union, the free inhabitants of each of these states, paupers, vagabonds, and fugitives from justice excepted, shall be entitled to all privileges and immunities of free citizens in the several states; and the people of each State shall have free ingress and regress to and from any other State, and shall enjoy therein all the privileges of trade and commerce, subject to the same duties, impositions, and restrictions, as the inhabitants thereof respectively; provided, that such restrictions shall not extend so far as to prevent the removal of property, imported into any State, to any other State of which the owner is an inhabitant; provided also, that no imposition, duties, or restriction, shall be laid by any State on the property of the United States, or either of them. If any person guilty of, or charged with treason, felony, or other high misdemeanor in any State, shall flee from justice and be found in any of the United States, he shall, upon demand of the governor or executive power of the State from which he fled, be delivered up and removed to the State having jurisdiction of his offence. Full faith and credit shall be given in each of these states to the records, acts, and judicial proceedings of the courts and magistrates of every other State.

Article 5

For the more convenient management of the general interests of the United States, delegates shall be annually appointed, in such manner as the legislature of each State shall direct, to meet in Congress, on the 1st Monday in November in every year, with a power reserved to each State to recall its delegates, or any of them, at any time within the year, and to send others in their stead for the remainder of the year.

No State shall be represented in Congress by less than two, nor by more than seven members; and no person shall be capable of being a delegate for more than three years in any term of six years; nor shall any person, being a delegate, be capable of holding any office under the United States, for which he, or any other for his benefit, receives any salary, fees, or emolument of any kind.

Each State shall maintain its own delegates in a meeting of the states, and while they act as members of the committee of the states.

In determining questions in the United States, in Congress assembled, each State shall have one vote.

Freedom of speech and debate in Congress shall not be impeached or questioned in any court or place out of Congress: and the members of Congress shall be protected in their persons from arrests and imprisonments, during the time of their going to and from, and attendance on Congress, except for treason, felony, or breach of the peace.

*This copy of the final draft of the Articles of Confederation is taken from the Journals, 9:907–925, November 15, 1777.

Article 6

No State, without the consent of the United States, in Congress assembled, shall send any embassy to, or receive any embassy from, or enter into any conference, agreement, alliance, or treaty with any king, prince, or state; nor shall any person, holding any office of profit or trust under the United States, or any of them, accept of any present, emolument, office or title, of any kind whatever, from any king, prince, or foreign state; nor shall the United States, in Congress assembled, or any of them, grant any title of nobility.

No two or more states shall enter into any treaty, confederation, or alliance, whatever, between them, without the consent of the United States, in Congress assembled, specifying accurately the purposes for which the same is to be entered into, and how long it shall continue.

No state shall lay any imposts or duties which may interfere with any stipulations in treaties entered into by the United States, in Congress assembled, with any king, prince, or state, in pursuance of any treaties already proposed by Congress to the courts of France and Spain.

No vessels of war shall be kept up in time of peace by any State, except such number only as shall be deemed necessary by the United States, in Congress assembled, for the defence of such State or its trade; nor shall any body of forces be kept up by any State, in time of peace, except such number only as, in the judgment of the United States, in Congress assembled, shall be deemed requisite to garrison the forts necessary for the defence of such State; but every State shall always keep up a well regulated and disciplined militia, sufficiently armed and accoutred, and shall provide, and constantly have ready for use, in public stores, a due number of field pieces and tents, and a proper quantity of arms, ammunition and camp equipage.

No State shall engage in any war without the consent of the United States, in Congress assembled, unless such State be actually invaded by enemies, or shall have received certain advice of a resolution being formed by some nation of Indians to invade such State, and the danger is so imminent as not to admit of a delay till the United States, in Congress assembled, can be consulted; nor shall any State grant commissions to any ships or vessels of war, nor letters of marque or reprisal, except it be after a declaration of war by the United States, in Congress assembled, and then only against the kingdom or state, and the subjects thereof, against which war has been so declared, and under such regulations as shall be established by the United States, in Congress assembled, unless such State be infested by pirates, in which case vessels of war may be fitted out for that occasion, and kept so long as the danger shall continue, or until the United States, in Congress assembled, shall determine otherwise.

Article 7

When land forces are raised by any State for the common defence, all officers of or under the rank of colonel, shall be appointed by the legislature of each State respectively, by whom such forces shall be raised, or in such manner as such State shall direct; and all vacancies shall be filled up by the State which first made the appointment.

Article 8

All charges of war and all other expences, that shall be incurred for the common defence or general welfare, and allowed by the United States, in Congress assembled, shall be defrayed out of a common treasury, which shall be supplied by the several states, in proportion to the value of all land within each State, granted to or surveyed for any person, as such land and the buildings and improvements thereon shall be estimated according to such mode as the United States, in Congress assembled, shall, from time to time, direct and appoint.

The taxes for paying that proportion shall be laid and levied by the authority and direction of the legislatures of the several states, within the time agreed upon by the United States, in Congress assembled.

Article 9

The United States, in Congress assembled, shall have the sole and exclusive right and power of determining on peace and war, except in the cases mentioned in the 6th article; of sending and receiving ambassadors; entering into treaties and alliances, provided that no treaty of commerce shall be made, whereby the legislative power of the respective states shall be restrained from imposing such imposts and duties on foreigners as their own people are subjected to, or from prohibiting the exportation or importation of any species of goods or commodities whatsoever; of establishing rules for deciding, in all cases, what captures on land or water shall be legal, and in what manner prizes, taken by land or naval forces in the service of the United States, shall be divided or appropriated; of granting letters of marque and reprisal in times of peace; appointing courts for the trial of piracies and felonies committed on the high seas, and establishing courts for receiving and determining, finally, appeals in all cases of captures; provided, that no member of Congress shall be appointed a judge of any of the said courts.

The United States, in Congress assembled, shall also be the last resort on appeal in all disputes and differences now subsisting, or that hereafter may arise between two or more states concerning boundary, jurisdiction or any other cause whatever; which authority shall always be exercised in the manner following: whenever the legislative or executive authority, or lawful agent of any State, in controversy with another, shall present a petition to Congress, stating the matter in question, and praying for a hearing, notice thereof shall be given, by order of Congress, to the legislative or executive authority of the other State in controversy, and a day assigned for the appearance of the parties by their lawful agents, who shall then be directed to appoint, by joint consent, commissioners or judges to constitute a court for hearing and determining the matter in question; but, if they cannot agree, Congress shall name three persons out of each of the United States, and from the list of such persons each party shall alternately strike out one, the petitioners beginning, until the number shall be reduced to thirteen; and from that number not less than seven, nor more than nine names, as Congress shall direct, shall, in the presence of Congress, be drawn out by lot; and the persons whose names shall be so drawn, or any five of them, shall be commissioners or judges to hear and finally determine the controversy, so always as a major part of the judges who shall hear the cause shall agree in the determination; and if either party shall neglect to attend at the day appointed, without shewing reasons which Congress shall judge sufficient, or, being present, shall refuse to strike, the Congress shall proceed to nominate three persons out of each State, and the secretary of Congress shall strike in behalf of such party absent or refusing; and the judgment and sentence of the court to be appointed, in the manner before prescribed, shall be final and conclusive; and if any of the parties shall refuse to submit to the authority of such court, or to appear or defend their claim or cause, the court shall nevertheless proceed to pronounce sentence or judgment, which shall, in like manner, be final and decisive, the judgment or sentence and other proceedings begin, in either case, transmitted to Congress, and lodged among the acts of Congress for the security of the parties concerned: provided, that every commissioner, before he sits in judgment, shall take an oath, to be administered by one of the judges of the supreme or superior court of the State where the cause shall be tried, "well and truly to hear and determine the matter in question, according to the best of his judgment, without favour, affection, or hope of reward:" provided, also, that no State shall be deprived of territory for the benefit of the United States.

All controversies concerning the private right of soil, claimed under different grants of two or more states, whose jurisdictions, as they may respect such lands and the states which passed such grants, are adjusted, the said grants, or either of them, being at the same time claimed to have originated antecedent to such settlement of jurisdiction, shall, on the petition of either party to the Congress of the United States, be finally determined, as near as may be, in the same manner as is before prescribed for deciding disputes respecting territorial jurisdiction between different states.

The United States, in Congress assembled, shall also have the sole and exclusive right and power of regulating the alloy and value of coin struck by their own authority, or by that of the respective states; fixing the standard of weights and measures throughout the United States; regulating the trade and managing all affairs with the Indians not members of any of the states; provided that the legislative right of any State within its own limits be not infringed or violated; establishing and regulating post offices from one State to another throughout all the United States, and exacting such postage on the papers passing through the same as may be requisite to defray the expences of the said office; appointing all officers of the land forces in the service of the United States, excepting regimental officers; appointing all the officers of the naval forces, and commissioning all officers whatever in the service of the United States; making rules for the government and regulation of the said land and naval forces, and directing their operations.

The United States, in Congress assembled, shall have authority to appoint a committee to sit in the recess of Congress, to be denominated "a Committee of the States," and to consist of one delegate from each State, and to appoint such other committees and civil officers as may be necessary for managing the general affairs of the United States, under their direction; to appoint one of their number to preside; provided that no person be allowed to serve in the office of president more than one year in any term of three years; to ascertain the necessary sums of money to be raised for the service of the United States, and to appropriate and apply the same for defraying the public expences; to borrow money or emit bills on the credit of the United States, transmitting, every half year, to the respective states, an account of the sums of money so borrowed or emitted; to build and equip a navy; to agree upon the number of land forces, and to make requisitions from each State for its quota, in proportion to the number of white inhabitants in such State; which requisitions shall be binding; and thereupon, the legislature of each State shall appoint the regimental officers, raise the men, and cloathe, arm, and equip them in a soldier-like manner, at the expence of the United States; and the officers and men so cloathed, armed, and equipped, shall march to the place appointed and within the time agreed on by the United States, in Congress assembled; but if the United States, in Congress assembled, shall, on consideration of circumstances, judge proper that any State should not raise men, or should raise a smaller number than its quota, and that any other State should raise a greater number of men than the quota thereof, such extra number shall be raised, officered, cloathed, armed, and equipped in the same manner as the quota of such State, unless the legislature of such State shall judge that such extra number cannot be safely spared out of the same, in which case they shall raise, officer, cloathe, arm, and equip as many of such extra number as they judge can be safely spared. And the officers and men so cloathed, armed, and equipped, shall march to the place appointed and within the time agreed on by the United States, in Congress assembled.

The United States, in Congress assembled, shall never engage in a war, nor grant letters of marque and reprisal in time of peace, nor enter into any treaties or alliances, nor coin money, nor regulate the value thereof, nor ascertain the sums and expences necessary for the defence and welfare of the United States, or any of them: nor emit bills, nor borrow money on the credit of the United States, nor appropriate money, nor agree upon the number of vessels of war to be built or purchased, or the number of land or sea forces to be raised, nor appoint a commander in chief of the army or navy, unless nine states assent to the same; nor shall a question on any other point, except for adjourning from day to day, be determined, unless by the votes of a majority of the United States, in Congress assembled.

The Congress of the United States shall have power to adjourn to any time within the year, and to any place within the United States, so that no period of adjournment be for a longer duration than the space of six months, and shall publish the journal of their proceedings monthly, except such parts thereof, relating to treaties, alliances or military operations, as, in their judgment, require secrecy; and the yeas and nays of the delegates of each State on any question shall be entered on the journal, when it is desired by any delegate; and the delegates of a State, or any of them, at his, or their request, shall be furnished with a transcript of the said journal, except such parts as are above excepted, to lay before the legislatures of the several states.

Article 10

The committee of the states, or any nine of them, shall be authorized to execute, in the recess of Congress, such of the powers of Congress as the United States, in Congress assembled, by the consent of nine states, shall, from time to time, think expedient to vest them with; provided, that no power be delegated to the said committee, for the exercise of which, by the articles of confederation, the voice of nine states, in the Congress of the United States assembled, is requisite.

Article 11

Canada acceding to this confederation, and joining in the measures of the United States, shall be admitted into and entitled to all the advantages of this union; but no other colony shall be admitted into the same, unless such admission be agreed to by nine states.

Article 12

All bills of credit emitted, monies borrowed and debts contracted by, or under the authority of Congress before the assembling of the United States, in pursuance of the present confederation, shall be deemed and considered as a charge against the United States, for payment and satisfaction whereof the said United States and the public faith are hereby solemnly pledged.

Article 13

Every State shall abide by the determinations of the United States, in Congress assembled, on all questions which, by this confederation, are submitted to them. And the articles of this confederation shall be inviolably observed by every State, and the union shall be perpetual; nor shall any alteration at any time hereafter be made in any of them, unless such alteration be agreed to in a Congress of the United States, and be afterwards confirmed by the legislatures of every State.

These articles shall be proposed to the legislatures of all the United States, to be considered, and if approved of by them, they are advised to authorize their delegates to ratify the same in the Congress of the United States; which being done, the same shall become conclusive.

THE CONSTITUTION OF THE UNITED STATES*

Agreed to by Philadelphia Convention, September 17, 1787. Implemented March 4, 1789.

Preamble

We the people of the United States, in order to form a more perfect union, establish justice, insure domestic tranquility, provide for the common defense, promote the general welfare, and secure the blessings of liberty to ourselves and our posterity, do ordain and establish this Constitution for the United States of America.

*Passages no longer in effect are in italic type.

Article I

Section 1 All legislative powers herein granted shall be vested in a Congress of the United States, which shall consist of a Senate and a House of Representatives.

Section 2 The House of Representatives shall be composed of members chosen every second year by the people of the several States, and the electors in each State shall have the qualifications requisite for electors of the most numerous branch of the State Legislature.

No person shall be a Representative who shall not have attained to the age of twenty-five years, and been seven years a citizen of the United States, and who shall not, when elected, be an inhabitant of that State in which he shall be chosen.

Representatives and direct taxes shall be apportioned among the several States which may be included within this Union, according to their respective numbers, *which shall be determined by adding to the whole number of free persons, including those bound to service for a term of years and excluding Indians not taxed, three-fifths of all other persons.* The actual enumeration shall be made within three years after the first meeting of the Congress of the United States, and within every subsequent term of ten years, in such manner as they shall by law direct. The number of Representatives shall not exceed one for every thirty thousand, but each State shall have at least one Representative; *and until such enumeration shall be made, the State of New Hampshire shall be entitled to choose three, Massachusetts eight, Rhode Island and Providence Plantations one, Connecticut five, New York six, New Jersey four, Pennsylvania eight, Delaware one, Maryland six, Virginia ten, North Carolina five, South Carolina five, and Georgia three.*

When vacancies happen in the representation from any State, the Executive authority thereof shall issue writs of election to fill such vacancies.

The House of Representatives shall choose their Speaker and other officers; and shall have the sole power of impeachment.

Section 3 The Senate of the United States shall be composed of two Senators from each State, *chosen by the legislature thereof,* for six years; and each Senator shall have one vote.

Immediately after they shall be assembled in consequence of the first election, they shall be divided as equally as may be into three classes. The seats of the Senators of the first class shall be vacated at the expiration of the second year, of the second class at the expiration of the fourth year, and of the third class at the expiration of the sixth year, so that one-third may be chosen every second year; *and if vacancies happen by resignation or otherwise, during the recess of the legislature of any State, the Executive thereof may make temporary appointments until the next meeting of the legislature, which shall then fill such vacancies.*

No person shall be a Senator who shall not have attained to the age of thirty years, and been nine years a citizen of the United States, and who shall not, when elected, be an inhabitant of that State for which he shall be chosen.

The Vice-President of the United States shall be President of the Senate, but shall have no vote, unless they be equally divided.

The Senate shall choose their other officers, and also a President pro tempore, in the absence of the Vice-President, or when he shall exercise the office of President of the United States.

The Senate shall have the sole power to try all impeachments. When sitting for that purpose, they shall be on oath or affirmation. When the President of the United States is tried, the Chief Justice shall preside: and no person shall be convicted without the concurrence of two-thirds of the members present.

Judgment in cases of impeachment shall not extend further than to removal from the office, and disqualification to hold and enjoy any office of honor, trust or profit under the United States: but the party convicted shall nevertheless be liable and subject to indictment, trial, judgment and punishment, according to law.

Section 4 The times, places and manner of holding elections for Senators and Representatives shall be prescribed in each State by the legislature thereof; but the Congress may at any time by law make or alter such regulations, except as to the places of choosing Senators.

The Congress shall assemble at least once in every year, and such meeting *shall be on the first Monday in December, unless they shall by law appoint a different day.*

Section 5 Each house shall be the judge of the elections, returns and qualifications of its own members, and a majority of each shall constitute a quorum to do business; but a smaller number may adjourn from day to day, and may be authorized to compel the attendance of absent members, in such manner, and under such penalties, as each house may provide.

Each house may determine the rules of its proceedings, punish its members for disorderly behavior, and with the concurrence of two-thirds, expel a member.

Each house shall keep a journal of its proceedings, and from time to time publish the same, excepting such parts as may in their judgment require secrecy; and the yeas and nays of the members of either house on any question shall, at the desire of one-fifth of those present, be entered on the journal.

Neither house, during the session of Congress, shall, without the consent of the other, adjourn for more than three days, nor to any other place than that in which the two houses shall be sitting.

Section 6 The Senators and Representatives shall receive a compensation for their services, to be ascertained by law and paid out of the treasury of the United States. They shall in all cases except treason, felony and breach of the peace, be privileged from arrest during their attendance at the session of their respective houses, and in going to and returning from the same; and for any speech or debate in either house, they shall not be questioned in any other place.

No Senator or Representative shall, during the time for which he was elected, be appointed to any civil office under the authority of the United States, which shall have been created, or the emoluments whereof shall have been increased, during such time; and no person holding any office under the United States shall be a member of either house during his continuance in office.

Section 7 All bills for raising revenue shall originate in the House of Representatives; but the Senate may propose or concur with amendments as on other bills.

Every bill which shall have passed the House of Representatives and the Senate, shall, before it become a law, be presented to the President of the United States; if he approve he shall sign it, but if not he shall return it with objections to that house in which it shall have originated, who shall enter the objections at large on their journal, and proceed to reconsider it. If after such reconsideration two-thirds of that house shall agree to pass the bill, it shall be sent, together with the objections, to the other house, by which it shall likewise be reconsidered, and, if approved by two-thirds of that house, it shall become a law. But in all such cases the votes of both houses shall be determined by yeas and nays, and the names of the persons voting for and against the bill shall be entered on the journal of each house respectively. If any bill shall not be returned by the President within ten days (Sundays excepted) after it shall have been presented to him, the same shall be a law, in like manner as if he had signed it, unless the Congress by their adjournment prevent its return, in which case it shall not be a law.

Every order, resolution, or vote to which the concurrence of the Senate and House of Representatives may be necessary (except on a question of adjournment) shall be presented to the President of the United States; and before the same shall take effect, shall be approved by him, or being disapproved by him, shall be repassed by two-thirds of the Senate and House of Representatives, according to the rules and limitations prescribed in the case of a bill.

Section 8 The Congress shall have power

To lay and collect taxes, duties, imposts, and excises, to pay the debts and provide for the common defense and general welfare of the United States; but all duties, imposts and excises shall be uniform throughout the United States;

To borrow money on the credit of the United States;

To regulate commerce with foreign nations, and among the several States, and with the Indian tribes;

To establish an uniform rule of naturalization, and uniform laws on the subject of bankruptcies throughout the United States;

To coin money, regulate the value thereof, and of foreign coin, and fix the standard of weights and measures;

To provide for the punishment of counterfeiting the securities and current coin of the United States;

To establish post offices and post roads;

To promote the progress of science and useful arts by securing for limited times to authors and inventors the exclusive right to their respective writings and discoveries;

To constitute tribunals inferior to the Supreme Court;

To define and punish piracies and felonies committed on the high seas and offences against the law of nations;

To declare war, grant letters of marque and reprisal, and make rules concerning captures on land and water;

To raise and support armies, but no appropriation of money to that use shall be for a longer term than two years;

To provide and maintain a navy;

To make rules for the government and regulation of the land and naval forces;

To provide for calling forth the militia to execute the laws of the Union, suppress insurrections and repel invasions;

To provide for organizing, arming, and disciplining the militia, and for governing such part of them as may be employed in the service of the United States, reserving to the States respectively the appointment of the officers, and the authority of training the militia according to the discipline prescribed by Congress;

To exercise exclusive legislation in all cases whatsoever, over such district (not exceeding ten miles square) as may, by cession of particular States, and the acceptance of Congress, become the seat of the government of the United States, and to exercise like authority over all places purchased by the consent of the legislature of the State, in which the same shall be, for erection of forts, magazines, arsenals, dockyards, and other needful buildings;—and

To make all laws which shall be necessary and proper for carrying into execution the foregoing powers, and all other powers vested by this Constitution in the government of the United States, or in any department or officer thereof.

Section 9 *The migration or importation of such persons as any of the States now existing shall think proper to admit shall not be prohibited by the Congress prior to the year one thousand eight hundred and eight; but a tax or duty may be imposed on such importation, not exceeding ten dollars for each person.*

The privilege of the writ of habeas corpus shall not be suspended, unless when in cases of rebellion or invasion the public safety may require it.

No bill of attainder or ex post facto law shall be passed.

No capitation, or other direct, tax shall be laid, unless in proportion to the census or enumeration herein before directed to be taken.

No tax or duty shall be laid on articles exported from any State.

No preference shall be given by any regulation of commerce or revenue to the ports of one State over those of another; nor shall vessels bound to, or from, one State be obliged to enter, clear, or pay duties in another.

No money shall be drawn from the treasury, but in consequence of appropriations made by law; and a regular statement and account of the receipts and expenditures of all public money shall be published from time to time.

No title of nobility shall be granted by the United States: and no person holding any office of profit or trust under them, shall, without the consent of the Congress, accept of any present, emolument, office, or title, of any kind whatever, from any king, prince, or foreign state.

Section 10 No State shall enter into any treaty, alliance, or confederation; grant letters of marque and reprisal; coin money; emit bills of credit; make anything but gold and silver coin a tender in payment of debts; pass any bill of attainder, ex post facto law, or law impairing the obligation of contracts, or grant any title of nobility.

No State shall, without the consent of Congress, lay any imposts or duties on imports or exports, except what may be absolutely necessary for executing its inspection laws: and the net produce of all duties and imposts, laid by any State on imports or exports, shall be for the use of the treasury of the United States; and all such laws shall be subject to the revision and control of the Congress.

No State shall, without the consent of Congress, lay any duty of tonnage, keep troops, or ships of war in time of peace, enter into any agreement or compact with another State, or with a foreign power, or engage in war, unless actually invaded, or in such imminent danger as will not admit of delay.

Article II

Section 1 The executive power shall be vested in a President of the United States of America. He shall hold his office during the term of four years, and, together with the Vice-President, chosen for the same term, be elected as follows:

Each State shall appoint, in such manner as the legislature thereof may direct, a number of electors, equal to the whole number of Senators and Representatives to which the State may be entitled in the Congress; but no Senator or Representative, or person holding an office of trust or profit under the United States, shall be appointed an elector.

The electors shall meet in their respective States, and vote by ballot for two persons, of whom one at least shall not be an inhabitant of the same State with themselves. And they shall make a list of all the persons voted for, and of the number of votes for each; which list they shall sign and certify, and transmit sealed to the seat of government of the United States, directed to the President of the Senate. The President of the Senate shall, in the presence of the Senate and House of Representatives, open all the certificates, and the votes shall then be counted. The person having the greatest number of votes shall be the President, if such number be a majority of the whole number of electors appointed; and if there be more than one who have such majority, and have an equal number of votes, then the House of Representatives shall immediately choose by ballot one of them for President; and if no person have a majority, then from the five highest on the list said house shall in like manner choose the President. But in choosing the President the votes shall be taken by States, the representation from each State having one vote; a quorum for this purpose shall consist of a member or members from two-thirds of the States, and a majority of all the States shall be necessary to a choice. In every case, after the choice of the President, the person having the greatest number of votes of the electors shall be the Vice-President. But if there should remain two or more who have equal votes, the Senate shall choose from them by ballot the Vice-President.

The Congress may determine the time of choosing the electors, and the day on which they shall give their votes; which day shall be the same throughout the United States.

No person except a natural-born citizen, *or a citizen of the United States at the time of the adoption of this Constitution*, shall be eligible to the office of President; neither shall any person be eligible to that office who shall not have attained to the age of thirty-five years, and been fourteen years a resident within the United States.

In cases of the removal of the President from office or of his death, resignation, or inability to discharge the powers and duties of the said office, the same shall devolve on the Vice-President, and the Congress may by law provide for the case of removal, death, resignation, or inability, both of the President and Vice-President, declaring what officer shall then act as President, and such officer shall act accordingly, until the disability be removed, or a President shall be elected.

The President shall, at stated times, receive for his services a compensation, which shall neither be increased nor diminished during the period for which he shall have been elected, and he shall not receive within that period any other emolument from the United States, or any of them.

Before he enter on the execution of his office, he shall take the following oath or affirmation:—"I do solemnly swear (or affirm) that I will faithfully execute the office of the President of the United States, and will to the best of my ability preserve, protect and defend the Constitution of the United States."

Section 2 The President shall be commander in chief of the army and navy of the United States, and of the militia of the several States, when called into the actual service of the United States; he may require the opinion, in writing, of the principal officer in each of the executive departments, upon any subject relating to the duties of their respective offices, and he shall have power to grant reprieves and pardons for offenses against the United States, except in cases of impeachment.

He shall have power, by and with the advice and consent of the Senate, to make treaties, provided two-thirds of the Senators present concur; and he shall nominate, and by and with the advice and consent of the Senate, shall appoint ambassadors, other public ministers and consuls, judges of the Supreme Court, and all other officers of the United States, whose appointments are not herein otherwise provided for, and which shall be established by law: but Congress may by law vest the appointment of such inferior officers, as they think proper, in the President alone, in the courts of law, or in the heads of departments.

The President shall have power to fill up all vacancies that may happen during the recess of the Senate, by granting commissions which shall expire at the end of their next session.

Section 3 He shall from time to time give to the Congress information of the state of the Union, and recommend to their consideration such measures as he shall judge necessary and expedient; he may, on extraordinary occasions, convene both houses, or either of them, and in case of disagreement between them, with respect to the time of adjournment, he may adjourn them to such time as he shall think proper; he shall receive ambassadors and other public ministers; he shall take care that the laws be faithfully executed, and shall commission all the officers of the United States.

Section 4 The President, Vice-President and all civil officers of the United States shall be removed from office on impeachment for, and on conviction of, treason, bribery, or other high crimes and misdemeanors.

Article III

Section 1 The judicial power of the United States shall be vested in one Supreme Court, and in such inferior courts as the Congress may from time to time ordain and establish. The judges, both of the Supreme and inferior courts, shall hold their offices during good behavior, and shall, at stated times, receive for their services a compensation which shall not be diminished during their continuance in office.

Section 2 The judicial power shall extend to all cases, in law and equity, arising under this Constitution, the laws of the United States, and treaties made, or which shall be made, under their authority;—to all cases affecting ambassadors, other public ministers and consuls;—to all cases of admiralty and maritime jurisdiction;—to controversies to which the United States shall be a party;—to controversies between two or more States;*—between a State and citizens of another State*;—between citizens of different States;— between citizens of the same State claiming lands under grants of different States, and between a State, or the citizens thereof, and foreign states, citizens or subjects.

In all cases affecting ambassadors, other public ministers and consuls, and those in which a State shall be party, the Supreme Court shall have original jurisdiction. In all the other cases before mentioned, the Supreme Court shall have appellate jurisdiction, both as to law and fact, with such exceptions, and under such regulations, as the Congress shall make.

The trial of all crimes, except in cases of impeachment, shall be by jury; and such trial shall be held in the State where said crimes shall have been committed; but when not committed within any State, the trial shall be at such place or places as the Congress may by Law have directed.

Section 3 Treason against the United States shall consist only in levying war against them, or in adhering to their enemies, giving them aid and comfort. No person shall be convicted of treason unless on the testimony of two witnesses to the same overt act, or on confession in open court.

The Congress shall have power to declare the punishment of treason, but no attainder of treason shall work corruption of blood, or forfeiture except during the life of the person attainted.

Article IV

Section 1 Full faith and credit shall be given in each State to the public acts, records, and judicial proceedings of every other State. And the Congress may by general laws prescribe the manner in which such acts, records, and proceedings shall be proved, and the effect thereof.

Section 2 The citizens of each State shall be entitled to all privileges and immunities of citizens in the several States.

A person charged in any State with treason, felony, or other crime, who shall flee from justice, and be found in another State, shall on demand of the executive authority of the State from which he fled, be delivered up, to be removed to the State having jurisdiction of the crime.

No Person held to service or labor in one State, under the laws thereof, escaping into another, shall, in consequence of any law or regulation therein, be discharged from such service or labor, but shall be delivered up on claim of the party to whom such service or labor may be due.

Section 3 New States may be admitted by the Congress into this Union; but no new State shall be formed or erected within the jurisdiction of any other State; nor any State be formed by the junction of two or more States, or parts of States, without the consent of the legislatures of the States concerned as well as of the Congress.

The Congress shall have power to dispose of and make all needful rules and regulations respecting the territory or other property belonging to the United States; and nothing in this Constitution shall be so construed as to prejudice any claims of the United States, or of any particular State.

Section 4 The United States shall guarantee to every State in this Union a republican form of government, and shall protect each of them against invasion; and on application of the legislature, or of the executive (when the legislature cannot be convened), against domestic violence.

Article V

The Congress, whenever two-thirds of both houses shall deem it necessary, shall propose amendments to this Constitution, or, on the application of the legislatures of two-thirds of the several States, shall call a convention for proposing amendments, which, in either case, shall be valid to all intents and purposes, as part of this Constitution, when ratified by the legislatures of three-fourths of the several States, or by conventions in three-fourths thereof, as the one or the other mode of ratification may be proposed by the Congress; provided *that no amendments which may be made prior to the year one thousand eight hundred and eight shall in any manner affect the first and fourth clauses in the ninth section of the first article*; and that no State, without its consent, shall be deprived of its equal suffrage in the Senate.

Article VI

All debts contracted and engagements entered into, before the adoption of this Constitution, shall be as valid against the United States under this Constitution, as under the Confederation.

This Constitution, and the laws of the United States which shall be made in pursuance thereof; and all treaties made, or which shall be made, under the authority of the United States, shall be the supreme law of the land; and the judges in every State shall be bound thereby, anything in the Constitution or laws of any State to the contrary notwithstanding.

The Senators and Representatives before mentioned, and the members of the several State legislatures, and all executive and judicial officers, both of the United States and of the several States, shall be bound by oath or affirmation to support this Constitution; but no religious test shall ever be required as a qualification to any office or public trust under the United States.

Article VII

The ratification of the conventions of nine States shall be sufficient for the establishment of this Constitution between the States so ratifying the same.

Done in convention by the unanimous consent of the States present, the seventeenth day of September in the year of our Lord one thousand seven hundred and eighty-seven and of the Independence of the United States of America the twelfth. In witness whereof we have hereunto subscribed our names.

GEORGE WASHINGTON
PRESIDENT AND DEPUTY FROM VIRGINIA

New Hampshire
John Langdon
Nicholas Gilman

Massachusetts
Nathaniel Gorham
Rufus King

Connecticut
William Samuel Johnson
Roger Sherman

New York
Alexander Hamilton

New Jersey
William Livingston
David Brearley
William Paterson
Jonathan Dayton

Pennsylvania
Benjamin Franklin
Thomas Mifflin
Robert Morris
George Clymer
Thomas FitzSimons
Jared Ingersoll
James Wilson
Gouverneur Morris

Delaware
George Read
Gunning Bedford, Jr.
John Dickinson
Richard Bassett
Jacob Broom

Maryland
James McHenry
Daniel of St. Thomas Jenifer
Daniel Carroll

Virginia
John Blair
James Madison, Jr.

North Carolina
William Blount
Richard Dobbs Spaight
Hugh Williamson

South Carolina
John Rutledge
Charles Cotesworth Pinckney
Charles Pinckney
Pierce Butler

Georgia
William Few
Abraham Baldwin

AMENDMENTS TO THE CONSTITUTION WITH ANNOTATIONS (including the six unratified amendments)

▶ *IN THEIR EFFORT TO GAIN Antifederalists' support for the Constitution, Federalists frequently pointed to the inclusion of Article 5, which provides an orderly method of amending the Constitution. In contrast, the Articles of Confederation, which were universally recognized as seriously flawed, offered no means of amendment. For their part, Antifederalists argued that the amendment process was so "intricate" that one might as easily roll "sixes an hundred times in succession" as change the Constitution.*

The system for amendment laid out in the Constitution requires that two-thirds of both houses of Congress agree to a proposed amendment, which must then be ratified by three-quarters of the legislatures of the states. Alternatively, an amendment may be proposed by a convention called by the legislatures of two-thirds of the states. Since 1789, members of Congress have proposed thousands of amendments. Besides the seventeen amendments added since 1789, only the six "unratified" ones included here were approved by two-thirds of both houses and sent to the states for ratification.

*Among the many amendments that never made it out of Congress have been proposals to declare dueling, divorce, and interracial marriage unconstitutional as well as proposals to establish a national university, to acknowledge the sovereignty of Jesus Christ, and to prohibit any person from possessing wealth in excess of $10 million.**

Among the issues facing Americans today that might lead to constitutional amendment are efforts to balance the federal budget, to limit the number of terms elected officials may serve, to limit access to or prohibit abortion, to establish English as the official language of the United States, and to prohibit flag burning. None of these proposed amendments has yet garnered enough support in Congress to be sent to the states for ratification.

Although the first ten amendments to the Constitution are commonly known as the Bill of Rights, only Amendments 1–8 actually provide guarantees of individual rights. Amendments 9 and 10 deal with the structure of power within the constitutional system. The Bill of Rights was promised to appease Antifederalists who refused to ratify the Constitution without guarantees of individual liberties and limitations to federal power. After studying more than two hundred amendments recommended by the ratifying conventions of the states, Federalist James Madison presented a list of seventeen to Congress, which used Madison's list as the foundation for the twelve amendments that were sent to the states for ratification. Ten of the twelve were adopted in 1791. The first on the list of twelve, known as the Reapportionment Amendment, was never adopted (see page A-15). The second proposed amendment was adopted in 1992 as Amendment 27 (see page A-24).

*Richard B. Bernstein, *Amending America* (New York: Times Books, 1993), 177–81.

Amendment I

Congress shall make no law respecting an establishment of religion, or prohibiting the free exercise thereof; or abridging the freedom of speech, or of the press; or the right of the people peaceably to assemble, and to petition the government for a redress of grievances.

♦♦♦

▶ *The First Amendment is a potent symbol for many Americans. Most are well aware of their rights to free speech, freedom of the press, and freedom of religion and their rights to assemble and to petition, even if they cannot cite the exact words of this amendment.*

The First Amendment guarantee of freedom of religion has two clauses: the "free exercise clause," which allows individuals to practice or not practice any religion, and the "establishment clause," which prevents the federal government from discriminating against or favoring any particular religion. This clause was designed to create what Thomas Jefferson referred to as "a wall of separation between church and state." In the 1960s, the Supreme Court ruled that the First Amendment prohibits prayer (see Engel v. Vitale, *online) and Bible reading in public schools.*

Although the rights to free speech and freedom of the press are established in the First Amendment, it was not until the twentieth century that the Supreme Court began to explore the full meaning of these guarantees. In 1919, the Court ruled in Schenck v. United States *(online) that the government could suppress free expression only where it could cite a "clear and present danger." In a decision that continues to raise controversies, the Court ruled in 1990, in* Texas v. Johnson, *that flag burning is a form of symbolic speech protected by the First Amendment.*

Amendment II

A well-regulated militia being necessary to the security of a free State, the right of the people to keep and bear arms shall not be infringed.

♦♦♦

▶ *Fear of a standing army under the control of a hostile government made the Second Amendment an important part of the Bill of Rights. Advocates of gun ownership claim that the amendment prevents the government from regulating firearms. Proponents of gun control argue that the amendment is designed only to protect the right of the states to maintain militia units.*

In 1939, the Supreme Court ruled in United States v. Miller *that the Second Amendment did not protect the right of an individual to own a sawed-off shotgun, which it argued was not ordinary militia equipment. Since then, the Supreme Court has refused to hear Second Amendment cases, while lower courts have upheld firearms regulations. Several justices currently on the bench seem to favor a narrow interpretation of the Second Amendment, which would allow gun control legislation. The controversy over the impact of the Second Amendment on gun owners and gun control legislation will certainly continue.*

Amendment III

No soldier shall, in time of peace, be quartered in any house without the consent of the owner, nor in time of war, but in a manner to be prescribed by law.

♦♦♦

▶ *The Third Amendment was extremely important to the framers of the Constitution, but today it is nearly forgotten. American colonists were especially outraged that they were forced to quarter British troops in the years before and during the American Revolution. The philosophy of the Third Amendment has been viewed by some justices and scholars as the foundation of the modern constitutional right to privacy. One example of this can be found in Justice William O. Douglas's opinion in* Griswold v. Connecticut *(online).*

Amendment IV

The right of the people to be secure in their persons, houses, papers, and effects, against unreasonable searches and seizures, shall not be violated, and no warrants shall issue but upon probable cause, supported by oath or affirmation, and particularly describing the place to be searched, and the persons or things to be seized.

♦♦♦

▶ *In the years before the Revolution, the houses, barns, stores, and warehouses of American colonists were ransacked by British authorities under "writs of assistance" or general warrants. The British, thus empowered, searched for seditious material or smuggled goods that could then be used as evidence against colonists who were charged with a crime only after the items were found. The first part of the Fourth Amendment protects citizens from "unreasonable" searches and seizures.*

The Supreme Court has interpreted this protection as well as the words search *and* seizure *in different ways at different times. At one time, the Court did not recognize electronic eavesdropping as a form of search and seizure, though it does today. At times, an "unreasonable" search has been almost any search carried out without a warrant, but in the two decades before 1969, the Court sometimes sanctioned warrantless searches that it considered reasonable based on "the total atmosphere of the case."*

The second part of the Fourth Amendment defines the procedure for issuing a search warrant and states the requirement of "probable cause," which is generally viewed as evidence indicating that a suspect has committed an offense.

The Fourth Amendment has been controversial because the Court has sometimes excluded evidence that has been seized in violation of constitutional standards. The justification is that excluding such evidence deters violations of the amendment, but doing so may allow a guilty person to escape punishment.

Amendment V

No person shall be held to answer for a capital, or otherwise infamous crime, unless on a presentment or indictment of a grand jury, except in cases arising in the land or naval forces, or in the militia, when in actual service in time of war or public danger; nor shall any person be subject for the same offence to be twice put in jeopardy of life or limb; nor shall be compelled in any criminal case to be a witness against himself, nor be deprived of life, liberty, or property, without due process of law; nor shall private property be taken for public use without just compensation.

♦♦♦

▶ *The Fifth Amendment protects people against government authority in the prosecution of criminal offenses. It prohibits the state, first, from charging a person with a serious crime without a grand jury hearing to decide whether there is sufficient evidence to support the charge and, second, from charging a person with the same crime twice. The best-known aspect of the Fifth Amendment is that it prevents a person from being "compelled . . . to be a witness against himself." The last clause, the "takings clause," limits the power of the government to seize property.*

Although invoking the Fifth Amendment is popularly viewed as a confession of guilt, a person may be innocent yet still fear prosecution. For example, during the Red-baiting era of the late 1940s and 1950s, many people who had participated in legal activities that were associated with the Communist Party claimed the Fifth Amendment privilege rather than testify before the House Un-American Activities Committee because the mood of the times cast those activities in a negative light. Since "taking the Fifth" was viewed as an admission of guilt, those people often lost their jobs or became unemployable. (See chapter 26.) Nonetheless, the right to protect oneself against self-incrimination plays an important role in guarding against the collective power of the state.

Amendment VI

In all criminal prosecutions, the accused shall enjoy the right to a speedy and public trial, by an impartial jury of the State and district wherein the crime shall have been committed, which district shall have been previously ascertained by law, and to be informed of the nature and cause of the accusation; to be confronted with the witnesses against him; to have compulsory process for obtaining witnesses in his favor, and to have the assistance of counsel for his defence.

♦♦♦

▶ *The original Constitution put few limits on the government's power to investigate, prosecute, and punish crime. This process was of great concern to the early Americans, however, and of the twenty-eight rights specified in the first eight amendments, fifteen have to do with it. Seven rights are specified in the Sixth Amendment. These include the right to a speedy trial, a public trial, a jury trial, a notice of accusation, confrontation by opposing witnesses, testimony by favorable witnesses, and the assistance of counsel.*

Although this amendment originally guaranteed these rights only in cases involving the federal government, the adoption of the Fourteenth Amendment began a process of applying the protections of the Bill of Rights to the states through court cases such as Gideon v. Wainwright *(online).*

Amendment VII

In suits at common law, where the value in controversy shall exceed twenty dollars, the right of trial by jury shall be preserved, and no fact tried by a jury shall be otherwise reexamined in any court of the United States, than according to the rules of the common law.

♦♦♦

▶ *This amendment guarantees people the same right to a trial by jury as was guaranteed by English common law in 1791. Under common law, in civil trials (those involving money damages) the role of the judge was to settle questions of law and that of the jury was to settle questions of fact. The amendment does not specify the size of the jury or its role in a trial, however. The Supreme Court has generally held that those issues be determined by English common law of 1791, which stated that a jury consists of twelve people, that a trial must be conducted before a judge who instructs the jury on the law and advises it on facts, and that a verdict must be unanimous.*

Amendment VIII

Excessive bail shall not be required, nor excessive fines imposed, nor cruel and unusual punishments inflicted.

♦♦♦

▶ *The language used to guarantee the three rights in this amendment was inspired by the English Bill of Rights of 1689. The Supreme Court has not had a lot to say about "excessive fines." In recent years it has agreed that, despite the provision against "excessive bail," persons who are believed to be dangerous to others can be held without bail even before they have been convicted.*

Although opponents of the death penalty have not succeeded in using the Eighth Amendment to achieve the end of capital punishment, the clause regarding "cruel and unusual punishments" has been used to prohibit capital punishment in certain cases (see Furman v. Georgia*, online) and to require improved conditions in prisons.*

Amendment IX

The enumeration in the Constitution, of certain rights, shall not be construed to deny or disparage others retained by the people.

♦♦♦

▶ *Some Federalists feared that inclusion of the Bill of Rights in the Constitution would allow later generations of interpreters to claim that the people had surrendered any rights not specifically enumerated there. To guard against this, Madison added language that became the Ninth Amendment. Interest in this heretofore largely ignored amendment revived in 1965 when it was used in a concurring opinion in* Griswold v. Connecticut *(online). While Justice William O. Douglas called on the Third Amendment to support the right to privacy in deciding that case, Justice Arthur Goldberg, in the concurring opinion, argued that the right to privacy regarding contraception was an unenumerated right that was protected by the Ninth Amendment.*

In 1980, the Court ruled that the right of the press to attend a public trial was protected by the Ninth Amendment. While some scholars argue that modern judges cannot identify the unenumerated rights that the framers were trying to protect, others argue that the Ninth Amendment should be read as providing a constitutional "presumption of liberty" that allows people to act in any way that does not violate the rights of others.

Amendment X

The powers not delegated to the United States by the Constitution, nor prohibited by it to the States, are reserved to the States respectively, or to the people.

♦♦♦

▶ *The Antifederalists were especially eager to see a "reserved powers clause" explicitly guaranteeing the states control over their internal affairs. Not surprisingly, the Tenth Amendment has been a frequent battleground in the struggle over states' rights and federal supremacy. Prior to the Civil War, the Democratic Republican Party and Jacksonian Democrats invoked the Tenth Amendment to prohibit the federal government from making decisions about whether people in individual states could own slaves. The Tenth Amendment was virtually suspended during Reconstruction following the Civil War. In 1883, however, the Supreme Court declared the Civil Rights Act of 1875 unconstitutional on the grounds that it violated the Tenth Amendment. Business interests also called on the amendment to block efforts at federal regulation.*

The Court was inconsistent over the next several decades as it attempted to resolve the tension between the restrictions of the Tenth Amendment and the powers the Constitution granted to Congress to regulate interstate commerce and levy taxes. The Court upheld the Pure Food and Drug Act (1906), the Meat Inspection Acts (1906 and 1907), and the White Slave Traffic Act (1910), all of which affected the states, but struck down an act prohibiting interstate shipment of goods produced through child labor. Between 1934 and 1935, a number of New Deal programs created by Franklin D. Roosevelt were declared unconstitutional on the grounds that they violated the Tenth Amendment. (See chapter 24.) As Roosevelt appointees changed the composition of the Court, the Tenth Amendment was declared to have no substantive meaning. Generally, the amendment is held to protect the rights of states to regulate internal matters such as local government, education, commerce, labor, and business, as well as matters involving families such as marriage, divorce, and inheritance within the state.

Unratified Amendment

Reapportionment Amendment (proposed by Congress September 25, 1789, along with the Bill of Rights)

After the first enumeration required by the first article of the Constitution, there shall be one Representative for every thirty thousand, until the number shall amount to one hundred, after which the proportion shall be so regulated by Congress, that there shall be not less than one hundred Representatives, nor less than one Representative for every forty thousand persons, until the number of Representatives shall amount to two hundred; after which the proportion shall be so regulated by Congress, that there shall not be less than two hundred Representatives, nor more than one Representative for every fifty thousand persons.

♦♦♦

▶ *If the Reapportionment Amendment had passed and remained in effect, the House of Representatives today would have more than 5,000 members rather than 435.*

Amendment XI

[Adopted 1798]

The judicial power of the United States shall not be construed to extend to any suit in law or equity, commenced or prosecuted against one of the United States by citizens of another State, or by citizens or subjects of any foreign state.

♦♦♦

▶ *In 1793, the Supreme Court ruled in favor of Alexander Chisholm, executor of the estate of a deceased South Carolina merchant. Chisholm was suing the state of Georgia because the merchant had never been paid for provisions he had supplied during the Revolution. Many regarded this Court decision as an error that violated the intent of the Constitution.*

Antifederalists had long feared a federal court system with the power to overrule a state court.

When the Constitution was being drafted, Federalists had assured worried Antifederalists that section 2 of Article 3, which allows federal courts to hear cases "between a State and citizens of another State," did not mean that the federal courts were authorized to hear suits against a state by citizens of another state or a foreign country. Antifederalists and many other Americans feared a powerful federal court system because they worried that it would become like the British courts of this period, which were accountable only to the monarch. Furthermore, Chisholm v. Georgia *prompted a series of suits against state governments by creditors and suppliers who had made loans during the war.*

In addition, state legislators and Congress feared that the shaky economies of the new states, as well as the country as a whole, would be destroyed, especially if loyalists who had fled to other countries sought reimbursement for land and property that had been seized. The day after the Supreme Court announced its decision, a resolution proposing the Eleventh Amendment, which overturned the decision in Chisholm v. Georgia, *was introduced in the U.S. Senate.*

Amendment XII

[Adopted 1804]

The electors shall meet in their respective States, and vote by ballot for President and Vice-President, one of whom, at least, shall not be an inhabitant of the same State with themselves; they shall name in their ballots the person voted for as President, and in distinct ballots the person voted for as Vice-President, and they shall make distinct lists of all persons voted for as President, and of all persons voted for as Vice-President, and of the number of votes for each, which lists they shall sign and certify, and transmit sealed to the seat of government of the United States, directed to the President of the Senate;—the President of the Senate shall, in the presence of the Senate and House of Representatives, open all the certificates and the votes shall then be counted;—the person having the greatest number of votes for President shall be the President, if such number be a majority of the whole number of electors appointed; and if no person have such majority, then from the persons having the highest numbers not exceeding three on the list of those voted for as President, the House of Representatives shall choose immediately, by ballot, the President. But in choosing the President, the votes shall be taken by States, the representation from each State having one vote; a quorum for this purpose shall consist of a member or members from two-thirds of the States, and a majority of all the States shall be necessary to a choice. And if the House of Representatives shall not choose a President whenever the right of choice shall devolve upon them, before the fourth day of March next following, then the Vice-President shall act as President, as in the case of the death or other constitutional disability of the President.

The person having the greatest number of votes as Vice-President shall be the Vice-President, if such number be a majority of the whole number of electors appointed; and if no person have a majority, then from the two highest numbers on the list the Senate shall choose the Vice-President; a quorum for the purpose shall consist of two-thirds of the whole number of Senators, and a majority of the whole number shall be necessary to a choice. But no person constitutionally ineligible to the office of President shall be eligible to that of Vice-President of the United States.

♦♦♦

▶ *The framers of the Constitution disliked political parties and assumed that none would ever form. Under the original system, electors chosen by the states would each vote for two candidates. The candidate who won the most votes would become president, while the person who won the second-highest number of votes would become vice president. Rivalries between Federalists and Antifederalists led to the formation of political parties, however, even before George Washington had left office. Though Washington was elected unanimously in 1789 and 1792, the elections of 1796 and 1800 were procedural disasters because of party maneuvering (see chapters 9 and 10). In 1796, Federalist John Adams was chosen as president, and his great rival, the Antifederalist Thomas Jefferson (whose party was called the Republican Party), became his vice president. In 1800, all the electors cast their two votes as one of two party blocs. Jefferson and his fellow Republican nominee, Aaron Burr, were tied with 73 votes each. The contest went to the House of Representatives, which finally elected Jefferson after 36 ballots. The Twelfth Amendment prevents these problems by requiring electors to vote separately for the president and vice president.*

Unratified Amendment

Titles of Nobility Amendment (proposed by Congress May 1, 1810)

If any citizen of the United States shall accept, claim, receive or retain any title of nobility or honor or shall, without the consent of Congress, accept and retain any present, pension, office or emolument of any kind whatever, from any emperor, king, prince or foreign power, such person shall cease to be a citizen of the United States, and shall be incapable of holding any office of trust or profit under them or either of them.

♦♦♦

▶ *This amendment would have extended Article 1, section 9, clause 8 of the Constitution, which prevents the awarding of titles by the United States and the acceptance of such awards from foreign powers without congressional consent. Historians speculate that general nervousness about the power of the emperor Napoleon, who was at that time extending France's empire throughout Europe, may have prompted the proposal. Though it fell one vote short of ratification, Congress and the American people thought the proposal had been ratified, and it was included in many nineteenth-century editions of the Constitution.*

The Civil War and Reconstruction Amendments (Thirteenth, Fourteenth, and Fifteenth Amendments)

▶ *In the four months between the election of Abraham Lincoln and his inauguration, more than 200 proposed constitutional amendments were presented to Congress as part of a desperate attempt to hold the rapidly dissolving Union together. Most of these were efforts to appease the southern states by protecting the right to own slaves or by disfranchising African Americans through constitutional amendment. None were able to win the votes required from Congress to send them to the states. The relatively innocuous Corwin Amendment seemed to be the only hope for preserving the Union by amending the Constitution.*

The northern victors in the Civil War tried to restructure the Constitution just as the war had restructured the nation. Yet they were often divided in their goals. Some wanted to end slavery; others hoped for social and economic equality regardless of race; others hoped that extending the power of the ballot box to former slaves would help create a new political order. The debates over the Thirteenth, Fourteenth, and Fifteenth Amendments were bitter. Few of those who fought for these changes were satisfied with the amendments themselves; fewer still were satisfied with their interpretation. Although the amendments put an end to the legal status of slavery, it took nearly a hundred years after the amendments' passage before most of the descendants of former slaves could begin to experience the economic, social, and political equality the amendments had been intended to provide.

Unratified Amendment

Corwin Amendment (proposed by Congress March 2, 1861)

No amendment shall be made to the Constitution which will authorize or give to Congress the power to abolish or interfere, within any State, with the domestic institutions thereof, including that of persons held to labor or service by the laws of said State.

♦♦♦

▶ *Following the election of Abraham Lincoln, Congress scrambled to try to prevent the secession of the slaveholding states. House member Thomas Corwin of Ohio proposed the "unamendable" amendment in the hope that by protecting slavery where it existed, Congress would keep the southern states in the Union. Lincoln indicated his support for the proposed amendment in his first inaugural address. Only Ohio and Maryland ratified the Corwin Amendment before it was forgotten.*

Amendment XIII

[Adopted 1865]

Section 1 Neither slavery nor involuntary servitude, except as a punishment for crime whereof the party shall have been duly convicted, shall exist within the United States, or any place subject to their jurisdiction.

Section 2 Congress shall have power to enforce this article by appropriate legislation.

♦♦♦

▶ *Although President Lincoln had abolished slavery in the Confederacy with the Emancipation Proclamation of 1863, abolitionists wanted to rid the entire country of slavery. The Thirteenth Amendment did this in a clear and straightforward manner. In February 1865, when the proposal was approved by the House, the gallery of the House was newly opened to black Americans who had a chance at last to see their government at work. Passage of the proposal was greeted by wild cheers from the gallery as well as tears on the House floor, where congressional representatives openly embraced one another.*

The problem of ratification remained, however. The Union position was that the Confederate states were part of the country of thirty-six states. Therefore, twenty-seven states were needed to ratify the amendment. When Kentucky and Delaware rejected it, backers realized that without approval from at least four former Confederate states, the amendment would fail. Lincoln's successor, President Andrew Johnson, made ratification of the Thirteenth Amendment a condition for southern states to rejoin the Union. Under those terms, all the former Confederate states except Mississippi accepted the Thirteenth Amendment, and by the end of 1865 the amendment had become part of the Constitution and slavery had been prohibited in the United States.

Amendment XIV

[Adopted 1868]

Section 1 All persons born or naturalized in the United States, and subject to the jurisdiction thereof, are citizens of the United States and of the State wherein they reside. No State shall make or enforce any law which shall abridge the privileges or immunities of citizens of the United States; nor shall any State deprive any person of life, liberty, or property, without due process of law; nor deny to any person within its jurisdiction the equal protection of the laws.

Section 2 Representatives shall be appointed among the several States according to their respective numbers, counting the whole number of persons in each State, excluding Indians not taxed. But when the right to vote at any election for the choice of Electors for President and Vice-President of the United States, Representatives in Congress, the executive and judicial officers of a State, or the members of the legislature thereof, is denied to any of the male inhabitants of such State, being twenty-one years of age and citizens of the United States, or in any way abridged, except for participation in rebellion, or other crime, the basis of representation therein shall be reduced in the proportion which the number of such male citizens shall bear to the whole number of male citizens twenty-one years of age in such State.

Section 3 No person shall be a Senator or Representative in Congress, or Elector of President and Vice-President, or hold any office, civil or military, under the United States, or under any State, who, having previously taken an oath, as a member of Congress, or as an officer of the United States, or as a member of any State legislature, or as an executive or judicial officer of any State, to support the Constitution of the United States, shall have engaged in insurrection or rebellion against the same, or given aid or comfort to the enemies thereof. Congress may, by a vote of two-thirds of each house, remove such disability.

Section 4 The validity of the public debt of the United States, authorized by law, including debts incurred for payment of pensions and bounties for services in suppressing insurrection or rebellion, shall not be questioned. But neither the United States nor any State shall assume or pay any debt or obligation incurred in aid of insurrection or rebellion against the United States, or any claim for the loss or emancipation of any slave; but all such debts, obligations, and claims shall be held illegal and void.

Section 5 The Congress shall have power to enforce, by appropriate legislation, the provisions of this article.

♦♦♦

▶ *Without Lincoln's leadership in the reconstruction of the nation following the Civil War, it soon became clear that the Thirteenth Amendment needed additional constitutional support. Less than a year after Lincoln's assassination, Andrew Johnson was ready to bring the former Confederate states back into the Union with few changes in their governments or politics. Anxious Republicans drafted the Fourteenth Amendment to prevent that from happening. The most important provisions of this complex amendment made all native-born or naturalized persons American citizens and prohibited states from abridging the "privileges or immunities" of citizens; depriving them of "life, liberty, or property, without due process of law"; and denying them "equal protection of the laws." In essence, it made all ex-slaves citizens and protected the rights of all citizens against violation by their own state governments.*

As occurred in the case of the Thirteenth Amendment, former Confederate states were forced to ratify the amendment as a condition of representation in the House and the Senate. The intentions of the Fourteenth Amendment, and how those intentions should be enforced, have been the most debated point of constitutional history. The terms due process *and* equal protection *have been especially troublesome. Was the amendment designed to outlaw racial segregation? Or was the goal simply to prevent the leaders of the rebellious South from gaining political power?*

The framers of the Fourteenth Amendment hoped Article 2 would produce black voters who would increase the power of the Republican Party. The federal government, however, never used its power to punish states for denying blacks their right to vote. Although the Fourteenth Amendment had an immediate impact in giving black Americans citizenship, it did nothing to protect blacks from the vengeance of whites once Reconstruction ended. In the late nineteenth and early twentieth centuries, section 1 of the Fourteenth Amendment was often used to protect business interests and strike down laws protecting workers on the grounds that the rights of "persons," that is, corporations, were protected by "due process." More recently, the Fourteenth Amendment has been used to justify school desegregation and affirmative action programs, as well as to dismantle such programs.

Amendment XV

[Adopted 1870]

Section 1 The right of citizens of the United States to vote shall not be denied or abridged by the United States or by any State on account of race, color, or previous condition of servitude.

Section 2 The Congress shall have power to enforce this article by appropriate legislation.

♦♦♦

▶ *The Fifteenth Amendment was the last major piece of Reconstruction legislation. While earlier Reconstruction acts had already required black suffrage in the South, the Fifteenth Amendment extended black voting rights to the entire nation. Some Republicans felt morally obligated to do away with the double standard between North and South since many northern states had stubbornly refused to enfranchise blacks. Others believed that the freedman's ballot required the extra protection of a constitutional amendment to shield it from white counterattack. But partisan advantage also played an important role in the amendment's passage, since Republicans hoped that by giving the ballot to northern blacks, they could lessen their political vulnerability.*

Many women's rights advocates had fought for the amendment. They had felt betrayed by the inclusion of the word "male" in section 2 of the Fourteenth Amendment and were further angered when the proposed Fifteenth Amendment failed to prohibit denial of the right to vote on the grounds of sex as well as "race, color, or previous condition of servitude." In this amendment, for the first time, the federal government claimed the power to regulate the franchise, or vote. It was also the first time the Constitution placed limits on the power of the states to regulate access to the franchise. Although ratified in 1870, the amendment was not enforced until the twentieth century.

The Progressive Amendments (Sixteenth–Nineteenth Amendments)

▶ *No amendments were added to the Constitution between the Civil War and the Progressive Era. America was changing, however, in fundamental ways. The rapid industrialization of the United States after the Civil War led to many social and economic problems. Hundreds of amendments were proposed, but none received enough support in Congress to be sent to the states. Some scholars believe that regional differences and rivalries were so strong during this period that it was almost impossible to gain a consensus on a constitutional amendment. During the Progressive Era, however, the Constitution was amended four times in seven years.*

Amendment XVI

[Adopted 1913]

The Congress shall have power to lay and collect taxes on incomes, from whatever source derived, without apportionment among the several States, and without regard to any census or enumeration.

♦♦♦

▶ *Until passage of the Sixteenth Amendment, most of the money used to run the federal government came from customs duties and taxes on specific items, such as liquor. During the Civil War, the federal government taxed incomes as an emergency measure. Pressure to enact an income tax came from those who were concerned about the growing gap between rich and poor in the United States. The Populist Party began campaigning for a graduated income tax in 1892, and support continued to grow. By 1909, thirty-three proposed income tax amendments had been presented in Congress, but lobbying by corporate and other special interests had defeated them all. In June 1909, the growing pressure for an income tax, which had been endorsed by Presidents Roosevelt and Taft, finally pushed an amendment through the Senate. The required thirty-six states had ratified the amendment by February 1913.*

Amendment XVII

[Adopted 1913]

Section 1 The Senate of the United States shall be composed of two Senators from each State, elected by the people thereof, for six years; and each Senator shall have one vote. The electors in each State shall have the qualifications requisite for electors of [voters for] the most numerous branch of the State legislatures.

Section 2 When vacancies happen in the representation of any State in the Senate, the executive authority of such State shall issue writs of election to fill such vacancies: Provided, that the Legislature of any State may empower the executive thereof to make temporary appointments until the people fill the vacancies by election as the Legislature may direct.

Section 3 This amendment shall not be so construed as to affect the election or term of any Senator chosen before it becomes valid as part of the Constitution.

♦♦♦

▶ *The framers of the Constitution saw the members of the House as the representatives of the people and the members of the Senate as the representatives of the states. Originally senators were to be chosen by the state legislators. According to reform advocates, however, the growth of private industry and transportation conglomerates during the Gilded Age had created a network of corruption in which wealth and power were exchanged for influence and votes in the Senate. Senator Nelson Aldrich, who represented Rhode Island in the late nineteenth and early twentieth centuries, for example, was known as "the senator from Standard Oil" because of his open support of special business interests.*

Efforts to amend the Constitution to allow direct election of senators had begun in 1826, but since any proposal had to be approved by the Senate, reform seemed impossible. Progressives tried to gain influence in the Senate by instituting party caucuses and primary elections, which gave citizens the chance to express their choice of a senator who could then be officially elected by the state legislature. By 1910, fourteen of the country's thirty senators received popular votes through a state primary before the state legislature made its selection. Despairing of getting a proposal through the Senate, supporters of a direct election amendment had begun in 1893 to seek a convention of representatives from two-thirds of the states to propose an amendment that could then be ratified. By 1905, thirty-one of forty-five states had endorsed such an amendment. Finally, in 1911, despite extraordinary opposition, a proposed amendment passed the Senate; by 1913, it had been ratified.

Amendment XVIII

[Adopted 1919; repealed 1933 by Amendment XXI]

Section 1 After one year from the ratification of this article the manufacture, sale, or transportation of intoxicating liquors within, the importation thereof into, or the exportation thereof from the United States and all territory subject to the jurisdiction thereof, for beverage purposes, is hereby prohibited.

Section 2 The Congress and the several States shall have concurrent power to enforce this article by appropriate legislation.

Section 3 This article shall be inoperative unless it shall have been ratified as an amendment to the Constitution by the legislatures of the several States, as provided by the Constitution, within seven years from the date of the submission thereof to the States by the Congress.

♦♦♦

▶ *The Prohibition Party, formed in 1869, began calling for a constitutional amendment to outlaw alcoholic beverages in 1872. A prohibition amendment was first proposed in the Senate in 1876 and was revived eighteen times before 1913. Between 1913 and 1919, another thirty-nine attempts were made to prohibit liquor in the United States through a constitutional amendment. Prohibition became a key element of the progressive agenda as reformers linked alcohol and drunkenness to numerous social problems, including the corruption of immigrant voters. While opponents of such an amendment argued that it was undemocratic, supporters claimed that their efforts had widespread public support. The admission of twelve "dry" western states to the Union in the early twentieth century and the spirit of sacrifice during World War I laid the groundwork for passage and ratification of the Eighteenth Amendment in 1919. Opponents added a time limit to the amendment in the hope that they could thus block ratification, but this effort failed. (See also Amendment XXI.)*

Amendment XIX

[Adopted 1920]

Section 1 The right of citizens of the United States to vote shall not be denied or abridged by the United States or by any State on account of sex.

Section 2 Congress shall have the power to enforce this article by appropriate legislation.

♦♦♦

▶ *Advocates of women's rights tried and failed to link woman suffrage to the Fourteenth and Fifteenth Amendments. Nonetheless, the effort for woman suffrage continued. Between 1878 and 1912, at least one and sometimes as many as four proposed amendments were introduced in Congress each year to grant women the right to vote. While over time women won very limited voting rights in some states, at both the state and federal levels opposition to an amendment for woman suffrage remained very strong. President Woodrow Wilson and other officials felt that the federal government should not interfere with the power of the states in this matter. Others worried that granting suffrage to women would encourage ethnic minorities to exercise their own right to vote. And many were concerned that giving women the vote would result in their abandoning traditional gender roles. In 1919, following a protracted and often bitter campaign of protest in which women went on hunger strikes and chained themselves to fences, an amendment was introduced with the backing of President Wilson. It narrowly passed the Senate (after efforts to limit the suffrage to white women failed) and was adopted in 1920 after Tennessee became the thirty-sixth state to ratify it.*

Unratified Amendment

Child Labor Amendment (proposed by Congress June 2, 1924)

Section 1 The Congress shall have power to limit, regulate, and prohibit the labor of persons under eighteen years of age.

Section 2 The power of the several States is unimpaired by this article except that the operation of State laws shall be suspended to the extent necessary to give effect to legislation enacted by Congress.

♦♦♦

▶ *Throughout the late nineteenth and early twentieth centuries, alarm over the condition of child workers grew. Opponents of child labor argued that children worked in dangerous and unhealthy conditions, that they took jobs from adult workers, that they depressed wages in certain industries, and that states that allowed child labor had an economic advantage over those that did not. Defenders of child labor claimed that children provided needed income in many families, that working at a young age developed character, and that the effort to prohibit the practice constituted an invasion of family privacy.*

In 1916, Congress passed a law that made it illegal to sell goods made by children through interstate commerce. The Supreme Court, however, ruled that the law violated the limits on the power of Congress to regulate interstate commerce. Congress then tried to penalize industries that used child labor by taxing such goods. This measure was also thrown out by the courts. In response, reformers set out to amend the Constitution. The proposed amendment was ratified by twenty-eight states, but by 1925, thirteen states had rejected it. Passage of the Fair Labor Standards Act in 1938, which was upheld by the Supreme Court in 1941, made the amendment irrelevant.

Amendment XX

[Adopted 1933]

Section 1 The terms of the President and Vice-President shall end at noon on the 20th day of January, and the terms of Senators and Representatives at noon on the 3rd day of January, of the years in which such terms would have ended if this article had not been ratified; and the terms of their successors shall then begin.

Section 2 The Congress shall assemble at least once in every year, and such meeting shall begin at noon on the 3rd day of January, unless they shall by law appoint a different day.

Section 3 If, at the time fixed for the beginning of the term of the President, the President-elect shall have died, the Vice-President-elect shall become President. If a President shall not have been chosen before the time fixed for the beginning of his term, or if the President-elect shall have failed to qualify, then the Vice-President-elect shall act as President until a President shall have qualified; and the Congress may by law provide for the case wherein neither a President-elect nor a Vice-President-elect shall have qualified, declaring who shall then act as President, or the manner in which one who is to act shall be selected, and such person shall act accordingly until a President or Vice-President shall have qualified.

Section 4 The Congress may by law provide for the case of the death of any of the persons from whom the House of Representatives may choose a President whenever the right of choice shall have devolved upon them, and for the case of the death of any of the persons from whom the Senate may choose a Vice-President whenever the right of choice shall have devolved upon them.

Section 5 Sections 1 and 2 shall take effect on the 15th day of October following the ratification of this article.

Section 6 This article shall be inoperative unless it shall have been ratified as an amendment to the Constitution by the Legislatures of three-fourths of the several States within seven years from the date of its submission.

♦♦♦

▶ *Until 1933, presidents took office on March 4. Since elections are held in early November and electoral votes are counted in mid-December, this meant that more than three months passed between the time a new president was elected and when he took office. Moving the inauguration to January shortened the transition period and allowed Congress to begin its term closer to the time of the president's inauguration. Although this seems like a minor change, an amendment was required because the Constitution specifies terms of office. This amendment also deals with questions of succession in the event that a president- or vice president-elect dies before assuming office. Section 3 also clarifies a method for resolving a deadlock in the electoral college.*

Amendment XXI

[Adopted 1933]

Section 1 The eighteenth article of amendment to the Constitution of the United States is hereby repealed.

Section 2 The transportation or importation into any State, Territory, or Possession of the United States for delivery or use therein of intoxicating liquors, in violation of the laws thereof, is hereby prohibited.

Section 3 This article shall be inoperative unless it shall have been ratified as an amendment to the Constitution by conventions in the several States, as provided in the Constitution, within seven years from the date of the submission thereof to the States by the Congress.

♦♦♦

▶ *Widespread violation of the Volstead Act, the law enacted to enforce prohibition, made the United States a nation of lawbreakers. Prohibition caused more problems than it solved by encouraging crime, bribery, and corruption. Further, a coalition of liquor and beer manufacturers, personal liberty advocates, and constitutional scholars joined forces to challenge the amendment. By 1929, thirty proposed repeal amendments had been introduced in Congress, and the Democratic Party made repeal part of its platform in the 1932 presidential campaign. The Twenty-first Amendment was proposed in February 1933 and ratified less than a year later. The failure of the effort to enforce prohibition through a constitutional amendment has often been cited by opponents to subsequent efforts to shape public virtue and private morality.*

Amendment XXII

[Adopted 1951]

Section 1 No person shall be elected to the office of the President more than twice, and no person who has held the office of President, or acted as President, for more than two years of a term to which some other person was elected President shall be elected to the office of President more than once. But this article shall not apply to any person holding the office of President when this Article was proposed by the Congress, and shall not prevent any person who may be holding the office of President, or acting as President, during the term within which this Article becomes operative from holding the office of President or acting as President during the remainder of such term.

Section 2 This article shall be inoperative unless it shall have been ratified as an amendment to the Constitution by the legislatures of three-fourths of the several States within seven years from the date of its submission to the States by the Congress.

♦♦♦

▶ *George Washington's refusal to seek a third term of office set a precedent that stood until 1912, when former president Theodore Roosevelt sought, without success, another term as an independent candidate. Democrat Franklin Roosevelt was the only president to seek and win a fourth term, though he did so amid great controversy. Roosevelt died in April 1945, a few months after the beginning of his fourth term. In 1946, Republicans won control of the House and the Senate, and early in 1947 a proposal for an amendment to limit future presidents to two four-year terms was offered to the states for ratification. Democratic critics of the Twenty-second Amendment charged that it was a partisan posthumous jab at Roosevelt.*

Since the Twenty-second Amendment was adopted, however, the only presidents who might have been able to seek a third term, had it not existed, were Republicans Dwight Eisenhower, Ronald Reagan, and George W. Bush, and Democrat Bill Clinton. Since 1826, Congress has entertained 160 proposed amendments to limit the president to one six-year term. Such amendments have been backed by fifteen presidents, including Gerald Ford and Jimmy Carter.

Amendment XXIII

[Adopted 1961]

Section 1 The District constituting the seat of Government of the United States shall appoint in such manner as the Congress may direct: A number of electors of President and Vice-President equal to the whole number of Senators and Representatives in Congress to which the District would be entitled if it were a State, but in no event more than the least populous State; they shall be in addition to those appointed by the States, but they shall be considered for the purposes of the election of President and Vice-President, to be electors appointed by a State; and they shall meet in the District and perform such duties as provided by the twelfth article of amendment.

Section 2 The Congress shall have the power to enforce this article by appropriate legislation.

♦♦♦

▶ *When Washington, D.C., was established as a federal district, no one expected that a significant number of people would make it their permanent and primary residence. A proposal to allow citizens of the district to vote in presidential elections was approved by Congress in June 1960 and was ratified on March 29, 1961.*

Amendment XXIV

[Adopted 1964]

Section 1 The right of citizens of the United States to vote in any primary or other election for President or Vice-President, for electors for President or Vice-President, or for Senator or Representative in Congress, shall not be denied or abridged by the United States or any State by reason of failure to pay any poll tax or other tax.

Section 2 The Congress shall have the power to enforce this article by appropriate legislation.

♦♦♦

▶ *In the colonial and Revolutionary eras, financial independence was seen as necessary to political independence, and the poll tax was used as a requirement for voting. By the twentieth century, however, the poll tax was used mostly to bar poor people, especially southern blacks, from voting. While conservatives complained that the amendment interfered with states' rights, liberals thought that the amendment did not go far enough because it barred the poll tax only in national elections and not in state or local elections. The amendment was ratified in 1964, however, and two years later, the Supreme Court ruled that poll taxes in state and local elections also violated the equal protection clause of the Fourteenth Amendment.*

Amendment XXV

[Adopted 1967]

Section 1 In case of the removal of the President from office or of his death or resignation, the Vice-President shall become President.

Section 2 Whenever there is a vacancy in the office of the Vice-President, the President shall nominate a Vice-President who shall take office upon confirmation by a majority vote of both Houses of Congress.

Section 3 Whenever the President transmits to the President pro tempore of the Senate and the Speaker of the House of Representatives his written declaration that he is unable to discharge the powers and duties of his office, and until he transmits to them a written declaration to the contrary, such powers and duties shall be discharged by the Vice-President as Acting President.

Section 4 Whenever the Vice-President and a majority of either the principal officers of the executive departments or of such other body as Congress may by law provide, transmit to the President pro tempore of the Senate and the Speaker of the House of Representatives their written declaration that the President is unable to discharge the powers and duties of his office, the Vice-President shall immediately assume the powers and duties of the office as Acting President.

Thereafter, when the President transmits to the President pro tempore of the Senate and the Speaker of the House of Representatives his written declaration that no inability exists, he shall resume the powers and duties of his office unless the Vice-President and a majority of either the principal officers of the executive department[s] or of such other body as Congress may by law provide, transmit within four days to the President pro tempore of the Senate and the Speaker of the House of Representatives their written declaration that the President is unable to discharge the powers and duties of his office. Thereupon Congress shall decide the issue, assembling within forty-eight hours for that purpose if not in session. If the Congress, within twenty-one days after receipt of the latter written declaration, or, if Congress is not in session, within twenty-one days after Congress is required to assemble, determines by two-thirds vote of both Houses that the President is unable to discharge the powers and duties of his office, the Vice-President shall continue to discharge the same as Acting President; otherwise, the President shall resume the powers and duties of his office.

♦♦♦

▶ *The framers of the Constitution established the office of vice president because someone was needed to preside over the Senate. The first president to die in office was William Henry Harrison, in 1841. Vice President John Tyler had himself sworn in as president, setting a precedent that was followed when seven later presidents died in office. The assassination of President James A. Garfield in 1881 posed a new problem, however. After he was shot, the president was incapacitated for two months before he died; he was unable to lead the country, while his vice president, Chester A. Arthur, was unable to assume leadership. Efforts to resolve questions of succession in the event of a presidential disability thus began with the death of Garfield.*

In 1963, the assassination of President John F. Kennedy galvanized Congress to action. Vice President Lyndon Johnson was a chain smoker with a history of heart trouble. According to the 1947 Presidential Succession Act, the two men who stood in line to succeed him were the seventy-two-year-old Speaker of the House and the eighty-six-year-old president of the Senate. There were serious concerns that any of these men might become incapacitated while serving as chief executive. The first time the Twenty-fifth Amendment was used, however, was not in the case of presidential death or illness, but during the Watergate crisis. When Vice President Spiro T. Agnew was forced to resign following allegations of bribery and tax violations, President Richard M. Nixon appointed House Minority Leader Gerald R. Ford vice president. Ford became president following Nixon's resignation eight months later and named Nelson A. Rockefeller as his vice president. Thus, for more than two years, the two highest offices in the country were held by people who had not been elected to them.

Amendment XXVI

[Adopted 1971]

Section 1 The right of citizens of the United States, who are eighteen years of age or older, to vote shall not be denied or abridged by the United States or by any State on account of age.

Section 2 The Congress shall have power to enforce this article by appropriate legislation.

♦♦♦

▶ *Efforts to lower the voting age from twenty-one to eighteen began during World War II. Recognizing that those who were old enough to fight a war should have some say in the government policies that involved them in the war, Presidents Eisenhower, Johnson, and Nixon endorsed the idea. In 1970, the combined pressure of the antiwar movement and the demographic pressure of the baby boom generation led to a Voting Rights Act lowering the voting age in federal, state, and local elections.*

In Oregon v. Mitchell *(1970), the state of Oregon challenged the right of Congress to determine the age at which people could vote in state or local elections. The Supreme Court agreed with Oregon. Since the Voting Rights Act was ruled unconstitutional, the Constitution had to be amended to allow passage of a law that would lower the voting age. The amendment was ratified in a little more than three months, making it the most rapidly ratified amendment in U.S. history.*

Unratified Amendment

Equal Rights Amendment (proposed by Congress March 22, 1972; seven-year deadline for ratification extended to June 30, 1982)

Section 1 Equality of rights under the law shall not be denied or abridged by the United States or by any State on account of sex.

Section 2 The Congress shall have the power to enforce, by appropriate legislation, the provisions of this article.

Section 3 This amendment shall take effect two years after the date of ratification.

♦♦♦

▶ *In 1923, soon after women had won the right to vote, Alice Paul, a leading activist in the woman suffrage movement, proposed an amendment requiring equal treatment of men and women. Opponents of the proposal argued that such an amendment would invalidate laws that protected women and would make women subject to the military draft. After the 1964 Civil Rights Act was adopted, protective workplace legislation was removed anyway.*

The renewal of the women's movement, as a byproduct of the civil rights and antiwar movements, led to a revival of the Equal Rights Amendment (ERA) in Congress. Disagreements over language held up congressional passage of the proposed amendment, but on March 22, 1972, the Senate approved the ERA by a vote of 84 to 8, and it was sent to the states. Six states ratified the amendment within two days, and by the middle of 1973 the amendment seemed well on its way to adoption, with thirty of the needed thirty-eight states having ratified it. In the mid-1970s, however, a powerful "Stop ERA" campaign developed. The campaign portrayed the ERA as a threat to "family values" and traditional relationships between men and women. Although thirty-five states ultimately ratified the ERA, five of those state legislatures voted to rescind ratification, and the amendment was never adopted.

Unratified Amendment

D.C. Statehood Amendment (proposed by Congress August 22, 1978)

Section 1 For purposes of representation in the Congress, election of the President and Vice-President, and article V of this Constitution, the District constituting the seat of government of the United States shall be treated as though it were a State.

Section 2 The exercise of the rights and powers conferred under this article shall be by the people of the District constituting the seat of government, and as shall be provided by Congress.

Section 3 The twenty-third article of amendment to the Constitution of the United States is hereby repealed.

Section 4 This article shall be inoperative, unless it shall have been ratified as an amendment to the Constitution by the legislatures of three-fourths of the several states within seven years from the date of its submission.

♦♦♦

▶ *The 1961 ratification of the Twenty-third Amendment, giving residents of the District of Columbia the right to vote for a president and vice president, inspired an effort to give residents of the district full voting rights. In 1966, President Lyndon Johnson appointed a mayor and city council; in 1971, D.C. residents were allowed to name a nonvoting delegate to the House; and in 1981, residents were allowed to elect the mayor and city council. Congress retained the right to overrule laws that might affect commuters, the height of federal buildings, and selection of judges and prosecutors. The district's nonvoting delegate to Congress, Walter Fauntroy, lobbied fiercely for a congressional amendment granting statehood to the district. In 1978, a proposed amendment was approved and sent to the states. A number of states quickly ratified the amendment, but, like the ERA, the D.C. Statehood Amendment ran into trouble.*

Opponents argued that section 2 created a separate category of "nominal" statehood. They argued that the federal district should be eliminated and that the territory should be reabsorbed into the state of Maryland. Although these theoretical arguments were strong, some scholars believe that racist attitudes toward the predominantly black population of the city were also a factor leading to the defeat of the amendment.

Amendment XXVII

[Adopted 1992]

No law, varying the compensation for the services of the Senators and Representatives, shall take effect, until an election of Representatives shall have intervened.

♦♦♦

▶ *While the Twenty-sixth Amendment was the most rapidly ratified amendment in U.S. history, the Twenty-seventh Amendment had the longest journey to ratification. First proposed by James Madison in 1789 as part of the package that included the Bill of Rights, this amendment had been ratified by only six states by 1791. In 1873, however, it was ratified by Ohio to protest a massive retroactive salary increase by the federal government. Unlike later proposed amendments, this one came with no time limit on ratification.*

In the early 1980s, Gregory D. Watson, a University of Texas economics major, discovered the "lost" amendment and began a single-handed campaign to get state legislators to introduce it for ratification. In 1983, it was accepted by Maine. In 1984, it passed the Colorado legislature. Ratifications trickled in slowly until May 1992, when Michigan and New Jersey became the thirty-eighth and thirty-ninth states, respectively, to ratify. This amendment prevents members of Congress from raising their own salaries without giving voters a chance to vote them out of office before they can benefit from the raises.

THE CONSTITUTION OF THE CONFEDERATE STATES OF AMERICA

▶ *In framing the Constitution of the Confederate States, the authors adopted, with numerous small but significant changes and additions, the language of the Constitution of the United States, and followed the same order of arrangement of articles and sections. The revisions that they made to the original Constitution are shown here. The parts stricken out are enclosed in brackets, and the new matter added in framing the Confederate Constitution is printed in italics.*

Adopted March 11, 1861

WE, the People of the [United States] *Confederated States, each State acting in its sovereign and independent character*, in order to form a [more perfect

Union] *permanent Federal government*, establish Justice, insure domestic Tranquillity [provide for the common defense, promote the general Welfare], and secure the Blessings of Liberty to ourselves and our Posterity, *invoking the favor and guidance of Almighty God*, do ordain and establish this Constitution for the [United] Confederate States of America.

Article I

Section I All legislative Powers herein [granted] *delegated*, shall be vested in a Congress of the [United] *Confederate* States, which shall consist of a Senate and House of Representatives.

Section II The House of Representatives shall be composed of Members chosen every second Year by the People of the several States, and the Electors in each State shall *be citizens of the Confederate States, and* have the Qualifications requisite for Electors of the most numerous Branch of the State Legislature; *but no person of foreign birth, and not a citizen of the Confederate States, shall be allowed to vote for any officer, civil or political, State or federal.*

No Person shall be a Representative who shall not have attained to the Age of twenty-five Years, and [been seven Years a Citizen of the United] *be a citizen of the Confederate States*, and who shall not, when elected, be an Inhabitant of that State in which he shall be chosen.

Representatives and direct Taxes shall be apportioned among the several States which may be included within this [Union] *Confederacy*, according to their respective Numbers, which shall be determined by adding to the whole Number of free Persons, including those bound to Service for a Term of Years, and excluding Indians not taxed, three-fifths of all [other Persons] *slaves*. The actual Enumeration shall be made within three Years after the first Meeting of the Congress of the [United] *Confederate States*, and within every subsequent Term of ten Years, in such Manner as they shall by Law direct. The Number of Representatives shall not exceed one for every [thirty] *fifty* Thousand, but each State shall have at Least one Representative; and until such enumeration shall be made, the State of [New Hampshire shall be entitled to choose three, Massachusetts eight, Rhode Island and Providence Plantations one, Connecticut five, New York six, New Jersey four, Pennsylvania eight, Delaware one, Maryland six, Virginia ten, North Carolina five, South Carolina five, and Georgia three] *South Carolina shall be entitled to choose six, the State of Georgia ten, the State of Alabama nine, the State of Florida two, the State of Mississippi seven, the State of Louisiana six, and the State of Texas six.*

When vacancies happen in the Representation from any State, the Executive Authority thereof shall issue Writs of Election to fill such Vacancies.

The House of Representatives shall choose their Speaker and other Officers; and shall have the sole Power of Impeachment; *except that any judicial or other federal officer resident and acting solely within the limits of any State, may be impeached by a vote of two-thirds of both branches of the Legislature thereof.*

Section III The Senate of the [United] *Confederate* States shall be composed of two Senators from each State, chosen by the Legislature thereof, for six Years, *at the regular session next immediately preceding the commencement of the term of service*; and each Senator shall have one Vote.

Immediately after they shall be assembled in Consequence of the first Election, they shall be divided as equally as may be into three Classes. The Seats of the Senators of the first Class shall be vacated at the Expiration of the second Year, of the second Class at the Expiration of the fourth Year, and of the third Class at the Expiration of the sixth Year, so that one-third may be chosen every second Year; and if Vacancies happen by Resignation, or otherwise, during the Recess of the Legislature of any State, the Executive thereof may make temporary Appointments until the next Meeting of the Legislature, which shall then fill such Vacancies.

No Person shall be a Senator who shall not have attained to the Age of thirty Years, and [been nine Years a Citizen of the United] *be a citizen of the Confederate* States, and who shall not, when elected, be an Inhabitant of that State for which he shall be chosen.

The Vice President of the [United] *Confederate* States shall be President of the Senate, but shall have no Vote, unless they be equally divided.

The Senate shall choose their other Officers, and also a President pro tempore, in the Absence of the Vice President, or when he shall exercise the Office of President of the United States.

The Senate shall have the sole Power to try all Impeachments. When sitting for that Purpose, they shall be on Oath or Affirmation. When the President of the [United] *Confederate* States is tried, the Chief Justice shall preside: And no Person shall be convicted without the Concurrence of two-thirds of the Members present.

Judgment in Cases of Impeachment shall not extend further than to removal from Office, and Disqualification to hold and enjoy any Office of honour, Trust or Profit under the [United] *Confederate* States; but the Party convicted shall nevertheless be liable and subject to Indictment, Trial, Judgment and Punishment, according to Law.

Section IV The Times, Places and Manner of holding Elections for Senators and Representatives, shall be prescribed in each State by the Legislature thereof, *subject to the provisions of this Constitution*; but the Congress may at any time by Law make or alter such Regulations, except as to the *times and* places of choosing Senators.

The Congress shall assemble at least once in every Year, and such Meeting shall be on the first Monday in December, unless they shall by Law appoint a different Day.

Section V Each House shall be the Judge of the Elections, Returns and Qualifications of its own Members, and a Majority of each shall constitute a Quorum to do Business; but a smaller Number may adjourn from day to day, and may be authorized to compel the Attendance of absent Members, in such Manner, and under such Penalties as each House may provide.

Each House may determine the Rules of its Proceedings, punish its Members for disorderly Behaviour, and, with the Concurrence of two-thirds *of the whole number* expel a Member.

Each House shall keep a Journal of its Proceedings, and from time to time publish the same, excepting such Parts as may in their Judgment require Secrecy; and the Yeas and Nays of the Members of either House on any question shall, at the Desire of one-fifth of those Present, be entered on the Journal.

Neither House, during the Session of Congress, shall, without the Consent of the other, adjourn for more than three days, nor to any other Place than that in which the two Houses shall be sitting.

Section VI The Senators and Representatives shall receive a Compensation for their Services, to be ascertained by Law, and paid out of the Treasury of the [United] *Confederate* States. They shall in all Cases, except Treason [Felony] and Breach of the Peace, be privileged from Arrest during their Attendance at the Session of their respective Houses, and in going to and returning from the same; and for any Speech or Debate in either House, they shall not be questioned in any other Place.

No Senator or Representative shall, during the Time for which he was elected, be appointed to any civil Office under the Authority of the [United] *Confederate* States, which shall have been created, or the Emoluments whereof shall have been increased during such time; and no Person holding any Office under the [United] *Confederate* States, shall be a Member of either House during his Continuance in Office. *But Congress may, by law, grant to the principal officers in each of the executive departments a seat upon the floor of either House, with the privilege of discussing any measures appertaining to his department.*

Section VII All Bills for raising Revenue shall originate in the House of Representatives; but the Senate may propose or concur with Amendments as on other Bills.

Every Bill which shall have passed [the House of Representatives and the Senate] *both Houses*, shall, before it become a Law, be presented to the President of the [United] *Confederate* States; If he approve he shall sign it, but if not he shall return it, with his Objections to that House in which it shall have originated, who shall enter the Objections at large on their Journal, and proceed to reconsider it. If after such Reconsideration two-thirds of that House shall agree to pass the Bill, it shall be sent, together with the Objections, to the other House, by which it shall likewise be reconsidered, and if approved by two-thirds of that House, it shall become a Law. But in all *such* Cases the Votes of both Houses shall be determined by Yeas and Nays, and the Names of the Persons voting for and against the Bill shall be entered on the Journal of each House respectively. If any Bill shall not be returned by the President within ten Days (Sundays excepted) after it shall have been presented to him, the Same shall be a law, in like Manner as if he had signed it, unless the Congress by their Adjournment prevent its return, in which Case it shall not be a Law. *The President may approve any appropriation and disapprove any other appropriation in the same bill. In such case he shall, in signing the bill, designate the appropriation disapproved, and shall return a copy of such appropriation, with his objections, to the House in which the bill shall have originated; and the same proceedings shall then be had as in case of other bills disapproved by the President.*

Every Order, Resolution, or Vote to which the Concurrence of [the Senate and House of Representatives] *both Houses* may be necessary (except on a question of Adjournment), shall be presented to the President of the [United] *Confederate* States; and before the Same shall take Effect, shall be approved by him, or being disapproved by him, [shall] *may* be repassed by two-thirds of [the Senate and House of Representatives] *both Houses*, according to the Rules and Limitations prescribed in the Case of a Bill.

Section VIII The Congress shall have Power.

To lay and collect Taxes, Duties, Imposts and *Excises, for revenue necessary* to pay the Debts [and], provide for the common Defense [and general Welfare of the United States; but], *and carry on the government of the Confederate States; but no bounties shall be granted from the treasury, nor shall any duties, or taxes, or importation from foreign nations be laid to promote or foster any branch of industry; and* all Duties, Imposts and Excises shall be uniform throughout the [United] Confederate States;

To borrow Money on the credit of the [United] Confederate States;

To regulate Commerce with foreign Nations, and among the several States, and with the Indian Tribes; *but neither this, nor any other clause contained in this Constitution, shall ever be construed to delegate the power to Congress to appropriate money for any internal improvement intended to facilitate commerce; except for the purpose of furnishing lights, beacons, and buoys, and other aids to navigation upon the coasts, and the improvement of harbors, and the removing of obstructions in river navigation; in all such cases such duties shall be laid on the navigation facilitated thereby, as may be necessary to pay the costs and expenses thereof;*

To establish an uniform Rule of Naturalization, and uniform Laws on the subject of Bankruptcies throughout the [United] *Confederate* States; *but no law of Congress shall discharge any debt contracted before the passage of the same;*

To coin Money, regulate the Value thereof, and of foreign Coin, and fix the Standard of Weights and Measures;

To provide for the Punishment of counterfeiting the Securities and current Coin of the [United] *Confederate* States;

To establish Post Offices and post [Roads] *routes; but the expenses of the Postoffice Department, after the first day of March, in the year of our Lord eighteen hundred and sixty-three, shall be paid out of its own revenues*;

To promote the progress of Science and useful Arts, by securing for limited Times to Authors and Inventors the exclusive Right to their respective Writings and Discoveries;

To constitute Tribunals inferior to the supreme Court;

To define and punish Piracies and Felonies committed on the high Seas, and Offences against the Law of Nations;

To declare War, grant Letters of Marque and Reprisal, and make Rules concerning Captures on Land and Water;

To raise and support Armies, but no Appropriation of Money to that Use shall be for a longer Term than two Years;

To provide and maintain a Navy;

To make Rules for the Government and Regulation of the land and naval Forces;

To provide for calling forth the Militia to execute the Laws of the [Union] *Confederate States*, suppress Insurrections and repel Invasions;

To provide for organizing, arming, and disciplining the Militia and for governing such Part of them as may be employed in the Service of the [United] *Confederate* States, reserving to the States respectively, the Appointment of the Officers, and the Authority of training the Militia according to the Discipline prescribed by Congress;

To exercise exclusive Legislation in all Cases whatsoever, over such District (not exceeding ten Miles square) as may, by Cession of particular States, and the Acceptance of Congress, become the Seat of the Government of the [United] *Confederate* States, and to exercise like Authority over all Places purchased by the Consent of the Legislature of the State in which the Same shall be, for the Erection of Forts, Magazines, Arsenals, Dock Yards, and other needful Buildings;—And

To make all Laws which shall be necessary and proper for carrying into Execution the foregoing Powers, and all other Powers vested by this Constitution in the Government of the [United] *Confederate* States or in any Department or Officer thereof.

Section IX [The Migration or Importation of such Persons as any of the States now existing shall think proper to admit, shall not be prohibited by the Congress prior to the Year one thousand eight hundred and eight, but a Tax or Duty may be imposed on such Importation, not exceeding ten dollars for each Person.] *The importation of negroes of the African race from any foreign country other than the slaveholding States or territories of the United States of America, is hereby forbidden; and Congress is required to pass such laws as shall effectually prevent the same. Congress shall also have power to prohibit the introduction of slaves from any State not a member of, or territory not belonging to, this Confederacy.*

The Privilege of the Writ of Habeas Corpus shall not be suspended, unless when in Cases of Rebellion or Invasion the public Safety may require it. No Bill of Attainder or ex post facto Law, *or law denying or impairing the right of property in negro slaves*, shall be passed.

No Capitation, or other direct, Tax shall be laid, unless in Proportion to the Census or Enumeration herein before directed to be taken.

No Tax or Duty shall be laid on Articles exported from any State, *except by a vote of two-thirds of both Houses*.

No Preference shall be given by any Regulation of Commerce or Revenue to the Ports of one State over those of another; nor shall Vessels bound to, or from, one State, be obliged to enter, clear, or pay Duties in another.

No Money shall be drawn from the Treasury, but in Consequence of Appropriations made by Law; and a regular Statement and Account of the Receipts and Expenditures of all public Money shall be published from time to time.

Congress shall appropriate no money from the Treasury except by a vote of two-thirds of both Houses, taken by yeas and nays, unless it be asked and estimated for by some one of the heads of departments and submitted to Congress by the President; or for the purpose of paying its own expenses and contingencies; or for the payment of claims against the Confederate States, the justice of which shall have been officially declared by a tribunal for the investigation of claims against the Government, which it is hereby made the duty of Congress to establish.

All bills appropriating money shall specify in Federal currency the exact amount of each appropriation and the purposes for which it is made; and Congress shall grant no extra compensation to any public contractor, officer, agent or servant, after such contract shall have been made or such service rendered.

No Title of Nobility shall be granted by the [United] *Confederate States*; and no Person holding any Office of Profit or Trust under them, shall, without the Consent of the Congress, accept of any present, Emolument, Office, or Title, of any kind whatever, from any King, Prince or foreign State.

[*Here the framers of the Confederate Constitution insert the U.S. Bill of Rights.*] Congress shall make no law respecting an establishment of religion, or prohibiting the free exercise thereof; or abridging the freedom of speech, or of the press; or the right of the people peaceably to assemble, and to petition the Government for a redress of grievances.

A well-regulated Militia, being necessary to the security of a free State, the right of the people to keep and bear Arms shall not be infringed.

No Soldier shall, in time of peace, be quartered in any house, without the consent of the Owner, nor in time of war, but in a manner to be prescribed by law.

The right of the people to be secure in their persons, houses, papers, and effects, against unreasonable searches and seizures, shall not be violated, and no Warrants shall issue, but upon probable cause, supported by Oath or affirmation, and particularly describing the place to be searched, and the persons or things to be seized.

No person shall be held to answer for a capital, or otherwise infamous crime, unless on a presentment or indictment of a Grand Jury, except in cases arising in the land or naval forces, or in the Militia, when in actual service in time of War or public danger; nor shall any person be subject for the same offence to be twice put in jeopardy of life or limb; nor shall be compelled in any Criminal Case to be a witness against himself, nor be deprived of life, liberty or property without due process of law; nor shall private property be taken for public use, without just compensation.

In all criminal prosecutions, the accused shall enjoy the right to a speedy and public trial, by an impartial jury of the State and district wherein the crime shall have been committed, which district shall have been previously ascertained by law, and to be informed of the nature and cause of the accusation; to be confronted with the witnesses against him; to have Compulsory process for obtaining Witnesses in his favour, and to have the Assistance of Counsel for his defence.

In Suits at common law, where the value in controversy shall exceed twenty dollars, the right of trial by jury shall be preserved, and no fact tried by a jury shall be otherwise reexamined in any Court of the [United] *Confederate* States, than according to the rules of the common law.

Excessive bail shall not be required, nor excessive fines imposed, nor cruel and unusual punishments inflicted.

Every law or resolution having the force of law, shall relate to but one subject, and that shall be expressed in the title.

Section X No State shall enter into any Treaty, Alliance, or Confederation; grant Letters of Marque and Reprisal; coin Money; [emit Bills of Credit;] make any Thing but gold and silver Coin a Tender in Payment of Debts; pass any Bill of Attainder, or ex post facto Law, or Law impairing the Obligation of Contracts, or grant any Title of Nobility.

No State shall, without the consent of the Congress, lay any Imposts or Duties on Imports or Exports, except what may be absolutely necessary for executing its inspection Laws: and the net Produce of all Duties and Imposts, laid by any State on Imports or Exports, shall be for the Use of the Treasury of the [United] *Confederate* States; and all such Laws shall be subject to the Revision and Control of the Congress.

No State shall, without the Consent of Congress, lay any Duty of Tonnage, *except on seagoing vessels, for the improvement of its rivers and harbors navigated by the said vessels; but such duties shall not conflict with any treaties of the Confederate States with foreign nations; and any surplus of revenue thus derived shall, after making such improvement, be paid into the common treasury; nor shall any State* keep Troops, or Ships of War in time of Peace, enter into any Agreement or Compact with another State, or with a foreign Power, or engage in War, unless actually invaded, or in such imminent Danger as will not admit of Delay. *But when any river divides or flows through two or more States, they may enter into compacts with each other to improve the navigation thereof.*

Article II

Section I [The executive Power shall be vested in a President of the United States of America. He shall hold his Office during the Term of four Years, and, together with the Vice President, chosen for the same Term, be elected, as follows:] *The executive power shall be vested in a President of the Confederate States of America. He and the Vice President shall hold their offices for the term of six years; but the President shall not be reeligible.*

The President and Vice President shall be elected as follows: Each State shall appoint in such Manner as the Legislature thereof may direct, a Number of Electors, equal to the whole Number of Senators and Representatives to which the State may be entitled in the Congress; but no Senator or Representative, or Person holding an Office of Trust or Profit under the [United] *Confederate* States, shall be appointed an Elector.

The Electors shall meet in their respective States, and vote by ballot for President and Vice President, one of whom, at least, shall not be an inhabitant of the same State with themselves; they shall name in their ballots the person voted for as President, and in distinct ballots the person voted for as Vice President, and they shall make distinct lists of all persons voted for as President, and of all persons voted for as Vice President, and of the number of votes for each, which lists they shall sign and certify, and transmit sealed to the seat of the government of the [United] *Confederate* States, directed to the President of the Senate;— The President of the Senate shall, in the presence of the Senate and House of Representatives, open all the certificates and the votes shall then be counted;—The person having the greatest number of votes for President shall be the President, if such number be a majority of the whole number of Electors appointed; and if no person have such majority, then from the persons having the highest numbers not exceeding three on the list of those voted for as President, the House of Representatives shall choose immediately, by ballot, the President. But in choosing the President, the votes shall be taken by States, the representation from each State having one vote; a quorum for this purpose shall consist of a member or members from two-thirds of the States, and a majority of all the States shall be necessary to a choice. And if the House of Representatives shall not choose a President whenever the right of choice shall devolve upon them, before the fourth day of March next following, then the Vice President shall act as President, as in the case of the death or other constitutional disability of the President. The person having the greatest number of votes as Vice President shall be the Vice President, if such number be a majority of the whole number of Electors appointed, and if no person have a majority, then from the two highest numbers on the list the Senate shall choose the Vice President; a quorum for the purpose shall consist of two-thirds of the whole number of Senators, and a majority of the whole number shall be necessary to a choice. But no person constitutionally ineligible to the office of President shall be eligible to that of Vice President of the [United] *Confederate* States.

The Congress may determine the Time of choosing the Electors, and the Day on which they shall give their Votes; which Day shall be the same throughout the [United] *Confederate* States.

No Person except a natural-born Citizen [or a Citizen of the United States] *of the Confederate States, or a citizen thereof,* at the time of the Adoption of this Constitution, *or a citizen thereof born in the United States prior to the 20th of December, 1860,* shall be eligible to the Office of President; neither shall any Person be eligible to that Office who shall not have attained to the Age of thirty-five Years, and been fourteen Years a Resident within the [United States] *limits of the Confederate States, as they may exist at the time of his election.*

In Cases of the Removal of the President from Office, or of his Death, Resignation, or Inability to discharge the Powers and Duties of the said Office, the same shall devolve on the Vice President, and the Congress may by Law provide for the Case of Removal, Death, Resignation, or Inability, both of the President and Vice President, declaring what Officer shall then act as President, and such Officer shall act accordingly, until the Disability be removed, or a President shall be elected.

The President shall, at stated Times, receive for his Services, a Compensation, which shall neither be increased nor diminished during the Period for which he shall have been elected, and he shall not receive within that Period any other Emolument from the [United] *Confederate* States or any of them.

Before he enters on the Execution of his Office, he shall take the following Oath or Affirmation—"I do solemnly swear (or affirm) that I will faithfully execute the Office of President of the [United] *Confederate* States, and will to the best of my Ability, preserve, protect and defend the Constitution [of the United States] *thereof.*"

Section II The President shall be Commander in Chief of the Army and Navy of the [United] *Confederate* States, and of the Militia of the several States, when called into the actual Service of the [United] *Confederate* States; he may require the Opinion, in writing, of the principal Officer in each of the executive Departments, upon any Subject relating to the Duties of their respective Offices, and he shall have Power to grant Reprieves and Pardons for Offenses against the [United] *Confederate* States, except in Cases of Impeachment.

He shall have Power, by and with the Advice and Consent of the Senate, to make Treaties, provided two-thirds of the Senators present concur; and he shall nominate, and by and with the Advice and Consent of the Senate, shall appoint Ambassadors, other public Ministers and Consuls, Judges of the supreme Court, and all other Officers of the [United] *Confederate* States, whose Appointments are not herein otherwise provided for, and which shall be established by Law: but the Congress may by Law vest the Appointment of such inferior Officers, as they think proper, in the President alone, in the Courts of Law, or in the Heads of Departments. *The principal officer in each of the executive departments, and all persons connected with the diplomatic service, may be removed from office at the pleasure of the President. All other civil officers of the executive department may be removed at any time by the President, or other appointing power, when their services are unnecessary, or for dishonesty, incapacity, inefficiency, misconduct, or neglect of duty; and when so removed, the removal shall be reported to the Senate, together with the reasons therefor.*

The President shall have Power to fill [up] all Vacancies that may happen during the Recess of the Senate, by granting Commissions which shall expire at the End of their next Session.

Section III [He] *The President* shall from time to time give to the Congress Information of the State of the [Union] *Confederacy,* and recommend to their Consideration such Measures as he shall judge necessary and expedient; he may, on extraordinary Occasions, convene both Houses, or either of them, and in Case of Disagreement between them, with Respect to the Time of Adjournment, he may adjourn them to such Time as he shall think proper; he shall receive Ambassadors and other public Ministers; he shall take Care that the Laws be faithfully executed, and shall Commission all the officers of the [United] *Confederate* States.

Section IV The President, Vice President and all civil Officers of the [United] *Confederate* States, shall be removed from Office or Impeachment for, and Conviction of, Treason, Bribery, or other high Crimes and Misdemeanors.

Article III

Section I The judicial Power of the [United] *Confederate* States shall be vested in one [supreme] *Superior* Court, and in such inferior Courts as the Congress may from time to time ordain and establish. The Judges, both of the supreme and inferior Courts, shall hold their Offices during good Behavior, and shall, at stated Times, receive for their Services a Compensation, which shall not be diminished during their Continuance in Office.

Section II The judicial Power shall extend to all cases [in Law and Equity, arising under this Constitution], *arising under this Constitution, in law and equity,* the Laws of the [United] Confederate States, and Treaties made, or which shall be made, under their Authority;—to all Cases affecting Ambassadors, other public Ministers, and Consuls;—to all Cases of admiralty and maritime Jurisdiction;—to Controversies to which the [United] *Confederate* States shall be a Party;—to Controversies between two or more States;—between a State and Citizens of another State *where the State is plaintiff;—between* Citizens *claiming lands under grants* of different States,—[between Citizens of the same State claiming Lands under Grants of different States,] and between a State, or the Citizens thereof, and foreign States, Citizens or Subjects; *but no State shall be sued by a citizen or subject of any foreign State.*

In all Cases affecting Ambassadors, other public Ministers and Consuls, and those in which a State shall be Party, the supreme Court shall have original Jurisdiction. In all the other Cases before mentioned, the supreme Court shall have appellate Jurisdiction, both as to Law and Fact, with such Exceptions, and under such Regulations as the Congress shall make.

The Trial of all Crimes, except in Cases of Impeachment, shall be by Jury; and such Trial shall be held in the State where the said Crime[s] shall have been committed; but when not committed within any State, the Trial shall be at such Place or Places as the Congress may by Law have directed.

Section III Treason against the [United] *Confederate* States shall consist only in levying War against them, or in adhering to their Enemies, giving them Aid and Comfort. No Person shall be convicted of Treason unless on the Testimony of two Witnesses to the same overt Act, or on Confession in open Court.

The Congress shall have Power to declare the Punishment of Treason, but no Attainder of Treason shall work Corruption of Blood, or Forfeiture except during the Life of the Person attainted.

Article IV

Section I Full Faith and Credit shall be given in each State to the public Acts, Records, and judicial Proceedings of every other State. And the Congress may by general Laws prescribe the Manner in which such Acts, Records and Proceedings shall be proved, and the Effect thereof.

Section II The Citizens of each State shall be entitled to all Privileges and Immunities of Citizens in the several States, *and shall have the right of transit and sojourn in any State of this Confederacy, with their slaves and other property; and the right of property in such slaves shall not be impaired.*

A Person charged in any State with Treason, Felony, or other Crime, who shall flee from Justice, and be found in another State, shall on Demand of the executive Authority of the State from which he fled, be delivered up, to be removed to the State having Jurisdiction of the Crime.

No *slave* or Person held to Service or Labor in [one State] *any State or Territory of the Confederate States* under the Laws thereof, escaping *or unlawfully carried* into another, shall, in Consequence of any Law or Regulation therein, be discharged from such Service or Labor, but shall be delivered up on Claim of the Party to whom such *slave belongs, or to whom such* Service or Labor may be due.

Section III [New States may be admitted by the Congress into this Union;] *Other States may be admitted into this Confederacy by a vote of two-thirds of the whole House of Representatives and two-thirds of the Senate, the Senate voting by States*; but no new State shall be formed or erected within the Jurisdiction of any other State; nor any State be formed by the Junction of two or more States, or Parts of States, without the Consent of the Legislatures of the States concerned as well as of the Congress.

The Congress shall have Power to dispose of and make all needful Rules and Regulations [respecting the Territory or other Property belonging to the United States; and nothing in this Constitution shall be so construed as to Prejudice any Claims of the United States, or of any particular State] *concerning the property of the Confederate States, including the lands thereof.*

The Confederate States may acquire new territory, and Congress shall have power to legislate and provide governments for the inhabitants of all territory belonging to the Confederate States lying without the limits of the several States, and may permit them, at such times and in such manner as it may by law provide, to form States to be admitted into the Confederacy. In all such territory the institution of negro slavery as it now exists in the Confederate States shall be recognized and protected by Congress and by the territorial government, and the inhabitants of the several Confederate States and territories shall have the right to take to such territory any slaves lawfully held by them in any of the States or Territories of the Confederate States.

Section IV The [United] *Confederate* States shall guarantee to every State [in this Union] *that now is, or hereafter may become, a member of this Confederacy,* a Republican Form of Government, and shall protect each of them against Invasion; and on Application of the Legislature, or of the Executive (when the Legislature [cannot be convened] *is not in session*) against domestic Violence.

Article V

[The Congress, whenever two-thirds of both Houses shall deem it necessary, shall propose Amendments to this Constitution, or on the Application of the Legislatures of two-thirds of the several States, shall call a Convention for proposing Amendments, which, in either Case, shall be valid to all Intents and Purposes, as Part of this Constitution, when ratified by the Legislatures of three-fourths of the several States, or by Conventions in three-fourths thereof, as the one or the other Mode of Ratification may be proposed by the Congress; Provided that no Amendment which may be made prior to the Year one thousand eight hundred and eight shall in any Manner affect the first and fourth Clauses in the Ninth Section of the first Article; and that no State, without its Consent, shall be deprived of its equal Suffrage in the Senate.] *Upon the demand of any three States, legally assembled in their several Conventions, the Congress shall summon a Convention of all the States, to take into consideration such amendments to the Constitution as the said States shall concur in suggesting at the time when the said demand is made; and should any of the proposed amendments to the Constitution be agreed on by the said Convention—voting by States—and the same be ratified by the Legislatures of two-thirds of the several States, or by Conventions in two-thirds thereof—as the one or the other mode of ratification may be proposed by the general Convention—they shall henceforward form a part of this Constitution. But no State shall, without its consent, be deprived of its equal representation in the Senate.*

Article VI

The Government established by this Constitution is the successor of the Provisional Government of the Confederate States of America, and all laws passed by the latter shall continue in force until the same shall be repealed or modified; and all the officers appointed by the same shall remain in office until their successors are appointed and qualified or the offices abolished.

All Debts contracted and Engagements entered into, before the Adoption of this Constitution, shall be as valid against the [United] *Confederate* States under this Constitution, as under the [Confederation] *Provisional Government.*

This Constitution and the Laws of the [United] *Confederate* States [which shall be] made in Pursuance thereof; and all Treaties made, or which shall be made, under the authority of the [United] *Confederate* States, shall be the supreme Law of the Land; and the Judges in every State shall be bound thereby, any Thing in the Constitution or Laws of any State to the Contrary notwithstanding.

The Senators and Representatives before mentioned, and the Members of the several State Legislatures, and all executive and judicial Officers, both of the [United] *Confederate* States and of the several States, shall be bound by Oath or Affirmation, to support this Constitution; but no religious Test shall ever be required as a Qualification to any Office or public Trust under the [United] *Confederate* States.

The enumeration in the Constitution, of certain rights, shall not be construed to deny or disparage others retained by the people *of the several States.*

The powers not delegated to the [United] *Confederate* States by the Constitution, nor prohibited by it to the States, are reserved to the States respectively, or to the people.

Article VII

The Ratification of the Conventions of [nine] *five* States shall be sufficient for the Establishment of this Constitution between the States so ratifying the same.

When five States shall have ratified this Constitution, in the manner before specified, the Congress under the Provisional Constitution shall prescribe the time for holding the election of President and Vice President; and for the meeting of the electoral college; and for counting the votes and inaugurating the President. They shall also prescribe the time for holding the first election of members of Congress under this Constitution, and the time for assembling the same. Until the assembling of such Congress, the Congress under the Provisional Constitution shall continue to exercise the legislative powers granted them, not extending beyond the time limited by the Constitution of the Provisional Government.

[Done in Convention by the Unanimous Consent of the States present, the Seventeenth Day of September in the Year of our Lord one thousand seven hundred and eighty-seven and of the Independence of the United States of America the Twelfth.] *Adopted unanimously March 11, 1861.*

APPENDIX II. Facts and Figures: Government, Economy, and Demographics

U.S. Politics and Government

PRESIDENTIAL ELECTIONS

Year	Candidates	Parties	Popular Vote	Percentage of Popular Vote	Electoral Vote	Percentage of Voter Participation
1789	**GEORGE WASHINGTON (Va.)***				69	
	John Adams				34	
	Others				35	
1792	**GEORGE WASHINGTON (Va.)**				132	
	John Adams				77	
	George Clinton				50	
	Others				5	
1796	**JOHN ADAMS (Mass.)**	Federalist			71	
	Thomas Jefferson	Democratic-Republican			68	
	Thomas Pinckney	Federalist			59	
	Aaron Burr	Dem.-Rep.			30	
	Others				48	
1800	**THOMAS JEFFERSON (Va.)**	Dem.-Rep.			73	
	Aaron Burr	Dem.-Rep.			73	
	John Adams	Federalist			65	
	C. C. Pinckney	Federalist			64	
	John Jay	Federalist			1	
1804	**THOMAS JEFFERSON (Va.)**	Dem.-Rep.			162	
	C. C. Pinckney	Federalist			14	
1808	**JAMES MADISON (Va.)**	Dem.-Rep.			122	
	C. C. Pinckney	Federalist			47	
	George Clinton	Dem.-Rep.			6	
1812	**JAMES MADISON (Va.)**	Dem.-Rep.			128	
	De Witt Clinton	Federalist			89	
1816	**JAMES MONROE (Va.)**	Dem.-Rep.			183	
	Rufus King	Federalist			34	
1820	**JAMES MONROE (Va.)**	Dem.-Rep.			231	
	John Quincy Adams	Dem.-Rep.			1	
1824	**JOHN Q. ADAMS (Mass.)**	Dem.-Rep.	108,740	30.5	84	26.9
	Andrew Jackson	Dem.-Rep.	153,544	43.1	99	
	William H. Crawford	Dem.-Rep.	46,618	13.1	41	
	Henry Clay	Dem.-Rep.	47,136	13.2	37	
1828	**ANDREW JACKSON (Tenn.)**	Democratic	647,286	56.0	178	57.6
	John Quincy Adams	National Republican	508,064	44.0	83	
1832	**ANDREW JACKSON (Tenn.)**	Democratic	687,502	55.0	219	55.4
	Henry Clay	National Republican	530,189	42.4	49	
	John Floyd	Independent			11	
	William Wirt	Anti-Mason	33,108	2.6	7	

*State of residence when elected president.

Year	Candidates	Parties	Popular Vote	Percentage of Popular Vote	Electoral Vote	Percentage of Voter Participation
1836	**MARTIN VAN BUREN (N.Y.)**	Democratic	765,483	50.9	170	57.8
	W. H. Harrison	Whig			73	
	Hugh L. White	Whig	739,795	49.1	26	
	Daniel Webster	Whig			14	
	W. P. Mangum	Independent			11	
1840	**WILLIAM H. HARRISON (Ohio)**	Whig	1,274,624	53.1	234	78.0
	Martin Van Buren	Democratic	1,127,781	46.9	60	
	J. G. Birney	Liberty	7,069		—	
1844	**JAMES K. POLK (Tenn.)**	Democratic	1,338,464	49.6	170	78.9
	Henry Clay	Whig	1,300,097	48.1	105	
	J. G. Birney	Liberty	62,300	2.3	—	
1848	**ZACHARY TAYLOR (La.)**	Whig	1,360,099	47.4	163	72.7
	Lewis Cass	Democratic	1,220,544	42.5	127	
	Martin Van Buren	Free-Soil	291,263	10.1	—	
1852	**FRANKLIN PIERCE (N.H.)**	Democratic	1,601,117	50.9	254	69.6
	Winfield Scott	Whig	1,385,453	44.1	42	
	John P. Hale	Free-Soil	155,825	5.0	—	
1856	**JAMES BUCHANAN (Pa.)**	Democratic	1,832,995	45.3	174	78.9
	John C. Frémont	Republican	1,339,932	33.1	114	
	Millard Fillmore	American	871,731	21.6	8	
1860	**ABRAHAM LINCOLN (Ill.)**	Republican	1,866,452	39.8	180	81.2
	Stephen A. Douglas	Democratic	1,375,157	29.4	12	
	John C. Breckinridge	Democratic	847,953	18.1	72	
	John Bell	Union	590,631	12.6	39	
1864	**ABRAHAM LINCOLN (Ill.)**	Republican	2,213,665	55.1	212	73.8
	George B. McClellan	Democratic	1,805,237	44.9	21	
1868	**ULYSSES S. GRANT (Ill.)**	Republican	3,012,833	52.7	214	78.1
	Horatio Seymour	Democratic	2,703,249	47.3	80	
1872	**ULYSSES S. GRANT (Ill.)**	Republican	3,597,132	55.6	286	71.3
	Horace Greeley	Democratic; Liberal Republican	2,834,125	43.9	66	
1876	**RUTHERFORD B. HAYES (Ohio)**	Republican	4,036,298	48.0	185	81.8
	Samuel J. Tilden	Democratic	4,288,590	51.0	184	
1880	**JAMES A. GARFIELD (Ohio)**	Republican	4,454,416	48.5	214	79.4
	Winfield S. Hancock	Democratic	4,444,952	48.1	155	
1884	**GROVER CLEVELAND (N.Y.)**	Democratic	4,874,986	48.5	219	77.5
	James G. Blaine	Republican	4,851,981	48.3	182	
1888	**BENJAMIN HARRISON (Ind.)**	Republican	5,439,853	47.9	233	79.3
	Grover Cleveland	Democratic	5,540,309	48.6	168	
1892	**GROVER CLEVELAND (N.Y.)**	Democratic	5,555,426	46.1	277	74.7
	Benjamin Harrison	Republican	5,182,690	43.0	145	
	James B. Weaver	People's	1,029,846	8.5	22	
1896	**WILLIAM McKINLEY (Ohio)**	Republican	7,104,779	51.1	271	79.3
	William J. Bryan	Democratic-People's	6,502,925	47.7	176	
1900	**WILLIAM McKINLEY (Ohio)**	Republican	7,207,923	51.7	292	73.2
	William J. Bryan	Dem.-Populist	6,358,133	45.5	155	
1904	**THEODORE ROOSEVELT (N.Y.)**	Republican	7,623,486	57.9	336	65.2
	Alton B. Parker	Democratic	5,077,911	37.6	140	
	Eugene V. Debs	Socialist	402,283	3.0	—	
1908	**WILLIAM H. TAFT (Ohio)**	Republican	7,678,908	51.6	321	65.4
	William J. Bryan	Democratic	6,409,104	43.1	162	
	Eugene V. Debs	Socialist	420,793	2.8	—	

Year	Candidates	Parties	Popular Vote	Percentage of Popular Vote	Electoral Vote	Percentage of Voter Participation
1912	**WOODROW WILSON (N.J.)**	Democratic	6,293,454	41.9	435	58.8
	Theodore Roosevelt	Progressive	4,119,538	27.4	88	
	William H. Taft	Republican	3,484,980	23.2	8	
	Eugene V. Debs	Socialist	900,672	6.1	—	
1916	**WOODROW WILSON (N.J.)**	Democratic	9,129,606	49.4	277	61.6
	Charles E. Hughes	Republican	8,538,221	46.2	254	
	A. L. Benson	Socialist	585,113	3.2	—	
1920	**WARREN G. HARDING (Ohio)**	Republican	16,143,407	60.5	404	49.2
	James M. Cox	Democratic	9,130,328	34.2	127	
	Eugene V. Debs	Socialist	919,799	3.4	—	
1924	**CALVIN COOLIDGE (Mass.)**	Republican	15,725,016	54.0	382	48.9
	John W. Davis	Democratic	8,386,503	28.8	136	
	Robert M. La Follette	Progressive	4,822,856	16.6	13	
1928	**HERBERT HOOVER (Calif.)**	Republican	21,391,381	57.4	444	56.9
	Alfred E. Smith	Democratic	15,016,443	40.3	87	
	Norman Thomas	Socialist	881,951	2.3	—	
	William Z. Foster	Communist	102,991	0.3	—	
1932	**FRANKLIN D. ROOSEVELT (N.Y.)**	Democratic	22,821,857	57.4	472	56.9
	Herbert Hoover	Republican	15,761,841	39.7	59	
	Norman Thomas	Socialist	881,951	2.2	—	
1936	**FRANKLIN D. ROOSEVELT (N.Y.)**	Democratic	27,751,597	60.8	523	61.0
	Alfred M. Landon	Republican	16,679,583	36.5	8	
	William Lemke	Union	882,479	1.9	—	
1940	**FRANKLIN D. ROOSEVELT (N.Y.)**	Democratic	27,244,160	54.8	449	62.5
	Wendell Willkie	Republican	22,305,198	44.8	82	
1944	**FRANKLIN D. ROOSEVELT (N.Y.)**	Democratic	25,602,504	53.5	432	55.9
	Thomas E. Dewey	Republican	22,006,285	46.0	99	
1948	**HARRY S. TRUMAN (Mo.)**	Democratic	24,105,695	49.5	303	53.0
	Thomas E. Dewey	Republican	21,969,170	45.1	189	
	J. Strom Thurmond	States'-Rights Democratic	1,169,021	2.4	38	
	Henry A. Wallace	Progressive	1,156,103	2.4	—	
1952	**DWIGHT D. EISENHOWER (N.Y.)**	Republican	33,936,252	55.1	442	63.3
	Adlai Stevenson	Democratic	27,314,992	44.4	89	
1956	**DWIGHT D. EISENHOWER (N.Y.)**	Republican	35,575,420	57.6	457	60.6
	Adlai Stevenson	Democratic	26,033,066	42.1	73	
	Other	—	—		1	
1960	**JOHN F. KENNEDY (Mass.)**	Democratic	34,227,096	49.9	303	62.8
	Richard M. Nixon	Republican	34,108,546	49.6	219	
	Other	—	—		15	
1964	**LYNDON B. JOHNSON (Texas)**	Democratic	43,126,506	61.1	486	61.7
	Barry M. Goldwater	Republican	27,176,799	38.5	52	
1968	**RICHARD M. NIXON (N.Y.)**	Republican	31,770,237	43.4	301	60.9
	Hubert H. Humphrey	Democratic	31,270,533	42.7	191	
	George Wallace	American Indep.	9,906,141	13.5	46	
1972	**RICHARD M. NIXON (N.Y.)**	Republican	47,169,911	60.7	520	55.2
	George S. McGovern	Democratic	29,170,383	37.5	17	
	Other	—	—		1	
1976	**JIMMY CARTER (Ga.)**	Democratic	40,830,763	50.0	297	53.5
	Gerald R. Ford	Republican	39,147,793	48.0	240	
	Other	—	1,575,459	2.1	—	
1980	**RONALD REAGAN (Calif.)**	Republican	43,901,812	51.0	489	54.0
	Jimmy Carter	Democratic	35,483,820	41.0	49	
	John B. Anderson	Independent	5,719,722	7.0	—	
	Ed Clark	Libertarian	921,188	1.1	—	

Year	Candidates	Parties	Popular Vote	Percentage of Popular Vote	Electoral Vote	Percentage of Voter Participation
1984	**RONALD REAGAN (Calif.)**	Republican	54,455,075	59.0	525	53.1
	Walter Mondale	Democratic	37,577,185	41.0	13	
1988	**GEORGE H. W. BUSH (Texas)**	Republican	47,946,422	54.0	426	50.2
	Michael S. Dukakis	Democratic	41,016,429	46.0	112	
1992	**WILLIAM J. CLINTON (Ark.)**	Democratic	44,908,254	43.0	370	55.9
	George H. W. Bush	Republican	39,102,282	38.0	168	
	H. Ross Perot	Independent	19,721,433	19.0	—	
1996	**WILLIAM J. CLINTON (Ark.)**	Democratic	47,401,185	49.2	379	49.0
	Robert Dole	Republican	39,197,469	40.7	159	
	H. Ross Perot	Independent	8,085,294	8.4	—	
2000	**GEORGE W. BUSH (Texas)**	Republican	50,456,062	47.8	271	51.2
	Al Gore	Democratic	50,996,862	48.4	267	
	Ralph Nader	Green Party	2,858,843	2.7	—	
	Patrick J. Buchanan	—	438,760	0.4	—	
2004	**GEORGE W. BUSH (Texas)**	Republican	61,872,711	50.7	286	60.3
	John F. Kerry	Democratic	58,894,584	48.3	252	
	Other	—	1,582,185	1.3	—	
2008	**BARACK OBAMA (Illinois)**	Democratic	69,456,897	52.9	365	56.8
	John McCain	Republican	59,934,314	45.7	173	

PRESIDENTS, VICE PRESIDENTS, AND SECRETARIES OF STATE

The Washington Administration (1789–1797)

Vice President	John Adams	1789–1797
Secretary of State	Thomas Jefferson	1789–1793
	Edmund Randolph	1794–1795
	Timothy Pickering	1795–1797

The John Adams Administration (1797–1801)

Vice President	Thomas Jefferson	1797–1801
Secretary of State	Timothy Pickering	1797–1800
	John Marshall	1800–1801

The Jefferson Administration (1801–1809)

Vice President	Aaron Burr	1801–1805
	George Clinton	1805–1809
Secretary of State	James Madison	1801–1809

The Madison Administration (1809–1817)

Vice President	George Clinton	1809–1813
	Elbridge Gerry	1813–1817
Secretary of State	Robert Smith	1809–1811
	James Monroe	1811–1817

The Monroe Administration (1817–1825)

Vice President	Daniel Tompkins	1817–1825
Secretary of State	John Quincy Adams	1817–1825

The John Quincy Adams Administration (1825–1829)

Vice President	John C. Calhoun	1825–1829
Secretary of State	Henry Clay	1825–1829

The Jackson Administration (1829–1837)

Vice President	John C. Calhoun	1829–1833
	Martin Van Buren	1833–1837
Secretary of State	Martin Van Buren	1829–1831
	Edward Livingston	1831–1833
	Louis McLane	1833–1834
	John Forsyth	1834–1837

The Van Buren Administration (1837–1841)

Vice President	Richard M. Johnson	1837–1841
Secretary of State	John Forsyth	1837–1841

The William Harrison Administration (1841)

Vice President	John Tyler	1841
Secretary of State	Daniel Webster	1841

The Tyler Administration (1841–1845)

Vice President	None	
Secretary of State	Daniel Webster	1841–1843
	Hugh S. Legaré	1843
	Abel P. Upshur	1843–1844
	John C. Calhoun	1844–1845

The Polk Administration (1845–1849)

Vice President	George M. Dallas	1845–1849
Secretary of State	James Buchanan	1845–1849

The Taylor Administration (1849–1850)

Vice President	Millard Fillmore	1849–1850
Secretary of State	John M. Clayton	1849–1850

The Fillmore Administration (1850–1853)

Vice President	None	
Secretary of State	Daniel Webster	1850–1852
	Edward Everett	1852–1853

The Pierce Administration (1853–1857)

Vice President	William R. King	1853–1857
Secretary of State	William L. Marcy	1853–1857

The Buchanan Administration (1857–1861)

Vice President	John C. Breckinridge	1857–1861
Secretary of State	Lewis Cass	1857–1860
	Jeremiah S. Black	1860–1861

The Lincoln Administration (1861–1865)

Vice President	Hannibal Hamlin	1861–1865
	Andrew Johnson	1865
Secretary of State	William H. Seward	1861–1865

The Andrew Johnson Administration (1865–1869)

Vice President	None	
Secretary of State	William H. Seward	1865–1869

The Grant Administration (1869–1877)

Vice President	Schuyler Colfax	1869–1873
	Henry Wilson	1873–1877
Secretary of State	Elihu B. Washburne	1869
	Hamilton Fish	1869–1877

The Hayes Administration (1877–1881)

Vice President	William A. Wheeler	1877–1881
Secretary of State	William M. Evarts	1877–1881

The Garfield Administration (1881)

Vice President	Chester A. Arthur	1881
Secretary of State	James G. Blaine	1881

The Arthur Administration (1881–1885)

Vice President	None	
Secretary of State	F. T. Frelinghuysen	1881–1885

The Cleveland Administration (1885–1889)

Vice President	Thomas A. Hendricks	1885–1889
Secretary of State	Thomas F. Bayard	1885–1889

The Benjamin Harrison Administration (1889–1893)

Vice President	Levi P. Morton	1889–1893
Secretary of State	James G. Blaine	1889–1892
	John W. Foster	1892–1893

The Cleveland Administration (1893–1897)

Vice President	Adlai E. Stevenson	1893–1897
Secretary of State	Walter Q. Gresham	1893–1895
	Richard Olney	1895–1897

The McKinley Administration (1897–1901)

Vice President	Garret A. Hobart	1897–1901
	Theodore Roosevelt	1901
Secretary of State	John Sherman	1897–1898
	William R. Day	1898
	John Hay	1898–1901

The Theodore Roosevelt Administration (1901–1909)

Vice President	Charles Fairbanks	1905–1909
Secretary of State	John Hay	1901–1905
	Elihu Root	1905–1909
	Robert Bacon	1909

The Taft Administration (1909–1913)

Vice President	James S. Sherman	1909–1913
Secretary of State	Philander C. Knox	1909–1913

The Wilson Administration (1913–1921)

Vice President	Thomas R. Marshall	1913–1921
Secretary of State	William J. Bryan	1913–1915
	Robert Lansing	1915–1920
	Bainbridge Colby	1920–1921

The Harding Administration (1921–1923)

Vice President	Calvin Coolidge	1921–1923
Secretary of State	Charles E. Hughes	1921–1923

The Coolidge Administration (1923–1929)

Vice President	Charles G. Dawes	1925–1929
Secretary of State	Charles E. Hughes	1923–1925
	Frank B. Kellogg	1925–1929

The Hoover Administration (1929–1933)

Vice President	Charles Curtis	1929–1933
Secretary of State	Henry L. Stimson	1929–1933

The Franklin D. Roosevelt Administration (1933–1945)

Vice President	John Nance Garner	1933–1941
	Henry A. Wallace	1941–1945
	Harry S. Truman	1945
Secretary of State	Cordell Hull	1933–1944
	Edward R. Stettinius Jr.	1944–1945

The Truman Administration (1945–1953)

Vice President	Alben W. Barkley	1949–1953
Secretary of State	Edward R. Stettinius Jr.	1945
	James F. Byrnes	1945–1947
	George C. Marshall	1947–1949
	Dean G. Acheson	1949–1953

The Eisenhower Administration (1953–1961)

Vice President	Richard M. Nixon	1953–1961
Secretary of State	John Foster Dulles	1953–1959
	Christian A. Herter	1959–1961

The Kennedy Administration (1961–1963)

Vice President	Lyndon B. Johnson	1961–1963
Secretary of State	Dean Rusk	1961–1963

The Lyndon Johnson Administration (1963–1969)

Vice President	Hubert H. Humphrey	1965–1969
Secretary of State	Dean Rusk	1963–1969

The Nixon Administration (1969–1974)

Vice President	Spiro T. Agnew	1969–1973
	Gerald R. Ford	1973–1974
Secretary of State	William P. Rogers	1969–1973
	Henry A. Kissinger	1973–1974

The Ford Administration (1974–1977)

Vice President	Nelson A. Rockefeller	1974–1977
Secretary of State	Henry A. Kissinger	1974–1977

The Carter Administration (1977–1981)

Vice President	Walter F. Mondale	1977–1981
Secretary of State	Cyrus R. Vance	1977–1980
	Edmund Muskie	1980–1981

The Reagan Administration (1981–1989)

Vice President	George H. W. Bush	1981–1989
Secretary of State	Alexander M. Haig	1981–1982
	George P. Shultz	1982–1989

The George H. W. Bush Administration (1989–1993)

Vice President	J. Danforth Quayle	1989–1993
Secretary of State	James A. Baker III	1989–1992
	Lawrence S. Eagleburger	1992–1993

The Clinton Administration (1993–2001)

Vice President	Albert Gore	1993–2001
Secretary of State	Warren M. Christopher	1993–1997
	Madeleine K. Albright	1997–2001

The George W. Bush Administration (2001–2009)

Vice President	Richard Cheney	2001–2009
Secretary of State	Colin Powell	2001–2005
	Condoleezza Rice	2005–2009

The Barack Obama Administration (2009–)

Vice President	Joseph Biden	2009–
Secretary of State	Hillary Clinton	2009–

ADMISSION OF STATES TO THE UNION

State	Date of Admission	State	Date of Admission
Delaware	December 7, 1787	Rhode Island	May 29, 1790
Pennsylvania	December 12, 1787	Vermont	March 4, 1791
New Jersey	December 18, 1787	Kentucky	June 1, 1792
Georgia	January 2, 1788	Tennessee	June 1, 1796
Connecticut	January 9, 1788	Ohio	March 1, 1803
Massachusetts	February 6, 1788	Louisiana	April 30, 1812
Maryland	April 28, 1788	Indiana	December 11, 1816
South Carolina	May 23, 1788	Mississippi	December 10, 1817
New Hampshire	June 21, 1788	Illinois	December 3, 1818
Virginia	June 25, 1788	Alabama	December 14, 1819
New York	July 26, 1788	Maine	March 15, 1820
North Carolina	November 21, 1789	Missouri	August 10, 1821

ADMISSION OF STATES TO THE UNION

State	Date of Admission	State	Date of Admission
Arkansas	June 15, 1836	Colorado	August 1, 1876
Michigan	January 16, 1837	North Dakota	November 2, 1889
Florida	March 3, 1845	South Dakota	November 2, 1889
Texas	December 29, 1845	Montana	November 8, 1889
Iowa	December 28, 1846	Washington	November 11, 1889
Wisconsin	May 29, 1848	Idaho	July 3, 1890
California	September 9, 1850	Wyoming	July 10, 1890
Minnesota	May 11, 1858	Utah	January 4, 1896
Oregon	February 14, 1859	Oklahoma	November 16, 1907
Kansas	January 29, 1861	New Mexico	January 6, 1912
West Virginia	June 19, 1863	Arizona	February 14, 1912
Nevada	October 31, 1864	Alaska	January 3, 1959
Nebraska	March 1, 1867	Hawaii	August 21, 1959

SUPREME COURT JUSTICES

Name	Service	Appointed by
John Jay*	1789–1795	Washington
James Wilson	1789–1798	Washington
John Blair	1789–1796	Washington
John Rutledge	1790–1791	Washington
William Cushing	1790–1810	Washington
James Iredell	1790–1799	Washington
Thomas Johnson	1791–1793	Washington
William Paterson	1793–1806	Washington
John Rutledge†	1795	Washington
Samuel Chase	1796–1811	Washington
Oliver Ellsworth	1796–1799	Washington
Bushrod Washington	1798–1829	J. Adams
Alfred Moore	1799–1804	J. Adams
John Marshall	1801–1835	J. Adams
William Johnson	1804–1834	Jefferson
Henry B. Livingston	1806–1823	Jefferson
Thomas Todd	1807–1826	Jefferson
Gabriel Duval	1811–1836	Madison
Joseph Story	1811–1845	Madison
Smith Thompson	1823–1843	Monroe
Robert Trimble	1826–1828	J. Q. Adams
John McLean	1829–1861	Jackson
Henry Baldwin	1830–1844	Jackson
James M. Wayne	1835–1867	Jackson
Roger B. Taney	1836–1864	Jackson
Philip P. Barbour	1836–1841	Jackson
John Catron	1837–1865	Van Buren
John McKinley	1837–1852	Van Buren
Peter V. Daniel	1841–1860	Van Buren
Samuel Nelson	1845–1872	Tyler
Levi Woodbury	1845–1851	Polk
Robert C. Grier	1846–1870	Polk
Benjamin R. Curtis	1851–1857	Fillmore
John A. Campbell	1853–1861	Pierce
Nathan Clifford	1858–1881	Buchanan
Noah H. Swayne	1862–1881	Lincoln
Samuel F. Miller	1862–1890	Lincoln
David Davis	1862–1877	Lincoln
Stephen J. Field	1863–1897	Lincoln
Salmon P. Chase	1864–1873	Lincoln
William Strong	1870–1880	Grant
Joseph P. Bradley	1870–1892	Grant
Ward Hunt	1873–1882	Grant
Morrison R. Waite	1874–1888	Grant
John M. Harlan	1877–1911	Hayes
William B. Woods	1880–1887	Hayes
Stanley Matthews	1881–1889	Garfield
Horace Gray	1882–1902	Arthur
Samuel Blatchford	1882–1893	Arthur
Lucius Q. C. Lamar	1888–1893	Cleveland
Melville W. Fuller	1888–1910	Cleveland
David J. Brewer	1889–1910	B. Harrison
Henry B. Brown	1890–1906	B. Harrison
George Shiras	1892–1903	B. Harrison
Howell E. Jackson	1893–1895	B. Harrison

***Chief Justices appear in bold type.**

†Acting Chief Justice; Senate refused to confirm appointment.

Name	Service	Appointed by
Edward D. White	1894–1910	Cleveland
Rufus W. Peckham	1896–1909	Cleveland
Joseph McKenna	1898–1925	McKinley
Oliver W. Holmes	1902–1932	T. Roosevelt
William R. Day	1903–1922	T. Roosevelt
William H. Moody	1906–1910	T. Roosevelt
Horace H. Lurton	1910–1914	Taft
Charles E. Hughes	1910–1916	Taft
Willis Van Devanter	1910–1937	Taft
Edward D. White	1910–1921	Taft
Joseph R. Lamar	1911–1916	Taft
Mahlon Pitney	1912–1922	Taft
James C. McReynolds	1914–1941	Wilson
Louis D. Brandeis	1916–1939	Wilson
John H. Clarke	1916–1922	Wilson
William H. Taft	1921–1930	Harding
George Sutherland	1922–1938	Harding
Pierce Butler	1923–1939	Harding
Edward T. Sanford	1923–1930	Harding
Harlan F. Stone	1925–1941	Coolidge
Charles E. Hughes	1930–1941	Hoover
Owen J. Roberts	1930–1945	Hoover
Benjamin N. Cardozo	1932–1938	Hoover
Hugo L. Black	1937–1971	F. Roosevelt
Stanley F. Reed	1938–1957	F. Roosevelt
Felix Frankfurter	1939–1962	F. Roosevelt
William O. Douglas	1939–1975	F. Roosevelt
Frank Murphy	1940–1949	F. Roosevelt
Harlan F. Stone	1941–1946	F. Roosevelt
James F. Byrnes	1941–1942	F. Roosevelt
Robert H. Jackson	1941–1954	F. Roosevelt
Wiley B. Rutledge	1943–1949	F. Roosevelt
Harold H. Burton	1945–1958	Truman
Frederick M. Vinson	1946–1953	Truman
Tom C. Clark	1949–1967	Truman
Sherman Minton	1949–1956	Truman
Earl Warren	1953–1969	Eisenhower
John Marshall Harlan	1955–1971	Eisenhower
William J. Brennan Jr.	1956–1990	Eisenhower
Charles E. Whittaker	1957–1962	Eisenhower
Potter Stewart	1958–1981	Eisenhower
Byron R. White	1962–1993	Kennedy
Arthur J. Goldberg	1962–1965	Kennedy
Abe Fortas	1965–1969	L. Johnson
Thurgood Marshall	1967–1991	L. Johnson
Warren E. Burger	1969–1986	Nixon
Harry A. Blackmun	1970–1994	Nixon
Lewis F. Powell Jr.	1972–1988	Nixon
William H. Rehnquist	1972–1986	Nixon
John Paul Stevens	1975–	Ford
Sandra Day O'Connor	1981–2006	Reagan
William H. Rehnquist	1986–2005	Reagan
Antonin Scalia	1986–	Reagan
Anthony M. Kennedy	1988–	Reagan
David H. Souter	1990–2009	G. H. W. Bush
Clarence Thomas	1991–	G. H. W. Bush
Ruth Bader Ginsburg	1993–	Clinton
Stephen Breyer	1994–	Clinton
John G. Roberts Jr.	2005–	G. W. Bush
Samuel Anthony Alito Jr.	2006–	G. W. Bush
Sonia Sotomayor	2009–	Obama
Elena Kagan	2010–	Obama

SIGNIFICANT SUPREME COURT CASES

Marbury v. Madison (1803)

This case established the right of the Supreme Court to review the constitutionality of laws. The decision involved judicial appointments made during the last hours of the administration of President John Adams. Some commissions, including that of William Marbury, had not yet been delivered when President Thomas Jefferson took office. Infuriated by the last-minute nature of Adams's Federalist appointments, Jefferson refused to send the undelivered commissions out, and Marbury decided to sue. The Supreme Court, presided over by John Marshall, a Federalist who had assisted Adams in the judicial appointments, ruled that although Marbury's commission was valid and the new president should have delivered it, the Court could not compel him to do so. The Court based its reasoning on a finding that the grounds of Marbury's suit, resting in the Judiciary Act of 1789, were in conflict with the Constitution.

For the first time, the Court had overturned a national law on the grounds that it was unconstitutional. John Marshall had quietly established the concept of judicial review: The Supreme Court had given itself the authority to nullify acts of the other branches of the federal government. Although the Constitution provides for judicial review, the Court had not exercised this power before and did not use it again until 1857. It seems likely that if the Court had waited until 1857 to use this power, it would have been difficult to establish.

McCulloch v. Maryland (1819)

In 1816, Congress authorized the creation of a national bank. To protect its own banks from competition with a branch of the national bank in Baltimore, the state legislature of Maryland placed a tax of 2 percent on all notes issued by any bank operating in Maryland that was not chartered by the state. McCulloch, cashier of the Baltimore branch of the Bank of the United States, was convicted for refusing to pay the tax. Under the leadership of Chief Justice John Marshall, the Court ruled that the federal government had the power to establish a bank, even though that specific authority was not mentioned in the Constitution.

Marshall maintained that the authority could be reasonably implied from Article 1, section 8, which gives Congress the power to make all laws that are necessary and proper to execute the enumerated powers. Marshall also held that Maryland could not tax the national bank because in a conflict between federal and state laws, the federal law must take precedence. Thus he established the principles of implied powers and federal supremacy, both of which set a precedent for subsequent expansion of federal power at the expense of the states.

Scott v. Sandford (1857)

Dred Scott was a slave who sued for his own and his family's freedom on the grounds that, with his master, he had traveled to and lived in free territory that did not allow slavery. When his case reached the Supreme Court, the justices saw an opportunity to settle once and for all the vexing question of slavery in the territories. The Court's decision in this case proved that it enjoyed no special immunity from the sectional and partisan passions of the time. Five of the nine justices were from the South and seven were Democrats.

Chief Justice Roger B. Taney hated Republicans and detested racial equality; his decision reflects those prejudices. He wrote an opinion not only declaring that Scott was still a slave but also claiming that the Constitution denied citizenship or rights to blacks, that Congress had no right to exclude slavery from the territories, and that the Missouri Compromise was unconstitutional. While southern Democrats gloated over this seven-to-two decision, sectional tensions were further inflamed, and the young Republican Party's claim that a hostile "slave power" was conspiring to destroy northern liberties was given further credence. The decision brought the nation closer to civil war and is generally regarded as the worst decision ever rendered by the Supreme Court.

Butchers' Benevolent Association of New Orleans v. Crescent City Livestock Landing and Slaughterhouse Co. (1873)

The *Slaughterhouse* cases, as the cases docketed under the *Butchers*' title were known, were the first legal test of the Fourteenth Amendment. To cut down on cases of cholera believed to be caused by contaminated water, the state of Louisiana prohibited the slaughter of livestock in New Orleans except in one slaughterhouse, effectively giving that slaughterhouse a monopoly. Other New Orleans butchers claimed that the state had deprived them of their occupation without due process of law, thus violating the Fourteenth Amendment.

In a five-to-four decision, the Court upheld the Louisiana law, declaring that the Fourteenth Amendment protected only the rights of federal citizenship, like voting in federal elections and interstate travel. The federal government thus was not obliged to protect basic civil rights from violation by state governments. This decision would have significant implications for African Americans and their struggle for civil rights in the twentieth century.

United States v. E. C. Knight Co. (1895)

Also known as the *Sugar Trust* case, this was among the first cases to reveal the weakness of the Sherman Antitrust Act in the hands of a pro-business Supreme Court. In 1895, American Sugar Refining Company purchased four other sugar producers, including the E. C. Knight Company, and thus took control of more than 98 percent of the sugar refining in the United States. In an effort to limit monopoly, the government brought suit against all five of the companies for violating the Sherman Antitrust Act, which outlawed trusts and other business combinations in restraint of trade. The Court dismissed the suit, however, arguing that the law applied only to commerce and not to manufacturing, defining the latter as a local concern and not part of the interstate commerce that the government could regulate.

Plessy v. Ferguson (1896)

African American Homer Plessy challenged a Louisiana law that required segregation on trains passing through the state. After ensuring that the railroad and the conductor knew that he was of mixed race (Plessy appeared to be white but under the racial code of Louisiana was classified as "colored" because he was one-eighth black), he refused to move to the "colored only" section of the coach. The Court ruled against Plessy by a vote of seven to one, declaring that "separate but equal" facilities were permissible according to section 1 of the Fourteenth Amendment, which calls upon the states to provide "equal protection of the laws" to anyone within their jurisdiction. Although the case was viewed as relatively insignificant at the time, it cast a long shadow over several decades.

Initially, the decision was viewed as a victory for segregationists, but in the 1930s and 1940s civil rights advocates referred to the doctrine of "separate but equal" in their efforts to end segregation. They argued that segregated institutions and accommodations were often not equal to those available to whites, and finally succeeded in overturning *Plessy* in *Brown v. Board of Education* in 1954 (see below).

Lochner v. New York (1905)

In this case, the Court ruled against a New York state law that prohibited employees from working in bakeries more than ten hours a day or sixty hours a week. The purpose of the law was to protect the health of workers, but the Court ruled that it was unconstitutional because it violated "freedom of contract" implicitly protected by the due process clause of the Fourteenth Amendment. Most of the justices believed strongly in a laissez-faire economic system that favored survival of the fittest. They felt that government protection of workers interfered with this system. In a dissenting opinion, Justice Oliver Wendell Holmes accused the majority of distorting the Constitution and of deciding the case on "an economic theory which a large part of the country does not entertain."

Muller v. Oregon (1908)

In 1905, Curt Muller, owner of a Portland, Oregon, laundry, demanded that one of his employees, Mrs. Elmer Gotcher, work more than the ten hours allowed as a maximum workday for women under Oregon law. Muller argued that the law violated his "freedom of contract" as established in prior Supreme Court decisions.

Progressive lawyer Louis D. Brandeis defended the Oregon law by arguing that a state could be justified in abridging freedom of contract when the health, safety, and welfare of workers was at issue. His innovative strategy drew on ninety-five pages of excerpts from factory and medical reports to substantiate his argument that there was a direct connection between long hours and the health of women and thus the health of the nation. In a unanimous decision, the Court upheld the Oregon law, but later generations of women fighting for equality would question the strategy of arguing that women's reproductive role entitled them to special treatment.

Schenck v. United States (1919)

During World War I, Charles Schenck and other members of the Socialist Party printed and mailed out flyers urging young men who were subject to the draft to oppose the war in Europe. In upholding the conviction of Schenck for publishing a pamphlet urging draft resistance, Justice Oliver Wendell Holmes established the "clear and present danger" test for freedom of speech. Such utterances as Schenck's during a time of national peril, Holmes wrote, could be considered the equivalent of shouting "Fire!" in a crowded theater. Congress had the right to protect the public against such an incitement to panic, the Court ruled in a unanimous decision. But the analogy was a false one. Schenck's pamphlet had little power to provoke a public firmly opposed to its message. Although Holmes later modified his position to state that the danger must relate to an immediate evil and a specific action, the "clear and present danger" test laid the groundwork for those who later sought to limit First Amendment freedoms.

Schechter Poultry Corp. v. United States (1935)

During the Great Depression, the National Industrial Recovery Act (NIRA), which was passed under President Franklin D. Roosevelt, established fair competition codes that were designed to help businesses. The Schechter brothers of New York City, who sold chickens, were convicted of violating the codes. The Supreme Court ruled that the NIRA unconstitutionally conferred legislative power on an administrative agency and overstepped the limits of federal power to regulate interstate commerce. The decision was a significant blow to the New Deal recovery program, demonstrating both historic American resistance to economic planning and the refusal of the business community to yield its autonomy unless it was forced to do so.

Brown v. Board of Education (1954)

In 1950, the families of eight Topeka, Kansas, children sued the Topeka Board of Education. The children were blacks who lived within walking distance of a whites-only school. The segregated school system required them to take a time-consuming, inconvenient, and dangerous route to get to a black school, and their parents argued that there was no reason their children should not be allowed to attend the nearest school. By the time the case reached the Supreme Court, it had been joined with similar cases regarding segregated schools in other states and the District of Columbia. A team of lawyers from the National Association for the Advancement of Colored People (NAACP), led by Thurgood Marshall (who would later be appointed to the Supreme Court), urged the Court to overturn the fifty-eight-year-old precedent established in *Plessy v. Ferguson*, which had enshrined "separate but equal" as the law of the land. A unanimous Court, led by Chief Justice Earl Warren, declared that "separate educational facilities are inherently unequal" and thus violate the Fourteenth Amendment. In 1955, the Court called for desegregation "with all deliberate speed" but established no deadline.

Roth v. United States (1957)

In 1957, New Yorker Samuel Roth was convicted of sending obscene materials through the mail in a case that ultimately reached the Supreme Court. With a six-to-three vote, the Court reaffirmed the historical view that obscenity is not protected by the First Amendment. Yet it broke new ground by declaring that a work could be judged obscene only if, "taken as a whole," it appealed to the "prurient interest" of "the average person."

Prior to this case, work could be judged obscene if portions were thought able to "deprave and corrupt" the most susceptible part of an audience (such as children). Thus, serious works of literature such as Theodore Dreiser's *An American Tragedy*, which was banned in Boston when first published, had received no protection. Although this decision continued to pose problems of definition, it did help to protect most works that attempt to convey ideas, even if those ideas have to do with sex, from the threat of obscenity laws.

Engel v. Vitale (1962)

In 1959, five parents with ten children in the New Hyde Park, New York, school system sued the school board. The parents argued that the so-called Regents' Prayer that public school students in New York recited at the start of every school day violated the doctrine of separation of church and state outlined in the First Amendment. In 1962, the Supreme Court voted six to one in favor of banning the Regents' Prayer.

The decision threw the religious community into an uproar. Many religious leaders expressed dismay and even shock; others welcomed the decision. Several efforts to introduce an amendment allowing school prayer have failed. Subsequent Supreme Court decisions have banned reading of the Bible in public schools. The Court has also declared mandatory flag saluting to be an infringement of religious and personal freedoms.

Gideon v. Wainwright (1963)

When Clarence Earl Gideon was tried for breaking into a poolroom, the state of Florida rejected his demand for a court-appointed lawyer as guaranteed by the Sixth Amendment. In 1963, the Court upheld his demand in a unanimous decision that established the obligation of states to provide attorneys for indigent defendants in felony cases. Prior to this decision, the right to an attorney had applied only to federal cases, not state cases. In its ruling in *Gideon v. Wainwright*, the Supreme Court applied the Sixth through the Fourteenth Amendments to the states. In 1972, the Supreme Court extended the right to legal representation to all cases, not just felony cases, in its decision in *Argersinger v. Hamlin*.

Griswold v. Connecticut (1965)

With a vote of seven to two, the Supreme Court reversed an "uncommonly silly law" (in the words of Justice Potter Stewart) that made it a crime for anyone in the state of Connecticut to use any drug, article, or instrument to prevent conception. *Griswold* became a landmark case because here, for the first time, the Court explicitly invested with full constitutional status "fundamental personal rights," such as the right to privacy, that were not expressly enumerated in the Bill of Rights. The majority opinion in the case held that the law infringed on the constitutionally protected right to privacy of married persons.

Although the Court had previously recognized fundamental rights not expressly enumerated in the Bill of Rights (such as the right to procreate in *Skinner v. Oklahoma* in 1942), *Griswold* was the first time the Court had justified, at length, the practice of investing such unenumerated rights with full constitutional status. Writing for the majority, Justice William O. Douglas explained that the First, Third, Fourth, Fifth, and Ninth Amendments imply "zones of privacy" that are the foundation for the general right to privacy affirmed in this case.

Miranda v. Arizona (1966)

In 1966, the Supreme Court, by a vote of five to four, upheld the case of Ernesto Miranda, who appealed a murder conviction on the grounds that police had gotten him to confess without giving him access to an attorney. The *Miranda* case was the culmination of the Court's efforts to find a meaningful way of determining whether police had used due process in extracting confessions from people accused of crimes. The *Miranda* decision upholds the Fifth Amendment protection against self-incrimination outside the courtroom and requires that suspects be given what came to be known as the "Miranda warning," which advises them of their right to remain silent and warns them that anything they say might be used against them in a court of law. Suspects must also be told that they have a right to counsel.

New York Times Co. v. United States (1971)

With a six-to-three vote, the Court upheld the right of the *New York Times* and the *Washington Post* to print materials from the so-called *Pentagon Papers*, a secret government study of U.S. policy in Vietnam, leaked by dissident Pentagon official Daniel Ellsberg. Since the papers revealed deception and secrecy in the conduct of the Vietnam War, the Nixon administration had quickly obtained a court injunction against their further publication, claiming that suppression was in the interests of national security. The Supreme Court's decision overturning the injunction strengthened the First Amendment protection of freedom of the press.

Furman v. Georgia (1972)

In this case, the Supreme Court ruled five to four that the death penalty for murder or rape violated the cruel and unusual punishment clause of the Eighth Amendment because the manner in which the death penalty was meted out was irregular, "arbitrary," and "cruel." In response, most states enacted new statutes that allow the death penalty to be imposed only after a postconviction hearing at which evidence must be presented to show that "aggravating" or "mitigating" circumstances were factors in the crime. If the post-conviction hearing hands down a death sentence, the case is automatically reviewed by an appellate court.

In 1976, the Court ruled in *Gregg v. Georgia* that these statutes were not unconstitutional. In 1977, the Court ruled in *Coker v. Georgia* that the death penalty for rape was "disproportionate and excessive," thus allowing the death penalty only in murder cases. Between 1977 and 1991, some 150 people were executed in the United States. Public opinion polls indicate that about 70 percent of Americans favor the death penalty for murder. Capital punishment continues to generate controversy, however, as opponents argue that there is no evidence that the death penalty deters crime and that its use reflects racial and economic bias.

Roe v. Wade (1973)

In 1973, the Court found, by a vote of seven to two, that state laws restricting access to abortion violated a woman's right to privacy guaranteed by the due process clause of the Fourteenth Amendment. The decision was based on the cases of two women living in Texas and Georgia, both states with stringent antiabortion laws. Upholding the individual rights of both women and physicians, the Court ruled that the Constitution protects the right to abortion and that states cannot prohibit abortions in the early stages of pregnancy.

The decision stimulated great debate among legal scholars as well as the public. Critics argued that since abortion was never addressed in the Constitution, the Court could not claim that legislation violated fundamental values of the Constitution. They also argued that since abortion was a medical procedure with an acknowledged impact on a fetus, it was inappropriate to invoke the kind of "privacy" argument that was used in *Griswold v. Connecticut* (see page A-43), which was about contraception. Defenders suggested that the case should be argued as a case of gender discrimination, which did violate the equal protection clause of the Fourteenth Amendment. Others said that the right to privacy in sexual matters was indeed a fundamental right.

Regents of the University of California v. Bakke (1978)

When Allan Bakke, a white man, was not accepted by the University of California Medical School at Davis, he filed a lawsuit alleging that the admissions program, which set up different standards for test scores and grades for members of certain minority groups, violated the Civil Rights Act of 1964, which outlawed racial or ethnic preferences in programs supported by federal funds. Bakke further argued that the university's practice of setting aside spaces for minority applicants denied him equal protection as guaranteed by the Fourteenth Amendment. In a five-to-four decision, the Court ordered that Bakke be admitted to the medical school, yet it sanctioned affirmative action programs to attack the results of past discrimination as long as strict quotas or racial classifications were not involved.

Webster v. Reproductive Health Services (1989)

By a vote of five to four, the Court upheld several restrictions on the availability of abortions as imposed by Missouri state law. It upheld restrictions on the use of state property, including public hospitals, for abortions. It also upheld a provision requiring physicians to perform tests to determine the viability of a fetus that a doctor judged to be twenty weeks of age or older. Although the justices did not go so far as to overturn the decision in *Roe v. Wade* (see at left), the ruling galvanized interest groups on both sides of the abortion issue. Opponents of abortion pressured state legislatures to place greater restrictions on abortions; those who favored availability of abortion tried to mobilize public action by presenting the decision as a major threat to the right to choose abortion.

Cipollone v. Liggett (1992)

In a seven-to-two decision, the Court ruled in favor of the family of Rose Cipollone, a woman who died of lung cancer after smoking for forty-two years. The Court rejected arguments that health warnings on cigarette packages protected tobacco manufacturers from personal injury suits filed by smokers who contract cancer and other serious illnesses.

Miller v. Johnson (1995)

In a five-to-four decision, the Supreme Court ruled that voting districts created to increase the voting power of racial minorities were unconstitutional. The decision threatens dozens of congressional, state, and local voting districts that were drawn to give minorities more representation as had been required by the Justice Department under the Voting Rights Act. If states are required to redraw voting districts, the number of black members of Congress could be sharply reduced.

Romer v. Evans (1996)

In a six-to-three decision, the Court struck down a Colorado amendment that forbade local governments from banning discrimination against homosexuals. Writing for the majority, Justice Anthony Kennedy said that forbidding communities from taking action to protect the rights of homosexuals and not of other groups unlawfully deprived gays and lesbians of opportunities that were available to others. Kennedy based the decision on the guarantee of equal protection under the law as provided by the Fourteenth Amendment.

Bush v. Palm Beach County Canvassing Board (2000)

In a bitterly argued five-to-four decision, the Court reversed the Florida Supreme Court's previous order for a hand recount of contested presidential election ballots in several counties of that battleground state, effectively securing the presidency for Texas Republican governor George W. Bush. The ruling ended a protracted legal dispute between presidential candidates Bush and Vice President Al Gore while inflaming public opinion: For the first time since 1888, a president who failed to win the popular vote took office. Critics charged that the Supreme Court had applied partisanship rather than objectivity to the case, pointing out that the decision went against this Court's customary interpretation of the Constitution to favor state over federal authority.

Lawrence v. Texas (2003)

In the 1986 case *Bowers v. Hardwick*, the Supreme Court upheld the constitutionality of a Georgia law that outlawed sodomy, ruling that sexual privacy was not protected by the Constitution. This decision came into question, however, when *Lawrence v. Texas* arrived at the Supreme Court in 2002, challenging the constitutionality of a Texas anti-sodomy statute. In this case, the Court voted six to three to strike down the statute, asserting that the 1986 decision was based on an interpretation of constitutional liberties that was too narrow. This decision thus overruled *Bowers v. Hardwick*, with the majority holding that the Texas law violated the Fourteenth Amendment's declaration that no state shall "deprive any person of life, liberty, or property, without due process of law." The decision in *Lawrence v. Texas* was hailed as a legal victory for the gay and lesbian community. It was landmark in its implication that laws cannot be made on the basis of morality, without proof of harm.

Hamdan v. Rumsfeld (2005)

In 2001, Salim Ahmed Hamdan, driver for al-Qaeda leader Osama bin Laden, was arrested in Afghanistan as a suspected terrorist. He was charged with conspiracy to commit terrorist offenses after being held in the U.S. military base in Guantanamo Bay, Cuba, for two years. It was decided that Hamdan would be tried by a military commission under an order from President George W. Bush that commissions be established for express non-citizens, including those with connections to al-Qaeda. Hamdan, however, claimed that trial by military commission was unlawful under the Geneva Conventions and Uniform Code of Military Justice (UCMJ).

In the case's first round through the courts, the U.S. District Court of the District of Columbia ruled in Hamdan's favor. Upon appeal, the decision was reversed, the new court ruling that the military commission was indeed lawful, and that the Geneva Conventions could not be enforced by the U.S. judicial systems. The Supreme Court issued a writ of certiorari in 2005 and ultimately upheld Hamdan's case by a vote of five to three, stating that the military commission was unlawful under both the Geneva Conventions and the UCMJ. This decision put a halt to all Guantanamo Bay tribunals, and was praised by human rights activists and lawyers.

Citizens United v. Federal Election Commission (2010)

In 2010, the Supreme Court overruled a ban on political spending by corporations in a vote of five to four. The case went to court after Citizens United, a conservative nonprofit organization, tried to air its critical documentary on Hillary Clinton, *Hillary: The Movie*, during the 2008 presidential campaign. *Citizens United v. Federal Election Commission* quickly became a matter of free speech and raised the sensitive question of whether corporations should be viewed as individuals under the First Amendment.

The Court's decision overturned two precedents and divided the nation in an already heated time in the political sphere. Advocates for the ruling felt that the previous ban would have given the Supreme Court power to prohibit other political outlets, such as newspapers and television programs. Dissenters, including President Barack Obama, believed that the vote created an opening for wealthy corporations to take advantage of the democratic system. In reversing years of policy, the ruling left all to speculate on its possible impact not only on the 2008 election, but also on American politics as a whole.

THE AMERICAN ECONOMY

THESE SIX "SNAPSHOTS" OF THE U.S. ECONOMY show significant changes over the past century and a half. In 1849, the agricultural sector was by far the largest contributor to the economy. By the turn of the century, with advances in technology and an abundance of cheap labor and raw materials, the country had experienced remarkable industrial expansion, and the manufacturing industries dominated. By 1950, the service sector had increased significantly, fueled by the consumerism of the 1920s and the post–World War II years, and the economy was becoming more diversified. Note that by 1990, the government's share in the economy had grown to more than 10 percent and activity in both the trade and manufacturing sectors had declined, partly as a result of competition from Western Europe and Asia. Manufacturing continued to decline, and by 2008 the service and finance, real estate, and insurance sectors had all grown steadily to eclipse it.

Main Sectors of the U.S. Economy: 1849, 1899, 1950, 1990, 2001, 2008

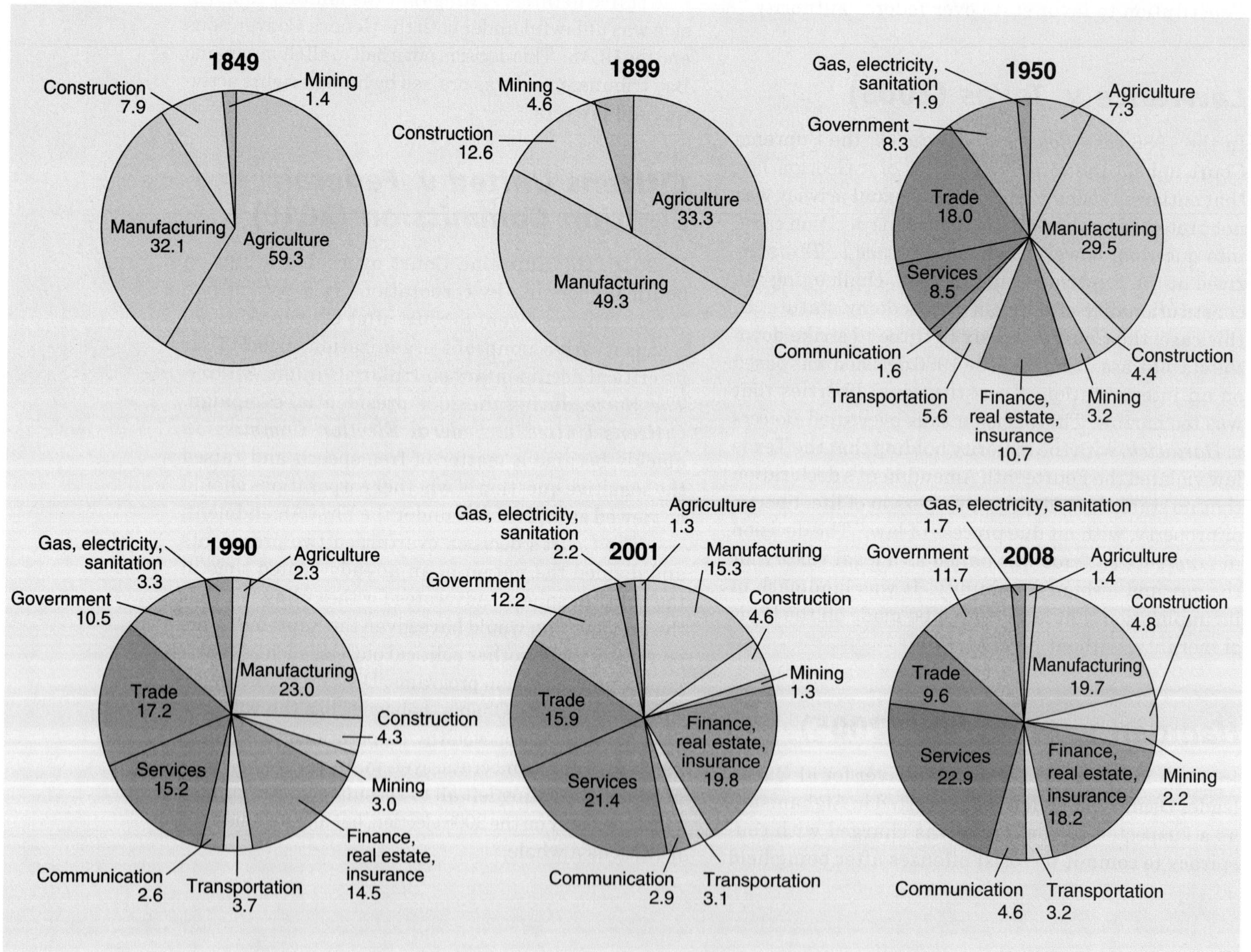

SOURCE: Data from *Historical Statistics of the United States, Colonial Times to 1970* (1975); *Statistical Abstract of the United States, 2010;* U.S. Bureau of Economic Analysis, *Industry Accounts Data, 2010.*

FEDERAL SPENDING AND THE ECONOMY, 1790–2009

Year	Gross Domestic Product (in billions)	Foreign Trade (in billions)		Federal Budget (in billions)	Federal Surplus/Deficit (in billions)	Federal Debt (in billions)
		Exports	Imports			
1790	4.03	0.43	0.50	0.09	0.0032	1.64
1800	7.40	1.10	1.41	0.17	0.0010	1.29
1810	10.6	1.02	1.29	0.12	0.0187	0.81
1820	14.4	1.44	1.52	0.37	−0.0078	1.87
1830	22.2	1.62	1.55	0.33	0.2120	1.07
1840	31.5	2.66	2.16	0.48	−0.0977	0.08
1850	49.6	2.95	3.45	0.78	0.0788	1.24
1860	82.1	7.56	6.84	1.19	−0.1340	1.23
1870	112	6.54	6.70	4.50	1.47	34.8
1880	192	15.8	14.1	4.96	1.22	38.9
1890	319	19.3	17.5	6.73	1.80	23.3
1900	423	30.8	19.1	10.7	0.95	26.7
1910	534	30.6	26.2	11.1	−0.29	17.6
1920	688	67.4	45.0	49.8	2.27	189
1930	893	39.3	34.3	33.7	7.22	159
1940	1,167	46.4	85.6	104	−41.50	495
1950	2,006	94.3	82.1	294	−14.30	257
1960	2,831	145	125	629	2.10	291
1970	4,270	270	246	983	−14.30	381
1980	5,839	470	513	1,369	−171	909
1990	8,034	545	686	1,832	−323	3,206
2000	11,226	1,071	1,449	2,041	270	5,269
2009	12,703	1,571	1,946	3,186	−1,280	11,876

NOTE: All Figures are in 2005 dollars.

SOURCE: *Historical Statistics of the U.S., 1789–1945* (1949), *Statistical Abstract of the U.S., 1965* (1965), *Statistical Abstract of the U.S., 1990* (1990), *Statistical Abstract of the U.S., 2011* (2011), and Louis Johnston and Samuel H. Williamson, "What Was the U.S. GDP Then?" MeasuringWorth, 2011, www.measuringworth.org/usgdp.

A DEMOGRAPHIC PROFILE OF THE UNITED STATES AND ITS PEOPLE

Population

FROM AN ESTIMATED 4,600 white inhabitants in 1630, the country's population grew to a total of more than 308 million in 2010. It is important to note that the U.S. census, first conducted in 1790 and the source of these figures, counted blacks, both free and slave, but did not include American Indians until 1860. The years 1790 to 1900 saw the most rapid population growth, with an average increase of 25 to 35 percent per decade. In addition to "natural" growth—birthrate exceeding death rate—immigration was also a factor in that rise, especially between 1840 and 1860, 1880 and 1890, and 1900 and 1910 (see table on page A-51). The twentieth century witnessed slower growth, partly a result of 1920s immigration restrictions and a decline in the birthrate, especially during the depression era and the 1960s and 1970s. The U.S. population is expected to pass 340 million by the year 2020.

POPULATION GROWTH, 1630–2010

Year	Population	Percent Increase	Year	Population	Percent Increase
1630	4,600	—	1830	12,866,020	33.5
1640	26,600	473.3	1840	17,069,453	32.7
1650	50,400	89.1	1850	23,191,876	35.9
1660	75,100	49.0	1860	31,443,321	35.6
1670	111,900	49.1	1870	39,818,449	26.6
1680	151,500	35.4	1880	50,155,783	26.0
1690	210,400	38.9	1890	62,947,714	25.5
1700	250,900	19.3	1900	75,994,575	20.7
1710	331,700	32.2	1910	91,972,266	21.0
1720	466,200	40.5	1920	105,710,620	14.9
1730	629,400	35.0	1930	122,775,046	16.1
1740	905,600	43.9	1940	131,669,275	7.2
1750	1,170,800	30.0	1950	150,697,361	14.5
1760	1,593,600	36.1	1960	179,323,175	19.0
1770	2,148,100	34.8	1970	203,302,031	13.4
1780	2,780,400	29.4	1980	226,542,199	11.4
1790	3,929,214	41.3	1990	248,718,302	9.8
1800	5,308,483	35.1	2000	281,422,509	13.1
1810	7,239,881	36.4	2010	308,745,538	9.7
1820	9,638,453	33.1			

SOURCE: *Historical Statistics of the U.S.* (1960), *Historical Statistics of the U.S., Colonial Times to 1970* (1975), *Statistical Abstract of the U.S., 1996* (1996), *Statistical Abstract of the U.S., 2003* (2003), and United States Census (2010).

Birthrate, 1820–2007

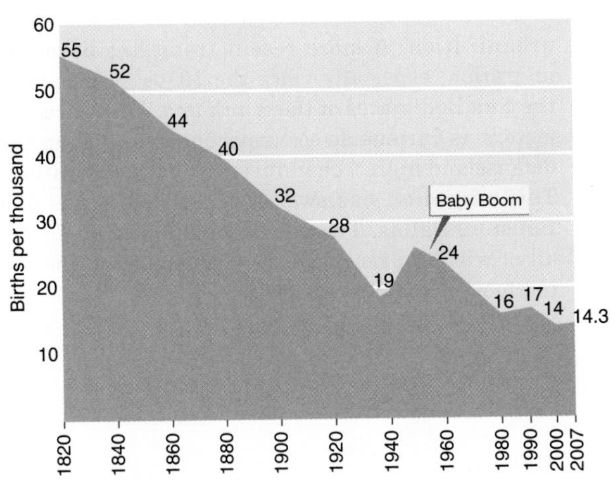

SOURCE: Data from *Historical Statistics of the U.S., Colonial Times to 1970* (1975) and *Statistical Abstract of the U.S., 2007* (2007).

Death Rate, 1900–2007

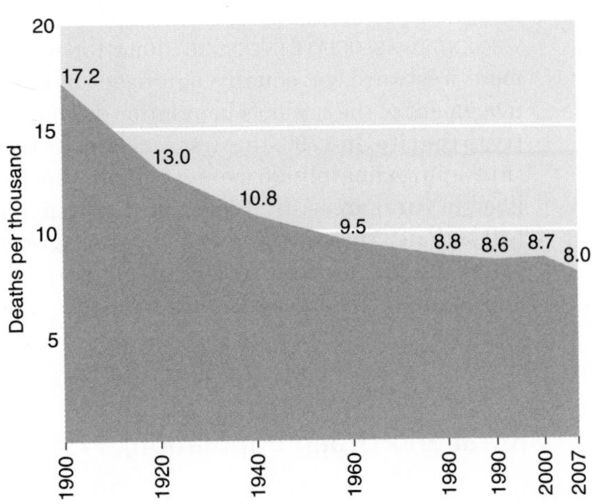

SOURCE: Data from *Historical Statistics of the U.S., Colonial Times to 1970* (1975) and *Statistical Abstract of the U.S., 2007* (2007).

Life Expectancy, 1900–2007

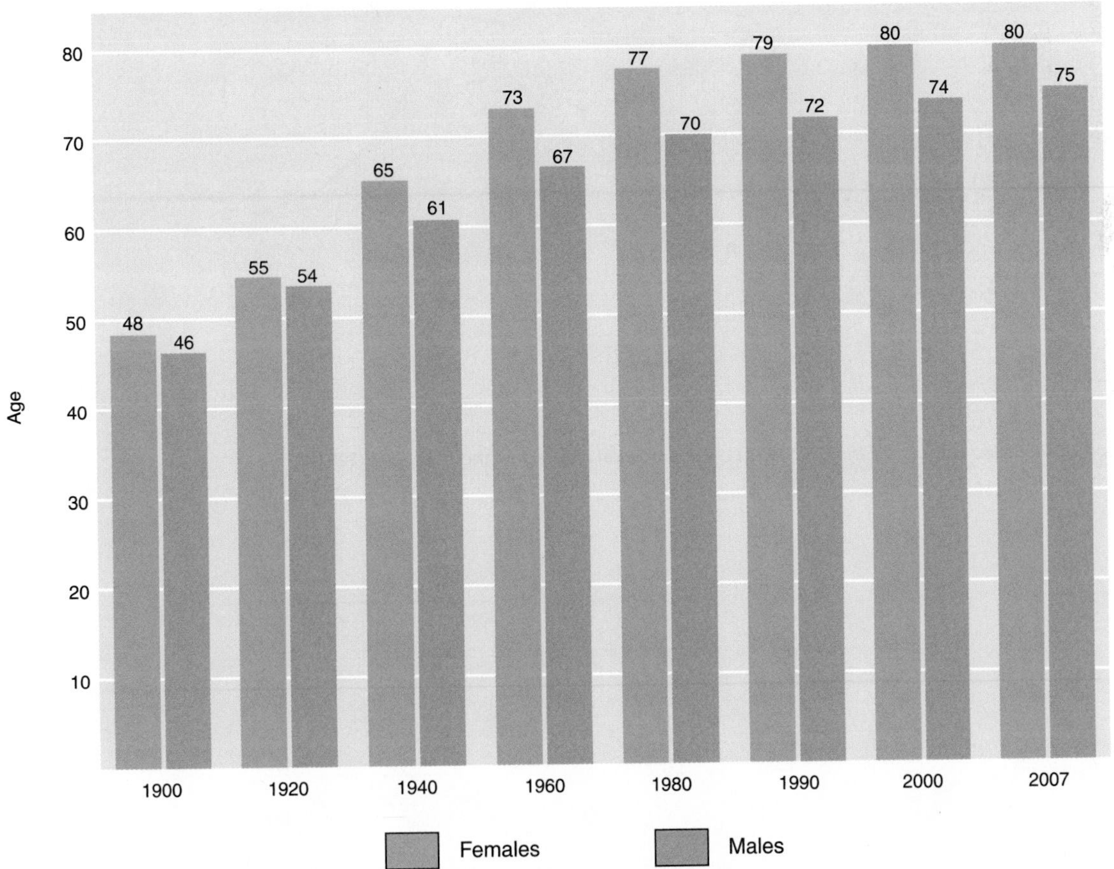

SOURCE: *Data from Historical Statistics of the U.S., Colonial Times to 1970* (1975) and *Statistical Abstract of the U.S., 2007* (2007).

MIGRATION AND IMMIGRATION

WE TEND TO ASSOCIATE INTERNAL MIGRATION with movement westward, yet equally significant has been the movement of the nation's population from the country to the city. In 1790, the first U.S. census recorded that approximately 95 percent of the population lived in rural areas. By 1990, that figure had fallen to less than 25 percent. The decline of the agricultural way of life, late-nineteenth-century industrialization, and immigration have all contributed to increased urbanization. A more recent trend has been the migration, especially since the 1970s, of people to the Sun Belt states of the South and West, lured by factors as various as economic opportunities in the defense and high-tech industries and good weather. This migration has swelled the size of cities like Houston, Dallas, Tucson, Phoenix, and San Diego, all of which in recent years ranked among the top ten most populous U.S. cities.

Rural and Urban Population, 1750–2000

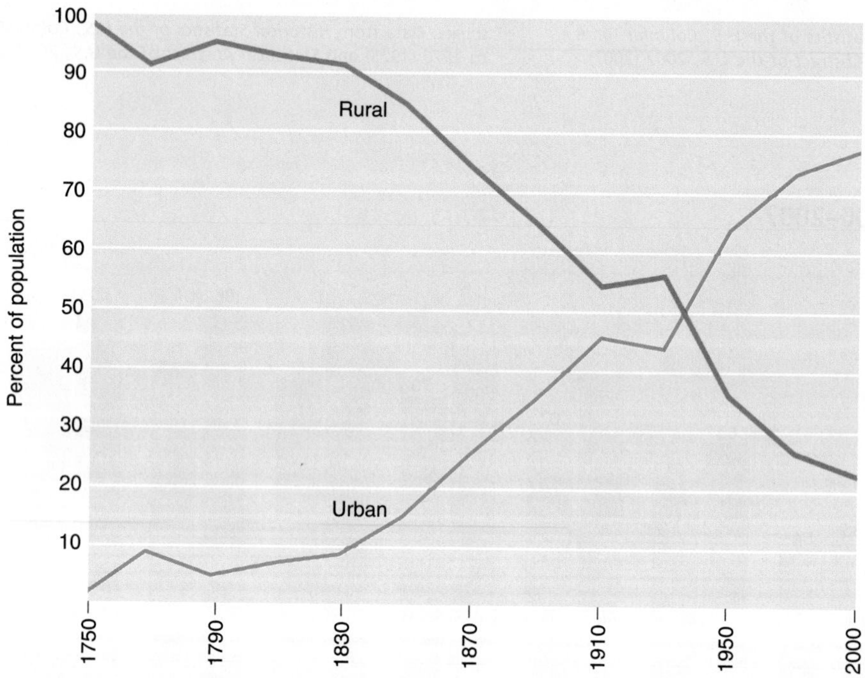

SOURCE: *Statistical Abstract of the U.S., 1991* (1991), *Statistical Abstract of the U.S., 2002* (2002).

THE QUANTITY AND CHARACTER OF IMMIGRATION to the United States has varied greatly over time. During the first major influx, between 1840 and 1860, newcomers hailed primarily from northern and western Europe. From 1880 to 1915, when rates soared even more dramatically, the profile changed, with 80 percent of the "new immigration" coming from central, eastern, and southern Europe. Following World War I, strict quotas reduced the flow considerably. Note also the significant falloff during the years of the Great Depression and World War II. The sources of immigration during the last half century have changed significantly, with the majority of people coming from Latin America, the Caribbean, and Asia. The latest surge during the 1980s and 1990s brought more immigrants to the United States than in any decade except 1901–1910.

RATES OF IMMIGRATION, 1821–2009

Year	Number	Rate per Thousand of Total Resident Population
1821–1830	151,824	1.6
1831–1840	599,125	4.6
1841–1850	1,713,521	10.0
1851–1860	2,598,214	11.2
1861–1870	2,314,824	7.4
1871–1880	2,812,191	7.1
1881–1890	5,246,613	10.5
1891–1900	3,687,546	5.8
1901–1910	8,795,386	11.6
1911–1920	5,735,811	6.2
1921–1930	4,107,209	3.9
1931–1940	528,431	0.4
1941–1950	1,035,039	0.7
1951–1960	2,515,479	1.6
1961–1970	3,321,677	1.8
1971–1980	4,493,300	2.2
1981–1990	7,338,100	3.0
1991	1,827,167	7.2
1992	973,977	3.8
1993	904,292	3.5
1994	804,416	3.1
1995	720,461	2.7
1996	915,900	3.4
1997	798,378	2.9
1998	654,451	2.4
1999	646,568	2.3
2000	849,807	3.0
2001	1,064,318	3.7
2002	1,063,732	3.7
2003	704,000	2.4
2004	958,000	3.3
2005	1,122,000	3.8
2006	1,266,129	4.2
2007	1,052,415	3.5
2008	1,107,126	3.6
2009	1,130,818	3.7

SOURCE: *Historical Statistics of the U.S., Colonial Times to 1970* (1975), *2002 Yearbook of Immigration Statistics* (2002), and *Statistical Abstract of the U.S., 1996, 1999, 2003, 2005,* and *2011* (1996, 1999, 2003, 2005, 2011).

Major Trends In Immigration, 1820–2010

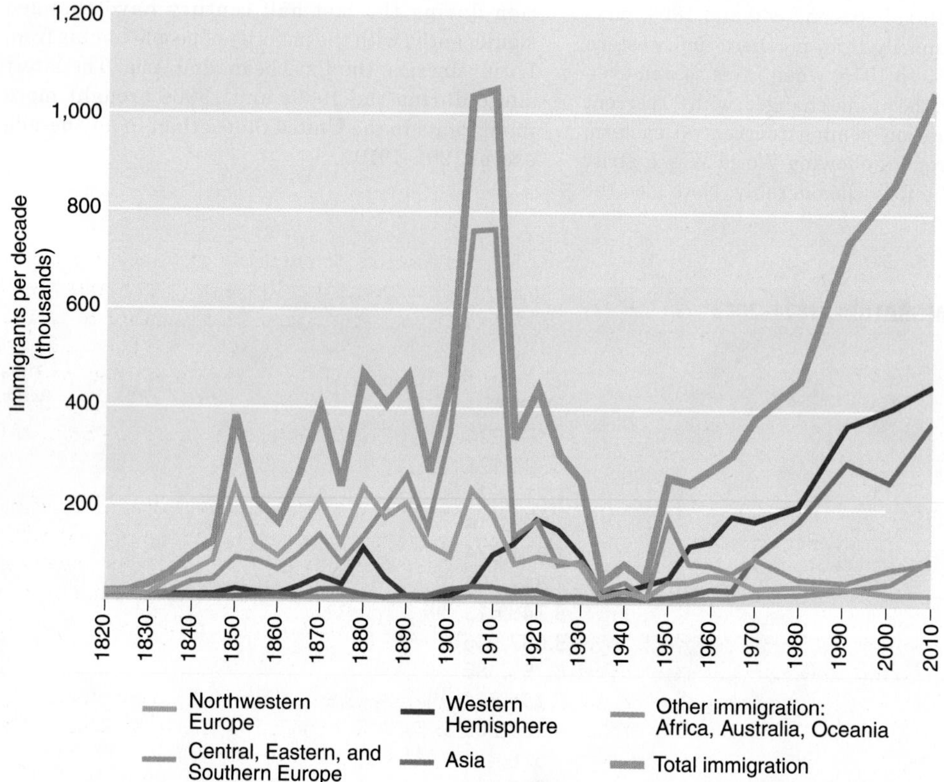

SOURCE: Data from *Historical Statistics of the U.S., Colonial Times to 1970* (1975), *Statistical Abstract of the U.S., 1999* (1999), and *Statistical Abstract of the U.S., 2011* (2011).

Glossary of Historical Vocabulary

A NOTE TO STUDENTS: This list of terms is provided to help you with historical and economic vocabulary. Many of these terms refer to broad, enduring concepts that you may encounter not only in further studies of history but also when following current events. The terms appear in bold at their first use in each chapter. In the glossary, the page numbers of those chapter-by-chapter appearances are provided so you can look up the terms' uses in various periods and contexts. For definitions and discussions of words not included here, consult a dictionary and the book's index, which will point you to topics covered at greater length in the book.

agribusiness Farming on a large scale, using the production, processing, and distribution methods of modern business. Farming became a big business, not just a way to feed a family and make a living, in the late nineteenth century as farms got larger and more mechanized. In the 1940s and 1950s, specialized commercial farms replaced many family-run operations and grew to an enormous scale. (p. 562)

antebellum A term that means "before a war" and commonly refers to the period prior to the Civil War. (pp. 373, 395, 493, 521)

artisan A term commonly used prior to 1900 to describe a skilled craftsman, such as a cabinetmaker. (p. 614)

bloody shirt A refrain used by Republicans in the late nineteenth century to remind the voting public that the Democratic Party, dominated by the South, was largely responsible for the Civil War and that the Republican Party had led the victory to preserve the Union. Republicans urged their constituents to "vote the way you shot." (pp. 524, 587)

capitalism An economic system in which private individuals and corporations own and operate most means of production. Free-market competition—in which supply and demand is minimally regulated by the state or not regulated at all—determines the prices of goods and services. There are three major aspects of capitalism. First, a capitalist system generally includes many workers who do not own what they produce, but instead perform labor for wages. Second, capitalist societies move beyond local trade to the specialized production of goods for large-scale cash markets. Third, people in a capitalist society internalize a social mentality that emphasizes rationality and the pursuit of profit as the primary goal of economic life. In the United States, most regions made the transition to capitalism by the early nineteenth century. Over the following two hundred years, the United States developed an industrial capitalist system, based on new technologies that allowed for self-sustaining economic growth. (pp. 570, 581, 632)

civil service The administrative service of a government. This term often applies to reforms following the passage of the Pendleton Act in 1883, which set qualifications for U.S. government jobs and sought to remove such jobs from political influence. (pp. 591, 592) *See also* spoils system.

colonization The process by which a country or society gains control over another, primarily through settlement. (pp. 343, 344, 388, 475, 476)

conscription Compulsory military service. Americans were first subject to conscription during the Civil War. The Selective Service Act of 1940 marked the first peacetime use of conscription. (p. 480) *See also* draft.

conservatism A political and moral outlook dating back to Alexander Hamilton's belief in a strong central government resting on a solid banking foundation. Currently associated with the Republican Party, conservatism today places a high premium on military preparedness, free market economics, low taxes, and strong sexual morality. (pp. 511, 517, 528, 586)

consumer culture (consumerism) A society that places high value on, and devotes substantial resources to, the purchase and display of material goods. Elements of American consumerism were evident in the nineteenth century but really took hold in the twentieth century with installment buying and advertising in the 1920s and again with the postwar prosperity of the 1950s. (pp. 755, 758, 799)

cult of domesticity The nineteenth-century belief that women's place was in the home, where they should create a haven for harried men working in the outside world. This ideal was made possible by the separation of the workplace and the home and was used to sentimentalize the home and women's role in it. (pp. 624, 625) *See also* separate spheres.

culture A term used here to connote what is commonly called "way of life." It refers not only to how a group of people supplied themselves with food and shelter but also to their family relationships, social groupings, religious ideas, and other features of their lives. (pp. 298, 482, 572, 574, 586, 587)

democracy A system of government in which the people have the power to rule, either directly or indirectly, through their elected representatives. Believing that direct democracy was dangerous, the framers of the Constitution created a government that gave direct voice to the people only in the House of Representatives and that placed a check on that voice in the Senate by offering unlimited six-year terms to senators, elected by the state legislatures to protect them from the whims of democratic majorities. The framers further curbed the perceived dangers of democracy by giving each of the three branches of government (legislative, executive, and judicial) the ability to check the power of the other two. (pp. 331, 332, 333, 474, 475, 505, 513, 529, 564) *See also* checks and balances.

disfranchisement The denial of suffrage to a group or individual through legal or other means. Beginning in 1890, southern progressives preached the disfranchisement of black voters as a "reform" of the electoral system. The most common means of eliminating black voters were poll taxes and literary tests. (pp. 455, 528)

draft (draftee) A system for selecting individuals for compulsory military service. A draftee is an individual selected through this process. (pp. 478, 480, 481, 482) *See also* conscription.

emancipation The act of freeing from slavery or bondage. The emancipation of American slaves, a goal shared by slaves and abolitionists alike, occurred with the passage of the Thirteenth Amendment in 1865. (pp. 343, 344, 388, 475, 476, 477, 485)

English Reformation *See* Reformation.

evangelicalism The trend in Protestant Christianity stressing salvation through conversion, repentance of sin, adherence to Scripture, and the importance of preaching over ritual. During the Second Great Awakening in the 1830s, evangelicals worshipped at camp meetings and religious revivals led by exuberant preachers. (pp. 322, 339, 341, 342) *See also* Second Great Awakening.

finance capitalism Refers to investment sponsored by banks and bankers and the profits garnered from the sale of financial assets such as stocks and bonds. The decades at the end of the twentieth century are known as a period of finance capitalism because banks and financiers increasingly took on the role of stabilizing markets and reorganizing industries. (p. 581)

franchise The right to vote. The franchise was gradually widened in the United States to include groups such as women and African Americans, who had no vote when the Constitution was ratified. (pp. 310, 516, 652) *See also* suffrage.

free labor Work conducted free from constraint and in accordance with the laborer's personal inclinations and will. Prior to the Civil War, free labor became an ideal championed by Republicans (who were primarily Northerners) to articulate individuals' right to work how and where they wished and to accumulate property in their own name. The ideal of free labor lay at the heart of the North's argument that slavery should not be extended into the western territories. (pp. 364, 365, 388, 397, 398)

free silver The late-nineteenth-century call by silver barons and poor American farmers for the widespread coinage of silver and for silver to be used as a base upon which to expand the paper money supply. The coinage of silver created a more inflationary monetary system that benefited debtors. (pp. 596, 643) *See also* gold standard.

free soil The idea advanced in the 1840s that Congress should prohibit slavery within the western territories. "Free soil, free speech, free labor, and free men" became the rallying cry of the short-lived Free-Soil Party. (pp. 430, 432)

gag rule A procedural rule invoked to prohibit discussion or debate on a particular subject in a legislative body. From 1836 to 1844, a series of gag rules prevented the House of Representatives from discussing the large number of antislavery petitions from abolitionist groups that flooded that chamber. (p. 347)

gold standard A monetary system in which any circulating currency was exchangeable for a specific amount of gold. Advocates for the gold standard believed that gold alone should be used for coinage and that the total value of paper banknotes should never exceed the government's supply of gold. The triumph of gold standard supporter William McKinley in the 1896 presidential election was a big victory for supporters of this policy. (pp. 597, 641) *See also* free silver.

gospel of wealth The idea that wealth garnered from earthly success should be used for good works. Andrew Carnegie promoted this view in an 1889 essay in which he maintained that the wealthy should serve as stewards and act in the best interests of society as a whole. (p. 585)

government bonds Promissory notes issued by a government in order to borrow money from members of the public. Such bonds are redeemable at a set future date. Bondholders earn interest on their investments. (p. 351)

guerrilla warfare Fighting carried out by an irregular military force usually organized into small, highly mobile groups. Guerrilla combat was common in the Vietnam War and during the American

Revolution. Guerrilla warfare is often effective against opponents who have greater material resources. (pp. 192, 445, 464, 471, 516, 663)

holding company A system of business organization whereby competing companies are combined under one central administration in order to curb competition and ensure profit. Pioneered in the late 1880s by John D. Rockefeller, holding companies, such as Standard Oil, exercised monopoly control even as the government threatened to outlaw trusts as a violation of free trade. (p. 577) *See also* monopoly; trust.

horizontal integration A system in which a single person or corporation creates several subsidiary businesses to sell a product in different markets. John D. Rockefeller pioneered the use of horizontal integration in the 1880s to control the refining process, giving him a virtual monopoly on the oil-refining business. (p. 577) *See also* vertical integration; monopoly.

impeachment The process by which formal charges of wrongdoing are brought against a president, a governor, or a federal judge. (pp. 514)

imperialism The system by which great powers gain control of overseas territories. The United States became an imperialist power by gaining control of Puerto Rico, Guam, the Philippines, and Cuba as a result of the Spanish-American War. (pp. 525, 537, 543, 544, 545, 667, 668, 669)

isolationism A foreign policy perspective characterized by a desire to have the United States withdraw from the conflicts of the world and enjoy the protection of two vast oceans. (pp. 658)

Jim Crow The system of racial segregation that developed in the post–Civil War South and extended well into the twentieth century; it replaced slavery as the chief instrument of white supremacy. Jim Crow laws segregated African Americans in public facilities such as trains and streetcars and denied them basic civil rights, including the right to vote. It was also at this time that the doctrine of "separate but equal" became institutionalized. (pp. 519, 588)

laissez-faire The doctrine, based on economic theory, that government should not interfere in business or the economy. Laissez-faire ideas guided American government policy in the late nineteenth century and conservative politics in the twentieth century. Business interests that supported laissez-faire in the late nineteenth century accepted government interference when it took the form of tariffs or subsidies that worked to their benefit. A broader use of the term refers to the simple philosophy of abstaining from interference. (pp. 585, 586, 640, 654)

land grant A gift of land from a government, usually intended to encourage settlement or development. The British government issued several land grants to encourage development in the American colonies. In the mid-nineteenth century, the U.S. government issued land grants to encourage railroad development and, through the passage of the Land-Grant College Act (also known as the Morrill Act) in 1862, set aside public land to support universities. (pp. 363, 552, 556, 560, 571, 573)

liberty The condition of being free or enjoying freedom from control. This term also refers to the possession of certain social, political, or economic rights, such as the right to own and control property. Eighteenth-century American colonists invoked the principle to argue for strict limitations on government's ability to tax its subjects. (pp. 378, 434, 452)

manifest destiny A term coined by journalist John O'Sullivan in 1845 to express the popular nineteenth-century belief that the United States was destined to expand westward to the Pacific Ocean and had an irrefutable right and God-given responsibility to do so. This idea provided an ideological shield for westward expansion and masked the economic and political motivations of many of those who championed it. (pp. 370, 382, 537)

miscegenation The sexual mixing of races. In slave states, despite the social stigma and legal restrictions on interracial sex, masters' almost unlimited power over their female slaves meant that liaisons inevitably occurred. Many states maintained laws against miscegenation into the 1950s. (pp. 397, 400, 588)

monopoly Exclusive control and domination by a single business entity over an entire industry through ownership, command of supply, or other means. Gilded Age businesses monopolized their industries quite profitably, often organizing holding companies and trusts to do so. (pp. 568, 571, 577, 581, 583, 596) *See also* holding company; trust.

Monroe Doctrine President James Monroe's 1823 declaration that the Western Hemisphere was closed to any further colonization or interference by European powers. In exchange, Monroe pledged that the United States would not become involved in European struggles. Although Monroe could not back his policy with action, it was an important formulation of national goals. (pp. 313, 314, 316)

nativism Bias against immigrants and in favor of native-born inhabitants. American nativists especially favor persons who come from white, Anglo-Saxon, Protestant lines over those from other racial, ethnic, and religious heritages. Nativists may include former immigrants who view new immigrants as incapable of assimilation. Many nativists, such as members of the Know-Nothing Party in the nineteenth century and the Ku Klux Klan through the contemporary period, voice anti-immigrant, anti-Catholic, and anti-Semitic sentiments. (p. 439)

New South A vision of the South, promoted after the Civil War by Henry Grady, editor of the *Atlanta Constitution*, that urged the South to abandon its dependence on agriculture and use its cheap labor and natural resources to compete with northern industry. Many Southerners migrated from farms to cities in the late nineteenth century, and Northerners and foreigners invested a significant amount of capital in railroads, cotton and textiles, mining, lumber, iron, steel, and tobacco in the region. (pp. 500, 587–588)

nullification The idea that states can disregard federal laws when those laws represent an overstepping of congressional powers. The controversial idea was first proposed by opponents of the Alien and Sedition Acts of 1798 and later by South Carolina politicians in 1828 as a response to the Tariff of Abominations. (pp. 337, 432)

oligopoly A competitive system in which several large corporations dominate an industry by dividing the market so each business has a share of it. More prevalent than outright monopolies during the late 1800s, the oligopolies of the Gilded Age successfully muted competition and benefited the corporations that participated in this type of arrangement. (pp. 550, 583)

paternalism The idea that slavery was a set of reciprocal obligations between masters and slaves, with slaves providing labor and obedience and masters providing basic care and direction. The concept of paternalism denied that the slave system was brutal and exploitative. Although paternalism did provide some protection against the worst brutality, it did not guarantee decent living conditions, reasonable work, or freedom from physical punishment. (pp. 404–406)

planters Owners of large farms (or, more specifically, plantations) that were worked by twenty or more slaves. By 1860, planters had accrued a great deal of local, statewide, and national political power in the South despite the fact that they represented a minority of the white electorate. Planters' dominance of southern politics demonstrated both the power of tradition and stability among southern voters and the planters' success at convincing white voters that the slave system benefited all whites, even those without slaves. (pp. 400, 404, 407, 408, 409, 416, 421–422, 482)

plutocracy A society ruled by the richest members. The excesses of the Gilded Age and the fact that just 1 percent of the population owned more than half the real and personal property in the country led many to question whether the United States was indeed a plutocracy. (p. 614)

pogrom An organized and often officially encouraged massacre of an ethnic minority; usually used in reference to attacks on Jews. (p. 608)

popular sovereignty The idea that government is subject to the will of the people. Before the Civil War, this was the idea that the residents of a territory should determine, through their legislatures, whether to allow slavery. (pp. 438, 444, 430–431)

Populism A political movement that led to the creation of the People's Party, primarily comprising southern and western farmers who railed against big business and advocated business and economic reforms, including government ownership of the railroads. The movement peaked in the late nineteenth century. The Populist ticket won more than 1 million votes in the presidential election of 1892 and 1.5 million in the congressional elections of 1894. The term *populism* has come to mean any political movement that advocates on behalf of the common person, particularly for government intervention against big business. (pp. 656, 657, 658)

predestination The idea that individual salvation or damnation is determined by God at, or just prior to, a person's birth. The concept of predestination invalidated the idea that salvation could be obtained through either faith or good works. (p. 98) *See also* Calvinism.

progressivism (progressive movement) A wide-ranging twentieth-century reform movement that advocated government activism to mitigate the problems created by urban industrialism. Progressivism reached its peak in 1912 with the creation of the Progressive Party, which ran Theodore Roosevelt for president. The term *progressivism* has come to mean any general effort advocating for social welfare programs. (pp. 614, 640, 643)

Protestantism A powerful Christian reform movement that began in the sixteenth century with Martin Luther's critiques of the Roman Catholic Church. Over the centuries, Protestantism has taken many different forms, branching into numerous denominations with differing systems of worship. (pp. 339, 347, 439, 587)

Protestant Reformation *See* Reformation.

Reformation The reform movement that began in 1517 with Martin Luther's critiques of the Roman Catholic Church, which led to the formation of Protestant Christian groups. The English Reformation began with Henry VIII's break with the Roman Catholic Church, which established the Protestant Church of England. Henry VIII's decision was politically motivated; he had no particular quarrel with Catholic theology and remained an orthodox Catholic in most matters of religious practice. (pp. 430–431, 437)

Second Great Awakening A popular religious revival that preached that salvation was available to anybody who chose to take it. The revival peaked in the 1830s, and its focus on social perfection inspired many of the reform movements of the Jacksonian era. (p. 339) *See also* evangelicalism.

separate spheres A concept of gender relations that developed in the Jacksonian era and continued well into the twentieth century, holding that women's proper place was in the world of hearth and home (the private sphere) and men's was in the world of commerce and politics (the public sphere). The doctrine of separate spheres eroded slowly over the nineteenth and twentieth centuries as women became more and more involved in public activities. (pp. 339–340, 588) *See also* cult of domesticity.

social Darwinism A social theory, based on Charles Darwin's theory of evolution, that argued that all progress in human society came as the result of competition and natural selection. Gilded Age proponents such as William Graham Sumner and Herbert Spencer claimed that reform was useless because the rich and poor were precisely where nature intended them to be and intervention would retard the progress of humanity. (pp. 583–586) *See also* reform Darwinism.

socialism A governing system in which the state owns and operates the largest and most important parts of the economy. (pp. 351, 611, 622, 643)

spoils system An arrangement in which party leaders reward party loyalists with government jobs. This slang term for *patronage* comes from the saying "To the victor go the spoils." Widespread government corruption during the Gilded Age spurred reformers to curb the spoils system through the passage of the Pendleton Act in 1883, which created the Civil Service Commission to award government jobs on the basis of merit. (pp. 333, 525, 586) *See also* civil service.

state sovereignty A state's autonomy or freedom from external control. The federal system adopted at the Constitutional Convention in 1787 struck a balance between state sovereignty and national control by creating a strong central government while leaving the states intact as political entities. The states remained in possession of many important powers on which the federal government cannot intrude. (p. 467)

states' rights A strict interpretation of the Constitution that holds that federal power over the states is limited and that the states hold ultimate sovereignty. First expressed in 1798 through the passage of the Virginia and Kentucky Resolutions, which were based on the assumption that the states have the right to judge the constitutionality of federal laws, the states' rights philosophy became a cornerstone of the South's resistance to federal control of slavery. (pp. 337, 480–481, 507, 508)

suffrage The right to vote. The term *suffrage* is most often associated with the efforts of American women to secure voting rights. (pp. 311–312, 443, 500, 554) *See also* franchise.

temperance movement The reform movement to end drunkenness by urging people to abstain from the consumption of alcohol. Begun in the 1820s, this movement achieved its greatest political victory with the passage of a constitutional amendment in 1919 that prohibited the manufacture, sale, and transportation of alcohol. That amendment was repealed in 1933. (pp. 589–590, 652–653)

third world Originally a cold war term linked to decolonization, *third world* was first used in the late 1950s to describe newly independent countries in Africa and Asia that were not aligned with either Communist nations (the second world) or non-Communist nations (the first world). Later, the term was applied to all poor, nonindustrialized countries, in Latin America as well as in Africa and Asia. Many international experts see *third world* as a problematic category when applied to such a large and disparate group of nations, and they criticize the discriminatory hierarchy suggested by the term. (pp. 605, 606)

trust A corporate system in which corporations give shares of their stock to trustees, who coordinate the industry to ensure profits to the participating corporations and curb competition. Pioneered by Standard Oil, such business practices were deemed unfair, were moderated by the Sherman Antitrust Act (1890), and were finally abolished by the combined efforts of Presidents Theodore Roosevelt and William Howard Taft and the sponsors of the 1914 Clayton Antitrust Act. The term *trust* is also loosely applied to all large business combinations. (pp. 568, 577, 595) *See also* holding company.

vertical integration A system in which a single person or corporation controls all processes of an industry from start to finished product. Andrew Carnegie first used vertical integration in the 1870s, controlling every aspect of steel production from the mining of iron ore to the manufacturing of the final product, thereby maximizing profits by eliminating the use of outside suppliers or services. (p. 576)

War Hawks Young Republicans elected to the U.S. Congress in the fall of 1810 who were eager for war with Britain in order to legitimize attacks on Indians, end impressment, and avenge foreign insults. (p. 303) *See also* hawks.

yeoman A farmer who owned a small plot of land that was sufficient to support a family and was tilled by family members and perhaps a few servants. (pp. 415–416, 421–422, 481–482, 518, 527–528)

Spot Artifact Credits

p. 296 (compass) National Museum of American History, Smithsonian Institution, Behring Center; p. 299 (headdress) National Museum of American Indian, Smithsonian Institution (2/1294) Photos by Photo Services; p. 304 (medal) © Collection of the New-York Historical Society; p. 351 (miniature log cabin) Smithsonian Institution, National Museum of American History, Behring Center; p. 359 (plow) Courtesy Deere & Company; p. 368 (sheet music) Special Collections, Milton S. Eisenhower Library, The Johns Hopkins University; p. 376 (flag) The Center for American History, The University of Texas at Austin; p. 405 (shoe) Archaeological Society of Virginia; p. 412 (whip) Louisiana State Museum; p. 418 (fiddle) National Museum of American History, Smithsonian Institution, Washington, D.C.; p. 431 (ticket) Courtesy, American Antiquarian Society; p. 434 (token) © Collection of the New-York Historical Society; p. 453 (revolver) Ohio Historical Society; p. 466 (Confederate flag) Smithsonian Institution, National Museum of American History, Behring Center; p. 468 (Confederate jacket) National Museum of American History, Smithsonian Institution, Behring Center; p. 472 (Union jacket) Chicago Historical Society; p. 501 (top hat) National Museum of American History, Smithsonian Institution, Behring Center; p. 514 (impeachment ticket) Collection of Janice L. and David J. Frent; p. 521 (plow) National Museum of American History, Smithsonian Institution, Behring Center; p. 524 (election artifact) Collection of Janice L. and David J. Frent; p. 546 (shirt) Image courtesy of National Park Service, Nez Perce National Historical Park. Catalogue #BIHO1256; p. 547 (moccasins) Photo Addison Doty, Santa Fe, NM; p. 549 (silver bar) Collection of the Oakland Museum of California, Museum Purchase; p. 560 (spurs) Courtesy of the High Desert Museum, Bend, Oregon, catalog number 0564AN.04; p. 573 (stock ticker) Collection of John D. Jenkins, www.sparkmanmuseum.com; p. 577 (kerosene lamp) Picture Research Consultants & Archives; p. 587 (cigarette box) Courtesy, Duke Homestead and Tobacco Museum; p. 616 (sewing machine) Smithsonian Institution, National Museum of American History, Behring Center; p. 625 (baseball glove with ball) Smithsonian Institution, National Museum of American History, Behring Center; p. 627 (faucet) Picture Research Consultants & Archives; p. 645 (dagger) Library & Archives Division, Historical Society of Western Pennsylvania; p. 656 (button) Collection of Janice L. and David J. Frent; p. 661 (magazine cover) The Granger Collection, NYC.

Index

A NOTE ABOUT THE INDEX:

Names of individuals appear in boldface.

Letters in parentheses following pages refer to:
(i) illustrations, including photographs and artifacts
(f) figures, including charts and graphs
(m) maps
(b) boxed features (such as "Historical Question")
(t) tables

ATLAS OF THE TERRITORIAL GROWTH OF THE UNITED STATES

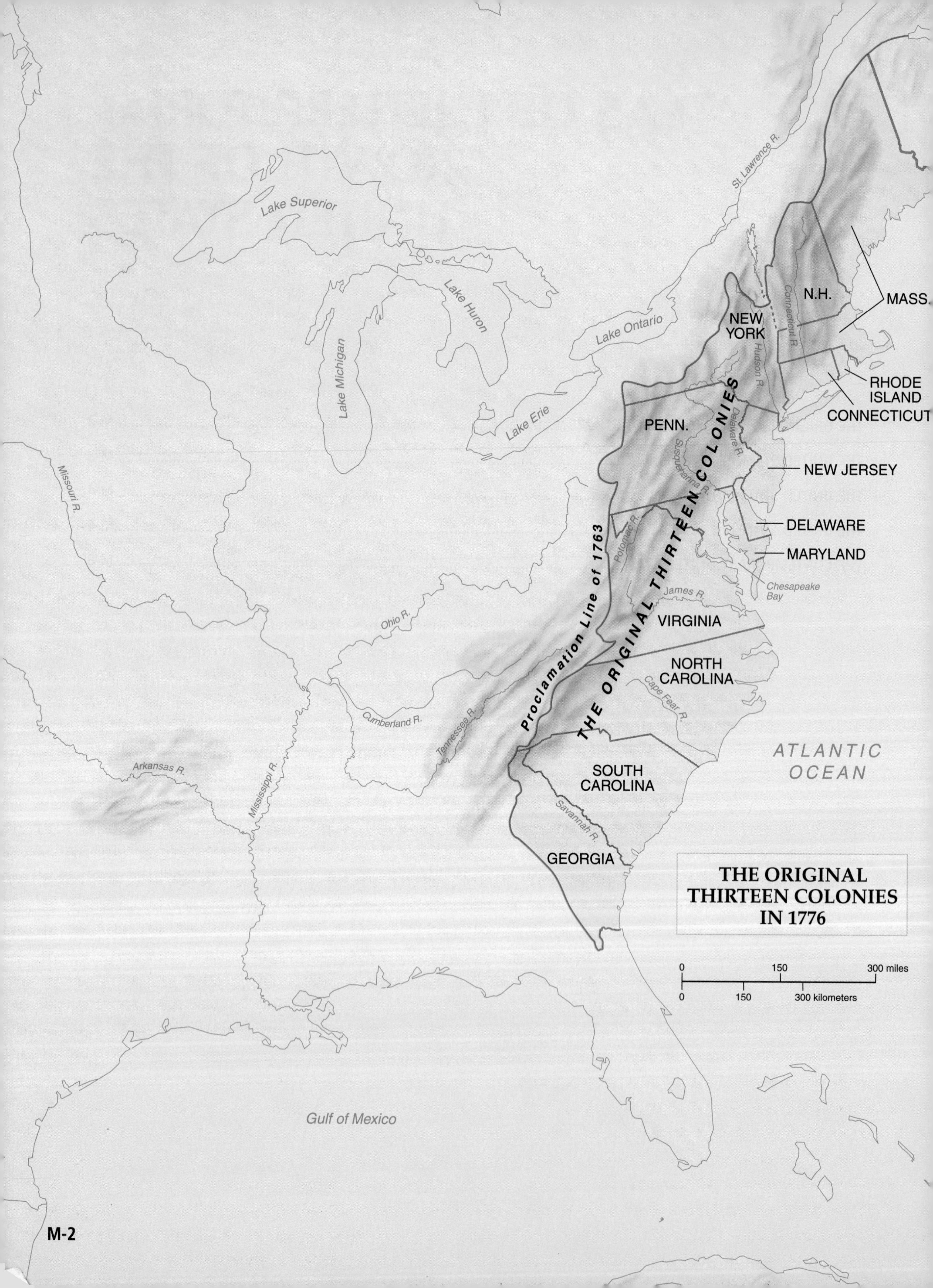
THE ORIGINAL THIRTEEN COLONIES IN 1776
THE ORIGINAL THIRTEEN COLONIES
Proclamation Line of 1763
N.H.
MASS.
NEW YORK
RHODE ISLAND
CONNECTICUT
PENN.
NEW JERSEY
DELAWARE
MARYLAND
VIRGINIA
NORTH CAROLINA
SOUTH CAROLINA
GEORGIA
ATLANTIC OCEAN
Gulf of Mexico
Lake Superior
Lake Michigan
Lake Huron
Lake Ontario
Lake Erie
St. Lawrence R.
Connecticut R.
Hudson R.
Delaware R.
Susquehanna R.
Potomac R.
James R.
Chesapeake Bay
Cape Fear R.
Savannah R.
Ohio R.
Cumberland R.
Tennessee R.
Mississippi R.
Missouri R.
Arkansas R.
0
150
300 miles
0
150
300 kilometers

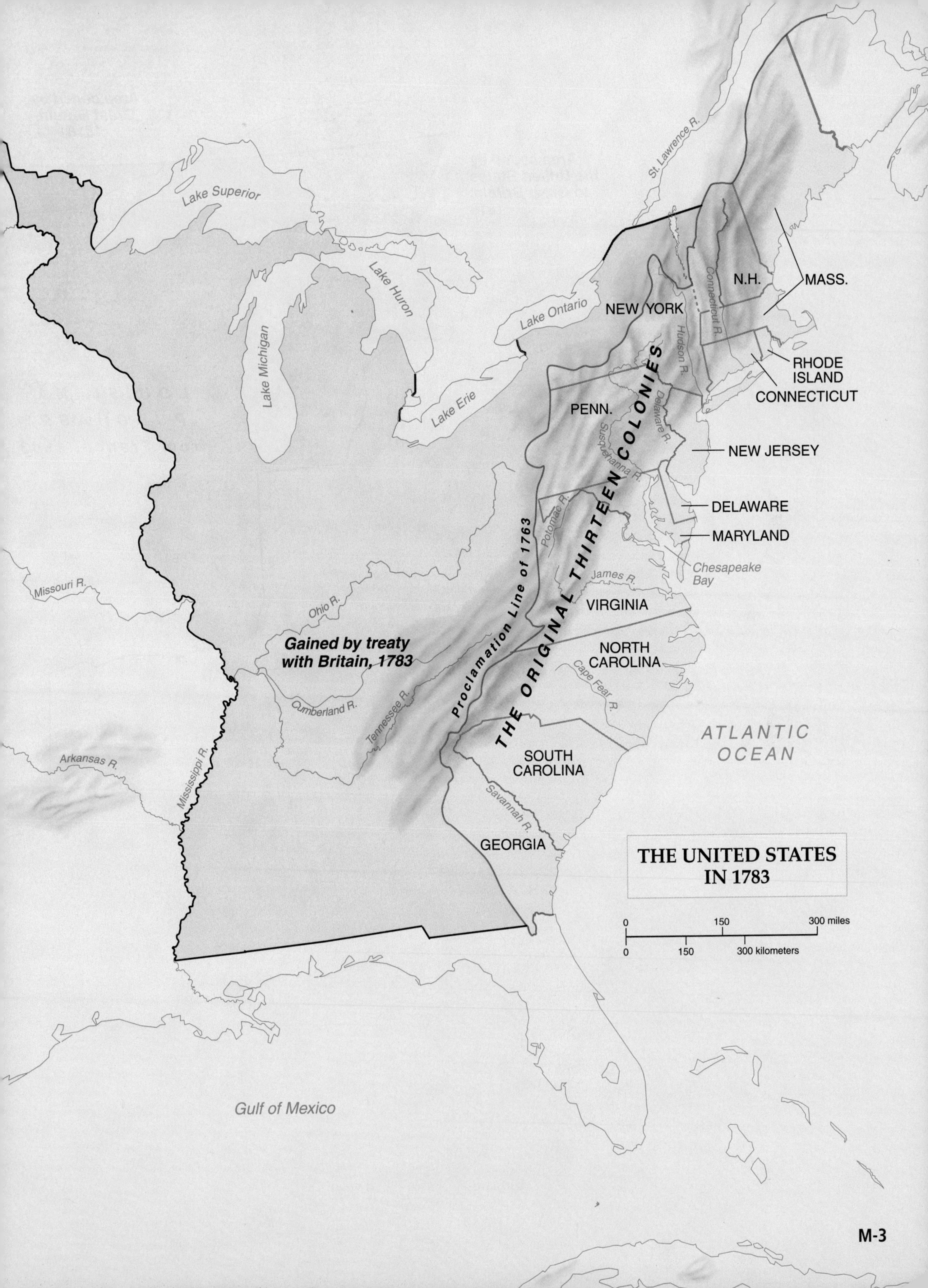
THE UNITED STATES IN 1783
Lake Superior
Lake Michigan
Lake Huron
Lake Ontario
Lake Erie
St. Lawrence R.
NEW YORK
N.H.
MASS.
Connecticut R.
Hudson R.
RHODE ISLAND
CONNECTICUT
PENN.
Delaware R.
Susquehanna R.
NEW JERSEY
DELAWARE
MARYLAND
Potomac R.
Chesapeake Bay
James R.
VIRGINIA
NORTH CAROLINA
Cape Fear R.
SOUTH CAROLINA
Savannah R.
GEORGIA
THE ORIGINAL THIRTEEN COLONIES
Proclamation Line of 1763
Gained by treaty with Britain, 1783
Ohio R.
Cumberland R.
Tennessee R.
Missouri R.
Arkansas R.
Mississippi R.
ATLANTIC OCEAN
Gulf of Mexico
0
150
300 miles
0
150
300 kilometers

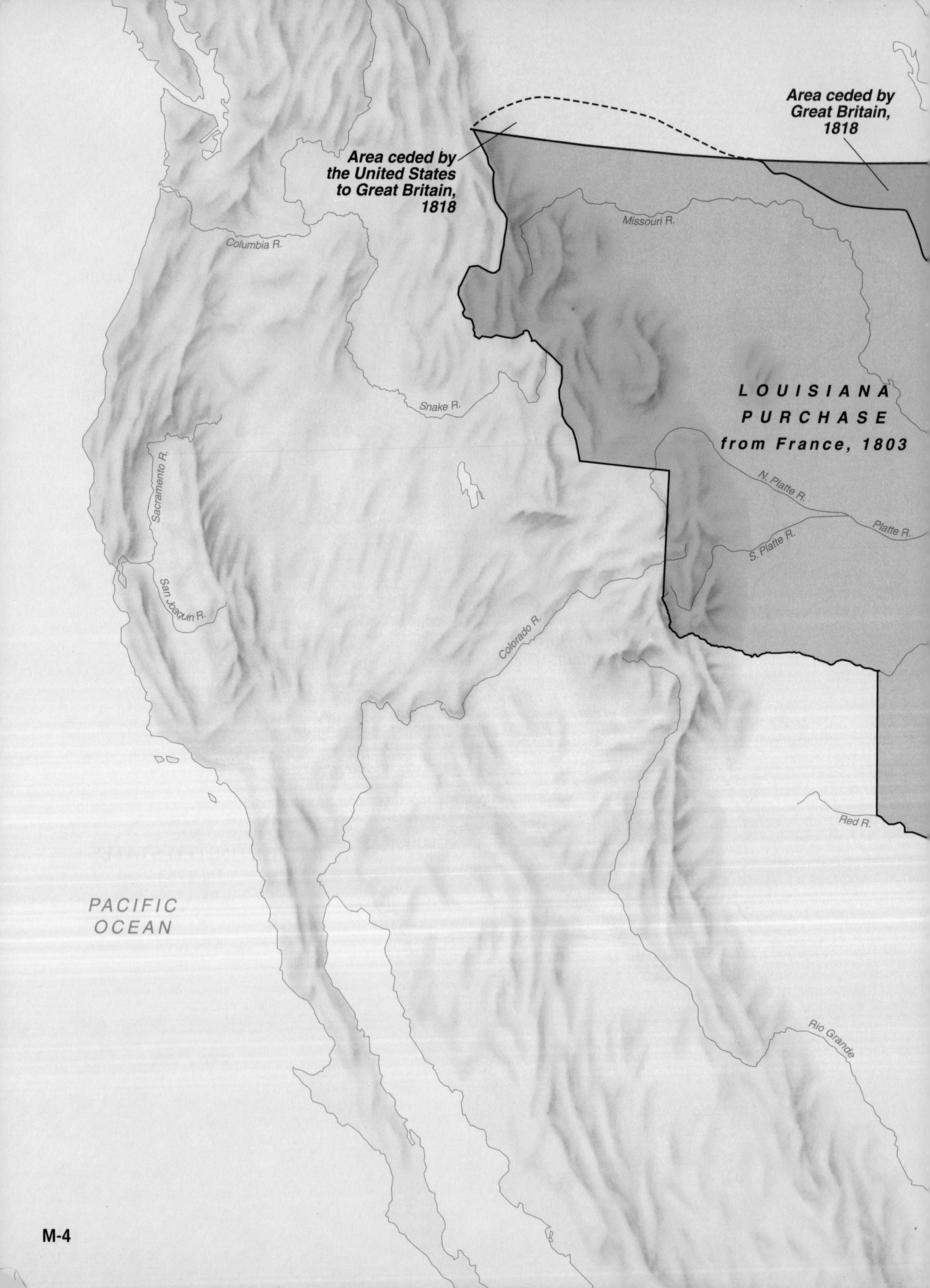

Area ceded by
Great Britain,
1818
Area ceded by
the United States
to Great Britain,
1818
Missouri R.
Columbia R.
LOUISIANA
PURCHASE
from France, 1803
Snake R.
Sacramento R.
N. Platte R.
Platte R.
S. Platte R.
San Joaquin R.
Colorado R.
Red R.
PACIFIC
OCEAN
Rio Grande

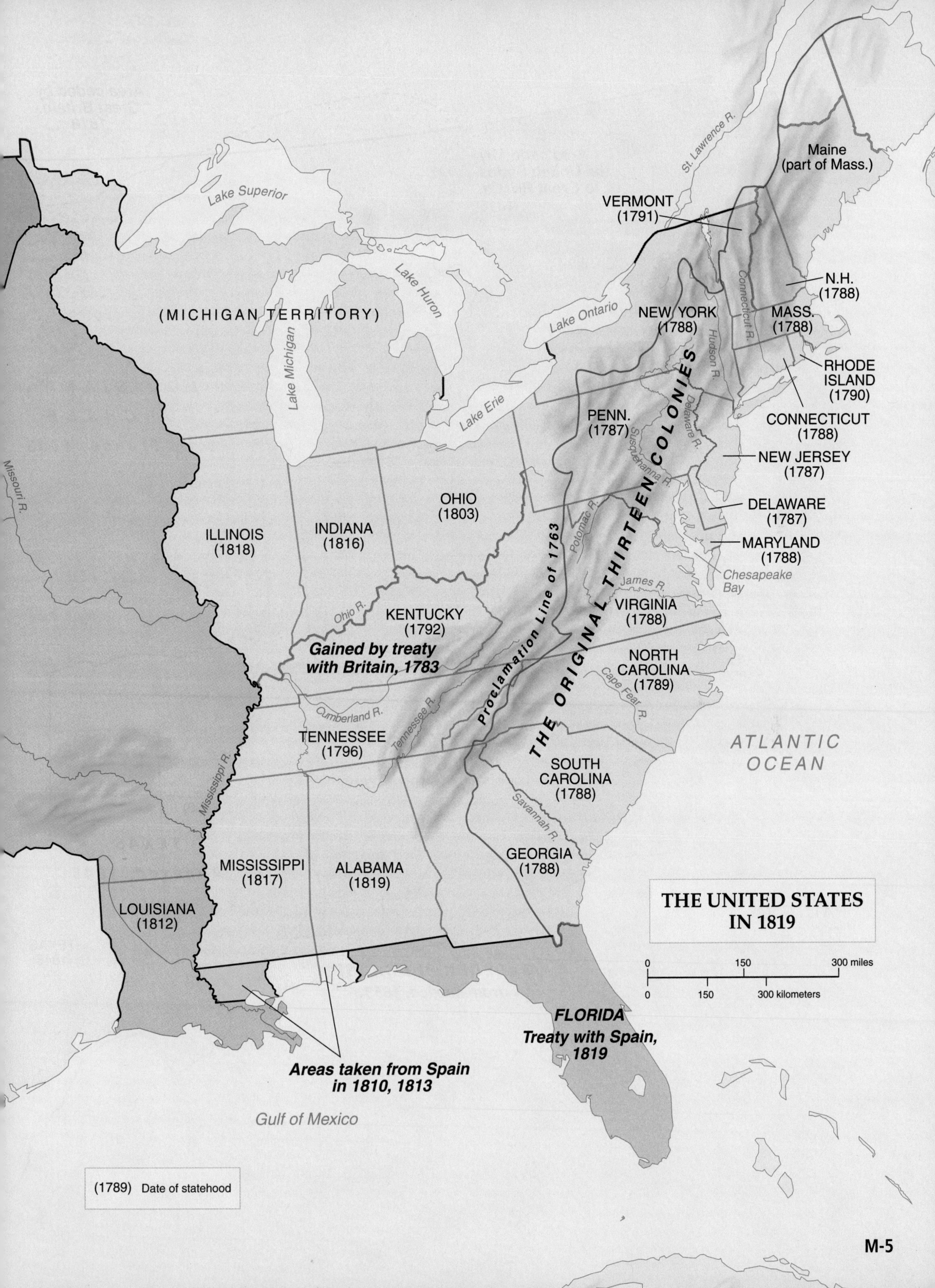
THE UNITED STATES IN 1819
(MICHIGAN TERRITORY)
Lake Superior
Lake Michigan
Lake Huron
Lake Ontario
Lake Erie
St. Lawrence R.
Maine (part of Mass.)
VERMONT (1791)
N.H. (1788)
MASS. (1788)
RHODE ISLAND (1790)
CONNECTICUT (1788)
NEW YORK (1788)
NEW JERSEY (1787)
DELAWARE (1787)
MARYLAND (1788)
PENN. (1787)
VIRGINIA (1788)
NORTH CAROLINA (1789)
SOUTH CAROLINA (1788)
GEORGIA (1788)
OHIO (1803)
INDIANA (1816)
ILLINOIS (1818)
KENTUCKY (1792)
TENNESSEE (1796)
MISSISSIPPI (1817)
ALABAMA (1819)
LOUISIANA (1812)
Gained by treaty with Britain, 1783
THE ORIGINAL THIRTEEN COLONIES
Proclamation Line of 1763
Connecticut R.
Hudson R.
Delaware R.
Susquehanna R.
Potomac R.
James R.
Chesapeake Bay
Cape Fear R.
Savannah R.
Ohio R.
Cumberland R.
Tennessee R.
Mississippi R.
Missouri R.
ATLANTIC OCEAN
FLORIDA Treaty with Spain, 1819
Areas taken from Spain in 1810, 1813
Gulf of Mexico
0 150 300 miles
0 150 300 kilometers
(1789) Date of statehood

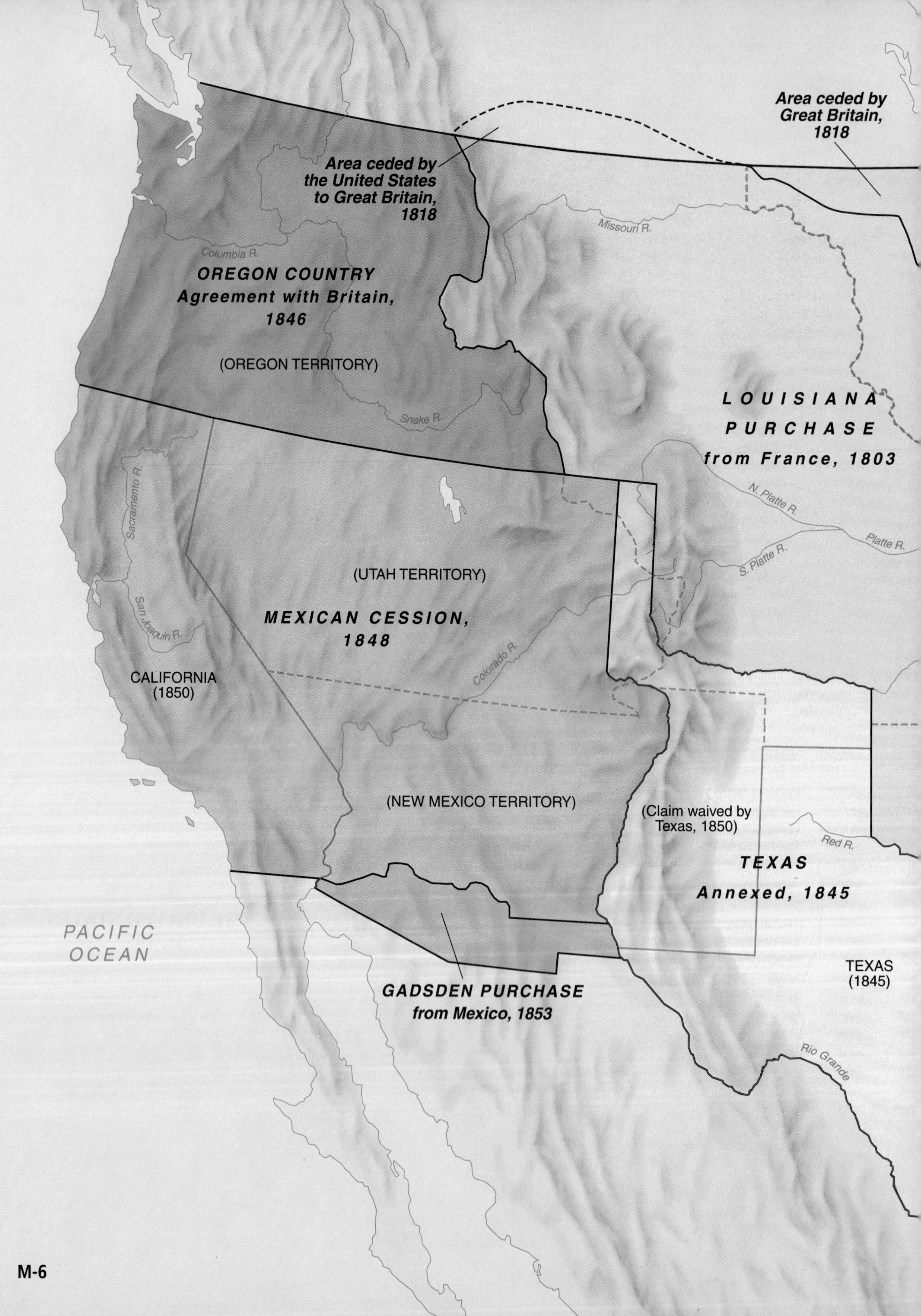

Area ceded by
Great Britain,
1818
Area ceded by
the United States
to Great Britain,
1818
Missouri R.
Columbia R.
OREGON COUNTRY
Agreement with Britain,
1846
(OREGON TERRITORY)
LOUISIANA
PURCHASE
from France, 1803
Snake R.
N. Platte R.
Platte R.
S. Platte R.
Sacramento R.
(UTAH TERRITORY)
San Joaquin R.
MEXICAN CESSION,
1848
Colorado R.
CALIFORNIA
(1850)
(NEW MEXICO TERRITORY)
(Claim waived by
Texas, 1850)
Red R.
TEXAS
Annexed, 1845
PACIFIC
OCEAN
TEXAS
(1845)
GADSDEN PURCHASE
from Mexico, 1853
Rio Grande

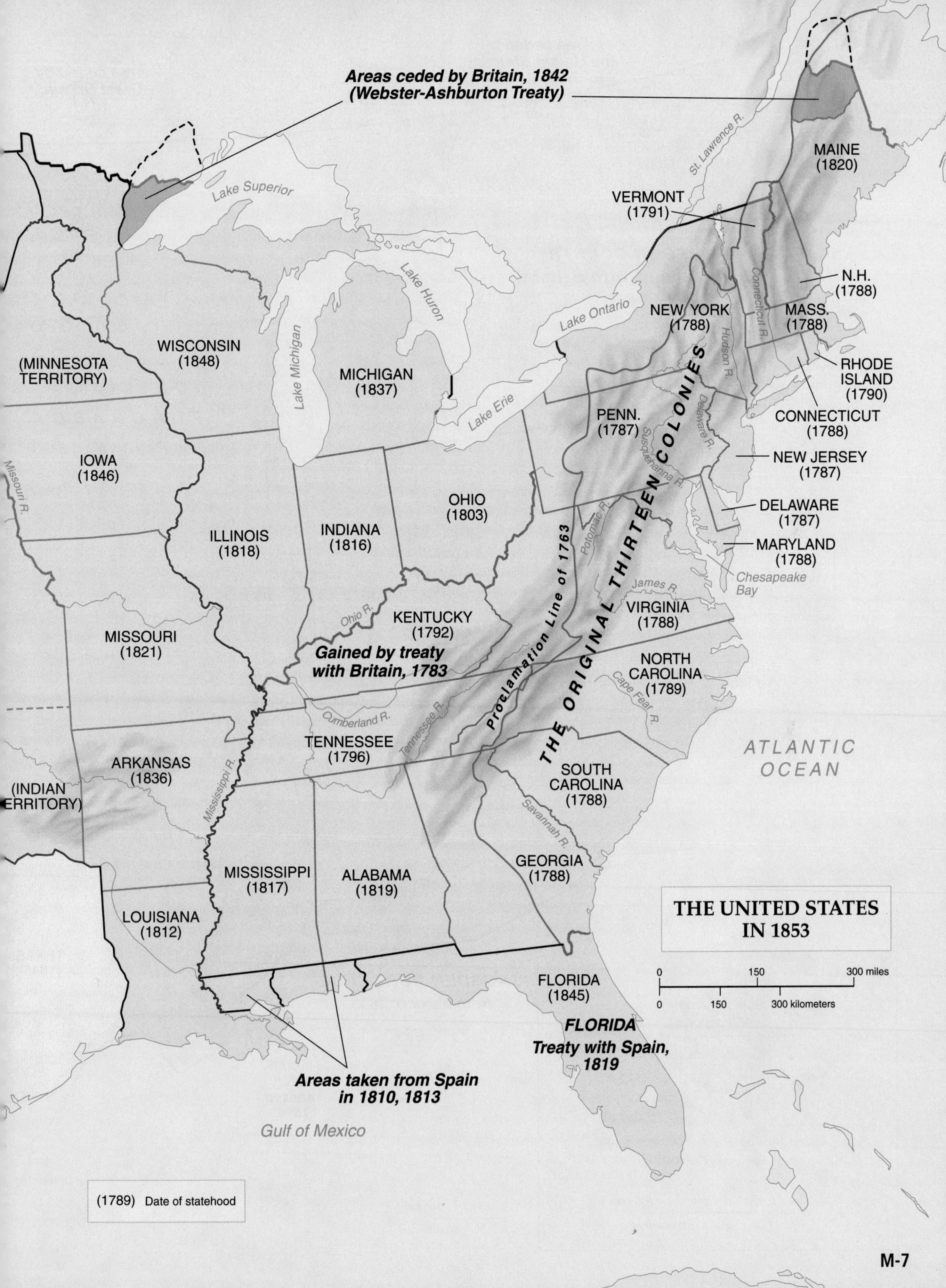

THE UNITED STATES IN 1853
Areas ceded by Britain, 1842
(Webster-Ashburton Treaty)
Gained by treaty with Britain, 1783
Areas taken from Spain in 1810, 1813
FLORIDA
Treaty with Spain, 1819
Proclamation Line of 1763
THE ORIGINAL THIRTEEN COLONIES
MAINE (1820)
VERMONT (1791)
N.H. (1788)
MASS. (1788)
RHODE ISLAND (1790)
CONNECTICUT (1788)
NEW YORK (1788)
NEW JERSEY (1787)
PENN. (1787)
DELAWARE (1787)
MARYLAND (1788)
VIRGINIA (1788)
NORTH CAROLINA (1789)
SOUTH CAROLINA (1788)
GEORGIA (1788)
FLORIDA (1845)
KENTUCKY (1792)
TENNESSEE (1796)
OHIO (1803)
INDIANA (1816)
ILLINOIS (1818)
MICHIGAN (1837)
WISCONSIN (1848)
IOWA (1846)
MISSOURI (1821)
ARKANSAS (1836)
LOUISIANA (1812)
MISSISSIPPI (1817)
ALABAMA (1819)
(MINNESOTA TERRITORY)
(INDIAN ERRITORY)
Lake Superior
Lake Michigan
Lake Huron
Lake Erie
Lake Ontario
St. Lawrence R.
Connecticut R.
Hudson R.
Delaware R.
Susquehanna R.
Potomac R.
James R.
Chesapeake Bay
Cape Fear R.
Savannah R.
Tennessee R.
Cumberland R.
Ohio R.
Mississippi R.
Missouri R.
ATLANTIC OCEAN
Gulf of Mexico
0 150 300 miles
0 150 300 kilometers
(1789) Date of statehood

Area ceded by the United States to Great Britain, 1818
Area ceded by Great Britain, 1818
WASHINGTON (1889)
Olympia
Missouri R.
Columbia R.
Helena
MONTANA (1889)
NORTH DAKOTA (1889)
Bismarck
Salem
OREGON COUNTRY
Agreement with Britain, 1846
OREGON (1859)
IDAHO (1890)
Boise
SOUTH DAKOTA (1889)
Pierre
Snake R.
WYOMING (1890)
LOUISIANA PURCHASE
from France, 1803
N. Platte R.
NEBRASKA (1867)
Cheyenne
Platte R.
Sacramento R.
Salt Lake City
Carson City
Sacramento
NEVADA (1864)
UTAH (1896)
S. Platte R.
Denver
San Joaquin R.
COLORADO (1876)
KANSAS (1861)
MEXICAN CESSION
1848
Colorado R.
CALIFORNIA (1850)
Santa Fe
ARIZONA (1912)
NEW MEXICO (1912)
Red R.
PACIFIC OCEAN
Phoenix
TEXAS
Annexed, 1845
ARCTIC OCEAN
RUSSIA
ALASKA (1959)
Purchased from Russia, 1867
Yukon R.
CANADA
Bering Sea
Gulf of Alaska
Juneau
0 250 500 miles
0 250 500 kilometers
TEXAS (1845)
GADSDEN PURCHASE
from Mexico, 1853
Rio Grande
HAWAII (1959)
Annexed, 1898
Honolulu
PACIFIC OCEAN
0 50 100 miles
0 50 100 kilometers
MEXICO

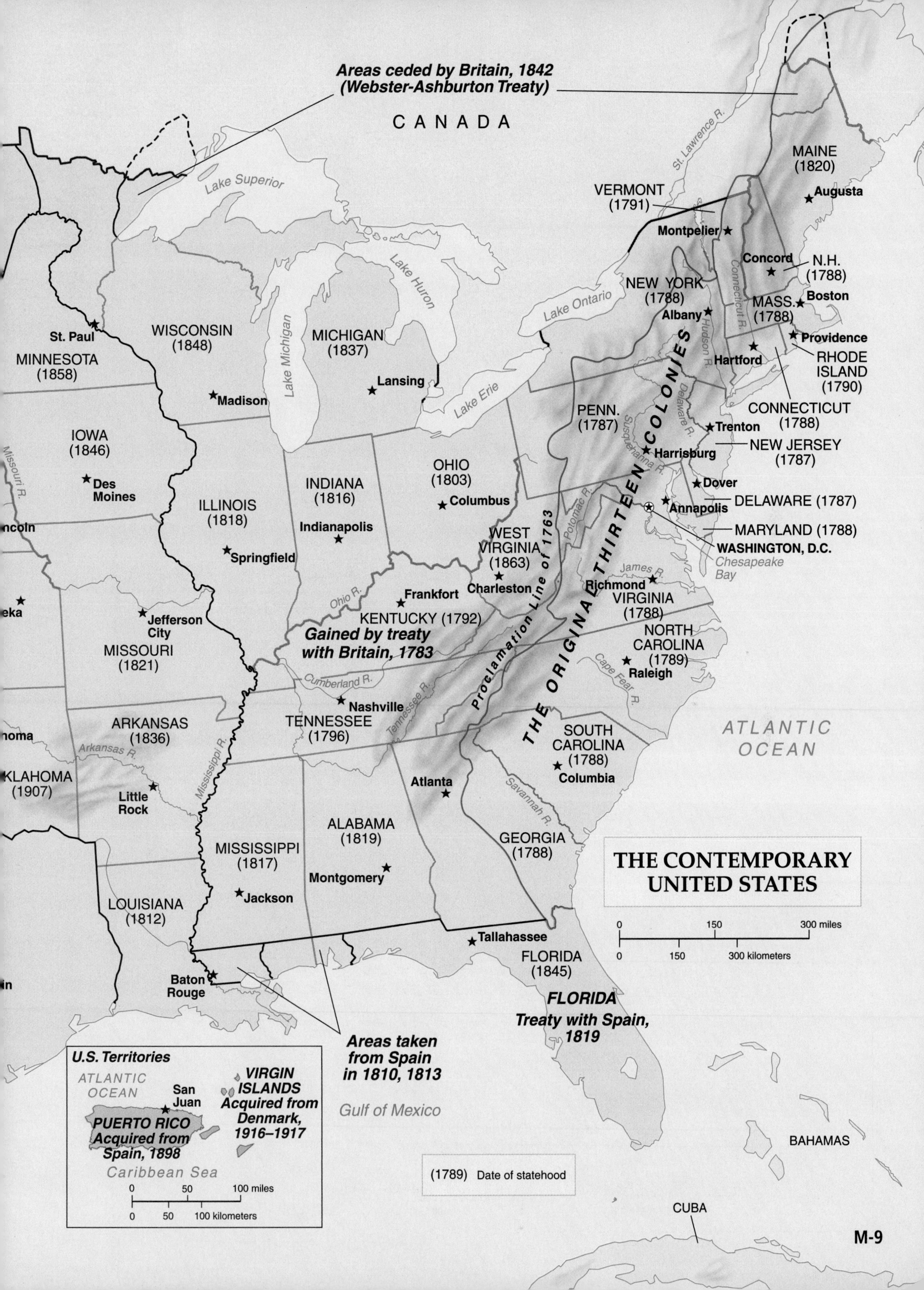
THE CONTEMPORARY UNITED STATES
Areas ceded by Britain, 1842 (Webster-Ashburton Treaty)
CANADA
Lake Superior
Lake Michigan
Lake Huron
Lake Ontario
Lake Erie
St. Lawrence R.
MAINE (1820)
Augusta
VERMONT (1791)
Montpelier
Concord
N.H. (1788)
NEW YORK (1788)
Albany
MASS. (1788)
Boston
Providence
RHODE ISLAND (1790)
Hartford
CONNECTICUT (1788)
Connecticut R.
Hudson R.
Delaware R.
Susquehanna R.
Trenton
NEW JERSEY (1787)
PENN. (1787)
Harrisburg
Dover
DELAWARE (1787)
Annapolis
MARYLAND (1788)
WASHINGTON, D.C.
Chesapeake Bay
Potomac R.
James R.
THE ORIGINAL THIRTEEN COLONIES
Proclamation Line of 1763
WEST VIRGINIA (1863)
Charleston
Richmond
VIRGINIA (1788)
NORTH CAROLINA (1789)
Raleigh
Cape Fear R.
SOUTH CAROLINA (1788)
Columbia
Savannah R.
GEORGIA (1788)
Atlanta
ATLANTIC OCEAN
MINNESOTA (1858)
St. Paul
WISCONSIN (1848)
Madison
MICHIGAN (1837)
Lansing
IOWA (1846)
Des Moines
Missouri R.
ILLINOIS (1818)
Springfield
INDIANA (1816)
Indianapolis
OHIO (1803)
Columbus
Ohio R.
Frankfort
KENTUCKY (1792)
Gained by treaty with Britain, 1783
MISSOURI (1821)
Jefferson City
Cumberland R.
Nashville
TENNESSEE (1796)
Tennessee R.
ARKANSAS (1836)
Arkansas R.
Little Rock
Mississippi R.
KLAHOMA (1907)
MISSISSIPPI (1817)
Jackson
ALABAMA (1819)
Montgomery
LOUISIANA (1812)
Baton Rouge
Tallahassee
FLORIDA (1845)
FLORIDA Treaty with Spain, 1819
Areas taken from Spain in 1810, 1813
Gulf of Mexico
BAHAMAS
CUBA
0 150 300 miles
0 150 300 kilometers
(1789) Date of statehood
U.S. Territories
ATLANTIC OCEAN
San Juan
PUERTO RICO Acquired from Spain, 1898
VIRGIN ISLANDS Acquired from Denmark, 1916–1917
Caribbean Sea
0 50 100 miles
0 50 100 kilometers

About the authors

JAMES L. ROARK (Ph.D., Stanford University) is Samuel Candler Dobbs Professor of American History at Emory University. In 1993, he received the Emory Williams Distinguished Teaching Award, and in 2001–2002 he was Pitt Professor of American Institutions at Cambridge University. He has written *Masters without Slaves: Southern Planters in the Civil War and Reconstruction* and coauthored *Black Masters: A Free Family of Color in the Old South* with Michael P. Johnson.

MICHAEL P. JOHNSON (Ph.D., Stanford University) is professor of history at Johns Hopkins University. His publications include *Toward a Patriarchal Republic: The Secession of Georgia*; *Abraham Lincoln, Slavery, and the Civil War: Selected Speeches and Writings*; and *Reading the American Past: Selected Historical Documents*, the documents reader for *The American Promise*. He has also coedited *No Chariot Let Down: Charleston's Free People of Color on the Eve of the Civil War* with James L. Roark.

PATRICIA CLINE COHEN (Ph.D., University of California, Berkeley) is professor of history at the University of California, Santa Barbara, where she received the Distinguished Teaching Award in 2005–2006. She has written *A Calculating People: The Spread of Numeracy in Early America* and *The Murder of Helen Jewett: The Life and Death of a Prostitute in Nineteenth-Century New York*, and she has coauthored *The Flash Press: Sporting Male Weeklies in 1840s New York.*

SARAH STAGE (Ph.D., Yale University) has taught U.S. history at Williams College and the University of California, Riverside, and she was visiting professor at Beijing University and Szechuan University. Currently she is professor of women's studies at Arizona State University. Her books include *Female Complaints: Lydia Pinkham and the Business of Women's Medicine* and *Rethinking Home Economics: Women and the History of a Profession.*

SUSAN M. HARTMANN (Ph.D., University of Missouri) is Arts and Humanities Distinguished Professor of History at Ohio State University. In 1995 she won the university's Exemplary Faculty Award in the College of Humanities. Her publications include *Truman and the 80th Congress*; *The Home Front and Beyond: American Women in the 1940s*; *From Margin to Mainstream: American Women and Politics since 1960*; and *The Other Feminists: Activists in the Liberal Establishment.*

About the cover image

***Woman and Men Posing with Giant Log,* ca. 1892**

During the second half of the twentieth century, the West promised land and opportunity, attracting thousands of migrants. Lumber was in short supply in other parts of the country but abundant in places such as Tulare County, California, where this photograph was taken around 1892. Logging enabled settlers, like those pictured here, to clear space and build homes as well as support themselves financially. Tulare County boasts some of the largest trees in the world. The tree in this picture measured 18 feet in diameter.